W ok

The firstwriter.com

Writers' Handbook

2018

EDITOR

J. PAUL DYSON

JP&A Dyson

Published in 2017 by JP&A Dyson
27 Old Gloucester Street, London WC1N 3AX, United Kingdom

https://www.firstwriter.com

ISBN 978-1-909935-18-1

Foreword

The firstwriter.com Writers' Handbook returns for its 2018 edition with over 1,400 listings of literary agents, publishers, and magazines, updated in firstwriter.com's online databases between 2015 and 2017, including revised and updated listings from the previous edition and over 25% new entries.

Previous editions of this handbook have been bought by writers across the United States, Canada, and Europe; and ranked in the United Kingdom as the number one bestselling writing and publishing directory on Amazon. The 2018 edition continues this international outlook, giving writers all over the English-speaking world access to the global publishing markets.

The handbook also provides free online access to the entire current firstwriter.com databases, including over 2,200 magazines, over 650 literary agencies, over 1,900 book publishers that don't charge fees, and constantly updated listings of current writing competitions, with typically more than 50 added each month.

For details on how to claim your free access please see the back of this book.

Included in the subscription

A subscription to the full website is not only free with this book, but comes packed with all the following features:

Advanced search features

- Save searches and save time – set up to 15 search parameters specific to your work, save them, and then access the search results with a single click whenever you log in. You can even save multiple different searches if you have different types of work you are looking to place.
- Add personal notes to listings, visible only to you and fully searchable – helping you to organise your actions.
- Set reminders on listings to notify you when to submit your work, when to follow up, when to expect a reply, or any other custom action.
- Track which listings you've viewed and when, to help you organise your search – any listings which have changed since you last viewed them will be highlighted for your attention.

Daily email updates

As a subscriber you will be able to take advantage of our email alert service, meaning you can specify your particular interests and we'll send you automatic email updates when we change or add a listing that matches them. So if you're interested in agents dealing in romantic fiction in the United States you can have us send you emails with the latest updates about them – keeping you up to date without even having to log in.

User feedback

Our agent, publisher, and magazine databases all include a user feedback feature that allows our subscribers to leave feedback on each listing – giving you not only the chance to have your say about the markets you contact, but giving a unique authors' perspective on the listings.

Save on copyright protection fees

If you're sending your work away to publishers, competitions, or literary agents, it's vital that you first protect your copyright. As a subscriber to firstwriter.com you can do this through our site and save 10% on the copyright registration fees normally payable for protecting your work internationally through the Intellectual Property Rights Office (https://www.CopyrightRegistrationService.com).

firstwriter.magazine

firstwriter.magazine showcases the best in new poetry and fiction from around the world. If you're interested in writing and want to get published, the most important thing you can do is read contemporary writing that's getting into print now. Our magazine helps you do that.

Monthly newsletter

When you subscribe to firstwriter.com you also receive our monthly email newsletter – described by one publishing company as "the best in the business" – including articles, news, and interviews for writers. And the best part is that you can continue to receive the newsletter even after you stop your paid subscription – at no cost!

For details on how to claim your free access please see the back of this book.

Contents

Foreword v

Contents vii

Glossary of Terms ix

Guidance

The Writer's Roadmap 1

Why Choose Traditional Publishing 5

Formatting Your Manuscript 9

Protecting Your Copyright 13

Should You Self-Publish? 19

The Self-Publishing Process 23

Magazines

US Magazines 27

UK Magazines 71

Canadian Magazines 109

Irish Magazines 113

Magazines Subject Index 117

Literary Agents

US Literary Agents 135

UK Literary Agents 187

Canadian Literary Agents 221

Irish Literary Agents 223

Literary Agents Subject Index 225

Publishers

US Publishers 269
UK Publishers 317
Canadian Publishers 369
Irish Publishers 373
Publishers Subject Index 377

Free Access

Get Free Access to the firstwriter.com Website 409

Glossary of Terms

This section explains common terms used in this handbook, and in the publishing industry more generally.

Academic

Listings in this book will be marked as targeting the academic market only if they publish material of an academic nature; e.g. academic theses, scientific papers, etc. The term is not used to indicate publications that publish general material aimed at people who happen to be in academia, or who are described as academic by virtue of being educated.

Adult

In publishing, "adult" simply refers to books that are aimed at adults, as opposed to books that are aimed at children, or young adults, etc. It is not a euphemism for pornographic or erotic content. Nor does it necessarily refer to content which is unsuitable for children; it is just not targeted at them. In this book, most ordinary mainstream publishers will be described as "adult", unless their books are specifically targeted at other groups (such as children, professionals, etc.).

Advance

Advances are up-front payments made by traditional publishers to authors, which are off-set against future royalties.

Agented

An *agented* submission is one which is submitted by a literary agent. If a publisher accepts only *agented* submissions then you will need a literary agent to submit the work on your behalf.

Author bio

A brief description of you and your life – normally in relation to your writing activity, but if intended for publication (particularly in magazines) may be broader in scope. May be similar to *Curriculum Vitae* (CV) or résumé, depending on context.

Bio

See *Author bio*.

Curriculum Vitae

A brief description of you, your qualifications, and accomplishments – normally in this context in relation to writing (any previous publications, or awards, etc.), but in the case of nonfiction proposals may also include relevant experience that qualifies you to write on the subject. Commonly abbreviated to "CV". May also be referred to as a résumé. May be similar to *Author bio*, depending on context.

CV

See *Curriculum Vitae*.

International Reply Coupon

When submitting material overseas you may be required to enclose *International Reply Coupons*, which will enable the recipient to send a response and/or return your material at your cost. Not applicable/available in all countries, so check with your local Post Office for more information.

IRC
See *International Reply Coupon*.

Manuscript
Your complete piece of work – be it a novel, short story, or article, etc. – will be referred to as your manuscript. Commonly abbreviated to "ms" (singular) or "mss" (plural).

MS
See *Manuscript*.

MSS
See *Manuscript*.

Professional
Listings in this book will be marked as targeting the professional market if they publish material serving a particular profession: e.g. legal journals, medical journals, etc. The term is not used to indicate publications that publish general material aimed at a notional "professional class".

Proposal
A proposal is normally requested for nonfiction projects (where the book may not yet have been completed, or even begun). Proposals can consist of a number of components, such as an outline, table of contents, CV, marketing information, etc. but the exact requirements will vary from one publisher to another.

Query
Many agents and publishers will prefer to receive a query in the first instance, rather than your full *manuscript*. A query will typically consist of a cover letter accompanied by a *synopsis* and/or sample chapter(s). Specific requirements will vary, however, so always check on a case by case basis.

Recommendation
If an agent is only accepting approaches by recommendation this means that they will only consider your work if it comes with a recommendation from an established professional in the industry, or an existing client.

RoW
Rest of world.

SAE
See *Stamped Addressed Envelope*. Can also be referred to as SASE.

SASE
Self-Addressed Stamped Envelope. Variation of SAE. See *Stamped Addressed Envelope*.

Simultaneous submission
A simultaneous submission is one which is sent to more than one market at the same time. Normally you will be sending your work to numerous different magazines, agents, and publishers at the same time, but some demand the right to consider it exclusively – i.e. they don't accept simultaneous submissions.

Stamped Addressed Envelope
Commonly abbreviated to "SAE". Can also be referred to as Self-Addressed Stamped Envelope, or SASE. When supplying an SAE, ensure that the envelope and postage is adequate for a reply or the return of your material, as required. If you are submitting overseas, remember that postage from your own country will not be accepted, and you may need to provide an *International Reply Coupon*.

Synopsis
A short outline of your story. This should cover all the main characters and events, including the ending. It is not the kind of "teaser" found on a book's back cover. The length of synopsis required can vary, but is generally between one and three pages.

TOC
Table of Contents. These are often requested as part of nonfiction proposals.

Unagented
An unagented submission is one which is not submitted through a literary agent. If a publisher accepts unagented submissions then you can approach them directly.

Unsolicited mss

A manuscript which has not been requested. Many agents and publishers will not accept unsolicited mss, but this does not necessarily mean they are closed to approaches – many will prefer to receive a short *query* in the first instance. If they like the idea, they will request the full work, which will then be a solicited manuscript.

Youth

The term "Youth" in this book is used to indicate the Young Adult market.

The Writer's Roadmap

With most objectives in life, people recognise that there is a path to follow. Whether it is career progression, developing a relationship, or chasing your dreams, we normally understand that there are foundations to lay and baby steps to take before we'll be ready for the main event.

But for some reason, with writing (perhaps because so much of the journey of a writer happens in private, behind closed doors), people often overlook the process involved. They often have a plan of action which runs something like this:

1. Write novel.

2. Get novel published.

This is a bit like having a plan for success in tennis which runs:

1. Buy tennis racket.

2. Win Wimbledon.

It misses out all the practice that is going to be required; the competing in the minor competitions and the learning of the craft that will be needed in order to succeed in the major events; the time that will need to be spent gaining reputation and experience.

In this roadmap we'll be laying out what we think is the best path to follow to try and give yourself the best shot of success in the world of writing. You don't necessarily have to jump through all the hoops, and there will always be people who, like Pop Idol or reality TV contestants, get a lucky break that propels them to stardom without laying any of the foundations laid out below, but the aim here is to limit your reliance on luck and maximise your ability to shape your destiny yourself.

1: Write short material

Writers will very often start off by writing a novel. We would advise strongly against this. It's like leaving school one day and applying for a job as a CEO of an international corporation the next. Novels are the big league. They are expensive to produce, market, and distribute. They require significant investment and pose a significant financial risk to publishers. They are not a good place for new writers to try and cut their teeth. If you've already written your novel that's great – it's great experience and you'll have learned a lot – but we'd recommend shelving it for now (you can always come back to it later) and getting stuck into writing some short form material, such as poetry and short fiction.

This is what novelist George R. R. Martin, author of *A Game of Thrones*, has to say on the subject:

> "I would also suggest that any aspiring writer begin with short stories. These days, I meet far too many young writers who try to start off with a novel right off, or a trilogy, or even a nine-book series. That's like starting in at rock climbing by tackling Mt Everest. Short stories help you learn your craft."

You will find that writing short material will improve your writing no end. Writing short fiction allows you to play with lots of different stories and characters very quickly. Because you will probably only spend a few days on any given story you will quickly gain a lot of experience with plotting stories and will learn a lot about what works, what doesn't work, and what you personally are good at. When you write a novel, by contrast, you may spend years on a single story and one set of characters, making this learning process much slower.

Your writing will also be improved by the need to stick to a word limit. Writers who start their career by writing a novel often produce huge epics, the word counts of which they wear as a badge of honour, as if they demonstrate their commitment to and enthusiasm for writing. What they actually demonstrate is a naivety about the realities of getting published. The odds are already stacked against new writers getting a novel published, because of the cost and financial risk of publishing a novel. The bigger the novel, the more it will cost to print, warehouse, and distribute. Publishers will not look at a large word count and be impressed – they will be terrified. The longer the novel, the less chance it has of getting published.

A lengthy first novel also suggests that the writer has yet to learn one of the most critical skills a writer must possess to succeed: brevity. By writing short stories that fit the limits imposed by competitions and magazines you will learn this critical skill. You will learn to remove unnecessary words and passages, and you will find that your writing becomes leaner, more engaging, and more exciting as a result. Lengthy first novels are often rambling and sometimes boring – but once you've been forced to learn how to "trim the fat" by writing short stories, the good habits you've got into will transfer across when you start writing long form works, allowing you to write novels that are pacier and better to read. They will stand a better chance of publication not just because they are shorter and cheaper to produce, but they are also likely to be better written.

2: Get a professional critique

It's a good idea to get some professional feedback on your work at some point, and it's probably better to do this sooner, rather than later. There's no point spending a long time doing something that doesn't quite work if a little advice early on could have got you on the right track sooner. It's also a lot cheaper to get a short story critiqued than a whole novel, and if you can learn the necessary lessons now it will both minimise the cost and maximise the benefit of the advice.

Should you protect the copyright of short works before showing them to anyone?

This is a matter of personal preference. We'd suggest that it certainly isn't as important to register short works as full novels, as your short works are unlikely to be of much financial value to you. Having said that, films do sometimes get made which are based on short stories, in which case you'd want to have all your rights in order. If you do choose to register your short works this can be done for a relatively small amount online at https://www.copyrightregistrationservice.com/register.

3: Submit to competitions and magazines, and build a list of writing credits

Once you have got some short works that you are happy with you can start submitting them to competitions and small magazines. You can search for competitions at https://www.firstwriter.com/competitions and magazines at https://www.firstwriter.com/magazines. Prize money may not be huge, and you probably won't be paid for having your work appear in the kind of small literary magazines you will probably be approaching at first, but the objective here is to build up a list of writing credits to give you more credibility when approaching agents and publishers. You'll be much more likely to grab their attention if you can reel off a list of places where you have already been published, or prizes you have won.

4: Finish your novel and protect your copyright

Okay – so you've built up a list of writing credits, and you've decided it's time to either write a novel, or go back to the one you had already started (in which case you'll probably find yourself cutting out large chunks and making it a lot shorter!). Once you've got your novel to the point where you're happy to start submitting it for publication you should get it registered for copyright. Unlike the registration of short works, which we think is a matter of personal preference, we'd definitely recommend registering a novel, and doing so before you show it to anybody. That *includes* family and friends. Don't worry that you might want to change it – as long as you don't rewrite it to the point where it's not recognisable it will still be protected – the important thing is to get it registered without delay. You can protect it online at https://www.
copyrightregistrationservice.com/register.

If you've already shown it to other people then just register it as soon as you can. Proving a claim to copyright is all about proving you had a copy of the work before anyone else, so time is of the essence.

5: Editing

These days, agents and publishers increasingly seem to expect manuscripts to have been professionally edited before being submitted to them – and no, getting your husband / wife / friend / relative to do it doesn't count. Ideally, you should have the whole manuscript professionally edited, but this can be expensive. Since most agents and publishers aren't going to want to see the whole manuscript in the first instance you can probably get away with just having the first three chapters edited. It may also be worth having your query letter and synopsis edited at the same time.

6: Submit to literary agents

There will be many publishers out there who will accept your submission directly, and on the face of it that might seem like a good idea, since you won't have to pay an agent 15% of your earnings.

However, all the biggest publishers are generally closed to direct submissions from authors, meaning that if you want the chance of getting a top publisher you're going to need a literary agent. You'll also probably find that their 15% fee is more than offset by the higher earnings you'll be likely to achieve.

To search for literary agents go to https://www.firstwriter.com/Agents. Start by being as specific in your search as possible. So if you've written a historical romance select "Fiction", "Romance", and "Historical". Once you've approached all the agents that specifically mention all three elements broaden your search to just "Fiction" and "Romance". As long as the new results don't specifically say they don't handle historical romance, these are still valid markets to approach. Finally, search for just "Fiction", as there are many agents who are willing to consider all kinds of fiction but don't specifically mention romance or historical.

Don't limit your approaches to just agents in your own country. With more and more agents accepting electronic queries it's now as easy to approach agents in other countries as in your own, and if you're ignoring either London or New York (the two main centres of English language publishing) you're cutting your chances of success in two.

7: Submit directly to publishers

Once you're certain that you've exhausted all potential agents for your work, you can start looking for publishers to submit your work directly to. You can search for publishers at https://www.firstwriter.com/publishers. Apply the same filtering as when you were searching for agents: start specific and gradually broaden, until you've exhausted all possibilities.

8: Self-publishing

In the past, once you got to the point where you'd submitted to all the publishers and agents who might be interested in your book, it would be time to pack away the manuscript in the attic, chalk it up to experience, and start writing another. However, these days writers have the option to take their book directly to market by publishing it themselves.

Before you decide to switch to self-publishing you must be sure that you've exhausted all traditional publishing possibilities – because once you've self-published your book you're unlikely to be able to submit it to agents and publishers. It will probably take a few years of exploring the world of traditional publishing to reach this point, but if you do then you've nothing to lose by giving self-publishing a shot. See our guide to self-publishing for details on how to proceed.

Why Choose Traditional Publishing

When **firstwriter.com** first started, back in 2001, there were only two games in town when it came to getting your book published: traditional publishing, and vanity publishing – and which you should pick was a no-brainer. Vanity publishing was little more than a scam that would leave you with an empty bank account and a house full of unsold books. If you were serious about being a writer, you had to follow the traditional publishing path.

Since then, there has been a self-publishing revolution, with new technologies and new printing methods giving writers a genuine opportunity to get their books into the market by themselves. So, is there still a reason for writers to choose traditional publishing?

The benefits of traditional publishing

Despite the allure and apparent ease of self-publishing, the traditional path still offers you the best chance of making a success of being a writer. There are rare cases where self-published writers make staggering fortunes and become internationally renowned on the back of their self-published books, but these cases are few and far between, and a tiny drop in the rapidly expanding ocean of self-published works. The vast majority of successful books – and the vast majority of successful writers – have their homes firmly in the established publishing houses. Even those self-published authors who find success usually end up moving to a traditional publisher in the end.

This is because the traditional publishers have the systems, the market presence, and the financial clout to *make* a book a bestseller. While successful self-published authors often owe their success in no small part to a decent dose of luck (a social media comment that goes viral; the right mention on the right media outlet at the right time), traditional publishers are in the business of engineering that success. They might not always succeed, but they have the marketing budgets and the distribution channels in place to give themselves, and the book they are promoting, the best possible chance.

And it's not just the marketing and the distribution. Getting signed with a traditional publisher brings a whole team of people with a wealth of expertise that will all work towards the success of the book. It will provide you with an editor who may have experience of working on previous bestsellers, who will not only help you get rid of mistakes in your work but may also help you refine it into a better book. They will help make sure that the quality of your content is good enough to make it in the marketplace.

The publishers will source a professional cover designer who will make your book look the part on the shelves and on the pages of the bookselling websites. They will have accountants who will handle the technicalities of tax regimes both home and abroad. They will have overseas contacts for establishing foreign publishing rights; translations; etc. They may even have contacts in the film industry, should there be a prospect of a movie adaptation. They will have experts working on every aspect of your book, right down to the printing and the warehousing and the shipping of the physical products. They will have people to manage the ebook conversion and the electronic distribution. As an author, you don't need to worry about any of this.

This means you get more time to simply be a writer. You may have to go on book tours, but even these will be organised for you by PR experts, who will also be handling all the press releases, etc.

And then there's the advances. Advances are up-front payments made by traditional publishers to authors, which are off-set against future royalties. So, an author might receive a $5,000 advance before their book is published. When the royalties start coming in, the publisher keeps the first $5,000 to off-set the advance. The good news for the author is that if the book flops and doesn't make $5,000 in royalties they still get to keep the full advance. In an uncertain profession, the security of an advance can be invaluable for an author – and of course it's not something available to self-published authors.

The drawbacks of traditional publishing

The main downside of traditional publishing is just that it's so hard to get into. If you choose to self-publish then – provided you have enough perseverance, the right help and advice, and perhaps a little bit of money – you are guaranteed to succeed and see your book in print and for sale. With traditional publishing, the cold hard fact is that most people who try will not succeed.

And for many of those people who fail it may not even be their fault. That aspect of traditional publishing which can bring so many benefits as compared to self-publishing – that of being part of a team – can also be part of its biggest drawback. It means that you have to get other people to buy into your book. It means that you have to rely on other people being competent enough to spot a bestseller. Many failed to spot the potential of the Harry Potter books. How many potential bestsellers never make it into print just because none of the professionals at the publishers' gates manage to recognise their potential?

So if you choose traditional publishing your destiny is not in your own hands – and for some writers the lack of exclusive control can also be a problem. Sometimes writers get defensive when editors try to tinker with their work, or annoyed when cover artists don't realise their vision the way they expect. But this is hardly a fair criticism of traditional publishing, as most writers (particularly when they are starting out) will benefit from advice from experienced professionals in the field, and will often only be shooting themselves in the foot if they insist on ignoring it.

The final main drawback with traditional publishing is that less of the sale price of each copy makes it to the writer. A typical royalty contract will give the writer 15%. With a self-published book, the author can expect to receive much more. So, all other things being equal, the self-published route can be more profitable – but, of course, all things are not equal. If self-publishing means lower sales (as is likely), then you will probably make less money overall. Remember, it's better to have 15% of something than 50% of nothing.

Conclusion

In conclusion, our advice to writers would be to aim for traditional publishing first. It might be a long shot, but if it works then you stand a much better chance of being successful. If you don't manage to get signed by an agent or a publisher then you still have the option of self-publishing, but make sure you don't get tempted to resort to self-publishing too soon – most agents and publishers won't consider self-published works, so this is a one-way street. Once you've self-published your work, you probably won't be able to change your mind and go back to the traditional publishers with your book unless it becomes a huge hit without them. It's therefore important that you exhaust all your traditional publishing options before making the leap to self-publishing. Be prepared for this to take perhaps a few years (lots of agents and publishers can take six months just to respond), and make sure you've submitted to everyone you can on *both* sides of the Atlantic (publishing is a global game these days, and you need to concentrate on the two main centres of English-language publishing (New York and London) equally) before you make the decision to self-publish instead.

Formatting Your Manuscript

Before submitting a manuscript to an agent, magazine, or publisher, it's important that you get the formatting right. There are industry norms covering everything from the size of your margins to the font you choose – get them wrong and you'll be marking yourself out as an amateur. Get them right, and agents and editors will be far more likely to take you seriously.

Fonts

Don't be tempted to "make your book stand out" by using fancy fonts. It *will* stand out, but not for any reason you'd want. Your entire manuscript should be in a monospaced font like Courier (not a proportional font, like Times Roman) at 12 points. (A monospaced font is one where each character takes up the same amount of space; a proportional font is where the letter "i" takes up less space than the letter "m".)

This goes for your text, your headings, your title, your name – everything. Your objective is to produce a manuscript that looks like it has been produced on a simple typewriter.

Italics / bold

Your job as the author is to indicate words that require emphasis, not to pick particular styles of font. This will be determined by the house style of the publisher in question. You indicate emphasis by underlining text; the publisher will decide whether they will use bold or italic to achieve this emphasis – you shouldn't use either in your text.

Margins

You should have a one inch (2.5 centimetre) margin around your entire page: top, bottom, left, and right.

Spacing

In terms of line spacing, your entire manuscript should be double spaced. Your word processor should provide an option for this, so you don't have to insert blank lines manually.

While line spacing should be double, spaces after punctuation should be single. If you're in the habit of putting two spaces after full stops this is the time to get out of that habit, and remove them from your manuscript. You're just creating extra work for the editor who will have to strip them all out.

Do not put blank lines between paragraphs. Start every paragraph (even those at the start of chapters) with an indent equivalent to five spaces. If you want a scene break then create a line with the "#" character centred in the middle. You don't need blank lines above or below this line.

Word count

You will need to provide an estimated word count on the front page of your manuscript. Tempting as it will be to simply use the word processor's word counting function to tell you exactly how many words there are in your manuscript, this is not what you should do. Instead, you should work out the maximum number of characters on a line, divide this number by six, and then multiply by the total number of lines in your manuscript.

Once you have got your estimated word count you need to round it to an approximate value. How you round will depend on the overall length of your manuscript:

- up to 1,500 words: round to the nearest 100;
- 1,500–10,000 words: round to the nearest 500;
- 10,000–25,000 words: round to the nearest 1,000;
- Over 25,000 words: round to the nearest 5,000.

The reason an agent or editor will need to know your word count is so that they can estimate how many pages it will make. Since actual pages include varying amounts of white space due to breaks in paragraphs, sections of speech, etc. the formula above will actually provide a better idea of how many pages will be required than an exact word count would.

And – perhaps more importantly – providing an exact word count will highlight you immediately as an amateur.

Layout of the front page

On the first page of the manuscript, place your name, address, and any other relevant contact details (such as phone number, email address, etc.) in the top left-hand corner. In the top right-hand corner write your approximate word count.

If you have registered your work for copyright protection, place the reference number two single lines (one double line) beneath your contact details. Since your manuscript will only be seen by agents or editors, not the public, this should be done as discreetly as possible, and you should refrain from using any official seal you may have been granted permissions to use. (For information on registering for copyright protection see "Protecting Your Copyright", below.)

Place your title halfway down the front page. Your title should be centred and would normally be in capital letters. You can make it bold or underlined if you want, but it should be the same size as the rest of the text.

From your title, go down two single lines (or one double line) and insert your byline. This should be centred and start with the word "By", followed by the name you are writing under. This can be your name or a pen name, but should be the name you want the work published under. However, make sure that the name in the top left-hand corner is your real, legal name.

From your byline, go down four single lines (or two double lines) and begin your manuscript.

Layout of the text

Print on only one side of the paper, even if your printer can print on both sides.

In the top right-hand corner of all pages except the first should be your running head. This should be comprised of the surname used in your byline; a keyword from your title, and the page number, e.g. "Myname / Mynovel Page 5".

Text should be left-aligned, *not* justified. This means that you should have a ragged right-hand edge to the text, with lines ending at different points. Make sure you don't have any sort of hyphenation function switched on in your word processor: if a word is too long to fit on a line it should be taken over to the next.

Start each new chapter a third of the way down the page with the centred chapter number / title, underlined. Drop down four single lines (two double lines) to the main text.

At the end of the manuscript you do not need to indicate the ending in any way: you don't need to write "The End", or "Ends", etc. The only exception to this is if your manuscript happens to end at the bottom of a page, in which case you can handwrite the word "End" at the bottom of the last page, after you have printed it out.

Protecting Your Copyright

Protecting your copyright is by no means a requirement before submitting your work, but you may feel that it is a prudent step that you would like to take before allowing strangers to see your material.

These days, you can register your work for copyright protection quickly and easily online. The Intellectual Property Rights Office operates a website called the "Copyright Registration Service" which allows you to do this:

- *https://www.CopyrightRegistrationService.com*

This website can be used for material created in any nation signed up to the Berne Convention. This includes the United States, United Kingdom, Canada, Australia, Ireland, New Zealand, and most other countries. There are around 180 countries in the world, and over 160 of them are part of the Berne Convention.

Provided you created your work in one of the Berne Convention nations, your work should be protected by copyright in all other Berne Convention nations. You can therefore protect your copyright around most of the world with a single registration, and because the process is entirely online you can have your work protected in a matter of minutes, without having to print and post a copy of your manuscript.

What is copyright?

Copyright is a form of intellectual property (often referred to as "IP"). Other forms of intellectual property include trade marks, designs, and patents. These categories refer to different kinds of ideas which may not exist in a physical form that can be owned as property in the traditional sense, but may nonetheless have value to the people who created them. These forms of intellectual property can be owned in the same way that physical property is owned, but – as with physical property – they can be subject to dispute and proper documentation is required to prove ownership.

The different types of intellectual property divide into these categories as follows:

- **Copyright:** copyright protects creative output such as books, poems, pictures, drawings, music, films, etc. Any work which can be recorded in some way can be protected by copyright, as long as it is original and of sufficient length. Copyright does not cover short phrases or names.

- **Trade marks:** trade marks cover words and/or images which distinguish the goods or services of one trader from another. Unlike copyright, trade marks can cover names and short phrases.

- **Designs:** designs cover the overall visual appearance of a product, such as its shape, etc.

- **Patents:** patents protect the technical or functional aspects of designs or inventions.

The specifics of the legal protection surrounding these various forms of intellectual property will vary from nation to nation, but there are also generally international conventions to which a lot if not most of the nations of the world subscribe. The information provided below outlines the common situation in many countries but you should be aware that this may not reflect the exact situation in every territory.

The two types of intellectual property most relevant to writers are copyright and trade marks. If a writer has written a novel, a short story, a poem, a script, or any other piece of writing then the contents themselves can be protected by copyright. The title, however, cannot be protected by copyright as it is a name. An author may therefore feel that they wish to consider protecting the title of their work by registering it as a trade mark, if they feel that it is particularly important and/or more valuable in itself than the cost of registering a trade mark.

If a writer wants to register the copyright for their work, or register the title of their work as a trade mark, there are generally registration fees to be paid. Despite the fact that copyright covers long works that could be hundreds of thousands of words long, while trade marks cover single words and short phrases, the cost for registering a trade mark is likely to be many times higher than that for registering a work for copyright protection. This is because trade marks must be unique and are checked against existing trade marks for potential conflicts. While works to be registered for copyright must also not infringe existing works, it is not practical to check the huge volume of new works to be registered for copyright against the even larger volume of all previously copyrighted works. Copyright registration therefore tends to simply archive the work in question as proof of the date at which the person registering the work was in possession of it.

In the case of both copyright and trade marks the law generally provides some protection even without any kind of registration, but registration provides the owner of the intellectual property with greater and more enforceable protection. In the case of copyright, the creator of a work usually automatically owns the copyright as soon as the work is recorded in some way (i.e. by writing it down or recording it electronically, etc.), however these rights can be difficult to prove if disputed, and therefore many countries (such as the United States) also offer an internal country-specific means of registering works. Some countries, like the United Kingdom, do not offer any such means of registration, however an international registration is available through the Intellectual Property Rights Office's Copyright Registration Service, and can be used regardless of any country-specific provisions. This can help protect copyright in all of the nations which are signatories of the Berne Convention.

In the case of trade marks, the symbol "TM" can be applied to any mark which is being used as a trade mark, however greater protection is provided if this mark is registered, in which case the symbol "®" can be applied to the mark. It is often illegal to apply the "®" symbol to a trade mark which has not been registered. There are also options for international registrations of trade marks, which are administered by the World Intellectual Property Organization, however applications cannot be made to the WIPO directly – applications must be made through the relevant office of the applicant's country.

Copyright law and its history

The modern concept of copyright can be traced back to 1710 and the "Statute of Anne", which applied to England, Scotland, and Wales. Prior to this Act, governments had granted monopoly rights to publishers to produce works, but the 1710 Act was the first time that a right of ownership was acknowledged for the actual creator of a work.

From the outset, the attempt to protect the creator's rights was beset with problems due to the local nature of the laws, which applied in Britain only. This meant that lots of copyrighted works were reproduced without the permission of the author in Ireland, America, and in European countries. This not only hindered the ability of the London publishers to sell their legitimate copies of their books in these territories, but the unauthorised reproductions would also find their way into Britain, harming the home market as well.

A natural progression for copyright law was therefore its internationalisation, beginning in 1846 with a reciprocal agreement between Britain and Prussia, and culminating in a series of international treaties, the principal of which is the Berne Convention, which applies to over 160 countries.

Traditionally in the United Kingdom and the United States there has been a requirement to register a work with an official body in order to be able to claim copyright over it (Stationers Hall and the US Library of Congress respectively), however this has been changed by the Berne Convention, which requires signatory countries to grant copyright as an automatic right: i.e. the creator of a work immediately owns its copyright by virtue of creating it and recording it in some physical way (for instance by writing it down or making a recording of it, etc.). The United Kingdom and the United States have both been slow to fully adopt this approach. Though the United Kingdom signed the Berne Convention in 1887, it took 100 years for it to be fully implemented by the Copyright Designs and Patents Act 1988. The United States did not even sign the convention until 1989.

In the United States the US Library of Congress continues to provide archiving services for the purposes of copyright protection, but these are now optional. US citizens no longer need to register their work in order to be able to claim copyright over it. It is necessary, however, to be able to prove when the person who created it did so, and this is essentially the purpose of the registration today. In the United Kingdom, Stationers Hall has ceased to exist, and there is no longer any state-run means of registering the copyright to unpublished works, leaving the only available options as independent and/or international solutions such as the copyright registration service provided by the IP Rights Office.

Registering your work for copyright protection

Registering your work for copyright protection can help you protect your rights in relation to your work. Generally (particularly if you live in a Berne Convention country, as most people do) registration will not be compulsory in order to have rights over your work. Any time you create a unique original work you will in theory own the copyright over it, however you will need to be able to prove when you created it, which is the purpose of registering your work for copyright protection. There are other ways in which you might attempt to prove this, but registration provides better evidence than most other forms.

There are a range of different options for protecting your copyright that vary depending on where you live and the kind of coverage you want. Some countries, like the United States, provide internal means of registering the copyright of unpublished works, however the scope of these will tend to be restricted to the country in question. Other countries, like the United

Kingdom, do not offer any specific government-sponsored system for registering the copyright of unpublished works. An international option is provided by the Intellectual Property Rights Office, which is not affiliated to any particular government or country. As long as you live in a Berne Convention country you should be able to benefit from using their Copyright Registration Service. You can register your work with the Intellectual Property Rights Office regardless of whether or not there are any specific arrangements in your home country (you may even choose to register with both to offer your work greater protection). Registration with the Intellectual Property Rights Office should provide you with protection throughout the area covered by the Berne Convention, which is most of the world.

Registering your work for copyright protection through the Intellectual Property Rights Office is an online process that can be completed in a few minutes, provided you have your file in an accepted format and your file isn't too large (if your file is too large and cannot be reduced you may have to split it and take out two or more registrations covering it). There is a registration fee to pay ($45 / £25 / €40 at the time of writing) per file for registration, however if you are a subscriber to **firstwriter.com** you can benefit from a 10% discount when you start the registration process on our site.

When registering your work, you will need to give some consideration to what your work actually consists of. This is a straightforward question if your work is a novel, or a screenplay, but if it is a collection of poetry or short stories then the issue is more difficult. Should you register your collection as one file, or register each poem separately, which would be more expensive? Usually, you can answer this question by asking yourself what you propose to do with your collection. Do you intend to submit it to publishers as a collection only? Or do you intend to send the constituent parts separately to individual magazines? If the former is the case, then register the collection as a single work under the title of the collection. If the latter is the case then this could be unwise, as your copyright registration certificate will give the name of the collection only – which will not match the names of the individual poems or stories. If you can afford to, you should therefore register them separately. If you have so many poems and / or stories to register that you cannot afford to register them all separately, then registering them as a collection will be better than nothing.

Proper use of the copyright symbol

The first thing to note is that for copyright there is only one form of the symbol (©), unlike trade marks, where there is a symbol for registered trade marks (®) and a symbol for unregistered trade marks (™).

To qualify for use of the registered trade mark symbol (®) you must register your trade mark with the appropriate authority in your country, whereas the trade mark symbol (™) can be applied to any symbol you are using as a trade mark. Use of the copyright symbol is more similar to use of the trade mark symbol, as work does not need to be registered in order to use it.

You can place the copyright symbol on any original piece of work you have created. The normal format would be to include alongside the copyright symbol the year of first publication and the name of the copyright holder, however there are no particular legal requirements regarding this. While it has historically been a requirement in some jurisdictions to include a copyright notice on a work in order to be able to claim copyright over it, the Berne Convention does not allow such restrictions, and so any country signed up to the convention no longer has this requirement. However, in some jurisdictions failure to include such a notice can affect the damages you may be able to claim if anyone infringes your copyright.

A similar situation exists in relation to the phrase "All Rights Reserved". This phrase was a requirement in order to claim international copyright protection in countries signed up to the 1910 Buenos Aires Convention. However, since all countries signed up to the Buenos Aires Convention are now also signed up to the Berne Convention (which grants automatic copyright) this phrase has become superfluous. The phrase continues to be used frequently but is unlikely to have any legal consequences.

The Berne Convention

The Berne Convention covers 162 of the approximately 190 countries in the world, including most major nations. Countries which are signed up to the convention are compelled to offer the same protection to works created in other signatory nations as they would to works created in their own. Nations not signed up to the Berne Convention may have their own arrangements regarding copyright protection.

You can check if your country is signed up to the Berne Convention at the following website:

- *https://www.CopyrightRegistrationService.com*

The status of your country should be shown automatically on the right side of the screen. If not, you can select your country manually from the drop-down menu near the top right of the page.

Should You Self-Publish?

Over recent years there has been an explosion in self-published books, as it has become easier and easier to publish your book yourself. This poses writers with a new quandary: continue to pursue publication through the traditional means, or jump into the world of self-publishing? As the rejections from traditional publishers pile up it can be tempting to reach for the control and certainty of self-publishing. Should you give into the temptation, or stick to your guns?

Isn't it just vanity publishing?

Modern self-publishing is quite different from the vanity publishing of times gone by. A vanity publisher would often pose or at least seek to appear to be a traditional publisher, inviting submissions and issuing congratulatory letters of acceptance to everyone who submitted – only slowly revealing the large fees the author would have to pay to cover the cost of printing the books.

Once the books were printed, the vanity publisher would deliver them to the author then cut and run. The author would be left with a big hole in their pocket and a mountain of boxes of books that they would be unlikely to ever sell a fraction of.

Modern self-publishing, on the other hand, is provided not by shady dealers but by some of the biggest companies involved in the publishing industry, including Penguin and Amazon. It doesn't have the large fees that vanity publishing did (depending on the path you choose and your own knowledge and technical ability it can cost almost nothing to get your book published); it *does* offer a viable means of selling your books (they can appear on the biggest bookselling websites around the world); and it *doesn't* leave you with a house full of unwanted books, because modern technology means that a copy of your book only gets printed when it's actually ordered.

That isn't to say that there aren't still shady characters out there trying to take advantage of authors' vanity by charging them enormous fees for publishing a book that stands very little chance of success, but it does mean that self-publishing – done right – can be a viable and cost effective way of an author taking their book to market.

The benefits of self-publishing

The main benefit of self-publishing, of course, is that the author gets control of whether their book is published or not. There is no need to spend years submitting to countless agents and publishers, building up countless heartbreaking rejection letters, and possibly accepting in the end that your dreams of publication will never come true – you can make them come true.

And this need not be pure vanity on the author's part. Almost every successful book – even such massive hits as *Harry Potter* – usually build up a string of rejections before someone finally accepts them. The professionals that authors rely on when going through the traditional publishing process – the literary agents and the editors – are often, it seems, just not that good at spotting what the public are going to buy. How many potential bestsellers might languish forever in the slush pile, just because agents and editors fail to spot them? What if your book is one of them? The traditional publishing process forces you to rely on the good judgment of others, but the self-publishing process enables you to sidestep that barrier and take your book directly to the public, so that readers can decide for themselves.

Self-publishing also allows you to keep control in other areas. You won't have an editor trying to change your text, and you'll have complete control over what kind of cover your book receives.

Finally, with no publisher or team of editors and accountants taking their slice, you'll probably get to keep a lot more of the retail price of every book you sell. So if you can sell the same amount of books as if you were traditionally published, you'll stand to make a lot more money.

The drawbacks of self-publishing

While self-publishing can guarantee that your book will be available for sale, it cannot guarantee that it will actually sell. Your self-published book will probably have a much lower chance of achieving significant sales than if it had been published traditionally, because it will lack the support that a mainstream publisher could bring. You will have no marketing support, no established position in the marketplace, and no PR – unless you do it yourself. You will have to arrange your own book tours; you will have to do your own sales pitches; you will have to set your own pricing structure; and you will have to manage your own accounts and tax affairs. If you're selling through Amazon or Smashwords or Apple (and if you're not, then why did you bother self-publishing in the first place?) you're going to need to fill in the relevant forms with the IRS (the US tax office) – whether you're a US citizen or not. If you're not a US citizen then you'll have to register with the IRS and complete the necessary tax forms, and potentially other forms for claiming treaty benefits so that you don't get taxed twice (in the US and your home country). And then of course you'll also have to register for tax purposes in your home nation and complete your own tax return there (though you would also have to do this as a traditionally published author).

It can all get very complicated, very confusing, and very lonely. Instead of being able to just be a writer you can find yourself writing less and less and becoming more and more embroiled in the business of publishing a book.

And while it's great to have control over your text and your cover, you'd be ill advised to ignore the value that professionals such as editors and cover designers can bring. It's tempting to think that you don't need an editor – that you've checked the book and had a friend or family member check it too, so it's probably fine – but a professional editor brings a totally different mindset to the process and will check things that won't have even occurred to you and your reader. Without a professional editor, you will almost certainly end up publishing a book which is full of embarrassing mistakes, and trust me – there is no feeling quite as deflating as opening up the first copy of your freshly printed book to see an obvious error jump out – or, even worse, to have it pointed out in an Amazon review, for all to see.

The cover is also incredibly important. Whether for sale on the shelf or on a website, the cover is normally the first point of contact your potential reader has with your book, and will cause them to form immediate opinions about it. A good cover can help a book sell well, but a bad one can kill its chances – and all too often self-published books have amateurish covers that will have readers flicking past them without a second glance.

Finally, the financial benefits of self-publishing can often be illusory. For starters, getting a higher proportion of the retail price is pretty irrelevant if you don't sell any copies. Fifty per cent of nothing is still nothing. Far better to have 15% of something. And then there's the advances. Advances are up-front payments made by traditional publishers to authors, which are off-set against future royalties. So, an author might receive a $5,000 advance before their book is published. When the royalties start coming in, the publisher keeps the first $5,000 to off-set the advance. The good news for the author is that if the book flops and doesn't make $5,000 in royalties they still get to keep the full advance. In an uncertain profession, the security of an advance can be invaluable for an author – and of course it's not something available to self-published authors.

Conclusion

Self-publishing can seem like a tempting shortcut to publication, but in reality it has its own challenges and difficulties. For the moment at least, traditional publishing still offers you the best shot of not only financial success, but also quality of life as a writer. With other people to handle all the other elements of publishing, you get to concentrate on doing what you love.

So we think that writers should always aim for traditional publishing first. It might be a long shot, but if it works then you stand a much better chance of being successful. If you don't manage to get signed by an agent or a publisher then you still have the option of self-publishing, but make sure you don't get tempted to resort to self-publishing too soon – most agents and publishers won't consider self-published works, so this is a one-way street. Once you've self-published your work, you probably won't be able to change your mind and go back to the traditional publishers with your book unless it becomes a huge hit without them. It's therefore important that you exhaust all your traditional publishing options before making the leap to self-publishing. Be prepared for this to take perhaps a few years (lots of agents and publishers can take six months just to respond), and make sure you've submitted to everyone you can on *both* sides of the Atlantic (publishing is a global game these days, and you need to concentrate on the two main centres of English-language publishing (New York and London) equally) before you make the decision to self-publish instead.

However, once you have exhausted all options for traditional publishing, modern self-publishing does offer a genuine alternative path to success, and there are a growing number of self-published authors who have managed to sell millions of copies of their books. If you don't think traditional publishing is going to be an option, we definitely think you should give self-publishing a shot.

For directions on your path through the traditional publishing process see our Writers' Roadmap, above.

If you're sure you've already exhausted all your options for traditional publishing then see below for our quick guide to the self-publishing process.

The Self-Publishing Process

Thinking about self-publishing your book? Make sure you go through all these steps first – and in the right order! Do them the wrong way round and you could find yourself wasting time and/or money.

1. Be sure you want to self-publish

You need to be 100% sure that you want to self-publish, because after you've done it there is no going back. Publishers and literary agents will not normally consider books that have been self-published, so if you wanted to get your book to print the old fashioned way you should stop now and rethink. Make absolutely sure that you've exhausted every possible opportunity for traditional publishing before you head down the self-publishing path.

For more information, see "Why choose traditional publishing?" and "Should you self-publish?", above.

2. Protect your copyright

Authors often wonder about what stage in the process they should protect their copyright – often thinking that it's best to leave it till the end so that there are no more changes to make to the book after it is registered.

However, this isn't the case. The key thing is to protect your work before you let other people see it – or, if you've already let other people see it, as soon as possible thereafter.

Don't worry about making small changes to your work after registering it – as long as the work is still recognisable as the same piece of work it will still be protected. Obviously, if you completely change everything you've written then you're going to need another registration, as it will effectively be a different book, but if you've just edited it and made minor alterations this won't affect your protection.

You can register you copyright online at https://www.copyrightregistrationservice.com.

3. Get your work edited

Editing is a vital step often overlooked by authors who self-publish. The result can often be an amateurish book littered with embarrassing mistakes. Any professionally published book will go through an editing process, and it's important that the same applies to your self-published book. It's also important to complete the editing process before beginning the layout, or you could find yourself having to start the layout again from scratch.

4. Choose your self-publishing path

Before you can go any further you are going to need to choose a size for your book, and in order to do that you are going to need to choose a self-publishing path.

There are various different ways of getting self-published, but in general these range from the expensive hands off approach, where you pay a company to do the hard work for you, to the cheap DIY approach, where you do as much as you can yourself.

At the top end, the hands off approach can cost you thousands. At the bottom end, the DIY approach allows you to publish your book for almost nothing.

5. Finalise your layout / typesetting

Before you can finalise your layout (often referred to in the industry as "typesetting") you need to be sure that you've finalised your content – which means having your full work professionally edited and all the necessary changes made. If you decide to make changes after this point it will be difficult and potentially costly, and will require you to go through many of the following steps all over again.

You also need to have selected your path to publication, so that you know what page sizes are available to you, and what page margins you are going to need to apply. If you create a layout that doesn't meet printing requirements (for instance, includes text too close to the edge of the page) then you will have to start the typesetting process all over again.

6. Organise your ISBN

Your book needs to have an ISBN. If you are using a self-publishing service then they may provide you with one of their own, but it is likely to come with restrictions, and the international record for your book will show your self-publishing service as the publisher.

You can acquire your own ISBNs directly from the ISBN issuer, but they do not sell them individually, so you will end up spending quite a lot of money buying more ISBNs than you need. You will, however, have control of the ISBN, and you will be shown as the publisher.

Alternatively, you can purchase a single ISBN at a lower price from an ISBN retailer. This should give you control over the ISBN, however the record for the book will show the ISBN retailer as the publisher, which you may not consider to be ideal.

Whatever you choose, you need to arrange your ISBN no later than this point, because it needs to appear in the preliminary pages (prelims) of your book.

7. Compile your prelims

Your prelims may include a variety of pages, but should always include a title page, a half title page, and an imprint/copyright page. You might then also include other elements, such as a foreword, table of contents, etc. You can only compile your table of contents at this stage, because you need to know your ISBN (this will be included on the copyright/imprint page) and the page numbers for your table of contents. You therefore need to make sure that you are happy with the typesetting and have no further changes to make before compiling your prelims.

8. Create your final press proof

Depending on the self-publishing path you have chosen, you may be able to use a Word file as your final document. However, you need to be careful. In order to print your book it will have to be converted into a press-ready PDF at some point. If a self-publishing service is doing this for you then you will probably find that they own the PDF file that is created, meaning you don't have control over your own press files. Some services will impose hefty charges (hundreds or even more than a thousand dollars) to release these press files.

It might also be the case that you won't get to see the final PDF, and therefore won't get chance to check it for any errors introduced by the conversion process. If it's an automated system, it may also be difficult to control the output you get from it.

We'd suggest that it's best to produce your own PDF files if possible. To do this you will need a copy of Adobe Acrobat Professional, and you will need to be familiar with the correct settings for creating print ready PDFs. Be careful to embed all fonts and make sure that all images are at 300 DPI.

9. Create your cover

Only once your press proof is finalised can you complete your cover design. That's because your cover includes not only the front cover and the back cover, but also (critically) the spine – and the width of the spine will vary according to the number of pages in your final press proof. In order to complete your cover design you therefore need to know your page size, your page count (including all prelims), and your ISBN, as this will appear on the back cover. You also need to get a barcode for your ISBN.

10. Produce your book

Once your cover and press proof are ready you can go through whichever self-publishing path you have chosen to create your book. With some pathways the production of a print proof can be an optional extra that is only available at an extra cost – but we'd recommend standing that cost and getting a print version of your book to check. You never know exactly how it's going to come out until you have a physical copy in your hand.

If you're happy with the proof you can clear your book for release. You don't need to do anything to get it on online retailers like Amazon – they will automatically pick up the ISBN and add your book to their websites themselves.

11. Create an ebook version

In the modern day, having an ebook version of your book is imperative. Ebooks account for a significant proportion of all book sales and are a particularly effective vehicle for unknown and self-published authors.

There are various different file formats used by the different platforms, but .epub is emerging as a standard, and having your book in .epub format should enable you to access all the platforms with a single file.

12. Distribute your ebook

Unlike with print books, you will need to act yourself to get your ebooks into sales channels. At a minimum, you need to ensure that you get your ebook available for sale through Amazon, Apple, and Google Play.

US Magazines

For the most up-to-date listings of these and hundreds of other magazines, visit https://www.firstwriter.com/magazines

*To claim your **free** access to the site, please see the back of this book.*

The Alembic

Providence College
English Department
Attn: The Alembic Editors
1 Cunningham Square
Providence, RI 02918-0001
Email: Alembic@providence.edu
Website: http://www.providence.edu/english/creative-writing/Pages/alembic.aspx

Publishes: Fiction; Poetry; Scripts; *Areas:* Drama; Short Stories; *Markets:* Adult; *Treatments:* Literary

Publishes poetry, drama, and fiction – including short stories and self-contained excerpts of novels. Send up to 5 poems or prose up to 6,000 words by post with return postage if return of material required. Accepts submissions from August 1 to November 30 annually.

A New Heart

PO Box 4004
San Clemente, CA 92474-4004
Email: HCFUSA@gmail.com
Website: http://www.hcfusa.com

Publishes: Articles; Nonfiction; Poetry; *Areas:* Health; Religious; *Markets:* Professional

Editors: Aubrey Beauchamp

Magazine aimed at healthcare workers, publishing articles with a Christian message. Also some limited space for poetry. Submit by email or by post with SASE. See website for full writers' guidelines.

A&U

Main Office
25 Monroe Street, Suite 205
Albany, New York 12210
Tel: +1 (518) 426-9010
Fax: +1 (518) 436-5354
Email: mailbox@aumag.org
Website: http://www.aumag.org

Articles; Essays; Fiction; Interviews; News; Nonfiction; Poetry; Reviews; *Areas:* Culture; Health; Medicine; Politics; Short Stories; *Markets:* Adult

Editors: David Waggoner

Publishes material covering the medical, cultural, and political responses to AIDS **only**. Does not publish material unconnected to AIDS so please do not send any. For fiction, and poetry, send complete MS. For nonfiction send query with published clips. Accepts approaches by email.

Able Muse

467 Saratoga Avenue, #602
San Jose, CA 95129
Email: submission@ablemuse.com
Website: http://www.ablemuse.com

Publishes: Essays; Fiction; Interviews; Nonfiction; Poetry; Reviews; *Areas:* Short Stories; Translations; *Markets:* Adult; *Treatments:* Light; Literary

Editors: Alex Pepple

Publishes mainly metrical poetry and poetry in translation. All forms of formal poetry welcome. Also publishes fiction, and nonfiction relating to metrical poetry, including book reviews and interviews. Accepts electronic submissions only – preferably using online submission system, but will also accept submissions by email. Welcomes humorous and light poetry. See website for full details.

The Account

Email: poetryprosethought@gmail.com
Website: http://theaccountmagazine.com

Publishes: Essays; Fiction; Nonfiction; Poetry; *Areas:* Short Stories; *Markets:* Adult; *Treatments:* Literary

Editors: Tyler Mills, Editor-in-Chief; Christina Stoddard, Managing Editor/ Publicist; Brianna Noll, Poetry Editor; Jennifer Hawe, Nonfiction Editor; M. Milks, Fiction Editor

Accepts poetry, fiction, and creative nonfiction, between May 1 and September 1, annually. Send 3-5 poems, essays up to 6,000 words, or fiction between 1,000 and 6,000 words, through online submission system. Each piece of work must be accompanied by an account between 150 and 500 words, giving voice to the artist's approach.

Adelaide Literary Magazine

1340 Stratford Avenue, Suite 3K
Bronx, NY 10472
Tel: +35 918 635 457
Email: info@adelaidemagazine.org
Website: http://www.adelaidemagazine.org

Publishes: Articles; Essays; Fiction; Interviews; News; Nonfiction; Poetry; Reviews; *Areas:* Arts; Criticism; Culture; Literature; Media; Short Stories; *Markets:* Academic; Adult; Professional; *Treatments:* Contemporary; Literary

Editors: Stevan V. Nikolic, Adelaide Franco Nikolic

An independent international quarterly publication, based in New York and Lisbon. Founded in 2015, the magazine'€™s aim is to publish quality poetry, fiction, nonfiction, artwork, and photography, as well as interviews, articles, and book reviews, written in English and Portuguese. Most of our content comes from unsolicited submissions.

We publish print, digital, and online editions of our magazine four times a year, in Fall (September), Winter (December), Spring (March), and Summer (June). The online edition is updated continuously. There are no charges for reading the magazine online.

The Adirondack Review

Email: editors@theadirondackreview.com
Website: http://adirondackreview.homestead.com

Publishes: Fiction; Nonfiction; Poetry; Reviews; *Areas:* Arts; Photography; Short Stories; Translations; Markets

Editors: Angela Leroux-Lindsey

Publishes poetry, fiction, translation, art, photography, and book reviews. Submit through online system via website.

Alebrijes

Email: alebrijesliterature@gmail.com
Website: http://www.alebrijeslit.org

Publishes: Essays; Fiction; Nonfiction; Poetry; *Markets:* Adult; *Treatments:* Experimental; Literary

Editors: Franco Strong; Anna Torres; Tiffany Ameline Zhu; Tyler Grinham

Publishes fiction, poetry, and lyrical essays. Particularly interested in pieces that play with form and structure, and surreal themes. In each reading period send up to one piece of fiction, one essay, or up to three poems, as Word file attachments. See website for full submission guidelines.

The Allegheny Review

Allegheny College Box 32
520 North Main Street
Meadville, PA 16335
Email: review@allegheny.edu
Website: https://alleghenyreview.wordpress.com

Publishes: Fiction; Nonfiction; Poetry; *Areas:* Short Stories; *Markets:* Adult; *Treatments:* Literary

National magazine publishing the work of enrolled undergraduate students. Submit fiction or creative nonfiction up to 20 double-spaced pages, or up to five poems. Submissions via online form only. See website for details.

Allegory

Email: submissions@allegoryezine.com
Website: http://www.allegoryezine.com

Publishes: Articles; Fiction; Nonfiction; *Areas:* Fantasy; Horror; Humour; Sci-Fi; Short Stories; *Markets:* Adult

Editors: Ty Drago

Online magazine specialising in science fiction, fantasy and horror, but also willing to consider humour and general interest fiction. No specific length restrictions for fiction, but stories under 500 words or over 5,000 may be hard sells. Also publishes articles up to 2,000 words on the art or business of writing. All submissions must be as attachments by email. See website for full guidelines.

Alligator Juniper

Prescott College
220 Grove Avenue
Prescott, AZ 86301
Email: alligatorjuniper@prescott.edu
Website: http://www.alligatorjuniper.org

Publishes: Fiction; Nonfiction; Poetry; *Areas:* Short Stories; *Markets:* Adult; *Treatments:* Literary

Annual magazine publishing winners and finalists from its annual competitions only. $18 entry fee. Open August 15 – October 15 each year. Submit through online submission system. Winner in each category receives $1,000. Submit up to 5 poems, or a piece of fiction or creative nonfiction up to 30 pages. No children's literature or strict genre work. All entrants receive a copy of the magazine.

Analog Science Fiction & Fact

44 Wall Street, Suite 904
New York, NY 10005-2401
Email: analog@dellmagazines.com
Website: http://www.analogsf.com

Publishes: Articles; Fiction; Poetry; *Areas:* Science; Sci-Fi; Short Stories; *Markets:* Adult

Editors: Trevor Quachri

Publishes short stories with few restrictions: the story must have some aspect of science or technology as an integral part of it (i.e. the story can't happen without it), and the characters must be believable (though not necassarily human), regardless of how fantastic the setting. For fiction, between 2,000 and 7,000 words for shorts is preferred, 10,000–20,000 words for novelettes, and 40,000–80,000 for serials. For serials, send query in first instance. Otherwise send complete MS.

Also publishes articles of current and future interest (i.e. at the cutting edge of research). Though subscribers tend to have a high level of technical knowledge they come from a wide variety of backgrounds, and therefore specialised jargon should be kept to a minimum. Contributors should also remember that the magazine is read largely for entertainment, and your style should reflect this.

Submit using online submission system on website. If absolutely necessary, accepts submissions by post with return postage. No submissions by fax or email. See website for full guidelines.

Ancient Paths

Email: skylarburris@yahoo.com
Website: http://www.editorskylar.com/magazine/table.html

Publishes: Fiction; Poetry; *Areas:* Religious; Short Stories; *Markets:* Adult; *Treatments:* Literary

Editors: Skylar Hamilton Burris

Contains writing and art that makes the reader both think and feel. The poems, stories, and art celebrate God, depict the consequences of sin, and explore man's struggle with faith. The editor favors works that convey a message subtly without directly telling the reader what to think. This magazine is a Christian publication, but works by non-Christian authors will be considered provided that the themes, values, and issues explored are appropriate in a Christian context.

As of 2012, this publication is online only.

Another Chicago Magazine (ACM)

Email: editors@anotherchicagomagazine.net
Website: http://www.anotherchicagomagazine.net

Publishes: Fiction; Nonfiction; Poetry; *Areas:* Short Stories; *Markets:* Adult; *Treatments:* Literary

Literary magazine publishing work by both new and established writers. Send up to 5 poems; fiction up to 7,500 words; or nonfiction up to 25 pages. Submit via website using online submission system only. $3 fee per submission.

Apalachee Review

PO Box 10469
Tallahassee, FL 32302
Email: ARsubmissions@gmail.com
Website: http://apalacheereview.org

Publishes: Fiction; Nonfiction; Poetry; *Areas:* Short Stories; *Markets:* Adult; *Treatments:* Literary

Editors: Michael Trammell; Jenn Bronson

Publishes fiction, poetry, and creative nonfiction. Send one story (or more, if very short), or 3-5 poems, with SASE. Will consider chapters of novels if they work by themselves, but no short story collections or novels. Accepts simultaneous submissions. Aims to reply within four months. Send query by email for details of submissions policies for writers outside the US. See website for full details.

Aphelion: The Webzine of Science Fiction and Fantasy

Alpharetta, GA
Email: editor@aphelion-webzine.com
Website: http://www.aphelion-webzine.com

Publishes: Essays; Features; Fiction; Interviews; Nonfiction; Poetry; Reviews; *Areas:* Adventure; Fantasy; Gothic; Horror; Humour; Literature; Sci-Fi; Short Stories; Suspense; Thrillers; *Markets:* Family; Professional; *Treatments:* Commercial; Contemporary; Cynical; Dark; Experimental; In-depth; Light; Literary; Mainstream; Niche; Popular; Positive; Progressive; Satirical; Serious; Traditional

Editors: Dan Hollifield, Nate Kailhofer, Curtis Manges, Iain Muir, Rob Wynne

Published since 1997. Free Science Fiction, Fantasy, and Horror Webzine which offers original fiction by new and established writers published on the first Sunday of every month except January. There is a double issue in December. The magazine includes poetry, short stories, serials and novellas, flash fiction, and reviews of interest to science fiction, fantasy, and horror fans. New writers are encouraged to submit their work to the webzine, and feedback to the authors is encouraged through the forum.

Appalachian Heritage

Borea College
101 Chestnut Street
Berea, KY 40403
Email: appalachianheritage@berea.edu
Website: http://appalachianheritage.net

Publishes: Essays; Fiction; Nonfiction; Poetry; Reviews; *Areas:* Short Stories; *Markets:* Adult; Youth; *Treatments:* Literary

Strives to be a literary sanctuary for the finest contemporary writing. Publishes previously unpublished fiction, creative nonfiction, poetry, writing for young adults, literary craft essays, book reviews, and visual art. No genre fiction.

Apple Valley Review

Email: editor@leahbrowning.net
Website: http://applevalleyreview.com

Publishes: Essays; Fiction; Nonfiction; Poetry; *Areas:* Short Stories; *Markets:* Adult; *Treatments:* Literary; Positive

Editors: Leah Browning

Online literary journal, publishing poetry, short fiction, and essays. Prose should be between 100 and 4,000 words. Preference is given to non-rhyming poetry under two pages in length. No genre fiction, scholarly, critical, inspirational, children's, erotica, explicit, violent, or depressing. Submit up to three prose pieces or up to six poems, by email. See website for full submission guidelines.

Aries

c/o Dr. Price
McMurray, General Editor
Texas Wesleyan University
Department of Languages and Literature
1201 Wesleyan
Fort Worth, TX 76105-1536
Email: aries@txwes.edu
Website: http://ariesjournal.wix.com/aries

Publishes: Essays; Fiction; Nonfiction; Poetry; Scripts; *Areas:* Drama; Short Stories; Theatre; *Markets:* Adult; *Treatments:* Literary

Editors: Dr Price McMurray (General Editor); Rolandra West (Managing Editor)

Literary journal inviting submissions of original, unpublished poetry (including poetry written by the author in Spanish and then translated to English); fiction; essays; one-act plays; and black-and-white photography and art. Submit up to 5 poems or one piece of prose up to 4,000 words, between August 15 and December 15 annually. See website for full submission guidelines.

Arsenic Lobster Poetry Journal

Email: lobster@magere.com
Website: http://arseniclobster.magere.com

Publishes: Poetry; *Markets:* Adult; *Treatments:* Literary

Send 3-5 poems of any length in the body of an email. No attachments. One submission per year. See website for more details.

Artifact Nouveau

Delta College, Shima 310
5151 Pacific Avenue
Stockton, CA 95207
Tel: +1 (209) 954-5533
Email: artifactsjdc@gmail.com
Website: https://www.deltacollege.edu/org/wrtrsgld/pubinfo.htm

Publishes: Essays; Fiction; Nonfiction; Poetry; *Areas:* Adventure; Arts; Autobiography; Criticism; Culture; Current Affairs; Drama; Entertainment; Erotic; Fantasy; Horror; Humour; Leisure; Lifestyle; Literature; Media; Music; Mystery; Nature; New Age; Philosophy; Photography; Politics; Romance; Sci-Fi; Short Stories; Spiritual; Suspense; Theatre; Thrillers; TV; Westerns; Women's Interests; *Markets:* Academic; Adult; *Treatments:* Contemporary; Experimental; In-depth; Literary; Popular; Progressive; Satirical; Serious; Traditional

A magazine of works by students, faculty, alumni, and employees of the college and Writers' Guild. Currently in its first year of publication, it is a re-branding of a previous publication (2007-2014). With a new advisor, officers, and editors, the magazine was re-booted to reflect its new beginnings. Its current format is 5.5 x 8.5 in a full color presentation. Works by writers and artists unaffiliated with the College may be selected for publication for up to 15% of the overall content. We accept submissions year round. All genres and mediums are welcome. Submit by email.

Asinine Poetry

Email: editor@asininepoetry.com
Website: http://www.asininepoetry.com

Publishes: Fiction; Poetry; *Areas:* Humour; Short Stories; *Markets:* Adult; *Treatments:* Satirical

Editors: Shay Tasaday

Online quarterly publishing humorous poetry and prose. Submit by email with material included in the body of the email. No attachments.

The Avalon Literary Review

PO Box 780696
Orlando, FL 32878
Email: submissions@avalonliteraryreview.com
Website: http://www.avalonliteraryreview.com

Publishes: Essays; Fiction; Nonfiction; Poetry; *Areas:* Short Stories; *Markets:* Adult; *Treatments:* Literary

Quarterly literary review. Submit up to three poems; one piece of fiction up to 2,500 words; up to two pieces of flash fiction up to 500 words each; or one personal essay up to 1,000 words, by email only. No query necessary. See website for full details.

The Baltimore Review

Email: editor@baltimorereview.org
Website: http://baltimorereview.org

Publishes: Essays; Fiction; Nonfiction; Poetry; *Areas:* Short Stories; *Markets:* Adult; *Treatments:* Literary

Editors: Barbara Westwood Diehl

Quarterly online literary journal. Submit 1-3 poems, or fiction or creative nonfiction up to 5,000 words, via online submission system. Also publishes annual collection in print. Reading periods are between August 1 and November 30, and February 1 and May 31.

Barbaric Yawp

3700 County Route 24
Russell, NY 13684
Website: http://www.boneworldpublishing.com

Publishes: Fiction; *Areas:* Adventure; Fantasy; Historical; Horror; Religious; Science; Sci-Fi; Short Stories; *Markets:* Adult; *Treatments:* Experimental; Literary; Mainstream

Send submissions by post, with SASE for reply.

Bartleby Snopes

Website: http://www.bartlebysnopes.com

Publishes: Fiction; *Areas:* Short Stories; *Markets:* Adult; *Treatments:* Literary

Publishes short stories between 1,000 and 3,000 words, and flash fiction up to 1,200 words (stories between 1,000 and 1,200 can be either). Submit online via website submission system.

Bayou Magazine

Department of English
University of New Orleans
2000 Lakeshore Drive
New Orleans, LA 70148
Email: bayou@uno.edu
Website: http://bayoumagazine.org

Publishes: Essays; Fiction; Nonfiction; Poetry; *Areas:* Short Stories; *Markets:* Adult; *Treatments:* Literary

Editors: Joanna Leake

National literary magazine. Publishes short stories, including flash fiction and short shorts; literary nonfiction, creative personal essays and lyric essays; and poetry. No gothic, horror, juvenile fiction, or scholarly articles. Submit a maximum of five poems at a time. Submit online via web system or by post with SASE for response only – mss will not be returned.

Bellevue Literary Review

NYU Langone Department of Medicine
550 First Avenue, OBV-A612
New York, NY 10016
Tel: +1 (212) 263-3973
Email: info@BLReview.org
Website: http://blr.med.nyu.edu

Publishes: Essays; Fiction; Nonfiction; Poetry; *Areas:* Short Stories; *Markets:* Adult; *Treatments:* Literary; Traditional

Publishes fiction, creative nonfiction, and poetry. Submit up to three poems maximum per submission. $5 reading fee for non-subscribers. Submit online using online submission system. Closed to submissions during July and August.

Berkeley Fiction Review

102 Hearst Gym MC: #4500
Berkeley, CA 94720
Email: berkeleyfictionreview@gmail.com
Website: http://berkeleyfictionreview.com

Publishes: Fiction; *Areas:* Short Stories; *Markets:* Adult; *Treatments:* Literary

Annual magazine of short fiction, inviting submissions from around the world. Send submissions as email attachments in .doc or .pdf format, double-spaced and up to 30 pages maximum. Do not paste stories into the body of the email. No hard copy submissions. Accepts multiple submissions, and also simultaneous submissions, provided notification is given of acceptance elsewhere. Response time varies between about three months and a year.

Best New Writing

PO Box 11
Titusville, NJ 08560
Email: info@bestnewwriting.com
Website: http://www.bestnewwriting.com

Publishes: Essays; Fiction; Nonfiction; *Areas:* Short Stories; *Markets:* Adult

Accepts unpublished fiction and creative nonfiction under 10,000 words. No simultaneous submissions. Maximum one submission per quarter.

Big Bridge

Email: walterblue@bigbridge.org
Website: http://www.bigbridge.org

Publishes: Essays; Fiction; Nonfiction; Poetry; *Areas:* Short Stories; *Markets:* Adult; *Treatments:* Literary

Editors: Michael Rothenberg and Terri Carrion

Publishes poetry, fiction, nonfiction, essays, journalism, and art of all kinds. Only open to submissions at specific times – see website for current status.

Big Pulp

Email: editors@bigpulp.com
Website: http://www.bigpulp.com

Publishes: Fiction; Poetry; *Areas:* Adventure; Fantasy; Horror; Mystery; Romance; Sci-Fi; Short Stories; *Markets:* Adult

Quarterly magazine of genre fiction and poetry, including horror, fantasy, science fiction, mystery and romance.

Bilingual Review

Hispanic Research Center
Arizona State University
PO Box 875303
Tempe, AZ 85287-5303
Tel: +1 (480) 965-3867
Fax: +1 (480) 965-0315
Email: brp@asu.edu
Website: https://www.asu.edu/brp/bilin/bilin.html

Publishes: Articles; Fiction; Nonfiction; Poetry; Reviews; Scripts; *Areas:* Criticism; Drama; Literature; Short Stories; *Markets:* Academic; Adult; *Treatments:* Literary

Scholarly/literary journal on the linguistics and literature of bilingualism and bilingual education. Publishes scholarly articles, literary criticism, book reviews, and creative literature: poetry, short stories, essays, and short theatre. Accepts material in English or Spanish. No previously published work. US Hispanic themes only. Response time is 2-3 months.

Blackbird

VCU Department of English
PO Box 843082
Richmond, VA 23284-3082
Email: blackbird@vcu.edu
Website: http://www.blackbird.vcu.edu

Publishes: Essays; Fiction; Nonfiction; Poetry; *Areas:* Short Stories; *Markets:* Adult; *Treatments:* Literary

Publishes, poetry, short stories, novel excerpts (if self-contained), personal essays, and memoir excerpts (if self-contained). Send up to six poems maximum at a time. Reading period runs from November 1 to April 15. Will consider long works, but query before submitting prose over 8,000 words or poems over 10 pages. No unsolicited books reviews or criticism.

Prefers to receive submissions through online submission system.

Blueline

120 Morey Hall, SUNY Potsdam
Potsdam, NY 13676
Email: blueline@potsdam.edu
Website: http://bluelinemagadk.com

Publishes: Essays; Fiction; Nonfiction; Poetry; *Areas:* Nature; Short Stories; *Markets:* Adult; *Treatments:* Literary

Publishes poems, stories and essays about the Adirondacks and regions similar in geography and spirit, focussing on nature's shaping influence. Accepts submissions from July to November. Submit by post, or by email with Word file attachments. See website for full details.

Bluestem

Email: info@bluestemmagazine.com
Website: http://www.bluestemmagazine.com

Publishes: Essays; Fiction; Nonfiction; Poetry; *Areas:* Short Stories; *Markets:* Adult; *Treatments:* Literary

Editors: Charlotte Pence

Submit one short story or creative nonfiction essay, or up to five poems at a time, via online submission system.

Boys' Quest

Fun For Kidz Magazines
ATTN: Submissions
PO Box 227
Bluffton, OH 45817
Tel: +1 (419) 358-4610
Website: http://funforkidzmagazines.com

Publishes: Articles; Fiction; Nonfiction; Poetry; *Areas:* Cookery; Entertainment; Hobbies; Nature; Science; Short Stories; Sport; *Markets:* Children's

Magazine aimed at boys aged 6-13 (focussing on ages 8-10), publishing articles, fiction, nonfiction, and poetry that deal with timeless topics, such as pets, nature, hobbies, science, games, sports, careers, simple cooking, and anything else likely to interest a 10-year-old boy. No submissions by email.

All issues are themed – see website for upcoming themes.

Bread for God's Children

PO Box 1017
Arcadia, FL 34265
Tel: +1 (863) 494-6214
Email: bread@breadministries.org
Website: http://www.breadministries.org

Publishes: Articles; Features; Fiction; Nonfiction; *Areas:* Religious; *Markets:* Children's; Youth

Christian magazine aimed at children and young adults. Looks for teaching stories that portray Christian lifestyles without preaching.

Brilliant Corners

Lycoming College
700 College Place
Williamsport, PA 17701
Email: feinstein@lycoming.edu
Website: http://www.lycoming.edu/brilliantcorners

Publishes: Fiction; Nonfiction; Poetry; *Areas:* Literature; Music; *Markets:* Adult; *Treatments:* Literary

Editors: Dr Sascha Feinstein

Publishes fiction, poetry, and nonfiction related to jazz. Send submissions by post with SASE. No fax or email submissions. Reading period runs from September 1 to May 15 annually.

Bryant Literary Review

Faculty Suite F
Bryant University
1150 Douglas Pike
Smithfield, RI 02917
Email: blr@bryant.edu
Website: http://bryantliteraryreview.org

Publishes: Fiction; Poetry; *Areas:* Short Stories; *Markets:* Adult; *Treatments:* Literary

Publishes poetry and fiction. Submit one story up to 5,000 words or up to five poems by post only with SASE. No submissions by email. Reading period runs from September 1 to December 1 annually.

Bugle

Rocky Mountain Elk Foundation
5705 Grant Creek
Missoula, MT 59808
Tel: (800) 225-5355
Email: bugle@rmef.org
Website: http://www.rmef.org/NewsandMedia/BugleMagazine.aspx

Publishes: Articles; Essays; Fiction; Nonfiction; Poetry; *Areas:* Adventure; Historical; Hobbies; Humour; Nature; *Markets:* Adult

Editors: PJ DelHomme

Magazine of elk hunting and conservation. Publishes relevant articles, essays, and also fiction and poetry on the subject.

Bust

253 36th Street, Suite C307
Brooklyn, NY 11232
Email: submissions@bust.com
Website: http://bust.com

Publishes: Articles; Features; Fiction; News; Nonfiction; *Areas:* Beauty and Fashion; Cookery; Crafts; Culture; Erotic; Health; Music; Travel; Women's Interests; *Markets:* Adult

Editors: Debbie Stoller

Magazine for women, publishing a variety of nonfiction, plus erotic fiction. No poetry or other forms of fiction considered. See website for full details and submission guidelines.

Cadet Quest

PO Box 7259
Grand Rapids, MI 49510-7259
Tel: +1 (616) 241-5616
Email: submissions@calvinistcadets.org
Website: http://www.calvinistcadets.org

Publishes: Articles; Fiction; Nonfiction; *Areas:* Adventure; Hobbies; Humour; Religious; Short Stories; *Markets:* Children's

Editors: G. Richard Broene

Publishes fiction and nonfiction for boys aged 9-14, presenting Christian life and helping boys relate to Christian values in their own lives. Issues are themed. View website for details or send request with SASE. Submit complete ms. Do not query first.

The Cafe Irreal

Email: editors@cafeirreal.com
Website: http://www.cafeirreal.com

Publishes: Fiction; *Areas:* Short Stories; *Markets:* Adult; *Treatments:* Literary

Quarterly webzine publishing fantastic fiction resembling the work of writers such as Franz Kafka and Jorge Luis Borges. Send stories up to 2,000 in the body of an email. No simultaneous submissions.

Callaloo

249 Blocker Hall, 4212 TAMU
College Station, TX 77843-4212
Tel: +1 (979) 458-3108
Fax: +1 (979) 458-3275
Email: callaloo@tamu.edu
Website: http://callaloo.tamu.edu

Publishes: Articles; Essays; Fiction; Interviews; Nonfiction; Poetry; Reviews; *Areas:* Arts; Culture; Literature; Short Stories; *Markets:* Academic; Adult; *Treatments:* Literary

Editors: Charles H. Rowell

Literary journal devoted to creative work by and critical studies of the work of African Americans and peoples of African descent throughout the African Diaspora. Submit via online submission system.

Camas

Email: camas@mso.umt.edu
Website: http://www.camasmagazine.org

Publishes: Essays; Fiction; Nonfiction; Poetry; *Areas:* Nature; *Markets:* Adult; *Treatments:* Literary

Publishes fiction, essays, and poetry that examines the relationships between individuals, communities, and the natural world in the American West. Issues are themed: see website for current theme and to submit via online submission system.

The Carolina Quarterly

510 Greenlaw Hall
CB# 3520
The University of North Carolina at Chapel Hill
Chapel Hill, NC 27599-3520
Tel: +1 (919) 408-7786
Email: carolina.quarterly@gmail.com
Website: http://thecarolinaquarterly.com

Publishes: Essays; Fiction; Nonfiction; Poetry; *Areas:* Autobiography; Short Stories; Travel; *Markets:* Adult; *Treatments:* Literary

Publishes poetry, fiction, nonfiction, and visual art. Submit by post or through online submission system from September to May. Send up to 6 poems, or one piece of prose. As well as fiction, increasingly looking for nonfiction, including personal essays, travel writing, memoirs, and other forms of creative nonfiction. Novel excerpts acceptable if self-contained.

Caveat Lector

400 Hyde St. #606
San Francisco, CA 94109
Email: caveatlectormagazine@gmail.com
Website: http://www.caveat-lector.org

Publishes: Essays; Fiction; Nonfiction; Poetry; *Areas:* Arts; Criticism; Literature; Short Stories; *Markets:* Adult; *Treatments:* Literary

Online magazine dedicated to literature, social and cultural criticism, philosophy, and the arts. Send poetry submissions by post only, between February 1 and June 30. Prose, art, and multimedia accepted year-round by post or by email (up to 5MB). Postal submissions should include brief bio and SASE.

The Chaffin Journal

Department of English
467 Case Annex
Eastern Kentucky University
Richmond, KY 40475
Email: robert.witt@eku.edu
Website: http://english.eku.edu/chaffin-journal

Publishes: Fiction; Poetry; *Areas:* Short Stories; *Markets:* Adult; *Treatments:* Literary

Editors: Robert W. Witt

Annual literary journal, open to all forms, subjects, schools, and styles. Send 3-5 poems, or short fiction up to 10,000 words, by post.

Chantarelle's Notebook

Email: chantarellesnotebook@yahoo.com
Website: http://www.chantarellesnotebook.com

Publishes: Poetry; *Markets:* Adult; *Treatments:* Literary

Poetry ezine. Submit 3-5 poems per reading period, pasted into the body of an email (no attachments) with cover letter and bio, up to 75 words.

The Chattahoochee Review

Georgia State University's Perimeter College
555 North Indian Creek Drive
Clarkston, GA 30021
Email: gpccr@gpc.edu
Website: http://thechattahoocheereview.gpc.edu

Publishes: Essays; Fiction; Interviews; Nonfiction; Poetry; Reviews; *Areas:* Arts; Short Stories; Translations; *Markets:* Adult; *Treatments:* Literary

Editors: Anna Schachner

Publishes fiction, poetry, reviews, essays, interviews, translations, and visual art. See website for details and for online submission system. No paper submissions.

Chicago Quarterly Review

517 Sherman Avenue
Evanston, IL 60202
Email: cqr@icogitate.com
Website: http://www.chicagoquarterlyreview.com

Publishes: Essays; Fiction; Nonfiction; Poetry; *Areas:* Short Stories; *Markets:* Adult; *Treatments:* Literary

Editors: S. Afzal Haider; Elizabeth McKenzie

Submit fiction or personal essays up to 5,000 words, or 3-5 poems, via online submission system.

Chicago Review

935 East 60th Street
Chicago, IL 60637
Email: chicagoreviewmail@gmail.com
Website: http://chicagoreview.org

Publishes: Essays; Fiction; Nonfiction; Poetry; Reviews; *Areas:* Criticism; Literature; Short Stories; *Markets:* Adult; *Treatments:* Literary

Send fiction up to 5,000 words, or poetry of any length (prefers to see at least three pages). Also publishes critical essays, books reviews, and review essays, but query by email before submitting nonfiction.

Cimarron Review

205 Morrill Hall
English Department
Oklahoma State University
Stillwater, OK 74078
Email: cimarronreview@okstate.edu
Website: https://cimarronreview.com

Publishes: Fiction; Poetry; *Areas:* Short Stories; *Markets:* Adult; *Treatments:* Literary

Editors: Toni Graham

Submit 3-6 poems or one piece of fiction by post or through online submission system. No fixed length restrictions, but rarely publishes short shorts or fiction over 25 pages. See website for full submission guidelines.

Cloud Rodeo

Email: submit@cloudrodeo.org
Website: https://cloudrodeo.org

Publishes: Fiction; Nonfiction; Poetry; *Markets:* Adult; *Treatments:* Experimental; Literary

Editors: Jake Syersak

Describes itself as a journal of the irregular. Send 3-5 short pieces or one longer piece of fiction, nonfiction, or poetry, as a Word or PDF attachment by email.

Cloudbank

PO Box 610,
Corvallis, OR 97339-0610
Tel: +1 (877) 782-6762
Email: michael@cloudbankbooks.com
Website: http://www.cloudbankbooks.com

Publishes: Fiction; Poetry; *Areas:* Short Stories; *Markets:* Adult; *Treatments:* Literary

Editors: Michael Malan

Publishes poetry and flash fiction. Submit up to five poems or up to five pieces of flash fiction by post or via online submission system. Online submissions require payment of a $3 fee.

Coal City Review

English Department
University of Kansas
Lawrence KS, 66045
Email: briandal@ku.edu
Website: https://coalcitypress.com

Publishes: Fiction; Poetry; *Areas:* Short Stories; *Markets:* Adult; *Treatments:* Literary

Editors: Brian Daldorph

Publishes poetry, short stories, and flash fiction. Send up to 6 poems, or one story up to 4,000 words, per year. Submissions by post only, with SASE for reply.

Cold Mountain Review

Attn: Poetry/Nonfiction/Fiction/Art Submission
Department of English
ASU Box 32052
Boone, NC 28608-2052

Email: coldmountain@appstate.edu
Website: http://coldmountain.appstate.edu

Publishes: Essays; Fiction; Interviews; Nonfiction; Poetry; *Areas:* Autobiography; Short Stories; *Markets:* Adult; *Treatments:* Literary

Send up to five poems, creative nonfiction up to 6,000 words, interviews up to five double-spaced pages, or fiction up to 6,000 words, by post or via online submission system. See website for full details and to submit.

The Collagist

Email: fiction@thecollagist.com
Website: http://thecollagist.com

Publishes: Essays; Fiction; Nonfiction; Poetry; Reviews; *Areas:* Literature; Short Stories; *Markets:* Adult; *Treatments:* Literary

Editors: Gabriel Blackwell (fiction and excerpts); Matthew Olzmann (poetry and nonfiction)

Online journal publishing short fiction, poetry, essays, book reviews, and excerpts from novels. Reads submissions from March 1-August 31 and from October 1-January 31. Poetry and nonfiction submissions closed until summer 2016.

Colorado Review

9105 Campus Delivery
Department of English
Colorado State University
Fort Collins, CO 80523-9105
Tel: +1 (970) 491-5449
Fax: +1 (970) 491-0283
Email: creview@colostate.edu
Website: http://coloradoreview.colostate.edu/colorado-review/

Publishes: Essays; Fiction; Nonfiction; Poetry; Reviews; *Areas:* Short Stories; *Markets:* Adult; *Treatments:* Literary

Send full MSS with cover letter through online submission system ($3 charge) or by post with SASE. Poetry and fiction read between August 1 and April 30 only. Nonfiction read year-round. No specific word limit, but generally publishes short stories and essays between 15 and 25 manuscript pages. Submit up to five poems in any style at one time. No unsolicited book reviews – query first. Simultaneous submissions are accepted if immediate notification is given of acceptance elsewhere. No previously published material.

Columbia: A Journal of Literature and Art

Email: info@columbiajournal.org
Website: http://columbiajournal.org

Publishes: Essays; Fiction; Poetry; *Areas:* Arts; Film; Music; Short Stories; Translations; *Markets:* Adult; *Treatments:* Literary

Publishes poetry, fiction, nonfiction, translations, art, film, and music. Submit via online submission system. Send up to 5 pages of poetry, or up to 7,500 words of prose. See website for details of specific reading periods for print and online editions.

Compose

Email: editor@composejournal.com
Website: http://composejournal.com

Publishes: Articles; Fiction; Interviews; Nonfiction; Poetry; *Areas:* How-to; Literature; Short Stories; *Markets:* Adult; *Treatments:* Literary

Online journal publishing fiction, poetry, creative nonfiction, articles on the craft of writing (both practical and inspirational), interviews with established writers, literary agents, editors, etc. excerpts from traditionally published works, photography and artwork. Submit online via website.

Conduit

788 Osceola Avenue
St Paul, MN 55105
Email: waltz@conduit.org
Website: http://www.conduit.org

Publishes: Fiction; Poetry; *Areas:* Short Stories; *Markets:* Adult; *Treatments:* Literary

Editors: William D. Waltz; Brett Astor

Publishes previously unpublished poetry and prose that demonstrates originality, intelligence, courage, irreverence, and humanity. Send 3-5 poems or 1 prose piece up to 3500 words with SASE. No online submissions.

Confrontation Magazine

English Department
LIU Post
Brookville, NY 11548
Email: confrontationmag@gmail.com
Website: http://confrontationmagazine.org

Publishes: Essays; Fiction; Nonfiction; Poetry; *Areas:* Autobiography; Culture; Politics; Short Stories; *Markets:* Adult; *Treatments:* Literary

Editors: Jonna G. Semeiks

Submit fiction up to 7,500 words; up to six pieces of flash fiction up to 500 words per piece; up to six poems up to two pages each; or cultural, political, or other types of essays or self-contained sections of memoirs up to 5,000 words. Will consider genre fiction if it has literary merit. Accepts email submissions from writers outside the US only.

Connecticut River Review

PO Box 516
Cheshire, CT 06410
Email: connpoetry@comcast.net
Website: http://www.ctpoetry.net/publications.html

Publishes: Poetry; *Markets:* Adult; *Treatments:* Literary

Editors: Pat Mottola

Poetry magazine accepting submissions nationally and internationally during the annual reading period from January 1 to April 15. Send 3-5 original unpublished poems on any topic (5 pages maximum) with SASE for response only (no poems will be returned). See website for full details.

Connotation Press

Website: http://www.connotationpress.com

Publishes: Fiction; Interviews; Nonfiction; Poetry; Reviews; Scripts; *Areas:* Drama; Literature; Music; Short Stories; *Markets:* Adult; *Treatments:* Literary

Editors: Ken Robidoux

Online journal publishing poetry, fiction, creative nonfiction, playwriting, screenplays, interviews, book reviews and music reviews. Send 3-5 poems, one story or chapter, 1-5 flash fiction pieces, one piece of creative nonfiction, or one script. Accepts unsolicited reviews, but also welcomes initial enquiries. For interviews, submit short treatment. See website for full guidelines.

Contemporary Haibun Online

Email: bob.lucky01@yahoo.com
Website: http://www.contemporaryhaibunonline.com

Publishes: Poetry; *Markets:* Adult; *Treatments:* Literary

Editors: Bob Lucky (Content Editor); Ray Rasmussen (Technical Editor)

Quarterly journal publishing haibun and tanka prose only. Send submissions by email during the following submission windows only:

Oct 15 – Nov 30
Jan 15 – Feb 28
April 15 – May 31
July 15 – Aug 31

Cottonwood

Room 400 Kansas Union
1301 Jayhawk Boulevard
University of Kansas
Lawrence, KS 66045
Email: tlorenz@ku.edu
Website: http://englishcw.ku.edu/cottonwood

Publishes: Essays; Fiction; Nonfiction; Poetry; *Areas:* Short Stories; *Markets:* Adult; *Treatments:* Literary

Editors: Tom Lorenz (Prose); Phil Wedge (Poetry)

Nationally circulated literary review. Send 4-6 poems or essays or short stories up to 8,500 words. Address material to appropriate editor.

Crab Creek Review

P.O. Box 840
Vashon, WA 98070
Tel: +1 (206) 463-5668
Email: crabcreekreview@gmail.com
Website: http://www.crabcreekreview.org

Publishes: Essays; Fiction; Nonfiction; Poetry; *Areas:* Short Stories; *Markets:* Adult; *Treatments:* Literary

Editors: Jenifer Lawrence

Submit fiction or creative nonfiction up to 3,500 words, or up to four poems, up to eight pages total, via online submission system. Only accepts material during specific reading periods. See website for details.

Crucible

Email: crucible@barton.edu
Website: https://www.barton.edu/crucible/

Publishes: Fiction; Poetry; *Areas:* Short Stories; *Markets:* Adult; *Treatments:* Literary

Send up to 5 poems or fiction up to 8,000 words by email. All submissions entered into poetry or fiction contest, with $150 prize and $100 runner-up prize in each.

Cruising Outpost Magazine

Box 100,
Berry Creek, 95916
Tel: +1 (510) 900-3616
Email: submissions@cruisingoutpost.com
Website: http://cruisingoutpost.com

Publishes: Articles; Essays; Interviews; Nonfiction; *Areas:* Cookery; How-to; Technology; Travel; *Markets:* Adult

Magazine covering boats/cruising. Submit via form on website.

The Cumberland River Review

Trevecca Nazarene University
Department of English
333 Murfreesboro Road
Nashville, TN 37210
Email: crr@trevecca.edu
Website: http://crr.trevecca.edu

Publishes: Essays; Fiction; Nonfiction; Poetry; *Areas:* Short Stories; *Markets:* Adult; *Treatments:* Literary

Quarterly online publication of new poetry, fiction, essays, and art. Submit 3-5 poems or one short story or one essay up to 5,000 words, between September and April only. Submissions accepted by post with SASE, but encourages submissions through online submission system via website.

The Daily Tea

Media40
1000 Germantown Pike, Suite F2
Plymouth Meeting, PA 19462
Tel: +1 (484) 688-0299
Email: alexis@thedailytea.com
Website: http://thedailytea.com

Publishes: Articles; Essays; Features; Interviews; Nonfiction; *Areas:* Historical; How-to; Humour; Travel; *Markets:* Adult

Magazine publishing material relating to tea. Send query with proposal or complete ms.

The Dark

Email: thedarkmagazine@gmail.com
Website: http://thedarkmagazine.com

Publishes: Fiction; *Areas:* Fantasy; Horror; *Markets:* Adult; *Treatments:* Dark

Publishes horror and dark fantasy stories between 2,000 and 6,000 words. No graphic, violent horror. Send submissions by email as .doc or .rtf attachment. See website for full guidelines.

Darkling

Darkling Publications
28780 318th Avenue
Colome, SD 57528
Email: darkling@mitchelltelecom.net
Website: http://darklingpublications.com

Publishes: Poetry; *Markets:* Adult; *Treatments:* Dark; Literary

Editors: James C. Van Oort

Open to submissions of dark poetry between October and May 15, annually. Submit up to 8 poems of any length by post with SASE or by email, either in the body of the email or as an attachment.

The Dead Mule School of Southern Literature

Email: deadmule@gmail.com
Website: http://www.deadmule.com

Publishes: Essays; Fiction; Nonfiction; Poetry; *Areas:* Short Stories; *Markets:* Adult; *Treatments:* Literary

Online journal of Southern literature. Submit online via website.

december

PO Box 16130
St Louis, MO 63105
Email: editor@decembermag.org
Website: http://decembermag.org

Publishes: Essays; Fiction; Nonfiction; Poetry; *Areas:* Autobiography; Biography; Culture; Short Stories; *Markets:* Adult; *Treatments:* Literary

Editors: Jennifer Goldring

Small magazine publishing poetry, fiction, and creative nonfiction (essays, memoirs, biography, literary journalism, social or cultural commentary or analysis). Original, unpublished work only (no self published or online published material). No simultaneous submissions. Submit online via website between October 1 and May 1 only.

Denver Quarterly

University of Denver
Department of English
2000 E. Asbury
Denver, CO 80208
Email: denverquarterly@gmail.com
Website: http://www.du.edu/denverquarterly

Publishes: Essays; Fiction; Interviews; Nonfiction; Poetry; Reviews; *Areas:* Short Stories; *Markets:* Adult; *Treatments:* Literary

Editors: Laird Hunt

Submit prose up to 15 pages, or 3-5 poems, between September 15 and May 15 annually, by post with SASE or via online submission system on website.

The Deronda Review

P.O. Box 55164
Madison, WI 53705
Email: derondareview@att.net
Website: http://www.derondareview.org

Publishes: Poetry; *Markets:* Adult; *Treatments:* Literary

Editors: Esther Cameron; Mindy Aber Barad (Co-editor for Israel)

Literary magazine publishing mainly poetry, but will consider reflective prose up to 500 words (especially expository blank verse). First-time contributors (unless in Israel) should submit by post with SASE.

Devil's Lake

600 North Park Street, Suite 6195
Madison, WI 53706
Email: devilslake.editor@gmail.com
Website: https://english.wisc.edu/devilslake

Publishes: Fiction; Nonfiction; Poetry; *Areas:* Short Stories; *Markets:* Adult; *Treatments:* Literary

Submit 3-5 poems, or fiction or nonfiction up to 4,500 words, via online submission system only. See website for full details, and to submit.

Diagram

Dept of English, PO Box 210067
University of Arizona
Tucson, AZ 85721-0067
Email: editor@thediagram.com
Website: http://thediagram.com

Publishes: Fiction; Nonfiction; Poetry; Reviews; *Areas:* Short Stories; *Markets:* Adult; *Treatments:* Literary

Editors: Ander Monson

Online literary journal publishing text, images, and new media. No material previously published in print or online (except personal websites). Submit material online through submission manager, or (if necessary) by post. See website for full guidelines.

The Dos Passos Review

Longwood University
Department of English and Modern Languages
201 High Street
Farmville, VA 23909
Email: dospassosreview@gmail.com
Website: https://brierycreekpress.wordpress.com/the-dos-passos-review/

Publishes: Fiction; Nonfiction; Poetry; *Markets:* Adult; *Treatments:* Literary

Publishes unpublished literary fiction, creative nonfiction, and poetry; particularly writing that explores specifically American themes. No genre fiction, experimentation for the sake of experimentation, or scholarly or critical nonfiction. Send submissions by email as Word attachments between April 1 and July 31, or between February 1 and May 31. See website for full details.

Down in the Dirt

Email: dirt@scars.tv
Website: http://scars.tv

Publishes: Essays; Fiction; Nonfiction; Poetry; *Areas:* Short Stories; *Markets:* Adult; *Treatments:* Literary

Editors: Janet Kuypers

Online and print magazine publishing poetry, prose, essays, and art work. Send submissions by email as .rtf or Word file attachments. No PDFs.

Dressing Room Poetry Journal

Email: dressingroompoetryjournal@gmail.com
Website: http://www.dressingroompoetryjournal.com

Publishes: Poetry; *Markets:* Adult; *Treatments:* Literary

Send 3-7 poems by email as an attachment.

Ducts

Email: vents@ducts.org
Website: http://www.ducts.org

Publishes: Fiction; Nonfiction; Poetry; *Areas:* Autobiography; Humour; Short Stories; *Markets:* Adult; *Treatments:* Literary; Satirical

Editors: Voichita Nachescu (Essays); Julie Wilkerson (Fiction); Mary Cool (Humour); Lisa Kirchner (Memoir); Amy Lemmon (Poetry)

Free online journal. Accepts submissions by email only. Send 3-5 poems, personal essays up to 3,000 words, fiction or humour (including satire and humorous short stories) up to 4,000 words, or memoir between 900 and 2,000 words. See website for specific submission email addresses and full submission guidelines.

Earthshine

C/O Ruminations
PO Box 245
Hummelstown, PA 17036
Email: poetry@earthshinepoetry.org
Website: http://www.earthshinepoetry.org

Publishes: Poetry; *Markets:* Adult; *Treatments:* Literary

Editors: Sally Zaino; Julie Moffitt

Poetry magazine with a voice of "illumination, compassion, humanity, and reason", publishing continually online and sporadically in print when a volume is full. Send submissions by post with SASE or by email (preferably pasted into the body of the email). See website for full guidelines.

Ellery Queen Mystery Magazine

44 Wall Street, Suite 904
New York, NY 10005-2401
Email: elleryqueenmm@dellmagazines.com
Website: http://www.themysteryplace.com

Publishes: Fiction; *Areas:* Crime; Mystery; Short Stories; *Markets:* Adult

Mystery magazine, publishing every kind of mystery short story: psychological suspense;

deductive puzzle; private eye case; realistic to imaginative; hard-boiled to "cozies". However, no explicit sex or violence, or true crime. Always seeking original detective stories, and especially happy to review first stories by authors who have never before published fiction professionally (submit to the "Department of First Stories). No need to send query – unsolicited MSS welcome. Submit through online system via website or by post (see website for details).

Emrys Journal

The Emrys Foundation
PO Box 8813
Greenville, SC 29604
Email: emrys.info@gmail.com
Website: http://www.emrys.org

Publishes: Fiction; Nonfiction; Poetry; *Areas:* Short Stories; *Markets:* Adult; *Treatments:* Literary

Editors: Katherine Burgess

Literary journal publishing fiction, poetry, and creative nonfiction. Submit up to three poems or prose up to 5,000 words between August 1 and November 1 annually, via online submission system. No postal submissions. $250 awarded to one piece selected from each category.

Epoch

251 Goldwin Smith Hall
Cornell University
Ithaca, NY 14853
Website: http://english.arts.cornell.edu/publications/epoch

Publishes: Essays; Fiction; Nonfiction; Poetry; Scripts; *Areas:* Drama; Film; Short Stories; TV; *Markets:* Adult; *Treatments:* Literary

Editors: Michael Koch

Publishes literary fiction, poetry, essays, screenplays, cartoons, graphic art, and graphic fiction. Previously unpublished material only. Accepts submissions between September 15 and April 15 annually. Submit up to 5 poems, one short story, or upt to three short short stories. Submit by post only. See website for full details.

Equal Opportunity

445 Broad Hollow Road, Suite 425
Melville, NY 11747
Tel: +1 (631) 421-9421
Fax: +1 (631) 421-1352
Email: jschneider@eop.com
Website: http://www.eop.com

Publishes: Articles; Nonfiction; *Areas:* Business; Finance; How-to; Self-Help; *Markets:* Academic; Professional

Editors: James Schneider (Director, Editorial & Production)

Career-guidance and recruitment magazine aimed at minority college students and professionals in career disciplines. Send complete ms.

Evansville Living

Tucker Publishing Group
223 NW Second Street, Suite 200
Evansville, IN 47708
Tel: +1 (812) 426-2115
Email: webmaster@evansvilleliving.com
Website: http://www.evansvilleliving.com

Publishes: Articles; Features; Nonfiction; *Areas:* Design; Gardening; Historical; Lifestyle; Sport; Travel; *Markets:* Adult

Regional magazine covering Evansville, Indiana, and the greater area. Send query with published clips.

The Evansville Review

University of Evansville Creative Writing Department
Room 416A, Olmsted Administration Hall
1800 Lincoln Avenue
Evansville, IN 47722
Tel: +1 (812) 488-2963
Email: evvreview@evansville.edu
Website: https://www.evansville.edu/majors/creativewriting/evansvilleReview.cfm

Publishes: Fiction; Interviews; Nonfiction; Poetry; Scripts; *Areas:* Drama; Short Stories; *Markets:* Adult; *Treatments:* Experimental; Literary; Traditional

Publishes poetry, fiction, nonfiction, plays, and interviews by a wide range of authors, from emerging writers to Nobel Prize recipients. Accepts submissions between September 1 and October 31 annually, through online submission system.

The Fabricator

833 Featherstone Road
Rockford, IL 61107
Tel: +1 (815) 227-8281
Email: dand@thefabricator.com
Website: http://www.thefabricator.com

Publishes: Articles; News; Nonfiction; *Areas:* How-to; Technology; *Markets:* Professional

Editors: Dan Davis

Magazine covering metal forming and the fabricating industry. Publishes news, technical articles, and case histories. Send query with published clips.

failbetter.com

2022 Grove Avenue
Richmond, VA 23220
Email: submissions@failbetter.com
Website: http://failbetter.com

Publishes: Fiction; Poetry; *Areas:* Short Stories; *Markets:* Adult; *Treatments:* Literary

Online literary journal. Publishes poetry, short stories, self-contained novel excerpts, and novellas. Send one piece of prose or between 4 and 6 poems at a time. Wait for response before sending more.

Fast Company

7 World Trade Center
New York, NY 10007-2195
Tel: +1 (212) 389-5300
Fax: +1 (212) 389-5496
Email: pr@fastcompany.com
Website: http://www.fastcompany.com

Publishes: Articles; Nonfiction; *Areas:* Business; Design; Finance; Technology; *Markets:* Professional

Publishes business articles, with a focus on innovation in technology, ethonomics (ethical economics), leadership, and design. See website for submission guidelines.

Feminist Studies

4137 Susquehanna Hall
University of Maryland
College Park, MD 20742
Tel: +1 (301) 405-7415
Fax: +1 (301) 405-8395
Email: info@feministstudies.org
Website: http://www.feministstudies.org

Publishes: Essays; Fiction; Nonfiction; Poetry; *Areas:* Criticism; Short Stories; Women's Interests; *Markets:* Academic; Adult

Feminist journal publishing research and criticism, creative writing, art, essays, and other forms of writing and visual expression. See website for submission guidelines and specific submission email addresses.

Field & Stream

Email: fsletters@bonniercorp.com
Website: http://www.fieldandstream.com

Publishes: Articles; Essays; Nonfiction; *Areas:* Hobbies; How-to; Leisure; Nature; Sport; *Markets:* Adult

Magazine aimed at hunters and fishermen. Send query by email to propose article ideas.

The Fifth Di...

Email: thefifthdi@yahoo.com
Website: http://www.nomadicdeliriumpress.com/fifth.htm

Publishes: Fiction; *Areas:* Fantasy; Sci-Fi; Short Stories; *Markets:* Adult

Publishes science fiction and fantasy stories up to 10,000 words. No horror or poetry. Flash fiction is unlikely to find favour unless exceptional. Send submissions by email as RTF attachments. No Word files. See website for full guidelines.

FineScale Modeler

21027 Crossroads Circle
PO Box 1612
Waukesha, WI 53187
Website: http://www.finescale.com

Publishes: Articles; Nonfiction; *Areas:* Crafts; Hobbies; How-to; *Markets:* Adult

Magazine for modeling enthusiasts. Most articles come from modelers, rather than professional writers. Prefers queries describing proposed article in first instance. See website for full guidelines.

Flint Hills Review

Dept. of English, Modern Languages, and Journalism
Emporia State University
1 Kellogg Circle
Emporia, KS 66801
Email: bluestem@emporia.edu
Website: http://www.emporia.edu/fhr

Publishes: Fiction; Nonfiction; Poetry; Scripts; *Areas:* Drama; Short Stories; *Markets:* Adult; *Treatments:* Literary

Annual literary magazine, publishing poetry, short stories, short plays, and creative nonfiction. Send 3-6 poems, short fiction 2,000-5,000 words (or one or two short pieces of flash fiction between 500 and 1,500 words), play scripts up to 10 minutes, or creative nonfiction between 2,000 and 5,000 words. Accepts work both by post and by email. See website for full details.

Floyd County Moonshine

720 Christiansburg Pike
Floyd, VA 24091-2440
Email: floydshine@gmail.com
Website: http://www.floydcountymoonshine.com

Publishes: Essays; Fiction; Nonfiction; Poetry; Reviews; *Areas:* Criticism; Literature; Short Stories; *Markets:* Adult; *Treatments:* Literary

Publishes short stories, poetry, essays, novel excerpts, literary criticism, book reviews, and interviews. Prose should be no longer than 8,000 words. No previously published submissions. See website for full guidelines.

Flyway: Journal of Writing & Environment

Email: flywayjournal@gmail.com
Website: https://flyway.org

Publishes: Essays; Fiction; Nonfiction; Poetry; *Areas:* Nature; Short Stories; *Markets:* Adult; *Treatments:* Literary

Online journal publishing poetry, fiction, nonfiction, and visual art that explores the many complicated facets of the word "environment". Submit online between August 15 and May 1 each year.

Fogged Clarity

Email: submissions@foggedclarity.com
Website: http://foggedclarity.com

Publishes: Essays; Fiction; Nonfiction; Poetry; Reviews; *Markets:* Adult; *Treatments:* Literary

Online journal publishing poetry, fiction, essays, reviews and visual art. Send up to five poems, or up to two pieces of prose up to 8,000 words, or one review between 300 and 1,000 words.

Food Product Design

Tel: +1 (480) 990-1101 ext. 1241
Email: lkuntz@vpico.com
Website: http://www.foodproductdesign.com

Publishes: Articles; News; Nonfiction; *Areas:* Business; Cookery; How-to; *Markets:* Professional

Editors: Lynn A. Kuntz

Magazine for professionals working in the food processing industry.

Fourteen Hills

Fourteen Hills Press
Department of Creative Writing
San Francisco State University
1600 Holloway Avenue
San Francisco, CA 94137
Email: hills@sfsu.edu
Website: http://www.14hills.net

Publishes: Fiction; Nonfiction; Poetry; *Areas:* Short Stories; *Markets:* Adult; *Treatments:* Literary

Publishes poetry, fiction, and creative nonfiction. Submit 1-3 poems (up to 7 pages max); or one short story or novel excerpt, or piece of creative nonfiction (up to 20 pages or 6,000 words). Submit via website using online submission system ($2 charge for non-subscribers). Accepts submissions between September 1 and December 1, and between March 1 and June 1, annually.

Freelance Writer's Report (FWR)

CNW Publishing, Editing & Promotion Inc.
PO Box A
North Stratford, NH 03590
Tel: +1 (603) 922-8338
Email: info@writers-editors.com
Website: http://www.writers-editors.com

Publishes: Articles; Nonfiction; *Areas:* Business; How-to; *Markets:* Professional

Magazine for freelance writers. Publishes how-to articles. No articles on freelancing basics. Submit complete ms by email.

Fruit Growers News Magazine

Great American Media Services
PO Box 128
Sparta, Michigan 49345
Tel: +1 (616) 887-9008
Fax: +1 (616) 887-2666
Email: fgnedit@fruitgrowersnews.com
Website: http://fruitgrowersnews.com

Publishes: Articles; Interviews; News; Nonfiction; *Areas:* Business; Nature; *Markets:* Professional

Magazine for commercial growers of fruit.

Fugue

Email: fugue@uidaho.edu
Website: http://www.fuguejournal.com

Publishes: Essays; Fiction; Nonfiction; Poetry; *Areas:* Short Stories; *Markets:* Adult; *Treatments:* Literary

Editors: Ash Goedker, Editor-in-Chief; Kat Lewis, Managing Editor

Submit up to 6 poems, up to two short shorts, one story, or one essay per submission. Accepts submissions online only, between September 1 and May 1. Submission service charges $3 per submission.

Garbled Transmissions

Email: editor@garbledtransmission.com
Website: http://garbledtransmission.com

Publishes: Fiction; News; Nonfiction; Reviews; *Areas:* Fantasy; Film; Sci-Fi; *Markets:* Adult; *Treatments:* Dark

Editors: James Robert Payne

Online magazine publishing science fiction and fantasy short stories between 500 and 15,000 words, and book, movie, and comic book reviews and news, slanted towards the science fiction and fantasy genres, between 500 and 3,000 words. Submit by email as .doc or OpenOffice documents. Responds in a month to all serious enquiries. Accepts simultaneous submissions, but no multiple submissions.

A Gathering of the Tribes

PO Box 20693
Tompkins Square Station
New York, NY 10009
Tel: +1 (212) 777-2038
Email: gatheringofthetribes@gmail.com
Website: http://www.tribes.org

Publishes: Essays; Fiction; Interviews; Nonfiction; Poetry; *Areas:* Arts; Short Stories; *Markets:* Adult; *Treatments:* Literary

Magazine focusing on excellence in the arts from a diverse perspective.

Gertrude

Email: EditorGertrudePress@gmail.com
Website: http://www.gertrudepress.org

Publishes: Essays; Fiction; Interviews; Nonfiction; Poetry; Reviews; *Markets:* Adult; *Treatments:* Literary

Editors: Tammy

Online LGBTQA journal publishing fiction, poetry, and creative nonfiction. Subject matter need not be LGBTQA-specific, and writers from all backgrounds are welcomed. Submit fiction or creative nonfiction up to 3,000 words, or up to five poems (no line limit, but under 40 lines preferred), via online submission system. For book reviews and interviews, email editor with proposal. See website for full guidelines.

The Gettysburg Review

Gettysburg College
300 N. Washington Street
Gettysburg, PA 17325-1491
Tel: +1 (717) 337-6770
Email: mdrew@gettysburg.edu
Website: http://www.gettysburgreview.com

Publishes: Essays; Fiction; Poetry; Reviews; *Areas:* Short Stories; *Markets:* Adult; *Treatments:* Literary

Editors: Mark Drew, Editor

Send submission by post with SASE for return, or through online submission system (small admin charge). Accepts submissions from September 1 to May 31 only: submissions received between June 1 and August 31 are returned unread. For poetry, submit up to five poems. Accepts both short poetry and longer narrative verse. Fiction is usually short stories, but will consider longer pieces for serialisation. No length limit. Accepts essays on any subject, so long as treated in a literary fashion. Simultaneous submissions accepted if immediate notification of acceptance elsewhere is given. No previously published material or submissions by fax or email.

Girlfriendz Magazine

6 Brookville Drive
Cherry Hill, NJ 08003
Tel: +1 (856) 751-2997
Email: tobi@girlfriendzmag.com
Website: http://www.girlfriendzmag.com

Publishes: Articles; *Areas:* Beauty and Fashion; Business; Health; Historical; How-to; Humour; Self-Help; Women's Interests; *Markets:* Adult

Editors: Tobi Schwartz-Cassell, Editor-in-Chief

Publishes well-researched articles for the thinking woman, from credentialed professionals. Aimed at women born between 1946 and 1964. Prefers not to be pitched ideas, but interested in baby-boom women writers who can be assigned to write articles, make-over tips, business articles, and fitness programmes. No poetry, personal essays, or community calendar announcements. Send query by email including published clips. No queries by fax. See website for full guidelines.

Golf News Magazine

PO Box 1040
Rancho Mirage, CA 92270
Tel: +1 (760) 321-8800
Fax: +1 (760) 328-3013
Email: dan@golfnewsmag.com
Website: http://golfnewsmag.com

Publishes: Articles; Features; Interviews; News; Nonfiction; *Areas:* Health; How-to; Sport; *Markets:* Adult

Magazine covering the sport of golf. Send query with published clips.

Grain Journal

Country Journal Publishing Co.
3065 Pershing Court
Decatur, IL 62526
Tel: +1 (800) 728-7511
Email: ed@grainnet.com
Website: http://www.grainnet.com

Publishes: Articles; Interviews; Nonfiction; *Areas:* Business; How-to; Technology; *Markets:* Professional

Editors: Ed Zdrojewski

Trade magazine for the North American grain industry.

Grasslimb

PO Box 420816
San Diego, CA 92142
Email: editor@grasslimb.com
Website: http://www.grasslimb.com

Publishes: Fiction; Nonfiction; Poetry; Reviews; *Areas:* Short Stories; *Markets:* Adult; *Treatments:* Literary

Editors: Valerie Polichar

Submit 4-6 poems, or prose up to 2,500 words, by email or by post. No submissions via links/downloads. See website for full details.

Green Hills Literary Lantern

Dept of English and Linguistics
Truman State University
Kirksville, MO 63501
Email: adavis@truman.edu
Website: http://ghll.truman.edu

Publishes: Fiction; Poetry; *Areas:* Short Stories; *Markets:* Adult; *Treatments:* Literary

Editors: Adam Brooke Davis; Joe Benevento

Online, open-access journal. Submit 3-7 poems, a short story or excerpt from a novel (15-18 double-spaced pages), or up to three short shorts, by email as a .doc, .rtf, or .txt attachment; or by post with SASE if return is required. See website for full details.

Green Mountains Review (GMR)

Johnson, VT 05656
Email: gmr@jsc.edu
Website: http://greenmountainsreview.com

Publishes: Essays; Fiction; Interviews; Nonfiction; Poetry; Reviews; *Areas:* Short Stories; *Markets:* Adult; *Treatments:* Literary

Editors: Jessica Hendry Nelson

Literary magazine publishing poetry, fiction, creative nonfiction, literary essays, interviews, and book reviews by both well-known writers and promising newcomers. Submit up to 5 poems, or prose up to 25 pages, via online submission system ($3 charge per submission).

The Griffin

Gwynedd Mercy University
1325 Sumneytown Pike
PO Box 901
Gwynedd Valley, PA 19437-9923
Email: allego.d@gmercyu.edu
Website: https://www.gmercyu.edu/griffin-literary-journal

Publishes: Essays; Fiction; Nonfiction; Poetry; *Areas:* Short Stories; *Markets:* Adult; *Treatments:* Literary

Editors: Dr Donna M. Allego

Publishes essays, short stories, and poetry, which explore universal qualities: truth, justice, integrity, compassion and mercy. Send submissions by email or on disk by post, with hard copy and SASE. See website for full guidelines.

GUD Magazine

Email: mike@ktf-design.com
Website: http://www.gudmagazine.com

Publishes: Articles; Essays; Features; Fiction; Interviews; Nonfiction; Poetry; *Areas:* Arts; Fantasy; Historical; Horror; Humour; Mystery; Romance; Sci-Fi; Short Stories; Suspense; *Markets:* Adult; *Treatments:* Literary

Editors: Kaolin Fire, Mike Coombes, Sue Miller, Sal Coraccio

Note: Closed to submissions as at November 2016. See website for current status.

What you've been looking for in a magazine. Published two times a year, we provoke with words and art. We bring you stories that engage. Essays and interviews that make you think harder. Poetry that bares reality, more subtly interprets what it means to be human.

We're aiming to make each issue roughly two hundred pages of content, 450 words (or a single poem or piece of art) per page.

Information for how to subscribe will be available shortly. Subscribe and discover a new magazine that looks good, feels good in the hand, and delivers content that will make you hungry for more.

Guernica

447 Broadway, 2nd Floor
New York, NY 10013
Email: editors@guernicamag.com
Website: https://www.guernicamag.com

Publishes: Essays; Fiction; Interviews; News; Nonfiction; Poetry; Reviews; *Areas:* Arts; Autobiography; Politics; Short Stories; Translations; *Markets:* Adult; *Treatments:* Literary

Editors: Hillary Brenhouse; Rachel Riederer

Non-profit online magazine focused on the intersection of arts and politics. Prefers work with a diverse international outlook – or, if it's American, from an underrepresented or alternative perspective. No stories about American tourists in other countries. Submit fiction between 1,200 and 4,500 words; up to five poems of any length (translations welcome); news, reviews, Q&A, and commentary up to 2,500 words; or memoirs, essays, reportage, or interviews between 2,500 and 7,500 words. Submit via online form on website only.

GuestLife

303 North Indian Canyon Drive
Palm Springs, CA 92262
Tel: +1 (760) 325-2333
Fax: +1 (760) 325-7008
Email: Sales@GuestLife.com
Website: http://www.guestlife.com

Publishes: Articles; Features; Nonfiction; *Areas:* Culture; Entertainment; Historical; Leisure; Travel; *Markets:* Adult

Magazine placed in hotel rooms, covering activities, attractions, and history of the specific area being covered. See website for details.

Gulf Coast: A Journal of Literature and Fine Arts

4800 Calhoun Road
Houston, TX 77204-3013
Email: gulfcoastea@gmail.com
Website: http://www.gulfcoastmag.org

Publishes: Essays; Fiction; Interviews; Nonfiction; Poetry; Reviews; *Markets:* Adult; *Treatments:* Literary

Editors: Luisa Muradyan Tannahill

Submit up to five poems, or fiction or essays up to 7,000 words, by post or via online submission manager. For other material, send query by email to address on website. $2.50 submission fee. Accepts material September 1 to March 1, annually.

Gyroscope Review

Website: http://www.gyroscopereview.com

Publishes: Poetry; *Markets:* Adult; *Treatments:* Contemporary; Literary

Publishes fine contemporary poetry in a variety of forms and themes. Welcomes both new and established writers. Submit online via website submission system.

Hard Hat News

PO Box 121
Palatine Bridge, NY 13428
Tel: +1 (717) 497-7616
Fax: +1 (518) 673-2381
Email: jcasey@leepub.com
Website: http://hardhat.com

Publishes: Articles; Interviews; News; Nonfiction; *Markets:* Professional

Editors: Jon Casey

Magazine for construction workers. Send complete ms.

Hill Country Sun

Email: melissa@hillcountrysun.com
Website: http://www.hillcountrysun.com

Publishes: Articles; Nonfiction; *Areas:* Travel; *Markets:* Adult

Editors: Melissa Maxwell Ball

Magazine covering interesting people, places, and things to do in Central Texas Hill Country from Austin to Leakey, from San Antonio to Burnet. Aimed at both residents and visitors. All topics must be pre-approved by editor. Send query by email.

Home Energy Magazine

1250 Addison Street, Suite 211B
Berkeley, CA 94702
Tel: +1 (510) 524-5405
Fax: +1 (510) 981-1406
Email: contact@homeenergy.org
Website: http://www.homeenergy.org

Publishes: Articles; Nonfiction; *Areas:* Architecture; Design; *Markets:* Professional

Editors: Jim Gunshinan

Magazine for the construction industry, publishing articles that disseminate objective and practical information on residential energy efficiency, performance, comfort, and affordability. Send query with published clips.

The Horn Book Magazine

300 The Fenway
Palace Road Building, Suite P-311
Boston, MA 02115
Tel: +1 (617) 628-0225
Fax: +1 (617) 628-0882
Email: magazine@hbook.com
Website: http://www.hbook.com

Publishes: Articles; Nonfiction; *Areas:* Criticism; Literature; *Markets:* Academic; Professional

Magazine aimed at professionals and academics involved with children's literature, publishing critical articles on the same. No fiction or work by children.

Houston Press

2603 La Branch Street
Houston, TX 77004
Tel: +1 (713) 280-2400
Fax: +1 (713) 280-2444
Website: http://www.houstonpress.com

Publishes: Articles; News; Nonfiction; *Areas:* Arts; Entertainment; *Markets:* Adult

Covers news, arts, and entertainment specific to Houston.

Hyde Park Living

179 Fairfield Avenue
Bellevue, KY 41073
Tel: +1 (859) 291-1412
Email: hydepark@livingmagazines.com
Website: http://www.livingmagazines.com/Hyde_Park_Living/Hyde_Park_Living.html

Publishes: Articles; Essays; Features; Interviews; Nonfiction; Poetry; Reviews; *Areas:* Historical; Humour; Travel; *Markets:* Adult

Editors: Grace DeGregorio

Publishes material related to Hyde Park, Ohio, only. Query in first instance.

Indianapolis Monthly

1 Emmis Plaza
40 Monument Circle Suite 100
Indianapolis, IN 46204
Tel: +1 (317) 237-9288
Fax: +1 (317) 684-2080
Email: khannel@indianapolismonthly.com
Website: http://www.indianapolismonthly.com

Publishes: Articles; Essays; Features; Interviews; Nonfiction; *Areas:* Lifestyle; *Markets:* Adult

Editors: Kim Hannel

Regional magazine publishing material related to Indiana. No fiction or poetry. Send query with published clips.

InTents

Industrial Fabrics Association International
1801 County Road, B W
Roseville MN 55113
Email: editorial@ifai.com
Website: http://intentsmag.com

Publishes: Interviews; Nonfiction; *Areas:* How-to; Technology; *Markets:* Professional

Magazine covering event tents, providing information on renting tents and staging tented events. Query in first instance.

Interweave Knits

201 East Fourth Street
Loveland, CO 80537
Website: http://www.knittingdaily.com

Publishes: Articles; Features; Nonfiction; *Areas:* Beauty and Fashion; Crafts; Design; Hobbies; How-to; *Markets:* Adult

Knitting magazine. Send query by post.

Iron Horse Literary Review

Texas Tech University
English Department
Mail Stop 43091
Lubbock, TX 79409-3091
Tel: +1 (806) 742-2500
Fax: +1 (806) 742-0989
Email: ihlr.mail@gmail.com
Website: http://www.ironhorsereview.com

Publishes: Essays; Fiction; Nonfiction; Poetry; *Areas:* Short Stories; *Markets:* Adult; *Treatments:* Literary

Publishes stories, poetry, and essays. Pays for published pieces, but submission fee charged. Subject matter, length restrictions, and submission fees vary from issue to issue. See website for details for upcoming issues.

The Journal of Adventist Education

12501 Old Columbia Pike
Silver Spring, MD 20904-6600
Tel: +1 (301) 680-5069
Fax: +1 (301) 622-9627
Email: mcgarrellf@gc.adventist.org
Website: http://jae.adventist.org

Publishes: Articles; Nonfiction; *Areas:* Religious; *Markets:* Professional

Editors: Faith-Ann McGarrell

Magazine aimed at Seventh-day Adventist teachers and educational administrators. See website for full submission guidelines.

Kashrus Magazine

PO Box 204
Brooklyn, NY 11204
Tel: +1 (718) 336-8544
Fax: +1 (718) 336-8550
Email: editorial@kashrusmagazine.com
Website: http://www.kashrusmagazine.com

Publishes: Articles; Nonfiction; *Areas:* Health; Religious; Travel; *Markets:* Adult

Magazine publishing information on Kosher.

KNOWAtlanta

9040 Roswell Road, Suite 210
Atlanta, GA 30350
Tel: +1 (770) 650-1102
Fax: +1 (770) 650.2848
Email: lindsay@knowatlanta.com
Website: http://www.knowatlanta.com

Publishes: Articles; Interviews; Nonfiction; *Areas:* Business; Culture; Finance; Health; How-to; Lifestyle; Self-Help; Travel; *Markets:* Adult; Professional

Magazine for businesses and individuals looking to relocate to Atlanta.

Lakeland Boating

O'Meara-Brown Publications
630 Davis Street, Suite 301
Evanston, IL 60201
Tel: +1 (312) 276-0610
Email: ljohnson@lakelandboating.com
Website: http://www.lakelandboating.com

Publishes: Articles; Essays; Features; Interviews; Nonfiction; *Areas:* Historical; How-to; Leisure; Technology; Travel; *Markets:* Adult

Editors: Lindsey Johnson

Magazine covering boating in the Great Lakes.

Leisure Group Travel

621 Plainfield Road, Suite 406
Willowbrook, IL 60527
Tel: +1 (630) 794-0696
Fax: +1 (630) 794-0652
Email: editor@ptmgroups.com
Website: http://leisuregrouptravel.com

Publishes: Articles; News; Nonfiction; *Areas:* Business; Travel; *Markets:* Professional

Magazine aimed at group travel buyers. Send query with published clips in first instance.

Little Patuxent Review

PO Box 6084
Columbia, MD 21045
Email: editor@littlepatuxentreview.org
Website: http://littlepatuxentreview.org

Publishes: Fiction; Nonfiction; Poetry; *Areas:* Short Stories; *Markets:* Adult; *Treatments:* Literary

Editors: Steven Leyva

A community-based publication focused on writers and artists from the Mid-Atlantic region, but will consider work originating from anywhere in the United States. Submit fiction up to 5,000 words; creative nonfiction up to 3,500 words, or up to three poems of up to 100 lines. No submissions from writers outside the US. Submit online using website submission system.

Longshot Island

Eugene, OR
Email: contact@longshotisland.com
Website: http://www.longshotisland.com

Publishes: Fiction; *Markets:* Adult; Youth; *Treatments:* Literary; Mainstream; Traditional

Editors: D. S. White

We are a small independent publisher. We create ebooks, paperbacks and magazines. Read more in our blog.

Work submitted that is considered good is published on the website as our 'short list'. From the website, we pick the best of the best and put those stories in a quarterly magazine. At the end of the year, we pick the best stories from the magazines and put them in a book. Everything gets sent off to various competitions. The magazines go to the O. Henry Awards and the best stories in the book go to the Pushcart Prizes.

Lost Treasure, Inc.

PO Box 451589
Grove, OK 74345
Tel: +1 (918) 786-2182
Email: managingeditor@losttreasure.com
Website: http://new.losttreasure.com

Publishes: Articles; Nonfiction; *Areas:* Hobbies; *Markets:* Adult

Editors: Carla Nielsen

Magazine for treasure hunting hobbyists.

Media Inc.

PO Box 24365
Seattle, WA 98124-0365
Tel: +1 (206) 382-9220
Fax: +1 (206) 382-9437
Email: ksauro@media-inc.com
Website: http://media-inc.com

Publishes: Articles; Features; News; Nonfiction; *Areas:* Business; Media; *Markets:* Professional

Editors: Katie Sauro

Magazine serving professionals in the US Northwest working in the media, including marketing, advertising, and creative services. Send query or complete ms.

Ms. Magazine

433 South Beverly Drive
Beverly Hills, CA 90212
Tel: +1 (310) 556-2515
Fax: +1 (310) 556-2514
Email: mkort@msmagazine.com
Website: http://www.msmagazine.com

Publishes: Articles; Fiction; News; Nonfiction; Poetry; Reviews; *Areas:* Arts; Culture; Legal; Nature; Politics; Short Stories; Sociology; Women's Interests; *Markets:* Adult

Editors: Michel Cicero

Publishes articles focussing on politics, social commentary, popular culture, law, education, art and the environment, through a feminist lens. Also publishes original fiction and poetry, but publishes these infrequently. See website for full submission guidelines.

Main Line Today

4645 West Chester Pike
Newtown Square, PA 19073
Tel: +1 (610) 325-4630
Fax: +1 (610) 325-4636
Email: hrowland@mainlinetoday.com
Website: http://www.mainlinetoday.com

Publishes: Articles; Features; Interviews; Nonfiction; *Areas:* Arts; Historical; How-to; Humour; Lifestyle; Travel; *Markets:* Adult

Editors: Hobart Rowland (Editorial Director)

Monthly magazine covering Philadelphia's main line and western suburbs. Send query with published clips.

Massage & Bodywork

25188 Genesee Trail Road, Suite 200
Golden, CO 80401
Tel: +1 (800) 458-2267
Email: editor@abmp.com

Website: http://www.massageandbodywork.com

Publishes: Articles; Interviews; Nonfiction; *Areas:* Health; How-to; Medicine; *Markets:* Professional

Editors: Leslie Young

Magazine aimed at professional massage therapists and bodyworkers. Send query with published clips.

Metro Parent

Metro Parent Publishing Group
22041 Woodward Avenue
Ferndale, MI 48220
Email: jelliott@metroparent.com
Website: http://www.metroparent.com

Publishes: Articles; Features; News; Nonfiction; *Areas:* Lifestyle; *Markets:* Adult

Editors: Julia Elliott

Regional lifestyle magazine aimed at Southeast Michigan. Publishes pieces on trends, local people, products of interest to parents / kids, child behaviour, etc. Must have a local focus. See website for full guidelines.

Midwest Meetings

Hennen Publishing
302 Sixth Street West
Brookings, SD 57006
Email: editor@midwestmeetings.com
Website: http://www.midwestmeetings.com

Publishes: Articles; News; Nonfiction; Reference; *Areas:* Business; *Markets:* Professional

Editors: Randy Hennen

Magazine for convention and meeting planners in the Midwest. Always looking for content from new authors, bloggers, industry experts and everyday professionals. Submit via online form on website.

Military Vehicles Magazine

700 East State Street
Iola, WI 54990-0001
Tel: +1 (888) 457-2873
Fax: +1 (715) 445-4087
Email: john.adams-graf@fwpubs.com
Website: http://www.militarytrader.com

Publishes: Articles; News; Nonfiction; *Areas:* Historical; How-to; Military; Technology; *Markets:* Adult

Editors: John Adams-Graf

Magazine aimed at people who own, restore, and collect historic military vehicles.

Mobile Bay

PMT Publishing
P.O.Box 66200
Mobile, AL 36660
Tel: +1 (251) 473-6269
Fax: +1 (251) 479-8822
Email: jculbreth@pmtpublishing.com
Website: http://www.mobilebaymag.com

Publishes: Articles; Nonfiction; *Areas:* Arts; Beauty and Fashion; Cookery; Culture; Historical; Lifestyle; *Markets:* Adult

Editors: Judy Culbreth, Editorial Director

Lifestyle magazine aimed at residents of Mobile and Baldwin counties. Send query with published clips. Material must have local relevance.

Model Engineer

MyTimeMedia Ltd
Enterprise House
Enterprise Way
Edenbridge
Kent
TN8 6HF
Email: diane.carney@mytimemedia.com
Website: http://www.model-engineer.co.uk

Publishes: Articles; Nonfiction; *Areas:* Hobbies; How-to; Technology; *Markets:* Adult

Editors: Diane Carney

Magazine for model-making enthusiasts.

More

Email: More@meredith.com
Website: http://www.more.com

Publishes: Articles; Features; Nonfiction; *Areas:* Beauty and Fashion; Entertainment;

Finance; Health; Lifestyle; Women's Interests; *Markets:* Adult

Editors: Lesley Jane Seymour

Women's lifestyle magazine celebrating women of style and substance who influence others. Aimed at sophisticated and accomplished readers.

Nails Magazine

Tel: +1 (310) 533-2552
Email: Erika.Kotite@bobit.com
Website: http://www.nailsmag.com

Publishes: Articles; Features; Interviews; News; Nonfiction; *Areas:* Business; Health; How-to; *Markets:* Professional

Editors: Erika Kotite

Magazine for nail salon professionals.

The National Jurist

7670 Opportunity Road, #105
San Diego, CA 92111
Tel: +1 (858) 300-3201
Email: Jack@cypressmagazines.com
Website: http://www.nationaljurist.com

Publishes: Articles; Interviews; News; Nonfiction; *Areas:* How-to; Legal; *Markets:* Academic

Editors: Jack Crittenden (Editor-In-Chief)

Magazine for law students. Contact by email.

New Mobility Magazine

United Spinal Association
120-34 Queens Boulevard #320
Kew Gardens, NY 11415
Email: info@unitedspinal.org
Website: http://www.spinalcord.org/new-mobility-magazine/

Publishes: Articles; Features; Interviews; News; Nonfiction; *Areas:* Health; Medicine; *Markets:* Adult; Professional

Editors: Ian Ruder

Magazine for people affected by spinal cord injuries and disorders, including sufferers, carers, and professionals in the field.

News Photographer

6677 Whitemarsh Valley Walk
Austin, TX 78746-6367
Email: magazine@nppa.org
Website: https://nppa.org/magazine

Publishes: Articles; Interviews; News; Nonfiction; *Areas:* Current Affairs; Historical; How-to; Photography; Technology; *Markets:* Professional

Editors: Donald R. Winslow

Magazine aimed at professional photo-journalists.

NFPA Journal

Tel: +1 (617) 770-3000
Email: nfpajournal@nfpa.org
Website: http://www.nfpa.org

Publishes: Articles; Features; News; Nonfiction; *Markets:* Professional

Association magazine covering fire protection and suppression.

Niche

3000 Chestnut Avenue, Suite 104
Baltimore, MD 21211
Tel: +1 (410) 889-3093
Email: info@nichemagazine.com
Website: http://www.nichemagazine.com/

Publishes: Articles; Nonfiction; *Areas:* Arts; Business; Crafts; Finance; *Markets:* Professional

Editors: Hope Daniels

Trade magazine aimed at craft gallery retailers. Send query with published clips.

Nob Hill Gazette

Fairmont Hotel
950 Mason Street, Mezzanine Level
San Francisco, CA 94108
Tel: +1 (415) 227-0190
Email: fred@nobhillgazette.com
Website: http://www.nobhillgazette.com

Publishes: Articles; Nonfiction; *Areas:* Arts; Beauty and Fashion; Cookery; Design; Finance; Health; Historical; Lifestyle; Travel; *Markets:* Adult

Editors: Fred Albert

Upscale lifestyle magazine for the San Francisco Bay area. Send query with published clips.

Northwest Quarterly Magazine

Hughes Media Corp.
728 North Prospect Street
Rockford, IL 61107
Tel: +1 (815) 316-2301
Email: clinden@northwestquarterly.com
Website: http://www.northwestquarterly.com

Publishes: Articles; Features; Interviews; Nonfiction; *Areas:* Business; Culture; Gardening; Health; Historical; Humour; Leisure; Lifestyle; Nature; *Markets:* Adult

Lifestyle magazine aimed at Northern Illinois, Southern Wisconsin, and Kane and McHenry counties.

Nostalgia Magazine

PO Box 8466
Spokane, WA 99203
Email: editor@nostalgiamagazine.net

Publishes: Essays; Nonfiction; *Areas:* Historical; *Markets:* Adult

Publishes nostalgic personal essays, illustrated with interesting photographs. At least one photo per 400 words. Accepts submissions in any format, but prefers stories and photos by email.

Nurseweek

Email: editor@nurse.com
Website: http://www.nurse.com

Publishes: Articles; Nonfiction; *Areas:* Medicine; *Markets:* Professional

Magazine provided free to registered nurses living in the United States.

NY Literary Magazine

Email: nyliterarymag@gmail.com
Website: https://nyliterarymagazine.com

Publishes: Articles; News; Poetry; *Areas:* Arts; *Markets:* Adult; Professional; Youth

Editors: Elizabeth Harding, Sandra Reynolds, Amanda Graham, Lara Wilson

Publishes the finest literary achievements in modern poetry. We are searching for outstanding talent, a beautiful play of words, emotionally stirring poems that have deep meaning and will withstand the test of time.

We strive to highlight talent and bring to light gifted poets of all ages and nationalities.
Publishes both poetry as well as striking visual art.

Our bimonthly magazine is available both as a free digital edition and in print.

O'Dwyer's

271 Madison Ave., #600
New York, NY 10016
Tel: +1 (212) 679-2471
Email: john@odwyerpr.com
Website: http://www.odwyerpr.com

Publishes: Articles; News; Nonfiction; *Areas:* Business; Legal; Technology; *Markets:* Professional

Editors: John O'Dwyer, Associate Publisher/Editor

Magazine aimed at PR professionals.

OfficePro

10502 N Ambassador Drive, Suite 100
Kansas City, MO 64153
Tel: +1 (816) 891-6600
Fax: +1 (816) 891-9118
Email: john.naatz@iaap-hq.org
Website: http://www.iaap-hq.org/page/OfficeProMagazine

Publishes: Articles; News; Nonfiction; *Areas:* Business; *Markets:* Professional

Editors: John Naatz

Publishes stories related to office life, from office politics to new software. Send query by email.

Onion World

Columbia Publishing
8405 Ahtanum Road

Yakima, WA 98903
Email: dkeller@columbiapublications.com
Website: http://www.onionworld.net

Publishes: Articles; Interviews; Nonfiction; *Areas:* Business; Nature; *Markets:* Professional

Editors: Denise Keller

Magazine for potential onion growers and sellers.

Opera News

70 Lincoln Center Plaza, 6th Floor
New York, NY 10023-6593
Tel: +1 (212) 769-7080
Fax: +1 (212) 769-8500
Email: info@operanews.com
Website: http://www.operanews.com

Publishes: Articles; News; Nonfiction; *Areas:* Music; *Markets:* Adult; Professional

Editors: Kitty March

Magazine for opera professionals and enthusiasts. Send queries, proposals, and unsolicited mss with published writing clips by email.

Oregon Coast

4969 Highway 101 N, Suite 2
Florence, OR 97439
Tel: +1 (541) 997-8401
Email: edit@nwmags.com
Website: http://www.oregoncoastmagazine.com

Publishes: Articles; Nonfiction; *Areas:* Historical; Leisure; Nature; *Markets:* Adult; Family

Publishes articles of regional interest. Send query or submit complete ms by email or by post. No fiction or poetry. See website for full details.

Organic Life

400 South 10th Street
Emmaus, PA 18049
Email: ROLsubmissions@rodale.com
Website: http://www.rodalesorganiclife.com

Publishes: Articles; Nonfiction; *Areas:* Gardening; Health; Lifestyle; Nature; *Markets:* Adult

Publishes articles that address some aspect of the magazine's focus on living naturally in the modern world.

Orson Scott Card's InterGalactic Medicine Show

Website: http://www.intergalacticmedicineshow.com

Publishes: Fiction; *Areas:* Fantasy; Sci-Fi; Short Stories; *Markets:* Adult; Youth

Online magazine publishing fantasy and science fiction of any length. Submit via online submission form.

The Ottawa Object

Email: threwlinebooks@gmail.com
Website: https://theottawaobject.wordpress.com

Publishes: Fiction; *Areas:* Short Stories; *Markets:* Adult; *Treatments:* Literary

Editors: Joshua Hjalmer Lind

Print literary journal with a particular interest in speculative fiction. Submit online through website.

Overtones

808 W. Melrose Avenue #802
Findlay, OH 45840
Email: jrsmith@handbellmusicians.org
Website: http://handbellmusicians.org/music-resources/overtones/

Publishes: Articles; Features; Interviews; News; Nonfiction; *Areas:* How-to; Music; *Markets:* Adult

Editors: J.R. Smith

Magazine for handbell musicians.

Painted Bride Quarterly

Drexel University
Department of English and Philosophy
3141 Chestnut Street
Philadelphia, PA 19104

Email: pbq@drexel.edu
Website: http://pbq.drexel.edu

Publishes: Essays; Fiction; Nonfiction; Poetry; *Areas:* Short Stories; *Markets:* Adult; *Treatments:* Literary

Submit up to 5 poems; fiction up to 5,000 words; or essays up to 3,000 words, via online submission system.

Painted Cave

Email: paintedcavesubmissions@gmail.com
Website: http://paintedcave.net

Publishes: Fiction; Nonfiction; Poetry; *Areas:* Short Stories; *Markets:* Adult; *Treatments:* Literary

Online literary magazine publishing submissions from community college students. Submit up to three pieces of flash fiction or flash creative nonfiction up to 750 words; one piece of fiction or creative nonfiction up to 5,000 words; or 3-5 poems up to 50 lines each. Include short, third-person biography. See website for full submission guidelines.

Palm Springs Life

303 North Indian Canyon Drive
Palm Springs, CA 92262
Tel: +1 (760) 325-2333
Website: http://www.palmspringslife.com

Publishes: Articles; Essays; Features; Interviews; Nonfiction; *Areas:* Arts; Beauty and Fashion; Culture; Design; Entertainment; Lifestyle; *Markets:* Adult

Editors: Kent Black

Magazine covering the Palm Springs-area desert resort communities. Send query with published clips.

Parents

805 3rd Ave #22
New York, NY 10022
Tel: +1 (212) 499-2000
Website: http://www.parents.com

Publishes: Articles; Features; Nonfiction; *Areas:* Beauty and Fashion; Health; Lifestyle; Women's Interests; *Markets:* Adult

Magazine aimed at mothers with small children. Query in first instance.

Pediatric Annals

Healio.com, c/o SLACK Incorporated
6900 Grove Road, Thorofare, NJ 08086
Tel: +1 (856) 848-1000
Fax: +1 (800) 257-8290
Email: editor@healio.com
Website: http://www.healio.com/pediatrics/journals/pedann

Publishes: Articles; News; Nonfiction; *Areas:* Medicine; *Markets:* Professional

Monthly online medical journal providing pediatricians and other clinicians with practical information on the diagnosis and treatment of pediatric diseases and disorders.

Pentecostal Evangel

1445 N. Boonville Avenue
Springfield, MO 65802
Email: pe@ag.org
Website: http://www.pe.ag.org

Publishes: Articles; Nonfiction; *Areas:* Religious; *Markets:* Adult

Christian magazine publishing inspirational articles. Prefers submissions by email. See website for full guidelines.

Pentecostal Messenger

701 Brown Trail
Bedford, TX 76021
Email: Communications@pcg.org
Website: http://www.pcg.org

Publishes: Articles; Essays; Nonfiction; *Areas:* Religious; *Markets:* Adult

Christian magazine acting as the official voice of the Pentecostal Church.

Pest Management Professional

North Coast Media
1360 E. 9th Street, Suite 1070
Cleveland, OH 44114
Tel: +1 (216) 706-3766

Fax: +1 (216) 706-3712
Email: mwhitford@northcoastmedia.net
Website: http://www.mypmp.net

Publishes: Articles; News; Nonfiction; *Areas:* Nature; *Markets:* Professional

Editors: Marty Whitford, Publisher & Editorial Director

Magazine for professionals working in the pest management industry. Send query by email with news or ideas for stories.

Philly Weekly

1617 JFK Boulevard, Suite 1005
Philadelphia, PA 19103
Tel: +1 (215) 563-7400
Fax: +1 (215) 563-6799
Email: mail@phillyweekly.com
Website: http://philadelphiaweekly.com

Publishes: News; Nonfiction; *Areas:* Arts; Current Affairs; Entertainment; *Markets:* Adult

Editors: Anastasia Barbalios

Local magazine publishing arts and entertainment news, dining reviews, and provocative current affairs coverage relating to Philadelphia.

Phoenix Magazine

15169 North Scottsdale Road, Suite 310
Scottsdale, AZ 85254
Website: http://www.phoenixmag.com

Publishes: Articles; Features; News; Nonfiction; *Areas:* Beauty and Fashion; Cookery; Finance; Health; Lifestyle; Travel; *Markets:* Adult

Publishes material of interest to the local area only. Send query by email with published clips.

Photonics & Imaging Technology

Tech Briefs Media Group
261 Fifth Avenue, Suite 1901
New York, NY 10016
Tel: +1 (212) 490-3999
Website: http://www.techbriefsmediagroup.com

Publishes: Articles; Nonfiction; *Areas:* Science; Technology; *Markets:* Academic; Professional

Technical magazine for the photonics / optics industry. Send query or submit complete ms.

Pizza Today

908 South 8th Street, Suite 200
Louisville, KY 40203
Tel: +1 (502) 736-9500
Email: jwhite@pizzatoday.com
Website: http://www.pizzatoday.com

Publishes: Articles; Features; News; Nonfiction; *Areas:* Business; Cookery; *Markets:* Professional

Editors: Jeremy White

Magazine aimed at the pizza industry. Send query by email, post, or fax.

Plain Truth Magazine

Plain Truth Ministries
Pasadena, CA 91129
Tel: +1 (800) 309-4466
Email: managing.editor@ptm.org
Website: http://www.ptm.org

Publishes: Articles; Interviews; Nonfiction; *Areas:* Religious; *Markets:* Adult

Christian magazine promoting a direct relationship with God, disintermediated by religion. Send query with SASE and published clips.

Play & Playground Magazine

Playground Professionals, LLC
10 North Bridge Street
Saint Anthony, ID 83445
Tel: +1 (208) 569-9189
Website: http://www.playgroundprofessionals.com

Publishes: Articles; Features; News; Nonfiction; *Areas:* Design; How-to; Leisure; Technology; *Markets:* Professional

Trade journal publishing material of relevance to the play and playground industry.

PN (Paraplegia News)
PVA Publications
2111 East Highland Avenue, Suite 180
Phoenix, AZ 85016-4702
Tel: +1 (602) 224-0500
Fax: +1 (602) 224-0507
Email: richard@pvamag.com
Website: http://pvamag.com/pn/

Publishes: Articles; Nonfiction; *Areas:* Health; Leisure; Lifestyle; Sport; *Markets:* Adult

Editors: Richard Hoover

Monthly magazine for people with spinal-cord injuries, family members and caregivers.

Police and Security News
1208 Juniper Street
Quakertown, PA 18951-1520
Tel: +1 (215) 538-1240
Fax: +1 (215) 538-1208
Email: dyaw@policeandsecuritynews.com
Website: http://policeandsecuritynews.com

Publishes: Articles; News; Nonfiction; *Areas:* How-to; Legal; *Markets:* Professional

Magazine for law enforcement professionals, covering new technology; training and tactics; new weaponry; management ideas; and more. Send query by email or through online form.

Popular Science
2 Park Avenue, 9th Floor
New York, NY 10016
Email: queries@popsci.com
Website: http://www.popsci.com

Publishes: Articles; News; Nonfiction; *Areas:* Science; Technology; *Markets:* Adult; *Treatments:* Popular

Magazine covering science and technology for a general adult readership. Welcomes queries by email. Send pitch with brief summary and links to past work, if available. No submission by post.

Postcard Poems and Prose
Website: https://postcardpoemsandprose.wordpress.com

Publishes: Fiction; Poetry; *Areas:* Short Stories; *Markets:* Adult

Publishes postcard-sized combinations of images and poems (12-20 lines) or prose (up to 190 words). Text and images should be sent as separate attachments. Will consider text without images.

PracticeLink Magazine
415 2nd Avenue
Hinton, WV 25951
Tel: +1 (800) 776-8383
Email: HelpDesk@PracticeLink.com
Website: http://www.practicelink.com

Publishes: Nonfiction; *Areas:* Medicine; *Markets:* Professional

Career advancement resource for physicians.

Preservation in Print
The Leeds-Davis Building
923 Tchoupitoulas Street
New Orleans, LA 70130
Tel: +1 (504) 636-3043
Email: ddelsol@prcno.org
Website: http://www.prcno.org

Publishes: Articles; Essays; Interviews; Nonfiction; *Areas:* Architecture; Historical; *Markets:* Adult

Editors: Danielle Del Sol

Louisiana publication covering architectural preservation and neighbourhood revitalisation issues.

The Produce News
800 Kinderkamack Road, Suite 100
Oradell, NJ 07649
Tel: +1 (201) 986-7990
Fax: +1 (201) 986-7996
Email: groh@theproducenews.com
Website: http://www.theproducenews.com

Publishes: Articles; News; Nonfiction; *Markets:* Professional

Editors: John Groh

Magazine for professionals in the fresh fruits and vegetables industry.

Properties Magazine

3826 W. 158th St.
Cleveland, OH 44111
Tel: +1 (216) 251-0035
Fax: +1 (216) 251-2655
Email: mwatt@propertiesmag.com
Website: http://www.propertiesmag.com

Publishes: Articles; News; Nonfiction; *Areas:* Architecture; Business; Design; *Markets:* Professional

Editors: Mark Watt, Managing Editor/Art Director

Monthly publication dedicated to realty, construction and architecture in Northeast Ohio.

QSR

Tel: +1 (919) 945-0703
Email: sam@qsrmagazine.com
Website: https://www.qsrmagazine.com

Publishes: Articles; News; Nonfiction; *Areas:* Business; Cookery; *Markets:* Professional

Editors: Sam Oches

Magazine for the limited-service restaurant industry.

Quill

3909 N. Meridian St.
Indianapolis, IN 46208
Tel: +1 (317) 927-8000 x211
Fax: +1 (317) 920-4789
Email: quill@spj.org
Website: http://www.spj.org/quillabout.asp

Publishes: Articles; Nonfiction; *Markets:* Professional

Editors: Scott Leadingham

Magazine covering professional journalism. Accepts unsolicited mss if sent by email only, but prefers topic pitches and queries to the editor.

Rain Taxi

PO Box 3840
Minneapolis, MN 55403
Email: info@raintaxi.com
Website: http://www.raintaxi.com

Publishes: Essays; Interviews; Nonfiction; Reviews; *Areas:* Culture; Literature; *Markets:* Adult; *Treatments:* Literary

Journal of literary culture. Publishes reviews, interviews, and essays. Prefers submissions by email, but will accept submissions by post, with SASE or email address for response. See website for full submission guidelines.

Rappahannock Review

University of Mary Washington
1301 College Avenue
Fredericksburg, VA 22401
Tel: +1 (540) 654-1033
Fax: +1 (540) 654-1569
Email: editor@rappahannockreview.com
Website: http://www.rappahannockreview.com

Publishes: Essays; Fiction; Nonfiction; Poetry; *Areas:* Short Stories; *Markets:* Adult; *Treatments:* Experimental; Literary

Editors: Avery Kopp; Sarah Palmer

Online literary journal publishing poetry of any length (submit up to five poems), plus creative nonfiction and fiction up to 8,000 words (or three pieces up to 1,000 words each). Encourages experimental pieces. See website for reading periods and any special topics.

Real Simple

Time Inc.
1271 Avenue of the Americas
New York, NY 10020
Tel: +1 (212)522-1212
Fax: +1 (212)467-1392
Email: publishing@realsimple.com
Website: http://www.realsimple.com

Publishes: Articles; Nonfiction; *Areas:* Cookery; Lifestyle; Women's Interests; *Markets:* Adult

Women's interest magazine. Send query in first instance.

Recommend Magazine

5979 NW 151st Street, Suite 120
Miami Lakes, FL 33014
Tel: +1 (305) 828-0123
Fax: +1 (305) 826-6950
Email: paloma@recommend.com
Website: http://www.recommend.com

Publishes: Articles; News; Nonfiction; *Areas:* Travel; *Markets:* Professional

Editors: Paloma Villaverde de Rico

Magazine for travel agents.

Red Paint Hill Poetry Journal

Email: submissions@redpainthill.com
Website: http://redpainthill.com

Publishes: Essays; Nonfiction; Poetry; Reviews; *Markets:* Adult; *Treatments:* Literary

Editors: Stephanie Bryant Anderson

Send 3-5 poems in a single Word document by email. No PDF files. Work must be unpublished. Simultaneous submissions accepted, provide immediate notification given of acceptance elsewhere. No rhyming poetry, poetry about poems or the writing process, or melodramatic love poems. Also publishes reviews, essays, and interviews. See website for full submission guidelines.

Referee

2017 Lathrop Avenue
Racine, WI 53405
Tel: +1 (800) 733-6100
Fax: +1 (262) 632-5460
Email: submissions@referee.com
Website: http://www.referee.com

Publishes: Articles; News; Nonfiction; *Areas:* Sport; *Markets:* Adult; Professional

Magazine for sports officiators from youth to professional level.

Remodeling

One Thomas Circle, N.W., Suite 600
Washington, DC 20005
Tel: +1 (202) 452-0800
Fax: +1 (202) 785-1974
Email: cwebb@hanleywood.com
Website: http://www.remodeling.hw.net

Publishes: Articles; Features; Interviews; News; Nonfiction; *Areas:* Business; Design; How-to; *Markets:* Professional

Editors: Craig Webb

Magazine publishing material relating to residential and light commercial remodelling.

Rider Magazine

1227 Flynn Road, Suite 304
Camarillo, CA 93012
Tel: +1 (763) 383-4400
Email: rider@ridermagazine.com
Website: http://ridermagazine.com

Publishes: Articles; Interviews; Nonfiction; *Areas:* How-to; Technology; Travel; *Markets:* Adult

Magazine written for, and by, mature, affluent and discerning motorcyclists. Query by email in first instance. Only buys stories with photos.

Rochester Business Journal

45 East Avenue, Suite 500
Rochester, NY 14604
Tel: +1 (585) 546-8303
Fax: +1 (585) 546-3398
Email: rbj@rbj.net
Website: http://www.rbj.net

Publishes: Articles; News; Nonfiction; *Areas:* Business; *Markets:* Professional

Local business magazine aimed at small business owners and corporate executives in the Rochester area. Send query with published clips.

Runner's World

400 South Tenth Street
Emmaus, PA 18098-0099
Tel: +1 (610) 967-8441
Fax: +1 (610) 967-8883
Email: rwedit@rodale.com
Website: http://www.runnersworld.com

Publishes: Articles; Interviews; Nonfiction; *Areas:* How-to; Leisure; Sport; *Markets:* Adult

Magazine for runners. Query in first instance.

San Diego Family Magazine

1475 6th Avenue, 5th Floor
San Diego, CA 92101-3200
Tel: +1 (619) 685-6970
Fax: +1 (619) 685-6978
Email: editor@sandiegofamily.com
Website: http://www.sandiegofamily.com

Publishes: Articles; Features; Nonfiction; *Areas:* Lifestyle; *Markets:* Adult

Magazine on parenting for caregivers in the San Diego area. Send articles by email with "Article submission" in the subject line. See website for full details.

Santa Barbara Magazine

2064 Alameda Padre Serra, Suite 120
Santa Barbara, CA 93103
Tel: +1 (805) 965-5999
Fax: +1 (805) 965-7627
Email: editorial@sbmag.com
Website: http://sbmag.com

Publishes: Articles; Nonfiction; *Areas:* Architecture; Arts; Gardening; Historical; Lifestyle; *Markets:* Adult

Magazine publishing articles on Santa Barbara lifestyle, people, homes, gardens, architecture, history, and more.

School Bus Fleet

3520 Challenger Street
Torrance, CA 90503
Tel: +1 (310) 533-2587
Email: info@schoolbusfleet.com
Website: http://www.schoolbusfleet.com

Publishes: Articles; News; Nonfiction; *Areas:* Travel; *Markets:* Professional

Editors: Nicole Schlosser

Magazine for school transportation professionals in the US and Canada. Query in first instance.

Scouting

1325 W. Walnut Hill Lane
PO Box 152401
Irving, TX 75015-2401
Tel: +1 (866) 584-6589
Website: http://scoutingmagazine.org

Publishes: Articles; Features; Interviews; Nonfiction; *Areas:* Adventure; Hobbies; Leisure; Nature; Travel; *Markets:* Adult

Magazine for scout leaders. Query with SASE.

Screen Printing

ST Media Group International
11262 Cornell Park Drive
Cincinnati, OH 45242
Email: kiersten.wones@stmediagroup.com
Website: http://www.screenweb.com

Publishes: Articles; Features; News; Nonfiction; *Areas:* Technology; *Markets:* Professional

Magazine for commercial and industrial screen printers. Query in first instance.

Self

Conde Nast
1 World Trade Center
New York, NY 10007
Tel: +1 (212) 286-2860
Email: letters@self.com
Website: http://www.self.com

Publishes: Articles; Nonfiction; *Areas:* Beauty and Fashion; Finance; Health; Lifestyle; Women's Interests; *Markets:* Adult

Women's healthy lifestyle magazine promoting self-expression and self-compassion as part of a path to personal well-being. Send query with published clips in first instance.

Sew Simple

741 Corporate Circle, Suite A
Golden, CO 80401
Email: sewnews@sewnews.com
Website: http://www.sewsimple.com

Publishes: Articles; Nonfiction; *Areas:* Crafts; Hobbies; How-to; *Markets:* Youth

Editors: Beth Bradley, Associate Editor

Sewing magazine for younger stitchers, providing fun ideas and quick, easy projects.

Shutterbug

PO Box 7
Titusville, FL 32781
Tel: +1 (321) 269-3212
Fax: +1 (321) 225-3146
Email: dhavlik@enthusiastnetwork.com
Website: http://www.shutterbug.com

Publishes: Articles; Features; News; Nonfiction; Reviews; *Areas:* How-to; Photography; Technology; *Markets:* Adult; Professional

Photography magazine for amateurs and professionals. No unsolicited mss. Send query by post or by email.

SignCraft Publishing Co., Inc.

PO Box 60031
Fort Myers, FL 33906
Tel: +1 (239) 939-4644
Fax: +1 (239) 939-0607
Email: signcraft@signcraft.com
Website: https://www.signcraft.com

Publishes: Articles; Interviews; News; Nonfiction; *Areas:* Business; How-to; *Markets:* Professional

Magazine for the sign industry. Welcomes photos, tips, article submissions, ideas, and suggestions.

Sixpenny Magazine

Email: elizabeth@sixpenny.org
Website: http://www.sixpenny.org

Publishes: Fiction; *Areas:* Arts; Literature; Short Stories; *Markets:* Adult; *Treatments:* Contemporary; Dark; Experimental; Literary; Popular; Progressive; Satirical; Serious; Traditional

Editors: Elizabeth Leonard, Kate Thomas

A digital and print magazine of illustrated short stories. Our stories will be classified as literary fiction, but they'll also be entertaining as a rule. Each issue has six stories that take six minutes to read: three by established authors, and three by emerging authors.

Ski Patrol Magazine

133 South Van Gordon Street, Suite 100
Lakewood, CO 80228
Tel: +1 (303) 988-1111
Email: chorgan@nsp.org
Website: http://www.nsp.org

Publishes: Articles; Nonfiction; *Areas:* Health; Sport; Travel; *Markets:* Professional

Editors: Candace Horgan

Magazine covering mountain rescue, skiing, snowboarding, and related sports.

Sling Magazine

Email: SlingMag@gmail.com
Website: http://www.slingmag.com

Publishes: Essays; Fiction; Interviews; Poetry; *Areas:* Short Stories; *Markets:* Adult; *Treatments:* Literary

Editors: Hope Johnson; Bonita Lee Penn; Kaela Danielle McNeil

Publishes essays, fiction, poetry, art / photography and interviews. See website for current requirements and deadlines. Submit one piece of prose, or up to two poems, by email.

Southern Boating

330 N. Andrews Ave, Suite 200
Fort Lauderdale, FL 33301
Tel: +1 (954) 522-5515
Fax: +1 (954) 522-2260
Email: liz@southernboating.com
Website: https://southernboating.com

Publishes: Articles; Nonfiction; Reviews; *Areas:* Hobbies; How-to; Leisure; Lifestyle; Sport; Travel; *Markets:* Adult

Magazine for boating and yachting enthusiasts, focused on the Southeast of the United States, Caribbean, Bahamas, and Gulf of Mexico.

Spin Off

F+W Media/Interweave Press
Attention: Spin Off
4868 Innovation Dr
Ft. Collins, CO 80525-5576
Email: spinoff@interweave.com
Website: http://www.interweave.com/spinning/

Publishes: Articles; Nonfiction; *Areas:* Crafts; Hobbies; *Markets:* Adult

Magazine covering a variety of spindles and spindle techniques.

SQL Server Pro

Penton Media
221 East 29th Street
Loveland, CO 80538
Email: articles@sqlmag.com
Website: http://sqlmag.com

Publishes: Articles; Features; News; Nonfiction; *Areas:* Technology; *Markets:* Professional

Magazine for SQL Server database administrators, developers, and architects, as well as BI professionals.

St Petersburg Review

Email: annejjames@gmail.com
Website: http://www.stpetersburgreview.com

Publishes: Essays; Fiction; Nonfiction; Poetry; Scripts; *Areas:* Short Stories; Theatre; *Markets:* Adult; *Treatments:* Literary

Send submissions of up to four poems, fiction, essays, or creative nonfiction up to 7,500 words, or plays up to 30 pages, via online submission system. Accepts submissions between September 1 and January 1 annually.

The Stampers' Sampler

22992 Mill Creek Drive
Laguna Hills, CA 92653
Email: thestamperssampler@stampington.com
Website: https://stampington.com/the-stampers-sampler

Publishes: Features; Nonfiction; *Areas:* Crafts; Hobbies; *Markets:* Adult

Rubber stamping magazine, publishing stamped project ideas.

Star 82 Review

Email: editor@star82review.com
Website: http://star82review.com

Publishes: Essays; Fiction; Nonfiction; *Areas:* Short Stories; *Markets:* Adult; *Treatments:* Literary

Publishes short fiction, creative fiction, mini essays, and work that combines words with visual art. Especially looks for humanity, humility and humour. Submit through website via online submission system.

State Journal

324 Hewes Avenue PO Box 2000
Clarksburg, WV 26301
Tel: +1 (800) 982-6034
Email: news@theet.com
Website: http://www.theet.com/statejournal/

Publishes: Articles; News; Nonfiction; *Areas:* Business; *Markets:* Professional

Magazine aimed at the West Virginia business community.

Stone World

2401 W. Big Beaver Rd., Suite 700
Troy, MI 48084-3333
Tel: +1 (248) 362-3700
Fax: +1 (248) 362-0317
Email: info@stoneworld.com
Website: http://www.stoneworld.com

Publishes: Articles; News; Nonfiction; *Areas:* Architecture; Design; Technology; *Markets:* Professional

Editors: Jennifer Richinelli

Magazine for professionals working with natural building stone.

Stormwater

Forester Media Inc.
PO Box 3100
Santa Barbara, CA 93130

Email: asantiago@forester.net
Website: http://foresternetwork.com/magazines/stormwater/

Publishes: Articles; Features; Interviews; News; Nonfiction; *Areas:* Architecture; Business; Design; *Markets:* Professional

Magazine aimed at professionals concerned with storm water management. Send query by email.

SuCasa

Bella Media, LLC
4100 Wolcott Avenue. NE, Suite B
Albuquerque, NM 87109
Tel: +1 (505) 344-1783
Fax: +1 (505) 345-3795
Email: amygross@sucasamagazine.com
Website: http://www.sucasamagazine.com

Publishes: Articles; Nonfiction; *Areas:* Architecture; Design; *Markets:* Adult; *Treatments:* Contemporary

Editors: Amy Gross

Magazine on contemporary home building in the South West. Send query with published clips.

Sunshine Artist

N7528 Aanstad Road
PO Box 5000
Iola, WI 54945
Tel: +1 (800) 597-2573
Email: editor@sunshineartist.com
Website: http://www.sunshineartist.com

Publishes: Nonfiction; Reviews; *Areas:* Arts; Crafts; *Markets:* Professional

Editors: Stephanie Hintz

Publishes reviews of fine art fairs, festivals, events, and small craft shows around the country, for professionals making a living through art shows.

Susquehanna Life

217 Market Street
Lewisburg, PA 17837
Tel: +1 (800) 232-1670
Fax: +1 (570) 524-7796
Email: susquehannalife@gmail.com
Website: http://www.susquehannalife.com

Publishes: Articles; Nonfiction; *Areas:* Arts; Beauty and Fashion; Business; Entertainment; Gardening; Health; Lifestyle; Nature; Travel; *Markets:* Adult

Lifestyle magazine covering central Pennsylvania.

Tallahassee Magazine

Rowland Publishing, Inc.
1932 Miccosukee Road
Tallahassee, FL 32308
Tel: +1 (850) 878-0554
Email: info@rowlandpublishing.com
Website: http://www.tallahasseemagazine.com

Publishes: Articles; Features; Interviews; Nonfiction; *Areas:* Business; Entertainment; Historical; Lifestyle; Sport; Travel; *Markets:* Adult

Publishes material for visitors to and residents of Florida's capital city. Send query with published clips.

Tech Directions

251 Jackson Plaza, Suite A
Ann Arbor, MI 48103-1955
Tel: +1 (734) 975-2800
Fax: +1 (734) 975-2787
Email: vanessa@techdirections.com
Website: http://www.techdirections.com

Publishes: Articles; Nonfiction; *Areas:* Science; Technology; *Markets:* Professional

Editors: Vanessa Revelli

Publishes articles about what is going on in the career-technical and STEM education fields; ideas teachers can use in the classroom; and anything that can help prepare students for a career. See website for submission guidelines.

Texas Co-op Power

1122 Colorado Street, 24th Floor
Austin, TX 78701
Email: info@texascooppower.com
Website: http://www.texascooppower.com

Publishes: Articles; Nonfiction; *Areas:* Technology; *Markets:* Adult

Magazine which aims to improve the quality of life of electric co-operative member-customers in Texas in an informative and engaging format. Potential contributors should familiarise themselves with the magazine, then submit query by email.

The Health Journal

4808 Courthouse Street, Suite 204
Williamsburg, VA 23188
Tel: +1 (757) 645-4475
Email: editorial@thehealthjournals.com
Website: http://www.thehealthjournals.com

Publishes: Articles; Nonfiction; *Areas:* Health; *Markets:* Adult

Health magazine focussing on Virginia, but willing to publish articles of both local and national interest.

This Old House

262 Harbor Drive
Stamford, CT 06902
Tel: +1 (475) 209-8665
Email: contact@thisoldhouse.com
Website: https://www.thisoldhouse.com

Publishes: Articles; Features; Nonfiction; *Areas:* Design; How-to; *Markets:* Adult

Home improvement magazine. Send query with published clips.

TimberWest

PO Box 610
Edmonds, WA 98020
Tel: +1 (425) 778-3388
Fax: +1 (425) 771-3623
Email: timberwest@forestnet.com
Website: http://forestnet.com/TimberWest.php

Publishes: Articles; Interviews; Nonfiction; *Areas:* Business; Historical; *Markets:* Professional

Magazine covering the logging industry in the Northwest. No material that puts a negative slant on the industry.

Tobacco International

Lockwood Publications, Inc.
3743 Crescent Street, 2nd Floor
Long Island City, NY 11101
Tel: +1 (212) 391-2060
Fax: +1 (212) 827-0945
Email: editor@tobaccointernational.com
Website: http://www.tobaccointernational.com

Publishes: Articles; News; Nonfiction; *Areas:* Business; *Markets:* Professional

Magazine publishing material relating to the tobacco industry.

Trailer Life Magazine

2750 Park View Ct., Suite 240
Oxnard, CA, 93036
Tel: +1 (800) 765-1912
Email: info@trailerlife.com
Website: http://www.trailerlife.com

Publishes: Articles; Features; News; Nonfiction; *Areas:* Hobbies; Leisure; Technology; Travel; *Markets:* Adult

Magazine written for, and by, mature and discerning RVers. No unsolicited submissions, or queries by email. Send queries by post only.

TravelWorld International Magazine

3579 Foothill Boulevard, #744
Pasadena, CA 91107
Tel: +1 (626) 376-9754
Fax: +1 (626) 628-1854
Website: http://www.travelworldmagazine.com

Publishes: Articles; Nonfiction; *Areas:* Travel; *Markets:* Adult

Editors: Dennis A. Britton

Travel magazine. Contributors must be members of NATJA.

Tropical Fish Hobbyist Magazine

Email: associateeditor@tfh.com
Website: http://www.tfhmagazine.com

Publishes: Articles; Nonfiction; *Areas:* Hobbies; Nature; *Markets:* Adult

Publishes articles of interest to keepers of tropical fish. Articles are normally between 10,000 and 20,000 words. See website for full submission guidelines.

Underground Construction

Oildom Publishing Company of Texas, Inc.
1160 Dairy Ashford Road, Suite 610
Houston, TX 77079
Tel: +1 (281) 558-6930
Email: rcarpenter@oildom.com
Website: https://ucononline.com

Publishes: Articles; News; Nonfiction; *Areas:* Business; Design; How-to; *Markets:* Professional

Publishes material for industries involved in the construction and maintenance of underground pipelines. Send query with published clips in first instance.

US Glass Magazine

Key Communications Inc.
20 PGA Drive, Suite 201
Stafford, VA 22554
Tel: +1 (540) 720-5584
Fax: +1 (540) 720-5687
Email: info@usglassmag.com
Website: http://www.usglassmag.com

Publishes: Articles; Nonfiction; *Areas:* Architecture; Business; *Markets:* Professional

Editors: Ellen Rogers

Magazine aimed at companies involved in the architectural class industry. Send query with published clips.

Vegetable Growers News Magazine

Great American Media Services
PO Box 128
Sparta, Michigan 49345
Tel: +1 (616) 887-9008
Fax: +1 (616) 887-2666
Email: vgnedit@vegetablegrowersnews.com
Website: http://vegetablegrowersnews.com

Publishes: Articles; Interviews; News; Nonfiction; Reviews; *Areas:* Nature; *Markets:* Professional

Magazine for professional vegetable growers. Send query with published clips and author CV.

VFW (Veterans of Foreign Wars) Magazine

406 West 34th Street
Kansas City, MO 64111
Tel: +1 (816) 756-3390
Email: magazine@vfw.org
Website: http://www.vfwmagazine.org

Publishes: Articles; News; Nonfiction; *Areas:* Current Affairs; Historical; Military; *Markets:* Adult

Magazine aimed at veterans of US overseas conflicts. Send query by email with published clips. No poetry, fiction, op-eds, reprints or book reviews.

Vogue Patterns

The McCall Pattern Company
Attn: Customer Service
120 Broadway, 34th floor
New York, New York 10271
Email: editor@voguepatterns.com
Website: https://voguepatterns.mccall.com

Publishes: Articles; Nonfiction; *Areas:* Crafts; Hobbies; How-to; *Markets:* Adult

Publishes sewing articles and patterns.

Walls & Ceilings

2401 West Big Beaver Road, Suite 700
Troy, MI 48084-3333
Tel: +1 (248) 362-3700
Fax: +1 (248) 362-5103
Email: wyattj@bnpmedia.com
Website: http://www.wconline.com

Publishes: Nonfiction; *Areas:* Architecture; Design; How-to; *Markets:* Professional

Editors: John Wyatt

Magazine aimed at interior and exterior wall and ceiling contractors, architects, manufacturers, suppliers and distributors. Send query or complete ms.

The Washington Pastime

Email: paulkaraffa@washingtonpastime.com
Website: http://www.
washingtonpastime.com

Publishes: Articles; Essays; Fiction; Nonfiction; Poetry; *Areas:* Adventure; Crime; Drama; Entertainment; Fantasy; Gothic; Horror; Humour; Literature; Mystery; Romance; Sci-Fi; Short Stories; Suspense; Thrillers; Westerns; *Markets:* Adult; Children's; Family; Professional; Youth; *Treatments:* Commercial; Contemporary; Cynical; Dark; Experimental; In-depth; Light; Literary; Mainstream; Niche; Popular; Positive; Progressive; Satirical; Serious; Traditional

Editors: Paul Karaffa, Laura Bolt

Note: Not accepting submissions as at November 2016. Check website for current status.

In 2010 a study from Central Connecticut State University found that the Washington DC area was the most well-read urban city in the United States. But Washington, DC did not have a professional literary magazine in the city representing its stake in contemporary American literature.

This magazine was founded as an electronic and print publication based in Washington, DC committed to publishing the best in literary and genre fiction. Work featured here will push literary limitations and take a new look at antiquated perspectives.

Authors will find a home here from all around the world, and in turn find themselves burrowing a place into the hearts of the readership in the United States, and specifically the DC metropolitan area.

Water Well Journal

National Ground Water Association
Attn: Water Well Journal
601 Dempsey Road
Westerville, OH 43081-8978
Email: tplumley@ngwa.org
Website: http://waterwelljournal.com

Publishes: Articles; Features; Interviews; Nonfiction; *Areas:* Business; How-to; Technology; *Markets:* Professional

Editors: Thad Plumley

Magazine serving the water well drilling industry. Send query with published clips.

Welding Design & Fabrication

1300 E. 9th St.
Cleveland, OH 44114-1503
Tel: +1 (216) 696-7000
Fax: +1 (216) 931-9524
Email: Robert.brooks@penton.com
Website: http://weldingdesign.com

Publishes: Articles; News; Nonfiction; *Areas:* Business; How-to; Technology; *Markets:* Professional

Magazine for welders, and those involved in the welding industry.

Western & Eastern Treasures

PO Box 647
Pacific Grove, CA 93950-0647
Tel: +1 (831) 920-2426
Email: editor@wetreasures.com
Website: http://www.wetreasures.com

Publishes: Articles; Nonfiction; *Areas:* Hobbies; Leisure; Sport; *Markets:* Adult

Magazine for metal detectorists, covering every aspect of the hobby. Articles must be between 1,500 and 2,500 words and must be accompanied by digital photos of at least 300 dpi.

Western Outdoor News

Email: pat@wonews.com
Website: http://www.wonews.com

Publishes: Articles; Nonfiction; *Areas:* Hobbies; Leisure; Sport; *Markets:* Adult

Editors: Pat McDonell

Magazine serving the interests of fishermen and hunters living in and around California. Submit articles via website or by email. See website for full details.

Wordpeace

Email: editors.wordpeace@gmail.com
Website: http://wordpeace.co

Publishes: Articles; Fiction; Interviews; Nonfiction; Poetry; *Areas:* Short Stories; *Markets:* Adult; *Treatments:* Literary

Editors: Monica A. Hand, Poetry; Joanna Eleftheriou, Nonfiction; Oonagh C. Doherty, Fiction

Online journal of literary response to world events in the spirit of promoting peace and hope for all people. Seeks poems, stories and articles or interviews that reflect or are in conversation with world events. Submit using online submission system.

Zeek

125 Maiden Lane, 8th Floor
New York, NY 10038
Email: zeek@zeek.net
Website: http://zeek.forward.com

Publishes: Articles; Essays; Fiction; Nonfiction; Poetry; *Areas:* Arts; Culture; Religious; Spiritual; *Markets:* Adult; *Treatments:* Progressive

Editors: Erica Brody

Jewish online magazine launched in 2001 and relaunched in 2013 as a hub for the domestic Jewish social justice movement. Publishes first-person essays, commentary, reporting, fiction, and poetry. Send query by email in first instance. Not accepting fiction submissions as at January 2015.

ZYZZYVA

57 Post Street, Suite 604
San Francisco, CA 94104
Tel: +1 (415) 752-4393
Fax: +1 (415) 752-4391
Email: editor@zyzzyva.org
Website: http://www.zyzzyva.org

Publishes: Fiction; Nonfiction; Poetry; *Areas:* Short Stories; Translations; *Markets:* Adult; *Treatments:* Literary

Publishes material by writers living on the West Coast, in Alaska and Hawaii only. Submit one piece of fiction or nonfiction or up to five poems at a time, with SASE for response. No restrictions as to length of item or number of items submitted. Accepts simultaneous submissions, but notify if accepted elsewhere. No submissions by email. Accepts submissions from January 1 to May 31 and from August 1 to November 30 only. See website for full guidelines.

UK Magazines

For the most up-to-date listings of these and hundreds of other magazines, visit https://www.firstwriter.com/magazines

*To claim your **free** access to the site, please see the back of this book.*

Acumen

6 The Mount
Higher Furzeham
Brixham
South Devon
TQ5 8QY
Tel: +44 (0) 1803 851098
Email: patriciaoxley6@gmail.com
Website: http://www.acumen-poetry.co.uk

Publishes: Articles; Features; Interviews; Nonfiction; Poetry; Reviews; *Areas:* Criticism; Literature; *Markets:* Adult; *Treatments:* Literary

Editors: Patricia Oxley

Magazine publishing poetry and articles, features, and reviews connected to poetry. Send submissions with SAE and author details on each page, or submit by email as Word attachment. See website for full submission guidelines.

Africa Confidential

37 John's Mews
London
WC1N 2NS
Tel: +44 (0) 20 7831 3511
Email: andrew@africa-confidential.com
Website: http://www.africa-confidential.com

Publishes: Articles; News; Nonfiction; *Areas:* Finance; Politics; *Markets:* Adult

Editors: Andrew Weir, Deputy Editor

Magazine publishing news and articles on African politics and economics. Welcomes unsolicited mss.

Africa-Asia Confidential

73 Farringdon Road
London
EC1M 3JQ
Tel: +44 (0) 20 7831 3511
Fax: +44 (0) 20 7831 6778
Email: editorial@africa-asia-confidential.com
Website: http://www.africa-asia-confidential.com

Publishes: Articles; Features; News; Nonfiction; *Areas:* Current Affairs; *Markets:* Adult

Editors: Clare Tauben

Publishes news articles and features focussing on the Africa-Asia axis. Welcomes unsolicited mss, but must be unpublished and offered exclusively.

African Business

IC Publications Ltd
7 Coldbath Square
EC1R 4LQ
London
Tel: +44 (0) 20 7841 3210
Fax: +44 (0) 20 7841 3211
Email: editorial@icpublications.com
Website: http://africanbusinessmagazine.com

Publishes: Articles; Nonfiction; *Areas:* Business; Finance; *Markets:* Professional

Editors: Anver Versi

Bestselling pan-African business magazine. Special reports profile a wide range of sectors and industries including transport, energy, mining, construction, aviation and agriculture.

Agenda

The Wheelwrights
Fletching Street
Mayfield
East Sussex
TN20 6TL
Tel: +44 (0) 1435 873703
Email: submissions@agendapoetry.co.uk
Website: http://www.agendapoetry.co.uk

Publishes: Essays; Poetry; Reviews; *Areas:* Criticism; Literature; *Markets:* Adult; *Treatments:* Literary

Editors: Patricia McCarthy

Publishes poems, critical essays, and reviews. Send up to five poems or up to two essays / reviews with email address, age, and short bio. No previously published material. Submit by email only, with each piece in a separate Word attachment. Accepts work only during specific submission windows – see website for current status.

All Out Cricket

TriNorth Ltd
Fourth Floor
Bedser Stand
Kia Oval
Kennington
London
SE11 5SS
Tel: +44 (0) 20 3696 5732
Email: comments@alloutcricket.com
Website: http://www.alloutcricket.com

Publishes: Articles; Interviews; News; Nonfiction; *Areas:* Sport; *Markets:* Adult

Editors: Phil Walker

Cricket magazine. Send query by email in first instance.

Ambit

Staithe House
Main Road
Brancaster Staithe
Norfolk
PE31 8BP
Tel: +44 (0) 7503 633601
Email: info@ambitmagazine.co.uk
Website: http://ambitmagazine.co.uk

Publishes: Fiction; Poetry; *Areas:* Arts; Short Stories; *Markets:* Adult; *Treatments:* Literary

An international magazine. Potential contributors are advised to read a copy before submitting work to us. Send up to 5 poems, a story up to 5,000 words, or flash fiction up to 1,000 words. Submit via online portal on website, or by post (see website for full details). No submissions by email. Two reading periods per year. For poetry: Feb 1 to April 1; and Sep 1 to Nov 1. For fiction: Feb 1 to March 1; and Sep 1 to Oct 1.

Android Magazine

Richmond House
33 Richmond Hill
Bournemouth
Dorset
BH2 6EZ
Tel: +44 (0) 1202 586200
Email: enquiries@imagine-publishing.co.uk
Website: http://www.littlegreenrobot.co.uk

Publishes: Articles; Features; News; Nonfiction; Reviews; *Areas:* How-to; Technology; *Markets:* Adult

Magazine covering the Android operating system, including news, features, reviews, and tips. Send query by email. No unsolicited mss.

Angler's Mail

Pinehurst 2
Pinehurst Road
Farnborough Business Park
Farnborough
Hampshire
GU14 7BF
Tel: +44 (0) 1252 555055
Email: anglersmail@timeinc.com
Website: http://www.anglersmail.co.uk

Publishes: Features; News; Nonfiction; *Areas:* Hobbies; Sport; *Markets:* Adult

Publishes pictures, stories, and features relating to angling news and matches.

Arc

c/o New Scientist
Lacon House
84 Theobald's Road
London
WC1X 8NS
Tel: +44 (0) 20 7611 1205
Email: simon.ings@arcfinity.org
Website: http://www.arcfinity.org

Publishes: Essays; Features; Fiction; Nonfiction; *Areas:* Science; Sci-Fi; Short Stories; *Markets:* Adult

Editors: Simon Ings

"Journal of the future". Publishes features, essays, and speculative fiction about the world to come. Most work is commissioned.

Architecture Today

34 Pentonville Road
London
N1 9HF
Tel: +44 (0) 20 7837 0143
Email: editorial@architecturetoday.co.uk
Website: http://www.architecturetoday.co.uk

Publishes: Articles; Features; Nonfiction; *Areas:* Architecture; *Markets:* Professional

Monthly magazine for architects, presenting the most important current projects in the UK and the rest of Europe.

Artificium

Email: editor@artificium.co.uk
Website: http://www.artificium.co.uk

Publishes: Fiction; Poetry; *Areas:* Short Stories; *Markets:* Adult; *Treatments:* Literary

Publishes short fiction between 2,000 and 6,000 words; three-part serials up to a total of 12,000 words; very short fiction between 400 and 1,250 words; and poetry of any length. All work must be in English and submitted by email during open reading periods: see website for details.

ArtReview

1 Honduras Street
London
EC1Y 0TH
Tel: +44 (0) 20 7490 8138
Email: artreview@abacusemedia.com
Website: http://artreview.com

Publishes: Articles; News; Nonfiction; Reviews; *Areas:* Arts; Criticism; *Markets:* Adult; *Treatments:* Contemporary

International contemporary art magazine, dedicated to expanding contemporary art's audience and reach.

Attitude

Attitude Media Ltd
33 Pear Tree Street
London
EC1V 3AG
Email: matthew.todd@attitude.co.uk
Website: http://attitude.co.uk

Publishes: Articles; Features; News; Nonfiction; *Areas:* Beauty and Fashion; Entertainment; Lifestyle; Men's Interests; Travel; *Markets:* Adult

Editors: Matthew Todd (Editorial Director)

Magazine for gay men.

The Author

84 Drayton Gardens
London
SW10 9SB
Tel: +44 (0) 207 7373 6642
Email: theauthor@societyofauthors.org
Website: http://www.societyofauthors.org

Publishes: Articles; Nonfiction; *Areas:* Business; How-to; Legal; *Markets:* Professional

Editors: James McConnachie

Magazine covering all aspects of the writing profession, including legal, technical, and commercial considerations. Query in writing in first instance.

Banipal

1 Gough Square
London
EC4A 3DE
Tel: +44 (0) 20 7832 1350
Fax: +44 (0) 20 8568 8509
Email: editor@banipal.co.uk
Website: http://www.banipal.co.uk

Publishes: Features; Fiction; Poetry; Reviews; *Areas:* Short Stories; Translations; *Markets:* Adult

Editors: Margaret Obank

Contemporary Arab authors in English translations. Publishes new and established writers, and diverse material including translations, poetry, short stories, novel excerpts, profiles, interviews, appreciations, book reviews, reports of literary festivals, conferences, and prizes.

The Beano

185 Fleet Street
London
EC4A 2HS
Tel: +44 (0) 1382 575580
Fax: +44 (0) 1382 575413
Email: beano@dcthomson.co.uk
Website: http://www.beano.com

Publishes: Fiction; *Areas:* Humour; Short Stories; *Markets:* Children's

Publishes comic strips for children aged 6-12. Accepts artwork and scripts.

The Big Issue

43 Bath Street
Glasgow
G2 1HW
Tel: +44 (0) 1413 527280
Email: editorial@bigissue.com
Website: http://www.bigissue.com

Publishes: Articles; Features; Interviews; News; Reviews; *Areas:* Arts; Culture; Sociology; *Markets:* Adult

General interest magazine focusing on social issues, culture, the arts, etc. No short stories or poetry.

Bizarre

Dennis Publishing
30 Cleveland Street
London
W1T 4JD
Tel: +44 (0) 20 7907 6000
Email: bizarre@dennis.co.uk
Website: http://www.bizarremag.com

Publishes: Articles; Features; Interviews; News; Nonfiction; *Markets:* Adult

Describes itself as one of the most shocking magazines in the world. Publishes features, interviews, and uncensored photos of the weird, freakish, and outrageous. No fiction.

Black Static

TTA Press
5 Martins Lane
Witcham
Ely
Cambs
CB6 2LB
Website: http://ttapress.com

Publishes: Fiction; *Areas:* Fantasy; Horror; Short Stories; *Markets:* Adult; *Treatments:* Dark

Editors: Andy Cox

Publishes short stories of horror and dark fantasy. See website for full guidelines and online submission system.

British Birds

4 Harlequin Gardens
St Leonards on Sea
East Sussex
TN37 7PF

EDITORIAL
Spindrift
Eastshore
Virkie
Shetland
ZE3 9JS
Tel: +44 (0) 1424 755155
Fax: +44 (0) 1424 755155
Email: editor@britishbirds.co.uk
Website: https://britishbirds.co.uk

Publishes: Articles; Nonfiction; *Areas:* Nature; *Markets:* Adult

Editors: Roger Riddington

Magazine for birdwatchers, publishing articles on behaviour, conservation, distribution, identification, status and taxonomy.

British Journalism Review

SAGE Publications
1 Oliver's Yard
55 City Road
London
EC1Y 1SP
Tel: +44 (0) 20 7324 8500
Fax: 20 7324 8600
Email: editor@bjr.org.uk
Website: http://www.bjr.org.uk

Publishes: Articles; Nonfiction; *Areas:* Media; *Markets:* Academic

Editors: Kim Fletcher

Quarterly peer-reviewed academic journal covering the field of journalism. Welcomes letters and articles, by post or by email.

Building

Ludgate House
245 Blackfriars Road
London
SE1 9UY
Tel: +44 (0) 20 7560 4000
Email: sarah.richardson@ubm.com
Website: http://www.building.co.uk

Publishes: Articles; News; Nonfiction; *Areas:* Architecture; Business; *Markets:* Professional

Editors: Sarah Richardson

Magazine for the construction industry.

Bunbury Magazine

Email: submissions@bunburymagazine.com
Website: https://bunburymagazine.com

Publishes: Articles; Fiction; Nonfiction; Poetry; Reviews; *Areas:* Short Stories; *Markets:* Adult; *Treatments:* Literary

Online literary magazine. Publishes anything from poetry to artwork, flash fiction to graphic story, life writing to photography, plus reviews and articles. Send submissions by email. See website for full guidelines, and for current issue theme.

Cambridge Magazine

Winship Road
Milton
Cambridge
Cambridgeshire
CB24 6BQ
Tel: +44 (0) 01223 434419
Email: alice.ryan@cambridge-news.co.uk
Website: http://www.cambridge-news.co.uk/CambridgeMagazine.html

Publishes: Features; Interviews; Nonfiction; *Areas:* Arts; Beauty and Fashion; Culture; Gardening; Lifestyle; Technology; *Markets:* Adult

Editors: Alice Ryan

Magazine covering Cambridge, including food and drink, arts and culture, homes and gardens, fashion and beauty, and gears and gadgets.

Carousel

The Saturn Centre
54-76 Bissell Street
Birmingham
B5 7HP
Tel: +44 (0) 1216 227458
Email: carousel.guide@virgin.net
Website: http://www.carouselguide.co.uk

Publishes: Articles; Interviews; Nonfiction; Reviews; *Areas:* Literature; *Markets:* Children's

Editors: David Blanch

Magazine publishing reviews of fiction, poetry, and nonfiction books for children. Also publishes articles, author profiles, and interviews.

The Casket of Fictional Delights

Email: joanna@thecasket.co.uk
Website: http://www.thecasket.co.uk

Publishes: Fiction; *Areas:* Short Stories; *Markets:* Adult

Editors: Joanna Sterling

Online magazine publishing flash fiction up to 300 words and short stories between 1,200 and 3,000 words. Submissions by invitation and recommendation only.

The Caterer

Travel Weekly Group Ltd
52 Grosvenor Gardens
London
SW1W 0AU
Tel: +44 (0) 20 7881 4803
Email: info@thecaterer.com
Website: https://www.thecaterer.com

Publishes: Articles; News; Nonfiction; *Areas:* Business; *Markets:* Professional

Editors: Amanda Afiya

Magazine for hotel, restaurant, foodservice and pub and bar operators.

The Catholic Herald

Herald House
15 Lamb's Passage
Bunhill Row
London
EC1Y 8TQ
Tel: +44 (0) 20 7448 3607
Fax: +44 (0) 20 7448 3603
Email: editorial@catholicherald.co.uk
Website: http://www.catholicherald.co.uk

Publishes: Articles; News; Nonfiction; *Areas:* Religious; *Markets:* Adult

Editors: Luke Coppen

Weekly magazine publishing articles and news for Catholics.

Central and Eastern European London Review

Email: ceel.org@gmail.com
Website: http://ceel.org.uk

Publishes: Articles; Nonfiction; Reviews; *Areas:* Arts; Culture; Film; Literature; Music; Theatre; Travel; *Markets:* Adult

Editors: Robin Ashenden

Online magazine covering all aspects of Central and Eastern European life in London. Send submissions by email.

Classic Cars

Bauer
Lynch Wood
Peterborough Business Park
Peterborough
Cambridgeshire
PE2 6EA
Tel: +44 (0) 1733 468582
Email: classic.cars@bauermedia.co.uk
Website: http://www.classiccarsmagazine.co.uk

Publishes: Articles; Nonfiction; *Areas:* Historical; Technology; Travel; *Markets:* Adult

Publishes articles on classic cars and related events.

Climb Magazine

Greenshires Publishing
160-164 Barkby Road
Leicester
LE16 8FZ
Tel: +44 (0) 1162 022600
Fax: +44 (0) 1162 769002
Email: climbmagazine@gmail.com
Website: http://www.climbmagazine.com

Publishes: Articles; Nonfiction; *Areas:* Hobbies; Leisure; Sport; *Markets:* Adult

Editors: David Pickford

Magazine aimed at climbers. Query editor in first instance.

Closer

Tel: +44 (0) 20 7859 8463
Email: closer@closermag.co.uk
Website: http://www.closeronline.co.uk

Publishes: Articles; Features; News; Nonfiction; *Areas:* Beauty and Fashion; Entertainment; Health; Lifestyle; Women's Interests; *Markets:* Adult

Women's lifestyle magazine publishing news, articles, and features on style and beauty, body and wellbeing, celebrities, and real life stories.

Coach

Email: editorial@coachmag.co.uk
Website: http://www.coachmag.co.uk

Publishes: Articles; News; Nonfiction; *Areas:* Health; Leisure; Sport; *Markets:* Adult

Free weekly health and fitness magazine.

Computeractive Magazine

800 Guillat Avenue
Kent Science Park
Sittingbourne
ME9 8GU
Tel: +44 (0) 1795 412882
Email: ca@servicehelpline.co.uk
Website: http://getcomputeractive.co.uk

Publishes: Articles; News; Nonfiction; Reviews; *Areas:* How-to; Technology; *Markets:* Adult

Magazine covering computers, smart phones, tablets, and the internet, providing news, reviews, and advice.

Cook Vegetarian

25 Phoenix Court
Hawkins Road
Colchester
Essex
CO2 8JY
Tel: +44 (0) 1206 508627
Email: fae@cookveg.co.uk
Website: http://www.vegetarianrecipesmag.com

Publishes: Nonfiction; *Areas:* Cookery; *Markets:* Adult

Editors: Fae Gilfillan

Publishes recipes for meat-free cooking.

Country Walking

Bauer Consumer Media Limited
Media House
Peterborough Business Park
Peterborough
PE2 6EA
Tel: +44 (0) 1733 468208
Email: guy.procter@lfto.com
Website: http://www.countrywalking.co.uk

Publishes: Articles; Features; News; Nonfiction; Reviews; *Areas:* Hobbies; Lifestyle; Nature; Travel; *Markets:* Adult

Editors: Guy Procter

Magazine on walking in the UK and Europe. Publishes news, product tests and reviews, features, and profiles of celebrity walkers.

craft&design Magazine

PO Box 5
Driffield
East Yorkshire
YO25 8JD
Tel: +44 (0) 1377 255213
Email: info@craftanddesign.net
Website: http://www.craftanddesign.net

Publishes: Articles; Features; News; Nonfiction; *Areas:* Crafts; Design; *Markets:* Adult

Editors: Angie Boyer

Publishes material for those interested in crafts and design. Ideas for articles and features welcome.

Critical Quarterly

Newbury
Crediton
Devon
EX17 5HA
Email: CQpoetry@gmail.com
Website: http://onlinelibrary.wiley.com/journal/10.1111/(ISSN)1467-8705

Publishes: Essays; Fiction; Nonfiction; Poetry; *Areas:* Criticism; Culture; Literature; Short Stories; *Markets:* Adult; *Treatments:* Literary

Editors: Colin MacCabe

Publishes literary criticism, cultural studies, poetry and fiction. Send submissions by email. See website for separate email address for submissions of criticism.

Crystal Magazine

3 Bowness Avenue
Prenton
Birkenhead
CH43 0SD
Tel: +44 (0) 1516 089736
Email: christinecrystal@hotmail.com
Website: http://www.christinecrystal.blogspot.com

Publishes: Articles; Fiction; Nonfiction; Poetry; *Areas:* Adventure; Fantasy; Humour; Literature; Mystery; Nature; Romance; Sci-Fi; Short Stories; Suspense; Thrillers; Travel; Westerns; *Markets:* Adult; *Treatments:* Light; Literary; Mainstream; Popular; Positive; Traditional

Editors: Christine Carr

For subscribers only. Work is only considered from subscribers. Handwritten material will be looked at.

Poems, stories, articles. A4, spiral-bound bi-monthly. Forty pages with colour images. Also includes the very popular 'Wordsmithing', a look into the lives of writers and writing. The magazine usually contains pages and pages of Readers' Letters. Subscribers' News provides an opportunity to share writing achievements.

The special 'golden' 100th issue (July 2017) is out now. More colour, more pages. Includes the winning poem in the Floral Poetry Competition.

Current Accounts

Apartment 2D
Beadshaw Hall
Hardcastle Gardens
Bolton
BL2 4NZ
Email: fjameshartnell@aol.com
Website: https://sites.google.com/site/bankstreetwriters/current-accounts-magazine

Publishes: Essays; Fiction; Nonfiction; Poetry; Scripts; *Areas:* Drama; Short Stories; Translations; *Markets:* Adult; *Treatments:* Literary

Editors: F. J. Hartnell

Web-based publication with one printed collection per year. Submit up to four poems or up to two stories, plays, or essays at a time, by email or by post with SAE /IRCs. Emailed submissions should be included in the body of the email, not as an attachment. Plays should be one act and no longer than 4 minutes when read aloud.

Custom Car

Kelsey Publishing Ltd
Cudham Tithe Barn
Berry's Hill
Cudham
Kent
TN16 3AG
Tel: +44 (0) 1959 543747
Email: cc.ed@kelseypb.co.uk
Website: http://www.customcarmag.co.uk

Publishes: Articles; Nonfiction; *Areas:* Hobbies; *Markets:* Adult

Editors: Dave Biggadyke

Magazine covering the UK drag racing scene and customised classics.

Dare

Ground Floor
16 Connaught Place
London
W2 2ES
Tel: +44 (0) 20 7420 7000
Email: info@therivergroup.co.uk
Website: http://www.therivergroup.co.uk

Publishes: Articles; Features; Nonfiction; *Areas:* Beauty and Fashion; Women's Interests; *Markets:* Adult

Free magazine published on behalf of high street chain.

The Dawntreader

24 Forest Houses
Halwill
Beaworthy
Devon
EX21 5UU
Email: dawnidp@gmail.com
Website: http://www.indigodreams.co.uk/the-dawntreader

Publishes: Articles; Features; Fiction; Nonfiction; Poetry; *Areas:* Fantasy; Nature; Short Stories; *Markets:* Adult

Editors: Ronnie Goodyer

A quarterly publication specialising in the landscape; myth and legend... nature; spirituality and pre-history... environment and ecology... the mystic.

Seeking poetry in all forms and also welcomes prose up to 1,000 words, articles and local legends.

Decanter

Blue Fin Building
110 Southwark Street
SE1 0SU
Tel: +44 (0) 20 3148 5000
Email: editor@decanter.com
Website: http://www.decanter.com

Publishes: Articles; Features; News; Nonfiction; *Areas:* Cookery; Travel; *Markets:* Adult

Magazine on wines publishing articles, features, and news relating to wine and related subjects of food, cookery, etc. Welcomes ideas by post or fax.

Decanto

PO Box 3257
Littlehampton
BN16 9AF
Email: masque_pub@btinternet.com
Website: http://www.masquepublishing.eu.pn

Publishes: Poetry; *Markets:* Adult

Editors: Lisa Stewart

On hiatus as of January 2015. Check website for current status.

Send up to six original poems, of which 1-3 may be published, by post with SAE or by email in the body of the message (no attachments). Poems of any subject or style are considered.

Diabetes Balance

Diabetes UK Central Office
Macleod House
10 Parkway
London
NW1 7AA
Tel: +44 (0) 345 123 2399
Fax: +44 (0) 20 7424 1001
Email: info@diabetes.org.uk
Website: https://www.diabetes.org.uk

Publishes: Articles; Interviews; News; Nonfiction; *Areas:* Health; Lifestyle; Medicine; Science; *Markets:* Adult

Lifestyle magazine for people with diabetes, publishing relevant news and research, as well as celebrity interviews, recipes, competitions, and regular free supplements.

Digital Camera World

Quay House
The Ambury
Bath
BA1 1UA
Tel: +44 (0) 1225 442244
Website: http://www.digitalcameraworld.com

Publishes: Articles; Features; Nonfiction; Reviews; *Areas:* How-to; Photography; *Markets:* Adult

How-to magazine for photographers, including reviews of equipment and software, etc.

Diva

Millivres Prowler Ltd.
Unit M,Spectrum House
32-34 Gordon House Road
London
NW5 1LP
Tel: +44 (0) 20 7424 7400
Fax: +44 (0) 20 7424 7401
Email: edit@divamag.co.uk
Website: http://www.divamag.co.uk

Publishes: Articles; Features; Nonfiction; *Areas:* Culture; Lifestyle; Women's Interests; *Markets:* Adult

Editors: Jane Czyzselska

Monthly glossy newsstand magazine for lesbians and bisexual women. Send query or submissions by email.

The Dolls' House

The Guild of Master Craftsmen
166 High Street
Lewes
East Sussex
BN7 1XU

Tel: +44 (0) 1273 477374
Website: https://www.thegmcgroup.com

Publishes: Articles; Features; Nonfiction; Reviews; *Areas:* Crafts; Hobbies; How-to; *Markets:* Adult

Magazine publishing material related to dolls' houses.

Drapers

Telephone House
69-77 Paul St
London
EC2A 4NQ
Tel: +44 (0) 20 3033 2600
Email: eric.musgrave@emap.com
Website: http://www.drapersonline.com

Publishes: Articles; Nonfiction; *Areas:* Beauty and Fashion; Business; Design; *Markets:* Professional

Editors: Eric Musgrave

Magazine for fashion retailers and suppliers.

Dream Catcher

Stairwell Books
161 Lowther Street
York
YO31 7LZ
Tel: +44 (0) 1904 733767
Email: rose@stairwellbooks.com
Website: http://www.dreamcatchermagazine.co.uk

Publishes: Fiction; Interviews; Nonfiction; Poetry; Reviews; *Areas:* Short Stories; Translations; *Markets:* Adult; *Treatments:* Literary

Editors: John Gilham

Send submissions by post, following guidelines on website. No electronic submissions.

Eat In Magazine

H Bauer Publishing
Academic House
24-28 Oval Road
London
NW1 7DT
Email: cookeryed@eatinmagazine.co.uk
Website: https://eatinmagazine.co.uk

Publishes: Articles; Nonfiction; *Areas:* Cookery; How-to; *Markets:* Adult

Editors: Margaret Nicholls

Cookery magazine.

Energy Engineering

Media Culture
Office 46
Pure Offices
Plato Close
Leamington Spa
Warwickshire
CV34 6WE
Tel: +44 (0) 1926 671338
Email: info@energyengineering.co.uk
Website: http://www.energyengineering.co.uk

Publishes: Articles; Features; News; Nonfiction; *Areas:* Design; Technology; *Markets:* Professional

Magazine covering the products and processes, innovation, technology and management of renewable energy and sustainability.

Engineering In Miniature

Warners Group Publications
The Maltings
West Street, Bourne
LINCS
PE10 9PH
Website: https://www.world-of-railways.co.uk/engineering-in-miniature

Publishes: Articles; Nonfiction; *Areas:* Hobbies; Technology; *Markets:* Adult

Editors: Martin Evans

Magazine publishing technical articles on model engineering. Send query via website.

The English Garden

The Chelsea Magazine Company
Third Floor Offices
Cumberland House
Oriel Road
Cheltenham

GL50 1BB
Email: theenglishgarden@chelseamagazines.com
Website: http://www.theenglishgarden.co.uk

Publishes: Articles; Features; Nonfiction; *Areas:* Gardening; How-to; *Markets:* Adult

Editors: Stephanie Mahon

Publishes features on gardens across the UK and Ireland, as well as gardening advice.

Envoi

Meirion House
Glan yr afon
Tanygrisiau
Blaenau Ffestiniog
LL41 3SU
Tel: +44 (0) 1766 832112
Email: envoi@cinnamonpress.com
Website: http://www.cinnamonpress.com/envoi

Publishes: Articles; Nonfiction; Poetry; Reviews; *Areas:* Literature; Translations; *Markets:* Adult; *Treatments:* Literary

Editors: Dr Jan Fortune-Wood

Magazine of poems, poetry sequences, reviews, and competitions, now more than 50 years old. Occasional poetry related articles and poetry in translation. Submit up to 6 poems up to 40 lines each or one or two longer poems by email only (in the body of the email; attachments will not be read). No submissions by post.

What others say:

"Probably the best poetry magazine currently available" – The Writers' College

"Without a grant and obviously well read, this poetry magazine excels itself." – Ore

"The policy of giving poets space to show their skills is the right one." – Haiku Quarterly

"Good quality, lots of bounce, poems, comps, reviews, reader comeback" – iota

"If you haven't tried it yet, do so, you'll get your money's worth." – New Hope International

Erotic Review

Email: editorial@ermagazine.org
Website: http://eroticreviewmagazine.com

Publishes: Articles; Features; Fiction; Nonfiction; Reviews; *Areas:* Erotic; Lifestyle; Short Stories; *Markets:* Adult

Editors: Jamie Maclean (Fiction)

Literary lifestyle publication about sex and sexuality aimed at sophisticated, intelligent and mature readers. Print version has been retired and is now online only. Publishes features, articles, short stories, and reviews. See website for full submission guidelines.

Evergreen

The Lypiatts
Lansdown Road
Cheltenham
Gloucestershire
GL50 2JA
Tel: +44 (0) 1242 225780
Email: editor@evergreenmagazine.co.uk
Website: https://www.thisengland.co.uk

Publishes: Articles; *Areas:* Culture; Historical; Nature; Travel; *Markets:* Adult

Magazine which "takes readers on a gentle journey around the highways and byways of Britain", covering British history, culture, people, and places. Publishes articles and poetry.

Everyday Practical Electronics

Wimborne Publishing Ltd
113 Lynwood Drive
Merley
Wimborne
Dorset
BH21 1UU
Tel: +44 (0) 1202 880299
Fax: +44 (0) 1202 843233
Email: editorial@wimborne.co.uk
Website: http://www.epemag.com

Publishes: Articles; Nonfiction; *Areas:* Hobbies; Technology; *Markets:* Academic; Adult

Editors: Matt Pulzer

Publishes articles on electronics for students and hobbyists.

Family Office Magazine

FOE Limited
27 Old Gloucester Street
London
WC1N 3AX
Tel: +44(0) 20 7193 8870
Email: contact@familyofficeelite.com
Website: http://www.familyofficemag.com

Publishes: Articles; *Areas:* Business; Finance; Leisure; *Markets:* Professional; *Treatments:* Mainstream

Editors: Ty Murphy

Caters for the ultra-wealthy Family Office sector. The publication is widely read by the world's leading experts from many of the World's leading institutions from the Family Office and the wealth sector. Many of these institutions are regular advertisers and sponsors while others are contributors who provide insightful interviews and contributions for the magazine.

Some of these institutions include Deloitte, Manulife Asset Management, Caplin & Drysdale, City Bank, BNY Mellon, PWC, Ernst & Young, BMO Private Bank, ING Private Bank, TSG Europe, Piraeus Bank, Global Family Offices, Trusted Family, Family Office Institute. Fuchs & AssociÃ©s Finance, Credit Suisse, Northwood Family Office, Lugen Family Office, Guernsey Finance, Family Office Association, FOSS Family Office Services Switzerland, Luxembourg For Family Office and many others. Family Office Elite also has publishing agreements in place with some these institutions including Deloitte which contribute expert articles in every issue.

Luxury brands include Heirloom, Tesla Cars, Heathrow Airport VIP , Luxury Channel, Ghurka Luggage, British Polo Day, 1066 Pianos, Holland & Holland, Burgess Yachts, DOMOS Fine Art, Signature Golf Events, Global Fine Arts Awards, Concierge-Aviation, Timeless Art Gallery, Charterworld, Alpha-Centauri Hydroplanes, Zimbali Costal Resorts, Chivas Luggage, Caprice Products, Polo & Tweed, Blenheim Palace, and more. Non – Profit Adverts include the Universal Film & Festival Organisation and Amnesty.

Feminist Review

c/o Women's Studies,
London Metropolitan University
166-220 Holloway Road
London
N7 8DB
Email: feminist-review@londonmet.ac.uk
Website: http://www.feminist-review.com

Publishes: Articles; Essays; Fiction; Interviews; Nonfiction; *Areas:* Politics; Sociology; Women's Interests; *Markets:* Academic; Adult; *Treatments:* Experimental

Editors: Joanna Hoare, Assistant Editor

Peer reviewed, interdisciplinary feminist journal. Publishes academic articles, experimental pieces, visual and textual media and political interventions, including, for example, interviews, short stories, poems and photographic essays. Submit via online submission system.

Fishing News

11th Floor
Nexus Place
25 Farringdon Street
London
EC4A 4AB
Tel: +44 (0) 1434 607375
Email: editor@fishingnews.co.uk
Website: http://fishingnews.co.uk

Publishes: Articles; News; Nonfiction; *Areas:* Business; Legal; Nature; *Markets:* Professional

Editors: Dave Linkie

Magazine for the fishing industry.

Flash: The International Short-Short Story Magazine

Department of English
University of Chester
Parkgate Road
Chester
CH1 4BJ
Email: flash.magazine@chester.ac.uk
Website: http://www.chester.ac.uk/flash.magazine

Publishes: Fiction; *Areas:* Short Stories; *Markets:* Adult; *Treatments:* Literary

Editors: Dr Peter Blair; Dr Ashley Chantler

Publishes flash fiction up to 360 words, including the title. Send up to four pieces per issue. Attach submissions to a single email. See website for full submission guidelines.

Flora International

Wimborne Publishing Ltd
113 Lynwood Drive
Merley
Wimborne
Dorset
BH21 1UU
Tel: +44 (0) 1202 880299
Fax: +44 (0) 1202 843233
Email: enquiries@flora-magazine.co.uk
Website: http://flora-magazine.co.uk

Publishes: Articles; Nonfiction; *Areas:* Crafts; Hobbies; How-to; Nature; *Markets:* Adult; Professional

Editors: Nina Tucknott

Magazine aimed at florists and flower arrangers.

Forage

Email: foragepoetry@gmail.com
Website: https://foragepoetry.com

Publishes: Essays; Nonfiction; Poetry; Reviews; *Markets:* Adult; *Treatments:* Literary

Publishes poetry, essays / creative nonfiction, reviews, art and photography. Submit up to five poems per issue. See website for upcoming issues and submit appropriate work by email.

The Friend

173 Euston Road
London
NW1 2BJ
Tel: +44 (0) 20 7663 1010
Email: editorial@thefriend.org
Website: https://thefriend.org

Publishes: Articles; Features; Nonfiction; *Areas:* Arts; Humour; Nature; Politics; Religious; Sociology; *Markets:* Adult

Unofficial magazine of Quaker interest intended to propogate their religious teaching, and promote interest in their work.

Frieze

1 Montclare Street
London
E2 7EU
Tel: +44 (0) 20 3372 6111
Email: editors@frieze.com
Website: https://frieze.com

Publishes: Articles; Essays; Nonfiction; Reviews; *Areas:* Arts; Culture; *Markets:* Adult; *Treatments:* Contemporary

Magazine of contemporary European arts and culture.

Geographical

3.20 Q West
1100 Great West Road
Brentford
Middlesex
TW8 0GP
Tel: +44 (0) 20 8332 8445
Fax: +44 (0) 20 8332 8438
Email: magazine@geographical.co.uk
Website: http://geographical.co.uk

Publishes: Articles; Nonfiction; *Areas:* Culture; Nature; Science; Travel; *Markets:* Adult

Publishes authoritative and educational material covering a wide range of subject areas, including geography, culture, wildlife and exploration.

Glamour

6-8 Old Bond Street
London

W1S 4PH
Tel: +44 (0) 20 7499 9080
Fax: +44 (0) 20 7491 2551
Email: glamoureditorialmagazine@condenast.co.uk
Website: http://www.glamourmagazine.co.uk

Publishes: Articles; Features; Nonfiction; *Areas:* Beauty and Fashion; Health; Lifestyle; Women's Interests; *Markets:* Adult

Editors: Jo Elvin; Rachel Pask (Features Editor)

Women's magazine publishing features on beauty, fashion, health, celebrities, love and relationships, gossip, etc. Send query to Features Editor with synopsis of idea. No unsolicited MSS.

Gold Dust
Email: sirat@davidgardiner.net
Website: http://www.golddustmagazine.co.uk

Publishes: Fiction; Poetry; Reviews; Scripts; *Areas:* Drama; Short Stories; *Markets:* Adult; *Treatments:* Literary

Editors: David Gardiner (Prose); Adele C Geraghty (Poetry)

Publishes short stories, flash fiction, and plays up to 3,000 words, poetry up to 50 lines, and book reviews up to 2,000 words. Submit up to 5 submissions at a time, by email. Accepts submissions December to February and June to August. No simultaneous submissions. See website for full guidelines.

Governance + Compliance
The Institute of Chartered Secretaries and Administrators
Saffron House
6–10 Kirby Street
London
EC1N 8TS
Tel: +44 (0) 20 7580 4741
Fax: +44 (0) 20 7323 1132
Email: ajones@icsa.org.uk
Website: https://www.icsa.org.uk/products-and-services/governance-and-compliance

Publishes: Articles; News; Nonfiction; *Areas:* Business; How-to; Legal; *Markets:* Professional

Editors: Alexandra Jones, Supervising Editor

Magazine publishing news, views and practical advice on the latest developments in the area of corporate governance and compliance.

GQ Magazine
Vogue House
1 Hanover Square
London
W1S 1JU
Email: onlineworkexperience@condenast.co.uk
Website: http://www.gq-magazine.co.uk

Publishes: Articles; News; Nonfiction; *Areas:* Beauty and Fashion; Culture; Lifestyle; Men's Interests; Technology; *Markets:* Adult

Magazine for men, covering fashion, culture, watches, grooming, lifestyle, and girls.

Granta
12 Addison Avenue
Holland Park
London
W11 4QR
Tel: +44 (0) 20 7605 1360
Fax: +44 (0) 20 7605 1361
Email: editorial@granta.com
Website: http://www.granta.com

Publishes: Fiction; Nonfiction; *Areas:* Autobiography; Culture; Politics; Short Stories; *Markets:* Adult; *Treatments:* Contemporary; Literary

Editors: Sigrid Rausing

Publishes fiction, memoirs, reportage, and photography. Issues tend to be themed and aim to be high-brow, diverse, and contemporary. No essays, book reviews, articles or news items that are topical and therefore transitory, genre fiction, poetry, or travel writing that does not have a particular focus. Accepts submissions between October 1 and March 31 only, except over the Christmas holidays. No length limits, but pieces are generally between 3,000 and

6,000 words. Submit online through website submission system.

Guitarist Magazine

Future Publishing Limited Quay House
The Ambury
Bath
BA1 1UA
Tel: +44 (0) 1225 442244
Email: futurenet-webmaster@futurenet.co.uk
Website: http://www.musicradar.com/guitarist

Publishes: Articles; Nonfiction; *Areas:* How-to; Music; *Markets:* Adult

Editors: Jamie Dickson

Magazine for guitar players, offering advice on what to buy and how to play. Welcomes ideas for articles.

Gutter Magazine

Email: info@guttermag.co.uk
Website: http://www.guttermag.co.uk

Publishes: Fiction; Poetry; Scripts; *Areas:* Drama; Short Stories; *Markets:* Adult; *Treatments:* Literary

Editors: Robbie Guillory; Colin Begg

Publishes poetry, short stories, and drama, by writers born or living in Scotland. Send up to five poems up to 120 lines total, or prose up to 3,500 words. Submit by email as Word attachment. See website for full guidelines.

H&E Naturist

Hawk Editorial Ltd
PO Box 545
Hull
HU9 9JF
Tel: +44 (0) 1482 342000
Email: editor@henaturist.net
Website: http://www.henaturist.net

Publishes: Articles; Essays; Features; News; Nonfiction; *Areas:* Arts; Culture; Historical; Lifestyle; Politics; Sociology; *Markets:* Adult

Editors: Sam Hawcroft

Publishes articles, essays, features, and opinion on life from a naturist angle. Send submissions by email as a .doc or .txt file, or by post on a CD or DVD, along with any images being supplied. See website for full guidelines.

Hortus

The Bryansground Press
Bryan's Ground
Stapleton (Nr Presteigne)
Herefordshire
LD8 2LP
Tel: +44 (0) 1544 260001
Email: all@hortus.co.uk
Website: http://www.hortus.co.uk

Publishes: Articles; Nonfiction; Reviews; *Areas:* Design; Gardening; Historical; Literature; *Markets:* Adult

Privately published quarterly journal aimed at intelligent and lively-minded gardeners throughout the English-speaking world. Publishes articles on gardens, plants, people and books; history design and ornament.

Housebuilder

Housebuilder Media Ltd
Ground Floor
HBF House
27 Broadwall
London
SE1 9PL
Tel: +44 (0) 20 7960 1630
Email: info@house-builder.co.uk
Website: http://www.house-builder.co.uk

Publishes: Articles; Nonfiction; *Areas:* Design; Technology; *Markets:* Professional

Professional journal for builders. Best to make initial contact in writing before submitting.

The Huffington Post (United Kingdom)

Shropshire House
11-20 Capper Street
London
WC1E 6JA
Email: HuffPostUK@huffingtonpost.com
Website: http://www.huffingtonpost.co.uk

Publishes: Articles; News; Nonfiction; *Areas:* Business; Current Affairs; Entertainment; Politics; Sport; Technology; *Markets:* Adult

UK branch of international online magazine of news and commentary. Send query by email to suggest news items or pitch ideas for a blog post. See website for specific contact details.

Index on Censorship

92-94 Tooley Street
London
SE1 2TH
Email: rachael@indexoncensorship.org
Website: https://www.indexoncensorship.org

Publishes: Articles; Nonfiction; *Areas:* Politics; *Markets:* Adult

Editors: Rachael Jolley

Magazine publishing material on censorship and the right to the freedom of expression.

Ink Sweat and Tears

Email: inksweatandtearssubmissions@gmail.com
Website: http://www.inksweatandtears.co.uk

Publishes: Poetry; Reviews; *Markets:* Adult; *Treatments:* Literary

Editors: Helen Ivory

UK-based webzine publishing poetry, prose, prose-poetry, word and image pieces, and poetry reviews. Send 4-6 pieces by email only. Also accepts unsolicited reviews of poetry and short story collections. See website for full guidelines.

Inside Soap

Hearst Magazines UK
72 Broadwick Street
London
W1F 9EP
Email: editor@insidesoap.co.uk
Website: http://www.insidesoap.co.uk

Publishes: Articles; Interviews; News; Nonfiction; *Areas:* Entertainment; Media; *Markets:* Adult

Editors: Steven Murphy

Magazine about UK soap operas. Query by email in first instance.

The Interpreter's House

36 College Bounds
Old Aberdeen
Aberdeen
AB24 3DS
Email: theinterpretershouse@aol.com
Website: http://www.theinterpretershouse.com

Publishes: Fiction; Poetry; *Areas:* Short Stories; *Markets:* Adult; *Treatments:* Literary

Editors: Martin Malone

Send up to five poems or up to two short stories by email in a single Word attachment, or by post with SAE. Accepts work in October, February, and June.

Interzone

TTA Press
5 Martins Lane
Witcham
Ely
Cambs
CB6 2LB
Website: http://ttapress.com

Publishes: Fiction; *Areas:* Fantasy; Sci-Fi; Short Stories; *Markets:* Adult

Editors: Andy Cox

Publishes science fiction and fantasy short stories up to about 10,000 words. No simultaneous submissions, multiple submissions or reprints. See website for full guidelines and online submission system.

Irish Pages

129 Ormeau Road
Belfast
BT7 1SH
Tel: +44 (0) 2890 434800
Email: editor@irishpages.org
Website: http://www.irishpages.org

Publishes: Essays; Fiction; Nonfiction; Poetry; Reviews; *Areas:* Autobiography; Historical; Nature; Science; Short Stories;

Translations; *Markets:* Adult; *Treatments:* Literary

Editors: Chris Agee

Non-partisan and non-sectarian literary journal publishing writing from the island of Ireland and elsewhere in equal measure. Publishes work in English, and in the Irish Language or Ulster Scots with English translations or glosses. Welcomes submissions throughout the year by post only with SAE or IRCs. See website for more details.

Jamie Magazine

Email: contact@jamiemagazine.com
Website: http://www.jamiemagazine.com

Publishes: Articles; Features; Nonfiction; *Areas:* Cookery; How-to; Markets

Cookery magazine publishing recipes, features, tips, etc.

Jewish Quarterly

28 St Albans Lane
London
NW11 7QE
Email: editor@jewishquarterly.org
Website: http://www.jewishquarterly.org

Publishes: Essays; Fiction; News; Nonfiction; Poetry; *Areas:* Arts; Culture; Current Affairs; Film; Historical; Literature; Music; Philosophy; Politics; Religious; Short Stories; *Markets:* Adult; *Treatments:* Contemporary; Literary

Says of itself it "leads the field in Jewish writing, covering a wide spectrum of subjects including art, criticism, fiction, film, history, Judaism, literature, poetry, philosophy, politics, theatre, the Shoah, Zionism and much more".

Kalyna Review

Email: editor@kalynareview.com
Website: http://www.kalynareview.com

Publishes: Fiction; Poetry; *Areas:* Short Stories; Translations; *Markets:* Adult; *Treatments:* Literary

Free online journal publishing poetry and fiction (including translations), photography, prints and art. Send submissions by email in the body of the email.

Kitchen Garden

Mortons Media Group Ltd
Media Centre
Morton Way
Horncastle
LN9 6JR
Tel: +44 (0) 1507 523456
Email: sott@mortons.co.uk
Website: http://www.kitchengarden.co.uk

Publishes: Articles; Features; Nonfiction; *Areas:* Cookery; Gardening; Hobbies; How-to; *Markets:* Adult

Editors: Steve Ott

Magazine for people who grow their own fresh fruit and vegetables.

The Lancet

125 London Wall
London
EC2Y 5AS
Tel: +44 (0) 20 7424 4922
Email: editorial@lancet.com
Website: http://www.thelancet.com

Publishes: Articles; Features; Nonfiction; *Areas:* Health; Medicine; Science; *Markets:* Professional

Journal of health and medical science and practice, with offices in London, Newy York, and Beijing. Publishes articles, commentaries, and research papers. See website for submission guidelines.

The Lawyer

Centaur Communications Ltd
Wells Point
79 Wells Street
London
W1T 3QN
Tel: +44 (0) 20 7970 4637
Email: editorial@thelawyer.com
Website: https://www.thelawyer.com

Publishes: Articles; Features; News; Nonfiction; *Areas:* Legal; *Markets:* Professional

Editors: Catrin Griffiths

Weekly magazine for the legal profession, publishing news, articles, and features.

Leopard Magazine

24 Cairnaquheen Gardens
Aberdeen
AB15 5HJ
Email: editor@leopardmag.co.uk
Website: http://www.leopardmag.co.uk

Publishes: Articles; Fiction; News; Nonfiction; Poetry; *Areas:* Culture; Historical; Short Stories; *Markets:* Adult

Editors: Judy Mackie

Magazine celebrating the people, places, history, and heritage of North-East Scotland. For articles, send query in first instance. For poetry and fiction, send complete ms.

Litro Magazine

1-15 Cremer Street
Studio 213
E2 8HD
Tel: +44 (0) 20 3371 9971
Email: online@litro.co.uk
Website: http://www.litro.co.uk

Publishes: Features; Fiction; Nonfiction; Poetry; Reviews; *Areas:* Arts; Autobiography; Literature; Short Stories; Travel; *Markets:* Adult; *Treatments:* Literary

Independent magazine distributing around 100,000 copies for free, across the UK and France. Publishes fiction and creative nonfiction; features; reviews; interviews; columns, and more. See website for upcoming themes and to submit using online submission system. Also publishes poetry and novel extracts, but no unsolicited submissions accepted for these.

Little White Lies

TCOLondon
71A Leonard Street
London
EC2A 4QS
Email: hello@tcolondon.com
Website: http://www.littlewhitelies.co.uk

Publishes: Articles; Features; Interviews; News; Reviews; *Areas:* Film; *Markets:* Adult

Publishes material relating to films, including articles, interviews, and reviews.

The London Magazine

11 Queen's Gate
London
SW7 5EL
Tel: +44 (0) 20 7584 5977
Fax: +44 (0) 20 7225 3273
Email: admin@thelondonmagazine.org
Website: http://thelondonmagazine.org

Publishes: Articles; Essays; Features; Fiction; Nonfiction; Poetry; Reviews; *Areas:* Arts; Autobiography; Criticism; Literature; Short Stories; *Markets:* Adult; *Treatments:* Literary

Send submissions by post with SAE, or through online submission system. Does not normally publish science fiction or fantasy writing, or erotica. See website for full guidelines.

London Review of Books

28 Little Russell Street
London
WC1A 2HN
Tel: +44 (0) 20 7209 1101
Fax: +44 (0) 20 7209 1102
Email: edit@lrb.co.uk
Website: http://www.lrb.co.uk

Publishes: Articles; Essays; Nonfiction; Poetry; Reviews; *Areas:* Arts; Culture; Film; Literature; Politics; Science; *Markets:* Adult; *Treatments:* Literary

Editors: Mary-Kay Wilmers

Contact editor in writing in first instance, including SAE. Publishes mainly reviews, essays, and articles, but also publishes poetry.

Lothian Life

4/8 Downfield Place
Edinburgh

EH11 2EW
Tel: +44 (0) 7905 614402
Email: anne@lothianlife.co.uk
Website: http://www.lothianlife.co.uk

Publishes: Articles; Features; News; Nonfiction; *Areas:* Arts; Cookery; Design; Gardening; Health; Travel; *Markets:* Adult

Editors: Anne Hamilton

Magazine relating to the Lothians. Publishes regular articles, news stories, local walks, and features relating to the area.

Magma

23 Pine Walk
Carshalton
SM5 4ES
Email: info@magmapoetry.com
Website: http://www.magmapoetry.com

Publishes: Nonfiction; Poetry; Reviews; *Areas:* Literature; *Markets:* Adult; *Treatments:* Literary

Editors: Laurie Smith

Prefers submissions through online submission system. Postal submissions accepted from the UK only, and must include SAE. No submissions by email. Accepts poems and artwork. Poems are considered for one issue only – they are not held over from one issue to the next. Seeks poems that give a direct sense of what it is to live today – honest about feelings, alert about world, sometimes funny, always well crafted. Also publishes reviews of books and pamphlets of poetry. See website for details.

marie claire

Time Inc. (UK) Ltd
Blue Fin Building
110 Southwark Street
London
SE1 0SU
Tel: +44 (0) 20 3148 5000
Email: marieclaire@timeinc.com
Website: http://www.timeincuk.com/brands/marie-claire-uk/

Publishes: Articles; Features; Nonfiction; *Areas:* Beauty and Fashion; Health; Lifestyle; Travel; Women's Interests; *Markets:* Adult; *Treatments:* Commercial

Editors: Trish Halpin

Glossy magazine for women.

Military Modelling Magazine

Email: kelvin.barber@mytimemedia.com
Website: http://www.militarymodelling.com

Publishes: Articles; Nonfiction; *Areas:* Crafts; Hobbies; How-to; Military; *Markets:* Adult

Editors: Kelvin Barber

Magazine for military model enthusiasts. Contact the editor in first instance.

Modern Poetry in Translation

The Queens College
Oxford
OX1 4AW
Tel: +44 (0) 1865 244701
Email: submissions@mptmagazine.com
Website: http://www.mptmagazine.com

Publishes: Essays; Nonfiction; Poetry; *Areas:* Literature; Translations; *Markets:* Adult

Editors: Sasha Dugdale

Respected poetry series originally founded by prominent poets in the sixties. New Series continues their editorial policy: translation of good poets by translators who are often themselves poets, fluent in the foreign language, and sometimes working with the original poet. See website for submission guidelines.

Currently closed to submissions as at March 2017

Mojo

Bauer Media
Endeavour House
189 Shaftesbury Avenue
London
WC2H 8JG
Tel: +44 (0) 20 7208 3443
Email: MOJO@bauermedia.co.uk
Website: http://www.mojo4music.com

Publishes: Articles; Interviews; News; Nonfiction; Reviews; *Areas:* Music; *Markets:* Adult; *Treatments:* Serious

Rock music magazine publishing news, reviews, and interviews.

Mslexia

PO Box 656
Newcastle upon Tyne
NE99 1PZ
Tel: +44 (0) 1912 048860
Email: postbag@mslexia.co.uk
Website: http://www.mslexia.co.uk

Publishes: Articles; Essays; Features; Fiction; Interviews; News; Nonfiction; Poetry; Reference; Reviews; *Areas:* Autobiography; Short Stories; Women's Interests; *Markets:* Adult

By women, for women who write, who want to write, who teach creative writing or who have an interest in women's literature and creativity. It is a mixture of original work, features, news, views, advice and listings. The UK's only magazine devoted to women writers and their writing.

See website for themes of upcoming issues / competitions.

Publishes features, columns, reviews, flash fiction, and literature listings. Some themes are open to subscribers only. Submit via online submission system on website.

Music Week

NewBay Media Europe Ltd
Emerson Studios
4th Floor
4-8 Emerson Street
London
SE1 9DU
Tel: +44 (0) 20 7226 7246
Email: msutherland@nbmedia.com
Website: http://www.musicweek.com

Publishes: Articles; News; Nonfiction; *Areas:* Business; Music; *Markets:* Adult; Professional

Editors: Mark Sutherland

Weekly magazine covering the music business, including production, marketing, and retailing.

Musical Opinion

1 Exford Road
London
SE12 9HD
Tel: +44 (0) 20 8857 1582
Email: musicalopinion@hotmail.co.uk
Website: http://www.musicalopinion.com

Publishes: Articles; Features; Nonfiction; Reviews; *Areas:* Music; *Markets:* Adult

Editors: Robert Matthew-Walker

Magazine publishing articles, features, and reviews on classical music. No unsolicited MSS, but welcomes ideas by phone or email.

The New Accelerator

Email: editors@thenewaccelerator.com
Website: http://thenewaccelerator.com

Publishes: Fiction; *Areas:* Entertainment; Fantasy; Horror; Religious; Science; Sci-Fi; Short Stories; Spiritual; Technology; Thrillers; *Markets:* Adult; *Treatments:* Commercial; Contemporary; Dark; Experimental; Literary; Positive; Progressive; Satirical; Serious; Traditional

Editors: Andy Coughlan and David Winstanley

A Science Fiction short story anthology. Published monthly through Apple's Newsstand app and Google Play, the anthology will be available to billions of iOS and Android users worldwide.

The aim of the anthology is to bring cutting-edge fiction to an eager and discerning global Science Fiction audience.

New Fairy Tales

Email: editor@newfairytales.co.uk
Website: http://www.newfairytales.co.uk

Publishes: Fiction; Poetry; *Areas:* Short Stories; *Markets:* Adult; Children's; Family; Youth

Editors: Claire Massey

Note: Closed to submissions as at January 2016

Publishes new original fairy tales, suitable for adults and children. Not looking for retellings or reimaginings of existing fairy tales. Send submissions and queries by email; see website for full guidelines.

New Musical Express (NME)

Time Inc. (UK)
The Blue Fin Building
110 Southwark Street
London
SE1 0SU
Tel: +44 (0) 20 3148 5000
Website: http://www.nme.com

Publishes: Articles; News; Nonfiction; Reviews; *Areas:* Film; Music; *Markets:* Adult; *Treatments:* Popular

Editors: Conor McNicholas

Publishes articles, news, and reviews on popular music, plus coverage of film.

New Statesman

John Carpenter House
7 Carmelite Street
Blackfriars
London
EC4Y 0BS
Tel: +44 (0) 20 7936 6400
Fax: +44 (0) 20 7305 7304
Email: editorial@newstatesman.co.uk
Website: http://www.newstatesman.com

Publishes: Articles; Features; News; Nonfiction; Poetry; Reviews; *Areas:* Arts; Current Affairs; Politics; *Markets:* Adult

Editors: Jason Cowley

Weekly political magazine. For nonfiction, send initial pitch by email to address provided on website. No fiction, but welcomes poems up to 30 lines, on any subject and in any style (do not need to be political). Send up to 4 poems by email in the body of the email or as a single Word attachment, to the specific poetry email address provided on the website.

New Welsh Reader

PO Box 170
Aberystwyth
SY23 1WZ
Tel: +44 (0) 1970 628410
Email: submissions@newwelshreview.com
Website: http://www.newwelshreview.com

Publishes: Features; Fiction; Nonfiction; Poetry; Reviews; *Areas:* Short Stories; *Markets:* Adult; *Treatments:* Literary

Editors: Gwen Davies

Focus is on Welsh writing in English, but has an outlook which is deliberately diverse, encompassing broader UK and international contexts. For feature articles, send 300-word query by email. Submit fiction or up to 6 poems by email or by post with cover letter and SAE. Full details available on website.

Note: Not accepting fiction submissions as at January 2017 due to high volume of submissions. See website for current status.

newbooks

1 Vicarage Lane
Stubbington
PO14 2JU
Email: info@newbooksmag.com
Website: http://www.newbooksmag.com

Publishes: Nonfiction; Reviews; *Areas:* Entertainment; Literature; *Markets:* Adult

Editors: Sheila Ferguson (Managing Editor)

Magazine aimed at readers and reading groups. Welcomes books for review from all publishers.

The North

Bank Street Arts
32-40 Bank Street
Sheffield
S1 2DS
Tel: +44 (0) 01143 463037
Email: office@poetrybusiness.co.uk
Website: http://www.poetrybusiness.co.uk

Publishes: Articles; Poetry; Reviews; *Areas:* Autobiography; Criticism; Literature;

Markets: Adult; *Treatments:* Contemporary; Literary

Editors: Peter Samson and Janet Fisher

Send up to 6 poems with SASE / return postage. We publish the best of contemporary poetry. No "genre" or derivative poetry. Submitters should be aware of, should preferably have read, the magazine before submitting. See our website for notes on submitting poems. No submissions by email.

Also publishes critical articles and reviews of contemporary poetry. Submit ideas/synopses only in first instance.

The Oldie

65 Newman Street
London
W1T 3EG
Tel: +44 (0) 20 7436 8801
Email: editorial@theoldie.co.uk
Website: http://www.theoldie.co.uk

Publishes: Articles; Features; *Areas:* Humour; *Markets:* Adult

Editors: Richard Ingrams

Prefers to receive completed articles by email (see website for specific email address). No commissions based on ideas. Publishes cartoons, letters, articles, and features on a range of topics, with a humorous slant, aimed at the older reader. No poetry.

Olive

Vineyard House
44 Brook Green
Hammersmith
London
W6 7BT
Tel: +44 (0) 020 7150 5000
Email: oliveweb@immediate.co.uk
Website: http://www.olivemagazine.com

Publishes: Articles; Features; Nonfiction; *Areas:* Cookery; *Markets:* Adult

Monthly food magazine. Welcomes unsolicited queries but responds only when interested.

Opera

36 Black Lion Lane
London
W6 9BE
Tel: +44 (0) 20 8563 8893
Fax: +44 (0) 20 8563 8635
Email: editor@opera.co.uk
Website: http://www.opera.co.uk

Publishes: Articles; Nonfiction; Reviews; *Areas:* Culture; Entertainment; *Markets:* Adult

Editors: John Allison

Review of the contemporary opera scene. Virtually all articles are commissioned so no unsolicited MSS. Approach in writing in first instance.

Oxford Poetry

Magdalen College
Oxford
OX1 4AU
Email: editors@oxfordpoetry.co.uk
Website: http://www.oxfordpoetry.co.uk

Publishes: Essays; Interviews; Nonfiction; Poetry; Reviews; *Areas:* Translations; *Markets:* Adult; *Treatments:* Literary

Editors: Nancy Campbell; Mary Jean Chan; and Theophilus Kwek

Publishes poems, interviews, reviews, and essays. Accepts unpublished poems on any theme and of any length. Send up to four poems. Prefers submissions by email, but will accept submissions by post. See website for full details.

People Management

Email: pmeditorial@haymarket.com
Website: http://www.peoplemanagement.co.uk

Publishes: Articles; Features; Nonfiction; *Areas:* Business; How-to; Legal; *Markets:* Professional

Editors: Robert Jeffery

Human resources magazine, publishing articles and features on all aspects of managing and developing people at work.

The People's Friend

80 Kingsway East
Dundee
DD4 8SL
Tel: +44 (0) 1382 462276
Fax: +44 (0) 1382 452491
Email: peoplesfriend@dcthomson.co.uk
Website: http://www.thepeoplesfriend.co.uk

Publishes: Articles; Features; Fiction; Nonfiction; Poetry; *Areas:* Adventure; Cookery; Crafts; Crime; Hobbies; Mystery; Nature; Romance; Short Stories; Thrillers; Travel; Women's Interests; *Markets:* Adult; Family; *Treatments:* Traditional

Publishes complete short stories (1,200-3,000 words (4,000 for specials)) and serials, focusing on character development rather than complex plots, plus 10,000-word crime thrillers. Also considers nonfiction from nature to nostalgia and from holidays to hobbies. Guidelines available on website.

People's Friend Pocket Novels

80 Kingsway East
Dundee
DD4 8SL
Tel: +44 (0) 1382 223131
Email: tsteel@dcthomson.co.uk
Website: http://www.thepeoplesfriend.co.uk

Publishes: Fiction; *Areas:* Romance; *Markets:* Adult; Family

Editors: Tracey Steel

Publishes romance and family fiction between 40,000 and 42,000 words, aimed at adults aged over 30. Send query by post or by email (preferred) with synopsis and first two chapters in first instance. See website for more information.

The Photographer

The British Institute of Professional Photography
The Coach House
The Firs
High Street
Whitchurch
Aylesbury
Buckinghamshire
HP22 4SJ
Tel: +44 (0) 1296 642020
Fax: +44 (0) 1296 641553
Email: editor@bipp.com
Website: http://www.bipp.com

Publishes: Articles; News; Nonfiction; Reviews; *Areas:* Photography; *Markets:* Professional

Photography magazine for professional photographers.

Planet

PO Box 44
Aberystwyth
Ceredigion
SY23 3ZZ
Tel: +44 (0) 1970 611255
Email: submissions@planetmagazine.org.uk
Website: http://www.planetmagazine.org.uk

Publishes: Articles; Features; Fiction; Nonfiction; Poetry; Reviews; *Areas:* Arts; Current Affairs; Literature; Music; Politics; Short Stories; Theatre; *Markets:* Adult; *Treatments:* Literary

Editors: Emily Trahair

Publishes mostly commissioned material, but will accept ideas for articles and reviews, and unsolicited submissions of fiction and poetry. Submit one piece of short fiction between 1,500 and 2,500 words, or 4-6 poems at a time. A range of styles and themes are accepted, but postal submissions will not be considered unless adequate return postage is provided. If you have an idea for a relevant article send a query with brief synopsis.

PN Review

4th Floor
Alliance House
Cross Street
Manchester
M2 7AP
Tel: +44 (0) 161 834 8730
Fax: +44 (0) 161 832 0084
Email: schmidt@carcanet.co.uk
Website: http://www.pnreview.co.uk

Publishes: Articles; Features; Interviews; News; Poetry; Reviews; *Areas:* Translations; *Markets:* Adult

Editors: Michael Schmidt

Send query with synopsis and sample pages, after having familiarised yourself with the magazine. Accepts prose up to 15 double-spaced pages or 4 poems / 5 pages of poetry.

Bimonthly magazine of poetry and poetry criticism. Includes editorial, letters, news, articles, interviews, features, poems, translations, and a substantial book review section. No short stories, children's prose / poetry, or non-poetry related work (academic, biography etc.). Accepts electronic submissions from individual subscribers only – otherwise only hard copy submissions are considered.

The Poetry Box

The Poetry Box
Ramshackles
2 Downview
Nyewood
Nyewood Road
Petersfield
Hampshire
GU31 5JA
Tel: +44 (0) 1730 821030
Email: FairyTaleRhymes@aol.com
Website: http://www.thepoetrybox.co.uk

Publishes: Poetry; *Areas:* Romance; *Markets:* Adult; *Treatments:* Literary

Poetry magazine publishing Romantic and Epic poetry in rhyming form. Also runs annual poetry award and live poetry events.

Poetry London

The Albany
Douglas Way
Deptford
London
SE8 4AG
Tel: +44 (0) 20 8691 7260
Email: admin@poetrylondon.co.uk
Website: http://www.poetrylondon.co.uk

Publishes: Features; Nonfiction; Poetry; Reviews; *Areas:* Translations; *Markets:* Adult; *Treatments:* Contemporary; Literary

Editors: Ahren Warner; Martha Kapos

Send up to six poems with SASE or adequate return postage. Considers poems by both new and established poets. Also publishes book reviews. No submissions by email.

The Poetry Review

The Poetry Society
22 Betterton Street
London
WC2H 9BX
Tel: +44 (0) 20 7420 9880
Fax: +44 (0) 20 7240 4818
Email: poetryreview@poetrysociety.org.uk
Website: http://www.poetrysociety.org.uk

Publishes: Essays; Nonfiction; Poetry; Reviews; *Areas:* Translations; *Markets:* Adult; *Treatments:* Literary

Describes itself as "one of the liveliest and most influential literary magazines in the world", and has been associated with the rise of the New Generation of British poets – Carol Ann Duffy, Simon Armitage, Glyn Maxwell, Don Paterson... though its scope extends beyond the UK, with special issues focusing on poetries from around the world. Poets from the UK must submit by post; those from elsewhere in the world may submit using online system. See website for details. Send up to 6 unpublished poems, or literary translations of poems.

Poetry Wales

57 Nolton Street
Bridgend
CF31 3AE
Tel: +44 (0) 1656 663018
Email: info@poetrywales.co.uk
Website: http://poetrywales.co.uk

Publishes: Essays; Nonfiction; Poetry; Reviews; *Markets:* Adult

Editors: Nia Davies

Publishes poetry, features, and reviews from Wales and beyond. Send up to six poems in one .doc file with your name, contact details, and short bio up to 50 words, via online submission system (see website).

The Police Journal

SAGE Publications Ltd
1 Oliver's Yard
55 City Road
London
EC1Y 1SP
Tel: +44 (0) 20 7324 8500
Fax: +44 (0) 20 7324 8600
Email: authorqueries@sagepub.co.uk
Website: https://uk.sagepub.com/en-gb/eur/the-police-journal/journal202314

Publishes: Articles; Nonfiction; *Areas:* Crime; Legal; *Markets:* Professional

Editors: Colin Rogers

Publishes articles aimed at police forces around the world. Submit using online submission manager only.

Poultry World

Quadrant House
The Quadrant
Sutton
Surrey
SM2 5AS
Tel: +44 (0) 20 8652 4921
Fax: +44 (0) 20 8652 4005
Email: poultry.world@rbi.co.uk
Website: http://www.fwi.co.uk/poultry

Publishes: Articles; News; Nonfiction; *Areas:* Business; Nature; *Markets:* Professional

Monthly magazine, catering for the whole poultry sector: eggs, broilers, turkeys, ducks and geese.

Practical Photography

Bauer Consumer Media Limited
Media House
Peterborough
PE2 6EA
Email: photoanswers@bauermedia.co.uk
Website: http://www.photoanswers.co.uk

Publishes: Articles; Features; Nonfiction; *Areas:* How-to; Photography; *Markets:* Adult

Magazine for photography enthusiasts. Send query in first instance.

The Practising Midwife

Medical Education Solutions Ltd
Monks Ridge
Burrows Lane
Gomshall
GU5 9QE
Tel: +44 (0) 20 8313 9617
Email: laurayeates@virginmedia.com
Website: http://www.practisingmidwife.co.uk

Publishes: Articles; News; Nonfiction; *Areas:* Health; Medicine; Women's Interests; *Markets:* Professional

Editors: Laura Yeates

Publishes accessible, authoritative and readable information for midwives, students and other professionals in the maternity services.

Private Eye

6 Carlisle Street
London
W1D 3BN
Tel: +44 (0) 20 7437 4017
Fax: +44 (0) 20 7437 0705
Email: strobes@private-eye.co.uk
Website: http://www.private-eye.co.uk

Publishes: Articles; Features; News; Nonfiction; *Areas:* Current Affairs; Humour; Politics; *Markets:* Adult; *Treatments:* Satirical

Editors: Ian Hislop

Satirical and investigative magazine publishing news stories, features, and cartoons.

Prole

Prolebooks
15 Maes-y-Dre
Abergele
Conwy
LL22 7HW
Email: submissionspoetry@prolebooks.co.uk
Website: http://www.prolebooks.co.uk

Publishes: Fiction; Nonfiction; Poetry; *Areas:* Short Stories; *Markets:* Adult; *Treatments:* Literary

Publishes accessible literature of high quality, including poetry, short fiction, and creative nonfiction. Seeks to appeal to a wide audience and avoid literary elitism (obscure references and highly stylised structures and forms are unlikely to find favour). No previously published material or simultaneous submissions. Submit one piece of prose or up to five poems in the body of an email, with your name, contact details, word count and third person author bio up to 100 words. See website for appropriate email addresses for prose and poetry submissions, and full submission guidelines. No attachments.

Psychologies

KELSEY Media Ltd
Cudham Tithe Barn
Berry's Hill
Cudham
Kent
TN16 3AG
Email: suzy.greaves@psychologies.co.uk
Website: https://www.psychologies.co.uk

Publishes: Articles; Nonfiction; *Areas:* Beauty and Fashion; Cookery; Culture; Health; Lifestyle; Travel; Women's Interests; *Markets:* Adult

Editors: Suzy Greaves

Grown up women's lifestyle magazine, seeking to enrich women's emotional lives. Covers self, relationships, family, work, beauty and wellbeing, culture, travel, food and more.

Radio Times

Vineyard House
44 Brook Green
London
W6 7BT
Tel: +44 (0) 20 7150 5800
Fax: +44 (0) 20 8433 3160
Email: feedback@radiotimes.com
Website: http://www.radiotimes.com

Publishes: Articles; Interviews; News; Nonfiction; *Areas:* Entertainment; Radio; TV; *Markets:* Adult

Articles and interviews relating to UK TV and radio. All articles are commissioned. Willing to consider synopses and ideas, but no unsolicited mss.

Rail

Media House
Lynch Wood
Peterborough
PE2 6EA
Email: rail@bauermedia.co.uk
Website: http://www.railmagazine.com

Publishes: Articles; Features; News; Nonfiction; *Areas:* Technology; Travel; *Markets:* Adult

Editors: Nigel Harris

Magazine of the modern railway. No fiction or accounts of personal journeys.

Reach

IDP
24 Forest Houses
Halwill
Beaworthy
Devon
EX21 5UU
Email: publishing@indigodreams.co.uk
Website: http://www.indigodreams.co.uk/reach-poetry/4563791643

Publishes: Poetry; *Markets:* Adult; *Treatments:* Literary

Editors: Ronnie Goodyer

Publishes quality poetry from both experienced and new poets. Formal or free verse, haiku... everything is considered. Subscribers can comment on and vote for poetry from the previous issue, the winner receiving £50, plus regular in-house anthologies and competitions. Receives no external funding and depends entirely on subscriptions.

Record Collector Magazine

The Perfume Factory
Room 101, Diamond Publishing Ltd
140 Wales Farm Road
London
W3 6UG
Tel: +44 (0) 870 732 8080
Email: ian.mccann@metropolis.co.uk

Website: http://www.recordcollectormag.com

Publishes: Articles; Features; Nonfiction; *Areas:* Hobbies; Music; *Markets:* Adult

Editors: Ian McCann

Magazine on record collecting. Most material is commissioned, but will consider unsolicited mss and welcomes ideas for articles and features.

Reform

86 Tavistock Place
London
WC1H 9RT
Tel: +44 (0) 20 7916 8630
Email: reform@urc.org.uk
Website: http://www.reform-magazine.co.uk

Publishes: Articles; Features; News; Nonfiction; *Areas:* Current Affairs; Religious; Sociology; Spiritual; *Markets:* Adult

Describes itself as a magazine for thinking people "who enjoy reading about Christian ideas from a range of viewpoints".

Restaurant Magazine

William Reed Business Media Ltd
Broadfield Park
Crawley
RH11 9RT
Tel: +44 (0) 1293 610342
Email: Stefan.chomka@wrbm.com
Website: http://www.restaurantmagazine.co.uk

Publishes: Articles; Features; News; Nonfiction; *Areas:* Business; Cookery; *Markets:* Professional

Editors: Stefan Chomka

Magazine publishing articles, features, and news for the restaurant trade.

Retail Week

EMAP Publishing Limited
Telephone House
69 – 77 Paul Street
London
EC2A 4NQ
Email: chris.brook-carter@emap.com
Website: http://www.retail-week.com

Publishes: Articles; Features; News; Nonfiction; *Areas:* Business; *Markets:* Professional

Magazine for the retail industry.

The Rialto

PO Box 309
Aylsham
Norwich
NR11 6LN
Email: info@therialto.co.uk
Website: http://www.therialto.co.uk

Publishes: Articles; Nonfiction; Poetry; Reviews; *Markets:* Adult; *Treatments:* Literary

Editors: Michael Mackmin

Send up to six poems with SASE or adequate return postage, or submit through online submission system. No submissions by email. Reviews and articles commissioned.

RUSI Journal

Royal United Services Institute
Whitehall
London
SW1A 2ET
Tel: +44 (0) 20 7747 2615
Email: publications@rusi.org
Website: https://rusi.org

Publishes: Articles; Nonfiction; Reviews; *Areas:* Historical; Military; Technology; *Markets:* Professional

Editors: Emma De Angelis

Journal publishing articles, book reviews, and letters to the editor, relating to defence, international security, military history, etc. See website for submission guidelines.

Sarasvati

24 Forest Houses
Halwill
Beaworthy
Devon
EX21 5UU
Email: dawnidp@gmail.com

Website: http://www.indigodreams.co.uk/sarasvati/4563791846

Publishes: Fiction; Poetry; *Areas:* Short Stories; *Markets:* Adult

Editors: Dawn Bauling

Showcases poetry and prose. Each contributor will have three to four A5 pages available to their work.

The Savage Kick

Murder Slim Press
22 Bridge Meadow
Hemsby
Norfolk
NR29 4NE
Email: murderslimpress@gmail.com
Website: http://www.murderslim.com/TheSavageKick.html

Publishes: Articles; Fiction; Interviews; Nonfiction; *Areas:* Crime; Literature; Military; Westerns; *Markets:* Adult; *Treatments:* Niche

Accepts only three or four stories per year. Publishes work dealing with any passionately held emotion and/or alternative viewpoints. Sleazy tales are encouraged. Prefers real-life stories. No genre fiction or poetry. See website for full submission guidelines. Also accepts articles and interviews relating to authors on the reading list provided on the website.

Scots Heritage Magazine

496 Ferry Road
Edinburgh
EH5 2DL
Tel: +44 (0) 1315 511000
Fax: +44 (0) 1315 517900
Email: editor@scotsheritagemagazine.com
Website: http://www.scotsheritagemagazine.com

Publishes: Articles; Features; Nonfiction; *Areas:* Historical; *Markets:* Adult

Editors: Richard Bath

Magazine of Scottish history, aimed at people of Scottish descent all over the world.

SelfBuild & Design

151 Station Street
Burton on Trent
DE14 1BG
Tel: +44 (0) 1584 841417
Email: ross.stokes@sbdonline.co.uk
Website: http://www.selfbuildanddesign.com

Publishes: Articles; Nonfiction; *Areas:* Design; How-to; *Markets:* Adult

Editors: Ross Stokes

Magazine aimed at those intending to build or manage the build of their own home, or any major building project.

The Sewing Directory

11a Tedders Close
Hemyock
Cullompton
EX15 3XD
Tel: +44 (0) 1823 680588
Email: fiona@thesewingdirectory.net
Website: http://www.thesewingdirectory.co.uk

Publishes: Articles; Features; Nonfiction; *Areas:* Crafts; Hobbies; *Markets:* Adult

Editors: Fiona Pullen

Online sewing directory, publishing articles on sewing and sewing projects.

SFX

Future Publishing Limited Quay House
The Ambury
Bath
BA1 1UA
Email: sfx@futurenet.com
Website: http://www.gamesradar.com/sfx/

Publishes: Articles; News; Nonfiction; *Areas:* Fantasy; Film; Hobbies; Sci-Fi; TV; *Markets:* Adult; Youth

Magazine covering science fiction and fantasy TV, films, comics, and games.

Shooter Literary Magazine

Email: submissions.shooterlitmag@gmail.com
Website: https://shooterlitmag.com

Publishes: Essays; Fiction; Nonfiction; Poetry; *Markets:* Adult; *Treatments:* Literary

Publishes literary fiction, poetry, creative nonfiction and narrative journalism relating to specific themes for each issue. Send one piece of prose between 2,000 and 7,500 words or up to three poems per issue, by email. See website for current theme and full submission guidelines.

Shoreline of Infinity

8 Craiglockhart Bank
Edinburgh
EH14 1JH
Email: editor@shorelineofinfinity.com
Website: https://www.shorelineofinfinity.com

Publishes: Fiction; Interviews; Nonfiction; Reviews; *Areas:* Literature; Music; Sci-Fi; Short Stories; *Markets:* Adult; Family; Youth

Editors: Noel Chidwick

Science Fiction magazine from Scotland. We want stories that explore our unknown future. We want to play around with the big ideas and the little ones. We want writers to tell us stories to inspire us, give us hope, provide some laughs. Or to scare the stuffing out of us. We want good stories: we want to be entertained. We want to read how people cope in our exotic new world, we want to be in their minds, in their bodies, in their souls.

ShortStorySunday.com

27 Old Gloucester Street
London
WC1N 3AX
Email: submissions@shortstorysunday.com
Website: http://www.shortstorysunday.com

Publishes: Fiction; *Areas:* Adventure; Crime; Fantasy; Gothic; Historical; Horror; Humour; Literature; Mystery; Nature; New Age; Philosophy; Romance; Sci-Fi; Short Stories; Suspense; Thrillers; Westerns; *Markets:* Adult; Children's; Family; Youth; *Treatments:* Commercial; Contemporary; Dark; Experimental; Light; Literary; Mainstream; Niche; Popular; Positive; Progressive; Satirical; Traditional

NOTE: On hiatus as at November 2016. Check website for current status.

A home for short stories and flash fiction online.

Launched in November 2014, this is a new 'boutique' experience for readers, authors, agents and publishers interested in reading and contributing world-class short stories. We wanted to create an experience for the reader so that every Sunday they can take half an hour and visit with a cup of tea and read through that week's story on their mobile, tablet or desktop either at home, at a coffee shop or on their lunch break.

To ensure we have the best stories we put together an editorial panel with an eye for a good story to pick the most interesting and original stories for our readers each Sunday.

Shropshire Magazine

Shropshire Newspapers Ltd
Ketley
Telford
TF1 5HU
Tel: +44 (0) 1952 241455
Email: neil.thomas@shropshirestar.co.uk
Website: http://www.shropshiremagazine.com

Publishes: Articles; Features; News; Nonfiction; Reviews; *Areas:* Beauty and Fashion; Entertainment; Historical; Leisure; Lifestyle; *Markets:* Adult

Glossy lifestyle magazine publishing features, profiles, news and reviews relating to the county.

Sky at Night Magazine

Immediate Media Co.
Vineyard House
44 Brook Green
Hammersmith
London
W6 7BT
Tel: +44 (0) 20 7150 5000
Email: skyatnight@bbcmagazines.com
Website: http://www.skyatnightmagazine.com

Publishes: Articles; Features; News; Nonfiction; Reviews; *Areas:* How-to; Science; Technology; *Markets:* Adult

Magazine for those interested in space, publishing space science stories and tips and advice for astronomers.

Slimming World

Clover Nook Road
Alfreton
Derbyshire
DE55 4SW
Email: editorial@slimming-world.co.uk
Website: http://www.slimmingworld.co.uk/magazine/latest-issue.aspx

Publishes: Articles; Features; Nonfiction; *Areas:* Health; How-to; *Markets:* Adult

Magazine covering slimming, healthy eating, and fitness.

Snooker Scene

Hayley Green Court
130 Hagley Road
Halesowen
B63 1DY
Tel: +44 (0) 1215 859188
Fax: +44 (0) 01215 857117
Email: info@snookerscene.co.uk
Website: http://www.snookerscene.co.uk

Publishes: Articles; News; Nonfiction; *Areas:* Sport; *Markets:* Adult

Editors: Clive Everton

Magazine covering the sports of snooker and billiards.

South

PO Box 4228
Bracknell
RG42 9PX
Email: south@southpoetry.org
Website: http://www.southpoetry.org

Publishes: Poetry; *Markets:* Adult

Editors: Anne Peterson, Andrew Curtis, Peter Keeble, Patrick Osada, and Chrissie Williams

Submit up to three poems by post (two copies of each), along with submission form available on website. No previously published poems (including poems that have appeared on the internet). Submissions are not returned. See website for full details. No submissions by email.

Spear's Magazine

Tel: +44 (0) 20 7936 6445
Email: alec.marsh@spearswms.com
Website: http://www.spearswms.com

Publishes: Articles; News; Nonfiction; *Areas:* Business; Finance; Lifestyle; *Markets:* Adult

Editors: Alec Marsh

Wealth management and luxury lifestyle magazine.

The Stage

Stage House
47 Bermondsey Street
London
SE1 3XT
Tel: +44 (0) 20 7403 1818
Email: alistair@thestage.co.uk
Website: http://www.thestage.co.uk

Publishes: Articles; Features; News; Nonfiction; *Areas:* Theatre; *Markets:* Professional

Editors: Alistair Smith

Query with ideas in first instance. Publishes material relating to the theatre: tabloid-style articles up to 800 words, profiles up to 1,200 words, and news items up to 300 words.

Stand Magazine

School of English
Leeds University
Leeds
LS2 9JT
Tel: +44 (0) 113 233 4794
Fax: +44 (0) 113 233 2791
Email: stand@leeds.ac.uk
Website: http://standmagazine.org

Publishes: Fiction; Poetry; *Areas:* Short Stories; Translations; *Markets:* Adult; *Treatments:* Literary

A well established magazine of poetry and literary fiction. Has previously published the work of, among others, Samuel Beckett, Angela Carter, Seamus Heaney, Geoffrey Hill, and Andrew Motion. No electronic submissions. See website for submission guidelines and alternative US address for American submissions.

Style at Home

Time Inc. (UK) Ltd
Blue Fin Building
110 Southwark Street
London
SE1 0SU
Tel: +44 (0) 20 3148 7112
Email: elizabeth.hudson@timeinc.com
Website: http://www.timeincuk.com/brands/style-at-home/

Publishes: Articles; Nonfiction; *Areas:* Design; How-to; Women's Interests; *Markets:* Adult

Editors: Elizabeth Hudson

Magazine offering practical advice for women taking a hands-on approach to styling, decorating, and revamping their homes on a budget.

Surrey Life

C/O Archant
28 Teville Road
Worthing
West Sussex
BN11 1UG
Tel: +44 (0) 1903 703730
Email: editor@surreylife.co.uk
Website: http://www.surreylife.co.uk

Publishes: Articles; Nonfiction; *Areas:* Arts; Cookery; Gardening; Lifestyle; Travel; *Markets:* Adult

Editors: Rebecca Younger

Magazine publishing articles on Surrey, covering such topics as home, gardens, popular destinations, history, food and drink, people, education, style, and motoring.

Television

Royal Television Society
3 Dorset Rise
London
EC4Y 8EN
Tel: +44 (0) 20 7822 2810
Email: info@rts.org.uk
Website: https://rts.org.uk

Publishes: Articles; Nonfiction; *Areas:* Technology; TV; *Markets:* Professional

Editors: Steve Clarke

Magazine covering the technical aspects of television and audio-visual equipment.

Tempo: A Quarterly Review of New Music

PO Box 171
Herne Bay
CT6 6WD
Email: tempoeditor@cambridge.org
Website: http://journals.cambridge.org/action/displayJournal?jid=TEM

Publishes: Articles; Nonfiction; Reviews; *Areas:* Music; *Markets:* Adult; *Treatments:* Contemporary

Editors: Christopher Fox; Juliet Fraser

Publishes articles and reviews on the new music scene. Emphasises musical developments of the 21st century, and developments of the late 20th century that have not yet received the deserved attention. Submit articles up to 5,000 words and reviews as Word format documents (no PDFs) with 100-word bio. See website for full guidelines.

TES (The Times Educational Supplement)

26 Red Lion Square
London
WC1R 4HQ
Tel: +44 (0) 20 3194 3000
Email: help@tesglobal.com
Website: https://www.tes.com

Publishes: Articles; Features; News; Nonfiction; Reviews; *Markets:* Academic; Adult

Weekly supplement of educational news and resources. Most material is commissioned, but accepts queries outlining ideas by email.

The Lady

39-40 Bedford Street
London
WC2E 9ER
Tel: +44 (0) 20 7379 4717
Email: editors@lady.co.uk
Website: http://www.lady.co.uk

Publishes: Articles; Features; Nonfiction; *Areas:* Arts; Beauty and Fashion; Cookery; Finance; Gardening; Health; Historical; Travel; Women's Interests; *Markets:* Adult

England's longest-running weekly magazine for women.

The Voice

GV Media Group Ltd
The Elephant & Castle Shopping Centre
Unit 236
London
SE1 6TE
Tel: +44 (0) 20 7510 0383
Email: newsdesk@gvmedia.co.uk
Website: http://voice-online.co.uk

Publishes: Articles; Features; Interviews; News; Nonfiction; *Areas:* Arts; Business; Culture; Entertainment; Politics; Sport; *Markets:* Adult

Weekly newspaper aimed at black Britons, publishing a mixture of news, features, sports and celebrity interviews.

This England

The Lypiatts
Lansdown Road
Cheltenham
Gloucestershire
GL50 2JA
Tel: +44 (0) 1242 225780
Email: thisengland@dcthomson.co.uk
Website: https://www.thisengland.co.uk

Publishes: Articles; Features; Nonfiction; Poetry; *Areas:* Crafts; Culture; Historical; Nature; *Markets:* Adult

Magazine celebrating English culture, history, people, nature, traditions, customs, legends, etc. Generally rural. Publishes articles between 250 and 2,000 words and poems 12-24 lines.

Times Higher Education

TES Global Limited
26 Red Lion Square
London
WC1R 4HQ
Tel: +44 (0) 20 3194 3300
Email: john.gill@timeshighereducation.com
Website: https://www.timeshighereducation.com

Publishes: Articles; Nonfiction; *Markets:* Academic; Adult

Magazine publishing articles on higher education.

The Times Literary Supplement (TLS)

1 London Bridge Street
London
SE1 9GF
Tel: +44 (0) 20 7782 5000
Email: letters@the-tls.co.uk
Website: http://www.the-tls.co.uk

Publishes: Articles; Features; News; Nonfiction; Poetry; Reviews; *Areas:* Arts; Film; Historical; Literature; Philosophy; Science; Theatre; *Markets:* Adult

Editors: Stig Abell

Publishes coverage of the latest and most important publications, as well as current theatre, opera, exhibitions and film. Also publishes letters to the editor and poetry. Send books for review by post. For poetry, submit up to six poems with SASE. Letters to the Editor may be sent by post or by email to the address provided on the website.

Top Sante

Bauer Media
Media House
Lynch Wood
Peterborough
PE2 6EA
Tel: +44 (0) 1733 468938

Email: nikki.dutton@bauermedia.co.uk
Website: http://www.topsante.co.uk

Publishes: Articles; Features; News; Nonfiction; *Areas:* Beauty and Fashion; Health; Women's Interests; *Markets:* Adult

Magazine publishing articles, features, and news on health and beauty.

Trail

Bauer Consumer Media Limited
Media House
Peterborough Business Park
Peterborough
PE2 6EA
Email: simon.ingram@lfto.com
Website: http://www.livefortheoutdoors.com

Publishes: Articles; Features; Nonfiction; *Areas:* Hobbies; Leisure; Travel; *Markets:* Adult

Editors: Simon Ingram

Monthly walking magazine, covering hillwalking, mountain climbing, gear, historic walks, and gentle strolls in the countryside.

Truck & Driver

Sixth Floor, Chancery House
St Nicholas Way
Sutton
SM1 1JB
Tel: +44 (0) 20 8912 2131
Email: pip.dunn@roadtransport.com
Website: http://truckanddriver.co.uk

Publishes: Articles; Features; News; Nonfiction; *Areas:* Travel; *Markets:* Professional

Editors: Pip Dunn

Magazine for truck drivers.

Vanity Fair

Conde Nast Publications
Vogue House
1-2 Hanover Square
London
W1S 1JU
Email: letters@vf.com
Website: http://www.vanityfair.com

Publishes: Articles; Nonfiction; *Areas:* Beauty and Fashion; Culture; Current Affairs; Entertainment; Media; Politics; *Markets:* Adult; *Treatments:* Popular

Magazine of glamour, popular culture, current affairs, fashion, and politics.

Vegan Life

Prime Impact Events & Media
Park House
The Business Centre
Earls Colne Business Park
Earls Colne
Colchester
CO6 2NS
Tel: +44 (0) 1787 224040
Email: info@veganlifemag.com
Website: http://www.veganlifemag.com

Publishes: Articles; Features; News; Nonfiction; *Areas:* Cookery; Health; Leisure; Lifestyle; Travel; *Markets:* Adult

Editors: Maria Chiorando

Vegan consumer magazine, aiming to bring about a change in attitudes by encouraging the adoption of a plant based diet.

Viz

30 Cleveland Street
London
W1T 4JD
Tel: +44 (0) 20 7907 6000
Fax: +44 (0) 20 7907 6020
Email: viz@viz.co.uk
Website: http://www.viz.co.uk

Publishes: Articles; Fiction; *Areas:* Humour; *Markets:* Adult

Editors: Russell Blackman

Magazine of adult humour, including cartoons, spoof articles, etc.

Wanderlust Magazine

PO Box 1832
Windsor
Berkshire
SL4 1YT
Tel: +44 (0) 1753 620426
Fax: +44 (0) 1753 620474

Email: submissions@wanderlust.co.uk
Website: http://www.wanderlust.co.uk

Publishes: Articles; Features; Nonfiction; *Areas:* Travel; *Markets:* Adult

Magazine covering all aspects of independent, semi-independent and special-interest travel. Particularly interested in local culture. No unsolicited mss. Send query by email with one-paragraph proposal.

Wasafiri

1-11 Hawley Crescent
Camden Town
London
NW1 8NP
Tel: +44 (0) 20 7556 6110
Fax: +44 (0) 20 7556 6187
Email: wasafiri@open.ac.uk
Website: http://www.wasafiri.org

Publishes: Articles; Essays; Fiction; Interviews; Nonfiction; Poetry; Reviews; *Areas:* Criticism; Culture; Literature; Short Stories; *Markets:* Adult; *Treatments:* Literary

Editors: Susheila Nasta

The indispensable journal of contemporary African, Asian Black British, Caribbean and transnational literatures.

In over fifteen years of publishing, this magazine has changed the face of contemporary writing in Britain. As a literary magazine primarily concerned with new and postcolonial writers, it continues to stress the diversity and range of black and diasporic writers world-wide. It remains committed to its original aims: to create a definitive forum for the voices of new writers and to open up lively spaces for serious critical discussion not available elsewhere. It is Britain's only international magazine for Black British, African, Asian and Caribbean literatures. Get the whole picture, get the magazine at the core of contemporary international literature today.

The Week

30 Cleveland Street
London
W1T 4JD
Tel: +44 (0) 20 7907 6000
Email: holden_frith@dennis.co.uk
Website: http://www.theweek.co.uk

Publishes: News; Nonfiction; *Markets:* Adult

Editors: Holden Frith

Weekly magazine condensing the best of the British and international news from the week into 35 succinct pages.

Weight Watchers Magazine

PO Box 326
Sittingbourne
Email: weightwatchers@servicehelpline.co.uk
Website: https://www.weightwatchers.co.uk

Publishes: Articles; Features; News; Nonfiction; *Areas:* Beauty and Fashion; Cookery; Health; *Markets:* Adult

Magazine covering slimming, health, beauty, etc.

What Car?

Teddington Studios
Teddington
Middlesex
TW11 9BE
Tel: +44 (0) 20 8267 5688
Fax: +44 (0) 20 8267 5750
Email: editorial@whatcar.com
Website: http://www.whatcar.com

Publishes: Articles; Features; News; Nonfiction; Reviews; *Areas:* Technology; Travel; *Markets:* Adult

Magazine providing new, reviews, articles and features on cars.

The White Review

243 Knightsbridge
London
SW7 1DN
Email: editors@thewhitereview.org
Website: http://www.thewhitereview.org

Publishes: Essays; Fiction; Nonfiction; Poetry; Reviews; *Areas:* Arts; Culture; Literature; Short Stories; *Markets:* Adult; *Treatments:* Literary; Serious

Print and online quarterly arts and literature magazine. Publishes cultural analysis, reviews, and new fiction and poetry. See website for guidelines and submit by email.

Woman

Time Inc. UK
Blue Fin Building
110 Southwark Street
London
SE1 0SU
Tel: +44 (0) 20 3148 5000
Email: woman@timeinc.com
Website: http://www.womanmagazine.co.uk

Publishes: Articles; Features; News; Nonfiction; *Areas:* Entertainment; Lifestyle; Women's Interests; *Markets:* Adult

Magazine for women, publishing celebrity and real-life features up to 1,000 words.

Woman & Home Feel Good Food

Email: wandhmail@ipcmedia.com
Website: http://www.womanandhome.com

Publishes: Articles; Nonfiction; *Areas:* Cookery; Women's Interests; *Markets:* Adult

Editors: Jane Curran

Magazine covering cookery, recipes, ingredients, etc.

Woman's Own

Time Inc. (UK) Ltd
Blue Fin Building
110 Southwark Street
London
SE1 0SU
Tel: +44 (0) 20 3148 6530
Email: womansown@timeinc.com
Website: http://www.timeinc.com/brands/womans-own/

Publishes: Articles; Features; Nonfiction; *Areas:* Beauty and Fashion; Entertainment; Lifestyle; Women's Interests; Markets

Editors: Karen Livermore

Magazine aimed at women aged 40 and older.

Woman's Weekly

Time Inc (UK)
161 Marsh Wall
London
E14 9AP
Email: womansweeklypostbag@timeinc.com
Website: http://www.womansweekly.com

Publishes: Features; Fiction; News; Nonfiction; *Areas:* Beauty and Fashion; Cookery; Crafts; Gardening; Health; Short Stories; Travel; Women's Interests; *Markets:* Adult; *Treatments:* Contemporary

Editors: Diane Kenwood; Sue Pilkington (Features); Gaynor Davies (Fiction)

Publishes features of interest to women over forty, plus fiction between 1,000 and 2,000 words and serials in three, four, or five parts of 3,300 words each. Only uses experienced journalists for nonfiction. No submissions by email. Submit by post with SAE.

Woman's Weekly Fiction Special

IPC Media Ltd
The Blue Fin Building
110 Southwark Street
London
SE1 0SU
Tel: +44 (0) 20 3148 6600
Email: womansweeklypostbag@timeinc.com
Website: http://www.womansweekly.com

Publishes: Fiction; *Areas:* Short Stories; Women's Interests; *Markets:* Adult

Editors: Gaynor Davies

Publishes short stories for women between 1,000 and 8,000 words. Send stories by post – no correspondence by email.

The World Today

The Royal Institute of International Affairs
Chatham House
10 St James's Square
London
SW1Y 4LE
Tel: +44 (0) 20 7957 5700
Fax: +44 (0) 20 7957 5710

Email: contact@chathamhouse.org
Website: http://www.theworldtoday.org

Publishes: Articles; News; Nonfiction; *Areas:* Current Affairs; Politics; *Markets:* Adult; *Treatments:* Serious

Bimonthly magazine providing authoritative analysis and commentary on current topics.

Yachts & Yachting

Email: Georgie.Corlett-Pitt@chelseamagazines.com
Website: http://www.yachtsandyachting.com

Publishes: Articles; Nonfiction; *Areas:* Hobbies; How-to; Sport; Travel; *Markets:* Adult

Editors: Georgie Corlett-Pitt

Magazine publishing articles on sailing techniques and lifestyle.

Yorkshire Ridings Magazine

Seasiders Way
Blackpool
Lancashire
FY1 6NZ
Tel: +44 (0) 1253 336588
Fax: +44 (0) 1253 336587
Website: http://www.yorkshireridingsmagazine.com

Publishes: Articles; News; *Areas:* Beauty and Fashion; Business; Cookery; Entertainment; Finance; Gardening; Historical; Leisure; Lifestyle; Sport; Travel; *Markets:* Adult

County magazine for Yorkshire. All material must be related to the people and places of Yorkshire.

Your Cat

1-6 Buckminster Yard
Main Street
Buckminster
Grantham
Lincs
NG33 5SB
Tel: +44 (0) 1476 859820
Email: editorial@yourcat.co.uk
Website: http://www.yourcat.co.uk

Publishes: Articles; Fiction; Nonfiction; *Areas:* How-to; Short Stories; *Markets:* Adult

Editors: Chloë Hukin

Practical magazine covering the care of cats and kittens. No poetry and no articles written from the cat's viewpoint. Fiction by commission only. Send query by email with outline by post or by email.

Your Dog Magazine

BPG Stamford Ltd
1-6 Buckminster Yard
Main Street
Buckminster
Grantham
Lincs
NG33 5SA
Tel: +44 (0) 1476 859830
Email: editorial@yourdog.co.uk
Website: http://www.yourdog.co.uk

Publishes: Articles; Features; News; Nonfiction; *Areas:* Hobbies; How-to; Leisure; Lifestyle; *Markets:* Adult

Editors: Sarah Wright

Publishes news articles (up to 400 words) and feature articles (up to 2,500 words) aimed at dog owners, offering practical advice and some personal experience pieces. No fiction. Approach by phone in first instance.

Yours

Media House
Peterborough Business Park
Peterborough
PE2 6EA
Tel: +44 (0) 1733 468000
Email: yours@bauermedia.co.uk
Website: http://www.yours.co.uk

Publishes: Articles; Features; Fiction; Nonfiction; *Areas:* Lifestyle; Short Stories; Women's Interests; *Markets:* Adult; *Treatments:* Positive

Editors: Sharon Red

Lifestyle magazine aimed at women over 55. Welcomes nonfiction articles. Uses one or two pieces of fiction each issue. Send complete MS with SAE.

Canadian Magazines

For the most up-to-date listings of these and hundreds of other magazines, visit https://www.firstwriter.com/magazines

*To claim your **free** access to the site, please see the back of this book.*

Alberta Views

208, 320 23rd Ave SW
Calgary AB, T2S 0J2
Tel: +1 (403) 243-5334
Fax: +1 (403) 243-8599
Email: queries@albertaviews.ab.ca
Website: https://albertaviews.ab.ca

Publishes: Articles; Features; Fiction; Nonfiction; Poetry; Reviews; *Areas:* Arts; Business; Culture; Finance; Politics; Short Stories; Sociology; *Markets:* Adult

Regional magazine for Alberta, publishing articles about the culture, politics and economy of Alberta; book reviews of books written or published in the province; poetry; and fiction. Accepted unsolicited poetry submissions. For nonfiction, query. Accepts fiction only through annual fiction competition. See website for full details.

Better Than Starbucks

605-190 Cosburn Avenue,
Toronto, Ontario
Tel: +1 (416) 425-1431
Email: betterthanstarbucks2@gmail.com
Website: http://www.betterthanstarbucks.org

Publishes: Fiction; Interviews; Poetry; *Areas:* Short Stories; Translations; *Markets:* Adult; Youth; *Treatments:* Contemporary; Literary; Popular; Traditional

Editors: Vera Ignatowitsch

Monthly poetry publication online, with separate pages of free verse, haiku and related forms, formal and rhyming poetry, poetry translations, short fiction, an interview with a personage in the world of poetry, and art.

The Capilano Review

281 Industrial Avenue
Vancouver, BC V6A 2P2
Email: contact@thecapilanoreview.ca
Website: https://www.thecapilanoreview.ca

Publishes: Fiction; Interviews; Nonfiction; Poetry; Reviews; *Markets:* Adult; *Treatments:* Experimental; Literary

Publishes experimental writing and art. Submit up to 8 pages of poetry; reviews up to 600 words; fiction up to 5,000 words; or interviews up to 4,000 words, through online submission system. No submissions by post or email.

The Claremont Review

Suite 101
1581-H Hillside Avenue
Victoria, BC V8T 2C1
Email: claremontreview@gmail.com
Website: http://www.theclaremontreview.ca

Publishes: Fiction; Poetry; Scripts; *Areas:* Drama; Short Stories; *Markets:* Children's; Youth

Publishes poetry, short stories, and short plays by young writers aged 13-19 from anywhere in the English-speaking world. Send submissions from September 1 to April 30 annually. See website for submission guidelines.

Event

PO Box 2503
New Westminster, BC
V3L 5B2
Tel: +1 (604) 527-5293
Fax: +1 (604) 527-5095
Email: event@douglascollege.ca
Website: http://event.douglas.bc.ca

Publishes: Fiction; Nonfiction; Poetry; Reviews; *Markets:* Adult; *Treatments:* Literary

Closed to fiction and poetry submissions until mid summer 2017, and closed to nonfiction submissions until autumn 2017

Send one story or up to eight poems via online submission system only. Occasional unsolicited reviews published – query before submitting.

Filling Station

filling Station Publications Society
Box 22135
Bankers Hall RPO
Calgary AB T2P 4J5
Email: mgmt@fillingstation.ca
Website: http://www.fillingstation.ca

Publishes: Articles; Fiction; Interviews; Nonfiction; Poetry; Reviews; *Areas:* Arts; Criticism; Literature; Short Stories; *Markets:* Adult; *Treatments:* Literary

Publishes previously unpublished poetry, fiction, creative nonfiction, and critical nonfiction (about literature and occasionally about visual art). Submit up to 10 pages of fiction; up to 6 pages of poetry; or up to two piece of nonfiction, via online submission system. See website for full details.

Flare

Rogers Communications
One Mt Pleasant Road, 8th Floor
Toronto
Ontario
M4Y 2Y5
Tel: +1 (416) 764-1829
Fax: +1 (416) 764-2866
Email: editors@flare.com
Website: http://www.flare.com/about/writers-guidelines/

Publishes: Articles; News; Nonfiction; *Areas:* Beauty and Fashion; Entertainment; Women's Interests; *Markets:* Adult

Canada's best-selling fashion magazine, celebrating "smart fashion, Canadian style". Publishes articles on the home, fashion, beauty, celebrity, and weddings. Welcomes pitches from experienced writers familiar with the magazine's tone and content. Send query by email with published writing samples.

The Grey Press

Email: editor@greypresspublishing.com
Website: https://greypresspublishing.com

Publishes: Fiction; Nonfiction; Poetry; *Areas:* Short Stories; *Markets:* Adult; *Treatments:* Literary

Online journal publishing short fiction up to 5,000 words, flash fiction up to 500 words, micro-fiction up to 100 words, short nonfiction up to 5,000 words, first chapters of graphic novels up to 5,000 words, and poetry (submit up to 5). Submissions must be sent by email with the subject line "Submission". See website for full details.

Quill & Quire

111 Queen Street East
Suite 320
Toronto, ON
M5C 1S2
Tel: +1 (416) 364-3333
Fax: +1 (416) 595-5415
Email: scflinn@quillandquire.com
Website: http://www.quillandquire.com

Publishes: Articles; News; Nonfiction; Reviews; *Areas:* Business; Literature; *Markets:* Professional

Editors: Sue Carter

Magazine of the Canadian book trade, including news, author profiles, and reviews of new titles.

Toronto Life

111 Queen St. E., Suite 320
Toronto, Ont. M5C 1S2
Email: editorial@torontolife.com
Website: http://torontolife.com

Publishes: Articles; News; Nonfiction; *Areas:* Lifestyle; *Markets:* Adult

Editors: Sarah Fulford

Local lifestyle magazine for Toronto. Send queries and unsolicited mss by email.

Irish Magazines

For the most up-to-date listings of these and hundreds of other magazines, visit https://www.firstwriter.com/magazines

*To claim your **free** access to the site, please see the back of this book.*

Books Ireland

Unit 9
78 Furze Road
Sandyford
Dublin 18
Tel: +353-1-2933568
Fax: +353-1-2939377
Email: office@wordwellbooks.com
Website: http://www.wordwellbooks.com

Publishes: Articles; Nonfiction; Reviews; *Areas:* Literature; *Markets:* Adult; Professional

Magazine publishing reviews of books by Irish authors or of Irish interest, plus articles aimed at booksellers, readers, and general readers.

Cyphers

3 Selskar Terrace
Ranelagh
Dublin 6
Email: letters@cyphers.ie
Website: http://www.cyphers.ie

Publishes: Fiction; Poetry; *Areas:* Short Stories; Translations; *Markets:* Adult; *Treatments:* Literary

Publishes poetry and fiction in English and Irish, from Ireland and around the world. Translations are welcome. No unsolicited critical articles. Submissions by post only. Attachments sent by email will be deleted. See website for full guidelines.

The Dublin Review

PO Box 7948
Dublin 1
Email: enquiry@thedublinreview.com
Website: http://thedublinreview.com

Publishes: Essays; Fiction; Nonfiction; *Areas:* Criticism; Literature; Short Stories; *Markets:* Adult; *Treatments:* Literary

Publishes essays, criticism, reportage, and fiction for a general, intelligent readership. No poetry. No official length limit, but rarely publishes pieces in excess of 12,000 words. Send submissions by post only with email address for response. Material is not returned, so do not include return postage. No response without email address.

EarthLines Magazine

Teach Dhoire an Easa
Meenderry
Falcarragh
Co Donegal
F92 W732
Email: info@earthlinesmagazine.org
Website: http://www.earthlinesmagazine.org

Publishes: Articles; Essays; Features; Fiction; Interviews; Nonfiction; Poetry; Reviews; *Areas:* Autobiography; Nature; Short Stories; Travel; *Markets:* Adult

Editors: David Knowles

Magazine publishing features, essays, poetry, and perhaps a little short fiction, exploring nature, place and the environment. Send query/submissions by email. Accepts attachments as Word or RTF files.

Hot Press

13 Trinity Street
Dublin 2
Tel: +353 (1) 241 1500
Email: info@hotpress.ie
Website: http://www.hotpress.com

Publishes: Articles; Nonfiction; *Areas:* Culture; Entertainment; Film; Lifestyle; Media; Music; Politics; Sport; *Markets:* Adult; Youth

Magazine aimed at readers aged 16-39.

Into The Void Magazine

Email: intothevoidmag@gmail.com
Website: https://intothevoidmagazine.com

Publishes: Essays; Fiction; Nonfiction; Poetry; *Areas:* Adventure; Anthropology; Arts; Crime; Current Affairs; Drama; Fantasy; Film; Gothic; Historical; Horror; Humour; Literature; Mystery; Nature; Philosophy; Politics; Psychology; Romance; Science; Sci-Fi; Short Stories; Sociology; Suspense; Thrillers; Westerns; *Markets:* Adult; *Treatments:* Commercial; Contemporary; Cynical; Dark; Experimental; Light; Literary; Mainstream; Niche; Popular; Positive; Progressive; Satirical; Serious; Traditional

Editors: Philip Elliott, Gabriela McAdams

A non-profit print and digital literary magazine dedicated to providing a platform for fantastic fiction, nonfiction and poetry from all over the world. We accept writing of all genres and styles, striving to publish work that we feel is heartfelt, genuine and screaming to be read. We adore beautiful and unique styles of writing but clarity is most important. We are committed to giving writers of all experience levels an opportunity. Unpublished writers have just as good a chance of getting published as established ones – it's all about the writing.

Ireland's Own

Channing House
Rowe Street
Wexford
Tel: 053 9140140
Email: info@irelandsown.ie
Website: https://irelandsown.ie

Publishes: Articles; Features; Fiction; Nonfiction; *Areas:* Short Stories; *Markets:* Adult; Children's; Family; Youth; *Treatments:* Literary; Traditional

Editors: Sean Nolan

Magazine publishing stories and articles of Irish interest for the whole family, plus puzzles and games.

Irish Arts Review

15 Harcourt Terrace
Dublin 2
Tel: +353 1 676 6711
Fax: +353 1 676 6700
Email: editorial@irishartsreview.com
Website: http://www.irishartsreview.com

Publishes: Articles; Nonfiction; *Areas:* Architecture; Arts; Design; Photography; *Markets:* Adult

Quarterly review of Irish arts and design, from pre-history to contemporary.

Irish Farmers Journal

Irish Farm Centre
Bluebell
Dublin 12
Tel: 01 419 9500
Email: jmccarthy@farmersjournal.ie
Website: http://www.farmersjournal.ie

Publishes: Articles; Nonfiction; *Areas:* Business; Nature; *Markets:* Professional

Editors: Justin McCarthy

Weekly magazine for Irish farmers.

The Moth

Ardan Grange
Milltown
Belturbet
Co. Cavan
Tel: 353 (0) 49 9522995

Email: editor@themothmagazine.com
Website: http://www.themothmagazine.com

Publishes: Fiction; Poetry; *Areas:* Short Stories; *Markets:* Adult; *Treatments:* Literary

Editors: Rebecca O'Connor

Submit up to six poems or up to two short stories by post or by email. See website for full submission guidelines.

The Penny Dreadful

Email: The.P.Dreadful@Gmail.com
Website: http://thepennydreadful.org

Publishes: Fiction; Poetry; *Areas:* Short Stories; *Markets:* Adult; *Treatments:* Literary

Editors: John Keating; Marc O'Connell

Publishes short stories up to 3,000 words (submit up to two at a time) and poems (submit up to six of any length). Include bio up to 100 words. Query by email in first instance. No submissions by email.

Poetry Ireland Review

11 Parnell Square East
Dublin 1
D01 ND60
Tel: +353 (0)1 6789815
Fax: +353 (0)1 6789782
Email: info@poetryireland.ie
Website: http://www.poetryireland.ie

Publishes: Articles; Nonfiction; Poetry; Reviews; *Areas:* Literature; *Markets:* Adult

Editors: Eavan Boland

Send up to 6 poems with SASE / IRCs or email address for response. Poetry is accepted from around the world, but must be previously unpublished. No sexism or racism. No submissions by email. Articles and reviews are generally commissioned, however proposals are welcome. No unsolicited reviews or articles.

U Magazine

Harmonia Ltd
Rosemount House
Dundrum Road
Dundrum
Dublin 14
Tel: +353 1 240 5300
Fax: +353 1 661 9486
Email: webmaster@harmonia.ie
Website: http://umagazine.ie

Publishes: Articles; Features; Interviews; Nonfiction; *Areas:* Beauty and Fashion; Cookery; Design; Entertainment; Film; Health; Lifestyle; Music; Travel; Women's Interests; *Markets:* Adult

Magazine aimed at Irish women aged 18-25. Most material is commissioned.

Woman's Way

Rosemount House
Dundrum Road
Dundrum
Dublin 14
Tel: +353 (0) 1 240 5318
Email: atoner@harmonia.ie
Website: http://womansway.ie

Publishes: Articles; Features; Interviews; Nonfiction; *Areas:* Beauty and Fashion; Entertainment; Lifestyle; Media; Women's Interests; *Markets:* Adult

Magazine for women aged 35-65. Describes itself as "Irelands best read and only Irish Woman's Weekly" [sic].

Magazines Subject Index

This section lists magazines by their subject matter, with directions to the section of the book where the full listing can be found.

You can create your own customised lists of magazines using different combinations of these subject areas, plus over a dozen other criteria, instantly online at https://www.firstwriter.com.

*To claim your **free** access to the site, please see the back of this book.*

Adventure
Aphelion: The Webzine of Science Fiction and Fantasy (*US*)
Artifact Nouveau (*US*)
Barbaric Yawp (*US*)
Big Pulp (*US*)
Bugle (*US*)
Cadet Quest (*US*)
Crystal Magazine (*UK*)
Into The Void Magazine (*Ire*)
The People's Friend (*UK*)
Scouting (*US*)
ShortStorySunday.com (*UK*)
The Washington Pastime (*US*)
Anthropology
Into The Void Magazine (*Ire*)
Architecture
Architecture Today (*UK*)
Building (*UK*)
Home Energy Magazine (*US*)
Irish Arts Review (*Ire*)
Preservation in Print (*US*)
Properties Magazine (*US*)
Santa Barbara Magazine (*US*)
Stone World (*US*)
Stormwater (*US*)
SuCasa (*US*)
US Glass Magazine (*US*)
Walls & Ceilings (*US*)
Arts
Adelaide Literary Magazine (*US*)
The Adirondack Review (*US*)
Alberta Views (*Can*)
Ambit (*UK*)
Artifact Nouveau (*US*)
ArtReview (*UK*)
The Big Issue (*UK*)
Callaloo (*US*)
Cambridge Magazine (*UK*)
Caveat Lector (*US*)
Central and Eastern European London Review (*UK*)
The Chattahoochee Review (*US*)
Columbia: A Journal of Literature and Art (*US*)
Filling Station (*Can*)
The Friend (*UK*)
Frieze (*UK*)
A Gathering of the Tribes (*US*)
GUD Magazine (*US*)
Guernica (*US*)
H&E Naturist (*UK*)
Houston Press (*US*)
Into The Void Magazine (*Ire*)
Irish Arts Review (*Ire*)
Jewish Quarterly (*UK*)
Litro Magazine (*UK*)
The London Magazine (*UK*)
London Review of Books (*UK*)
Lothian Life (*UK*)
Ms. Magazine (*US*)
Main Line Today (*US*)
Mobile Bay (*US*)
New Statesman (*UK*)
Niche (*US*)
Nob Hill Gazette (*US*)
NY Literary Magazine (*US*)
Palm Springs Life (*US*)
Philly Weekly (*US*)

Planet (*UK*)
Santa Barbara Magazine (*US*)
Sixpenny Magazine (*US*)
Sunshine Artist (*US*)
Surrey Life (*UK*)
Susquehanna Life (*US*)
The Lady (*UK*)
The Voice (*UK*)
The Times Literary Supplement (TLS) (*UK*)
The White Review (*UK*)
Zeek (*US*)

Autobiography

Artifact Nouveau (*US*)
The Carolina Quarterly (*US*)
Cold Mountain Review (*US*)
Confrontation Magazine (*US*)
december (*US*)
Ducts (*US*)
EarthLines Magazine (*Ire*)
Granta (*UK*)
Guernica (*US*)
Irish Pages (*UK*)
Litro Magazine (*UK*)
The London Magazine (*UK*)
Mslexia (*UK*)
The North (*UK*)

Beauty and Fashion

Attitude (*UK*)
Bust (*US*)
Cambridge Magazine (*UK*)
Closer (*UK*)
Dare (*UK*)
Drapers (*UK*)
Flare (*Can*)
Girlfriendz Magazine (*US*)
Glamour (*UK*)
GQ Magazine (*UK*)
Interweave Knits (*US*)
marie claire (*UK*)
Mobile Bay (*US*)
More (*US*)
Nob Hill Gazette (*US*)
Palm Springs Life (*US*)
Parents (*US*)
Phoenix Magazine (*US*)
Psychologies (*UK*)
Self (*US*)
Shropshire Magazine (*UK*)
Susquehanna Life (*US*)
The Lady (*UK*)
Top Sante (*UK*)
U Magazine (*Ire*)
Vanity Fair (*UK*)
Weight Watchers Magazine (*UK*)
Woman's Own (*UK*)
Woman's Way (*Ire*)
Woman's Weekly (*UK*)
Yorkshire Ridings Magazine (*UK*)

Biography

december (*US*)

Business

African Business (*UK*)
Alberta Views (*Can*)
The Author (*UK*)
Building (*UK*)
The Caterer (*UK*)
Drapers (*UK*)
Equal Opportunity (*US*)
Family Office Magazine (*UK*)
Fast Company (*US*)
Fishing News (*UK*)
Food Product Design (*US*)
Freelance Writer's Report (FWR) (*US*)
Fruit Growers News Magazine (*US*)
Girlfriendz Magazine (*US*)
Governance + Compliance (*UK*)
Grain Journal (*US*)
The Huffington Post (United Kingdom) (*UK*)
Irish Farmers Journal (*Ire*)
KNOWAtlanta (*US*)
Leisure Group Travel (*US*)
Media Inc. (*US*)
Midwest Meetings (*US*)
Music Week (*UK*)
Nails Magazine (*US*)
Niche (*US*)
Northwest Quarterly Magazine (*US*)
O'Dwyer's (*US*)
OfficePro (*US*)
Onion World (*US*)
People Management (*UK*)
Pizza Today (*US*)
Poultry World (*UK*)
Properties Magazine (*US*)
QSR (*US*)
Quill & Quire (*Can*)
Remodeling (*US*)
Restaurant Magazine (*UK*)
Retail Week (*UK*)
Rochester Business Journal (*US*)
SignCraft Publishing Co., Inc. (*US*)
Spear's Magazine (*UK*)
State Journal (*US*)
Stormwater (*US*)
Susquehanna Life (*US*)
Tallahassee Magazine (*US*)
The Voice (*UK*)
TimberWest (*US*)
Tobacco International (*US*)
Underground Construction (*US*)
US Glass Magazine (*US*)
Water Well Journal (*US*)
Welding Design & Fabrication (*US*)
Yorkshire Ridings Magazine (*UK*)

Cookery

Boys' Quest (*US*)
Bust (*US*)
Cook Vegetarian (*UK*)
Cruising Outpost Magazine (*US*)
Decanter (*UK*)
Eat In Magazine (*UK*)
Food Product Design (*US*)
Jamie Magazine (*UK*)
Kitchen Garden (*UK*)
Lothian Life (*UK*)
Mobile Bay (*US*)

Nob Hill Gazette (*US*)
Olive (*UK*)
The People's Friend (*UK*)
Phoenix Magazine (*US*)
Pizza Today (*US*)
Psychologies (*UK*)
QSR (*US*)
Real Simple (*US*)
Restaurant Magazine (*UK*)
Surrey Life (*UK*)
The Lady (*UK*)
U Magazine (*Ire*)
Vegan Life (*UK*)
Weight Watchers Magazine (*UK*)
Woman & Home Feel Good Food (*UK*)
Woman's Weekly (*UK*)
Yorkshire Ridings Magazine (*UK*)

Crafts
Bust (*US*)
craft&design Magazine (*UK*)
The Dolls' House (*UK*)
FineScale Modeler (*US*)
Flora International (*UK*)
Interweave Knits (*US*)
Military Modelling Magazine (*UK*)
Niche (*US*)
The People's Friend (*UK*)
Sew Simple (*US*)
The Sewing Directory (*UK*)
Spin Off (*US*)
The Stampers' Sampler (*US*)
Sunshine Artist (*US*)
This England (*UK*)
Vogue Patterns (*US*)
Woman's Weekly (*UK*)

Crime
Ellery Queen Mystery Magazine (*US*)
Into The Void Magazine (*Ire*)
The People's Friend (*UK*)
The Police Journal (*UK*)
The Savage Kick (*UK*)
ShortStorySunday.com (*UK*)
The Washington Pastime (*US*)

Criticism
Acumen (*UK*)
Adelaide Literary Magazine (*US*)
Agenda (*UK*)
Artifact Nouveau (*US*)
ArtReview (*UK*)
Bilingual Review (*US*)
Caveat Lector (*US*)
Chicago Review (*US*)
Critical Quarterly (*UK*)
The Dublin Review (*Ire*)
Feminist Studies (*US*)
Filling Station (*Can*)
Floyd County Moonshine (*US*)
The Horn Book Magazine (*US*)
The London Magazine (*UK*)
The North (*UK*)
Wasafiri (*UK*)

Culture
A&U (*US*)
Adelaide Literary Magazine (*US*)
Alberta Views (*Can*)
Artifact Nouveau (*US*)
The Big Issue (*UK*)
Bust (*US*)
Callaloo (*US*)
Cambridge Magazine (*UK*)
Central and Eastern European London Review (*UK*)
Confrontation Magazine (*US*)
Critical Quarterly (*UK*)
december (*US*)
Diva (*UK*)
Evergreen (*UK*)
Frieze (*UK*)
Geographical (*UK*)
GQ Magazine (*UK*)
Granta (*UK*)
GuestLife (*US*)
H&E Naturist (*UK*)
Hot Press (*Ire*)
Jewish Quarterly (*UK*)
KNOWAtlanta (*US*)
Leopard Magazine (*UK*)
London Review of Books (*UK*)
Ms. Magazine (*US*)
Mobile Bay (*US*)
Northwest Quarterly Magazine (*US*)
Opera (*UK*)
Palm Springs Life (*US*)
Psychologies (*UK*)
Rain Taxi (*US*)
The Voice (*UK*)
This England (*UK*)
Vanity Fair (*UK*)
Wasafiri (*UK*)
The White Review (*UK*)
Zeek (*US*)

Current Affairs
Africa-Asia Confidential (*UK*)
Artifact Nouveau (*US*)
The Huffington Post (United Kingdom) (*UK*)
Into The Void Magazine (*Ire*)
Jewish Quarterly (*UK*)
New Statesman (*UK*)
News Photographer (*US*)
Philly Weekly (*US*)
Planet (*UK*)
Private Eye (*UK*)
Reform (*UK*)
Vanity Fair (*UK*)
VFW (Veterans of Foreign Wars) Magazine (*US*)
The World Today (*UK*)

Design
craft&design Magazine (*UK*)
Drapers (*UK*)
Energy Engineering (*UK*)
Evansville Living (*US*)
Fast Company (*US*)
Home Energy Magazine (*US*)
Hortus (*UK*)
Housebuilder (*UK*)

Interweave Knits (*US*)
Irish Arts Review (*Ire*)
Lothian Life (*UK*)
Nob Hill Gazette (*US*)
Palm Springs Life (*US*)
Play & Playground Magazine (*US*)
Properties Magazine (*US*)
Remodeling (*US*)
SelfBuild & Design (*UK*)
Stone World (*US*)
Stormwater (*US*)
Style at Home (*UK*)
SuCasa (*US*)
This Old House (*US*)
U Magazine (*Ire*)
Underground Construction (*US*)
Walls & Ceilings (*US*)

Drama
The Alembic (*US*)
Aries (*US*)
Artifact Nouveau (*US*)
Bilingual Review (*US*)
The Claremont Review (*Can*)
Connotation Press (*US*)
Current Accounts (*UK*)
Epoch (*US*)
The Evansville Review (*US*)
Flint Hills Review (*US*)
Gold Dust (*UK*)
Gutter Magazine (*UK*)
Into The Void Magazine (*Ire*)
The Washington Pastime (*US*)

Entertainment
Artifact Nouveau (*US*)
Attitude (*UK*)
Boys' Quest (*US*)
Closer (*UK*)
Flare (*Can*)
GuestLife (*US*)
Hot Press (*Ire*)
Houston Press (*US*)
The Huffington Post (United Kingdom) (*UK*)
Inside Soap (*UK*)
More (*US*)
The New Accelerator (*UK*)
newbooks (*UK*)
Opera (*UK*)
Palm Springs Life (*US*)
Philly Weekly (*US*)
Radio Times (*UK*)
Shropshire Magazine (*UK*)
Susquehanna Life (*US*)
Tallahassee Magazine (*US*)
The Voice (*UK*)
U Magazine (*Ire*)
Vanity Fair (*UK*)
The Washington Pastime (*US*)
Woman (*UK*)
Woman's Own (*UK*)
Woman's Way (*Ire*)
Yorkshire Ridings Magazine (*UK*)

Erotic
Artifact Nouveau (*US*)
Bust (*US*)
Erotic Review (*UK*)

Fantasy
Allegory (*US*)
Aphelion: The Webzine of Science Fiction and Fantasy (*US*)
Artifact Nouveau (*US*)
Barbaric Yawp (*US*)
Big Pulp (*US*)
Black Static (*UK*)
Crystal Magazine (*UK*)
The Dark (*US*)
The Dawntreader (*UK*)
The Fifth Di... (*US*)
Garbled Transmissions (*US*)
GUD Magazine (*US*)
Interzone (*UK*)
Into The Void Magazine (*Ire*)
The New Accelerator (*UK*)
Orson Scott Card's InterGalactic Medicine Show (*US*)
SFX (*UK*)
ShortStorySunday.com (*UK*)
The Washington Pastime (*US*)

Fiction
The Alembic (*US*)
A&U (*US*)
Able Muse (*US*)
The Account (*US*)
Adelaide Literary Magazine (*US*)
The Adirondack Review (*US*)
Alberta Views (*Can*)
Alebrijes (*US*)
The Allegheny Review (*US*)
Allegory (*US*)
Alligator Juniper (*US*)
Ambit (*UK*)
Analog Science Fiction & Fact (*US*)
Ancient Paths (*US*)
Another Chicago Magazine (ACM) (*US*)
Apalachee Review (*US*)
Aphelion: The Webzine of Science Fiction and Fantasy (*US*)
Appalachian Heritage (*US*)
Apple Valley Review (*US*)
Arc (*UK*)
Aries (*US*)
Artifact Nouveau (*US*)
Artificium (*UK*)
Asinine Poetry (*US*)
The Avalon Literary Review (*US*)
The Baltimore Review (*US*)
Banipal (*UK*)
Barbaric Yawp (*US*)
Bartleby Snopes (*US*)
Bayou Magazine (*US*)
The Beano (*UK*)
Bellevue Literary Review (*US*)
Berkeley Fiction Review (*US*)
Best New Writing (*US*)
Better Than Starbucks (*Can*)
Big Bridge (*US*)
Big Pulp (*US*)

Bilingual Review (*US*)
Black Static (*UK*)
Blackbird (*US*)
Blueline (*US*)
Bluestem (*US*)
Boys' Quest (*US*)
Bread for God's Children (*US*)
Brilliant Corners (*US*)
Bryant Literary Review (*US*)
Bugle (*US*)
Bunbury Magazine (*UK*)
Bust (*US*)
Cadet Quest (*US*)
The Cafe Irreal (*US*)
Callaloo (*US*)
Camas (*US*)
The Capilano Review (*Can*)
The Carolina Quarterly (*US*)
The Casket of Fictional Delights (*UK*)
Caveat Lector (*US*)
The Chaffin Journal (*US*)
The Chattahoochee Review (*US*)
Chicago Quarterly Review (*US*)
Chicago Review (*US*)
Cimarron Review (*US*)
The Claremont Review (*Can*)
Cloud Rodeo (*US*)
Cloudbank (*US*)
Coal City Review (*US*)
Cold Mountain Review (*US*)
The Collagist (*US*)
Colorado Review (*US*)
Columbia: A Journal of Literature and Art (*US*)
Compose (*US*)
Conduit (*US*)
Confrontation Magazine (*US*)
Connotation Press (*US*)
Cottonwood (*US*)
Crab Creek Review (*US*)
Critical Quarterly (*UK*)
Crucible (*US*)
Crystal Magazine (*UK*)
The Cumberland River Review (*US*)
Current Accounts (*UK*)
Cyphers (*Ire*)
The Dark (*US*)
The Dawntreader (*UK*)
The Dead Mule School of Southern Literature (*US*)
december (*US*)
Denver Quarterly (*US*)
Devil's Lake (*US*)
Diagram (*US*)
The Dos Passos Review (*US*)
Down in the Dirt (*US*)
Dream Catcher (*UK*)
The Dublin Review (*Ire*)
Ducts (*US*)
EarthLines Magazine (*Ire*)
Ellery Queen Mystery Magazine (*US*)
Emrys Journal (*US*)
Epoch (*US*)
Erotic Review (*UK*)
The Evansville Review (*US*)
Event (*Can*)
failbetter.com (*US*)
Feminist Review (*UK*)
Feminist Studies (*US*)
The Fifth Di... (*US*)
Filling Station (*Can*)
Flash: The International Short-Short Story Magazine (*UK*)
Flint Hills Review (*US*)
Floyd County Moonshine (*US*)
Flyway: Journal of Writing & Environment (*US*)
Fogged Clarity (*US*)
Fourteen Hills (*US*)
Fugue (*US*)
Garbled Transmissions (*US*)
A Gathering of the Tribes (*US*)
Gertrude (*US*)
The Gettysburg Review (*US*)
Gold Dust (*UK*)
Granta (*UK*)
Grasslimb (*US*)
Green Hills Literary Lantern (*US*)
Green Mountains Review (GMR) (*US*)
The Grey Press (*Can*)
The Griffin (*US*)
GUD Magazine (*US*)
Guernica (*US*)
Gulf Coast: A Journal of Literature and Fine Arts (*US*)
Gutter Magazine (*UK*)
The Interpreter's House (*UK*)
Interzone (*UK*)
Into The Void Magazine (*Ire*)
Ireland's Own (*Ire*)
Irish Pages (*UK*)
Iron Horse Literary Review (*US*)
Jewish Quarterly (*UK*)
Kalyna Review (*UK*)
Leopard Magazine (*UK*)
Litro Magazine (*UK*)
Little Patuxent Review (*US*)
The London Magazine (*UK*)
Longshot Island (*US*)
Ms. Magazine (*US*)
The Moth (*Ire*)
Mslexia (*UK*)
The New Accelerator (*UK*)
New Fairy Tales (*UK*)
New Welsh Reader (*UK*)
Orson Scott Card's InterGalactic Medicine Show (*US*)
The Ottawa Object (*US*)
Painted Bride Quarterly (*US*)
Painted Cave (*US*)
The Penny Dreadful (*Ire*)
The People's Friend (*UK*)
People's Friend Pocket Novels (*UK*)
Planet (*UK*)
Postcard Poems and Prose (*US*)
Prole (*UK*)
Rappahannock Review (*US*)
Sarasvati (*UK*)

The Savage Kick (*UK*)
Shooter Literary Magazine (*UK*)
Shoreline of Infinity (*UK*)
ShortStorySunday.com (*UK*)
Sixpenny Magazine (*US*)
Sling Magazine (*US*)
St Petersburg Review (*US*)
Stand Magazine (*UK*)
Star 82 Review (*US*)
Viz (*UK*)
Wasafiri (*UK*)
The Washington Pastime (*US*)
The White Review (*UK*)
Woman's Weekly (*UK*)
Woman's Weekly Fiction Special (*UK*)
Wordpeace (*US*)
Your Cat (*UK*)
Yours (*UK*)
Zeek (*US*)
ZYZZYVA (*US*)

Film
Central and Eastern European London Review (*UK*)
Columbia: A Journal of Literature and Art (*US*)
Epoch (*US*)
Garbled Transmissions (*US*)
Hot Press (*Ire*)
Into The Void Magazine (*Ire*)
Jewish Quarterly (*UK*)
Little White Lies (*UK*)
London Review of Books (*UK*)
New Musical Express (NME) (*UK*)
SFX (*UK*)
The Times Literary Supplement (TLS) (*UK*)
U Magazine (*Ire*)

Finance
Africa Confidential (*UK*)
African Business (*UK*)
Alberta Views (*Can*)
Equal Opportunity (*US*)
Family Office Magazine (*UK*)
Fast Company (*US*)
KNOWAtlanta (*US*)
More (*US*)
Niche (*US*)
Nob Hill Gazette (*US*)
Phoenix Magazine (*US*)
Self (*US*)
Spear's Magazine (*UK*)
The Lady (*UK*)
Yorkshire Ridings Magazine (*UK*)

Gardening
Cambridge Magazine (*UK*)
The English Garden (*UK*)
Evansville Living (*US*)
Hortus (*UK*)
Kitchen Garden (*UK*)
Lothian Life (*UK*)
Northwest Quarterly Magazine (*US*)
Organic Life (*US*)
Santa Barbara Magazine (*US*)
Surrey Life (*UK*)
Susquehanna Life (*US*)
The Lady (*UK*)
Woman's Weekly (*UK*)
Yorkshire Ridings Magazine (*UK*)

Gothic
Aphelion: The Webzine of Science Fiction and Fantasy (*US*)
Into The Void Magazine (*Ire*)
ShortStorySunday.com (*UK*)
The Washington Pastime (*US*)

Health
A New Heart (*US*)
A&U (*US*)
Bust (*US*)
Closer (*UK*)
Coach (*UK*)
Diabetes Balance (*UK*)
Girlfriendz Magazine (*US*)
Glamour (*UK*)
Golf News Magazine (*US*)
Kashrus Magazine (*US*)
KNOWAtlanta (*US*)
The Lancet (*UK*)
Lothian Life (*UK*)
marie claire (*UK*)
Massage & Bodywork (*US*)
More (*US*)
Nails Magazine (*US*)
New Mobility Magazine (*US*)
Nob Hill Gazette (*US*)
Northwest Quarterly Magazine (*US*)
Organic Life (*US*)
Parents (*US*)
Phoenix Magazine (*US*)
PN (Paraplegia News) (*US*)
The Practising Midwife (*UK*)
Psychologies (*UK*)
Self (*US*)
Ski Patrol Magazine (*US*)
Slimming World (*UK*)
Susquehanna Life (*US*)
The Health Journal (*US*)
The Lady (*UK*)
Top Sante (*UK*)
U Magazine (*Ire*)
Vegan Life (*UK*)
Weight Watchers Magazine (*UK*)
Woman's Weekly (*UK*)

Historical
Barbaric Yawp (*US*)
Bugle (*US*)
Classic Cars (*UK*)
The Daily Tea (*US*)
Evansville Living (*US*)
Evergreen (*UK*)
Girlfriendz Magazine (*US*)
GUD Magazine (*US*)
GuestLife (*US*)
H&E Naturist (*UK*)
Hortus (*UK*)
Hyde Park Living (*US*)
Into The Void Magazine (*Ire*)
Irish Pages (*UK*)
Jewish Quarterly (*UK*)

Lakeland Boating (*US*)
Leopard Magazine (*UK*)
Main Line Today (*US*)
Military Vehicles Magazine (*US*)
Mobile Bay (*US*)
News Photographer (*US*)
Nob Hill Gazette (*US*)
Northwest Quarterly Magazine (*US*)
Nostalgia Magazine (*US*)
Oregon Coast (*US*)
Preservation in Print (*US*)
RUSI Journal (*UK*)
Santa Barbara Magazine (*US*)
Scots Heritage Magazine (*UK*)
ShortStorySunday.com (*UK*)
Shropshire Magazine (*UK*)
Tallahassee Magazine (*US*)
The Lady (*UK*)
This England (*UK*)
TimberWest (*US*)
The Times Literary Supplement (TLS) (*UK*)
VFW (Veterans of Foreign Wars) Magazine (*US*)
Yorkshire Ridings Magazine (*UK*)

Hobbies

Angler's Mail (*UK*)
Boys' Quest (*US*)
Bugle (*US*)
Cadet Quest (*US*)
Climb Magazine (*UK*)
Country Walking (*UK*)
Custom Car (*UK*)
The Dolls' House (*UK*)
Engineering In Miniature (*UK*)
Everyday Practical Electronics (*UK*)
Field & Stream (*US*)
FineScale Modeler (*US*)
Flora International (*UK*)
Interweave Knits (*US*)
Kitchen Garden (*UK*)
Lost Treasure, Inc. (*US*)
Military Modelling Magazine (*UK*)
Model Engineer (*US*)
The People's Friend (*UK*)
Record Collector Magazine (*UK*)
Scouting (*US*)
Sew Simple (*US*)
The Sewing Directory (*UK*)
SFX (*UK*)
Southern Boating (*US*)
Spin Off (*US*)
The Stampers' Sampler (*US*)
Trail (*UK*)
Trailer Life Magazine (*US*)
Tropical Fish Hobbyist Magazine (*US*)
Vogue Patterns (*US*)
Western & Eastern Treasures (*US*)
Western Outdoor News (*US*)
Yachts & Yachting (*UK*)
Your Dog Magazine (*UK*)

Horror

Allegory (*US*)
Aphelion: The Webzine of Science Fiction and Fantasy (*US*)
Artifact Nouveau (*US*)
Barbaric Yawp (*US*)
Big Pulp (*US*)
Black Static (*UK*)
The Dark (*US*)
GUD Magazine (*US*)
Into The Void Magazine (*Ire*)
The New Accelerator (*UK*)
ShortStorySunday.com (*UK*)
The Washington Pastime (*US*)

How-to

Android Magazine (*UK*)
The Author (*UK*)
Compose (*US*)
Computeractive Magazine (*UK*)
Cruising Outpost Magazine (*US*)
The Daily Tea (*US*)
Digital Camera World (*UK*)
The Dolls' House (*UK*)
Eat In Magazine (*UK*)
The English Garden (*UK*)
Equal Opportunity (*US*)
The Fabricator (*US*)
Field & Stream (*US*)
FineScale Modeler (*US*)
Flora International (*UK*)
Food Product Design (*US*)
Freelance Writer's Report (FWR) (*US*)
Girlfriendz Magazine (*US*)
Golf News Magazine (*US*)
Governance + Compliance (*UK*)
Grain Journal (*US*)
Guitarist Magazine (*UK*)
InTents (*US*)
Interweave Knits (*US*)
Jamie Magazine (*UK*)
Kitchen Garden (*UK*)
KNOWAtlanta (*US*)
Lakeland Boating (*US*)
Main Line Today (*US*)
Massage & Bodywork (*US*)
Military Modelling Magazine (*UK*)
Military Vehicles Magazine (*US*)
Model Engineer (*US*)
Nails Magazine (*US*)
The National Jurist (*US*)
News Photographer (*US*)
Overtones (*US*)
People Management (*UK*)
Play & Playground Magazine (*US*)
Police and Security News (*US*)
Practical Photography (*UK*)
Remodeling (*US*)
Rider Magazine (*US*)
Runner's World (*US*)
SelfBuild & Design (*UK*)
Sew Simple (*US*)
Shutterbug (*US*)
SignCraft Publishing Co., Inc. (*US*)
Sky at Night Magazine (*UK*)
Slimming World (*UK*)

Southern Boating (*US*)
Style at Home (*UK*)
This Old House (*US*)
Underground Construction (*US*)
Vogue Patterns (*US*)
Walls & Ceilings (*US*)
Water Well Journal (*US*)
Welding Design & Fabrication (*US*)
Yachts & Yachting (*UK*)
Your Cat (*UK*)
Your Dog Magazine (*UK*)

Humour

Allegory (*US*)
Aphelion: The Webzine of Science Fiction and Fantasy (*US*)
Artifact Nouveau (*US*)
Asinine Poetry (*US*)
The Beano (*UK*)
Bugle (*US*)
Cadet Quest (*US*)
Crystal Magazine (*UK*)
The Daily Tea (*US*)
Ducts (*US*)
The Friend (*UK*)
Girlfriendz Magazine (*US*)
GUD Magazine (*US*)
Hyde Park Living (*US*)
Into The Void Magazine (*Ire*)
Main Line Today (*US*)
Northwest Quarterly Magazine (*US*)
The Oldie (*UK*)
Private Eye (*UK*)
ShortStorySunday.com (*UK*)
Viz (*UK*)
The Washington Pastime (*US*)

Legal

The Author (*UK*)
Fishing News (*UK*)
Governance + Compliance (*UK*)
The Lawyer (*UK*)
Ms. Magazine (*US*)
The National Jurist (*US*)
O'Dwyer's (*US*)
People Management (*UK*)
Police and Security News (*US*)
The Police Journal (*UK*)

Leisure

Artifact Nouveau (*US*)
Climb Magazine (*UK*)
Coach (*UK*)
Family Office Magazine (*UK*)
Field & Stream (*US*)
GuestLife (*US*)
Lakeland Boating (*US*)
Northwest Quarterly Magazine (*US*)
Oregon Coast (*US*)
Play & Playground Magazine (*US*)
PN (Paraplegia News) (*US*)
Runner's World (*US*)
Scouting (*US*)
Shropshire Magazine (*UK*)
Southern Boating (*US*)
Trail (*UK*)
Trailer Life Magazine (*US*)
Vegan Life (*UK*)
Western & Eastern Treasures (*US*)
Western Outdoor News (*US*)
Yorkshire Ridings Magazine (*UK*)
Your Dog Magazine (*UK*)

Lifestyle

Artifact Nouveau (*US*)
Attitude (*UK*)
Cambridge Magazine (*UK*)
Closer (*UK*)
Country Walking (*UK*)
Diabetes Balance (*UK*)
Diva (*UK*)
Erotic Review (*UK*)
Evansville Living (*US*)
Glamour (*UK*)
GQ Magazine (*UK*)
H&E Naturist (*UK*)
Hot Press (*Ire*)
Indianapolis Monthly (*US*)
KNOWAtlanta (*US*)
Main Line Today (*US*)
marie claire (*UK*)
Metro Parent (*US*)
Mobile Bay (*US*)
More (*US*)
Nob Hill Gazette (*US*)
Northwest Quarterly Magazine (*US*)
Organic Life (*US*)
Palm Springs Life (*US*)
Parents (*US*)
Phoenix Magazine (*US*)
PN (Paraplegia News) (*US*)
Psychologies (*UK*)
Real Simple (*US*)
San Diego Family Magazine (*US*)
Santa Barbara Magazine (*US*)
Self (*US*)
Shropshire Magazine (*UK*)
Southern Boating (*US*)
Spear's Magazine (*UK*)
Surrey Life (*UK*)
Susquehanna Life (*US*)
Tallahassee Magazine (*US*)
Toronto Life (*Can*)
U Magazine (*Ire*)
Vegan Life (*UK*)
Woman (*UK*)
Woman's Own (*UK*)
Woman's Way (*Ire*)
Yorkshire Ridings Magazine (*UK*)
Your Dog Magazine (*UK*)
Yours (*UK*)

Literature

Acumen (*UK*)
Adelaide Literary Magazine (*US*)
Agenda (*UK*)
Aphelion: The Webzine of Science Fiction and Fantasy (*US*)
Artifact Nouveau (*US*)
Bilingual Review (*US*)
Books Ireland (*Ire*)

Brilliant Corners (*US*)
Callaloo (*US*)
Carousel (*UK*)
Caveat Lector (*US*)
Central and Eastern European London Review (*UK*)
Chicago Review (*US*)
The Collagist (*US*)
Compose (*US*)
Connotation Press (*US*)
Critical Quarterly (*UK*)
Crystal Magazine (*UK*)
The Dublin Review (*Ire*)
Envoi (*UK*)
Filling Station (*Can*)
Floyd County Moonshine (*US*)
The Horn Book Magazine (*US*)
Hortus (*UK*)
Into The Void Magazine (*Ire*)
Jewish Quarterly (*UK*)
Litro Magazine (*UK*)
The London Magazine (*UK*)
London Review of Books (*UK*)
Magma (*UK*)
Modern Poetry in Translation (*UK*)
newbooks (*UK*)
The North (*UK*)
Planet (*UK*)
Poetry Ireland Review (*Ire*)
Quill & Quire (*Can*)
Rain Taxi (*US*)
The Savage Kick (*UK*)
Shoreline of Infinity (*UK*)
ShortStorySunday.com (*UK*)
Sixpenny Magazine (*US*)
The Times Literary Supplement (TLS) (*UK*)
Wasafiri (*UK*)
The Washington Pastime (*US*)
The White Review (*UK*)

Media
Adelaide Literary Magazine (*US*)
Artifact Nouveau (*US*)
British Journalism Review (*UK*)
Hot Press (*Ire*)
Inside Soap (*UK*)
Media Inc. (*US*)
Vanity Fair (*UK*)
Woman's Way (*Ire*)

Medicine
A&U (*US*)
Diabetes Balance (*UK*)
The Lancet (*UK*)
Massage & Bodywork (*US*)
New Mobility Magazine (*US*)
Nurseweek (*US*)
Pediatric Annals (*US*)
PracticeLink Magazine (*US*)
The Practising Midwife (*UK*)

Men's Interests
Attitude (*UK*)
GQ Magazine (*UK*)

Military
Military Modelling Magazine (*UK*)
Military Vehicles Magazine (*US*)
RUSI Journal (*UK*)
The Savage Kick (*UK*)
VFW (Veterans of Foreign Wars) Magazine (*US*)

Music
Artifact Nouveau (*US*)
Brilliant Corners (*US*)
Bust (*US*)
Central and Eastern European London Review (*UK*)
Columbia: A Journal of Literature and Art (*US*)
Connotation Press (*US*)
Guitarist Magazine (*UK*)
Hot Press (*Ire*)
Jewish Quarterly (*UK*)
Mojo (*UK*)
Music Week (*UK*)
Musical Opinion (*UK*)
New Musical Express (NME) (*UK*)
Opera News (*US*)
Overtones (*US*)
Planet (*UK*)
Record Collector Magazine (*UK*)
Shoreline of Infinity (*UK*)
Tempo: A Quarterly Review of New Music (*UK*)
U Magazine (*Ire*)

Mystery
Artifact Nouveau (*US*)
Big Pulp (*US*)
Crystal Magazine (*UK*)
Ellery Queen Mystery Magazine (*US*)
GUD Magazine (*US*)
Into The Void Magazine (*Ire*)
The People's Friend (*UK*)
ShortStorySunday.com (*UK*)
The Washington Pastime (*US*)

Nature
Artifact Nouveau (*US*)
Blueline (*US*)
Boys' Quest (*US*)
British Birds (*UK*)
Bugle (*US*)
Camas (*US*)
Country Walking (*UK*)
Crystal Magazine (*UK*)
The Dawntreader (*UK*)
EarthLines Magazine (*Ire*)
Evergreen (*UK*)
Field & Stream (*US*)
Fishing News (*UK*)
Flora International (*UK*)
Flyway: Journal of Writing & Environment (*US*)
The Friend (*UK*)
Fruit Growers News Magazine (*US*)
Geographical (*UK*)
Into The Void Magazine (*Ire*)
Irish Farmers Journal (*Ire*)
Irish Pages (*UK*)
Ms. Magazine (*US*)
Northwest Quarterly Magazine (*US*)
Onion World (*US*)

Oregon Coast (*US*)
Organic Life (*US*)
The People's Friend (*UK*)
Pest Management Professional (*US*)
Poultry World (*UK*)
Scouting (*US*)
ShortStorySunday.com (*UK*)
Susquehanna Life (*US*)
This England (*UK*)
Tropical Fish Hobbyist Magazine (*US*)
Vegetable Growers News Magazine (*US*)

New Age

Artifact Nouveau (*US*)
ShortStorySunday.com (*UK*)

Nonfiction

A New Heart (*US*)
A&U (*US*)
Able Muse (*US*)
The Account (*US*)
Acumen (*UK*)
Adelaide Literary Magazine (*US*)
The Adirondack Review (*US*)
Africa Confidential (*UK*)
Africa-Asia Confidential (*UK*)
African Business (*UK*)
Alberta Views (*Can*)
Alebrijes (*US*)
All Out Cricket (*UK*)
The Allegheny Review (*US*)
Allegory (*US*)
Alligator Juniper (*US*)
Android Magazine (*UK*)
Angler's Mail (*UK*)
Another Chicago Magazine (ACM) (*US*)
Apalachee Review (*US*)
Aphelion: The Webzine of Science Fiction and Fantasy (*US*)
Appalachian Heritage (*US*)
Apple Valley Review (*US*)
Arc (*UK*)
Architecture Today (*UK*)
Aries (*US*)
Artifact Nouveau (*US*)
ArtReview (*UK*)
Attitude (*UK*)
The Author (*UK*)
The Avalon Literary Review (*US*)
The Baltimore Review (*US*)
Bayou Magazine (*US*)
Bellevue Literary Review (*US*)
Best New Writing (*US*)
Big Bridge (*US*)
Bilingual Review (*US*)
Bizarre (*UK*)
Blackbird (*US*)
Blueline (*US*)
Bluestem (*US*)
Books Ireland (*Ire*)
Boys' Quest (*US*)
Bread for God's Children (*US*)
Brilliant Corners (*US*)
British Birds (*UK*)
British Journalism Review (*UK*)
Bugle (*US*)
Building (*UK*)
Bunbury Magazine (*UK*)
Bust (*US*)
Cadet Quest (*US*)
Callaloo (*US*)
Camas (*US*)
Cambridge Magazine (*UK*)
The Capilano Review (*Can*)
The Carolina Quarterly (*US*)
Carousel (*UK*)
The Caterer (*UK*)
The Catholic Herald (*UK*)
Caveat Lector (*US*)
Central and Eastern European London Review (*UK*)
The Chattahoochee Review (*US*)
Chicago Quarterly Review (*US*)
Chicago Review (*US*)
Classic Cars (*UK*)
Climb Magazine (*UK*)
Closer (*UK*)
Cloud Rodeo (*US*)
Coach (*UK*)
Cold Mountain Review (*US*)
The Collagist (*US*)
Colorado Review (*US*)
Compose (*US*)
Computeractive Magazine (*UK*)
Confrontation Magazine (*US*)
Connotation Press (*US*)
Cook Vegetarian (*UK*)
Cottonwood (*US*)
Country Walking (*UK*)
Crab Creek Review (*US*)
craft&design Magazine (*UK*)
Critical Quarterly (*UK*)
Cruising Outpost Magazine (*US*)
Crystal Magazine (*UK*)
The Cumberland River Review (*US*)
Current Accounts (*UK*)
Custom Car (*UK*)
The Daily Tea (*US*)
Dare (*UK*)
The Dawntreader (*UK*)
The Dead Mule School of Southern Literature (*US*)
Decanter (*UK*)
december (*US*)
Denver Quarterly (*US*)
Devil's Lake (*US*)
Diabetes Balance (*UK*)
Diagram (*US*)
Digital Camera World (*UK*)
Diva (*UK*)
The Dolls' House (*UK*)
The Dos Passos Review (*US*)
Down in the Dirt (*US*)
Drapers (*UK*)
Dream Catcher (*UK*)
The Dublin Review (*Ire*)
Ducts (*US*)
EarthLines Magazine (*Ire*)

Eat In Magazine (*UK*)
Emrys Journal (*US*)
Energy Engineering (*UK*)
Engineering In Miniature (*UK*)
The English Garden (*UK*)
Envoi (*UK*)
Epoch (*US*)
Equal Opportunity (*US*)
Erotic Review (*UK*)
Evansville Living (*US*)
The Evansville Review (*US*)
Event (*Can*)
Everyday Practical Electronics (*UK*)
The Fabricator (*US*)
Fast Company (*US*)
Feminist Review (*UK*)
Feminist Studies (*US*)
Field & Stream (*US*)
Filling Station (*Can*)
FineScale Modeler (*US*)
Fishing News (*UK*)
Flare (*Can*)
Flint Hills Review (*US*)
Flora International (*UK*)
Floyd County Moonshine (*US*)
Flyway: Journal of Writing & Environment (*US*)
Fogged Clarity (*US*)
Food Product Design (*US*)
Forage (*UK*)
Fourteen Hills (*US*)
Freelance Writer's Report (FWR) (*US*)
The Friend (*UK*)
Frieze (*UK*)
Fruit Growers News Magazine (*US*)
Fugue (*US*)
Garbled Transmissions (*US*)
A Gathering of the Tribes (*US*)
Geographical (*UK*)
Gertrude (*US*)
Glamour (*UK*)
Golf News Magazine (*US*)
Governance + Compliance (*UK*)
GQ Magazine (*UK*)
Grain Journal (*US*)
Granta (*UK*)
Grasslimb (*US*)
Green Mountains Review (GMR) (*US*)
The Grey Press (*Can*)
The Griffin (*US*)
GUD Magazine (*US*)
Guernica (*US*)
GuestLife (*US*)
Guitarist Magazine (*UK*)
Gulf Coast: A Journal of Literature and Fine Arts (*US*)
H&E Naturist (*UK*)
Hard Hat News (*US*)
Hill Country Sun (*US*)
Home Energy Magazine (*US*)
The Horn Book Magazine (*US*)
Hortus (*UK*)
Hot Press (*Ire*)
Housebuilder (*UK*)
Houston Press (*US*)
The Huffington Post (United Kingdom) (*UK*)
Hyde Park Living (*US*)
Index on Censorship (*UK*)
Indianapolis Monthly (*US*)
Inside Soap (*UK*)
InTents (*US*)
Interweave Knits (*US*)
Into The Void Magazine (*Ire*)
Ireland's Own (*Ire*)
Irish Arts Review (*Ire*)
Irish Farmers Journal (*Ire*)
Irish Pages (*UK*)
Iron Horse Literary Review (*US*)
Jamie Magazine (*UK*)
Jewish Quarterly (*UK*)
The Journal of Adventist Education (*US*)
Kashrus Magazine (*US*)
Kitchen Garden (*UK*)
KNOWAtlanta (*US*)
Lakeland Boating (*US*)
The Lancet (*UK*)
The Lawyer (*UK*)
Leisure Group Travel (*US*)
Leopard Magazine (*UK*)
Litro Magazine (*UK*)
Little Patuxent Review (*US*)
The London Magazine (*UK*)
London Review of Books (*UK*)
Lost Treasure, Inc. (*US*)
Lothian Life (*UK*)
Media Inc. (*US*)
Ms. Magazine (*US*)
Magma (*UK*)
Main Line Today (*US*)
marie claire (*UK*)
Massage & Bodywork (*US*)
Metro Parent (*US*)
Midwest Meetings (*US*)
Military Modelling Magazine (*UK*)
Military Vehicles Magazine (*US*)
Mobile Bay (*US*)
Model Engineer (*US*)
Modern Poetry in Translation (*UK*)
Mojo (*UK*)
More (*US*)
Mslexia (*UK*)
Music Week (*UK*)
Musical Opinion (*UK*)
Nails Magazine (*US*)
The National Jurist (*US*)
New Mobility Magazine (*US*)
New Musical Express (NME) (*UK*)
New Statesman (*UK*)
New Welsh Reader (*UK*)
newbooks (*UK*)
News Photographer (*US*)
NFPA Journal (*US*)
Niche (*US*)
Nob Hill Gazette (*US*)
Northwest Quarterly Magazine (*US*)
Nostalgia Magazine (*US*)
Nurseweek (*US*)

O'Dwyer's (*US*)
OfficePro (*US*)
Olive (*UK*)
Onion World (*US*)
Opera (*UK*)
Opera News (*US*)
Oregon Coast (*US*)
Organic Life (*US*)
Overtones (*US*)
Oxford Poetry (*UK*)
Painted Bride Quarterly (*US*)
Painted Cave (*US*)
Palm Springs Life (*US*)
Parents (*US*)
Pediatric Annals (*US*)
Pentecostal Evangel (*US*)
Pentecostal Messenger (*US*)
People Management (*UK*)
The People's Friend (*UK*)
Pest Management Professional (*US*)
Philly Weekly (*US*)
Phoenix Magazine (*US*)
The Photographer (*UK*)
Photonics & Imaging Technology (*US*)
Pizza Today (*US*)
Plain Truth Magazine (*US*)
Planet (*UK*)
Play & Playground Magazine (*US*)
PN (Paraplegia News) (*US*)
Poetry Ireland Review (*Ire*)
Poetry London (*UK*)
The Poetry Review (*UK*)
Poetry Wales (*UK*)
Police and Security News (*US*)
The Police Journal (*UK*)
Popular Science (*US*)
Poultry World (*UK*)
Practical Photography (*UK*)
PracticeLink Magazine (*US*)
The Practising Midwife (*UK*)
Preservation in Print (*US*)
Private Eye (*UK*)
The Produce News (*US*)
Prole (*UK*)
Properties Magazine (*US*)
Psychologies (*UK*)
QSR (*US*)
Quill (*US*)
Quill & Quire (*Can*)
Radio Times (*UK*)
Rail (*UK*)
Rain Taxi (*US*)
Rappahannock Review (*US*)
Real Simple (*US*)
Recommend Magazine (*US*)
Record Collector Magazine (*UK*)
Red Paint Hill Poetry Journal (*US*)
Referee (*US*)
Reform (*UK*)
Remodeling (*US*)
Restaurant Magazine (*UK*)
Retail Week (*UK*)
The Rialto (*UK*)
Rider Magazine (*US*)
Rochester Business Journal (*US*)
Runner's World (*US*)
RUSI Journal (*UK*)
San Diego Family Magazine (*US*)
Santa Barbara Magazine (*US*)
The Savage Kick (*UK*)
School Bus Fleet (*US*)
Scots Heritage Magazine (*UK*)
Scouting (*US*)
Screen Printing (*US*)
Self (*US*)
SelfBuild & Design (*UK*)
Sew Simple (*US*)
The Sewing Directory (*UK*)
SFX (*UK*)
Shooter Literary Magazine (*UK*)
Shoreline of Infinity (*UK*)
Shropshire Magazine (*UK*)
Shutterbug (*US*)
SignCraft Publishing Co., Inc. (*US*)
Ski Patrol Magazine (*US*)
Sky at Night Magazine (*UK*)
Slimming World (*UK*)
Snooker Scene (*UK*)
Southern Boating (*US*)
Spear's Magazine (*UK*)
Spin Off (*US*)
SQL Server Pro (*US*)
St Petersburg Review (*US*)
The Stage (*UK*)
The Stampers' Sampler (*US*)
Star 82 Review (*US*)
State Journal (*US*)
Stone World (*US*)
Stormwater (*US*)
Style at Home (*UK*)
SuCasa (*US*)
Sunshine Artist (*US*)
Surrey Life (*UK*)
Susquehanna Life (*US*)
Tallahassee Magazine (*US*)
Tech Directions (*US*)
Television (*UK*)
Tempo: A Quarterly Review of New Music (*UK*)
TES (The Times Educational Supplement) (*UK*)
Texas Co-op Power (*US*)
The Health Journal (*US*)
The Lady (*UK*)
The Voice (*UK*)
This England (*UK*)
This Old House (*US*)
TimberWest (*US*)
Times Higher Education (*UK*)
The Times Literary Supplement (TLS) (*UK*)
Tobacco International (*US*)
Top Sante (*UK*)
Toronto Life (*Can*)
Trail (*UK*)
Trailer Life Magazine (*US*)
TravelWorld International Magazine (*US*)
Tropical Fish Hobbyist Magazine (*US*)

Truck & Driver (*UK*)
U Magazine (*Ire*)
Underground Construction (*US*)
US Glass Magazine (*US*)
Vanity Fair (*UK*)
Vegan Life (*UK*)
Vegetable Growers News Magazine (*US*)
VFW (Veterans of Foreign Wars) Magazine (*US*)
Vogue Patterns (*US*)
Walls & Ceilings (*US*)
Wanderlust Magazine (*UK*)
Wasafiri (*UK*)
The Washington Pastime (*US*)
Water Well Journal (*US*)
The Week (*UK*)
Weight Watchers Magazine (*UK*)
Welding Design & Fabrication (*US*)
Western & Eastern Treasures (*US*)
Western Outdoor News (*US*)
What Car? (*UK*)
The White Review (*UK*)
Woman (*UK*)
Woman & Home Feel Good Food (*UK*)
Woman's Own (*UK*)
Woman's Way (*Ire*)
Woman's Weekly (*UK*)
Wordpeace (*US*)
The World Today (*UK*)
Yachts & Yachting (*UK*)
Your Cat (*UK*)
Your Dog Magazine (*UK*)
Yours (*UK*)
Zeek (*US*)
ZYZZYVA (*US*)

Philosophy

Artifact Nouveau (*US*)
Into The Void Magazine (*Ire*)
Jewish Quarterly (*UK*)
ShortStorySunday.com (*UK*)
The Times Literary Supplement (TLS) (*UK*)

Photography

The Adirondack Review (*US*)
Artifact Nouveau (*US*)
Digital Camera World (*UK*)
Irish Arts Review (*Ire*)
News Photographer (*US*)
The Photographer (*UK*)
Practical Photography (*UK*)
Shutterbug (*US*)

Poetry

The Alembic (*US*)
A New Heart (*US*)
A&U (*US*)
Able Muse (*US*)
The Account (*US*)
Acumen (*UK*)
Adelaide Literary Magazine (*US*)
The Adirondack Review (*US*)
Agenda (*UK*)
Alberta Views (*Can*)
Alebrijes (*US*)
The Allegheny Review (*US*)
Alligator Juniper (*US*)
Ambit (*UK*)
Analog Science Fiction & Fact (*US*)
Ancient Paths (*US*)
Another Chicago Magazine (ACM) (*US*)
Apalachee Review (*US*)
Aphelion: The Webzine of Science Fiction and Fantasy (*US*)
Appalachian Heritage (*US*)
Apple Valley Review (*US*)
Aries (*US*)
Arsenic Lobster Poetry Journal (*US*)
Artifact Nouveau (*US*)
Artificium (*UK*)
Asinine Poetry (*US*)
The Avalon Literary Review (*US*)
The Baltimore Review (*US*)
Banipal (*UK*)
Bayou Magazine (*US*)
Bellevue Literary Review (*US*)
Better Than Starbucks (*Can*)
Big Bridge (*US*)
Big Pulp (*US*)
Bilingual Review (*US*)
Blackbird (*US*)
Blueline (*US*)
Bluestem (*US*)
Boys' Quest (*US*)
Brilliant Corners (*US*)
Bryant Literary Review (*US*)
Bugle (*US*)
Bunbury Magazine (*UK*)
Callaloo (*US*)
Camas (*US*)
The Capilano Review (*Can*)
The Carolina Quarterly (*US*)
Caveat Lector (*US*)
The Chaffin Journal (*US*)
Chantarelle's Notebook (*US*)
The Chattahoochee Review (*US*)
Chicago Quarterly Review (*US*)
Chicago Review (*US*)
Cimarron Review (*US*)
The Claremont Review (*Can*)
Cloud Rodeo (*US*)
Cloudbank (*US*)
Coal City Review (*US*)
Cold Mountain Review (*US*)
The Collagist (*US*)
Colorado Review (*US*)
Columbia: A Journal of Literature and Art (*US*)
Compose (*US*)
Conduit (*US*)
Confrontation Magazine (*US*)
Connecticut River Review (*US*)
Connotation Press (*US*)
Contemporary Haibun Online (*US*)
Cottonwood (*US*)
Crab Creek Review (*US*)
Critical Quarterly (*UK*)
Crucible (*US*)
Crystal Magazine (*UK*)
The Cumberland River Review (*US*)

Current Accounts (*UK*)
Cyphers (*Ire*)
Darkling (*US*)
The Dawntreader (*UK*)
The Dead Mule School of Southern Literature (*US*)
Decanto (*UK*)
december (*US*)
Denver Quarterly (*US*)
The Deronda Review (*US*)
Devil's Lake (*US*)
Diagram (*US*)
The Dos Passos Review (*US*)
Down in the Dirt (*US*)
Dream Catcher (*UK*)
Dressing Room Poetry Journal (*US*)
Ducts (*US*)
EarthLines Magazine (*Ire*)
Earthshine (*US*)
Emrys Journal (*US*)
Envoi (*UK*)
Epoch (*US*)
The Evansville Review (*US*)
Event (*Can*)
failbetter.com (*US*)
Feminist Studies (*US*)
Filling Station (*Can*)
Flint Hills Review (*US*)
Floyd County Moonshine (*US*)
Flyway: Journal of Writing & Environment (*US*)
Fogged Clarity (*US*)
Forage (*UK*)
Fourteen Hills (*US*)
Fugue (*US*)
A Gathering of the Tribes (*US*)
Gertrude (*US*)
The Gettysburg Review (*US*)
Gold Dust (*UK*)
Grasslimb (*US*)
Green Hills Literary Lantern (*US*)
Green Mountains Review (GMR) (*US*)
The Grey Press (*Can*)
The Griffin (*US*)
GUD Magazine (*US*)
Guernica (*US*)
Gulf Coast: A Journal of Literature and Fine Arts (*US*)
Gutter Magazine (*UK*)
Gyroscope Review (*US*)
Hyde Park Living (*US*)
Ink Sweat and Tears (*UK*)
The Interpreter's House (*UK*)
Into The Void Magazine (*Ire*)
Irish Pages (*UK*)
Iron Horse Literary Review (*US*)
Jewish Quarterly (*UK*)
Kalyna Review (*UK*)
Leopard Magazine (*UK*)
Litro Magazine (*UK*)
Little Patuxent Review (*US*)
The London Magazine (*UK*)
London Review of Books (*UK*)
Ms. Magazine (*US*)
Magma (*UK*)
Modern Poetry in Translation (*UK*)
The Moth (*Ire*)
Mslexia (*UK*)
New Fairy Tales (*UK*)
New Statesman (*UK*)
New Welsh Reader (*UK*)
The North (*UK*)
NY Literary Magazine (*US*)
Oxford Poetry (*UK*)
Painted Bride Quarterly (*US*)
Painted Cave (*US*)
The Penny Dreadful (*Ire*)
The People's Friend (*UK*)
Planet (*UK*)
PN Review (*UK*)
The Poetry Box (*UK*)
Poetry Ireland Review (*Ire*)
Poetry London (*UK*)
The Poetry Review (*UK*)
Poetry Wales (*UK*)
Postcard Poems and Prose (*US*)
Prole (*UK*)
Rappahannock Review (*US*)
Reach (*UK*)
Red Paint Hill Poetry Journal (*US*)
The Rialto (*UK*)
Sarasvati (*UK*)
Shooter Literary Magazine (*UK*)
Sling Magazine (*US*)
South (*UK*)
St Petersburg Review (*US*)
Stand Magazine (*UK*)
This England (*UK*)
The Times Literary Supplement (TLS) (*UK*)
Wasafiri (*UK*)
The Washington Pastime (*US*)
The White Review (*UK*)
Wordpeace (*US*)
Zeek (*US*)
ZYZZYVA (*US*)

Politics

A&U (*US*)
Africa Confidential (*UK*)
Alberta Views (*Can*)
Artifact Nouveau (*US*)
Confrontation Magazine (*US*)
Feminist Review (*UK*)
The Friend (*UK*)
Granta (*UK*)
Guernica (*US*)
H&E Naturist (*UK*)
Hot Press (*Ire*)
The Huffington Post (United Kingdom) (*UK*)
Index on Censorship (*UK*)
Into The Void Magazine (*Ire*)
Jewish Quarterly (*UK*)
London Review of Books (*UK*)
Ms. Magazine (*US*)
New Statesman (*UK*)
Planet (*UK*)
Private Eye (*UK*)
The Voice (*UK*)

Vanity Fair (*UK*)
The World Today (*UK*)
Psychology
Into The Void Magazine (*Ire*)
Radio
Radio Times (*UK*)
Reference
Midwest Meetings (*US*)
Mslexia (*UK*)
Religious
A New Heart (*US*)
Ancient Paths (*US*)
Barbaric Yawp (*US*)
Bread for God's Children (*US*)
Cadet Quest (*US*)
The Catholic Herald (*UK*)
The Friend (*UK*)
Jewish Quarterly (*UK*)
The Journal of Adventist Education (*US*)
Kashrus Magazine (*US*)
The New Accelerator (*UK*)
Pentecostal Evangel (*US*)
Pentecostal Messenger (*US*)
Plain Truth Magazine (*US*)
Reform (*UK*)
Zeek (*US*)
Romance
Artifact Nouveau (*US*)
Big Pulp (*US*)
Crystal Magazine (*UK*)
GUD Magazine (*US*)
Into The Void Magazine (*Ire*)
The People's Friend (*UK*)
People's Friend Pocket Novels (*UK*)
The Poetry Box (*UK*)
ShortStorySunday.com (*UK*)
The Washington Pastime (*US*)
Science
Analog Science Fiction & Fact (*US*)
Arc (*UK*)
Barbaric Yawp (*US*)
Boys' Quest (*US*)
Diabetes Balance (*UK*)
Geographical (*UK*)
Into The Void Magazine (*Ire*)
Irish Pages (*UK*)
The Lancet (*UK*)
London Review of Books (*UK*)
The New Accelerator (*UK*)
Photonics & Imaging Technology (*US*)
Popular Science (*US*)
Sky at Night Magazine (*UK*)
Tech Directions (*US*)
The Times Literary Supplement (TLS) (*UK*)
Sci-Fi
Allegory (*US*)
Analog Science Fiction & Fact (*US*)
Aphelion: The Webzine of Science Fiction and Fantasy (*US*)
Arc (*UK*)
Artifact Nouveau (*US*)
Barbaric Yawp (*US*)
Big Pulp (*US*)
Crystal Magazine (*UK*)
The Fifth Di... (*US*)
Garbled Transmissions (*US*)
GUD Magazine (*US*)
Interzone (*UK*)
Into The Void Magazine (*Ire*)
The New Accelerator (*UK*)
Orson Scott Card's InterGalactic Medicine Show (*US*)
SFX (*UK*)
Shoreline of Infinity (*UK*)
ShortStorySunday.com (*UK*)
The Washington Pastime (*US*)
Scripts
The Alembic (*US*)
Aries (*US*)
Bilingual Review (*US*)
The Claremont Review (*Can*)
Connotation Press (*US*)
Current Accounts (*UK*)
Epoch (*US*)
The Evansville Review (*US*)
Flint Hills Review (*US*)
Gold Dust (*UK*)
Gutter Magazine (*UK*)
St Petersburg Review (*US*)
Self-Help
Equal Opportunity (*US*)
Girlfriendz Magazine (*US*)
KNOWAtlanta (*US*)
Short Stories
The Alembic (*US*)
A&U (*US*)
Able Muse (*US*)
The Account (*US*)
Adelaide Literary Magazine (*US*)
The Adirondack Review (*US*)
Alberta Views (*Can*)
The Allegheny Review (*US*)
Allegory (*US*)
Alligator Juniper (*US*)
Ambit (*UK*)
Analog Science Fiction & Fact (*US*)
Ancient Paths (*US*)
Another Chicago Magazine (ACM) (*US*)
Apalachee Review (*US*)
Aphelion: The Webzine of Science Fiction and Fantasy (*US*)
Appalachian Heritage (*US*)
Apple Valley Review (*US*)
Arc (*UK*)
Aries (*US*)
Artifact Nouveau (*US*)
Artificium (*UK*)
Asinine Poetry (*US*)
The Avalon Literary Review (*US*)
The Baltimore Review (*US*)
Banipal (*UK*)
Barbaric Yawp (*US*)
Bartleby Snopes (*US*)
Bayou Magazine (*US*)
The Beano (*UK*)
Bellevue Literary Review (*US*)

Berkeley Fiction Review (*US*)
Best New Writing (*US*)
Better Than Starbucks (*Can*)
Big Bridge (*US*)
Big Pulp (*US*)
Bilingual Review (*US*)
Black Static (*UK*)
Blackbird (*US*)
Blueline (*US*)
Bluestem (*US*)
Boys' Quest (*US*)
Bryant Literary Review (*US*)
Bunbury Magazine (*UK*)
Cadet Quest (*US*)
The Cafe Irreal (*US*)
Callaloo (*US*)
The Carolina Quarterly (*US*)
The Casket of Fictional Delights (*UK*)
Caveat Lector (*US*)
The Chaffin Journal (*US*)
The Chattahoochee Review (*US*)
Chicago Quarterly Review (*US*)
Chicago Review (*US*)
Cimarron Review (*US*)
The Claremont Review (*Can*)
Cloudbank (*US*)
Coal City Review (*US*)
Cold Mountain Review (*US*)
The Collagist (*US*)
Colorado Review (*US*)
Columbia: A Journal of Literature and Art (*US*)
Compose (*US*)
Conduit (*US*)
Confrontation Magazine (*US*)
Connotation Press (*US*)
Cottonwood (*US*)
Crab Creek Review (*US*)
Critical Quarterly (*UK*)
Crucible (*US*)
Crystal Magazine (*UK*)
The Cumberland River Review (*US*)
Current Accounts (*UK*)
Cyphers (*Ire*)
The Dawntreader (*UK*)
The Dead Mule School of Southern Literature (*US*)
december (*US*)
Denver Quarterly (*US*)
Devil's Lake (*US*)
Diagram (*US*)
Down in the Dirt (*US*)
Dream Catcher (*UK*)
The Dublin Review (*Ire*)
Ducts (*US*)
EarthLines Magazine (*Ire*)
Ellery Queen Mystery Magazine (*US*)
Emrys Journal (*US*)
Epoch (*US*)
Erotic Review (*UK*)
The Evansville Review (*US*)
failbetter.com (*US*)
Feminist Studies (*US*)
The Fifth Di... (*US*)
Filling Station (*Can*)
Flash: The International Short-Short Story Magazine (*UK*)
Flint Hills Review (*US*)
Floyd County Moonshine (*US*)
Flyway: Journal of Writing & Environment (*US*)
Fourteen Hills (*US*)
Fugue (*US*)
A Gathering of the Tribes (*US*)
The Gettysburg Review (*US*)
Gold Dust (*UK*)
Granta (*UK*)
Grasslimb (*US*)
Green Hills Literary Lantern (*US*)
Green Mountains Review (GMR) (*US*)
The Grey Press (*Can*)
The Griffin (*US*)
GUD Magazine (*US*)
Guernica (*US*)
Gutter Magazine (*UK*)
The Interpreter's House (*UK*)
Interzone (*UK*)
Into The Void Magazine (*Ire*)
Ireland's Own (*Ire*)
Irish Pages (*UK*)
Iron Horse Literary Review (*US*)
Jewish Quarterly (*UK*)
Kalyna Review (*UK*)
Leopard Magazine (*UK*)
Litro Magazine (*UK*)
Little Patuxent Review (*US*)
The London Magazine (*UK*)
Ms. Magazine (*US*)
The Moth (*Ire*)
Mslexia (*UK*)
The New Accelerator (*UK*)
New Fairy Tales (*UK*)
New Welsh Reader (*UK*)
Orson Scott Card's InterGalactic Medicine Show (*US*)
The Ottawa Object (*US*)
Painted Bride Quarterly (*US*)
Painted Cave (*US*)
The Penny Dreadful (*Ire*)
The People's Friend (*UK*)
Planet (*UK*)
Postcard Poems and Prose (*US*)
Prole (*UK*)
Rappahannock Review (*US*)
Sarasvati (*UK*)
Shoreline of Infinity (*UK*)
ShortStorySunday.com (*UK*)
Sixpenny Magazine (*US*)
Sling Magazine (*US*)
St Petersburg Review (*US*)
Stand Magazine (*UK*)
Star 82 Review (*US*)
Wasafiri (*UK*)
The Washington Pastime (*US*)
The White Review (*UK*)
Woman's Weekly (*UK*)
Woman's Weekly Fiction Special (*UK*)
Wordpeace (*US*)

Your Cat (*UK*)
Yours (*UK*)
ZYZZYVA (*US*)

Sociology
Alberta Views (*Can*)
The Big Issue (*UK*)
Feminist Review (*UK*)
The Friend (*UK*)
H&E Naturist (*UK*)
Into The Void Magazine (*Ire*)
Ms. Magazine (*US*)
Reform (*UK*)

Spiritual
Artifact Nouveau (*US*)
The New Accelerator (*UK*)
Reform (*UK*)
Zeek (*US*)

Sport
All Out Cricket (*UK*)
Angler's Mail (*UK*)
Boys' Quest (*US*)
Climb Magazine (*UK*)
Coach (*UK*)
Evansville Living (*US*)
Field & Stream (*US*)
Golf News Magazine (*US*)
Hot Press (*Ire*)
The Huffington Post (United Kingdom) (*UK*)
PN (Paraplegia News) (*US*)
Referee (*US*)
Runner's World (*US*)
Ski Patrol Magazine (*US*)
Snooker Scene (*UK*)
Southern Boating (*US*)
Tallahassee Magazine (*US*)
The Voice (*UK*)
Western & Eastern Treasures (*US*)
Western Outdoor News (*US*)
Yachts & Yachting (*UK*)
Yorkshire Ridings Magazine (*UK*)

Suspense
Aphelion: The Webzine of Science Fiction and Fantasy (*US*)
Artifact Nouveau (*US*)
Crystal Magazine (*UK*)
GUD Magazine (*US*)
Into The Void Magazine (*Ire*)
ShortStorySunday.com (*UK*)
The Washington Pastime (*US*)

Technology
Android Magazine (*UK*)
Cambridge Magazine (*UK*)
Classic Cars (*UK*)
Computeractive Magazine (*UK*)
Cruising Outpost Magazine (*US*)
Energy Engineering (*UK*)
Engineering In Miniature (*UK*)
Everyday Practical Electronics (*UK*)
The Fabricator (*US*)
Fast Company (*US*)
GQ Magazine (*UK*)
Grain Journal (*US*)
Housebuilder (*UK*)
The Huffington Post (United Kingdom) (*UK*)
InTents (*US*)
Lakeland Boating (*US*)
Military Vehicles Magazine (*US*)
Model Engineer (*US*)
The New Accelerator (*UK*)
News Photographer (*US*)
O'Dwyer's (*US*)
Photonics & Imaging Technology (*US*)
Play & Playground Magazine (*US*)
Popular Science (*US*)
Rail (*UK*)
Rider Magazine (*US*)
RUSI Journal (*UK*)
Screen Printing (*US*)
Shutterbug (*US*)
Sky at Night Magazine (*UK*)
SQL Server Pro (*US*)
Stone World (*US*)
Tech Directions (*US*)
Television (*UK*)
Texas Co-op Power (*US*)
Trailer Life Magazine (*US*)
Water Well Journal (*US*)
Welding Design & Fabrication (*US*)
What Car? (*UK*)

Theatre
Aries (*US*)
Artifact Nouveau (*US*)
Central and Eastern European London Review (*UK*)
Planet (*UK*)
St Petersburg Review (*US*)
The Stage (*UK*)
The Times Literary Supplement (TLS) (*UK*)

Thrillers
Aphelion: The Webzine of Science Fiction and Fantasy (*US*)
Artifact Nouveau (*US*)
Crystal Magazine (*UK*)
Into The Void Magazine (*Ire*)
The New Accelerator (*UK*)
The People's Friend (*UK*)
ShortStorySunday.com (*UK*)
The Washington Pastime (*US*)

Translations
Able Muse (*US*)
The Adirondack Review (*US*)
Banipal (*UK*)
Better Than Starbucks (*Can*)
The Chattahoochee Review (*US*)
Columbia: A Journal of Literature and Art (*US*)
Current Accounts (*UK*)
Cyphers (*Ire*)
Dream Catcher (*UK*)
Envoi (*UK*)
Guernica (*US*)
Irish Pages (*UK*)
Kalyna Review (*UK*)
Modern Poetry in Translation (*UK*)
Oxford Poetry (*UK*)
PN Review (*UK*)
Poetry London (*UK*)

The Poetry Review (*UK*)
Stand Magazine (*UK*)
ZYZZYVA (*US*)

Travel

Attitude (*UK*)
Bust (*US*)
The Carolina Quarterly (*US*)
Central and Eastern European London Review (*UK*)
Classic Cars (*UK*)
Country Walking (*UK*)
Cruising Outpost Magazine (*US*)
Crystal Magazine (*UK*)
The Daily Tea (*US*)
Decanter (*UK*)
EarthLines Magazine (*Ire*)
Evansville Living (*US*)
Evergreen (*UK*)
Geographical (*UK*)
GuestLife (*US*)
Hill Country Sun (*US*)
Hyde Park Living (*US*)
Kashrus Magazine (*US*)
KNOWAtlanta (*US*)
Lakeland Boating (*US*)
Leisure Group Travel (*US*)
Litro Magazine (*UK*)
Lothian Life (*UK*)
Main Line Today (*US*)
marie claire (*UK*)
Nob Hill Gazette (*US*)
The People's Friend (*UK*)
Phoenix Magazine (*US*)
Psychologies (*UK*)
Rail (*UK*)
Recommend Magazine (*US*)
Rider Magazine (*US*)
School Bus Fleet (*US*)
Scouting (*US*)
Ski Patrol Magazine (*US*)
Southern Boating (*US*)
Surrey Life (*UK*)
Susquehanna Life (*US*)
Tallahassee Magazine (*US*)
The Lady (*UK*)
Trail (*UK*)
Trailer Life Magazine (*US*)
TravelWorld International Magazine (*US*)
Truck & Driver (*UK*)
U Magazine (*Ire*)
Vegan Life (*UK*)
Wanderlust Magazine (*UK*)
What Car? (*UK*)
Woman's Weekly (*UK*)
Yachts & Yachting (*UK*)
Yorkshire Ridings Magazine (*UK*)

TV

Artifact Nouveau (*US*)
Epoch (*US*)
Radio Times (*UK*)
SFX (*UK*)
Television (*UK*)

Westerns

Artifact Nouveau (*US*)
Crystal Magazine (*UK*)
Into The Void Magazine (*Ire*)
The Savage Kick (*UK*)
ShortStorySunday.com (*UK*)
The Washington Pastime (*US*)

Women's Interests

Artifact Nouveau (*US*)
Bust (*US*)
Closer (*UK*)
Dare (*UK*)
Diva (*UK*)
Feminist Review (*UK*)
Feminist Studies (*US*)
Flare (*Can*)
Girlfriendz Magazine (*US*)
Glamour (*UK*)
Ms. Magazine (*US*)
marie claire (*UK*)
More (*US*)
Mslexia (*UK*)
Parents (*US*)
The People's Friend (*UK*)
The Practising Midwife (*UK*)
Psychologies (*UK*)
Real Simple (*US*)
Self (*US*)
Style at Home (*UK*)
The Lady (*UK*)
Top Sante (*UK*)
U Magazine (*Ire*)
Woman (*UK*)
Woman & Home Feel Good Food (*UK*)
Woman's Own (*UK*)
Woman's Way (*Ire*)
Woman's Weekly (*UK*)
Woman's Weekly Fiction Special (*UK*)
Yours (*UK*)

US Literary Agents

For the most up-to-date listings of these and hundreds of other literary agents, visit https://www.firstwriter.com/Agents

*To claim your **free** access to the site, please see the back of this book.*

A+B Works

Email: query@aplusbworks.com
Website: http://www.aplusbworks.com

Handles: Fiction; *Markets:* Children's; Youth

Specialises in young adult and middle grade fiction, women's fiction, and select narrative nonfiction. No thrillers, literary fiction, erotica, cook books, picture books, poetry, short fiction, or screenplays. Query by email only, or using form on website. Response not guaranteed. Accepts very few new clients.

Aaron M. Priest Literary Agency

200 West 41st Street, 21st Floor, New York, NY 10036
Tel: +1 (212) 818-0344
Fax: +1 (212) 573-9417
Email: querypriest@aaronpriest.com
Website: http://www.aaronpriest.com

Handles: Fiction; Nonfiction; *Areas:* Autobiography; Biography; Crime; Culture; Current Affairs; Fantasy; Gothic; Historical; How-to; Mystery; Politics; Science; Suspense; Thrillers; Translations; Women's Interests; *Markets:* Adult; Youth; *Treatments:* Commercial; Contemporary; Literary; Popular

Send one-page query by email, describing your work and your background. No attachments, but you may paste the first chapter into the body of the email. Query one agent only. See website for specific agent interests and email addresses. No poetry, screenplays, sci-fi, or horror.

Dominick Abel Literary Agency, Inc

146 W. 82nd Street, #1B, New York, NY 10024
Tel: +1 (212) 877-0710
Fax: +1 (212) 595-3133
Email: agency@dalainc.com
Website: http://dalainc.com

Handles: Fiction; Nonfiction; *Markets:* Adult

Handles adult fiction and nonfiction. Not accepting submissions as at September 2016.

Above the Line Agency

468 N. Camden Drive, #200, Beverly Hills, CA 90210
Tel: +1 (310) 859-6115
Fax: +1 (310) 859-6119
Website: http://www.abovethelineagency.com

Handles: Scripts; *Areas:* Film; TV; *Markets:* Adult; Children's

Send query via online web system only. Represents writers and directors; feature films, movies of the week, animation. Offers consultations at a rate of $200 per hour.

Abrams Artists Agency

275 Seventh Ave, 26th Floor, New York, NY 10001
Tel: +1 (646) 486-4600
Fax: +1 (646) 486-2358
Email: literary@abramsartny.com
Website: http://www.abramsartists.com

Handles: Scripts; *Areas:* Drama; Film; Humour; Music; Mystery; Romance; Suspense; TV; *Markets:* Adult

Send query with SASE via industry professional only. Specialises in film, TV, theatre, and publishing.

Bret Adams Ltd

448 West 44th Street, New York, NY 10036
Tel: +1 (212) 765-5630
Fax: +1 (212) 265-2212
Email: bretadamsltd@bretadamsltd.net
Website: http://www.bretadamsltd.net

Handles: Scripts; *Areas:* Film; Theatre; TV; *Markets:* Adult

Handles projects for theatre, film, and TV only. No books. No unsolicited submissions. Accepts approaches by referral only.

Adams Literary

7845 Colony Road, C4 #215, Charlotte, NC 28226
Tel: +1 (704) 542-1440
Fax: +1 (704) 542-1450
Email: info@adamsliterary.com
Website: http://www.adamsliterary.com

Handles: Fiction; *Markets:* Children's; Youth

Handles books for children and young adults, from picture books to teen novels. No unsolicited MSS. Send query with complete ms via webform. See website for full submission guidelines.

Adler & Robin Books, Inc

3000 Connecticut Avenue, NW, Suite 317, Washington DC, 20008
Tel: +1 (202) 986-9275
Fax: +1 (202) 986-9485
Email: submissions@adlerrobin.com
Website: http://www.adlerrobin.com

Handles: Nonfiction; Reference; *Areas:* Autobiography; Biography; Culture; Historical; How-to; Humour; Lifestyle; Self-Help; *Markets:* Adult; Children's

Interested in biography/memoir, careers, gift books, how-to, humour, lifestyle, local history, pop culture, reference books, self-help, and children's books. Send queries by email only.

Agency for the Performing Arts (APA)

405 S. Beverly Dr, Beverly Hills, CA 90212
Tel: +1 (310) 888-4200
Fax: +1 (310) 888-4242
Website: http://www.apa-agency.com

Handles: Fiction; Nonfiction; Scripts; *Areas:* Film; Theatre; TV; *Markets:* Adult

Handles nonfiction, novels, scripts for film, theatre, and TV, as well as musicians and other performing artists.

The Ahearn Agency, Inc

2021 Pine Street, New Orleans, LA 70118
Tel: +1 (504) 861-8395
Fax: +1 (504) 866-6434
Email: pahearn@aol.com
Website: http://www.ahearnagency.com

Handles: Fiction; Nonfiction; *Areas:* Autobiography; Biography; Crime; Current Affairs; Health; Historical; Humour; Lifestyle; Mystery; Nature; Romance; Short Stories; Suspense; Thrillers; Women's Interests; *Markets:* Adult; *Treatments:* Literary

Send one page query with SASE, description, length, market info, and any writing credits. Accepts email queries without attachments. Response in 2-3 months.

Specialises in women's fiction and suspense. No nonfiction, poetry, juvenile material or science fiction.

Aimee Entertainment Agency

15840 Ventura Blvd., Ste. 215, Encino, CA 91436
Tel: +1 (818) 783-3831
Fax: +1 (818) 783-4447
Email: info@onlinemediapublications.com
Website: http://www.aimeeentertainment.com

Handles: Fiction; Scripts; *Areas:* Film; *Markets:* Adult

Handles film scripts and book-length works.

Alive Communications, Inc

7680 Goodard Street, Suite 200, Colorado Springs, CO 80920
Tel: +1 (719) 260-7080
Fax: +1 (719) 260-8223
Email: Submissions@aliveliterary.com
Website: http://aliveliterary.com

Handles: Fiction; Nonfiction; *Areas:* Adventure; Autobiography; Biography; Business; Crime; Historical; How-to; Humour; Lifestyle; Mystery; Religious; Self-Help; Short Stories; Spiritual; Sport; Suspense; Thrillers; Westerns; Women's Interests; *Markets:* Adult; Children's; *Treatments:* Commercial; Literary; Mainstream; Popular

Accepts queries from referred authors only. Works primarily with well-established, best-selling, and career authors. Referred authors may submit query by email with bio, name of the client referring you, synopsis, and first three chapters. See website for full details.

Miriam Altshuler Literary Agency

53 Old Post Road North, Red Hook, NY 12571
Tel: +1 (845) 758-9408
Fax: +1 (845) 758-3118
Email: query@maliterary.com
Website: http://www.miriamaltshulerliteraryagency.com

Handles: Fiction; Nonfiction; *Areas:* Autobiography; Culture; Fantasy; How-to; Psychology; Self-Help; Sociology; Spiritual; *Markets:* Adult; Children's; Youth; *Treatments:* Commercial; Literary

Send query by post or by email. If submitting by post, include email address for reply. Only include SASE if no email address available, but note that a response is not guaranteed, even with an SASE. Include brief author bio, synopsis, and the first chapter, pasted into the body of the email (no attachments). See website for full guidelines. No Mystery, Romance, Poetry, Fantasy, Science Fiction, Thrillers, Screenplays, Horror, or Westerns.

Ambassador Speakers Bureau & Literary Agency

PO Box 50358, Nashville, TN 37205
Tel: +1 (615) 370-4700
Email: info@ambassadorspeakers.com
Website: http://www.ambassadorspeakers.com

Handles: Fiction; Nonfiction; *Areas:* Adventure; Autobiography; Biography; Culture; Current Affairs; Finance; Health; Historical; How-to; Legal; Lifestyle; Medicine; Politics; Religious; Self-Help; Women's Interests; *Markets:* Adult; *Treatments:* Contemporary; Literary; Mainstream

Represents select authors and writers who are published by religious and general market publishers in the US and Europe. No short stories, children's books, screenplays, or poetry. Send query by email with short description. Submit work on invitation only.

Ann Rittenberg Literary Agency

15 Maiden Lane, Suite 206, New York, NY 10038
Email: info@rittlit.com
Website: http://www.rittlit.com

Handles: Fiction; Nonfiction; *Areas:* Autobiography; Biography; Culture; Historical; Mystery; Sociology; Thrillers; Women's Interests; *Markets:* Adult; *Treatments:* Literary

Send three sample chapters with outline by email (pasted into the body of the email) or by post with SASE. Email queries receive a response only if interested. No Screenplays,

Genre fiction, Poetry, or Self-help. No queries by fax.

Anonymous Content

155 Spring St, 3rd Floor, New York, NY 10012
Tel: +1 (212) 925-0055
Fax: +1 (212) 925-5030
Email: litmanagement@anonymouscontent.com
Website: http://www.anonymouscontent.com

Handles: Scripts; *Areas:* Film; TV; *Markets:* Adult

Works in the areas of film, TV, adverts, and music videos.

Aponte Literary

Email: agents@aponteliterary.com
Website: http://aponteliterary.com

Handles: Fiction; Nonfiction; *Areas:* Fantasy; Historical; Politics; Science; Sci-Fi; Women's Interests; *Markets:* Adult; *Treatments:* Commercial; Mainstream

Handles any genre of mainstream fiction and nonfiction, but particularly women's novels, historical novels, supernatural and paranormal fiction, fantasy novels, political and science thrillers. Closed to submissions as at June 2017. See website for current situation.

Arcadia

31 Lake Place North, Danbury, CT 06810
Email: arcadialit@sbcglobal.net

Handles: Nonfiction; *Areas:* Autobiography; Biography; Current Affairs; Health; Historical; Lifestyle; Music; Nature; Politics; Psychology; Science; Self-Help; Spiritual; Technology; Women's Interests; *Markets:* Adult; *Treatments:* Commercial; Literary

Send query with proposal or up to 50 sample pages by email (no attachments) or by post with SASE. No fiction.

Audrey A. Wolf Literary Agency

2510 Virginia Avenue NW, #702N, Washington, DC 20037
Email: audreyrwolf@gmail.com

Handles: Nonfiction; *Areas:* Autobiography; Biography; Business; Current Affairs; Finance; Health; Historical; Lifestyle; Politics; Self-Help; Sport; *Markets:* Adult

Send query by post or email, including synopsis up to two pages long showing the full structure of the book: beginning, middle, and end. Also include chapter outline.

The August Agency LLC

Email: submissions@augustagency.com
Website: http://www.augustagency.com

Handles: Fiction; Nonfiction; *Areas:* Arts; Autobiography; Biography; Business; Culture; Current Affairs; Entertainment; Finance; Historical; Media; Politics; Sociology; Technology; Women's Interests; *Markets:* Adult; Family; Literary

Accepts queries by referral or by request at a writers' conference only.

The Axelrod Agency

55 Main Street, P.O. Box 357, Chatham, NY 12037
Tel: +1 (518) 392-2100
Fax: +1 (518) 392-2944
Email: steve@axelrodagency.com
Website: http://axelrodagency.com

Handles: Fiction; *Areas:* Crime; Erotic; Mystery; Romance; Thrillers; Women's Interests; *Markets:* Adult

Send query by email only. No nonfiction, African-American, Christian, comedy, humour, comics, graphic novels, gay/lesbian, historical, horror, literary, poetry, puzzles, games, science fiction, fantasy, or westerns.

Ayesha Pande Literary

128 West 132 Street, New York, NY 10027
Tel: +1 (212) 283-5825
Email: queries@pandeliterary.com
Website: http://pandeliterary.com

Handles: Fiction; Nonfiction; *Areas:* Autobiography; Biography; Crime; Culture; Fantasy; Finance; Historical; Humour; Mystery; Romance; Sci-Fi; Thrillers; Women's Interests; *Markets:* Adult; Youth; *Treatments:* Commercial; Literary; Popular

A New York based boutique literary agency with a small and eclectic roster of clients. Submit queries via form on website. No poetry, business books, screenplays, illustrated children's books or middle grade fiction.

B.J. Robbins Literary Agency

5130 Bellaire Avenue, North Hollywood, CA 91607
Tel: +1 (818) 760-6602
Fax: +1 (818) 760-6616
Email: Robbinsliterary@gmail.com

Handles: Fiction; Nonfiction; *Areas:* Autobiography; Biography; Culture; Health; Historical; Mystery; Science; Sport; Suspense; Thrillers; Travel; *Markets:* Adult

Send query with outline / proposal and first 50 pages (fiction) or three sample chapters (nonfiction) by post with SASE or by email (no attachments). No screenplays, plays, poetry, science fiction, horror, westerns, romance, techno-thrillers, religious tracts, dating books or anything with the word "unicorn" in the title.

Baldi Agency

233 West 99th Street, 19C, New York, NY 10025
Tel: +1 (212) 222-3213
Email: info@baldibooks.com
Website: http://www.baldibooks.com

Handles: Fiction; Nonfiction; Reference; *Areas:* Autobiography; Biography; Business; Cookery; Culture; Finance; Historical; How-to; Lifestyle; Literature; Science; Self-Help; Spiritual; Technology; Travel; *Markets:* Adult

Send one page query by email, or by post with SASE. See website for full guidelines.

Barbara Hogenson Agency

165 West End Ave., Suite 19-C, New York, NY 10023
Tel: +1 (212) 874-8084
Fax: +1 (212) 362-3011
Email: Bhogenson@aol.com

Handles: Fiction; Nonfiction; Scripts; *Areas:* Theatre; *Markets:* Adult

Represents fiction, nonfiction, and stage plays. Send query by email only. No unsolicited MSS.

Baror International, Inc.

P.O. Box 868, Armonk, NY 10504-0868
Email: Heather@Barorint.com
Website: http://www.barorint.com

Handles: Fiction; Nonfiction; *Areas:* Fantasy; Sci-Fi; *Markets:* Adult; Youth; *Treatments:* Commercial; Literary

Specialises in the international and domestic representation of literary works in both fiction and nonfiction, including commercial fiction, literary, science fiction, fantasy, young adult and more. Send query by post or by email with a few sample chapters. Taking on very few authors as at July 2017. Check website for current situation.

Belcastro Agency

721 Virginia Ave, Tarpon Springs, FL 34689
Tel: +1 (330) 766-4885
Email: queries@belcastroagency.com
Website: http://www.belcastroagency.com

Handles: Fiction; *Areas:* Adventure; Crime; Erotic; Fantasy; Mystery; Romance; Sci-Fi; Suspense; Thrillers; Women's Interests; *Markets:* Adult; Children's; Youth; *Treatments:* Commercial; Contemporary; Literary; Mainstream

We are a passionate, hands-on, editorially-focused boutique agency with a focus on women's fiction and YA. We work closely with our writers in developing manuscripts and proposals for submission. Queries welcome by email.

Betsy Amster Literary Enterprises

6312 SW Capitol Hwy. #503, Portland, OR 97239
Email: b.amster.assistant@gmail.com
Website: http://amsterlit.com

Handles: Fiction; Nonfiction; *Areas:* Autobiography; Biography; Cookery; Culture; Gardening; Health; Historical; Lifestyle; Medicine; Mystery; Psychology; Self-Help; Sociology; Thrillers; Travel; Women's Interests; *Markets:* Adult; *Treatments:* Literary; Popular

Send query by email only. For fiction and narrative nonfiction include the first three pages in the body of your email; for nonfiction include your proposal, again in the body of the email. See website for different email addresses for adult and children's/YA submissions. No unsolicited attachments or queries by phone or fax.

No romances, screenplays, adult poetry, westerns, adult fantasy, horror, science fiction, techno thrillers, spy capers, apocalyptic scenarios, political or religious arguments, self-published books, or children's nonfiction.

Bidnick & Company

Email: bidnick@comcast.net

Handles: Nonfiction; *Areas:* Cookery; *Markets:* Adult; *Treatments:* Commercial

Handles cookbooks and commercial nonfiction. Send query by email only.

Vicky Bijur Literary Agency

27 West 20th Street, Suite 1003, New York, NY 10011
Email: queries@vickybijuragency.com
Website: http://www.vickybijuragency.com

Handles: Fiction; Nonfiction; *Areas:* Biography; Cookery; Health; Historical; Politics; Psychology; Science; Self-Help; Sociology; *Markets:* Adult

Send query by email or by post with SASE. For fiction include synopsis and first chapter (pasted into the body of the email if submitting electronically). For nonfiction include proposal. No attachments or queries by phone or fax. No picture books, poetry, self-help, science fiction, fantasy, horror, or romance.

David Black Literary Agency

335 Adams Street, Suite 2707, Brooklyn, NY 11201
Tel: +1 (718) 852-5500
Fax: +1 (718) 852-5539
Email: dblack@dblackagency.com
Website: http://www.davidblackagency.com

Handles: Fiction; Nonfiction; *Areas:* Autobiography; Biography; Business; Cookery; Crafts; Current Affairs; Entertainment; Finance; Health; Historical; Humour; Legal; Lifestyle; Military; Mystery; Politics; Psychology; Romance; Science; Self-Help; Spiritual; Sport; Thrillers; Women's Interests; *Markets:* Adult; Children's; Youth; *Treatments:* Commercial; Literary; Mainstream

See website for details of different agents, and specific interests and submission guidelines of each. Otherwise, query the agency generally by post only and allow 8 weeks for a response. See website for full details.

Bleecker Street Associates, Inc.

217 Thompson Street, #519, New York, NY 10012
Tel: +1 (212) 677-4492
Fax: +1 (212) 388-0001
Email: bleeckerst@hotmail.com

Handles: Fiction; Nonfiction; *Areas:* Autobiography; Biography; Business; Cookery; Crime; Culture; Current Affairs; Entertainment; Erotic; Finance; Health; Historical; Horror; How-to; Humour; Lifestyle; Military; Mystery; Nature; New Age; Politics; Psychology; Religious; Romance; Science; Self-Help; Sociology; Spiritual; Sport; Technology; Thrillers; Women's Interests; *Markets:* Adult; Youth; *Treatments:* Literary

Send query with SASE for response. No poetry, plays, scripts, short stories, academic, scholarly, professional, science fiction, westerns, children's books, or phone calls, faxes, or emails.

The Blumer Literary Agency, Inc.

809 West 181 Street, Suite 201, New York, NY 10033
Tel: +1 (212) 947-3040
Email: livblumer@earthlink.net

Handles: Fiction; Nonfiction; *Areas:* Anthropology; Archaeology; Architecture; Arts; Autobiography; Biography; Business; Cookery; Crafts; Crime; Criticism; Culture; Design; Entertainment; Finance; Health; Historical; Hobbies; How-to; Humour; Literature; Medicine; Mystery; Nature; New Age; Photography; Psychology; Religious; Self-Help; Suspense; Thrillers; Travel; Women's Interests; *Markets:* Adult; *Treatments:* Contemporary; Literary; Mainstream

Send query by email or by post with SASE. One page or two pages maximum. Include summary and bio. No sample chapters or attachments. Queries by post are more likely to be read and receive a response.

The Book Group

20 West 20th Street, Suite 601, New York, NY 10011
Tel: +1 (212) 803-3360
Email: submissions@thebookgroup.com
Website: http://www.thebookgroup.com

Handles: Fiction; Nonfiction; *Areas:* Autobiography; Biography; Cookery; Historical; Lifestyle; Psychology; *Markets:* Adult; Children's; Youth; *Treatments:* Commercial; Literary

Represents a broad range of fiction and nonfiction. No poetry or screenplays. Send query by email only with ten sample pages and the first and last name of the agent you are querying in the subject line (see website for individual agent interests). No attachments. Include all material in the body of the email. See website for full guidelines. Response only if interested.

BookEnds, LLC

Tel: +1 (908) 362-0090
Email: submissions@bookends-inc.com
Website: http://www.bookends-inc.com

Handles: Fiction; Nonfiction; Reference; *Areas:* Business; Culture; Current Affairs; Erotic; Fantasy; Historical; Lifestyle; Mystery; Romance; Sci-Fi; Suspense; Women's Interests; *Markets:* Adult; Youth; *Treatments:* Contemporary

Accepts queries from both published and unpublished authors by email only. No postal approaches. Send query directly to specific agent (see website for specific interests and email addresses). No children's picture books, short fiction, poetry, screenplays, or techno-thrillers.

Brandt & Hochman Literary Agents, Inc.

1501 Broadway, Suite 2310, New York, NY 10036
Tel: +1 (212) 840-5760
Fax: +1 (212) 840-5776
Email: ghochman@bromasite.com
Website: http://brandthochman.com

Handles: Fiction; Nonfiction; *Areas:* Arts; Autobiography; Culture; Current Affairs; Health; Historical; Lifestyle; Mystery; Science; Thrillers; *Markets:* Adult; Children's; Youth; *Treatments:* Commercial; Literary; Popular

Send query by post with SASE or by email with query letter up to two pages long, including overview and author details and writing credits. See website for full submission guidelines and for details of individual agents' interests and direct contact details, then approach one agent specifically. No screenplays or textbooks. Response to email queries not guaranteed.

Barbara Braun Associates, Inc.

7 East 14th St #19F, New York, NY 10003
Email: bbasubmissions@gmail.com
Website: http://www.barbarabraunagency.com

Handles: Fiction; Nonfiction; *Areas:* Architecture; Arts; Beauty and Fashion; Biography; Criticism; Culture; Design; Film; Historical; Mystery; Photography; Politics; Psychology; Sociology; Thrillers; Women's Interests; *Markets:* Adult; *Treatments:* Commercial; Literary; Serious

Send query by email only, with "Query" in the subject line, including brief summary, word count, genre, any relevant publishing experience, and the first five pages pasted into the body of the email. No attachments. No poetry, science fiction, fantasy, horror, or screenplays. Particularly interested in stories for women, art-related fiction, historical and multicultural stories, and to a lesser extent mysteries and thrillers. Also interested in narrative nonfiction and current affairs books by journalists.

Bresnick Weil Literary Agency, LLC

115 West 29th Street, 3rd Floor, New York, NY 10001
Tel: +1 (212) 239-3166
Fax: +1 (212) 239-3165
Email: query@bresnickagency.com
Website: http://bresnickagency.com

Handles: Fiction; Nonfiction; *Areas:* Autobiography; Biography; Crime; Culture; Health; Historical; Humour; Lifestyle; Music; Politics; Psychology; Science; Sport; Travel; Women's Interests; *Markets:* Adult; *Treatments:* Commercial; Literary; Popular

Send query by email only, with two sample chapters (fiction) or proposal (nonfiction).

Marie Brown Associates, Inc.

412 W. 154th Street, New York, NY 10032
Tel: +1 (212) 939-9725
Fax: +1 (212) 939-9728
Email: mbrownlit@aol.com

Handles: Fiction; Nonfiction; *Areas:* Biography; Business; Culture; Historical; Music; Religious; Women's Interests; *Markets:* Adult; Youth; *Treatments:* Literary; Mainstream

Send query with SASE. Particularly interested in multicultural and African-American writers. MSS should preferably not be submitted elsewhere simultaneously.

Browne & Miller Literary Associates

410 S. Michigan Avenue, Suite 460, Chicago, IL 60605
Tel: +1 (312) 922-3063
Fax: +1 (312) 922-1905
Email: mail@browneandmiller.com
Website: http://www.browneandmiller.com

Handles: Fiction; Nonfiction; *Areas:* Anthropology; Archaeology; Autobiography; Biography; Business; Cookery; Crafts; Crime; Culture; Current Affairs; Finance; Health; Historical; Hobbies; How-to; Humour; Lifestyle; Medicine; Mystery; Nature; Psychology; Religious; Science; Self-Help; Sociology; Sport; Technology; Women's Interests; *Markets:* Adult; Youth; *Treatments:* Commercial; Literary; Satirical

Particularly interested in literary/commercial fiction/women's fiction, women's historical fiction, literary-leaning crime fiction, romance, Amish fiction, time travel stories, Christian/inspirational fiction by established authors, literary and commercial Young Adult fiction, nonfiction by nationally-recognised, platformed author/experts. No children's picture books, horror or sci-fi novels, short stories, poetry, original screenplays, articles, or software. Send query by email with synopsis and first five chapters for fiction, or proposal and three chapters for nonfiction, in the body of the email (attachments will not be opened). See website for full details.

Kelvin C. Bulger and Associates

4540 W. Washington Blvd, Suite 101, Chicago, IL 60624
Tel: +1 (312) 218-1943
Fax: +1 (773) 261-5950
Email: bulgerassociates@gmail.com
Website: http://bulgerandassociates.biz

Handles: Scripts; *Areas:* Adventure; Film; Humour; Religious; TV; *Markets:* Adult

Send query by post with SASE, or by fax or email. Include first ten pages of your screenplay, one-page plot synopsis and one-page logline.

Carnicelli Literary Management

7 Kipp Road, Rhinebeck, NY 12572
Email: queries@carnicellilit.com
Website: http://www.carnicellilit.com

Handles: Fiction; Nonfiction; *Areas:* Autobiography; Biography; Business; Culture; Current Affairs; Health; Historical; Psychology; Science; Spiritual; Sport; *Markets:* Adult; *Treatments:* Commercial; Literary; Popular; Serious

Handles mainly nonfiction. Send query by email, or using form on website. Restrict queries to one page. If approaching by email, include the word "Query" in the subject line and do not include attachments. See website for full guidelines. No poetry, plays, screenplays, or books for children.

Carol Mann Agency

55 Fifth Avenue, New York, NY 10003
Tel: +1 (212) 206-5635
Fax: +1 (212) 674-4809
Email: submissions@carolmannagency.com
Website: http://www.carolmannagency.com

Handles: Fiction; Nonfiction; *Areas:* Anthropology; Archaeology; Architecture; Arts; Autobiography; Biography; Business; Culture; Current Affairs; Design; Finance; Health; Historical; Humour; Legal; Lifestyle; Medicine; Music; Nature; Politics; Psychology; Religious; Self-Help; Sociology; Spiritual; Sport; Women's Interests; *Markets:* Adult; Youth; *Treatments:* Commercial; Literary

Send query by email only, including synopsis, brief bio, and first 25 pages, all pasted into the body of your email. No attachments. No submissions by post, or phone calls. Allow 3-4 weeks for response.

Chalberg & Sussman

115 West 29th St, Third Floor, New York, NY 10001
Email: rachel@chalbergsussman.com
Website: http://www.chalbergsussman.com

Handles: Fiction; Nonfiction; *Areas:* Autobiography; Culture; Historical; Psychology; Science; Self-Help; Suspense; Thrillers; Women's Interests; *Markets:* Adult; Children's; *Treatments:* Commercial; Dark; Literary; Popular

Send query by email. See website for specific agent interests and email addresses.

Elyse Cheney Literary Associates, LLC

78 Fifth Avenue, 3rd Floor, New York, NY 10011
Tel: +1 (212) 277-8007
Fax: +1 (212) 614-0728
Email: submissions@cheneyliterary.com
Website: http://www.cheneyliterary.com

Handles: Fiction; Nonfiction; *Areas:* Autobiography; Biography; Business; Culture; Current Affairs; Finance; Historical; Horror; Literature; Politics; Romance; Science; Sport; Suspense; Thrillers; Women's Interests; *Markets:* Adult; *Treatments:* Commercial; Contemporary; Literary

Send query with up to three chapters of sample material by post with SASE, or by email (no attachments). Response not guaranteed.

The Choate Agency, LLC

1320 Bolton Road, Pelham, NY 10803
Tel: +1 (917) 446-2694
Email: mickey@thechoateagency.com
Website: http://www.thechoateagency.com

Handles: Fiction; Nonfiction; *Areas:* Biography; Cookery; Current Affairs; Historical; Military; Mystery; Nature; Politics; Science; Thrillers; *Markets:* Adult; *Treatments:* Commercial

Handles commercial fiction and narrative nonfiction. Send query with brief synopsis/outline by post with SASE, or by email. Strongly prefers submissions by email. No genre fiction, romance, self-help, confessional memoirs, spirituality, pop psychology, religion, how-to, New Age titles, children's books poetry, self-published works or screenplays. See website for full details.

The Chudney Agency

72 North State Road, Suite 501, Briarcliff Manor, NY 10510
Tel: +1 (201) 758-8739
Fax: +1 (201) 758-8739
Email: steven@thechudneyagency.com
Website: http://www.thechudneyagency.com

Handles: Fiction; *Areas:* Historical; Humour; Mystery; Suspense; *Markets:* Adult; Children's; Youth; *Treatments:* Commercial; Literary; Mainstream

Handles children's and young adult books. Send query only in first instance. Happy to accept queries by email. Submit material upon invitation only. No fantasy, science fiction, early readers, or scripts. See website for full guidelines.

Cine/Lit Representation

PO Box 802918, Santa Clarita, CA 91380-2918
Tel: +1 (661) 513-0268
Fax: +1 (661) 513-0915
Email: cinelit@att.net
Website: http://www.cinelitrepresentation.com

Handles: Fiction; Nonfiction; *Areas:* Adventure; Biography; Culture; Horror; Mystery; Nature; Thrillers; Travel; *Markets:* Adult; *Treatments:* Mainstream; Popular

Handles nonfiction and novels. Send query with SASE or by email. No romance, westerns, or science fiction.

The Cowles-Ryan Literary Agency

Email: katherine@cowlesryan.com
Website: http://www.cowlesryan.com

Handles: Fiction; Nonfiction; *Areas:* Arts; Autobiography; Biography; Cookery; Culture; Current Affairs; Historical; Literature; Mystery; Nature; Psychology; Science; Self-Help; Spiritual; *Markets:* Adult; Children's; *Treatments:* Commercial; Contemporary; Literary; Mainstream; Popular; Satirical

We specialise in quality fiction and nonfiction. Our primary areas of interest include literary and selected commercial fiction, history, journalism, culture, biography, memoir, science, natural history, spirituality, cooking, gardening, building and design, and young adult and children's books. We also work with institutions and organisations to develop books and book programs. We do not represent authors in a number of categories, e.g. romance and westerns, and we do not represent screenplays. See website for full submission guidelines.

Creative Trust, Inc.

210 Jamestown Park Drive, Suite 200, Brentwood, TN 37027
Tel: +1 (615) 297-5010
Fax: +1 (615) 297-5020
Email: info@creativetrust.com
Website: http://www.creativetrust.com

Handles: Fiction; Nonfiction; Scripts; *Areas:* Autobiography; Film; *Markets:* Adult

Literary division founded in 2001 to handle authors with particular potential in cross-media development, including movie scripts, graphic novels, etc. Accepts queries by email from previously published authors only. No attachments.

The Culinary Entertainment Agency (CEA)

53 W 36, #706, New York, NY 10018
Tel: +1 (212) 380-1264
Email: info@the-cea.com
Website: http://www.the-cea.com

Handles: Nonfiction; *Areas:* Cookery; Lifestyle; *Markets:* Adult

Literary agency focused on the cooking and lifestyle markets.

Richard Curtis Associates, Inc.

171 East 74th Street, Floor 2, New York, NY 10021
Tel: +1 (212) 772-7363
Fax: +1 (212) 772-7393
Email: info@curtisagency.com
Website: http://www.curtisagency.com

Handles: Fiction; Nonfiction; *Areas:* Autobiography; Biography; Business;

Fantasy; Finance; Health; Historical; Medicine; Mystery; Romance; Science; Sci-Fi; Technology; Thrillers; Westerns; *Markets:* Adult; Children's; Youth

Accepts approaches from authors previously published with national publishing houses only.

Curtis Brown Ltd

10 Astor Place, New York, NY 10003
Tel: +1 (212) 473-5400
Fax: +1 (212) 598-0917
Email: info@cbltd.com
Website: http://www.curtisbrown.com

Handles: Fiction; Nonfiction; *Markets:* Adult; Children's; Youth

Handles material for adults and children in all genres. See website for individual agent interests and submission policies. No unsolicited MSS. No scripts.

Laura Dail Literary Agency

350 Seventh Avenue, Suite 2003, New York, NY 10001
Tel: +1 (212) 239-7477
Fax: +1 (212) 947-0460
Email: queries@ldlainc.com
Website: http://www.ldlainc.com

Handles: Fiction; Nonfiction; *Areas:* Autobiography; Biography; Cookery; Crime; Fantasy; Historical; Humour; Mystery; Science; Sci-Fi; Technology; Thrillers; Women's Interests; *Markets:* Adult; Children's; Youth; *Treatments:* Commercial; Light; Literary; Serious

Send query by email (preferred) with the word "query" in the subject line, or by post with SASE. You may optionally include a synopsis and up to 10 pages. Particularly interested in historical and high-concept fiction, funny YA, humour, and serious nonfiction. Also considers graphical novels. No children's picture books, new age, screenplays, poetry, or unsolicited Spanish material.

Daniel Literary Group

601 Old Hickory Boulevard, #56, Brentwood, TN 37027
Tel: +1 (615) 730-8207
Email: submissions@danielliterarygroup.com
Website: http://www.danielliterarygroup.com

Handles: Nonfiction; *Markets:* Adult; *Treatments:* Popular

Specialises in nonfiction and is closed to submissions of fiction. Query by email only, including brief synopsis, key selling points, author biography, and publishing history, all pasted into the body of the email. No attachments, or queries by post or telephone. Response not guaranteed if guidelines are not adhered to.

Darhansoff & Verrill Literary Agents

133 West 72nd Street, Room 304, New York, NY 10023
Tel: +1 (917) 305-1300
Fax: +1 (917) 305-1400
Email: submissions@dvagency.com
Website: http://www.dvagency.com

Handles: Fiction; Nonfiction; *Areas:* Mystery; Suspense; *Markets:* Adult; Children's; Youth; *Treatments:* Literary

Particularly interested in literary fiction, narrative nonfiction, memoir, sophisticated suspense, and fiction and nonfiction for younger readers. No theatrical plays or film scripts. Send queries by post or email. See website for full submission guidelines.

Liza Dawson Associates

350 Seventh Avenue, Suite 2003, New York, NY 10001
Tel: +1 (212) 465-9071
Fax: +1 (212) 947-0460
Email: queryliza@LizaDawsonAssociates.com
Website: http://www.lizadawsonassociates.com

Handles: Fiction; Nonfiction; *Areas:* Autobiography; Business; Culture; Current Affairs; Fantasy; Historical; Humour; Lifestyle; Medicine; Military; Mystery; Politics; Psychology; Religious; Romance; Science; Sci-Fi; Self-Help; Sociology; Spiritual; Suspense; Theatre; Thrillers; Women's Interests; *Markets:* Academic;

Adult; Children's; Youth; *Treatments:* Commercial; Literary; Mainstream; Popular

See website for specific agent interests and query appropriate agent directly. Specific agent submission guidelines and contact details are available on website.

Deal Points Ent.

Tel: +1 (424) 652-4411
Email: ak@dealpointsent.com
Website: http://www.dealpointsent.com

Handles: Fiction; Nonfiction; Scripts; *Areas:* Crime; *Markets:* Academic; Adult; Professional; *Treatments:* Commercial; Literary

A strictly literary focused agency for writers, producers, and directors.

The Jennifer DeChiara Literary Agency

31 East 32nd Street, Suite 300, New York, NY 10016
Tel: +1 (212) 481-8484
Fax: +1 (212) 481-9582
Email: jenndec@aol.com
Website: http://www.jdlit.com

Handles: Fiction; Nonfiction; *Areas:* Autobiography; Biography; Cookery; Culture; Fantasy; Film; Health; Historical; How-to; Humour; Lifestyle; Literature; Mystery; Science; Self-Help; Sociology; Sport; Suspense; Theatre; Thrillers; Travel; Women's Interests; *Markets:* Adult; Children's; Youth; *Treatments:* Commercial; Contemporary; Literary; Mainstream; Popular

Send query by email only. Posted submissions will be discarded. See website for full guidelines and for specific agent interests and email addresses.

DeFiore and Company

47 East 19th Street, 3rd Floor, New York, NY 10003
Tel: +1 (212) 925-7744
Fax: +1 (212) 925-9803
Email: submissions@defioreandco.com
Website: http://www.defioreandco.com

Handles: Fiction; Nonfiction; *Areas:* Arts; Biography; Culture; Current Affairs; Historical; Lifestyle; Literature; Medicine; Military; Music; Nature; Philosophy; Politics; Psychology; Romance; Science; Short Stories; Sociology; Technology; Thrillers; *Markets:* Adult; Children's; Youth; *Treatments:* Commercial; Literary; Mainstream

Always looking for exciting, fresh, new talent, and currently accepting queries for both fiction and nonfiction. Send query with summary, description of why you're writing the book, any specific credentials, and (for fiction) first five pages. Send by email (with all material in the body of the text; no attachments; and the word "Query" in the subject line) or post with SASE. See website for specific agent interests and methods of approach. No scripts for film, TV, or theatre.

Joëlle Delbourgo Associates, Inc.

101 Park St., Montclair, Montclair, NJ 07042
Tel: +1 (973) 773-0836
Email: submissions@delbourgo.com
Website: http://www.delbourgo.com

Handles: Fiction; Nonfiction; Reference; *Areas:* Autobiography; Biography; Business; Culture; Current Affairs; Fantasy; Health; Historical; Lifestyle; Mystery; Psychology; Science; Sci-Fi; Thrillers; Women's Interests; *Markets:* Adult; Children's; Youth; *Treatments:* Commercial; Popular

We are a highly selective agency, broad in our interests. No category romance, Westerns, early readers, or picture books. Send query by email to specific agent (see website for interests and email addresses) or to generic submissions address. Submissions must include the word "QUERY" in the subject line. See website for full guidelines.

Don Congdon Associates, Inc.

110 William St. Suite 2202, New York, NY 10038
Tel: +1 (212) 645-1229
Fax: +1 (212) 727-2688
Email: dca@doncongdon.com
Website: http://doncongdon.com

Handles: Fiction; Nonfiction; *Areas:* Adventure; Anthropology; Archaeology; Arts; Autobiography; Biography; Cookery; Crime; Criticism; Culture; Current Affairs; Fantasy; Film; Health; Historical; Humour; Legal; Lifestyle; Literature; Medicine; Military; Music; Mystery; Nature; Politics; Psychology; Science; Sport; Suspense; Technology; Theatre; Thrillers; Travel; Women's Interests; *Markets:* Adult; Children's; Youth; *Treatments:* Commercial; Literary; Mainstream

Send query by email (no attachments) or by post with SASE. Include one-page synopsis, relevant background info, and first chapter, all within the body of the email if submitting by email. Include the word "Query" in the subject line. See website for full guidelines. No unsolicited MSS.

Donadio & Olson, Inc.

40 West 27th Street, 5th Floor, New York, NY 10001
Tel: +1 (212) 691-8077
Fax: +1 (212) 633-2837
Email: mail@donadio.com
Website: http://donadio.com

Handles: Fiction; Nonfiction; *Areas:* Arts; Biography; Culture; Historical; Literature; Nature; Science; *Markets:* Adult; Children's; Youth; *Treatments:* Commercial; Literary; Mainstream

Send query by email with first three chapters or first 25 pages. Allow at least one month for reply.

Jim Donovan Literary

5635 SMU Boulevard, Suite 201, Dallas, TX 75206
Email: jdliterary@sbcglobal.net

Handles: Fiction; Nonfiction; Reference; *Areas:* Adventure; Autobiography; Biography; Business; Crime; Culture; Current Affairs; Finance; Health; Historical; How-to; Legal; Lifestyle; Medicine; Military; Music; Mystery; Nature; Politics; Science; Sport; Suspense; Thrillers; Westerns; Women's Interests; *Markets:* Adult; *Treatments:* Commercial; Contemporary; Literary; Mainstream; Popular

Send query with SASE or by email. For fiction, include first 30-50 pages and a 2-5 page outline. Handles mainly nonfiction, and specialises in commercial fiction and nonfiction. No poetry, children's, science fiction, fantasy short stories, autobiography, or inspirational.

The Dravis Agency, Inc.

4370 Tujunga AVE, Suite 145, Studio City, CA 91604
Tel: +1 (818) 501-1177
Fax: +1 (818) 501-1194
Email: monrose@monteiro-rose.com
Website: http://www.monteiro-rose.com

Handles: Scripts; *Areas:* Adventure; Crime; Drama; Film; Historical; Humour; Mystery; Romance; Sci-Fi; Suspense; Thrillers; TV; *Markets:* Adult; Children's; Family; Youth; *Treatments:* Contemporary; Mainstream

Handles for TV, film, and animation. No unsolicited mss. Accepts new clients by referral only.

Dunham Literary, Inc.

110 William Street, Suite 2202, New York, NY 10038
Tel: +1 (212) 929-0994
Fax: +1 (212) 929-0904
Email: query@dunhamlit.com
Website: http://www.dunhamlit.com

Handles: Fiction; Nonfiction; *Areas:* Autobiography; Biography; Culture; Current Affairs; Fantasy; Historical; Lifestyle; Music; Mystery; Nature; Politics; Science; Sci-Fi; Spiritual; Technology; Thrillers; Travel; Women's Interests; *Markets:* Adult; Children's; Youth; *Treatments:* Literary

Handles quality fiction and nonfiction for adults and children. Send query by email or by post with SASE. See website for full guidelines. No genre romance, Christian, erotica, Westerns, poetry, cookery, proeffesional, reference, textbooks, plays, or approaches by phone or fax. No email attachments.

Dunow, Carlson & Lerner Agency

27 West 20th Street, Suite 1107, New York, NY 10011
Tel: +1 (212) 645-7606
Email: mail@dclagency.com
Website: http://www.dclagency.com

Handles: Fiction; Nonfiction; *Areas:* Arts; Autobiography; Biography; Criticism; Culture; Current Affairs; Health; Historical; Humour; Music; Mystery; Science; Sport; Suspense; Thrillers; Women's Interests; *Markets:* Adult; Children's; Youth; *Treatments:* Commercial; Literary

Send query by post with SASE or by email. No attachments. Does not respond to all email queries.

Dystel & Goderich Literary Management

One Union Square West, Suite 904, New York, NY 10003
Tel: +1 (212) 627-9100
Fax: +1 (212) 627-9313
Email: miriam@dystel.com
Website: http://www.dystel.com

Handles: Fiction; Nonfiction; *Areas:* Adventure; Anthropology; Archaeology; Autobiography; Biography; Business; Cookery; Crime; Culture; Current Affairs; Fantasy; Finance; Health; Historical; Humour; Lifestyle; Military; Mystery; New Age; Politics; Psychology; Religious; Romance; Science; Sci-Fi; Spiritual; Suspense; Technology; Thrillers; Women's Interests; *Markets:* Adult; Children's; Youth; *Treatments:* Commercial; Contemporary; Literary; Mainstream; Popular

Prefers email approaches, but will also still accept queries by post with brief synopsis and sample chapter with SASE. Email queries should include the cover letter in the body of the email, and synopsis and sample material (a chapter or the first 25 pages) either below the query letter or in an attached document. Attachments to blank emails will not be opened.. Queries should be brief, devoid of gimmicks, and professionally presented, including author details and any writing credits. See website for more details.

East West Literary Agency LLC

1158 26th Street, Suite 462, Santa Monica, CA 90403
Tel: +1 (310) 573-9303
Fax: +1 (310) 453-9008
Email: dwarren@eastwestliteraryagency.com
Website: http://eastwestliteraryagency.com

Handles: Fiction; Nonfiction; *Markets:* Children's; Youth; *Treatments:* Niche

Specialises in children's books of all genres: from concept, novelty and picture books toh young adult literature. Represents both authors and illustrators.

Accepts queries via email only and by referral only. See website for current details.

Ebeling & Associates

PO Box 2529, Lyons, CO 80540
Tel: +1 (808) 579-6414
Fax: +1 (808) 579-9294
Email: michael@ebelingagency.com
Website: http://www.ebelingagency.com

Handles: Nonfiction; *Areas:* Business; Health; Self-Help; *Markets:* Adult; *Treatments:* Commercial

Accepts queries and proposals by email only. Write "Inquiry for Author Representation" in subject line and outline your book in up to 200 words in the body of the email. Attach proposal as Word or PDF document. See website for proposal requirements. Submissions by post are not accepted. No fiction, poetry, or children's.

Anne Edelstein Literary Agency

404 Riverside Drive, New York, NY 10025
Tel: +1 (212) 414-4923
Fax: +1 (212) 414-2930
Email: info@aeliterary.com
Website: http://www.aeliterary.com

Handles: Fiction; Nonfiction; *Areas:* Autobiography; Historical; Psychology; Religious; *Markets:* Adult; *Treatments:* Commercial; Literary

Note: Note accepting approaches as at June 2017

Send query letter with SASE and for fiction a summary of your novel plus the first 25 pages, or for nonfiction an outline of your book and one or two sample chapters. No queries by email.

Judith Ehrlich Literary Management

146 Central Park West, 20E, New York, NY 10023
Tel: +1 (646) 505-1570
Email: jehrlich@judithehrlichliterary.com
Website: http://www.judithehrlichliterary.com

Handles: Fiction; Nonfiction; *Areas:* Arts; Autobiography; Biography; Business; Culture; Current Affairs; Fantasy; Health; Historical; How-to; Humour; Legal; Lifestyle; Medicine; Mystery; Politics; Psychology; Romance; Science; Self-Help; Sociology; Sport; Thrillers; Women's Interests; *Markets:* Adult; Children's; Youth; *Treatments:* Commercial; Literary; Mainstream

Send query by email only. No attachments. For nonfiction give details of your book, your qualifications for writing it, and any existing platform. For fiction include synopsis, writing credentials, and 7-10 sample pages, pasted into the body of the email. No poetry, textbooks, plays or screenplays. See website for full guidelines and individual agent details and email addresses. Response not guaranteed.

Einstein Literary Management

27 West 20th Street, Suite 1003, New York, NY 10011
Tel: +1 (212) 221-8797
Fax: +1 (212) 221-8722
Email: submissions@einsteinliterary.com
Website: http://einsteinliterary.com

Handles: Fiction; Nonfiction; *Areas:* Autobiography; Biography; Historical; Mystery; Romance; Thrillers; Women's Interests; *Markets:* Adult; Children's; Youth; *Treatments:* Literary

No picture books, poetry, textbooks, or screenplays. Accepts submissions by email only. See website for full submission guidelines. No queries by post or by phone.

Elaine Markson Literary Agency

450 Seventh Ave, Suite 1408, New York, NY 10123
Tel: +1 (212) 243-8480
Fax: +1 (212) 691-9014
Email: gary@marksonagency.com
Website: http://www.marksonagency.com

Handles: Fiction; Nonfiction; *Markets:* Adult; *Treatments:* Literary

New York literary agency working with co-agents in the UK, Germany, France, and Italy.

Energy Entertainment

729 Seward Street, 2nd Floor, Los Angeles, CA 90038
Tel: +1 (323) 785-5370
Email: info@energyentertainment.net
Website: http://www.energyentertainment.net

Handles: Scripts; *Areas:* Film; TV; *Markets:* Adult

Agency specialising in discovering new and edgy screenwriters. No unsolicited MSS or calls; send query only.

Elaine P. English, Attorney & Literary Agent

4710 41st Street, NW, Suite D, Wahington, DC 20016
Tel: +1 (202) 362-5190
Fax: +1 (202) 362-5192
Email: queries@elaineenglish.com
Website: http://www.elaineenglish.com

Handles: Fiction; *Areas:* Erotic; Fantasy; Gothic; Historical; Humour; Mystery; Romance; Women's Interests; *Markets:* Adult; *Treatments:* Commercial; Contemporary; Dark; Light; Serious; Traditional

Closed to approaches as at September 2015. Check website for current status.

Handles women's fiction, mysteries, and thrillers. Handles romance ranging from historical to contemporary, funny to erotic, and paranormal. No memoirs, science fiction, fantasy (unless romance fantasy), children's, young adult, horror, thrillers, short stories, screenplays, or nonfiction. Send query by email in first instance – see website for full guidelines. No attachments or unsolicited materials.

Felicia Eth Literary Representation

555 Bryant Street, Suite 350, Palo Alto, CA 94301
Tel: +1 (650) 375-1276
Fax: +1 (650)401-8892
Email: feliciaeth.literary@gmail.com
Website: http://ethliterary.com

Handles: Fiction; Nonfiction; *Areas:* Anthropology; Autobiography; Biography; Business; Crime; Culture; Current Affairs; Finance; Health; Historical; Legal; Lifestyle; Medicine; Nature; Politics; Psychology; Science; Sociology; Spiritual; Technology; Travel; Women's Interests; *Markets:* Adult; *Treatments:* Commercial; Contemporary; Literary; Mainstream

Send query by email or by post with SASE, including details about yourself and your project. Send sample pages upon invitation only.

Ethan Ellenberg Literary Agency

155 Suffolk Street, #2R, New York, NY 10002
Tel: +1 (212) 431-4554
Fax: +1 (212) 941-4652
Email: agent@ethanellenberg.com
Website: http://www.ethanellenberg.com

Handles: Fiction; Nonfiction; *Areas:* Adventure; Autobiography; Biography; Cookery; Crime; Culture; Current Affairs; Fantasy; Health; Historical; Mystery; New Age; Psychology; Romance; Science; Sci-Fi; Spiritual; Thrillers; Women's Interests; *Markets:* Adult; Children's; *Treatments:* Commercial; Literary

Send query by email (no attachments; paste material into the body of the email) or by post with SASE. For fiction send synopsis and first 50 pages. For nonfiction send proposal, author bio, and sample chapters. For picture books send complete MS. No poetry, short stories, scripts, or queries by fax.

We have been in business for over 17 years. We are a member of the AAR. We accept unsolicited submissions and, of course, do not charge reading fees.

Mary Evans, Inc.

242 East Fifth Street, New York, NY 10003
Tel: +1 (212) 979-0880
Fax: +1 (212) 979-5344
Email: info@maryevansinc.com
Website: http://www.maryevansinc.com

Handles: Fiction; Nonfiction; *Areas:* Culture; Historical; Medicine; Politics; Science; Sociology; Technology; *Markets:* Adult; Children's; Youth; *Treatments:* Commercial; Literary

Send query by email or by with SASE. Does not represent scriptwriters, unless they also write books. See website for full submission guidelines.

Fairbank Literary Representation

P.O. Box 6, Hudson, NY 12534-0006
Tel: +1 (617) 576-0030
Fax: +1 (617) 576-0030
Email: queries@fairbankliterary.com
Website: http://www.fairbankliterary.com

Handles: Fiction; Nonfiction; Reference; *Areas:* Architecture; Biography; Cookery; Culture; Design; Humour; Lifestyle; Mystery; Science; Sport; Thrillers; *Markets:* Adult; *Treatments:* Literary; Mainstream

No romance, poetry, screenplays, science fiction or fantasy, paranormal, young adult, children's books, or novels set before 1900. Send one-page query outlining work by post or email. If sending by post a sample chapter may be included, plus SASE if return is required. If sending by email, do not include attachments, but you may include up to the first three pages pasted into the email. No queries by fax, or phone calls. Works over 120,000 by unpublished authors are probably too long to be accepted.

Diana Finch Literary Agency

116 West 23rd Street, Suite 500, New York, NY 10011
Tel: +1 (917) 544-4470
Email: diana.finch@verizon.net
Website: http://dianafinchliteraryagency.blogspot.com

Handles: Fiction; Nonfiction; *Areas:* Adventure; Autobiography; Biography; Business; Crime; Culture; Current Affairs; Film; Finance; Health; Historical; How-to; Humour; Legal; Lifestyle; Medicine; Military; Music; Nature; Photography; Politics; Psychology; Science; Self-Help; Sport; Technology; Theatre; Thrillers; Translations; Women's Interests; *Markets:* Academic; Adult; Youth; *Treatments:* Literary; Mainstream; Satirical

Approach using online submission system – see website for link. Particularly interested in narrative nonfiction, health, and popular science, however actively looking for new fiction to balance the list. No children's picture books, romance, or mysteries.

FinePrint Literary Management

207 West 106th Street, Suite 1D, New York, NY 10025
Tel: +1 (212) 279-1282
Email: peter@fineprintlit.com
Website: http://www.fineprintlit.com

Handles: Fiction; Nonfiction; Reference; *Areas:* Autobiography; Beauty and Fashion; Biography; Business; Cookery; Crime; Culture; Entertainment; Fantasy; Health; Historical; Horror; How-to; Humour; Lifestyle; Military; Music; Mystery; Nature; Religious; Romance; Science; Sci-Fi; Self-Help; Spiritual; Suspense; Technology; Thrillers; Travel; Women's Interests; *Markets:* Adult; Children's; Youth; *Treatments:* Contemporary; Dark; Literary; Serious

Consult agent profiles on website for individual interests and approach appropriate agent for your work.

The James Fitzgerald Agency

118 Waverly Pl., #1B, New York, NY 10011
Tel: +1 (212) 308-1122
Email: submissions@jfitzagency.com
Website: http://www.jfitzagency.com

Handles: Fiction; Nonfiction; *Areas:* Culture; *Markets:* Adult

Primarily represents books reflecting the popular culture of the day, in fiction, nonfiction, graphic and packaged books. No poetry or screenplays. All information must be submitted in English, even if the manuscript is in another language. See website for detailed submission guidelines.

Fletcher & Company

78 Fifth Avenue, Third Floor, New York, NY 10011
Tel: +1 (212) 614-0778
Fax: +1 (212) 614-0728
Email: info@fletcherandco.com
Website: http://www.fletcherandco.com

Handles: Fiction; Nonfiction; *Areas:* Autobiography; Biography; Business; Crime; Culture; Current Affairs; Health; Historical; Humour; Lifestyle; Politics; Science; Self-Help; Sport; Travel; Women's Interests; *Markets:* Adult; Youth; *Treatments:* Commercial; Literary

Full-service literary agency representing writers of nonfiction and commercial and literary fiction. Send query by email only with brief synopsis and first 5-10 pages of your manuscript / proposal pasted into the body of the email. No attachments. Query only one agent at a time (see website for list of individual agent interests). Response normally in 4-6 weeks. No queries by post.

Folio Literary Management, LLC

630 9th Avenue, Suite 1101, New York, NY 10036
Tel: +1 (212) 400-1494
Fax: +1 (212) 967-0977

Email: jeff@foliolit.com
Website: http://www.foliolit.com

Handles: Fiction; Nonfiction; Reference; *Areas:* Autobiography; Business; Cookery; Crime; Culture; Entertainment; Fantasy; Health; Historical; Horror; How-to; Humour; Lifestyle; Media; Military; Music; Mystery; Politics; Psychology; Religious; Romance; Science; Sci-Fi; Self-Help; Spiritual; Sport; Suspense; Technology; Thrillers; Women's Interests; *Markets:* Adult; Children's; Youth; *Treatments:* Commercial; Contemporary; Dark; Literary; Popular; Serious

Read agent bios on website and decide which agent to approach. Do not submit to multiple agents simultaneously. Each agent has different submission requirements: consult website for details. No unsolicited MSS or multiple submissions.

Foundry Literary + Media

33 West 17th Street, PH, New York, NY 10011
Tel: +1 (212) 929-5064
Fax: +1 (212) 929-5471
Email: info@foundrymedia.com
Website: http://www.foundrymedia.com

Handles: Fiction; Nonfiction; *Areas:* Adventure; Autobiography; Biography; Business; Cookery; Culture; Current Affairs; Health; Historical; How-to; Humour; Lifestyle; Music; Psychology; Religious; Science; Sci-Fi; Spiritual; Sport; Thrillers; Travel; Women's Interests; *Markets:* Adult; Children's; Youth; *Treatments:* Commercial; Literary; Niche; Popular

Queries should be addressed to a specific agent (see website) and sent by email or by post with SASE, according to requirements of individual agent (see website). For fiction queries, send letter with synopsis, First Three Chapters of Manuscript, and Author Bio. For nonfiction approaches send letter with Sample Chapters, Table of Contents, and Author Bio.

Frances Collin Literary Agent

PO Box 33, Wayne, PA 19087-0033
Tel: +1 (610) 254-0555
Fax: +1 (610) 254-5029
Email: queries@francescollin.com
Website: http://www.francescollin.com

Handles: Fiction; Nonfiction; *Areas:* Autobiography; Biography; Culture; Fantasy; Historical; Nature; Sci-Fi; Travel; Women's Interests; *Markets:* Adult; *Treatments:* Literary

Send query by email (no attachments) or by post with SASE, or IRCs if outside the US. No queries by phone or fax.

Samuel French, Inc.

235 Park Avenue South, Fifth Floor, New York, NY 10003
Tel: +1 (212) 206-8990
Fax: +1 (212) 206-1429
Email: info@samuelfrench.com
Website: http://www.samuelfrench.com

Handles: Scripts; *Areas:* Crime; Fantasy; Horror; Humour; Mystery; Theatre; Thrillers; *Markets:* Adult

Note: Not accepting unsolicited submissions as at March 2015

Publishes plays and represents writers of plays. Deals in well-known plays from Broadway and London's West End.

Fresh Books Literary Agency

231 Diana Street, Placerville, CA 95667
Email: matt@fresh-books.com
Website: http://www.fresh-books.com

Handles: Nonfiction; Reference; *Areas:* Business; Design; Finance; Health; How-to; Humour; Lifestyle; Photography; Science; Self-Help; Technology; *Markets:* Adult; *Treatments:* Popular

Handles narrative non-fiction, lifestyle and reference titles on subjects such as popular science, technology, health, fitness, photography, design, computing, gadgets, social media, career development, education, business, leadership, personal finance, how-to, and humour. No fiction, children's books, screenplays, or poetry. Send query by email. No attachments. Send further material upon request only.

Sarah Jane Freymann Literary Agency

59 West 71st Street, New York, NY 10023
Tel: +1 (212) 362-9277
Fax: +1 (212) 501-8240
Email: Submissions@SarahJaneFreymann.com
Website: http://www.sarahjanefreymann.com

Handles: Fiction; Nonfiction; *Areas:* Autobiography; Business; Cookery; Crime; Culture; Health; Historical; Humour; Lifestyle; Men's Interests; Nature; Psychology; Science; Self-Help; Spiritual; Sport; Thrillers; Travel; Women's Interests; *Markets:* Adult; Youth; *Treatments:* Literary; Mainstream

Prefers to receive queries by email. Include pitch letter and first ten pages pasted into the body of the email (no attachments). See website for full details.

Fredrica S. Friedman and Co. Inc.

857 Fifth Avenue, New York, NY 10065
Tel: +1 (212) 829-9600
Fax: +1 (212) 829-9669
Email: submissions@fredricafriedman.com
Website: http://www.fredricafriedman.com

Handles: Fiction; Nonfiction; *Areas:* Arts; Autobiography; Biography; Business; Cookery; Crime; Culture; Current Affairs; Design; Film; Finance; Health; Historical; How-to; Humour; Lifestyle; Music; Photography; Politics; Psychology; Self-Help; Sociology; Women's Interests; *Markets:* Adult; *Treatments:* Literary

Send query with synopsis by email. For fiction, include ten-page sample. All material must be in the body of the email – no attachments. No poetry, plays, screenplays, children's books, sci-fi/fantasy, or horror.

Nancy Gallt Literary Agency

273 Charlton Avenue, South Orange , NJ 07079
Tel: +1 (973) 761-6358
Fax: +1 (973) 761-6318
Email: nancy@nancygallt.com
Website: http://www.nancygallt.com

Handles: Fiction; *Markets:* Children's; Youth

Handles children's books only. Use submission form on website or submit by post with SASE and appropriate postage if return of material required. All online submissions must go through the submission form on the website.

Gelfman Schneider / ICM Partners

850 Seventh Avenue, Suite 903, New York, NY 10019
Tel: +1 (212) 245-1993
Email: mail@gelfmanschneider.com
Website: http://www.gelfmanschneider.com

Handles: Fiction; Nonfiction; *Areas:* Autobiography; Culture; Current Affairs; Historical; Mystery; Politics; Science; Suspense; Thrillers; Women's Interests; *Markets:* Adult; Youth; *Treatments:* Commercial; Literary; Mainstream; Popular

Different agents within the agency have different submission guidelines. See website for full details. No screenplays, or poetry.

Georges Borchardt, Inc.

136 East 57th Street, New York, NY 10022
Tel: +1 (212) 753-5785
Email: anne@gbagency.com
Website: http://www.gbagency.com

Handles: Fiction; Nonfiction; *Areas:* Arts; Biography; Current Affairs; Historical; Literature; Philosophy; Politics; Religious; Science; Short Stories; *Markets:* Adult; Youth; *Treatments:* Commercial; Literary

New York based literary agency founded in 1967. No unsolicited MSS or screenplays.

The Gernert Company

136 East 57th Street, New York, NY 10022
Tel: +1 (212) 838-7777
Fax: +1 (212) 838-6020
Email: info@thegernertco.com
Website: http://www.thegernertco.com

Handles: Fiction; Nonfiction; *Areas:* Adventure; Arts; Autobiography; Biography; Crafts; Crime; Current Affairs; Fantasy;

Historical; Politics; Science; Sci-Fi; Sociology; Sport; Thrillers; Women's Interests; *Markets:* Academic; Adult; Children's; Youth; *Treatments:* Commercial; Literary; Popular

Send query describing work by post with SASE or email with author info and sample chapter. If querying by email, send to generic email and indicate which agent you would like to query. No queries by fax. Response only if interested.

Gina Maccoby Agency

PO Box 60, Chappaqua, NY 10514
Tel: +1 (914) 238-5630
Email: query@maccobylit.com

Handles: Fiction; Nonfiction; *Areas:* Autobiography; Biography; Culture; Current Affairs; Entertainment; Health; Historical; Lifestyle; Mystery; Nature; Politics; Self-Help; Suspense; Thrillers; Women's Interests; *Markets:* Adult; Children's; Youth; *Treatments:* Literary; Mainstream

Send query by email only. Response not guaranteed.

Glass Literary Management LLC

138 West 25th Street, 10th Floor, New York, NY 10001
Tel: +1 (646) 237-4881
Email: alex@glassliterary.com
Website: http://www.glassliterary.com

Handles: Fiction; Nonfiction; *Areas:* Autobiography; Biography; Business; Culture; Entertainment; Health; Historical; Media; Sport; *Markets:* Adult; Children's; *Treatments:* Literary; Mainstream; Popular

Send query by email only, directly to one of the two agents -- see website for both email addresses. No attachments, picture books for children, or approaches by post. No response to queries not directly addressed to either one of the agents. Send query letter in the body of your email. Response not guaranteed unless interested.

Global Lion Intellectual Property Management, Inc.

PO BOX 669238, Pompano Beach, FL 33066
Email: queriesgloballionmgt@gmail.com
Website: http://www.globallionmanagement.com

Handles: Fiction; Nonfiction; *Markets:* Adult

Looks for cutting-edge authors of both fiction and nonfiction with global marketing and motion picture/television production potential. Authors must not only have a great book and future, but also a specific game-plan of how to use social media to grow their fan base. Send query by email only with synopsis, up to 20 pages if available (otherwise, chapter synopsis), author bio, and any social media outlets. See website for full details.

Barry Goldblatt Literary Agency, Inc.

320 7th Avenue, #266, Brooklyn, NY 11215
Email: query@bgliterary.com
Website: http://www.bgliterary.com

Handles: Fiction; *Areas:* Fantasy; Sci-Fi; *Markets:* Children's; Youth

Handles books for young people; from picture books to middle grade and young adult. Send query by email including the word "Query" in the subject line and synopsis and first five pages in the body of the email. No attachments. Emails with attachments will be ignored. See website for full details.

Frances Goldin Literary Agency, Inc.

57 E. 11th Street, Suite 5B, New York, NY 10003
Tel: +1 (212) 777-0047
Fax: +1 (212) 228-1660
Email: agency@goldinlit.com
Website: http://www.goldinlit.com

Handles: Fiction; Nonfiction; *Areas:* Arts; Autobiography; Culture; Current Affairs; Entertainment; Film; Historical; Nature; Philosophy; Science; Sociology; Sport;

Technology; *Markets:* Adult; Children's; Youth; *Treatments:* Commercial; Literary; Progressive

Submit through online system available at website. No screenplays, illustrated books, genre fiction, romance, science fiction, cookery, business, diet, racism, sexism, ageism, homophobia, or pornography.

Goodman Associates

500 West End Avenue, New York, NY 10024
Tel: +1 (212) 873-4806

Handles: Fiction; Nonfiction; *Areas:* Adventure; Anthropology; Archaeology; Autobiography; Biography; Business; Cookery; Crime; Criticism; Culture; Current Affairs; Erotic; Film; Finance; Health; Historical; Legal; Leisure; Literature; Medicine; Military; Music; Mystery; Nature; Philosophy; Politics; Psychology; Science; Sociology; Sport; Suspense; Technology; Theatre; Thrillers; Translations; Travel; Women's Interests; *Markets:* Adult; *Treatments:* Contemporary; Literary; Mainstream

Send query with SASE. Accepting new clients by recommendation only. No poetry, articles, children's, young adult, or individual stories.

Irene Goodman Literary Agency

27 W. 24 Street, Suite 700B, New York, NY 10010
Tel: +1 (212) 604-0330
Fax: +1 (212) 675-1381
Email: irene.queries@irenegoodman.com
Website: http://www.irenegoodman.com

Handles: Fiction; Nonfiction; *Areas:* Autobiography; Cookery; Culture; Fantasy; Historical; Lifestyle; Mystery; Romance; Science; Sociology; Suspense; Thrillers; Women's Interests; *Markets:* Adult; Children's; Youth; *Treatments:* Commercial; Literary; Popular

Select specific agent to approach based on details given on website (specific agent email addresses on website). Send query by email only with synopsis, bio, and first ten pages in the body of the email. No poetry, inspirational fiction, screenplays, or children's picture books. Response only if interested. See website for further details.

Grace Freedson's Publishing Network

7600 Jericho Turnpike, Suite 300, Woodbury, NY 11797
Tel: +1 (516) 931-7757
Fax: +1 (516) 931-7759
Email: gfreedson@gmail.com

Handles: Nonfiction; *Areas:* Autobiography; Business; Cookery; Crafts; Crime; Culture; Current Affairs; Design; Finance; Gardening; Health; Historical; Hobbies; How-to; Humour; Legal; Leisure; Lifestyle; Medicine; Military; Nature; Philosophy; Psychology; Religious; Science; Self-Help; Sport; Technology; Women's Interests; *Markets:* Adult; Children's; Youth

Literary agency and book packager. Handles nonfiction from qualified authors with credentials and platforms only. No fiction. Send query with synopsis and SASE.

Kathryn Green Literary Agency, LLC

250 West 57th Street, Suite 2302, New York, NY 10107
Tel: +1 (212) 245-4225
Fax: +1 (212) 245-4042
Email: query@kgreenagency.com

Handles: Fiction; Nonfiction; *Areas:* Autobiography; Biography; Business; Cookery; Crime; Culture; Current Affairs; Design; Finance; Health; Historical; How-to; Humour; Lifestyle; Psychology; Romance; Self-Help; Sport; Suspense; Thrillers; Women's Interests; *Markets:* Adult; Children's; Youth; *Treatments:* Contemporary; Literary; Mainstream; Satirical

Send query by email. Do not send samples unless requested. No science fiction, fantasy, or queries by fax.

Blanche C. Gregory Inc.

2 Tudor City Place, New York, NY 10017
Tel: +1 (212) 697-0828
Email: info@bcgliteraryagency.com
Website: http://www.bcgliteraryagency.com

Handles: Fiction; Nonfiction; *Markets:* Adult; Children's

Specialises in adult fiction and nonfiction, but will also consider children's literature. Send query describing your background with SASE and synopsis. No stage, film or TV scripts, or queries by fax or email.

Greyhaus Literary Agency

3021 20th St. Pl. SW, Puyallup, WA 98373
Email: submissions@greyhausagency.com
Website: http://www.greyhausagency.com

Handles: Fiction; *Areas:* Romance; Women's Interests; *Markets:* Adult; *Treatments:* Contemporary; Traditional

Small agency focussing only on romance and women's fiction. To query, send query by email (no attachments); complete online form on website; or send query by post with 3-5 page synopsis, first three pages, and SASE.

Laura Gross Literary Agency

PO Box 610326, Newton Highlands, MA 02461
Tel: +1 (617) 964-2977
Fax: +1 (617) 964-3023
Email: query@lg-la.com
Website: http://lauragrossliteraryagency.com

Handles: Fiction; Nonfiction; *Areas:* Autobiography; Biography; Culture; Current Affairs; Health; Historical; Legal; Lifestyle; Medicine; Mystery; Politics; Psychology; Sport; Suspense; Thrillers; Women's Interests; *Markets:* Adult; *Treatments:* Literary; Mainstream

Submit query using online web form, including your book's genre and a synopsis or plot summary. No sample chapters in first instance.

Hannigan Salky Getzler (HSG) Agency

37 West 28th St, 8th floor, New York, NY 10001
Tel: +1 (646) 442-5770
Email: channigan@hsgagency.com
Website: http://hsgagency.com

Handles: Fiction; Nonfiction; *Areas:* Adventure; Autobiography; Business; Cookery; Crafts; Culture; Current Affairs; Design; Finance; Gardening; Health; Historical; Humour; Lifestyle; Mystery; Photography; Politics; Psychology; Science; Sociology; Suspense; Thrillers; Travel; Women's Interests; *Markets:* Adult; Children's; Youth; *Treatments:* Commercial; Literary; Popular

Send query by email only with first five pages pasted into the body of the email (no attachments), or the full ms for picture books. See website for agent interests and individual email addresses, and contact one agent only. No screenplays, romance fiction, science fiction, or religious fiction.

Harold Ober Associates, Inc.

425 Madison Avenue, New York, NY 10017
Tel: +1 (212) 759-8600
Fax: +1 (212) 759-9428
Email: phyllis@haroldober.com
Website: http://www.haroldober.com

Handles: Fiction; Nonfiction; *Markets:* Adult; Children's

Send query addressed to a specific agent by post only, including first five pages and SASE for reply. No plays, screenplays, or queries by fax.

Joy Harris Literary Agency, Inc.

381 Park Avenue South, Suite 428, New York, NY 10016
Tel: +1 (212) 924-6269
Fax: +1 (212) 725-5275
Email: submissions@joyharrisliterary.com
Website: http://www.joyharrisliterary.com

Handles: Fiction; Nonfiction; *Areas:* Autobiography; Biography; Culture; Historical; Humour; Media; Mystery; Short

Stories; Spiritual; Suspense; Translations; Women's Interests; *Markets:* Adult; Youth; *Treatments:* Experimental; Literary; Mainstream; Satirical

Send query by post with SASE or by email, including sample chapter or outline. Prefers submissions by email. No poetry, screenplays, genre fiction, self-help, or unsolicited mss.

The Helen Brann Agency, Inc.

94 Curtis Road, Bridgewater, CT 06752
Fax: +1 (860) 355-2572
Email: helenbrannagency@earthlink.net

Handles: Fiction; Nonfiction; *Markets:* Adult

Works mostly with established writers and referrals.

The Jeff Herman Agency, LLC

PO Box 1522, Stockbridge, MA 01262
Tel: +1 (413) 298-0077
Fax: +1 (413) 298-8188
Email: submissions@jeffherman.com
Website: http://www.jeffherman.com

Handles: Nonfiction; Reference; *Areas:* Autobiography; Business; Crime; Culture; Health; Historical; How-to; Lifestyle; Psychology; Self-Help; Spiritual; *Markets:* Academic; Adult

Send query by post with SASE, or by email. With few exceptions, handles nonfiction only, with particular interest in the genres given above. No scripts or unsolicited MSS.

Hidden Value Group

27758 Santa Margarita Pkwy #361, Mission Viejo, CA 92691
Tel: +1 (951) 549-8891
Fax: +1 (951) 549-8891
Email: bookquery@hiddenvaluegroup.com
Website: http://www.hiddenvaluegroup.com

Handles: Fiction; Nonfiction; *Areas:* Business; Lifestyle; Men's Interests; Religious; Self-Help; Women's Interests; *Markets:* Adult; Youth; *Treatments:* Literary

Represents previously published Christian authors (not including self-published authors). Send one-page summary, marketing information, author bio, and two or three sample chapters by email or by post with SASE. Cannot guarantee a response to all email queries. No poetry or short stories, or queries by phone.

Hill Nadell Literary Agency

6442 Santa Monica Blvd, Suite 201, Los Angeles, CA 90038
Tel: +1 (310) 860-9605
Fax: +1 (323) 380-5206
Email: queries@hillnadell.com
Website: http://www.hillnadell.com

Handles: Fiction; Nonfiction; *Areas:* Autobiography; Biography; Cookery; Culture; Current Affairs; Health; Historical; Legal; Nature; Politics; Science; Thrillers; Women's Interests; *Markets:* Adult; Youth; *Treatments:* Literary; Mainstream

Handles current affairs, food, memoirs and other narrative nonfiction, fiction, thrillers, upmarket women's fiction, literary fiction, genre fiction, graphic novels, and occasional young adult novels. No scripts or screenplays. Accepts queries both by post and by email. See website for full submission guidelines.

Hopkins Literary Associates

2117 Buffalo Road, Ste. 327, Rochester, NY 14624
Tel: +1 (585) 352-6268
Email: hlasubmissions@rochester.rr.com

Handles: Fiction; *Areas:* Historical; Romance; Women's Interests; *Markets:* Adult; Youth; *Treatments:* Contemporary; Mainstream

Send query by email only. Specialises in women's fiction, particularly historical and contemporary romance. No queries by fax or email.

Hudson Agency

3 Travis Lane, Montrose, NY 10548
Tel: +1 (914) 737-1475
Fax: +1 (914) 736-3064
Email: Sue@hudsonagency.net
Website: http://www.hudsonagency.net

Handles: Scripts; *Areas:* Crime; Drama; Fantasy; Film; Humour; Mystery; Romance; TV; Westerns; *Markets:* Adult; Children's; Family; Youth; *Treatments:* Contemporary

Send query with SASE. Most new clients taken on by recommendation from industry professionals.

Andrea Hurst Literary Management

PO Box 1467, Coupeville, WA 98239
Email: info@andreahurst.com
Website: http://www.andreahurst.com

Handles: Fiction; Nonfiction; *Areas:* Adventure; Autobiography; Business; Cookery; Crime; Current Affairs; Fantasy; Historical; How-to; Humour; Politics; Psychology; Religious; Romance; Science; Sci-Fi; Self-Help; Thrillers; Westerns; Women's Interests; *Markets:* Adult; Youth; *Treatments:* Commercial; Contemporary

Agent has semi-retired from the agent division of her business and is now accepting queries by referral through an existing client, agent, or publisher only.

InkWell Management

521 Fifth Avenue, 26th Floor, New York, NY 10175
Tel: +1 (212) 922-3500
Fax: +1 (212) 922-0535
Email: submissions@inkwellmanagement.com
Website: http://www.inkwellmanagement.com

Handles: Fiction; Nonfiction; Business; Crime; Current Affairs; Finance; Health; Historical; Medicine; Mystery; Psychology; Self-Help; Thrillers; *Markets:* Adult; *Treatments:* Contemporary; Literary; Mainstream

Send query by email with up to two sample chapters. No large attachments. Response not guaranteed. Response within two months if interested. See website for full guidelines.

International Transactions, Inc.

PO Box 97, Gila, NM 88038-0097
Tel: +1 (845) 373-9696
Fax: +1 (480) 393-5162
Email: info@intltrans.com
Website: http://www.intltrans.com

Handles: Fiction; Nonfiction; *Areas:* Adventure; Arts; Biography; Crime; Historical; Medicine; Mystery; Short Stories; Thrillers; Women's Interests; *Markets:* Academic; Adult; Youth; *Treatments:* Contemporary; Literary; Mainstream

Send query with outline or synopsis by email. No nonfiction enquiries from unpublished authors. No queries by fax, or material which is too influenced by TV or other successful novels. See website for full submission guidelines.

J de S Associates Inc.

9 Shagbark Road, Wilson Point, South Norwalk, CT 06854
Tel: +1 (203) 838-7571
Fax: +1 (203) 866-2713
Email: jdespoel@aol.com
Website: http://www.jdesassociates.com

Handles: Fiction; *Areas:* Autobiography; Biography; Business; Crime; Culture; Current Affairs; Finance; Health; Historical; How-to; Legal; Lifestyle; Medicine; Military; Mystery; New Age; Politics; Self-Help; Sociology; Sport; Suspense; Thrillers; Translations; Westerns; *Markets:* Adult; Children's; Youth; *Treatments:* Commercial; Literary; Mainstream

Welcomes brief queries by post and by email, but no samples or other material unless requested.

Jabberwocky Literary Agency

49 West 45th Street, 12th Floor North, New York, NY 10036
Tel: +1 (917) 388-3010
Fax: +1 (917) 388-2998
Email: queryeddie@awfulagent.com
Website: http://awfulagent.com

Handles: Fiction; Nonfiction; *Areas:* Fantasy; Historical; Science; Sci-Fi;

Markets: Adult; Children's; Youth;
Treatments: Literary

Handles a broad range of fiction and nonfiction intended for general audiences, but no series romance or poetry. Book-length material only. Also considers graphic novels and comics. Send query by post with SASE or IRC, or by email. No queries by phone or by fax. See website for full guidelines.

Jane Rotrosen Agency

85 Broad Street, 28th Floor, New York, NY 10004
Tel: +1 (212) 593-4330
Fax: +1 (212) 935-6985
Email: acirillo@janerotrosen.com
Website: http://www.janerotrosen.com

Handles: Fiction; Nonfiction; *Areas:* Autobiography; Historical; Mystery; Romance; Suspense; Thrillers; Women's Interests; *Markets:* Adult; Youth; *Treatments:* Commercial; Mainstream

Send query by email to one of the agent email addresses provided on the agency bios page of the website, or by post with SASE, describing your work and giving relevant biographical details and publishing history, along with synopsis and the first three chapters in the case of fiction, or proposal in the case of nonfiction. Submissions without an SASE will be recycled without response. Attachments to a blank email will not be opened. See website for full guidelines and individual agent details.

The Jean V. Naggar Literary Agency

216 East 75th Street, New York, NY 10021
Tel: +1 (212) 794-1082
Email: jvnla@jvnla.com
Website: http://www.jvnla.com

Handles: Fiction; Nonfiction; *Areas:* Adventure; Autobiography; Biography; Culture; Current Affairs; Fantasy; Gothic; Health; Historical; Horror; Humour; Lifestyle; Music; Mystery; Psychology; Romance; Science; Suspense; Thrillers; *Markets:* Adult; Children's; Youth; *Treatments:* Commercial; Dark; Literary; Mainstream; Popular

Accepts queries via online submission system only. See website for more details.

Jeanne Fredericks Literary Agency, Inc.

221 Benedict Hill Road, New Canaan, CT 06840
Tel: +1 (203) 972-3011
Fax: +1 (203) 972-3011
Email: jeanne.fredericks@gmail.com
Website: http://jeannefredericks.com

Handles: Nonfiction; Reference; *Areas:* Antiques; Arts; Biography; Business; Cookery; Crafts; Design; Finance; Gardening; Health; Historical; How-to; Legal; Leisure; Lifestyle; Medicine; Nature; Photography; Psychology; Science; Self-Help; Sport; Travel; Women's Interests; *Markets:* Adult; *Treatments:* Popular

Send query by email (no attachments) or post with SASE. Specialises in adult nonfiction by authorities in their fields. No fiction, true crime, juvenile, textbooks, poetry, essays, screenplays, short stories, science fiction, pop culture, guides to computers and software, politics, horror, pornography, books on overly depressing or violent topics, romance, teacher's manuals, or memoirs. See website for full guidelines.

Jill Grinberg Literary Management LLC

392 Vanderbilt Avenue, Brooklyn, NY 11238
Tel: +1 (212) 620-5883
Email: info@jillgrinbergliterary.com
Website: http://www.jillgrinbergliterary.com

Handles: Fiction; Nonfiction; *Areas:* Autobiography; Biography; Business; Culture; Current Affairs; Entertainment; Fantasy; Finance; Health; Historical; Humour; Legal; Lifestyle; Medicine; Nature; Politics; Psychology; Romance; Science; Sci-Fi; Spiritual; Sport; Technology; Travel; Women's Interests; *Markets:* Adult; Children's; Youth; *Treatments:* Commercial; Literary

Send query with synopsis and first 50 pages for fiction, or proposal and author bio for nonfiction.

Jill Grosjean Literary Agency

1390 Millstone Road, Sag Harbor, NY 11963-2214
Tel: +1 (631) 725-7419
Email: JillLit310@aol.com

Handles: Fiction; *Areas:* Crime; Gardening; Historical; Humour; Mystery; Nature; Romance; Suspense; Thrillers; Travel; Women's Interests; *Markets:* Adult; *Treatments:* Literary; Mainstream

Prefers email queries. No attachments. Particularly interested in literary novels and mysteries.

The Joan Brandt Agency

788 Wesley Drive, Atlanta, GA 30305-3933
Tel: +1 (404) 351-8877

Handles: Fiction; Nonfiction; *Areas:* How-to; Mystery; Suspense; Women's Interests; *Markets:* Adult; *Treatments:* Literary; Mainstream

Send query with SASE. Simultaneous submissions are accepted.

Kathi J. Paton Literary Agency

PO Box 2236, Radio City Station, New York, NY 10101-2236
Tel: +1 (212) 265-6586
Email: kjplitbiz@optonline.net
Website: http://www.PatonLiterary.com

Handles: Fiction; Nonfiction; *Areas:* Biography; Business; Culture; Current Affairs; Finance; Health; Historical; Humour; Lifestyle; Politics; Religious; Science; Sport; Technology; *Markets:* Adult; *Treatments:* Literary; Mainstream; Popular

Send query with brief description by email only. No attachments or referrals to websites. Specialises in adult nonfiction. No science fiction, fantasy, horror, category romance, juvenile, young adult or self-published books. Response only if interested. Also offers editorial services.

Ken Sherman & Associates

1275 N. Hayworth, Suite 103, Los Angeles, CA 90046
Tel: +1 (310) 273-8840
Fax: +1 (310) 271-2875
Email: ken@kenshermanassociates.com
Website: http://www.kenshermanassociates.com

Handles: Fiction; Nonfiction; Scripts; *Areas:* Film; TV; *Markets:* Adult

Handles fiction, nonfiction, and writers for film and TV. Query by referral only.

Virginia Kidd Agency, Inc

PO Box 278, Milford, PA 18337
Tel: +1 (570) 296-6205
Fax: +1 (570) 296-7266
Email: subs@vk-agency.com
Website: http://www.vk-agency.com

Handles: Fiction; *Areas:* Fantasy; Historical; Mystery; Sci-Fi; Suspense; Women's Interests; *Markets:* Adult; *Treatments:* Mainstream

Specialises in science fiction and fantasy. Send query by post or email with brief synopsis and a few sample pages (not necessarily the opening). See website for full details.

Harvey Klinger, Inc

300 West 55th Street, Suite 11V, New York, NY 10019
Tel: +1 (212) 581-7068
Fax: +1 (212) 315-3823
Email: david@harveyklinger.com
Website: http://www.harveyklinger.com

Handles: Fiction; Nonfiction; *Areas:* Adventure; Autobiography; Biography; Cookery; Crime; Culture; Fantasy; Health; How-to; Humour; Medicine; Music; Mystery; Psychology; Romance; Science; Sci-Fi; Self-Help; Spiritual; Sport; Suspense; Technology; Thrillers; Women's Interests; *Markets:* Adult; Children's; Youth; *Treatments:* Literary; Mainstream; Popular

Send query by email or through submission form on website. No submissions by post. Include short synopsis, author bio, and first five pages, pasted into the body of your email. No attachments. Do not query more than one agent at the agency at a time. See website for individual agent interests and email addresses. No screenplays, or queries by phone or fax. See website for full submission guidelines.

Kneerim & Williams

90 Canal Street, Boston, MA 02114
Tel: +1 (617) 303-1650
Fax: +1 (617) 542-1660
Email: jill@kwlit.com
Website: http://www.kwlit.com

Handles: Fiction; Nonfiction; *Areas:* Adventure; Anthropology; Archaeology; Autobiography; Biography; Business; Crime; Culture; Current Affairs; Finance; Health; Historical; Legal; Lifestyle; Literature; Medicine; Nature; Politics; Psychology; Religious; Science; Sociology; Sport; Technology; Women's Interests; *Markets:* Adult; *Treatments:* Commercial; Literary; Mainstream; Serious

Send query by email to individual agent. See website for specific agent interests and email addresses.

The Knight Agency

Email: submissions@knightagency.net
Website: http://www.knightagency.net

Handles: Fiction; *Areas:* Autobiography; Beauty and Fashion; Business; Cookery; Crime; Culture; Entertainment; Fantasy; Finance; Health; Historical; How-to; Lifestyle; Media; Mystery; Psychology; Religious; Romance; Sci-Fi; Self-Help; Suspense; Thrillers; Women's Interests; *Markets:* Adult; Children's; Youth; *Treatments:* Commercial; Contemporary; Literary; Popular

Send one-page query by email, with the first five pages of your manuscript in the body of the email. No attachments or paper or phone queries. Paper queries will not be returned.

Not accepting Screen Plays, Short Story Collections, Poetry Collections, Essay Collections, Photography, Film Treatments, Picture Books (excluding graphic novels), Children's Books (excluding young adult and middle grade), Biographies, Nonfiction Historical Treatments.

Linda Konner Literary Agency

10 West 15 Street, Suite 1918, New York, NY 10011
Email: ldkonner@cs.com
Website: http://www.lindakonnerliteraryagency.com

Handles: Nonfiction; Reference; *Areas:* Biography; Business; Cookery; Culture; Entertainment; Finance; Health; How-to; Lifestyle; Psychology; Science; Self-Help; Women's Interests; *Markets:* Adult; *Treatments:* Popular

Send one to two page query by email or by post with SASE, synopsis, and author bio. Attachments from unknown senders will be deleted unread. Nonfiction only. Books must be written by or with established experts in their field. No Fiction, Memoir, Religion, Spiritual/Christian, Children's/young adult, Games/puzzles, Humour, History, Politics, or unsolicited MSS. See website for full guidelines.

Barbara S. Kouts, Literary Agent

PO Box 560, Bellport, NY 11713
Tel: +1 (631) 286-1278
Fax: +1 (631) 286-1538
Email: bkouts@aol.com

Handles: Fiction; *Areas:* Autobiography; Biography; Crime; Current Affairs; Health; Historical; Lifestyle; Mystery; Nature; Psychology; Suspense; Thrillers; Women's Interests; *Markets:* Adult; Children's; *Treatments:* Literary

Note: Not accepting submissions as at January 2017.

Send query with SASE. Postal queries only. Particularly interested in adult fiction and nonfiction and children's books.

Bert P. Krages

6665 S.W. Hampton Street, Suite 200, Portland, Oregon 97223
Tel: +1 (503) 597-2525
Fax: +1 (503) 597-2549
Email: krages@onemain.com
Website: http://www.krages.com/lvaserv.htm

Handles: Nonfiction; *Areas:* Health; Historical; Psychology; Science; *Markets:* Adult

Send query by email, with outline, similar books and how yours will compete with them, and your relevant qualifications and writing experience. Query letters should not exceed one page. Particularly interested in science, health, psychology, and history. Not currently accepting fiction. Do not call or send MS instead of query.

Edite Kroll Literary Agency, Inc.

20 Cross Street, Saco, ME 04072
Tel: +1 (207) 283-8797
Fax: +1 (207) 283-8799
Email: ekroll@maine.rr.com

Handles: Fiction; Nonfiction; *Areas:* Autobiography; Biography; Culture; Current Affairs; Health; Humour; Legal; Medicine; Politics; Psychology; Religious; Self-Help; Women's Interests; *Markets:* Academic; Adult; Children's; Youth; *Treatments:* Literary

Handles mainly nonfiction so very selective about fiction. Particularly interested in international feminists and women writers and artists. No genre books such as mysteries, romance, or thrillers; no diet, cookery, etc.; no photography books, coffee table books, or commercial fiction. Send query by email, fax, or by post with SASE, including synopsis, author bio, and one or two sample chapters. For picture books, send complete MS. No queries by phone.

Kuhn Projects

19 West 21st Street., Suite 501, New York, NY 10010
Tel: +1 (212) 929-2227
Fax: +1 (212) 929-2583
Email: submissions@kuhnprojects.com
Website: http://www.kuhnprojects.com

Handles: Fiction; Nonfiction; *Areas:* Arts; Autobiography; Beauty and Fashion; Business; Cookery; Culture; Current Affairs; Design; Health; Historical; Humour; Politics; Psychology; Science; Spiritual; Technology; *Markets:* Adult; Children's; Youth

Handles mainly adult nonfiction. Send query by email with description of the project, author bio, and sample pages up to one chapter, if included in the body of the email. See website for full details.

L. Perkins Associates

5800 Arlington Ave, Riverdale, NY 10471
Tel: +1 (718) 543-5344
Fax: +1 (718) 543-5354
Email: submissions@lperkinsagency.com
Website: http://lperkinsagency.com

Handles: Fiction; Nonfiction; *Areas:* Arts; Autobiography; Biography; Cookery; Crime; Culture; Erotic; Fantasy; Film; Historical; Horror; How-to; Humour; Music; Mystery; Psychology; Romance; Science; Sci-Fi; Theatre; Thrillers; Westerns; *Markets:* Adult; Children's; Youth; *Treatments:* Commercial; Dark; Literary; Popular

Send query by email with synopsis, bio, and first five pages of your novel / proposal in the body of the email. No email attachments and no queries by post or any other means apart from email. Pitch only one book at a time, and to only one agent. Specific agent email addresses are available at website, or use general address provided below. No screenplays, short story collections, or poetry.

The LA Literary Agency

PO Box 46370, Los Angeles, CA 90046
Tel: +1 (323) 654-5288
Email: ann@laliteraryagency.com
Website: http://www.laliteraryagency.com

Handles: Fiction; Nonfiction; *Areas:* Autobiography; Biography; Business; Cookery; Health; Historical; Lifestyle; Psychology; Science; Sport; *Markets:* Adult; *Treatments:* Commercial; Contemporary; Literary; Mainstream

Send query with proposal (nonfiction) or full ms (fiction) by email. Response only if interested. Sister company offers editorial services.

Peter Lampack Agency, Inc

The Empire State Building, 350 Fifth Avenue, Suite 5300, New York, NY 10118

Tel: +1 (212) 687-9106
Fax: +1 (212) 687-9109
Email: andrew@peterlampackagency.com
Website: http://www.peterlampackagency.com

Handles: Fiction; Nonfiction; *Markets:* Adult; *Treatments:* Commercial; Literary; Mainstream

Specialises in commercial and literary fiction as well as nonfiction by recognised experts in a given field. Send query by email only, with cover letter, author bio, sample chapter, and 1-2 page synopsis. No children's books, horror, romance, westerns, science fiction or screenplays.

Laura Langlie, Literary Agent

147-149 Green Street, Hudson, NY 12534
Tel: +1 (518) 828-4708
Fax: +1 (518) 828-4787
Email: laura@lauralanglie.com

Handles: Fiction; Nonfiction; *Areas:* Autobiography; Biography; Crime; Culture; Current Affairs; Film; Historical; Humour; Legal; Literature; Mystery; Nature; Politics; Psychology; Suspense; Theatre; Thrillers; Women's Interests; *Markets:* Adult; Children's; Youth; *Treatments:* Literary; Mainstream

Send query by post with SASE, or by fax. No poetry, children's picture books, hardcore science fiction, men's adventure, how-to, or erotica. Simultaneous submissions accepted.

Larsen Pomada Literary Agents

1029 Jones Street, San Francisco, CA 94109-5023
Tel: +1 (415) 673-0939
Fax: +1 (415) 673-0367
Email: larsenpoma@aol.com
Website: http://www.larsenpomada.com

Handles: Fiction; Nonfiction; *Areas:* Anthropology; Architecture; Arts; Autobiography; Biography; Business; Cookery; Crime; Culture; Current Affairs; Design; Fantasy; Film; Finance; Health; Historical; How-to; Humour; Legal; Lifestyle; Medicine; Music; Mystery; Nature; New Age; Politics; Psychology; Religious; Romance; Science; Self-Help; Sociology; Sport; Suspense; Thrillers; Travel; Women's Interests; *Markets:* Adult; Children's; *Treatments:* Commercial; Literary; Mainstream; Satirical

Not accepting new clients as at August 2016. Check website for current status.

The Steve Laube Agency

5025 N. Central Ave., #635, Phoenix, AZ 85012-1502
Email: krichards@stevelaube.com
Website: http://www.stevelaube.com

Handles: Fiction; Nonfiction; *Areas:* Religious; *Markets:* Adult; Youth

Handles quality Christian fiction and nonfiction in all genres, except poetry, personal biographies, personal stories, end-times literature (either fiction or nonfiction), and children's picture books. Accepts submissions by post or by email. See website for extensive information on making submissions.

LaunchBooks Literary Agency

Tel: +1 (760) 944-9909
Email: david@launchbooks.com
Website: http://www.launchbooks.com

Handles: Fiction; Nonfiction; *Areas:* Adventure; Business; Culture; Current Affairs; Humour; Politics; Science; Sci-Fi; Sociology; Sport; Technology; Thrillers; *Markets:* Adult; *Treatments:* Contemporary; Mainstream; Popular

Handles nonfiction and fiction. Send query or proposal with one sample chapter and author bio by email.

Sarah Lazin Books

19 West 21st Street, Suite 501, New York, NY 10001
Tel: +1 (212) 989-5757
Fax: +1 (212) 989-1393
Email: slazin@lazinbooks.com
Website: http://lazinbooks.com

Handles: Fiction; Nonfiction; *Areas:* Autobiography; Biography; Culture; Current

Affairs; Historical; Music; Politics; *Markets:* Adult

Accepting queries via referral only. No queries by email.

Levine Greenberg Rostan Literary Agency

307 Seventh Ave., Suite 2407, New York, NY 10001
Tel: +1 (212) 337-0934
Fax: +1 (212) 337-0948
Email: submit@lgrliterary.com
Website: http://lgrliterary.com

Handles: Fiction; Nonfiction; *Areas:* Arts; Autobiography; Beauty and Fashion; Biography; Business; Cookery; Crafts; Crime; Culture; Finance; Gardening; Health; Historical; Hobbies; Humour; Leisure; Lifestyle; Mystery; Nature; New Age; Politics; Psychology; Religious; Romance; Science; Self-Help; Sociology; Spiritual; Sport; Suspense; Technology; Thrillers; Travel; Women's Interests; *Markets:* Adult; Children's; Youth; *Treatments:* Commercial; Literary; Mainstream; Popular

No queries by post. Send query using online form at website, or send email attaching no more than 50 pages. See website for detailed submission guidelines. No response to submissions by post.

Linda Chester & Associates

630 Fifth Avenue, Suite 2000, Rockefeller Center, New York, NY 10111
Tel: +1 (212) 218-3350
Email: submissions@lindachester.com
Website: http://www.lindachester.com

Handles: Fiction; Nonfiction; *Markets:* Adult; *Treatments:* Commercial; Literary

Send query by email only with short bio and first five pages pasted directly into the body of the email. Response within 4 weeks if interested only. No submissions by post.

Linda Roghaar Literary Agency, Inc.

133 High Point Drive, Amherst, MA 01002
Email: contact@lindaroghaar.com
Website: http://www.LindaRoghaar.com

Handles: Fiction; Nonfiction; *Areas:* Anthropology; Autobiography; Biography; Business; Crafts; Culture; Gardening; Health; Historical; Hobbies; How-to; Lifestyle; Music; Nature; Religious; Self-Help; Spiritual; Women's Interests; *Markets:* Adult

Send query by email (mentioning "query" in the subject line) or by post with SASE. For fiction, include the first five pages. Specialises in nonfiction. No romance, science fiction, fantasy, westerns, children's, young adult, or horror. Scripts handled through sub-agents.

Linn Prentis, Literary Agent

c/o Trodayne Northern, Acquisitions Director, for: Amy Hayden, Acquisitions, Linn Prentis Literary, 3 Inverness Drive, New Hartford, NY 13413
Tel: +1 (315) 790-5174
Email: ahayden@linnprentis.com
Website: http://www.linnprentis.com

Handles: Fiction; Nonfiction; *Areas:* Autobiography; Fantasy; Mystery; Sci-Fi; Women's Interests; *Markets:* Adult; Children's; Youth; *Treatments:* Contemporary; Literary; Mainstream

Not accepting submissions as at January 2017, but expects to resume shortly. See website for current status.

Send query by email or by post with SASE, including synopsis and first ten pages. No books for small children, or queries by fax or phone.

Lippincott Massie McQuilkin

27 West 20th Street, Suite 305, New York, NY 10011
Tel: +1 (212) 352-2055
Fax: +1 (212) 352-2059
Email: info@lmqlit.com
Website: http://www.lmqlit.com

Handles: Fiction; Nonfiction; *Areas:* Autobiography; Biography; Crime; Culture; Current Affairs; Fantasy; Health; Historical; Humour; Politics; Psychology; Science; Sociology; Sport; Suspense; Thrillers; Women's Interests; *Markets:* Adult;

Children's; Youth; *Treatments:* Commercial; Literary

See website for specific agent interests and contact details. Query only one agent at a time.

The Lisa Ekus Group, LLC

57 North Street, Hatfield, MA 01038
Tel: +1 (413) 247-9325
Email: info@lisaekus.com
Website: http://www.lisaekus.com

Handles: Nonfiction; *Areas:* Cookery; *Markets:* Adult

Send query with table of contents, summary of chapters, one complete sample chapter, author bio, explanation of concept, potential market, and potential competition. Handles cookery books only. See website for full submission guidelines.

Literary Management Group, Inc.

16970 San Carlos Boulevard, Suite 160-100, Ft Myers, FL 33908
Tel: +1 (615) 812-4445
Email: BruceBarbour@LiteraryManagementGroup.com
Website: http://literarymanagementgroup.com

Handles: Nonfiction; *Areas:* Biography; Business; Lifestyle; Religious; Spiritual; *Markets:* Adult

Handles Christian books (defined as books which are consistent with the historical, orthodox teachings of the Christian fathers). Handles adult nonfiction only. No children's or illustrated books, poetry, memoirs, YA Fiction or text/academic books. Download proposal from website then complete and send with sample chapters.

Literary & Creative Artists Inc.

3543 Albemarle Street NW, Washington, DC 20008-4213
Tel: +1 (202) 362-4688
Fax: +1 (202) 362-8875
Email: lca9643@lcadc.com
Website: http://www.lcadc.com

Handles: Fiction; Nonfiction; *Areas:* Arts; Autobiography; Biography; Business; Cookery; Crime; Current Affairs; Drama; Health; Historical; How-to; Legal; Lifestyle; Medicine; Nature; Philosophy; Politics; Religious; Spiritual; *Markets:* Adult

Send query by post with SASE, or by email without attachments. No poetry, academic / educational textbooks, or unsolicited MSS. Currently only accepts projects from established authors.

The Literary Group International

1357 Broadway, Suite 316, New York, NY 10018
Tel: +1 (212) 400-1494
Email: fweimann@theliterarygroup.com
Website: http://www.theliterarygroup.com

Handles: Fiction; Nonfiction; *Areas:* Adventure; Anthropology; Autobiography; Biography; Business; Crime; Culture; Fantasy; Historical; How-to; Humour; Lifestyle; Military; Music; Mystery; Psychology; Religious; Romance; Science; Self-Help; Sociology; Sport; Thrillers; Travel; Women's Interests; *Markets:* Adult; Youth; *Treatments:* Contemporary; Experimental; Literary

Send query by email only, with writing credentials, 2 page synopsis, and 50-page writing sample. Response only if interested. Asks for a 30-day exclusivity period, beginning from the date the material is received.

Julia Lord Literary Management

38 W. Ninth Street, New York, NY 10011
Tel: +1 (212) 995-2333
Fax: +1 (212) 995-2332
Email: query@julialordliterary.com
Website: http://julialordliterary.com

Handles: Fiction; Nonfiction; Reference; *Areas:* Adventure; Autobiography; Biography; Crafts; Crime; Current Affairs; Entertainment; Health; Historical; Hobbies; Humour; Lifestyle; Music; Mystery; Politics; Science; Self-Help; Sport; Technology;

Thrillers; Women's Interests; *Markets:* Adult; Youth

Send query by post or by email. If sending by email, include synopsis and first five pages in the body of the email. Responds only if interested and does not open or respond to emails with attachments.

If sending by post include synopsis, first five pages, and SASE for response. Responds to all postal submissions.

Lowenstein Associates, Inc.

115 East 23rd Street, 4th Floor, New York, NY 10010
Tel: +1 (212) 206-1630
Email: assistant@bookhaven.com
Website: http://www.lowensteinassociates.com

Handles: Fiction; Nonfiction; *Areas:* Autobiography; Business; Crime; Fantasy; Health; Lifestyle; Literature; Psychology; Science; Sci-Fi; Sociology; Spiritual; Thrillers; Women's Interests; *Markets:* Adult; *Treatments:* Commercial; Literary

Send query by email with one-page query letter and first ten pages pasted into the body of the email (fiction) or table of contents and (if available) proposal. See website for full guidelines. No Westerns, textbooks, children's picture books, or books in need of translation.

The Jennifer Lyons Literary Agency, LLC

151 West 19th Street 3rd floor, New York, NY 10011
Tel: +1 (212) 368-2812
Email: jenniferlyonsagency@gmail.com
Website: http://www.jenniferlyonsliteraryagency.com

Handles: Fiction; Nonfiction; *Areas:* Autobiography; Biography; Current Affairs; Finance; Historical; Science; Sport; Thrillers; *Markets:* Adult; Children's; Youth

See website for agent preferences and submission policies, plus specific email addresses.

Donald Maass Literary Agency

Suite 801, 121 West 27th Street, New York, NY 10001
Tel: +1 (212) 727-8383
Fax: +1 (212) 727-3271
Email: info@maassagency.com
Website: http://www.maassagency.com

Handles: Fiction; *Areas:* Crime; Fantasy; Historical; Horror; Humour; Mystery; Romance; Sci-Fi; Suspense; Westerns; Women's Interests; *Markets:* Adult; Youth; *Treatments:* Dark; Literary; Mainstream

Welcomes all genres, in particular science fiction, fantasy, mystery, suspense, horror, romance, historical, literary and mainstream novels. Send query to a specific agent, by email, with "query" in the subject line, or by post with SASE, with synopsis and first five pages. Prefers electronic approaches, but no attachments (include all material within the body of the email). No screenplays, poetry or picture books. See website for individual agent interests and email addresses.

MacGregor Literary

PO Box 1316, Manzanita, OR 97130
Tel: +1 (503) 389-4803
Email: chip@macgregorliterary.com
Website: http://www.macgregorliterary.com

Handles: Fiction; Nonfiction; *Areas:* Autobiography; Biography; Business; Crime; Culture; Current Affairs; Finance; Historical; How-to; Humour; Lifestyle; Mystery; Religious; Romance; Self-Help; Short Stories; Sport; Suspense; Thrillers; Women's Interests; *Markets:* Academic; Adult; *Treatments:* Contemporary; Mainstream

Handles work in a variety of genres, but all from a Christian perspective. Not accepting unpublished authors, except through conferences and referrals from current clients. Unsolicited MSS will not be returned, even if an SASE is provided.

Kirsten Manges Literary Agency, LLC

115 West 29th Street, 3rd Floor, New York, NY 10001

Email: kirsten@mangeslit.com
Website: http://www.mangeslit.com

Handles: Fiction; Nonfiction; *Areas:* Autobiography; Cookery; Culture; Health; Historical; Psychology; Science; Spiritual; Sport; Technology; Travel; Women's Interests; *Markets:* Adult; Youth; *Treatments:* Commercial; Literary

Particularly interested in women's issues. Most new clients by recommendation.

Manus & Associates Literary Agency, Inc.

425 Sherman Avenue, Suite 200, Palo Alto, CA 94306
Tel: +1 (650) 470-5151
Fax: +1 (650) 470-5159
Email: ManusLit@ManusLit.com
Website: http://www.ManusLit.com

Handles: Fiction; Nonfiction; *Areas:* Autobiography; Biography; Business; Culture; Current Affairs; Finance; Health; How-to; Lifestyle; Mystery; Nature; Psychology; Romance; Science; Self-Help; Suspense; Thrillers; Women's Interests; *Markets:* Adult; *Treatments:* Literary; Mainstream

Send query letter describing your project and giving pertinent biographical info only by fax or email, or send query letter by post with SASE and include complete proposal (nonfiction), or first 30 pages (fiction). When querying by email use one of the direct personal emails of a specific agent as given on the website, not the generic inbox shown on this page. Approach only one agent. No screenplays, academic, romance, science fiction, fantasy, western, young adult, children's, poetry, cookbooks, or magazine articles. See website for full guidelines.

Maria Carvainis Agency, Inc.

1270 Avenue of the Americas, Suite 2915, New York, NY 10020
Tel: +1 (212) 245-6365
Fax: +1 (212) 245-7196
Email: mca@mariacarvainisagency.com
Website: http://mariacarvainisagency.com

Handles: Fiction; Nonfiction; *Areas:* Adventure; Autobiography; Biography; Business; Crime; Culture; Finance; Historical; Horror; Humour; Mystery; Psychology; Romance; Science; Suspense; Technology; Thrillers; Women's Interests; *Markets:* Adult; Children's; Youth; *Treatments:* Commercial; Contemporary; Literary; Mainstream; Popular

Send query with synopsis, two sample chapters, and details of any previous writing credits, by post or by email. If sending by post and return of the material is required, include SASE; otherwise include email address for response, usually within 5-10 days. If submitting by email, all documents must be Word or PDF. No screenplays, children's picture books, science fiction, or poetry.

Marly Russoff & Associates

PO Box 524, Bronxville, NY 10708
Tel: +1 (914) 961-7939
Website: http://www.rusoffagency.com

Handles: Fiction; Nonfiction; *Markets:* Adult

Note: Note accepting submissions as at August 2015. Check website for current status.

Send 1-2 page query by post or email, with synopsis and relevant author info, plus word or page count and email address for response. All email queries must have the word "query" in the subject line.

Material is never returned so do not send return postage.

The Martell Agency

1350 Avenue of the Americas, Suite 1205, New York, NY 10019
Tel: +1 (212) 317-2672
Email: submissions@themartellagency.com
Website: http://www.themartellagency.com

Handles: Fiction; Nonfiction; *Areas:* Autobiography; Business; Finance; Health; Historical; Medicine; Mystery; Psychology; Self-Help; Suspense; Thrillers; Women's Interests; *Markets:* Adult; *Treatments:* Commercial

Send query by post or by email, including summary, short bio, any information, if appropriate, as to why you are qualified to write on the subject of your book, any publishing credits, the year of publication and the publisher. No original screenplays or poetry.

Martin Literary Management

Email: Sharlene@martinliterarymanagement.com
Website: http://www.martinliterarymanagement.com

Handles: Fiction; Nonfiction; *Areas:* Autobiography; Biography; Business; Crime; Culture; Current Affairs; Entertainment; Health; How-to; Lifestyle; Media; Religious; Self-Help; Women's Interests; *Markets:* Adult; Children's; Youth; *Treatments:* Commercial; Literary; Mainstream; Popular; Positive; Traditional

This agency has strong ties to film/TV. Interested in nonfiction that is highly commercial and that can be adapted to film. Please review our website carefully to make sure we're a good match for your work. How to contact: Completely electronic: emails and MS Word only. No attachments on queries. Place letter in body of email. See submission requirements on website. Do not send materials unless requested. We give very serious consideration to the material requested.

No adult fiction. Principal agent handles adult nonfiction only. See website for submission guidelines and separate email address for submissions of picture books, middle grade, and young adult fiction and nonfiction.

Margret McBride Literary Agency

PO Box 9128, La Jolla, CA 92037
Tel: +1 (858) 454-1550
Email: staff@mcbridelit.com
Website: http://www.mcbrideliterary.com

Handles: Fiction; Nonfiction; *Areas:* Autobiography; Biography; Business; Culture; Health; Historical; Humour; Legal; Medicine; Music; Sci-Fi; Self-Help; Suspense; Thrillers; Travel; Westerns; Women's Interests; *Markets:* Adult; Youth; *Treatments:* Commercial; Dark

Accepts submissions by email only. See website for full submission guidelines.

McIntosh & Otis, Inc

353 Lexington Avenue, New York, NY 10016
Tel: +1 (212) 687-7400
Fax: +1 (212) 687-6894
Email: info@mcintoshandotis.com
Website: http://www.mcintoshandotis.com

Handles: Fiction; Nonfiction; *Areas:* Adventure; Culture; Current Affairs; Fantasy; Historical; Horror; Humour; Music; Mystery; Nature; Psychology; Romance; Sci-Fi; Self-Help; Spiritual; Sport; Suspense; Thrillers; Travel; Women's Interests; *Markets:* Adult; Children's; Youth; *Treatments:* Commercial; Contemporary; Literary; Mainstream; Popular

Submissions by email only. See website for specific agent interests and email addresses, and query appropriate agent. No longer accepts submissions by post. See website for full details.

Meredith Bernstein Literary Agency, Inc.

2095 Broadway, Suite 505, New York, NY 10023
Tel: +1 (212) 799-1007
Fax: +1 (212) 799-1145
Email: mgoodbern@aol.com
Website: http://www.meredithbernsteinliteraryagency.com

Handles: Fiction; Nonfiction; *Areas:* Mystery; Romance; Thrillers; *Markets:* Adult; Youth; *Treatments:* Literary

An eclectic agency which does not specialise in any one particular area. Accepts queries by post with SASE, or via form on website. No poetry or screenplays. See website for full guidelines.

Martha Millard Literary Agency

50 West 67th Street #1G, New York, NY 10023
Tel: +1 (212) 662-1030
Email: marmillink@aol.com

Handles: Fiction; Nonfiction; *Areas:* Architecture; Arts; Autobiography; Biography; Business; Cookery; Crime; Culture; Current Affairs; Design; Fantasy; Film; Finance; Health; Historical; Horror; How-to; Lifestyle; Music; Mystery; New Age; Photography; Psychology; Romance; Sci-Fi; Self-Help; Short Stories; Suspense; Theatre; Thrillers; Women's Interests; *Markets:* Adult; Children's; Youth

No unsolicited queries or queries by fax or email. Authors wishing to approach this agency will need to be recommended to the agent by someone else in the profession.

Patricia Moosbrugger Literary Agency

Email: pm@pmagency.net
Website: http://www.pmagency.net

Handles: Fiction; Nonfiction; *Areas:* Literature; *Markets:* Adult; Youth

Accepts submissions of adult fiction and nonfiction and young adult literature. No science fiction, fantasy or category romance. Send query by email with brief synopsis.

Howard Morhaim Literary Agency

30 Pierrepont Street, Brooklyn, NY 11201
Tel: +1 (718) 222-8400
Fax: +1 (718) 222-5056
Email: kmckean@morhaimliterary.com
Website: http://morhaimliterary.com

Handles: Fiction; Nonfiction; *Areas:* Autobiography; Biography; Business; Cookery; Crafts; Culture; Design; Fantasy; Finance; Health; Historical; Horror; Humour; Romance; Sci-Fi; Sport; Thrillers; Women's Interests; *Markets:* Adult; Children's; Youth; *Treatments:* Contemporary; Literary

Enthusiastically accept unsolicited submissions. Send query by email only with outline / proposal for nonfiction, or three sample chapters for fiction. Attachments are accepted. See website for specific agent interests and contact details.

Nappaland Literary Agency

PO Box 1674, Loveland, CO 80539-1674
Fax: +1 (970) 635-9869
Email: Literary@nappaland.com
Website: http://www.nappaland.com/literary

Handles: Fiction; Nonfiction; *Areas:* Culture; Historical; Humour; Lifestyle; Religious; Suspense; Women's Interests; *Markets:* Adult; Youth; *Treatments:* Literary; Popular

Deliberately small boutique-sized agency. Send query letter only by email during specific submission windows (see website). No children's books, memoirs, screenplays, poetry, or anything about cats.

Nelson Literary Agency, LLC

1732 Wazee Street, Suite 207, Denver, CO 80202
Tel: +1 (303) 292-2805
Email: querykristin@nelsonagency.com
Website: http://www.nelsonagency.com

Handles: Fiction; *Areas:* Fantasy; Historical; Romance; Sci-Fi; Women's Interests; *Markets:* Adult; Children's; Youth; *Treatments:* Commercial; Literary; Mainstream

Handles young adult, upper-level middle grade, "big crossover novels with one foot squarely in genre", literary commercial novels, upmarket women's fiction, single-title romances (especially historicals), and lead title or hardcover science fiction and fantasy. No nonfiction, screenplays, short story collections, poetry, children's picture books or chapter books, or material for the Christian/inspirational market. No queries by post, phone, in person, or through Facebook. No email attachments. See website for full submission guidelines.

New Leaf Literary & Media, Inc.

110 West 40th Street, Suite 410, New York, NY 10018
Tel: +1 (646) 248-7989
Fax: +1 (646) 861-4654
Email: query@newleafliterary.com
Website: http://www.newleafliterary.com

Handles: Fiction; Nonfiction; *Areas:* Culture; Entertainment; Erotic; Fantasy; Historical; Romance; Sci-Fi; Technology; Thrillers; Women's Interests; *Markets:* Adult; Children's; Youth; *Treatments:* Mainstream

Send query by email only, with the word "Query" along with the specific agent's name in the subject line. Do not query more than one agent. Include up to five double-spaced sample pages in the body of the email -- no attachments. Response only if interested.

Niad Management

15021 Ventura Blvd. #860, Sherman Oaks, CA 91403
Tel: +1 (818) 774-0051
Fax: +1 (818) 774-1740
Email: queries@niadmanagement.com
Website: http://www.niadmanagement.com

Handles: Fiction; Nonfiction; Scripts; *Areas:* Adventure; Autobiography; Biography; Crime; Culture; Drama; Film; Humour; Mystery; Romance; Sport; Suspense; Theatre; Thrillers; TV; *Markets:* Adult; Youth; *Treatments:* Contemporary; Literary; Mainstream

Manages mainly Hollywood writers, actors, and directors, although does also handle a very small number of books. Send query by email or by post with SASE. Responds only if interested.

Northern Lights Literary Services

762 State Road 458, Bedford, IN 47421
Email: queries@northernlightsls.com
Website: http://www.northernlightsls.com

Handles: Fiction; Nonfiction; *Areas:* Biography; Business; Health; Historical; How-to; Lifestyle; Medicine; Mystery; New Age; Psychology; Romance; Self-Help; Suspense; Women's Interests; *Markets:* Adult

Our goal is to provide personalized service to clients and create a bond that will endure throughout your career. We seriously consider each query we receive and will accept hardworking new authors who are willing to develop their talents and skills.

Encourages email queries but responds only if interested (within 5 working days). No horror or books for children.

Paradigm Talent and Literary Agency

360 Park Avenue South, 16th Floor, New York, NY 10010
Tel: +1 (212) 897-6400
Fax: +1 (212) 764-8941
Email: books@paradigmagency.com
Website: http://www.paradigmagency.com

Handles: Scripts; *Areas:* Film; Theatre; TV; *Markets:* Adult

Talent agency with offices in Los Angeles, New York City, Monterey, California and Nashville, Tennessee, representing actors, musical artists, directors, writers and producers. No unsolicited approaches unless by referral or through meeting an agent at an event.

The Park Literary Group LLC

270 Lafayette Street, Suite 1504, New York, NY 10012
Tel: +1 (212) 691-3500
Fax: +1 (212) 691-3540
Email: queries@parkliterary.com
Website: http://www.parkliterary.com

Handles: Fiction; Nonfiction; *Areas:* Adventure; Arts; Autobiography; Culture; Current Affairs; Historical; Politics; Science; Women's Interests; *Markets:* Adult; *Treatments:* Commercial; Literary

Send query by email only, with all materials in the body of the email (no attachments). See website for individual agent details and query one specific agent with their first and last name in the subject line of your email.

See website for full guidelines. No poetry or screenplays.

Pavilion Literary Management

660 Massachusetts Avenue, Suite 4, Boston, MA 02118
Tel: +1 (617) 792-5218
Email: jeff@pavilionliterary.com
Website: http://www.pavilionliterary.com

Handles: Fiction; Nonfiction; *Areas:* Adventure; Autobiography; Fantasy; Historical; Mystery; Science; Thrillers; *Markets:* Adult; Children's; Youth; *Treatments:* Popular

Only accepting approaches for fiction work by previously published authors or client referral. Send query by email specifying fiction or nonfiction and title of work in the subject line. No attachments. See website for full details.

Peregrine Whittlesey Agency

279 Central Park West, New York, NY 10024
Tel: +1 (212) 787-1802
Fax: +1 (212) 787-4985
Email: pwwagy@aol.com

Handles: Scripts; *Areas:* Film; Theatre; TV; *Markets:* Adult

Handles mainly theatre scripts, plus a small number of film/TV scripts by playwrights who also write for screen. Send query with SASE. No simultaneous submissions.

Pippin Properties, Inc

110 West 40th Street, Suite 1704, New York, NY 10016
Tel: +1 (212) 338-9310
Fax: +1 (212) 338-9579
Email: info@pippinproperties.com
Website: http://www.pippinproperties.com

Handles: Fiction; *Markets:* Adult; Children's; Youth

Devoted primarily to picture books, middle-grade, and young adult novels, but also represents adult projects on occasion. Send query by email with synopsis, first chapter, or entire picture book manuscript in the body of your email. No attachments. See website for full guidelines.

Prospect Agency

551 Valley Rd., PMB 377, Upper Montclair, NJ 07043
Tel: +1 (718) 788-3217
Fax: +1 (718) 360-9582
Email: esk@prospectagency.com
Website: http://www.prospectagency.com

Handles: Fiction; Nonfiction; *Areas:* Adventure; Autobiography; Crime; Erotic; Fantasy; Mystery; Romance; Science; Sci-Fi; Suspense; Thrillers; Westerns; Women's Interests; *Markets:* Adult; Children's; Youth; *Treatments:* Contemporary; Literary; Mainstream

Handles very little nonfiction. Specialises in romance, women's fiction, literary fiction, young adult/children's literature, and science fiction. Send submissions via website submission system **only** (no email queries – **email queries are not accepted or responded to** – or queries by post (these will be recycled). No poetry, short stories, text books, screenplays, or most nonfiction.

Queen Literary Agency, Inc.

30 East 60th Street, Suite 1004, New York, NY 10024
Tel: +1 (212) 974-8333
Fax: +1 (212) 974-8347
Email: submissions@queenliterary.com
Website: http://www.queenliterary.com

Handles: Fiction; Nonfiction; *Areas:* Business; Cookery; Historical; Mystery; Psychology; Science; Sport; Thrillers; *Markets:* Adult; *Treatments:* Commercial; Literary

Founded by a former publishing executive, most recently head of IMG WORLDWIDE'S literary division. Handles a wide range of nonfiction titles, with a particular interest in business books, food writing, science and popular psychology, as well as books by well-known chefs, radio and television personalities and sports figures. Also handles commercial and literary fiction, including historical fiction, mysteries, and thrillers.

Lynne Rabinoff Agency

72-11 Austin Street, No. 201, Forest Hills, NY 11375
Tel: +1 (718) 459-6894
Email: lynne@lynnerabinoff.com

Handles: Nonfiction; *Areas:* Anthropology; Archaeology; Autobiography; Biography; Business; Culture; Current Affairs; Finance; Historical; Legal; Military; Politics; Psychology; Religious; Science; Technology; Women's Interests; *Markets:* Adult

Particularly interested in politics, history, current affairs, and religion. Send query by email or by post with SASE, including proposal, sample chapter, and author bio. No queries by fax.

Raines & Raines

103 Kenyon Road, Medusa, NY 12120
Tel: +1 (518) 239-8311
Fax: +1 (518) 239-6029

Handles: Fiction; Nonfiction; *Areas:* Adventure; Autobiography; Biography; Crime; Fantasy; Finance; Historical; Military; Mystery; Psychology; Sci-Fi; Suspense; Thrillers; Westerns; *Markets:* Adult

Handles nonfiction in all areas, and fiction in the areas specified above. Send query with SASE.

Rebecca Friedman Literary Agency

Email: brandie@rfliterary.com
Website: http://rfliterary.com

Handles: Fiction; Nonfiction; *Areas:* Autobiography; Fantasy; Mystery; Romance; Sci-Fi; Suspense; Thrillers; Women's Interests; *Markets:* Adult; Youth; *Treatments:* Commercial; Contemporary; Literary

See website for full submission guidelines and specific agent interests and contact details. Aims to respond in 6-8 weeks, but may take longer.

Rees Literary Agency

14 Beacon St., Suite 710, Boston, MA 02108
Tel: +1 (617) 227-9014
Fax: +1 (617) 227-8762
Email: reesagency@reesagency.com
Website: http://www.reesagency.com

Handles: Fiction; *Areas:* Autobiography; Biography; Business; Historical; Military; Mystery; Psychology; Romance; Science; Self-Help; Suspense; Thrillers; Women's Interests; *Markets:* Adult; Children's; Youth; *Treatments:* Commercial; Literary

See website for specific agents' interests and submission requirements.

Renee Zuckerbrot Literary Agency

115 West 29th Street, 10th floor, New York, NY 10001
Tel: +1 (212) 967-0072
Fax: +1 (212) 967-0073
Email: Submissions@rzagency.com
Website: http://rzagency.com

Handles: Fiction; Nonfiction; *Areas:* Culture; Historical; Literature; Mystery; Science; Short Stories; Thrillers; Women's Interests; *Markets:* Adult; *Treatments:* Commercial; Literary; Popular

Send query by email only, with synopsis, publication history, brief bio, contact information, and excerpt (up to three sample chapters) as a Word document attachment (for novels, should be the first three chapters). See website for full details. No screenplays.

The Amy Rennert Agency, Inc.

1550 Tiburon Boulevard #302, Tiburon, CA 94920
Email: queries@amyrennert.com
Website: http://www.amyrennert.com

Handles: Fiction; Nonfiction; *Areas:* Autobiography; Biography; Business; Finance; Health; Historical; Lifestyle; Literature; Mystery; Spiritual; Sport; *Markets:* Adult; *Treatments:* Literary

Not accepting unsolicited mss, but referrals still welcome. Send query by email, with cover letter in body of email and a Word file attachment containing proposal and first chapter (nonfiction) or first 10-20 pages (fiction). For picture books, send cover letter in the body of the email and attach file with the text. Include phone number. Response only if interested.

Rita Rosenkranz Literary Agency

440 West End Ave, Suite 15D, New York, NY 10024
Tel: +1 (212) 873-6333
Email: rrosenkranz@mindspring.com
Website: http://www.ritarosenkranzliteraryagency.com

Handles: Nonfiction; Reference; *Areas:* Cookery; Health; Historical; How-to; Humour; Lifestyle; Music; Science; Spiritual; *Markets:* Adult; *Treatments:* Commercial; Niche; Popular

Send query only by post or email. Submit proposal on request only. Deals specifically in adult nonfiction. No screenplays, poetry, fiction, children's or YA books. Response within two weeks.

Riverside Literary Agency

41 Simon Keets Road, Leyden, MA 01337
Tel: +1 (413) 772-0067
Fax: +1 (413) 772-0969
Email: rivlit@sover.net

Handles: Fiction; Nonfiction; *Markets:* Adult

Send query with outline by email. Usually obtains new clients by referral.

RLR Associates

Literary Department, 7 West 51st Street, New York, NY 10019
Tel: +1 (212) 541-8641
Email: website.info@rlrassociates.net
Website: http://www.rlrliterary.net

Handles: Fiction; Nonfiction; *Areas:* Biography; Culture; Historical; Humour; Romance; Sport; Women's Interests; *Markets:* Adult; Children's; Youth; *Treatments:* Commercial; Literary; Mainstream; Popular

Represents literary and commercial fiction, genre fiction, and narrative nonfiction. Particularly interested in history, pop culture, humour, food and beverage, biography, and sports. Also represents all types of children's literature. Send query or proposal by post or by email. For fiction, include writing sample (normally the first few chapters). If no response after three months, assume rejection.

Robin Straus Agency, Inc.

229 East 79th Street, Suite 5A, New York, NY 10075
Tel: +1 (212) 472-3282
Fax: +1 (212) 472-3833
Email: info@robinstrausagency.com
Website: http://www.robinstrausagency.com

Handles: Fiction; Nonfiction; *Areas:* Autobiography; Biography; Cookery; Culture; Current Affairs; Historical; Lifestyle; Nature; Psychology; Science; Women's Interests; *Markets:* Adult; *Treatments:* Commercial; Literary

Prefers submissions by email. Send query with bio, synopsis or outline, submission history, and market information. You may also include the opening chapter. All material must be in the body of the email. No attachments. Approaches by post are accepted, but no response without SASE. No juvenile, young adult, science fiction/fantasy, horror, romance, westerns, poetry or screenplays. No metered postage. If no response after 6 weeks, assume rejection.

Andy Ross Agency

767 Santa Ray Avenue, Oakland, CA 94610
Tel: +1 (510) 238-8965
Email: andyrossagency@hotmail.com
Website: http://www.andyrossagency.com

Handles: Fiction; Nonfiction; *Areas:* Culture; Current Affairs; Historical; Religious; Science; *Markets:* Adult; Children's; Youth; *Treatments:* Commercial; Contemporary; Literary

We encourage queries for material in our fields of interest. No poetry, short stories, adult romance, science fiction and fantasy, adult and teen paranormal, or film scripts.

The agent has worked in the book business for 36 years, all of his working life. He was owner and general manager of Cody's Books in Berkeley, California from 1977-2006. Cody's has been recognised as one of America's great independent book stores.

During this period, the agent was the primary trade book buyer. This experience has given him a unique understanding of the retail book market, of publishing trends and, most importantly and uniquely, the hand selling of books to book buyers.

The agent is past president of the Northern California Booksellers Association, a board member and officer of the American Booksellers Association and a national spokesperson for issues concerning independent businesses. He has had significant profiles in the Wall Street Journal, Time Magazine, and the San Francisco Chronicle.

Queries by email only. See website for full guidelines.

Ross Yoon Agency

1666 Connecticut Avenue, NW, Suite 500, Washington, DC 20009
Tel: +1 (202) 328-3282
Email: submissions@rossyoon.com
Website: http://www.rossyoon.com

Handles: Nonfiction; *Areas:* Autobiography; Biography; Business; Culture; Current Affairs; Historical; Psychology; Science; *Markets:* Adult; *Treatments:* Commercial; Popular; Serious

Handles adult nonfiction only. Send query or complete book proposal by email only with proposal in body of email or as .doc or .docx attachment. No unsolicited MSS or approaches by post or phone. See website for full guidelines.

The Rudy Agency

825 Wildlife Lane, Estes Park, CO 80517
Tel: +1 (970) 577-8500
Fax: +1 (970) 577-8600
Email: mak@rudyagency.com
Website: http://www.rudyagency.com

Handles: Fiction; Nonfiction; *Areas:* Autobiography; Biography; Business; Culture; Current Affairs; Health; Historical; Lifestyle; Medicine; Military; Politics; Science; Technology; Thrillers; *Markets:* Adult; Children's

Concentrates on adult nonfiction in the areas listed above. In fiction, accepts only historical fiction and thrillers. See website for full guidelines, and appropriate email addresses for different types of submissions.

Marly Rusoff & Associates, Inc.

PO Box 524, Bronxville, NY 10708
Tel: +1 (914) 961-7939
Email: mra_queries3@rusoffagency.com
Website: http://www.rusoffagency.com

Handles: Fiction; Nonfiction; *Areas:* Architecture; Arts; Autobiography; Biography; Business; Culture; Design; Finance; Health; Historical; Medicine; Psychology; *Markets:* Adult; *Treatments:* Commercial; Literary

Note: Not accepting new clients as at January 2016. See website for current status

Send 1-2 page query by post or email, including synopsis and relevant author info and page or word count. Queries sent by email should include the word "query" in the subject line. Changes email address regularly to avoid spam, so check website before querying and notify firstwriter.com via the "Report an Error" button if address has changed from that displayed. May not respond if not interested. No PDFs, CDs, or directions to view material on websites.

The Sagalyn Literary Agency

2 Wisconsin Circle, Suite 650, Chevy Chase, MD 20815
Email: query@sagalyn.com
Website: http://www.sagalyn.com

Handles: Fiction; Nonfiction; *Areas:* Biography; Business; Culture; Finance; Historical; Science; Technology; *Markets:* Adult; *Treatments:* Mainstream

Specialises in quality nonfiction and mainstream fiction. No romance, westerns, science fiction, poetry, children's books, or screenplays. Query by email only, but no attachments. Visit website for details on submissions.

Salkind Literary Agency

62 Nassau Drive, Great Neck, NY 11021
Tel: +1 (785) 371-0101
Fax: +1 (516) 706-2369
Email: neil@studiob.com
Website: http://www.salkindagency.com

Handles: Fiction; Nonfiction; *Areas:* Adventure; Arts; Autobiography; Biography; Business; Cookery; Crafts; Crime; Culture; Current Affairs; Design; Fantasy; Finance; Health; Historical; How-to; Humour; Lifestyle; Mystery; Photography; Politics; Psychology; Religious; Science; Sci-Fi; Self-Help; Spiritual; Suspense; Technology; Thrillers; Travel; Women's Interests; *Markets:* Academic; Adult; *Treatments:* Commercial

Handles general nonfiction trade, fiction, and textbook authors. Query by email or telephone.

Sandra Dijkstra Literary Agency

PMB 515, 1155 Camino Del Mar, Del Mar, CA 92014
Tel: +1 (858) 755-3115
Fax: +1 (858) 794-2822
Email: queries@dijkstraagency.com
Website: http://www.dijkstraagency.com

Handles: Fiction; Nonfiction; *Areas:* Autobiography; Biography; Business; Cookery; Culture; Current Affairs; Design; Fantasy; Health; Historical; Humour; Lifestyle; Music; Mystery; Nature; Politics; Religious; Romance; Science; Sci-Fi; Self-Help; Short Stories; Sociology; Sport; Suspense; Thrillers; Travel; Women's Interests; *Markets:* Adult; Children's; Youth; *Treatments:* Commercial; Contemporary; Literary

Check author bios on website and submit query by email to one agent only. For fiction, include a one-page synopsis, brief bio, and first 10-15 pages. For nonfiction, include overview, chapter outline, brief bio, and first 10-15 pages. All material must be in the body of the email. No attachments. See website for full submission guidelines.

Sanford J. Greenburger Associates, Inc.

15th Floor, 55 Fifth Avenue, New York, NY 10003
Tel: +1 (212) 206-5600
Fax: +1 (212) 463-8718
Email: queryHL@sjga.com
Website: http://www.greenburger.com

Handles: Fiction; Nonfiction; Reference; *Areas:* Arts; Autobiography; Biography; Business; Entertainment; Fantasy; Health; Historical; Humour; Lifestyle; Music; Mystery; Nature; Politics; Psychology; Romance; Science; Sci-Fi; Self-Help; Sociology; Sport; Thrillers; Women's Interests; *Markets:* Adult; Children's; Youth; *Treatments:* Commercial; Literary; Popular

Check website for specific agent interests, guidelines, and contact details. Most will not accept submissions by post. Aims to respond to queries within 6-8 weeks.

Susan Schulman, A Literary Agency

454 West 44th Street, New York, NY 10036
Tel: +1 (212) 713-1633
Fax: +1 (212) 581-8830
Email: queries@schulmanagency.com
Website: http://schulmanagency.com

Handles: Fiction; Nonfiction; Scripts; *Areas:* Adventure; Anthropology; Archaeology; Arts; Autobiography; Biography; Business; Cookery; Crafts; Crime; Culture; Current Affairs; Entertainment; Film; Finance; Health; Historical; Hobbies; How-to; Humour; Legal; Lifestyle; Literature; Medicine; Music; Mystery; Nature; Photography; Politics; Psychology; Religious; Science; Self-Help; Sociology; Spiritual; Sport; Suspense; Technology; Theatre; Thrillers; Travel; Women's Interests; *Markets:* Adult; Children's; Youth; *Treatments:* Commercial; Literary; Mainstream

Send query with synopsis by email in the body of the email or by post with SASE.

Include author resume and outline. For fiction, include three sample chapters. For nonfiction, include at least one. No poetry, TV scripts, concepts for TV, email attachments, submissions via UPS or FedEx, or unsolicited MSS.

Scott Treimel NY

434 Lafayette Street, New York, NY 10003
Tel: +1 (212) 505-8353
Email: general@scotttreimelny.com
Website: http://www.scotttreimelny.com

Handles: Fiction; Nonfiction; *Markets:* Children's; Youth

Children's books only – from concept / board books to teen fiction. Accepts submissions only from published authors, or by referral from contacts, or from attendees at conferences.

Scovil Galen Ghosh Literary Agency, Inc.

276 Fifth Avenue, Suite 708, New York, NY 10001
Tel: +1 (212) 679-8686
Fax: +1 (212) 679-6710
Email: info@sgglit.com
Website: http://www.sgglit.com

Handles: Fiction; Nonfiction; *Areas:* Adventure; Arts; Autobiography; Biography; Business; Cookery; Culture; Health; Historical; Nature; Politics; Psychology; Religious; Science; Sociology; Sport; Women's Interests; *Markets:* Adult; Children's; Youth; *Treatments:* Commercial; Contemporary; Literary

Send query letter only in first instance. Prefers contact by email, but no attachments. If contacting by post include letter only, with email address for response rather than an SASE.

Scribe Agency LLC

5508 Joylynne Drive, Madison, WI 53716
Tel: +1 (608) 259-0491
Email: submissions@scribeagency.com
Website: http://www.scribeagency.com

Handles: Fiction; *Areas:* Fantasy; Literature; Sci-Fi; Short Stories; *Markets:* Adult; *Treatments:* Commercial; Literary; Mainstream

Handles science fiction, fantasy, and literary fiction. No nonfiction, humour, cozy mysteries, faith-based fiction, screenplays, poetry, or works based on another's ideas. Send query in body of email, with synopsis and first three chapters as Word docs, RTFs, or PDFs. No hard copy approaches. If unable to submit material electronically, send email query in first instance.

Secret Agent Man

PO Box 1078, Lake Forest, CA 92609-1078
Tel: +1 (949) 698-6987
Email: query@secretagentman.net
Website: http://www.secretagentman.net

Handles: Fiction; Nonfiction; *Areas:* Crime; Mystery; Religious; Suspense; Thrillers; Westerns; *Markets:* Adult

Send query by email only (no postal submissions) with the word "Query" in the subject line, sample consecutive chapter(s), synopsis and/or outline. No first contact by phone. Not interested in vampire; sci-fi; fantasy; horror; cold war, military or political thrillers; children's or young adult; short stories; screenplays; poetry collections; romance; or historical. Christian nonfiction should be based on Biblical theology, not speculative. No self-published works.

Lynn Seligman, Literary Agent

400 Highland Avenue, Upper Montclair, NJ 07043
Tel: +1 (973) 783-3631

Handles: Fiction; Nonfiction; *Areas:* Anthropology; Arts; Biography; Business; Cookery; Crime; Culture; Current Affairs; Design; Fantasy; Film; Finance; Health; Historical; Horror; How-to; Humour; Lifestyle; Music; Mystery; Nature; Photography; Politics; Psychology; Romance; Science; Sci-Fi; Self-Help; Sociology; Women's Interests; *Markets:* Adult; *Treatments:* Contemporary; Literary; Mainstream

Send query with SASE.

Denise Shannon Literary Agency, Inc.

20 West 22nd Street, Suite 1603, New York, NY 10010
Tel: +1 (212) 414-2911
Fax: +1 (212) 414-2930
Email: submissions@deniseshannonagency.com
Website: http://deniseshannonagency.com

Handles: Fiction; Nonfiction; *Areas:* Autobiography; Biography; Business; Current Affairs; Health; Historical; Politics; Sociology; *Markets:* Adult; *Treatments:* Literary

Send query by email, or by post with SASE, including outline and bio listing any previous publishing credits. Notify if simultaneous submission. No unsolicited MSS, or queries for incomplete fiction MSS.

Sheree Bykofsky Associates, Inc.

4326 Harbor Beach Boulevard, PO Box 706, Brigantine, NJ 08203
Email: submitbee@aol.com
Website: http://www.shereebee.com

Handles: Fiction; Nonfiction; Reference; *Areas:* Biography; Business; Cookery; Culture; Current Affairs; Film; Hobbies; Humour; Lifestyle; Mystery; Psychology; Self-Help; Spiritual; Women's Interests; *Markets:* Adult; *Treatments:* Commercial; Literary

Send query by email only. Include one page query, and for fiction a one page synopsis, and first page of manuscript, all in the body of the email. No attachments. Always looking for a bestseller in any category, but generally not interested in poetry, thrillers, westerns, romances, occult, science fiction, fantasy, children's or young adult.

Signature Literary Agency

4200 Wisconsin Ave, NW #106-233, Washington, DC 20016
Email: gary@signaturelit.com
Website: http://www.signaturelit.com

Handles: Fiction; Nonfiction; Reference; *Areas:* Autobiography; Biography; Criticism; Culture; Fantasy; Health; Historical; Mystery; Politics; Psychology; Religious; Romance; Science; Sci-Fi; Spiritual; Technology; *Markets:* Adult; *Treatments:* Commercial; Literary

Agency established in Washington DC. The principal agent formerly worked at the Graybill and English Literary Agency. She has a law degree from George Washington University and extensive editorial experience.

Send query by email to specific agent (see website for individual contact details and "wishlists").

Offices in both New York and Washington DC.

SLW Literary Agency

4100 Ridgeland Avenue, Northbrook, IL 60062
Tel: +1 (847) 207-2075
Email: shariwenk@swenkagency.com

Handles: Nonfiction; *Areas:* Sport; *Markets:* Adult

Handles sports celebrities and sports writers only.

Solow Literary Enterprises, Inc.

769 Center Blvd., #148, Fairfax, CA 94930
Email: info@solowliterary.com
Website: http://www.solowliterary.com

Handles: Nonfiction; *Areas:* Autobiography; Business; Culture; Finance; Health; Historical; Nature; Psychology; Science; *Markets:* Adult

Handles nonfiction in the stated areas only. Send single-page query by email or by post with SASE, providing information on what your book is about; why you think it has to be written; and why you are the best person to write it. Response only if interested.

Spectrum Literary Agency

320 Central Park West, Suite 1-D, New York, NY 10025
Tel: +1 (212) 362-4323

Fax: +1 (212) 362-4562
Email: ruddigore1@aol.com
Website: http://www.spectrumliteraryagency.com

Handles: Fiction; Nonfiction; *Areas:* Fantasy; Historical; Mystery; Romance; Sci-Fi; Suspense; *Markets:* Adult; *Treatments:* Contemporary; Mainstream

Send query with SASE describing your book and providing background information, publishing credits, and relevant qualifications. The first 10 pages of the work may also be included. Response within three months. No unsolicited MSS or queries by fax, email, or phone.

Spencerhill Associates

8131 Lakewood Main Street, #205, Lakewood Ranch, FL 34202
Tel: +1 (941) 907-3700
Email: submission@spencerhillassociates.com
Website: http://spencerhillassociates.com

Handles: Fiction; Nonfiction; *Areas:* Erotic; Fantasy; Historical; Mystery; Romance; Thrillers; *Markets:* Adult; Youth; *Treatments:* Commercial; Literary

Handles commercial, general-interest fiction, romance including historical romance, paranormal romance, urban fantasy, erotic fiction, category romance, literary fiction, thrillers and mysteries, young adult, and nonfiction. No children's. Send query by email with synopsis and first three chapters attached in .doc / .rtf / .txt format. See website for full details.

The Spieler Agency

27 West 20th Street, Suite 305, New York, NY 10011
Tel: +1 (212) 757-4439, ext.1
Fax: +1 (212) 333-2019
Email: joe@TheSpielerAgency.com
Website: http://thespieleragency.com

Handles: Fiction; Nonfiction; Poetry; *Areas:* Architecture; Autobiography; Biography; Business; Cookery; Crime; Culture; Current Affairs; Film; Finance; Gardening; Health; Historical; Humour; Legal; Lifestyle; Music; Mystery; Nature; Photography; Politics; Science; Sociology; Spiritual; Theatre; Thrillers; Travel; Women's Interests; *Markets:* Adult; Children's; Youth; *Treatments:* Literary; Popular

Consult website for details of specific agents' interests and contact details. Send query by email or by post with SASE. Response not guaranteed if not interested. No response to postal submissions without SASE.

Philip G. Spitzer Literary Agency, Inc.

50 Talmage Farm Lane, East Hampton, NY 11937
Tel: +1 (631) 329-3650
Fax: +1 (631) 329-3651
Email: kim.lombardini@spitzeragency.com
Website: http://spitzeragency.com

Handles: Fiction; Nonfiction; *Areas:* Biography; Current Affairs; Fantasy; Historical; Mystery; Politics; Sci-Fi; Short Stories; Sport; Suspense; Thrillers; Travel; *Markets:* Adult; Children's; *Treatments:* Literary

Full client list, but will consider queries by email with proposal and first chapter. No telephone calls.

Sterling Lord Literistic, Inc.

115 Broadway, New York, NY 10006
Tel: +1 (212) 780-6050
Fax: +1 (212) 780-6095
Email: info@sll.com
Website: http://www.sll.com

Handles: Fiction; Nonfiction; *Areas:* Autobiography; Beauty and Fashion; Biography; Business; Cookery; Culture; Current Affairs; Health; Historical; Lifestyle; Nature; Politics; Science; Self-Help; Technology; Travel; Women's Interests; *Markets:* Adult; Children's; Youth; *Treatments:* Commercial; Literary; Popular

Send query with SASE, synopsis, brief author bio, and first three chapters. Literary value considered above all else. No response to unsolicited email queries.

Sternig & Byrne Literary Agency

2370 S. 107th Street, Apt 4, Milwaukee, Wisconsin 53227-2036
Tel: +1 (414) 328-8034
Fax: +1 (414) 328-8034
Email: jackbyrne@hotmail.com
Website: http://sff.net/people/jackbyrne

Handles: Fiction; Nonfiction; *Areas:* Fantasy; Horror; Mystery; Sci-Fi; Suspense; *Markets:* Adult; Youth

Send brief query by post or email in first instance (if sending by email send in the body of the mail, do not send attachments). Will request further materials if interested. Currently only considering science fiction, fantasy, and mysteries. Preference given to writers with a publishing history.

Stone Manners Salners Agency

6100 Wilshire Boulevard, Suite 1400, Los Angeles, CA 90048
Tel: +1 (323) 655-1313 / +1 (212) 505-1400
Email: info@smsagency.com
Website: http://www.smsagency.com

Handles: Scripts; *Areas:* Film; TV; *Markets:* Adult

Handles movie and TV scripts. Send query by email or post with SASE. No queries by fax.

Stonesong

270 West 39th Street #201, New York, NY 10018
Tel: +1 (212) 929-4600
Email: submissions@stonesong.com
Website: http://stonesong.com

Handles: Fiction; Nonfiction; *Areas:* Autobiography; Beauty and Fashion; Business; Cookery; Crafts; Culture; Current Affairs; Design; Finance; Health; Lifestyle; Psychology; Science; Self-Help; *Markets:* Adult; Children's; Youth; *Treatments:* Commercial; Literary

Send query by email with the word "Query" in the subject line, and the first chapter or 10 pages pasted into the body of the email. See website for specific agent interests and approach one agent only. No plays, screenplays, or poetry. Also offers self-publishing services.

The Strothman Agency

63 East 9th Street, 10X, New York, NY 10003
Email: strothmanagency@gmail.com
Website: http://www.strothmanagency.com

Handles: Fiction; Nonfiction; *Areas:* Business; Current Affairs; Finance; Historical; Nature; Science; *Markets:* Adult; Children's; Youth

Send query by email only. Postal approaches will be recycled or returned unread. Include query, details about yourself, a synopsis, and (for fiction) 2-10 sample pages. All material must be in the body of the email – no attachments. No romance, science fiction, picture books, or poetry.

Stuart Krichevsky Literary Agency, Inc.

6 East 39th Street, Suite 500, New York, NY 10016
Tel: +1 (212) 725-5288
Fax: +1 (212) 725-5275
Email: query@skagency.com
Website: http://www.skagency.com

Handles: Fiction; Nonfiction; *Areas:* Adventure; Autobiography; Biography; Business; Culture; Current Affairs; Fantasy; Historical; Nature; Politics; Science; Sci-Fi; Technology; *Markets:* Adult; Youth; *Treatments:* Commercial; Literary

Send query by email with first few pages of your manuscript (up to 10) pasted into body of the email (no attachments). See website for complete submission guidelines and appropriate submission addresses for each agent.

The Stuart Agency

260 West 52 Street, Suite #25C, New York, NY 10019
Tel: +1 (212) 586-2711
Email: andrew@stuartagency.com
Website: http://www.stuartagency.com

Handles: Fiction; Nonfiction; *Areas:* Arts; Autobiography; Business; Culture; Current Affairs; Design; Health; Historical; Horror; Humour; Lifestyle; Music; Psychology; Religious; Science; Sport; Thrillers; *Markets:* Adult; *Treatments:* Commercial; Literary

Send query using submission form on website.

Susan Rabiner, Literary Agent, Inc.

315 West 39th Street, Suite 1501, New York, NY 10018
Email: susan@rabiner.net
Website: http://www.rabinerlit.com

Handles: Fiction; Nonfiction; *Areas:* Arts; Autobiography; Entertainment; Finance; Historical; Humour; Politics; Science; Sport; *Markets:* Adult

Send query by email only. Response within two weeks if interested. See website for details and email addresses of individual agents.

The Swetky Agency and Associates

Trinindad, CO 81082
Tel: +1 (435) 313-8006
Email: fayeswetky@amsaw.org
Website: http://www.amsaw.org/swetkyagency/

Handles: Fiction; Nonfiction; Scripts; *Areas:* Adventure; Anthropology; Archaeology; Architecture; Arts; Autobiography; Business; Cookery; Crime; Criticism; Culture; Current Affairs; Design; Erotic; Fantasy; Film; Finance; Gardening; Gothic; Health; Historical; How-to; Humour; Legal; Leisure; Literature; Medicine; Military; Mystery; Nature; Philosophy; Photography; Politics; Psychology; Religious; Romance; Science; Sci-Fi; Self-Help; Short Stories; Sociology; Sport; Suspense; Technology; Theatre; Thrillers; Translations; Travel; TV; Westerns; Women's Interests; *Markets:* Adult; Children's; Youth; *Treatments:* Contemporary; Experimental; Literary; Mainstream

Submit query using submission form on website only. Do not send any portion of your work until requested to do so. Follow guidelines on website precisely. Failure to do so results in automatic rejection. Willing to consider anything marketable, except short stories, poetry and children's picture books (but accepts children's fiction and nonfiction).

Talcott Notch Literary

31 Cherry Street, Suite 104, Milford, CT 06460
Fax: +1 (203) 876-9517
Email: editorial@talcottnotch.net
Website: http://www.talcottnotch.net

Handles: Fiction; Nonfiction; *Areas:* Autobiography; Business; Cookery; Crafts; Crime; Fantasy; Gardening; Historical; Horror; Lifestyle; Mystery; Nature; Science; Sci-Fi; Suspense; Technology; Thrillers; Women's Interests; *Markets:* Adult; Children's; Family; Youth; *Treatments:* Mainstream

Currently closed to unsolicited queries and submissions. Will continue to consider works requested as a result of meeting writers through conferences, pitch slams, writing workshops, bootcamps, and client referrals.

Tessler Literary Agency

27 West 20th Street, Suite 1003, New York, NY 10011
Tel: +1 (212) 242-0466
Fax: +1 (212) 242-2366
Website: http://www.tessleragency.com

Handles: Fiction; Nonfiction; *Areas:* Autobiography; Biography; Business; Cookery; Culture; Health; Historical; Psychology; Science; Travel; Women's Interests; *Markets:* Adult; *Treatments:* Commercial; Literary; Popular

Welcomes appropriate queries. Handles quality nonfiction and literary and commercial fiction. No genre fiction or children's fiction. Send query via form on website only.

Thompson Literary Agency

115 West 29th St, Third Floor, New York, NY 10001
Tel: +1 (347) 281-7685
Email: submissions@thompsonliterary.com
Website: http://thompsonliterary.com

Handles: Fiction; Nonfiction; *Areas:* Arts; Autobiography; Beauty and Fashion; Biography; Cookery; Culture; Health; Historical; Music; Politics; Science; Spiritual; Sport; *Markets:* Adult; Children's; Youth; *Treatments:* Commercial; Literary; Popular

Always on the lookout for commercial and literary fiction, but specialises in nonfiction. See website for list of agent interests and address submission by email to specific agent.

Tracy Brown Literary Agency

PO Box 772, Nyack, NY 10960
Tel: +1 (914) 400-4147
Fax: +1 (914) 931-1746
Email: tracy@brownlit.com

Handles: Fiction; Nonfiction; *Areas:* Biography; Current Affairs; Health; Historical; Psychology; Travel; Women's Interests; *Markets:* Adult; *Treatments:* Literary; Popular; Serious

Particularly interested in serious nonfiction and fiction. Send query with author bio, outline/proposal, and synopsis. Queries accepted by email but not by fax. No Young Adult, Science Fiction, or Romance.

TriadaUS Literary Agency, Inc.

P.O.Box 561, Sewickley, PA 15143
Tel: +1 (412) 401-3376
Email: uwe@triadaus.com
Website: http://www.triadaus.com

Handles: Fiction; Nonfiction; *Areas:* Adventure; Autobiography; Biography; Business; Cookery; Crafts; Crime; Culture; Current Affairs; Fantasy; Finance; Gardening; Health; Historical; How-to; Humour; Lifestyle; Music; Mystery; Politics; Psychology; Romance; Science; Sci-Fi; Self-Help; Sport; Suspense; Thrillers; Travel; Women's Interests; *Markets:* Adult; Children's; Youth; *Treatments:* Commercial; Literary; Mainstream

Prefers email queries. No attachments, unless requested. Accepts submissions by post, but no response without SASE. No response to queries that do not follow the guidelines.

Trident Media Group, LLC

41 Madison Avenue, 36th Fl., New York, NY 10010
Tel: +1 (212) 333-1511
Email: info@tridentmediagroup.com
Website: http://www.tridentmediagroup.com

Handles: Fiction; Nonfiction; *Areas:* Adventure; Autobiography; Biography; Business; Crime; Criticism; Culture; Current Affairs; Fantasy; Film; Health; Historical; Humour; Lifestyle; Music; Mystery; Politics; Religious; Romance; Science; Sci-Fi; Sport; Suspense; Technology; Thrillers; Women's Interests; *Markets:* Adult; Children's; Youth; *Treatments:* Commercial; Literary; Popular

Send query using form on website. Check website for details and interests of specific agents and approach one agent only. Do not approach more than one agent at a time. No unsolicited MSS.

2M Literary Agency Ltd

19 West 21 Street Suite 501, New York, NY 10010
Tel: +1 (212) 741-1509
Fax: +1 (212) 691-4460
Email: morel@2mcommunications.com
Website: http://www.2mcommunications.com

Handles: Nonfiction; *Areas:* Autobiography; Beauty and Fashion; Business; Cookery; Crime; Culture; Film; Health; Lifestyle; Medicine; Music; Politics; Psychology; Science; Sport; *Markets:* Adult; Family; *Treatments:* Contemporary; Mainstream; Niche; Popular; Progressive; Traditional

Only accepts queries from established ghostwriters, collaborators, and editors with experience in the fields of business; film, music and television; health and fitness; medicine and psychology; parenting; politics; science; sport; true crime; or the world of food.

United Talent Agency

142 West 57th Street, Sixth Floor, New York, NY 10019
Tel: +1 (212) 581-3100
Fax: +1 (212) 581-0015
Email: Sasha.Raskin@Unitedtalent.com
Website: http://www.theagencygroup.com

Handles: Fiction; Nonfiction; *Areas:* Business; Historical; Science; Sci-Fi; *Markets:* Adult; *Treatments:* Literary

Multimedia agency representing recording artists, celebrities, and with a literary agency operating out of the New York and London offices. Send query letter with synopsis and first 100 pages.

Veritas Literary Agency

601 Van Ness Avenue, Opera Plaza Suite E, San Francisco, CA 94102
Tel: +1 (415) 647-6964
Fax: +1 (415) 647-6965
Email: submissions@veritasliterary.com
Website: http://www.veritasliterary.com

Handles: Fiction; Nonfiction; *Areas:* Autobiography; Business; Crime; Culture; Erotic; Fantasy; Health; Historical; Lifestyle; Mystery; Nature; Science; Sci-Fi; Self-Help; Thrillers; Women's Interests; *Markets:* Adult; Children's; Youth; *Treatments:* Commercial; Literary; Popular

Send query or proposal by email only. Submit further information on request only. For fiction, include cover letter listing previously published work, one-page summary and first two chapters. For nonfiction, include author bio, overview, chapter-by-chapter summary, and analysis of competing titles.

Victoria Sanders & Associates LLC

440 Buck Road, Stone Ridge, NY 12484
Tel: +1 (212) 633-8811
Email: queriesvsa@gmail.com
Website: http://www.victoriasanders.com

Handles: Fiction; Nonfiction; *Areas:* Adventure; Arts; Autobiography; Biography; Crime; Culture; Current Affairs; Fantasy; Film; Historical; Humour; Legal; Literature; Music; Mystery; Politics; Psychology; Sociology; Suspense; Theatre; Thrillers; Translations; Women's Interests; *Markets:* Adult; Children's; Youth; *Treatments:* Commercial; Contemporary; Light; Literary; Mainstream; Satirical

Send one-page query describing the work and the author by email only, with the first 25 pages pasted into the body of the email. No attachments or submissions by post. Response usually between 1 and 4 weeks.

Watkins / Loomis Agency, Inc.

PO Box 20925, New York, NY 10025
Tel: +1 (212) 532-0080
Fax: +1 (646) 383-2449
Email: assistant@watkinsloomis.com
Website: http://www.watkinsloomis.com

Handles: Fiction; Nonfiction; *Areas:* Autobiography; Biography; Culture; Current Affairs; Historical; Nature; Politics; Short Stories; Technology; Travel; *Markets:* Adult; Youth; *Treatments:* Contemporary; Literary; Popular

Specialises in literary fiction, memoir, biography, essay, travel, and political journalism. No unsolicited MSS and does not guarantee a response to queries.

Waxman Leavell Literary Agency

443 Park Ave South, #1004, New York, NY 10016
Tel: +1 (212) 675-5556
Fax: +1 (212) 675-1381
Email: scottsubmit@waxmanleavell.com
Website: http://www.waxmanleavell.com

Handles: Fiction; Nonfiction; *Areas:* Adventure; Autobiography; Biography; Business; Cookery; Fantasy; Health; Historical; Humour; Mystery; Romance; Science; Self-Help; Sport; Suspense; Women's Interests; *Markets:* Adult; Children's; Youth; *Treatments:* Commercial; Contemporary; Literary

Send query by email to one of the agent-specific addresses on the website. Do not query more than one agent at a time. For details of what each agent is looking for, see details on website. No attachments, but for fiction include 5-10 pages in the body of the email.

The Weingel-Fidel Agency

310 East 46th Street, Suite 21-E, New York, NY 10017
Tel: +1 (212) 599-2959

Handles: Fiction; Nonfiction; *Areas:* Arts; Autobiography; Biography; Music; Psychology; Science; Sociology; Technology; Women's Interests; *Markets:* Adult; *Treatments:* Commercial; Literary; Mainstream

Accepts new clients by referral only – approach only via an existing client or industry contact. Specialises in commercial and literary fiction and nonfiction. Particularly interested in investigative journalism. No children's books, science fiction, fantasy, or self-help.

Wendy Sherman Associates, Inc.

138 West 25th Street, Suite 1018, New York, NY 10001
Tel: +1 (212) 279-9027
Email: submissions@wsherman.com
Website: http://www.wsherman.com

Handles: Fiction; Nonfiction; *Areas:* Autobiography; Biography; Cookery; Culture; Entertainment; Health; Historical; Lifestyle; Nature; Psychology; Self-Help; Spiritual; Sport; Suspense; Women's Interests; *Markets:* Adult; Youth; *Treatments:* Literary

Send queries by email only, including query letter and (for fiction) first ten pages pasted into the body of the email, or (for nonfiction) author bio. No unsolicited attachments. Do not send emails to personal agent addresses (these are deleted unread). Response only if interested. Does not handle poetry, screenplays, cozy mysteries, genre romance, westerns, science fiction, horror, fantasy, or children's picture books

Wernick & Pratt Agency

1207 North Avenue, Beacon, NY 12508
Email: submissions@wernickpratt.com
Website: http://www.wernickpratt.com

Handles: Fiction; Nonfiction; *Markets:* Children's; Youth; *Treatments:* Commercial; Literary

Handles children's books of all genres, from picture books to young adult literature. Particularly interested in authors who also illustrate their picture books; humorous young chapter books; literary and commercial middle grade / young adult books.

Not interested in picture book manuscripts of more than 750 words, mood pieces, work specifically targeted to the educational market, or fiction about the American Revolution, Civil War, or World War II (unless told from a very unique perspective). Accepts queries by email only. See website for full guidelines. Response only if interested.

William Morris Endeavor Entertainment

11 Madison Avenue, New York, NY 10010
Tel: +1 (212) 586-5100
Fax: +1 (212) 246-3583
Email: jrw@wmeentertainment.com
Website: http://www.wma.com

Handles: Fiction; Nonfiction; Scripts; *Areas:* Film; TV; *Markets:* Adult

Accepts unsolicited submissions through conferences or by referral only.

Wm Clark Associates

186 Fifth Avenue, 2nd Floor, New York, NY 10010
Tel: +1 (212) 675-2784
Fax: +1 (347) 649-9262
Email: general@wmclark.com
Website: http://www.wmclark.com

Handles: Fiction; Nonfiction; *Areas:* Architecture; Arts; Autobiography; Biography; Culture; Current Affairs; Design; Film; Historical; Music; Philosophy; Religious; Science; Sociology; Technology; Theatre; Translations; *Markets:* Adult; *Treatments:* Contemporary; Literary; Mainstream

Query through online form on website only. No simultaneous submissions or screenplays.

Wolfson Literary Agency

Email: query@wolfsonliterary.com
Website: http://www.wolfsonliterary.com

Handles: Fiction; Nonfiction; *Areas:* Culture; Health; How-to; Humour; Lifestyle; Medicine; Mystery; Romance; Suspense; Thrillers; Women's Interests; *Markets:* Adult; Youth; *Treatments:* Mainstream; Popular

Accepts queries by email only. Response only if interested. See website for full submission guidelines.

Writers' Representatives, LLC

116 W. 14th St., 11th Fl., New York, NY 10011-7305
Tel: +1 (212) 620-0023
Fax: +1 (212) 620-0023
Email: transom@writersreps.com
Website: http://www.writersreps.com

Handles: Fiction; Nonfiction; Poetry; Reference; *Areas:* Autobiography; Biography; Business; Cookery; Criticism; Current Affairs; Finance; Historical; Humour; Legal; Literature; Mystery; Philosophy; Politics; Science; Self-Help; Thrillers; *Markets:* Adult; *Treatments:* Literary; Serious

Send email describing your project and yourself, or send proposal, outline, CV, and sample chapters, or complete unsolicited MS, with SASE. See website for submission requirements in FAQ section. Specialises in serious and literary fiction and nonfiction. No screenplays. No science fiction or children's or young adult fiction unless it aspires to serious literature.

Writers House, LLC

21 West 26th Street, New York, NY 10010
Tel: +1 (212) 685-2400
Fax: +1 (212) 685-1781
Email: Azuckerman@writershouse.com
Website: http://writershouse.com

Handles: Fiction; Nonfiction; *Areas:* Autobiography; Biography; Business; Cookery; Fantasy; Finance; Historical; How-to; Lifestyle; Psychology; Science; Sci-Fi; Self-Help; Women's Interests; *Markets:* Adult; Children's; Youth; *Treatments:* Commercial; Literary

Handles adult and juvenile fiction and nonfiction, commercial and literary, including picture books. Policies of individual agents vary, but most prefer email queries. Postal submissions with an SASE are still accepted, however. Do not query more than one agent at a time. See website for full details.

Yates & Yates

1551 North Tustin Avenue, Suite 710, Santa Ana, CA 92705
Tel: +1 (714) 480-4000
Email: email@yates2.com
Website: http://www.yates2.com

Handles: Fiction; Nonfiction; *Areas:* Autobiography; Biography; Business; Current Affairs; Legal; Politics; Religious; Sport; Thrillers; Women's Interests; *Markets:* Adult; *Treatments:* Literary

Literary agency based in California, representing "gifted Christian communicators". Takes a holistic approach, combining agency representation, expert legal advice, marketing guidance, career coaching, creative counseling, and business management consulting.

The Zack Company, Inc

PMB 525, 4653 Carmel Mountain Rd, Ste 308, San Diego, CA 92130-6650
Website: http://www.zackcompany.com

Handles: Fiction; Nonfiction; Reference; *Areas:* Adventure; Autobiography; Biography; Cookery; Crime; Culture; Current Affairs; Erotic; Fantasy; Film; Finance; Gardening; Health; Historical; Horror; How-to; Humour; Medicine; Military; Music; Mystery; Nature; Politics; Religious; Romance; Science; Sci-Fi; Self-Help; Spiritual; Sport; Suspense; Technology; Thrillers; TV; Women's Interests; *Markets:* Adult; *Treatments:* Popular

Requirements change frequently, so check the agency website before approaching. Please note that approaches are not accepted to the former submissions email address (submissions@zackcompany.com). Electronic approaches must be made via the form on the website. Also accepts approaches by post.

Karen Gantz Zahler Literary Agency

860 Fifth Ave Suite 7J, New York, NY 10021
Tel: +1 (212) 734-3619
Email: karen@karengantzlit.com
Website: http://www.karengantzlit.com

Handles: Fiction; Nonfiction; *Areas:* Autobiography; Cookery; Design; Entertainment; Historical; Lifestyle; Politics; Psychology; Religious; Sociology; Spiritual; *Markets:* Adult

Considers all genres but specialises in nonfiction. Send query and summary by email only.

Helen Zimmermann Literary Agency

58 South Manheim Boulevard, Suite 25, New Paltz, NY 12561
Tel: +1 (845) 256-0977
Fax: +1 (845) 256-0979
Email: Submit@ZimmAgency.com
Website: http://www.zimmagency.com

Handles: Fiction; Nonfiction; *Areas:* Autobiography; Biography; Cookery; Culture; Health; Historical; How-to; Humour; Lifestyle; Music; Mystery; Nature; Science; Spiritual; Sport; Suspense; Technology; Thrillers; Women's Interests; *Markets:* Adult; *Treatments:* Literary

Particularly interested in health and wellness, relationships, popular culture, women's issues, lifestyle, sports, and music. No poetry, science fiction, horror, or romance. Prefers email queries, but no attachments unless requested. Send pitch letter – for fiction include summary, bio, and first chapter in the body of the email.

Zoë Pagnamenta Agency, LLC

20 West 22nd Street, Suite 1603, New York, NY 10010
Tel: +1 (212) 253-1074
Fax: +1 (212) 253-1075
Email: mail@zpagency.com
Website: http://www.zpagency.com

Handles: Fiction; Nonfiction; *Areas:* Autobiography; Biography; Business; Historical; Science; Short Stories; *Markets:* Adult; *Treatments:* Commercial; Literary; Popular

No screenplays, poetry, self-help, or genre fiction, including mystery, romance or science fiction. Send queries by post only, with SASE (or return email address) and up to 25 pages of sample material.

UK Literary Agents

For the most up-to-date listings of these and hundreds of other literary agents, visit https://www.firstwriter.com/Agents

*To claim your **free** access to the site, please see the back of this book.*

A for Authors

73 Hurlingham Road, Bexleyheath, Kent
DA7 5PE
Email: enquiries@aforauthors.co.uk
Website: http://aforauthors.co.uk

Handles: Fiction; Nonfiction; *Markets:* Adult; *Treatments:* Commercial; Literary

Query by email only. Include synopsis and first three chapters (or up to 50 pages) and short author bio. All attachments must be Word format documents. No scripts, poetry, fantasy, SF, horror, short stories, adult illustrated books on art, architecture, design, visual culture, or submissions by post, hand delivery, or on discs, memory sticks, or other electronic devices. No longer accepting young adult or children's. See website for full details.

A & B Personal Management Ltd

PO Box 64671, London, NW3 9LH
Tel: +44 (0) 20 7794 3255
Email: b.ellmain@aandb.co.uk

Handles: Fiction; Nonfiction; Scripts; *Areas:* Film; Theatre; TV; *Markets:* Adult

Handles full-length mss and scripts for film, TV, and theatre. No unsolicited mss. Query by email or by phone in first instance.

Abner Stein

10 Roland Gardens, London, SW7 3PH
Tel: +44 (0) 20 7373 0456
Email: caspian@abnerstein.co.uk
Website: http://www.abnerstein.co.uk

Handles: Fiction; Nonfiction; *Markets:* Adult; Children's

Agency based in London. Handles fiction, general nonfiction, and children's.

The Agency (London) Ltd

24 Pottery Lane, Holland Park, London, W11 4LZ
Tel: +44 (0) 20 7727 1346
Email: info@theagency.co.uk
Website: http://www.theagency.co.uk

Handles: Fiction; Nonfiction; Scripts; *Areas:* Film; Radio; Theatre; TV; *Markets:* Adult; Children's

Closed to submissions as at April 2017. Check website for current status.

Represents writers and authors for film, television, radio and the theatre. Also represents directors, producers, composers, and film and television rights in books, as well as authors of children's books from picture books to teen fiction. **Handles adult fiction and nonfiction for existing clients only**. Does not consider adult fiction or nonfiction from writers who are not already clients. For script writers, only considers unsolicited material if it has been recommended by a producer, development executive or course tutor. If this is the case send CV, covering letter and details of your referee to the relevant agent, or to the email address below. Do not email more than one agent at a time. For directors, send CV, showreel and cover letter by email. For children's authors, send query by email with synopsis and first three chapters (middle grade and teen) or complete ms (picture books) to address given on website.

AHA Talent Ltd

74 Clerkenwell Road, London, EC1M 5QA
Tel: +44 (0) 20 7250 1760
Email: mail@ahacreatives.co.uk
Website: http://www.ahatalent.co.uk

Handles: Nonfiction; Scripts; *Areas:* Autobiography; How-to; Humour; *Markets:* Adult; *Treatments:* Popular

Handles actors, writers, creatives, and voice-over artists. Send query with return postage, CV/bio, and 10-page writing sample. No poetry.

Aitken Alexander Associates

291 Gray's Inn Road, Kings Cross, London, WC1X 8QJ
Tel: +44 (0) 20 7373 8672
Fax: +44 (0) 20 7373 6002
Email: submissions@aitkenalexander.co.uk
Website: http://www.aitkenalexander.co.uk

Handles: Fiction; Nonfiction; *Markets:* Adult

Send query by email, with short synopsis, and first 30 pages as a Word document. See website for list of agents and their interests and indicate in the subject line which agent you would like to query. No illustrated children's books, poetry or screenplays. No submissions or queries by post.

Alan Brodie Representation Ltd

Paddock Suite, The Courtyard, 55 Charterhouse Street, London, EC1M 6HA
Tel: +44 (0) 20 7253 6226
Fax: +44 (0) 20 7183 7999
Email: ABR@alanbrodie.com
Website: http://www.alanbrodie.com

Handles: Scripts; *Areas:* Film; Radio; Theatre; TV; *Markets:* Adult

Handles scripts only. No books. Approach with preliminary letter, recommendation from industry professional, and CV. Do not send a sample of work unless requested. No fiction, nonfiction, or poetry.

The Ampersand Agency Ltd

Ryman's Cottages, Little Tew, Chipping Norton, Oxfordshire OX7 4JJ
Tel: +44 (0) 1608 683677 / 683898
Fax: +44 (0) 1608 683449
Email: submissions@theampersandagency.co.uk
Website: http://www.theampersandagency.co.uk

Handles: Fiction; Nonfiction; *Areas:* Autobiography; Biography; Crime; Current Affairs; Fantasy; Historical; Horror; Science; Sci-Fi; Sport; Thrillers; Women's Interests; *Markets:* Adult; Youth; *Treatments:* Commercial; Contemporary; Literary

We handle literary and commercial fiction and nonfiction, including contemporary and historical novels, crime, thrillers, biography, women's fiction, history, current affairs, and memoirs. Send query by post or email with brief bio, outline, and first two chapters. Also accepts science fiction, fantasy, horror, and Young Adult material to separate email address listed on website. No scripts except those by existing clients, no poetry, self-help or illustrated children's books. No unpublished American writers, because in our experience British and European publishers aren't interested unless there is an American publisher on board. And we'd like to make it clear that American stamps are no use outside America!

Andlyn

Tel: +44 (0) 20 3290 5638
Email: submissions@andlyn.co.uk
Website: http://www.andlyn.co.uk

Handles: Fiction; Nonfiction; *Markets:* Children's; Youth

Specialises in children's/teen fiction and content. Handles picture books, middle-grade, young adult, and cross-over. Send query by email with one-page synopsis and first three chapters (fiction) or proposal and market analysis (nonfiction). Not accepting picture book submissions as at February 2017. Check website for current status.

Andrew Lownie Literary Agency Ltd

36 Great Smith Street, London, SW1P 3BU
Tel: +44 (0) 20 7222 7574
Fax: +44 (0) 20 7222 7576
Email: mail@andrewlownie.co.uk
Website: http://www.andrewlownie.co.uk

Handles: Fiction; Nonfiction; *Areas:* Autobiography; Biography; Crime; Culture; Current Affairs; Fantasy; Finance; Health; Historical; Horror; How-to; Lifestyle; Literature; Media; Medicine; Men's Interests; Military; Music; Mystery; Politics; Psychology; Romance; Science; Sci-Fi; Self-Help; Sport; Suspense; Technology; Thrillers; Translations; Westerns; *Markets:* Academic; Adult; Family; Professional; *Treatments:* Commercial; Mainstream; Popular; Serious; Traditional

This agency, founded in 1988, is now one of the UK's leading boutique literary agencies with some two hundred nonfiction and fiction authors and is actively building its fiction list through its new agent (see website for specific contact address for fiction submissions). It prides itself on its personal attention to its clients and specialises both in launching new writers and taking established writers to a new level of recognition.

Andrew Nurnberg Associates, Ltd

20-23 Greville Street, London, EC1N 8SS
Tel: +44 (0) 20 3327 0400
Fax: +44 (0) 20 7430 0801
Email: submissions@andrewnurnberg.com
Website: http://www.andrewnurnberg.com

Handles: Fiction; Nonfiction; *Markets:* Adult; Children's

Handles adult fiction and nonfiction, and children's fiction. No poetry, children's picture books, or scripts for film, TV, radio or theatre. Send query with one-page synopsis and first three chapters by post with SAE (if return required) or by email as attachments.

Anne Clark Literary Agency

PO Box 1221, Harlton, Cambridge, CB23 1WW
Tel: +44 (0) 1223 262160
Email: submissions@anneclarkliteraryagency.co.uk
Website: http://www.anneclarkliteraryagency.co.uk

Handles: Fiction; *Markets:* Children's; Youth

Handles fiction and picture books for children and young adults. Send query by email only with the following pasted into the body of the email (not as an attachment): for fiction, include brief synopsis and first 3,000 words; for picture books, send complete ms; for nonfiction, send short proposal and the text of three sample pages. No submissions by post. See website for full guidelines.

Anthony Sheil in Association with Aitken Alexander Associates

291 Gray's Inn Road, Kings Cross, London, WC1X 8QJ
Tel: +44 (0) 20 7373 8672
Fax: +44 (0) 20 7373 6002
Website: http://www.aitkenalexander.co.uk/agents/anthony-sheil/

Handles: Fiction; Nonfiction; *Markets:* Adult

Handles fiction and nonfiction. No scripts, poetry, short stories, or children's fiction. Send query by post with SAE, synopsis up to half a page, and first 30 pages.

Anubis Literary Agency

6 Birdhaven Close, Lighthorne Heath, CV35 0BE
Tel: +44 (0) 1926 642588
Fax: +44 (0) 1926 642588
Email: writerstuff2@btopenworld.com

Handles: Fiction; *Areas:* Fantasy; Horror; Sci-Fi; *Markets:* Adult

No children's books, poetry, short stories, journalism, TV or film scripts, academic or nonfiction. Only considers genre fiction as listed above. Send a covering letter with one-page synopsis and 50-page sample. SAE essential. No telephone calls, or email / fax queries. Simultaneous queries accepted, but no material returned without SAE. Usually responds in six weeks to queries and three months to MSS. Runs regular writers' workshops/seminars to help writers. Email for details.

Artellus Limited

30 Dorset House, Gloucester Place, London, NW1 5AD
Tel: +44 (0) 20 7935 6972
Fax: +44 (0) 20 8609 0347
Email: artellussubmissions@gmail.com
Website: http://www.artellusltd.co.uk

Handles: Fiction; Nonfiction; *Areas:* Arts; Beauty and Fashion; Biography; Crime; Culture; Current Affairs; Entertainment; Fantasy; Historical; Military; Science; Sci-Fi; *Markets:* Adult; Youth; *Treatments:* Contemporary; Literary

Welcomes submissions from new fiction and nonfiction writers. Send first three chapters and synopsis in first instance, or send query by email. No film or TV scripts. If you would prefer to submit electronically send query by email in advance.

The Authors Care Service ltd

50 Cecil Road, Croydon, Surrey CR0 3BG
Tel: +44 (0) 7984 316734
Email: vanessa@theauthorscare.co.uk
Website: http://www.theauthorscare.co.uk

Handles: Fiction; Nonfiction; *Areas:* Autobiography; Business; Religious; Self-Help; *Markets:* Adult; Children's; Youth; *Treatments:* Positive

This is a Christian based agency. In nonfiction, handles bible studies and Christian based testimonial memoirs. You must be established and have a strong platform to submit a memoir. Occasionally also represents nonfiction that is not Christian based such as motivational, business books, educational, or children's books. In fiction, handles Christian-themed allegory type manuscripts, and edgy Christian fiction. No obscene language, exotic or dark paranormal. Also represents children's and young adult fiction which has positive messages.Currently open only to approaches from established authors – no new authors. We are looking for authors who either already have a vast platform, or strong marketing skills. We also require authors to have strong writing skills. It is advised for authors to get their work checked by a professional editor before they submit. As we want to submit high quality work to publishers.

AVAnti Productions & Management

Units 2-8, 31 St. Aubyns, Brighton, BN3 2TH
Tel: +44 (0) 07999 193311
Email: avantiproductions@live.co.uk
Website: http://www.avantiproductions.co.uk

Handles: Fiction; Nonfiction; Poetry; Scripts; *Areas:* Film; Theatre; *Markets:* Adult; *Treatments:* Contemporary

Talent and literary representation – also, a film and theatre production company. Open to screenplay submissions, but no unsolicited theatre scripts.

Bath Literary Agency

5 Gloucester Road, Bath, BA1 7BH
Email: submissions@bathliteraryagency.com
Website: http://bathliteraryagency.com

Handles: Fiction; Nonfiction; *Markets:* Children's; Youth

Handles fiction and nonfiction for children, from picture books to Young Adult. Send query by email or by post with SAE for reply and return of materials if required, along with the first three chapters (fiction) or the full manuscript (picture books). See website for full details.

Bell Lomax Moreton Agency

Suite C, 131 Queensway, Petts Wood, Kent BR5 1DG
Tel: +44 (0) 20 7930 4447
Fax: +44 (0) 1689 820061
Email: agency@bell-lomax.co.uk
Website: http://www.belllomaxmoreton.co.uk

Handles: Fiction; Nonfiction; *Areas:* Biography; Business; Sport; *Markets:* Adult; Children's

Considers most fiction, nonfiction, and children's book proposals. No poetry, short stories, novellas, textbooks, film scripts, stage plays, or science fiction. Send query by email with details of any previous work, short synopsis, and first three chapters (up to 50 pages). For children's picture books send complete ms. Also accepts postal submissions. See website for full guidelines.

Berlin Associates

7 Tyers Gate, London, SE1 3HX
Tel: +44 (0) 20 7836 1112
Fax: +44 (0) 20 7632 5296
Email: submissions@berlinassociates.com
Website: http://www.berlinassociates.com

Handles: Scripts; *Areas:* Film; Radio; Theatre; TV; *Markets:* Adult

Most clients through recommendation or invitation, but accepts queries by email with CV, experience, and outline of work you would like to submit.

The Blair Partnership

PO Box, 7828, London, W1A 4GE
Tel: +44 (0) 20 7504 2520
Email: submissions@theblairpartnership.com
Website: http://www.theblairpartnership.com

Handles: Fiction; Nonfiction; *Markets:* Adult; Children's; Family; Youth

Open to all genres of fiction and nonfiction. Send query by email with one-page synopsis and first ten pages, including some detail about yourself.

Blake Friedmann Literary Agency Ltd

First Floor, Selous House, 5-12 Mandela Street, London, NW1 0DU
Tel: +44 (0) 20 7387 0842
Email: info@blakefriedmann.co.uk
Website: http://www.blakefriedmann.co.uk

Handles: Fiction; Nonfiction; Scripts; *Areas:* Autobiography; Biography; Cookery; Crime; Culture; Current Affairs; Film; Finance; Historical; Military; Mystery; Politics; Psychology; Radio; Science; Sociology; Suspense; Technology; Thrillers; Travel; TV; Women's Interests; *Markets:* Adult; Children's; Youth; *Treatments:* Commercial; Contemporary; Literary; Popular

Send query by email to a specific agent best suited to your work. See website for full submission guidelines, details of agents, and individual agent contact details.

No poetry or plays. Short stories and journalism for existing clients only.

Media department currently only accepting submissions from writers with produced credits.

Reply not guaranteed. If no response within 8 weeks, assume rejection.

Luigi Bonomi Associates Ltd

91 Great Russell Street, London, WC1 3PS
Tel: +44 (0) 20 7637 1234
Fax: +44 (0) 20 7637 2111
Email: info@lbabooks.com
Website: http://www.lbabooks.com

Handles: Fiction; Nonfiction; *Areas:* Adventure; Cookery; Crime; Fantasy; Health; Historical; Lifestyle; Romance; Science; Sci-Fi; Thrillers; TV; Women's Interests; *Markets:* Adult; Children's; Youth; *Treatments:* Commercial; Literary

Send query with synopsis and first three chapters by post with SAE (if return of material required) or email address for response, or by email (Word or PDF attachments only). See website for specific agents' interests and email addresses. No scripts or poetry.

BookBlast Ltd.

PO Box 20184, London, W10 5AU
Tel: +44 (0) 20 8968 3089
Fax: +44 (0) 20 8932 4087
Email: gen@bookblast.com
Website: http://www.bookblast.com

Handles: Fiction; Nonfiction; *Areas:* Autobiography; Culture; Travel; *Markets:* Adult

Handles adult fiction and nonfiction. Currently reading very selectively. Send query with one-page synopsis for fiction, or full outline for nonfiction, with first three chapters and SAE. No scripts or children's books. Film, TV, and radio rights normally sold for works by existing clients. Also offers translation consultancy service. No submissions on fax, email, or disc. Notification must be given of any other agencies previously or currently submitted to.

Bookseeker Agency

PO Box 7535, Perth, PH2 1AF
Tel: +44 (0) 1738 620688
Email: bookseeker@blueyonder.co.uk
Website: http://bookseekeragency.com

Handles: Fiction; Poetry; *Markets:* Adult

Handles fiction and (under some circumstances) poetry. No nonfiction. Send query by post or email outlining what you have written and your current projects, along with synopsis and sample chapter (novels).

The Bright Literary Academy

Studio 102, 250 York Road, London, SW11 1RJ
Tel: +44 (0) 20 7326 9140
Email: literarysubmissions@brightgroupinternational.com
Website: http://brightliteraryagency.com

Handles: Fiction; *Areas:* Autobiography; Entertainment; Literature; Mystery; Sci-Fi; Self-Help; Short Stories; Thrillers; TV; Women's Interests; *Markets:* Children's; Youth; *Treatments:* Commercial; Contemporary; Mainstream; Positive

A boutique literary agency representing the most fabulous new talent to grace the publishing industry in recent years. Born out of the success of a leading illustration agency with an outstanding global client list this agency aims to produce sensational material across all genres of children's publishing, including novelty, picture books, fiction and adult autobiographies, in order to become a one-stop-shop for publishers looking for something extra special to fit into their lists.

Prides itself on nurturing the creativity of its authors and illustrators so that they can concentrate on their craft rather than negotiate their contracts. As a creative agency we develop seeds of ideas into something extraordinary, before searching for the right publisher with which to develop them further to create incredible and unforgettable books.

We are fortunate enough to have a never-ending source of remarkable material at our fingertips and a stable of exceptional creators who are all united by one common goal – a deep passion and dedication to children's books and literature in all its shapes and forms.

Send query by email only, with synopsis and first three chapters, or whole text for picture books.

Caroline Davidson Literary Agency

5 Queen Anne's Gardens, London, W4 1TU
Tel: +44 (0) 20 8995 5768
Email: enquiries@cdla.co.uk
Website: http://www.cdla.co.uk

Handles: Fiction; Nonfiction; Reference; *Areas:* Archaeology; Architecture; Arts; Biography; Cookery; Culture; Design; Gardening; Health; Historical; Lifestyle; Medicine; Nature; Politics; Psychology; Science; *Markets:* Adult

Send query with CV, SAE, outline and history of work, and (for fiction) the first 50 pages and last 10 pages of novel. For nonfiction, include table of contents, detailed chapter-by-chapter synopsis, description of sources and / or research for the book, market and competition analysis, and (if possible) one or two sample chapters.

Submissions without adequate return postage are neither returned or considered. No Chick lit, romance, erotica, Crime and thrillers, Science fiction, fantasy, Poetry, Individual short stories, Children's, Young Adult, Misery memoirs or fictionalised autobiography. Completed and polished first novels positively welcomed. See website for more details. No submissions by fax and only in exceptional circumstances accepts submissions by email.

See website for full details.

Caroline Sheldon Literary Agency

71 Hillgate Place, London, W8 7SS
Tel: +44 (0) 20 7727 9102
Email: carolinesheldon@carolinesheldon.co.uk
Website: http://www.carolinesheldon.co.uk

Handles: Fiction; Nonfiction; *Areas:* Autobiography; Fantasy; Historical; Humour; Suspense; Women's Interests; *Markets:* Adult; Children's; Youth; *Treatments:* Commercial; Contemporary; Literary

Send query by email only. Do not query both agents. See website for both email addresses and appropriate subject line to include. Handles fiction and human-interest nonfiction for adults, and fiction for children, including full-length and picture books.

The Catchpole Agency

53 Cranham Street, Oxford, OX2 6DD
Tel: +44 (0) 7789 588070
Email: submissions@thecatchpoleagency.co.uk
Website: http://www.thecatchpoleagency.co.uk

Handles: Fiction; *Markets:* Children's

Works on children's books with both artists and writers. Send query by email with sample pasted directly into the body of the email (the whole text of a picture book or a couple of chapters of a novel). No attachments. See website for full guidelines.

Catherine Pellegrino & Associates

148 Russell Court, Woburn Place, London, WC1H 0LR
Email: catherine@catherinepellegrino.co.uk
Website: http://catherinepellegrino.co.uk

Handles: Fiction; *Markets:* Children's; Youth; *Treatments:* Commercial; Literary

Handles children's books, from picture books to young adult. Send query by email with some background on you and the book, plus synopsis and first three chapters or approximately 50 pages, up to a natural break. See website for full details.

Cecily Ware Literary Agents

19C John Spencer Square, London, N1 2LZ
Tel: +44 (0) 20 7359 3787
Fax: +44 (0) 20 7226 9828
Email: info@cecilyware.com
Website: http://www.cecilyware.com

Handles: Scripts; *Areas:* Drama; Film; Humour; TV; *Markets:* Adult; Children's

Handles film and TV scripts only. No books or theatre scripts. Submit complete script with covering letter, CV, and SAE. No email submissions or return of material without SAE and correct postage.

Chartwell

14 Gray's Inn Road, London, WC1X 8HN
Tel: +44 (0) 20 7293 0864
Email: hello@chartwellspeakers.com
Website: http://www.chartwellspeakers.com

Handles: Fiction; Nonfiction; *Areas:* Autobiography; Biography; Cookery; Crime; Health; Historical; Lifestyle; Mystery; Psychology; Science; Suspense; Technology; Thrillers; Women's Interests; *Markets:* Adult; Children's; Youth

Agency handling speakers and authors. Will consider all fiction and nonfiction, but particularly interested in General fiction, Mystery/suspense/thriller/crime, Women's fiction, Children's and YA (fiction); and Biography/memoir, Technology, Science, History, Personal development, Health (including popular psychology), Cookery and lifestyle (nonfiction). Send query by email only. See website for full guidelines.

Mic Cheetham Literary Agency

50 Albemarle Street, London, W1S 4BD
Tel: +44 (0) 20 7495 2002
Fax: +44 (0) 20 7399 2801
Email: simon@miccheetham.com
Website: http://www.miccheetham.com

Handles: Fiction; Nonfiction; *Areas:* Crime; Fantasy; Historical; Sci-Fi; Thrillers; *Markets:* Adult; *Treatments:* Commercial; Literary; Mainstream

Send query with SAE, first three chapters, and publishing history. Focuses on fiction, and is not elitist about genre or literary fiction, providing it combines good writing, great storytelling, intelligence, imagination, and (as a bonus) anarchic wit. Film and TV scripts handled for existing clients only. No poetry, children's, illustrated books, or unsolicited MSS. Do not send manuscripts by email. Approach in writing in the first instance (no email scripts accepted).

The Christopher Little Literary Agency

48 Walham Grove, London, SW6 1QR
Tel: +44 (0) 20 7736 4455
Fax: +44 (0) 20 7736 4490
Email: submissions@christopherlittle.net
Website: http://www.christopherlittle.net

Handles: Fiction; Nonfiction; *Markets:* Adult; *Treatments:* Commercial; Literary

Closed to submissions as at June 2016

Handles commercial and literary full-length fiction and nonfiction. Film scripts handled for existing clients only (no submissions of film scripts). Send query by email (preferred) or by post with SAE or IRCs. Attach one-page synopsis and three consecutive chapters (fiction) or proposal (nonfiction). No poetry, plays, textbooks, short stories, illustrated children's books, science fiction, fantasy, or submissions by email.

Clare Hulton Literary Agency

Email: info@clarehulton.co.uk
Website: http://www.clarehulton.com

Handles: Fiction; Nonfiction; *Areas:* Autobiography; Cookery; Culture; Historical; Humour; Lifestyle; Music; Philosophy; Self-Help; TV; *Markets:* Adult; Children's; *Treatments:* Commercial; Popular

Specialises in nonfiction, but also has a small commercial fiction and children's list. Finds most authors through recommendation, but open to brief queries by email, explaining what your book is about. No attachments.

Conville & Walsh Ltd

5th Floor, Haymarket House, 28-29 Haymarket, London, SW1Y 4SP
Tel: +44 (0) 20 7393 4200
Email: sue@cwagency.co.uk
Website: http://cwagency.co.uk

Handles: Fiction; Nonfiction; *Areas:* Autobiography; Biography; Crime; Current Affairs; Fantasy; Historical; Humour; Leisure; Lifestyle; Men's Interests; Military; Mystery; Psychology; Science; Sci-Fi; Sport; Suspense; Thrillers; Travel; Women's Interests; *Markets:* Adult; Children's; Youth; *Treatments:* Commercial; Literary

See website for agent profiles and submit to one particular agent only. Send submissions by email as Word .doc files only. No postal submissions. For fiction, please submit the first three sample chapters of the completed manuscript (or about 50 pages) with a one to two page synopsis. For nonfiction, send 30-page proposal. No poetry or scripts, or picture books. See website for full guidelines.

Coombs Moylett & Maclean Literary Agency

120 New Kings Road, London, SW6 4LZ
Email: zoe@cmm.agency
Website: http://cmm.agency

Handles: Fiction; Nonfiction; *Areas:* Biography; Cookery; Crime; Current Affairs; Historical; Mystery; Suspense; Thrillers; Women's Interests; *Markets:* Adult;

Children's; Youth; *Treatments:* Commercial; Contemporary; Literary

Handles historical fiction, crime/mystery/suspense and thrillers, women's fiction from chick-lit to sagas to contemporary and literary fiction. Also looking to build a children's list concentrating on Young Adult fiction. In nonfiction, considers history, biography, current affairs and cookery.

Send query with synopsis and first three chapters via online form. No submissions by fax. No poetry, plays or scripts for film and TV.

The Creative Rights Agency

17 Prior Street, London, SE10 8SF
Tel: +44 (0) 20 3371 7673
Email: info@creativerightsagency.co.uk
Website: http://www.creativerightsagency.co.uk

Handles: Fiction; Nonfiction; *Areas:* Autobiography; Culture; Men's Interests; Sport; Thrillers; *Markets:* Adult; *Treatments:* Contemporary

Specialises in men's interests. Send query by email with sample chapters, synopsis, and author bio.

Creative Authors Ltd

11A Woodlawn Street, Whitstable, Kent CT5 1HQ
Tel: +44 (0) 01227 770947
Email: write@creativeauthors.co.uk
Website: http://www.creativeauthors.co.uk

Handles: Fiction; Nonfiction; *Areas:* Arts; Autobiography; Biography; Business; Cookery; Crafts; Crime; Culture; Health; Historical; Humour; Nature; Women's Interests; *Markets:* Adult; Children's; *Treatments:* Commercial; Literary

As at June 2017, not accepting new fiction clients. See website for current situation.

We are a dynamic literary agency – established to provide an attentive and unique platform for writers and scriptwriters and representing a growing list of clients. We're on the lookout for fresh talent and books with strong commercial potential. No unsolicited MSS, but considers queries by email. No paper submissions. Do not telephone regarding submissions.

Rupert Crew Ltd

6 Windsor Road, London, N3 3SS
Tel: +44 (0) 20 8346 3000
Fax: +44 (0) 20 8346 3009
Email: info@rupertcrew.co.uk
Website: http://www.rupertcrew.co.uk

Handles: Fiction; Nonfiction; *Markets:* Adult

Send query with SAE, synopsis, and first two or three consecutive chapters. International representation, handling volume and subsidiary rights in fiction and nonfiction properties. No Short Stories, Science Fiction, Fantasy, Horror, Poetry or original scripts for Theatre, Television and Film. Email address for correspondence only. No response by post and no return of material with insufficient return postage.

Curtis Brown Group Ltd

Haymarket House, 28/29 Haymarket, London, SW1Y 4SP
Tel: +44 (0) 20 7393 4400
Fax: +44 (0) 20 7393 4401
Email: info@curtisbrown.co.uk
Website: http://www.curtisbrowncreative.co.uk

Handles: Fiction; Nonfiction; Scripts; *Areas:* Biography; Crime; Fantasy; Film; Historical; Radio; Science; Suspense; Theatre; Thrillers; TV; *Markets:* Adult; Children's; Youth; *Treatments:* Literary; Mainstream; Popular

Renowned and long established London agency. Handles general fiction and nonfiction, and scripts. Also represents directors, designers, and presenters. No longer accepts submissions by post or email – all submissions must be made using online submissions manager. Also offers services such as writing courses for which authors are charged.

The Darley Anderson Agency

Estelle House, 11 Eustace Road, London, SW6 1JB

Tel: +44 (0) 20 7385 6652
Email: camilla@darleyanderson.com
Website: http://www.darleyanderson.com

Handles: Fiction; *Areas:* Crime; Romance; Suspense; Thrillers; Women's Interests; *Markets:* Adult; Children's; Youth; *Treatments:* Commercial; Literary

Accepts submissions by email and by post. See website for individual agent requirements, submission guidelines, and contact details. No poets or short story writers.

David Luxton Associates

23 Hillcourt Avenue, London, N12 8EY
Tel: +44 (0) 20 8922 3942
Email: nick@davidluxtonassociates.co.uk
Website: http://www.davidluxtonassociates.co.uk

Handles: Nonfiction; Reference; *Areas:* Autobiography; Biography; Culture; Historical; Politics; Sport; *Markets:* Adult; *Treatments:* Popular

Specialises in nonfiction, including sports, memoir, history, popular reference and politics. No scripts or screenplays. Most clients by recommendation, but will consider email queries. See website for correct email addresses for different subjects. No submissions by post.

David Godwin Associates

55 Monmouth Street, London, WC2H 9DG
Tel: +44 (0) 20 7240 9992
Email: sebastiangodwin@davidgodwinassociates.co.uk
Website: http://www.davidgodwinassociates.com

Handles: Fiction; Nonfiction; *Markets:* Adult; *Treatments:* Literary

Handles a range of nonfiction and fiction. Send query by email with synopsis and first 30 pages. No poetry. No picture books, except for existing clients.

DHH Literary Agency Ltd

23-27 Cecil Court, London, WC2N 4EZ
Tel: +44 (0) 20 7836 7376
Email: enquiries@dhhliteraryagency.com
Website: http://www.dhhliteraryagency.com

Handles: Fiction; Nonfiction; Scripts; *Areas:* Adventure; Archaeology; Autobiography; Biography; Crime; Fantasy; Film; Historical; Sci-Fi; Theatre; Thrillers; TV; Women's Interests; *Markets:* Adult; Children's; Youth; *Treatments:* Literary

Accepts submissions by email only. No postal submissions. See website for specific agent interests and email addresses and approach one agent only. Do not send submissions to generic "enquiries" email address.

Diamond Kahn and Woods (DKW) Literary Agency Ltd

Top Floor, 66 Onslow Gardens, London, N10 3JX
Tel: +44 (0) 20 3514 6544
Email: info@dkwlitagency.co.uk
Website: http://dkwlitagency.co.uk

Handles: Fiction; Nonfiction; *Areas:* Adventure; Archaeology; Biography; Crime; Culture; Fantasy; Gothic; Historical; Humour; Politics; Sci-Fi; Sociology; Suspense; Thrillers; *Markets:* Adult; Children's; Youth; *Treatments:* Commercial; Contemporary; Literary

Send submissions by email. See website for specific agent interests and contact details. Do not send submissions to general agency email address.

Diane Banks Associates Literary Agency

Email: submissions@dianebanks.co.uk
Website: http://www.dianebanks.co.uk

Handles: Fiction; Nonfiction; *Areas:* Autobiography; Beauty and Fashion; Business; Crime; Culture; Current Affairs; Entertainment; Health; Historical; Lifestyle; Psychology; Science; Self-Help; Thrillers; Women's Interests; *Markets:* Adult; Youth; *Treatments:* Commercial; Literary; Popular

Send query with author bio, synopsis, and the first three chapters by email as Word or Open Document attachments. No poetry, plays, scripts, academic books, short stories or children's books, with the exception of young adult fiction. Hard copy submissions are not accepted will not be read or returned.

Dinah Wiener Ltd

12 Cornwall Grove, Chiswick, London, W4 2LB
Tel: +44 (0) 20 8994 6011
Email: dinah@dwla.co.uk

Handles: Fiction; Nonfiction; *Areas:* Autobiography; Biography; Cookery; Science; *Markets:* Adult

Note: Not taking on new clients as at January 2017.

Send preliminary query letter with SAE. No poetry, scripts, or children's books.

Toby Eady Associates Ltd

Third Floor, 9 Orme Court, London, W2 4RL
Tel: +44 (0) 20 7792 0092
Fax: +44 (0) 20 7792 0879
Email: submissions@tobyeadyassociates.co.uk
Website: http://www.tobyeadyassociates.co.uk

Handles: Fiction; Nonfiction; *Markets:* Adult

Send first 50 pages of your fiction or nonfiction work by email, with a synopsis, and a letter including biographical information. If submitting by post, include SAE for return of material, if required. No film / TV scripts or poetry. Particular interest in China, Middle East, India, and Africa.

Eddison Pearson Ltd

West Hill House, 6 Swains Lane, London, N6 6QS
Tel: +44 (0) 20 7700 7763
Fax: +44 (0) 20 7700 7866
Email: enquiries@eddisonpearson.com
Website: http://www.eddisonpearson.com

Handles: Fiction; Nonfiction; Poetry; *Markets:* Children's; Youth; *Treatments:* Literary

Send query by email only (or even blank email) for auto-response containing up-to-date submission guidelines and email address for submissions. No unsolicited MSS. No longer accepts submissions or enquiries by post. Send query with first two chapters by email only to address provided in auto-response. Response in 6-10 weeks. If no response after 10 weeks send email query.

Edwards Fuglewicz

49 Great Ormond Street, London, WC1N 3HZ
Tel: +44 (0) 20 7405 6725
Fax: +44 (0) 20 7405 6726
Email: info@efla.co.uk

Handles: Fiction; Nonfiction; *Areas:* Biography; Crime; Culture; Historical; Humour; Mystery; Romance; Thrillers; *Markets:* Adult; *Treatments:* Commercial; Literary

Handles literary and commercial fiction, and nonfiction. No children's, science fiction, horror, or email submissions.

Elaine Steel

49 Greek Street, London, W1D 4EG
Tel: +44 (0) 1273 739022
Email: info@elainesteel.com
Website: http://www.elainesteel.com

Handles: Fiction; Nonfiction; Scripts; *Areas:* Film; Radio; TV; *Markets:* Adult

Send query by email with CV and outline, along with details of experience. No unsolicited mss.

Elise Dillsworth Agency (EDA)

9 Grosvenor Road, London, N10 2DR
Email: submissions@elisedillsworthagency.com
Website: http://elisedillsworthagency.com

Handles: Fiction; Nonfiction; *Areas:* Autobiography; Biography; Cookery; Travel; *Markets:* Adult; *Treatments:* Commercial; Literary

Represents writers from around the world. Looking for literary and commercial fiction, and nonfiction (especially memoir, autobiography, biography, cookery and travel writing). No science fiction, fantasy, poetry, film scripts, plays, young adult, or children's. Send query by email only (postal submissions no longer accepted). For fiction, include synopsis up to two pages and first three chapters, up to about 50 pages, as Word or PDF attachments. For nonfiction, send details of expertise / credentials, proposal, chapter outline, and writing sample of around 30 pages as a Word file attachment. See website for full guidelines. Response in 6-8 weeks.

Elizabeth Roy Literary Agency

White Cottage, Greatford, Stamford, Lincolnshire PE9 4PR
Tel: +44 (0) 1778 560672
Website: http://www.elizabethroy.co.uk

Handles: Fiction; Nonfiction; *Markets:* Children's

Handles fiction and nonfiction for children. Particularly interested in funny fiction, gentle romance for young teens, picture book texts for pre-school children, and books with international market appeal. Send query by post with return postage, synopsis, and sample chapters. No science fiction, poetry, plays or adult books.

Emily Sweet Associates

Website: http://www.emilysweetassociates.com

Handles: Fiction; Nonfiction; *Areas:* Biography; Cookery; Current Affairs; Historical; *Markets:* Adult; *Treatments:* Commercial; Literary

No Young Adult or children's. Query through form on website in first instance.

Faith Evans Associates

27 Park Avenue North, London, N8 7RU
Tel: +44 (0) 20 8340 9920
Fax: +44 (0) 20 8340 9410
Email: faith@faith-evans.co.uk

Handles: Fiction; Nonfiction; *Markets:* Adult

Small agency with full list. Not accepting new clients as at January 2016. No phone calls, or unsolicited MSS.

Eve White: Literary Agent

54 Gloucester Street, London, SW1V 4EG
Tel: +44 (0) 20 7630 1155
Email: eve@evewhite.co.uk
Website: http://www.evewhite.co.uk

Handles: Fiction; Nonfiction; *Markets:* Adult; Children's; Youth; *Treatments:* Commercial; Literary

Important! Check and follow website submission guidelines before contacting!

DO NOT send submissions to email address listed on this page – see website for specific submission email addresses for different areas.

QUERIES ONLY to the email address on this page.

This agency requests that you go to their website for up-to-date submission procedure.

Commercial and literary fiction, nonfiction, children's fiction and picture books ages 7+ (home 15%, overseas 20%). No reading fee. No poetry, short stories, novellas, screenplays, or science fiction/fantasy for adults. Does not consider approaches from US writers. See website for detailed submission guidelines. Submission by email only.

The Feldstein Agency

54 Abbey Street, Bangor, Northern Ireland BT20 4JB
Tel: +44 (0) 2891 472823
Email: submissions@thefeldsteinagency.co.uk
Website: http://www.thefeldsteinagency.co.uk

Handles: Fiction; Nonfiction; *Areas:* Adventure; Autobiography; Biography; Business; Cookery; Crime; Criticism; Current Affairs; Historical; Humour; Leisure; Lifestyle; Media; Military; Music; Mystery; Philosophy; Politics; Sociology; Sport; Thrillers; Travel; Women's Interests;

Markets: Adult; *Treatments:* Commercial; Literary

Handles adult fiction and nonfiction only. No children's, young adult, romance, science fiction, fantasy, poetry, scripts, or short stories. Send query by email with 1-2 pages synopsis. No reading fees or evaluation fees. The only instance in which an author would be charged a fee is for ghost-writing.

Felicity Bryan Associates

2a North Parade Avenue, Banbury Road, Oxford, OX2 6LX
Tel: +44 (0) 1865 513816
Fax: +44 (0) 1865 310055
Email: agency@felicitybryan.com
Website: http://www.felicitybryan.com

Handles: Fiction; Nonfiction; *Areas:* Biography; Current Affairs; Historical; Science; *Markets:* Adult; Children's; Youth; *Treatments:* Commercial; Literary

Particularly interested in commercial and literary fiction and nonfiction for the adult market, children's fiction for 8+, and Young Adult. Send query by post with sufficient postage, or via submission form on website. See website for detailed submission guidelines. No science fiction, horror, adult fantasy, light romance, self-help, gardening, film and TV scripts, plays, poetry or picture/illustrated books.

Felix de Wolfe

20 Old Compton Street, London, W1D 4TW
Tel: +44 (0) 20 7242 5066
Fax: +44 (0) 20 7242 8119
Email: info@felixdewolfe.com
Website: http://www.felixdewolfe.com

Handles: Fiction; Scripts; *Areas:* Film; Radio; Theatre; TV; *Markets:* Adult

Send query letter with SAE, short synopsis, and CV by post only, unless alternative arrangements have been made with the agency in advance. Quality fiction and scripts only. No nonfiction, children's books, or unsolicited MSS.

Film Rights Ltd in association with Laurence Fitch Ltd

11 Pandora Road, London, NW6 1TS
Tel: +44 (0) 20 8001 3040
Fax: +44 (0) 20 8711 3171
Email: information@filmrights.ltd.uk
Website: http://filmrights.ltd.uk

Handles: Fiction; Scripts; *Areas:* Film; Horror; Radio; Theatre; TV; *Markets:* Adult; Children's

Represents films, plays, and novels, for adults and children.

Jill Foster Ltd (JFL)

48 Charlotte Street, London, W1T 2NS
Tel: +44 (0) 20 3137 8182
Email: agents@jflagency.com
Website: http://www.jflagency.com

Handles: Scripts; *Areas:* Drama; Film; Humour; Radio; Theatre; TV; *Markets:* Adult

Handles scripts only (for television, film, theatre and radio). Considers approaches from established writers with broadcast experience, but only accepts submissions from new writers during specific periods – consult website for details.

Fox & Howard Literary Agency

39 Eland Road, London, SW11 5JX
Tel: +44 (0) 20 7352 8691
Email: enquiries@foxandhoward.co.uk
Website: http://www.foxandhoward.co.uk

Handles: Nonfiction; Reference; *Areas:* Biography; Business; Culture; Health; Historical; Lifestyle; Psychology; Self-Help; Spiritual; *Markets:* Adult

Closed to submissions as at February 2016. Please check website for current status and use Report an Error function above if it has changed.

Send query with synopsis and SAE for response. Small agency specialising in nonfiction that works closely with its authors. No unsolicited MSS.

Fraser Ross Associates

6/2 Wellington Place, Edinburgh, Scotland EH6 7EQ
Tel: +44 (0) 01315 532759
Email: fraserrossassociates@gmail.com
Website: http://www.fraserross.co.uk

Handles: Fiction; *Markets:* Adult; Children's; *Treatments:* Commercial; Literary; Mainstream

Send query by email or by post with SAE, including CV, the first three chapters and synopsis for fiction, or a one page proposal and the opening and a further two chapters for nonfiction. For picture books, send complete MS, without illustrations. Rarely accept poetry, playscripts or short stories.

Furniss Lawton

James Grant Group Ltd, 94 Strand on the Green, Chiswick, London, W4 3NN
Tel: +44 (0) 20 8987 6804
Email: info@furnisslawton.co.uk
Website: http://www.jamesgrant.com/furniss-lawton/

Handles: Fiction; Nonfiction; *Areas:* Autobiography; Biography; Business; Cookery; Crime; Fantasy; Historical; Humour; Politics; Psychology; Science; Sociology; Sport; Suspense; Thrillers; Women's Interests; *Markets:* Adult; Children's; Youth; *Treatments:* Commercial; Contemporary; Literary; Popular

Send query with synopsis and first 10,000 words / three chapters as a Word or PDF document by email. Include the word "Submission" in the subject line, and your name and the title of the work in any attachments. No submissions by post. Does not handle screenwriters for film or TV. See website for full details.

Noel Gay

19 Denmark Street, London, WC2H 8NA
Tel: +44 (0) 20 7836 3941
Email: info@noelgay.com
Website: http://www.noelgay.com

Handles: Scripts; *Markets:* Adult

Agency representing writers, directors, performers, presenters, comedians, etc. Send query with SASE.

Georgina Capel Associates Ltd

29 Wardour Street, London, W1D 6PS
Tel: +44 (0) 20 7734 2414
Email: georgina@georginacapel.com
Website: http://www.georginacapel.com

Handles: Fiction; Nonfiction; *Areas:* Biography; Film; Historical; Radio; TV; *Markets:* Adult; *Treatments:* Commercial; Literary

Handles general fiction and nonfiction. Send query outlining writing history (for nonfiction, what qualifies you to write your book), with synopsis around 500 words and first three chapters, plus SAE or email address for reply. Submissions are not returned. Mark envelope for the attention of the Submissions Department. Accepts submissions by email, but prefers them by post. Response only if interested, normally within 6 weeks. Film and TV scripts handled for established clients only.

Eric Glass Ltd

25 Ladbroke Crescent, London, W11 1PS
Tel: +44 (0) 20 7229 9500
Fax: +44 (0) 20 7229 6220
Email: eglassltd@aol.com

Handles: Fiction; Nonfiction; Scripts; *Areas:* Film; Theatre; TV; *Markets:* Adult

Handles full-length mss and scripts for film, TV, and theatre. Send query with SAE. No children's books, short stories, poetry, or unsolicited MSS.

Graham Maw Christie Literary Agency

37 Highbury Place, London, N5 1QP
Tel: +44 (0) 7971 268342
Email: submissions@grahammawchristie.com
Website: http://www.grahammawchristie.com

Handles: Nonfiction; Reference; *Areas:* Autobiography; Business; Cookery; Crafts;

Gardening; Health; Historical; Humour; Lifestyle; Philosophy; Science; Self-Help; *Markets:* Adult; Children's

No fiction, poetry, or scripts. Send query with one-page summary, a paragraph on the contents of each chapter, your qualifications for writing it, details of your online presence, market analysis, what you could do to help promote your book, and a sample chapter. Accepts approaches by email.

Christine Green Authors' Agent

LSBU Technopark, 90 London Road, London, SE1 6LN
Tel: +44 (0) 20 7401 8844
Email: info@christinegreen.co.uk
Website: http://www.christinegreen.co.uk

Handles: Fiction; Nonfiction; *Markets:* Adult; Youth; *Treatments:* Commercial; Literary

Focusses on fiction for adult and young adult, and also considers narrative nonfiction. No children's books, genre science-fiction/fantasy, poetry or scripts. Send query by email (preferred) or by post with SAE. No submissions by fax or CD. See website for full submission guidelines.

Louise Greenberg Books Ltd

The End House, Church Crescent, London, N3 1BG
Tel: +44 (0) 20 8349 1179
Email: louisegreenberg@msn.com

Handles: Fiction; Nonfiction; *Markets:* Adult; *Treatments:* Literary; Serious

Handles full-length literary fiction and serious nonfiction only. All approaches must be accompanied by SAE. No approaches by telephone.

Greene & Heaton Ltd

37 Goldhawk Road, London, W12 8QQ
Tel: +44 (0) 20 8749 0315
Fax: +44 (0) 20 8749 0318
Email: submissions@greeneheaton.co.uk
Website: http://www.greeneheaton.co.uk

Handles: Fiction; Nonfiction; *Areas:* Arts; Autobiography; Biography; Cookery; Crime; Culture; Current Affairs; Gardening; Health; Historical; Humour; Philosophy; Politics; Romance; Science; Sci-Fi; Thrillers; Travel; *Markets:* Adult; Children's; *Treatments:* Commercial; Contemporary; Literary; Traditional

Send query by email or by post with SAE, including synopsis and three chapters or approximately 50 pages. No response to unsolicited MSS with no SAE or inadequate means of return postage provided. No response to email submissions unless interested. Handles all types of fiction and nonfiction, but no scripts.

The Greenhouse Literary Agency

Tel: +44 (0) 20 7841 3959
Email: submissions@greenhouseliterary.com
Website: http://www.greenhouseliterary.com

Handles: Fiction; *Markets:* Children's; Youth

Transatlantic agency with offices in the US and London. Handles children's and young adult fiction only. For novels, send query by email with first five pages pasted into the body of the email. For picture books (maximum 1,000 words) paste full text into the boxy of the email. No illustrations required at this stage, unless you are an author/illustrator. No attachments or hard copy submissions.

Gregory & Company, Authors' Agents

3 Barb Mews, London, W6 7PA
Tel: +44 (0) 20 7610 4676
Fax: +44 (0) 20 7610 4686
Email: maryjones@gregoryandcompany.co.uk
Website: http://www.gregoryandcompany.co.uk

Handles: Fiction; *Areas:* Crime; Historical; Thrillers; *Markets:* Adult; *Treatments:* Commercial

Particularly interested in Crime, Family Sagas, Historical Fiction, Thrillers and Upmarket Commercial Fiction.
Send query with CV, one-page synopsis, future writing plans, and first ten pages, by post with SAE, or by email. No unsolicited MSS, Business Books, Children's, Young Adult Fiction, Plays, Screenplays, Poetry, Science Fiction, Future Fiction, Fantasy, Self Help, Lifestyle books, Short Stories, Spiritual, New Age, Philosophy, Supernatural, Paranormal, Horror, Travel, or True Crime.

David Grossman Literary Agency Ltd

118b Holland Park Avenue, London, W11 4UA
Tel: +44 (0) 20 7221 2770
Email: david@dglal.co.uk

Handles: Fiction; Nonfiction; *Markets:* Adult

Send preliminary letter before making a submission. No approaches or submissions by fax or email. Usually works with published fiction writers, but well-written and original work from beginners considered. No poetry, scripts, technical books for students, or unsolicited MSS.

Gunn Media Associates

50 Albemarle Street, London, W1S 4BD
Tel: +44 (0) 20 7529 3745
Website: http://www.gunnmedia.co.uk

Handles: Fiction; Nonfiction; *Areas:* Autobiography; Entertainment; Thrillers; *Markets:* Adult; *Treatments:* Commercial; Literary

Handles commercial fiction and nonfiction, including literary, thrillers, and celebrity autobiographies.

Hardman & Swainson

4 Kelmscott Road, London, SW11 6QY
Tel: +44 (0) 20 7223 5176
Email: submissions@hardmanswainson.com
Website: http://www.hardmanswainson.com

Handles: Fiction; Nonfiction; *Areas:* Autobiography; Crime; Historical; Horror; Philosophy; Science; Thrillers; Women's Interests; *Markets:* Adult; Children's; Youth; *Treatments:* Literary; Popular

Agency launched June 2012 by former colleagues at an established agency. Welcomes submissions of fiction and nonfiction. No poetry, plays / screenplays / scripts, or very young children's / picture books. No submissions by post. See website for full submission guidelines.

Antony Harwood Limited

103 Walton Street, Oxford, OX2 6EB
Tel: +44 (0) 1865 559615
Fax: +44 (0) 1865 310660
Email: mail@antonyharwood.com
Website: http://www.antonyharwood.com

Handles: Fiction; Nonfiction; *Areas:* Adventure; Anthropology; Antiques; Archaeology; Architecture; Arts; Autobiography; Beauty and Fashion; Biography; Business; Cookery; Crafts; Crime; Criticism; Culture; Current Affairs; Design; Drama; Entertainment; Erotic; Fantasy; Film; Finance; Gardening; Gothic; Health; Historical; Hobbies; Horror; How-to; Humour; Legal; Leisure; Lifestyle; Literature; Media; Medicine; Men's Interests; Military; Music; Mystery; Nature; New Age; Philosophy; Photography; Politics; Psychology; Radio; Religious; Romance; Science; Sci-Fi; Self-Help; Short Stories; Sociology; Spiritual; Sport; Suspense; Technology; Theatre; Thrillers; Translations; Travel; TV; Westerns; Women's Interests; *Markets:* Adult; Children's; Youth

Handles fiction and nonfiction in every genre and category, except for screenwriting and poetry. Send brief outline and first 50 pages by email, or by post with SASE.

A M Heath & Company Limited, Author's Agents

6 Warwick Court, Holborn, London, WC1R 5DJ
Tel: +44 (0) 20 7242 2811
Fax: +44 (0) 20 7242 2711
Email: enquiries@amheath.com
Website: http://www.amheath.com

Handles: Fiction; Nonfiction; *Areas:* Biography; Cookery; Crime; Historical; Nature; Psychology; Sport; Suspense; Thrillers; Women's Interests; *Markets:* Adult; Children's; Youth; *Treatments:* Commercial; Literary

Handles general commercial and literary fiction and nonfiction. Submit work with cover letter and synopsis via online submission system only. No paper submissions. Aims to respond within six weeks.

Rupert Heath Literary Agency

50 Albemarle Street, London, W1S 4BD
Tel: +44 (0) 20 7060 3385
Email: emailagency@rupertheath.com
Website: http://www.rupertheath.com

Handles: Fiction; Nonfiction; *Areas:* Arts; Autobiography; Biography; Crime; Culture; Current Affairs; Historical; Humour; Nature; Politics; Science; Sci-Fi; Thrillers; *Markets:* Adult; *Treatments:* Commercial; Literary; Popular

Send query giving some information about yourself and the work you would like to submit. Prefers queries by email. Response only if interested.

David Higham Associates Ltd

7th Floor, Waverley House, 7–12 Noel Street, London, W1F 8GQ
Tel: +44 (0) 20 7434 5900
Fax: +44 (0) 20 7437 1072
Email: dha@davidhigham.co.uk
Website: http://www.davidhigham.co.uk

Handles: Fiction; Nonfiction; Scripts; *Areas:* Autobiography; Biography; Cookery; Crime; Current Affairs; Drama; Film; Historical; Humour; Nature; Theatre; Thrillers; TV; *Markets:* Adult; Children's; *Treatments:* Commercial; Literary; Serious

For adult fiction and nonfiction contact "Adult Submissions Department" by post only with SASE, covering letter, CV, and synopsis (fiction)/proposal (nonfiction) and first two or three chapters. For children's fiction submit by email to the specific children's submission address given on the website, with covering letter, synopsis, CV, and first two or three chapters (or complete MS if a picture book). See website for complete guidelines. Scripts by referral only.

Vanessa Holt Ltd

59 Crescent Road, Leigh-on-Sea, Essex SS9 2PF
Tel: +44 (0) 1702 473787
Email: v.holt791@btinternet.com

Handles: Fiction; Nonfiction; *Markets:* Adult

General fiction and nonfiction. No unsolicited mss or overseas approaches.

Kate Hordern Literary Agency

18 Mortimer Road, Clifton, Bristol, BS8 4EY
Tel: +44 (0) 117 923 9368
Email: katehordern@blueyonder.co.uk
Website: http://www.katehordern.co.uk

Handles: Fiction; Nonfiction; Reference; *Areas:* Autobiography; Business; Crime; Culture; Current Affairs; Historical; Sociology; Thrillers; Women's Interests; *Markets:* Adult; Children's; Youth; *Treatments:* Commercial; Contemporary; Literary; Popular

Send query by email only with pitch, outline or synopsis, and first three chapters. No submissions by post, or from authors not resident in the UK.

Valerie Hoskins Associates

20 Charlotte Street, London, W1T 2NA
Tel: +44 (0) 20 7637 4490
Fax: +44 (0) 20 7637 4493
Email: info@vhassociates.co.uk
Website: http://www.vhassociates.co.uk

Handles: Scripts; *Areas:* Film; Radio; TV; *Markets:* Adult

Always on the lookout for screenwriters with an original voice and creatives with big ideas. Query by email or by phone. Allow up to eight weeks for response to submissions.

Hunter Profiles

London,
Email: info@hunterprofiles.com
Website: http://www.hunterprofiles.com

Handles: Fiction; Nonfiction; *Markets:* Adult; *Treatments:* Commercial

We specialise in commercial and narrative fiction and nonfiction. We only accept proposals by email. See website for submission guidelines.

Independent Talent Group Ltd

40 Whitfield Street, London, W1T 2RH
Tel: +44 (0) 20 7636 6565
Fax: +44 (0) 20 7323 0101
Email: laurarourke@independenttalent.com
Website: http://www.independenttalent.com

Handles: Scripts; *Areas:* Film; Radio; Theatre; TV; *Markets:* Adult

Specialises in scripts and works in association with agencies in Los Angeles and New York. No unsolicited MSS. Materials submitted will not be returned.

Intercontinental Literary Agency

5 New Concordia Wharf, Mill Street, London, SE1 2BB
Tel: +44 (0) 20 7379 6611
Fax: +44 (0) 20 7240 4724
Email: ila@ila-agency.co.uk
Website: http://www.ila-agency.co.uk

Handles: Fiction; Nonfiction; *Areas:* Translations; *Markets:* Adult; Children's

Handles translation rights only for, among others, the authors of LAW Ltd, London; Harold Matson Co. Inc., New York; PFD, London. Submissions accepted via client agencies and publishers only – no submissions from writers seeking agents.

Isabel White Literary Agent

Tel: +44 (0) 20 3070 1602
Email: query.isabelwhite@googlemail.com
Website: http://www.isabelwhite.co.uk

Handles: Fiction; Nonfiction; *Markets:* Adult

Selective one-woman agency, not taking on new clients as at January 2017.

Jane Conway-Gordon Ltd

38 Cromwell Grove, London, W6 7RG
Tel: +44 (0) 20 7371 6939
Email: jane@conway-gordon.co.uk
Website: http://www.janeconwaygordon.com

Handles: Fiction; Nonfiction; *Markets:* Adult

Handles fiction and general nonfiction. Prefers to receive queries by post with SASE, synopsis, and first 3 chapters or 40 pages; but will also accept short email describing the book (no attachments). No poetry, children's or science fiction.

Jane Turnbull

Barn Cottage, Veryan, Truro TR2 5QA
Tel: +44 (0) 20 7727 9409 / +44 (0) 1872 501317
Email: jane@janeturnbull.co.uk
Website: http://www.janeturnbull.co.uk

Handles: Fiction; Nonfiction; *Areas:* Biography; Current Affairs; Entertainment; Gardening; Historical; Humour; Lifestyle; Nature; TV; *Markets:* Adult; Youth; *Treatments:* Commercial; Literary; Mainstream

Agency with offices in London and Cornwall. New clients always welcome and a few taken on every year. Will occasionally take on fiction for older children, but no science fiction, fantasy, or "misery memoirs". Send query by post to Cornwall office with short description of your book or idea. No unsolicited MSS.

Janet Fillingham Associates

52 Lowther Road, London, SW13 9NU
Tel: +44 (0) 20 8748 5594
Fax: +44 (0) 20 8748 7374
Email: info@janetfillingham.com
Website: http://www.janetfillingham.com

Handles: Scripts; *Areas:* Film; Theatre; TV; *Markets:* Adult; Children's; Youth

Represents writers and directors for stage, film and TV, as well as librettists, lyricists and composers in musical theatre. Does not represent books. Prospective clients may register via website.

Jenny Brown Associates

31 Marchmont Road, Edinburgh, Scotland
EH9 1HU
Tel: +44 (0) 1312 295334
Email: submissions@jennybrownassociates.com
Website: http://www.jennybrownassociates.com

Handles: Fiction; Nonfiction; *Areas:* Autobiography; Biography; Crime; Culture; Finance; Historical; Humour; Music; Romance; Science; Sport; Thrillers; Women's Interests; *Markets:* Adult; Children's; *Treatments:* Commercial; Literary; Popular

Strongly prefers queries by email. Approach by post only if not possible to do so by email. Send query with market information, bio, synopsis and first 50 pages in one document (fiction) or sample chapter and info on market and your background (nonfiction). No academic, poetry, short stories, science fiction, or fantasy. Responds only if interested. If no response in 8 weeks assume rejection. Different agents are open to queries at different times. See website for individual agent interests, submission status, and email addresses.

Jo Unwin Literary Agency

West Wing, Somerset House, London,
WC2R 1LA
Tel: +44 (0) 20 7257 9599
Email: submissions@jounwin.co.uk
Website: http://www.jounwin.co.uk

Handles: Fiction; Nonfiction; *Areas:* Humour; Women's Interests; *Markets:* Adult; Children's; Youth; *Treatments:* Commercial; Literary

Handles literary fiction, commercial women's fiction, comic writing, narrative nonfiction, Young Adult fiction and fiction for children aged 9+. No poetry, picture books, or screenplays, except for existing clients. Accepts submissions by email. Mainly represents authors from the UK and Ireland, and sometimes Australia and New Zealand. Only represents US authors in very exceptional circumstances. See website for full guidelines.

Johnson & Alcock

Clerkenwell House, 45/47 Clerkenwell
Green, London, EC1R 0HT
Tel: +44 (0) 20 7251 0125
Fax: +44 (0) 20 7251 2172
Email: info@johnsonandalcock.co.uk
Website: http://www.johnsonandalcock.co.uk

Handles: Fiction; Nonfiction; Poetry; *Areas:* Arts; Autobiography; Biography; Crime; Culture; Current Affairs; Design; Film; Health; Historical; Lifestyle; Music; Nature; Psychology; Science; Sci-Fi; Self-Help; Sport; Suspense; Thrillers; Women's Interests; *Markets:* Adult; Children's; Youth; *Treatments:* Commercial; Literary; Popular

Send query by email (response only if interested), or by post with SASE. Include synopsis and first three chapters (approximately 50 pages). Email submissions should go to specific agents. See website for list of agents and full submission guidelines. No poetry, screenplays, children's books 0-7, or board or picture books.

Jonathan Clowes Ltd

10 Iron Bridge House, Bridge Approach,
London, NW1 8BD
Tel: +44 (0) 20 7722 7674
Fax: +44 (0) 20 7722 7677
Email: cara@jonathanclowes.co.uk
Website: http://www.jonathanclowes.co.uk

Handles: Fiction; Nonfiction; Scripts; *Areas:* Film; Radio; Theatre; TV; *Markets:* Adult; *Treatments:* Commercial; Literary

Send query with synopsis and three chapters (or equivalent sample) by email. No science fiction, poetry, short stories, academic. Only considers film/TV clients with previous success in TV/film/theatre. If no response within six weeks, assume rejection.

Jonathan Pegg Literary Agency

67 Wingate Square, London, SW4 OAF
Tel: +44 (0) 20 7603 6830
Email: submissions@jonathanpegg.com
Website: http://www.jonathanpegg.com

Handles: Fiction; Nonfiction; *Areas:* Arts; Autobiography; Biography; Culture; Current Affairs; Historical; Lifestyle; Nature; Psychology; Science; Thrillers; *Markets:* Adult; *Treatments:* Commercial; Literary; Popular

Established by the agent after twelve years at Curtis Brown. The agency's main areas of interest are:

Fiction: literary fiction, thrillers and quality commercial in general
Non-Fiction: current affairs, memoir and biography, history, popular science, nature, arts and culture, lifestyle, popular psychology

Rights:
Aside from the UK market, the agency will work in association with translation, US, TV & film agents according to each client's best interests.

If you're looking for an agent:
I accept submissions by email. See website for full submission guidelines.

Juliet Burton Literary Agency

2 Clifton Avenue, London, W12 9DR
Tel: +44 (0) 20 8762 0148
Email: juliet.burton@btinternet.com

Handles: Fiction; Nonfiction; *Areas:* Crime; Women's Interests; *Markets:* Adult

Particularly interested in crime and women's fiction. Send query with SAE, synopsis, and two sample chapters. No poetry, plays, film scripts, children's, articles, academic material, science fiction, fantasy, unsolicited MSS, or email submissions.

Michelle Kass Associates

85 Charing Cross Road, London, WC2H 0AA
Tel: +44 (0) 20 7439 1624
Fax: +44 (0) 20 7734 3394
Email: office@michellekass.co.uk
Website: http://www.michellekass.co.uk

Handles: Fiction; Scripts; *Areas:* Film; Literature; TV; *Markets:* Adult; *Treatments:* Literary

No email submissions. Approach by telephone in first instance.

Keane Kataria Literary Agency

1 Queen Square, Bath, BA1 2HA
Email: info@keanekataria.co.uk
Website: http://www.keanekataria.co.uk

Handles: Fiction; Nonfiction; *Areas:* Biography; Crime; Historical; Romance; Women's Interests; *Markets:* Adult; *Treatments:* Commercial

Actively seeking commercial fiction and nonfiction. In fiction, handles crime, romance, women's, sagas, historical and general. In nonfiction, handles narrative nonfiction, biography, and subjects with wide general appeal. No science fiction, fantasy or children's books. Send query by email only with synopsis and first three chapters. Attachments in PDF format only.

Frances Kelly

111 Clifton Road, Kingston upon Thames, Surrey KT2 6PL
Tel: +44 (0) 20 8549 7830
Fax: +44 (0) 20 8547 0051

Handles: Nonfiction; Reference; *Areas:* Arts; Biography; Business; Cookery; Finance; Health; Historical; Lifestyle; Medicine; Self-Help; *Markets:* Academic; Adult; Professional

Send query with SAE, CV, and synopsis or brief description of work. Scripts handled for existing clients only. No unsolicited MSS.

Ki Agency Ltd

Studio 315, Screenworks, 22 Highbury Grove, London, N5 2ER
Tel: +44 (0) 20 3214 8287
Email: meg@ki-agency.co.uk
Website: http://www.ki-agency.co.uk

Handles: Fiction; Nonfiction; Scripts; *Areas:* Culture; Film; Historical; Politics; Science; Self-Help; Sport; Theatre; TV; *Markets:* Adult; *Treatments:* Popular

Represents novelists and scriptwriters in all media. No children's or YA novels, humorous science fiction or commercial women's fiction. Send synopsis and first three chapters by email. See website for individual agent interests.

Barbara Levy Literary Agency

64 Greenhill, Hampstead High Street, London, NW3 5TZ
Tel: +44 (0) 20 7435 9046
Fax: +44 (0) 20 7431 2063
Email: blevysubmissions@gmail.com

Handles: Fiction; Nonfiction; *Markets:* Adult

Send query with synopsis by email or by post with SAE.

Limelight Management

10 Filmer Mews, 75 Filmer Road, London, SW6 7JF
Tel: +44 (0) 20 7384 9950
Fax: +44 (0) 20 7384 9955
Email: mail@limelightmanagement.com
Website: http://www.limelightmanagement.com

Handles: Fiction; Nonfiction; *Areas:* Arts; Autobiography; Biography; Business; Cookery; Crafts; Crime; Health; Historical; Lifestyle; Mystery; Nature; Science; Sport; Suspense; Thrillers; Travel; Women's Interests; *Markets:* Adult; *Treatments:* Commercial; Literary

Always looking for exciting new authors. Send query by email with the word "Submission" in the subject line and synopsis and first three chapters as Word or Open Document attachments. Also include market info, and details of your professional life and writing ambitions. Film and TV scripts for existing clients only. See website for full guidelines.

Linda Seifert Management

Screenworks, Room 315, 22 Highbury Grove, Islington, London, N5 2ER
Tel: +44 (0) 20 3214 8293
Email: contact@lindaseifert.com
Website: http://www.lindaseifert.com

Handles: Scripts; *Areas:* Film; TV; *Markets:* Adult; Children's

A London-based management company representing screenwriters and directors for film and television. Our outstanding client list ranges from the highly established to the new and exciting emerging talent of tomorrow. Represents UK-based writers and directors only. Not currently accepting unsolicited submissions as at October 2016.

Lindsay Literary Agency

East Worldham House, East Worldham, Alton GU34 3AT
Tel: +44 (0) 0142 083143
Email: info@lindsayliteraryagency.co.uk
Website: http://www.lindsayliteraryagency.co.uk

Handles: Fiction; Nonfiction; *Markets:* Adult; Children's; *Treatments:* Literary; Serious

Send query by post with SASE or by email, including single-page synopsis and first three chapters. For picture books send complete ms.

London Independent Books

26 Chalcot Crescent, London, NW1 8YD
Tel: +44 (0) 20 7722 7160

Handles: Fiction; Nonfiction; *Areas:* Fantasy; *Markets:* Adult; Youth; *Treatments:* Commercial

Send query with synopsis, SASE, and first two chapters. All fiction and nonfiction subjects considered if treatment is strong and saleable, but no computer books, young children's, or unsolicited MSS. Particularly interested in commercial fiction, fantasy, and teen fiction. Scripts handled for existing clients only.

Lorella Belli Literary Agency (LBLA)

54 Hartford House, 35 Tavistock Crescent, Notting Hill, London, W11 1AY
Tel: +44 (0) 20 7727 8547
Fax: +44 (0) 870 787 4194
Email: info@lorellabelliagency.com
Website: http://www.lorellabelliagency.com

Handles: Fiction; Nonfiction; *Markets:* Adult; *Treatments:* Literary

Send query by post or by email in first instance. No attachments. Particularly interested in multicultural / international writing, and books relating to Italy, or written in Italian; first novelists, and journalists; successful sel-published authors. Welcomes queries from new authors and will suggest revisions where appropriate. No poetry, children's, original scripts, academic, SF, or fantasy.

Lutyens and Rubinstein

21 Kensington Park Road, London, W11 2EU
Tel: +44 (0) 20 7792 4855
Email: submissions@lutyensrubinstein.co.uk
Website: http://www.lutyensrubinstein.co.uk

Handles: Fiction; Nonfiction; *Areas:* Cookery; *Markets:* Adult; Children's; Youth; *Treatments:* Commercial; Literary

Send up to 5,000 words or first three chapters by email with covering letter and short synopsis. No film or TV scripts, or unsolicited submissions by hand or by post.

Macnaughton Lord Representation

44 South Molton Street, London, W1K 5RT
Tel: +44 (0) 20 7499 1411
Email: info@mlrep.com
Website: http://www.mlrep.com

Handles: Scripts; *Areas:* Arts; Film; Theatre; TV; *Markets:* Adult

Theatrical and literary agency representing established names and emerging talent in theatre, film, tv and the performing arts. Send query by email with CV and a sample of your work.

Madeleine Milburn Literary, TV & Film Agency

10 Shepherd Market, Mayfair, London, W1J 7QF
Tel: +44 (0) 20 7499 7550
Email: submissions@madeleinemilburn.com
Website: http://madeleinemilburn.co.uk

Handles: Fiction; Nonfiction; Scripts; *Areas:* Autobiography; Crime; Fantasy; Film; Historical; Horror; Humour; Mystery; Psychology; Romance; Science; Sci-Fi; Self-Help; Suspense; Thrillers; Translations; TV; Women's Interests; *Markets:* Adult; Children's; Youth; *Treatments:* Literary

Send query by email only, with 1-2 page synopsis and first three chapters for fiction, or proposal and 30-page writing sample for nonfiction. See website for full submission guidelines. Film and TV scripts for established clients only.

Maggie Pearlstine Associates Ltd

31 Ashley Gardens, Ambrosden Avenue, London, SW1P 1QE
Tel: +44 (0) 20 7828 4212
Fax: +44 (0) 20 7834 5546
Email: maggie@pearlstine.co.uk

Handles: Fiction; Nonfiction; *Areas:* Biography; Current Affairs; Health; Historical; *Markets:* Adult

Small, selective agency, not currently taking on new clients.

Andrew Mann Ltd

39 – 41 North Road, London, N7 9DP
Tel: +44 (0) 20 7609 6218
Email: info@andrewmann.co.uk
Website: http://www.andrewmann.co.uk

Handles: Fiction; *Areas:* Crime; Historical; Thrillers; *Markets:* Adult; *Treatments:* Commercial; Literary

Interested in literary and commercial fiction, historical, and crime/thriller. Send query by email, or by post if absolutely necessary with SAE, with brief synopsis and first three chapters or 30 pages. See website for specific email address for crime/thriller submissions. No children's, screenplays or theatre, misery memoirs, new age philosophy, nonfiction, fantasy, science fiction, poetry, short stories, vampires, or dystopian fiction. See website for full submission guidelines.

Marjacq Scripts Ltd

Box 412, 19/21 Crawford St, London, W1H 1PJ
Tel: +44 (0) 20 7935 9499
Fax: +44 (0) 20 7935 9115
Email: subs@marjacq.com
Website: http://www.marjacq.com

Handles: Fiction; Nonfiction; Scripts; *Areas:* Biography; Crime; Film; Health; Historical; Radio; Sci-Fi; Sport; Thrillers; Travel; TV; Women's Interests; *Markets:* Adult; Children's; *Treatments:* Commercial; Literary

For books, send query with synopsis and three sample chapters. For scripts, send short treatment and entire screenplay. All queries must include an SAE for response, if sent by post. If sent by email send only Word or PDF documents less than 2MB. Do not paste work into the body of the email. See website for full details. No poetry, short stories, or stage plays. Do not send queries without including samples of the actual work.

Mary Clemmey Literary Agency

6 Dunollie Road, London, NW5 2XP
Tel: +44 (0) 20 7267 1290
Fax: +44 (0) 20 7813 9757
Email: mcwords@googlemail.com

Handles: Fiction; Nonfiction; Scripts; *Areas:* Film; Radio; Theatre; TV; *Markets:* Adult

Send query with SAE and description of work only. Handles high-quality work with an international market. No children's books, science fiction, fantasy, or unsolicited MSS or submissions by email. Scripts handled for existing clients only. Do not submit a script or idea for a script unless you are already a client.

MBA Literary Agents Ltd

62 Grafton Way, London, W1T 5DW
Tel: +44 (0) 20 7387 2076
Email: submissions@mbalit.co.uk
Website: http://www.mbalit.co.uk

Handles: Fiction; Nonfiction; Scripts; *Areas:* Arts; Biography; Crafts; Film; Health; Historical; Lifestyle; Radio; Self-Help; Theatre; TV; *Markets:* Adult; Children's; Youth; *Treatments:* Commercial; Literary

For books, send query with CV, synopsis and first three chapters. Not currently accepting unsolicited film and television submissions. Submissions by email only, in Word, PDF or Final Draft format. No submissions by post. See website for full submission guidelines. Works in conjunction with agents in most countries.

Duncan McAra

28 Beresford Gardens, Edinburgh, Scotland EH5 3ES
Tel: +44 (0) 131 552 1558
Email: duncanmcara@mac.com

Handles: Fiction; Nonfiction; *Areas:* Archaeology; Architecture; Arts; Biography; Historical; Military; Travel; *Markets:* Adult; *Treatments:* Literary

Also interested in books of Scottish interest. Send query letter with SAE in first instance.

The Michael Greer Literary Agency

51 Aragon Court, 8 Hotspur Street, Kennington, London SE11 6BX
Tel: +44 (0) 777 592 0885
Email: mmichaelgreer@yahoo.co.uk
Website: http://www.wix.com/mmichaelgreer/mgla

Handles: Fiction; Nonfiction; Scripts; *Areas:* Business; Lifestyle; Psychology; Sport; *Markets:* Adult; Children's; Professional; Youth; *Treatments:* Commercial; Contemporary; Literary; Mainstream; Popular; Positive

Currently, represents writing mainly in the Sports genre – be that covering certain players, or covering certain games and the philosophy of sports.

We also accept manuscripts in the Young Adult / Teen Fiction category, and in the

Literary Fiction category – the latter with an emphasis on work set in a City environment.

Miles Stott Children's Literary Agency

East Hook Farm, Lower Quay Road, Hook, Haverfordwest, Pembrokeshire SA62 4LR
Tel: +44 (0) 1437 890570
Email: submissions@milesstottagency.co.uk
Website: http://www.milesstottagency.co.uk

Handles: Fiction; *Markets:* Children's

Handles picture books, novelty books, and children's fiction. No poetry or nonfiction. Not accepting new fiction submissions as at July 2015, however this is due to be reviewed in late 2015. Check website for current status. For picture book submissions, send query by email only, with short covering letter, details about you and your background, and up to three stories a Word or PDF attachments. See website for full guidelines.

Mulcahy Associates

First Floor, 7 Meard Street, London, W1F 0EW
Email: submissions@ma-agency.com
Website: http://www.ma-agency.com

Handles: Fiction; Nonfiction; *Areas:* Biography; Crime; Finance; Historical; Lifestyle; Sport; Thrillers; Women's Interests; *Markets:* Adult; Children's; Youth; *Treatments:* Commercial; Literary

Send query with synopsis and first three chapters by email only. See website for full guidelines.

Judith Murdoch Literary Agency

19 Chalcot Square, London, NW1 8YA
Tel: +44 (0) 20 7722 4197
Email: jmlitag@btinternet.com
Website: http://www.judithmurdoch.co.uk

Handles: Fiction; *Areas:* Crime; Women's Interests; *Markets:* Adult; *Treatments:* Commercial; Literary; Popular

Send query by post with SAE or email address for response, brief synopsis, and and first three chapters. Provides editorial advice. No short stories, children's books, science fiction, email submissions, or unsolicited MSS.

MNLA (Maggie Noach Literary Agency)

Hop Hill Cottage, Harmston Road, Aubourn, Lincoln, LN5 9DZ
Tel: +44 (0) 1522 788110
Email: info@mnla.co.uk
Website: http://www.mnla.co.uk

Handles: Fiction; Nonfiction; *Areas:* Biography; Historical; Travel; *Markets:* Adult; Children's

Note: As at June 2013 not accepting submissions. Check website for current situation.

Deals with UK residents only. Send query with SAE, outline, and two or three sample chapters. No email attachments or fax queries. Very few new clients taken on. Deals in general adult nonfiction and non-illustrated children's books for ages 8 and upwards. No poetry, scripts, short stories, cookery, gardening, mind, body, and spirit, scientific, academic, specialist nonfiction, or unsolicited MSS.

Deborah Owen Ltd

78 Narrow Street, Limehouse, London, E14 8BP
Tel: +44 (0) 20 7987 5119 / 5441

Handles: Fiction; Nonfiction

Represents only two authors worldwide. Not accepting any new authors.

John Pawsey

8 Snowshill Court, Giffard Park, Milton Keynes, MK14 5QG
Tel: +44 (0) 1908 611841
Email: john.pawsey@virgin.net

Handles: Nonfiction; *Areas:* Biography; Sport; *Markets:* Adult

No fiction, poetry, scripts, journalism, academic, or children's books. Particularly interested in sport and biography. Send query by email only, with synopsis and opening chapter.

PBJ and JBJ Management

22 Rathbone Street, London, W1T 1LA
Tel: +44 (0) 20 7287 1112
Fax: +44 (0) 20 7637 0899
Email: general@pbjmanagement.co.uk
Website: http://www.pbjmgt.co.uk

Handles: Scripts; *Areas:* Drama; Film; Humour; Radio; Theatre; TV; *Markets:* Adult

Handles scripts for film, TV, theatre, and radio. Particularly interested in comedy.

The Peters Fraser & Dunlop Group Ltd (PFD)

Drury House, 34-43 Russell Street, London, WC2B 5HA
Tel: +44 (0) 20 7344 1000
Fax: +44 (0) 20 7836 9539
Email: submissions@pfd.co.uk
Website: http://www.pfd.co.uk

Handles: Fiction; Nonfiction; Scripts; *Areas:* Autobiography; Cookery; Crime; Culture; Film; Finance; Historical; Horror; Nature; Psychology; Radio; Science; Suspense; Theatre; Thrillers; TV; *Markets:* Adult; Children's; Youth; *Treatments:* Commercial; Literary; Popular

Send query by email or by post with SAE, CV, synopsis and first three chapters (or around 50 pages). For nonfiction, send detailed proposal with cover letter and CV. Film, stage, and TV department is accepting new writers by referral only. No unsolicited scripts or pitches.

Shelley Power Literary Agency Ltd

20 Powell Gardens, South Heighton, Newhaven, BN9 0PS
Tel: +44 (0) 1273 512347
Email: sp@shelleypower.co.uk

Handles: Fiction; Nonfiction; *Markets:* Adult

Send query by email or by post with return postage. No attachments. No poetry, scripts, science fiction, fantasy, young adult, or children's books.

Puttick Literary Agency

Email: editorial@puttick.com
Website: http://www.puttick.com

Handles: Nonfiction; *Areas:* Biography; Culture; Current Affairs; Health; Historical; Philosophy; Science; Self-Help; *Markets:* Adult

Closed to submissions as at May 2017. See website for current situation.

Send query with short two or three page synopsis and CV by email (by preference), or by post with SAE. No fiction, poetry, drama, screenplays, children's books, or submissions by email (enquiries only). Enquiries only should be clearly marked in the subject line to avoid being deleted as spam. Make sure it is made clear if the material is under consideration elsewhere at the same time. Owing to the large volume of submissions we receive, we are only able to reply to those we wish to take further.

Redhammer

186 Bickenhall Mansions, Bickenhall Street, London, W1U 6BX
Tel: +44 (0) 20 7486 3465
Fax: +44 (0) 20 7000 1249
Email: admin@redhammer.info
Website: http://redhammer.info

Handles: Fiction; Nonfiction; *Areas:* Autobiography; Crime; Entertainment; Mystery; Thrillers; *Markets:* Adult

Handles fiction and nonfiction. Would love to discover a big, sprawling crime / mystery / thriller with international blockbuster potential. Also keen on autobiographies, whistleblowers, and celebrity tales. Submit first ten pages of manuscript using online form on website only.

Richford Becklow Literary Agency

Tel: +44 (0) 20 3737 1068 / + 44 (0) 7510 023823
Email: enquiries@richfordbecklow.co.uk
Website: http://www.richfordbecklow.com

Handles: Fiction; Nonfiction; *Areas:* Arts; Autobiography; Biography; Cookery; Crime; Fantasy; Gardening; Gothic; Historical; Horror; Lifestyle; Literature; Romance; Sci-Fi; Self-Help; Women's Interests; *Markets:* Adult; Youth; *Treatments:* Commercial; Contemporary; Literary; Satirical; Serious

Company founded in 2011 by an experienced agent, previously at the longest established literary agency in the world. Interested in fiction and nonfiction. Email submissions only. Does not accept postal submissions and cannot currently offer to represent American or Australian authors. No picture book texts for babies and toddlers, or erotica. No submissions in April or October. See website for full submission guidelines.

Robert Dudley Agency

135A Bridge Street, Ashford, Kent TN25 5DP
Email: info@robertdudleyagency.co.uk
Website: http://www.robertdudleyagency.co.uk

Handles: Nonfiction; *Areas:* Adventure; Biography; Business; Current Affairs; Historical; Medicine; Military; Self-Help; Sport; Technology; Travel; *Markets:* Adult; *Treatments:* Popular

Specialises in nonfiction. No fiction submissions. Send submissions by email, preferably in Word format, as opposed to PDF.

Robin Jones Literary Agency

6b Marmora Road, London, SE22 0RX
Tel: +44 (0) 20 8693 6062
Email: robijones@gmail.com

Handles: Fiction; Nonfiction; *Markets:* Adult; *Treatments:* Commercial; Literary

London-based literary agency founded in 2007 by an agent who has previously worked at four other agencies, and was the UK scout for international publishers in 11 countries. Handles commercial and literary fiction and nonfiction for adults, and occasional children's for ages 8 and over. Welcomes Russian language fiction and nonfiction. No poetry, young adult, academic, religious, or original scripts. Accepts full mss or query with synopsis and 50-page sample.

Rochelle Stevens & Co.

2 Terretts Place, Upper Street, London, N1 1QZ
Tel: +44 (0) 20 7359 3900
Email: info@rochellestevens.com
Website: http://www.rochellestevens.com

Handles: Scripts; *Areas:* Film; Radio; Theatre; TV; *Markets:* Adult

Handles script writers for film, television, theatre, and radio. No longer handles writers of fiction, nonfiction, or children's books. Submit by post only. See website for full submission guidelines.

Rocking Chair Books

2 Rudgwick Terrace, St Stephens Close, London, NW8 6BR
Tel: +44 (0) 7809 461342
Email: representme@rockingchairbooks.com
Website: http://www.rockingchairbooks.com

Handles: Fiction; Nonfiction; *Areas:* Adventure; Arts; Crime; Culture; Current Affairs; Entertainment; Historical; Horror; Lifestyle; Literature; Mystery; Nature; Romance; Thrillers; Translations; Travel; Women's Interests; *Markets:* Adult; *Treatments:* Commercial; Contemporary; Cynical; Dark; Experimental; In-depth; Light; Literary; Mainstream; Popular; Positive; Progressive; Satirical; Serious; Traditional

Founded in 2011 after the founder worked for five years as a Director at an established London literary agency. Send complete ms or a few chapters by email only. No Children's, YA or Science Fiction / Fantasy.

Roger Hancock Ltd

44 South Grove House, London, N6 6LR
Tel: +44 (0) 20 8341 7243
Email: enquiries@rogerhancock.com
Website: http://www.rogerhancock.com

Handles: Scripts; *Areas:* Drama; Entertainment; Humour; *Markets:* Adult; *Treatments:* Light

Enquire by phone in first instance. Handles scripts only. Interested in comedy dramas and light entertainment. No books or unsolicited MSS.

Rosica Colin Ltd

1 Clareville Grove Mews, London, SW7 5AH
Tel: +44 (0) 20 7370 1080

Handles: Fiction; Nonfiction; Scripts; *Areas:* Autobiography; Beauty and Fashion; Biography; Cookery; Crime; Current Affairs; Erotic; Fantasy; Film; Gardening; Health; Historical; Horror; Humour; Leisure; Lifestyle; Men's Interests; Military; Mystery; Nature; Psychology; Radio; Religious; Romance; Science; Sport; Suspense; Theatre; Thrillers; Travel; TV; Women's Interests; *Markets:* Academic; Adult; Children's; *Treatments:* Literary

Send query with SAE, CV, synopsis, and list of other agents and publishers where MS has already been sent. Considers any full-length mss (except science fiction and poetry), but send synopsis only in initial query.

Sarah Such Literary Agency

81 Arabella Drive, London, SW15 5LL
Tel: +44 (0) 20 8876 4228
Email: info@sarah-such.com
Website: http://www.sarahsuch.com

Handles: Fiction; Nonfiction; *Areas:* Autobiography; Biography; Culture; Historical; Humour; *Markets:* Adult; Children's; Youth; *Treatments:* Commercial; Literary; Popular

Handles literary and commercial nonfiction and fiction for adults, young adults and children. Particularly interested in debut novels, biography, memoir, history, popular culture and humour. Works mainly by recommendation, but does also accept unsolicited approaches, by email only. Send synopsis, author bio, and sample chapter as Word attachment. No unsolicited mss or queries by phone. Handles TV and film scripts for existing clients, but no radio or theatre scripts. No poetry, fantasy, self-help or short stories.

The Sayle Literary Agency

1 Petersfield, Cambridge, CB1 1BB
Tel: +44 (0) 1223 303035
Fax: +44 (0) 1223 301638
Email: info@sayleliteraryagency.com
Website: http://www.sayleliteraryagency.com

Handles: Fiction; Nonfiction; *Areas:* Biography; Crime; Current Affairs; Historical; Music; Science; Travel; *Markets:* Adult; *Treatments:* Literary

Note: Not accepting new manuscripts as at August 2015. See website for current status.

Send query with CV, synopsis, and three sample chapters. No text books, technical, legal, medical, children's, plays, poetry, unsolicited MSS, or approaches by email. Do not include SAE as all material submitted is recycled. If no response after three months assume rejection.

Sayle Screen Ltd

11 Jubilee Place, London, SW3 3TD
Tel: +44 (0) 20 7823 3883
Fax: +44 (0) 20 7823 3363
Email: info@saylescreen.com
Website: http://www.saylescreen.com

Handles: Scripts; *Areas:* Film; Radio; Theatre; TV; *Markets:* Adult

Only considers material which has been recommended by a producer, development executive or course tutor. In this case send query by email with cover letter and details of your referee to the relevant agent. Query only one agent at a time.

The Science Factory

Scheideweg 34C, Hamburg, Germany 20253
Tel: +44 (0) 20 7193 7296 (Skype)
Email: info@sciencefactory.co.uk
Website: http://www.sciencefactory.co.uk

Handles: Fiction; Nonfiction; *Areas:* Autobiography; Biography; Current Affairs; Historical; Medicine; Music; Politics; Science; Technology; Travel; *Markets:* Adult

Specialises in science, technology, medicine, and natural history, but will also consider other areas of nonfiction. Novelists handled only occasionally, and if there is some special relevance to the agency (e.g. a thriller about scientists, or a novel of ideas). See website for full submission guidelines.

Please note that the agency address is in Germany, but the country is listed as United Kingdom, as the company is registered in the United Kingdom.

Sheil Land Associates Ltd

52 Doughty Street, London, WC1N 2LS
Tel: +44 (0) 20 7405 9351
Fax: +44 (0) 20 7831 2127
Email: info@sheilland.co.uk
Website: http://www.sheilland.co.uk

Handles: Fiction; Nonfiction; Scripts; *Areas:* Autobiography; Biography; Cookery; Crime; Drama; Fantasy; Film; Gardening; Historical; Humour; Lifestyle; Military; Mystery; Politics; Psychology; Radio; Romance; Science; Sci-Fi; Self-Help; Theatre; Thrillers; Travel; TV; Women's Interests; *Markets:* Adult; Children's; Youth; *Treatments:* Commercial; Contemporary; Literary

Send query with synopsis, CV, and first three chapters (or around 50 pages), by post addressed to "The Submissions Dept", or by email. If posting mss, do not send only copy as submissions are recycled and responses sent by email. If you require response by post, include SAE.

Sheila Ableman Literary Agency

36 Duncan House, Fellows Road, London, NW3 3LZ
Tel: +44 (0) 20 7586 2339
Email: sheila@sheilaableman.co.uk
Website: http://www.sheilaableman.com

Handles: Nonfiction; *Areas:* Autobiography; Biography; Historical; Science; TV; *Markets:* Adult; *Treatments:* Commercial; Popular

Not taking on new clients as at February 2017

Send query with SAE, brief bio, one-page synopsis, and two sample chapters. Specialises in popular history, science, biography, autobiography, general narrative and 'quirky' nonfiction with strong commercial appeal, TV tie-ins and celebrity ghost writing. No poetry, children's books, gardening, or sport.

Dorie Simmonds Agency

Riverbank House, 1 Putney Bridge Approach, London, SW6 3JD
Tel: +44 (0) 20 7736 0002
Fax: +44 (0) 20 7736 0010
Email: info@doriesimmonds.com
Website: http://doriesimmonds.com

Handles: Fiction; Nonfiction; *Areas:* Biography; Historical; Women's Interests; *Markets:* Adult; Children's; *Treatments:* Commercial; Contemporary

Send query by email as Word or PDF attachments or by post with SAE. Include details on your background and relevant writing experience, and first three chapters or fifty pages. See website for full details.

Jeffrey Simmons

15 Penn House, Mallory Street, London, NW8 8SX
Tel: +44 (0) 20 7224 8917
Email: jasimmons@unicombox.co.uk

Handles: Fiction; Nonfiction; *Areas:* Autobiography; Biography; Crime; Current Affairs; Entertainment; Film; Historical; Legal; Politics; Psychology; Sport; Theatre; *Markets:* Adult; *Treatments:* Commercial; Literary

Send query with brief bio, synopsis, history of any prior publication, and list of any publishers or agents to have already seen the MSS. Particularly interested in personality books of all kinds and fiction from young writers (under 40) with a future. No children's books, science fiction, fantasy, cookery, crafts, gardening, or hobbies. Film scripts handled for existing book clients only.

Sinclair-Stevenson

3 South Terrace, London, SW7 2TB
Tel: +44 (0) 20 7581 2550
Fax: +44 (0) 20 7581 2550

Handles: Fiction; Nonfiction; *Areas:* Arts; Biography; Current Affairs; Historical; Travel; *Markets:* Adult

Send query with synopsis and SAE. No children's books, scripts, academic, science fiction, or fantasy.

Robert Smith Literary Agency Ltd

12 Bridge Wharf, 156 Caledonian Road, London, N1 9UU
Tel: +44 (0) 20 7278 2444
Fax: +44 (0) 20 7833 5680
Email: robertsmith.literaryagency@virgin.net
Website: http://www.robertsmithliteraryagency.com

Handles: Nonfiction; *Areas:* Autobiography; Biography; Crime; Culture; Current Affairs; Health; Historical; Humour; Lifestyle; Military; Self-Help; *Markets:* Adult; *Treatments:* Mainstream; Popular

Send query with synopsis initially and sample chapter if available, by post or by email. No poetry, fiction, scripts, children's books, academic, or unsolicited MSS. Will suggest revision. See website for full guidelines.

Sophie Hicks Agency

60 Gray's Inn Road, London, WC1X 8AQ
Email: submissions@sophiehicksagency.com
Website: http://www.sophiehicksagency.com

Handles: Fiction; Nonfiction; *Markets:* Adult; Children's; Youth

Welcomes submissions for fiction and nonfiction for adults, young adults, teens, and children 9+. Send query by email only with sample pages attached as Word or PDF documents. See website for full guidelines.

Standen Literary Agency

12 Tetherdown, London, N10 1NB
Tel: +44 (0) 20 8245 2606
Fax: +44 (0) 20 8245 2606
Email: yasmin@standenliteraryagency.com
Website: http://www.standenliteraryagency.com

Handles: Fiction; Nonfiction; *Markets:* Adult; Children's; Youth; *Treatments:* Commercial; Literary

Based in London. For fiction, send synopsis and first three chapters by email only. No picture books. Responds if interested only. If no response in 6 weeks assume rejection. For nonfiction, query in first instance.

Steph Roundsmith Agent and Editor

3 Bowes Road, Billingham, Stockton-on-Tees TS23 2BU
Email: agent@stephroundsmith.co.uk
Website: http://www.stephroundsmith.co.uk

Handles: Fiction; *Areas:* Adventure; Fantasy; Historical; Humour; Literature; Mystery; Sci-Fi; *Markets:* Children's; *Treatments:* Commercial; Literary; Mainstream

I only represent children's authors and I am currently looking for new clients. If you would like to submit your work for consideration then please send me a one page synopsis (including age range and word count), a paragraph or two about yourself, and your first three chapters. Please send everything by email and I will endeavour to get back to you within two weeks.

Ideally, I'm looking for writers who write for children (up to 12 years) in any genre. Whether it's a picture book or a full-length novel, I'd love to see your work. If you'd like to ask any questions then please don't hesitate to contact me.

Susanna Lea Associates (UK)

55 Monmouth Street, London, WC2H 9DG
Tel: +44 (0) 20 7287 7757
Fax: +44 (0) 20 7287 7775
Email: uk-submission@susannalea.com
Website: http://www.susannalea.com

Handles: Fiction; Nonfiction; *Markets:* Adult

Literary agency with offices in Paris, London, and New York. Always on the lookout for exciting new talent. No poetry, plays, screen plays, science fiction, educational text books, short stories or illustrated works. No queries by fax or post. Accepts queries by email only. Include cover letter, synopsis, and first three chapters or proposal. Response not guaranteed.

The Susijn Agency

820 Harrow Road, London, NW10 5JU
Tel: +44 (0) 20 8968 7435
Email: submissions@thesusijnagency.com
Website: http://www.thesusijnagency.com

Handles: Fiction; Nonfiction; *Markets:* Adult; *Treatments:* Literary

Send query with synopsis and three sample chapters only by post or by email. Include SASE if return of material required. Response in 8-10 weeks. Specialises in selling rights worldwide and also represents non-English language authors and publishers for US, UK, and translation rights worldwide. No self-help, science-fiction, fantasy, romance, children's, illustrated, business, screenplays, or theatre plays.

SYLA – Susan Yearwood Literary Agency

2 Knebworth House, Londesborough Road, Stoke Newington, London N16 8RL
Tel: +44 (0) 20 7503 0954
Email: submissions@susanyearwood.com
Website: http://www.susanyearwood.com

Handles: Fiction; Nonfiction; *Areas:* Autobiography; Biography; Business; Crime; Lifestyle; Psychology; Thrillers; Women's Interests; *Markets:* Adult; Children's; Youth; *Treatments:* Commercial; Literary; Popular

Send query by email, including synopsis and sample thirty pages (fiction) or ten pages (nonfiction) in one Word file attachment. No poetry or screenwriting, or submissions by post.

The Tennyson Agency

109 Tennyson Avenue, New Malden, Surrey KT3 6NA
Tel: +44 (0) 20 8543 5939
Email: agency@tenagy.co.uk
Website: http://www.tenagy.co.uk

Handles: Scripts; *Areas:* Drama; Film; Radio; Theatre; TV; *Markets:* Adult

Mainly deals in scripts for film, TV, theatre, and radio, along with related material on an ad-hoc basis. Handles writers in the European Union only. Send query with CV and outline of work. Prefers queries by email. No nonfiction, poetry, short stories, science fiction and fantasy or children's writing, or unsolicited MSS.

Teresa Chris Literary Agency Ltd

43 Musard Road, London, W6 8NR
Tel: +44 (0) 20 7386 0633
Email: teresachris@litagency.co.uk
Website: http://www.teresachrisliteraryagency.co.uk

Handles: Fiction; Nonfiction; *Areas:* Biography; Cookery; Crafts; Crime; Gardening; Historical; Lifestyle; Women's Interests; *Markets:* Adult; *Treatments:* Commercial; Literary

Welcomes submissions. Overseas authors may approach by email, otherwise hard copy submissions preferred. For fiction, send query with SAE, first three chapters, and one-page synopsis. For nonfiction, send overview with two sample chapters. Specialises in crime fiction and commercial women's fiction. No poetry, short stories, fantasy, science fiction, horror, children's fiction or young adult.

Toby Mundy Associates Ltd

6 Bayley Street, Bedford Square, London, WC1B 3HE
Tel: +44 (0) 20 3713 0067
Email: submissions@tma-agency.com
Website: http://tma-agency.com

Handles: Fiction; Nonfiction; *Areas:* Autobiography; Biography; Crime; Current Affairs; Historical; Politics; Science;

Thrillers; *Markets:* Adult; *Treatments:* Literary

Send query by email with brief synopsis, first chapter, and a note about yourself, all pasted into the body of the email. No poetry, plays, short stories, science fiction, horror, attachments or hard copy submissions.

Lavinia Trevor Agency

29 Addison Place, London, W11 4RJ
Tel: +44 (0) 20 7603 0895
Email: info@laviniatrevor.co.uk
Website: http://www.laviniatrevor.co.uk

Handles: Fiction; Nonfiction; *Areas:* Science; *Markets:* Adult; *Treatments:* Commercial; Literary

Does not handle poetry, children's, technical, academic, fantasy, science fiction, or scripts. No unsolicited material.

Uli Rushby-Smith Literary Agency

72 Plimsoll Road, London, N4 2EE
Tel: +44 (0) 20 7354 2718
Email: uli.rushby-smith@btconnect.com

Handles: Fiction; Nonfiction; *Markets:* Adult; *Treatments:* Commercial; Literary

Send query with SAE, outline, and two or three sample chapters. Film and TV rights handled in conjunction with a sub-agent. No disks, poetry, picture books, films, or plays.

United Agents

12--26 Lexington Street, London, W1F 0LE
Tel: +44 (0) 20 3214 0800
Fax: +44 (0) 20 3214 0801
Email: info@unitedagents.co.uk
Website: http://unitedagents.co.uk

Handles: Fiction; Nonfiction; Scripts; *Areas:* Biography; Film; Radio; Theatre; TV; *Markets:* Adult; Children's; Youth

Do not approach the book department generally. Consult website and view details of each agent before selecting a specific agent to approach personally. Accepts submissions by email only. Submissions by post will not be returned or responded to.

Ed Victor Ltd

6 Bayley Street, Bedford Square, London, WC1B 3HE
Tel: +44 (0) 20 7304 4100
Fax: +44 (0) 20 7304 4111
Email: linda@edvictor.com
Website: http://www.edvictor.com

Handles: Fiction; Nonfiction; *Areas:* Autobiography; Biography; Cookery; Historical; Politics; Travel; *Markets:* Adult; Children's; *Treatments:* Commercial; Literary

Handles authors of both literary and commercial fiction, as well as children's books and nonfiction in areas including biography, memoir, politics, travel, food and history. Send query by email with synopsis/outline and first five chapters as an attachment – do not include in the body of the email. Response not guaranteed unless interested.

Wade & Co Literary Agency

33 Cormorant Lodge, Thomas More Street, London, E1W 1AU
Tel: +44 (0) 20 7488 4171
Fax: +44 (0) 20 7488 4172
Email: rw@rwla.com
Website: http://www.rwla.com

Handles: Fiction; Nonfiction; *Markets:* Adult; Youth

New full-length proposals for adult and young adult fiction and nonfiction always welcome. Send query with detailed 1--6 page synopsis, brief biography, and first 10,000 words via email as Word documents (.doc) or PDF; or by post with SAE if return required. We much prefer to correspond by email. Actively seeking new writers across the literary spectrum. No poetry, children's, short stories, scripts or plays.

Watson, Little Ltd

Suite 315, ScreenWorks, 22 Highbury Grove, London, N5 2ER
Tel: +44 (0) 20 7388 7529
Email: submissions@watsonlittle.com
Website: http://www.watsonlittle.com

Handles: Fiction; Nonfiction; *Areas:* Business; Crime; Film; Historical; Humour;

Leisure; Music; Psychology; Science; Self-Help; Sport; Technology; Women's Interests; *Markets:* Adult; Children's; Youth; *Treatments:* Commercial; Literary; Popular

Send query by email only with synopsis and sample material, addressed to a specific agent. See website for full guidelines and details of specific agents. No scripts, poetry, or unsolicited MSS.

Whispering Buffalo Literary Agency Ltd

97 Chesson Road, London, W14 9QS
Tel: +44 (0) 20 7565 4737
Email: info@whisperingbuffalo.com
Website: http://www.whisperingbuffalo.com

Handles: Fiction; Nonfiction; *Areas:* Adventure; Anthropology; Arts; Autobiography; Beauty and Fashion; Design; Entertainment; Film; Health; Humour; Lifestyle; Music; Nature; Politics; Romance; Sci-Fi; Self-Help; Thrillers; *Markets:* Adult; Children's; Youth; *Treatments:* Commercial; Literary

Handles commercial/literary fiction/nonfiction and children's/YA fiction with special interest in book to film adaptations. No TV, film, radio or theatre scripts, or poetry or academic. Accepts submissions by email only. For fiction, send query with CV, synopsis, and first three chapters. For nonfiction, send proposal and sample chapter. Response only if interested. Aims to respond within 6-8 weeks.

William Morris Endeavor (WME) London

100 New Oxford Street, London, WC1A 1HB
Tel: +44 (0) 20 7534 6800
Fax: +44 (0) 20 7534 6900
Email: ldnsubmissions@wmeentertainment.com
Website: http://www.wmeentertainment.com

Handles: Fiction; Nonfiction; *Areas:* Autobiography; Biography; Crime; Culture; Historical; Thrillers; *Markets:* Adult; Youth; *Treatments:* Commercial; Literary

London office of a worldwide theatrical and literary agency, with offices in New York, Beverly Hills, Nashville, Miami, and Shanghai, as well as associates in Sydney. Always on the lookout for exciting new work and welcomes submissions across all genres. Send query by email, using link on website. See website for full guidelines.

Writers House UK

7th Floor, Waverley House, 7-12 Noel Street, London, W1F 8GQ
Email: akowal@writershouse.com
Website: http://www.writershouse.com

Handles: Fiction; Nonfiction; *Areas:* Autobiography; Biography; Business; Cookery; Fantasy; Finance; Historical; How-to; Lifestyle; Psychology; Science; Sci-Fi; Self-Help; Women's Interests; *Markets:* Adult; Children's; Youth; *Treatments:* Commercial; Literary

UK branch of established US agency with offices in New York and California. Actively seeking new material.

The Writers' Practice

6 Denmark Street, London, WC2H 8LX
Tel: +44 (0) 845 680 6578
Email: jemima@thewriterspractice.com
Website: http://www.thewriterspractice.com

Handles: Fiction; Nonfiction; *Markets:* Adult; *Treatments:* Commercial; Literary

Send query by email with for fiction a synopsis, brief bio, and first three chapters; and for nonfiction a pitch, brief bio, chapter outline, and at least one sample chapter. Also offers consultancy services to writers.

The Wylie Agency (UK) Ltd

17 Bedford Square, London, WC2B 3JA
Tel: +44 (0) 20 7908 5900
Fax: +44 (0) 20 7908 5901
Email: mail@wylieagency.co.uk
Website: http://www.wylieagency.co.uk

Handles: Fiction; Nonfiction; *Markets:* Adult

Note: Not accepting unsolicited mss as at January 2017

Send query by post or email before submitting. All submissions must include adequate return postage. No scripts, children's books, or unsolicited MSS.

Zeno Agency Ltd

Primrose Hill Business Centre, 110 Gloucester Avenue, London, NW1 3LH
Tel: +44 (0) 20 7096 0927
Email: info@zenoagency.com
Website: http://zenoagency.com

Handles: Fiction; *Areas:* Crime; Fantasy; Historical; Horror; Sci-Fi; Thrillers; Women's Interests; *Markets:* Adult; Children's; Youth; *Treatments:* Commercial

Not accepting new clients as at May 2017. Check website for current status

London-based literary agency specialising in Science Fiction, Fantasy, and Horror, but expanding into other areas such as crime, thrillers, women's fiction, and young adult fiction. Adult fiction must be at least 75,000 words and children's fiction should be at least 50,000 words. Send query by email with synopsis up to two pages, and first three chapters (or approximately 50 double-spaced pages) as attachments in .doc or .rtf format. No submissions by post.

Canadian Literary Agents

For the most up-to-date listings of these and hundreds of other literary agents, visit https://www.firstwriter.com/Agents

*To claim your **free** access to the site, please see the back of this book.*

Rick Broadhead & Associates Literary Agency

47 St. Clair Avenue West, Suite 501, Toronto, Ontario M4V 3A5
Tel: +1 (416) 929-0516
Fax: +1 (416) 927-8732
Email: submissions@rbaliterary.com
Website: http://www.rbaliterary.com

Handles: Nonfiction; *Areas:* Biography; Business; Culture; Current Affairs; Health; Historical; Humour; Lifestyle; Medicine; Military; Nature; Politics; Science; Self-Help; *Markets:* Adult; *Treatments:* Popular

Prefers queries by email. Send brief query outlining your project and your credentials. Responds only if interested. No screenplays, poetry, children's books, or fiction.

The Characters Talent Agency

8 Elm Street, Toronto, Ontario M3H 1Y9
Tel: +1 (416) 964-8522
Fax: +1 (416) 964-8206
Email: litsubmissionsto@thecharacters.com
Website: http://www.thecharacters.com

Handles: Scripts; *Areas:* Biography; Drama; Erotic; Fantasy; Film; Historical; Horror; Humour; Mystery; Romance; Science; Sport; Thrillers; TV; Westerns; Women's Interests; *Markets:* Adult; Children's; Youth; *Treatments:* Contemporary; Mainstream

Approach by email. Response only if interested.

The Cooke Agency

75 Sherbourne Street., Suite 501, Toronto, Ontario M5A 2P9
Tel: +1 (647) 788-4010
Email: egriffin@cookeagency.ca
Website: http://www.cookeagency.ca

Handles: Fiction; Nonfiction; *Areas:* Crime; Culture; Fantasy; Historical; Nature; Politics; Romance; Science; Sci-Fi; Spiritual; *Markets:* Adult; Children's; Youth; *Treatments:* Commercial; Literary

Send query by email only with "Author Query" in the subject line (no attachments). No illustrated, photographic or children's picture books, US political thrillers, or poetry. No queries or submissions by post. Consult website before making contact.

The Helen Heller Agency

4-216 Heath Street West, Toronto, ON M5P 1N7
Tel: +1 (416) 489-0396
Email: info@helenhelleragency.com
Website: http://www.helenhelleragency.com

Handles: Fiction; Nonfiction; *Areas:* Historical; Thrillers; *Markets:* Adult; Youth; *Treatments:* Commercial

Handles adult and young adult nonfiction and fiction. No children's, screenplays, or genre fiction (sci-fi / fantasy etc.). Send query by email including synopsis, bio, and recent writing sample, pasted into the body of the email. No attachments or postal submission.

Robert Lecker Agency

4055 Melrose Avenue, Montréal, Québec H4A 2S5
Tel: +1 (514) 830-4818
Fax: +1 (514) 483-1644
Email: robert.lecker@gmail.com
Website: http://www.leckeragency.com

Handles: Fiction; Nonfiction; *Areas:* Adventure; Autobiography; Biography; Cookery; Crime; Culture; Entertainment; Erotic; Film; Historical; How-to; Literature; Music; Mystery; Science; Suspense; Theatre; Thrillers; Travel; *Markets:* Academic; Adult; *Treatments:* Contemporary; Literary; Mainstream

Specialises in books about entertainment, music, popular culture, popular science, intellectual and cultural history, food, and travel, but willing to consider any original and well presented material. No children's literature, screenplays, poetry, self-help books, or spiritual guides. Send query by email in first instance with brief description of your project. No proposals or attachments unless requested. No response unless interested.

P.S. Literary Agency

20033-520 Kerr Street, Oakville, Ontario L6K 3C7
Tel: +1 (416) 907-8325
Email: query@psliterary.com
Website: http://www.PSLiterary.com

Handles: Fiction; Nonfiction; *Areas:* Autobiography; Business; Cookery; Current Affairs; Design; Fantasy; Health; Historical; Humour; Lifestyle; Literature; Mystery; Nature; Photography; Politics; Psychology; Romance; Science; Sci-Fi; Sport; Suspense; Thrillers; Women's Interests; *Markets:* Adult; Children's; Youth; *Treatments:* Commercial; Contemporary; Literary; Mainstream; Popular

A literary agency representing both fiction and nonfiction for adults, young adults, and children. Does not handle poetry or screenplays. Send one-page query by email only. No attachments. See website for full submission guidelines and address query to the agent best matched to your work.

Seventh Avenue Literary Agency

2052 – 124th Street, South Surrey, BC V4A 9K3
Tel: +1 (604) 538-7252
Fax: +1 (604) 538-7252
Email: info@seventhavenuelit.com
Website: http://www.seventhavenuelit.com

Handles: Nonfiction; *Markets:* Adult

Handles nonfiction only and takes on few new clients. Send query by email with 2-3 paragraph description of your project and one paragraph about you; or by post with description of your book and its category, its potential market, table of contents with short description of each chapter, one sample chapter, and author bio, including previously published material and your qualifications on the subject you have written on.

Westwood Creative Artists

94 Harbord Street, Toronto, Ontario M5S 1G6
Tel: +1 (416) 964-3302
Fax: +1 (416) 975-9209
Email: wca_office@wcaltd.com
Website: http://www.wcaltd.com

Handles: Fiction; Nonfiction; *Areas:* Autobiography; Biography; Current Affairs; Historical; Mystery; Science; Thrillers; *Markets:* Adult; Children's; Youth; *Treatments:* Commercial; Literary

Send query by email with your credentials, a synopsis, and short sample up to ten pages in the body of the email. No attachments

Irish Literary Agents

For the most up-to-date listings of these and hundreds of other literary agents, visit https://www.firstwriter.com/Agents

*To claim your **free** access to the site, please see the back of this book.*

Author Rights Agency

20 Victoria Road, Dublin, D06 DR02
Tel: +353 1 4922112
Email: submissions@authorrightsagency.com
Website: http://www.authorrightsagency.com

Handles: Fiction; Nonfiction; *Areas:* Crime; Historical; *Markets:* Adult; Children's; Youth; *Treatments:* Contemporary; Literary

Currently concentrating on literary fiction and genre fiction of literary quality (particularly crime and Noir). Welcomes submissions in English, particularly from Ireland, UK, and the US. Send query by email only with synopsis, ideally one page long, and writing sample up to 10 pages or about 3,000 words, as a Word or RTF attachment. Do not include in the body of the email, or send full manuscripts. See website for full guidelines. No phone calls.

The Book Bureau Literary Agency

7 Duncairn Avenue, Bray, Co. Wicklow
Tel: +353 (0) 1276 4996
Fax: +353 (0) 1276 4834
Email: thebookbureau@oceanfree.net

Handles: Fiction; Nonfiction; *Areas:* Crime; Thrillers; Women's Interests; *Markets:* Adult; *Treatments:* Commercial; Literary

Handles mainly general and literary fiction, plus some nonfiction. Particularly interested in women's, crime, Irish novels, and thrillers. Send query by email (preferred) or by post with SAE, synopsis, and first three chapters. Prefers single line spacing. No poetry, children's, horror, or science fiction. Strong editorial support provided before submission to publishers.

Frank Fahy

129 Delwood Close, Castleknock, Dublin 15
Tel: +353 (0) 86 226 9330
Email: submissions@frank-fahy.com
Website: http://www.frank-fahy.com

Handles: Fiction; *Markets:* Adult; Youth

Handles adult and young adult fiction. No picture books, poetry, or nonfiction. Send query by email with author profile, synopsis, and first three chapters by email. No hard copy submissions.

Marianne Gunn O'Connor Literary Agency

Morrison Chambers, Suite 17, 32 Nassau Street, Dublin, 2
Tel: 353 1 677 9100
Fax: 353 1 677 9101
Email: mgoclitagency@eircom.net

Handles: Fiction; Nonfiction; *Areas:* Biography; Health; *Markets:* Adult;

Children's; *Treatments:* Commercial; Literary

Send query with half-page synopsis by email.

The Lisa Richards Agency

108 Upper Leeson Street, Dublin, 4
Tel: +353 1 637 5000
Fax: +353 1 667 1256
Email: info@lisarichards.ie
Website: http://www.lisarichards.ie

Handles: Fiction; Nonfiction; Scripts; *Areas:* Autobiography; Biography; Culture; Historical; Humour; Lifestyle; Self-Help; Sport; Theatre; *Markets:* Adult; Children's; *Treatments:* Commercial; Literary; Popular

Send query by email or by post with SASE, including three or four sample chapters in the case of fiction, or proposal and sample chapter for nonfiction. No horror, science fiction, screenplays, or children's picture books.

Literary Agents Subject Index

This section lists literary agents by their subject matter, with directions to the section of the book where the full listing can be found.

You can create your own customised lists of literary agents using different combinations of these subject areas, plus over a dozen other criteria, instantly online at https://www.firstwriter.com.

*To claim your **free** access to the site, please see the back of this book.*

Adventure
Alive Communications, Inc (*US*)
Ambassador Speakers Bureau & Literary Agency (*US*)
Belcastro Agency (*US*)
Luigi Bonomi Associates Ltd (*UK*)
Kelvin C. Bulger and Associates (*US*)
Cine/Lit Representation (*US*)
DHH Literary Agency Ltd (*UK*)
Diamond Kahn and Woods (DKW) Literary Agency Ltd (*UK*)
Don Congdon Associates, Inc. (*US*)
Jim Donovan Literary (*US*)
The Dravis Agency, Inc. (*US*)
Dystel & Goderich Literary Management (*US*)
Ethan Ellenberg Literary Agency (*US*)
The Feldstein Agency (*UK*)
Diana Finch Literary Agency (*US*)
Foundry Literary + Media (*US*)
The Gernert Company (*US*)
Goodman Associates (*US*)
Hannigan Salky Getzler (HSG) Agency (*US*)
Antony Harwood Limited (*UK*)
Andrea Hurst Literary Management (*US*)
International Transactions, Inc. (*US*)
The Jean V. Naggar Literary Agency (*US*)
Harvey Klinger, Inc (*US*)
Kneerim & Williams (*US*)
LaunchBooks Literary Agency (*US*)
Robert Lecker Agency (*Can*)
The Literary Group International (*US*)
Julia Lord Literary Management (*US*)
Maria Carvainis Agency, Inc. (*US*)
McIntosh & Otis, Inc (*US*)
Niad Management (*US*)
The Park Literary Group LLC (*US*)
Pavilion Literary Management (*US*)
Prospect Agency (*US*)
Raines & Raines (*US*)
Robert Dudley Agency (*UK*)
Rocking Chair Books (*UK*)
Salkind Literary Agency (*US*)
Susan Schulman, A Literary Agency (*US*)
Scovil Galen Ghosh Literary Agency, Inc. (*US*)
Steph Roundsmith Agent and Editor (*UK*)
Stuart Krichevsky Literary Agency, Inc. (*US*)
The Swetky Agency and Associates (*US*)
TriadaUS Literary Agency, Inc. (*US*)
Trident Media Group, LLC (*US*)
Victoria Sanders & Associates LLC (*US*)
Waxman Leavell Literary Agency (*US*)
Whispering Buffalo Literary Agency Ltd (*UK*)
The Zack Company, Inc (*US*)
Anthropology
The Blumer Literary Agency, Inc. (*US*)
Browne & Miller Literary Associates (*US*)
Carol Mann Agency (*US*)
Don Congdon Associates, Inc. (*US*)
Dystel & Goderich Literary Management (*US*)
Felicia Eth Literary Representation (*US*)
Goodman Associates (*US*)
Antony Harwood Limited (*UK*)
Kneerim & Williams (*US*)
Larsen Pomada Literary Agents (*US*)
Linda Roghaar Literary Agency, Inc. (*US*)
The Literary Group International (*US*)
Lynne Rabinoff Agency (*US*)
Susan Schulman, A Literary Agency (*US*)

Lynn Seligman, Literary Agent (*US*)
The Swetky Agency and Associates (*US*)
Whispering Buffalo Literary Agency Ltd (*UK*)

Antiques

Antony Harwood Limited (*UK*)
Jeanne Fredericks Literary Agency, Inc. (*US*)

Archaeology

The Blumer Literary Agency, Inc. (*US*)
Browne & Miller Literary Associates (*US*)
Carol Mann Agency (*US*)
Caroline Davidson Literary Agency (*UK*)
DHH Literary Agency Ltd (*UK*)
Diamond Kahn and Woods (DKW) Literary Agency Ltd (*UK*)
Don Congdon Associates, Inc. (*US*)
Dystel & Goderich Literary Management (*US*)
Goodman Associates (*US*)
Antony Harwood Limited (*UK*)
Kneerim & Williams (*US*)
Duncan McAra (*UK*)
Lynne Rabinoff Agency (*US*)
Susan Schulman, A Literary Agency (*US*)
The Swetky Agency and Associates (*US*)

Architecture

The Blumer Literary Agency, Inc. (*US*)
Barbara Braun Associates, Inc. (*US*)
Carol Mann Agency (*US*)
Caroline Davidson Literary Agency (*UK*)
Fairbank Literary Representation (*US*)
Antony Harwood Limited (*UK*)
Larsen Pomada Literary Agents (*US*)
Duncan McAra (*UK*)
Martha Millard Literary Agency (*US*)
Marly Rusoff & Associates, Inc. (*US*)
The Spieler Agency (*US*)
The Swetky Agency and Associates (*US*)
Wm Clark Associates (*US*)

Arts

Artellus Limited (*UK*)
The August Agency LLC (*US*)
The Blumer Literary Agency, Inc. (*US*)
Brandt & Hochman Literary Agents, Inc. (*US*)
Barbara Braun Associates, Inc. (*US*)
Carol Mann Agency (*US*)
Caroline Davidson Literary Agency (*UK*)
The Cowles-Ryan Literary Agency (*US*)
Creative Authors Ltd (*UK*)
DeFiore and Company (*US*)
Don Congdon Associates, Inc. (*US*)
Donadio & Olson, Inc. (*US*)
Dunow, Carlson & Lerner Agency (*US*)
Judith Ehrlich Literary Management (*US*)
Fredrica S. Friedman and Co. Inc. (*US*)
Georges Borchardt, Inc. (*US*)
The Gernert Company (*US*)
Frances Goldin Literary Agency, Inc. (*US*)
Greene & Heaton Ltd (*UK*)
Antony Harwood Limited (*UK*)
Rupert Heath Literary Agency (*UK*)
International Transactions, Inc. (*US*)
Jeanne Fredericks Literary Agency, Inc. (*US*)
Johnson & Alcock (*UK*)
Jonathan Pegg Literary Agency (*UK*)
Frances Kelly (*UK*)
Kuhn Projects (*US*)
L. Perkins Associates (*US*)
Larsen Pomada Literary Agents (*US*)
Levine Greenberg Rostan Literary Agency (*US*)
Limelight Management (*UK*)
Literary & Creative Artists Inc. (*US*)
Macnaughton Lord Representation (*UK*)
MBA Literary Agents Ltd (*UK*)
Duncan McAra (*UK*)
Martha Millard Literary Agency (*US*)
The Park Literary Group LLC (*US*)
Richford Becklow Literary Agency (*UK*)
Rocking Chair Books (*UK*)
Marly Rusoff & Associates, Inc. (*US*)
Salkind Literary Agency (*US*)
Sanford J. Greenburger Associates, Inc. (*US*)
Susan Schulman, A Literary Agency (*US*)
Scovil Galen Ghosh Literary Agency, Inc. (*US*)
Lynn Seligman, Literary Agent (*US*)
Sinclair-Stevenson (*UK*)
The Stuart Agency (*US*)
Susan Rabiner, Literary Agent, Inc. (*US*)
The Swetky Agency and Associates (*US*)
Thompson Literary Agency (*US*)
Victoria Sanders & Associates LLC (*US*)
The Weingel-Fidel Agency (*US*)
Whispering Buffalo Literary Agency Ltd (*UK*)
Wm Clark Associates (*US*)

Autobiography

Aaron M. Priest Literary Agency (*US*)
Adler & Robin Books, Inc (*US*)
AHA Talent Ltd (*UK*)
The Ahearn Agency, Inc (*US*)
Alive Communications, Inc (*US*)
Miriam Altshuler Literary Agency (*US*)
Ambassador Speakers Bureau & Literary Agency (*US*)
The Ampersand Agency Ltd (*UK*)
Andrew Lownie Literary Agency Ltd (*UK*)
Ann Rittenberg Literary Agency (*US*)
Arcadia (*US*)
Audrey A. Wolf Literary Agency (*US*)
The August Agency LLC (*US*)
The Authors Care Service ltd (*UK*)
Ayesha Pande Literary (*US*)
B.J. Robbins Literary Agency (*US*)
Baldi Agency (*US*)
Betsy Amster Literary Enterprises (*US*)
David Black Literary Agency (*US*)
Blake Friedmann Literary Agency Ltd (*UK*)
Bleecker Street Associates, Inc. (*US*)
The Blumer Literary Agency, Inc. (*US*)
The Book Group (*US*)
BookBlast Ltd. (*UK*)
Brandt & Hochman Literary Agents, Inc. (*US*)
Bresnick Weil Literary Agency, LLC (*US*)
The Bright Literary Academy (*UK*)
Browne & Miller Literary Associates (*US*)
Carnicelli Literary Management (*US*)
Carol Mann Agency (*US*)
Caroline Sheldon Literary Agency (*UK*)
Chalberg & Sussman (*US*)

Chartwell (*UK*)
Elyse Cheney Literary Associates, LLC (*US*)
Clare Hulton Literary Agency (*UK*)
Conville & Walsh Ltd (*UK*)
The Cowles-Ryan Literary Agency (*US*)
The Creative Rights Agency (*UK*)
Creative Trust, Inc. (*US*)
Creative Authors Ltd (*UK*)
Richard Curtis Associates, Inc. (*US*)
Laura Dail Literary Agency (*US*)
David Luxton Associates (*UK*)
Liza Dawson Associates (*US*)
The Jennifer DeChiara Literary Agency (*US*)
Joëlle Delbourgo Associates, Inc. (*US*)
DHH Literary Agency Ltd (*UK*)
Diane Banks Associates Literary Agency (*UK*)
Dinah Wiener Ltd (*UK*)
Don Congdon Associates, Inc. (*US*)
Jim Donovan Literary (*US*)
Dunham Literary, Inc. (*US*)
Dunow, Carlson & Lerner Agency (*US*)
Dystel & Goderich Literary Management (*US*)
Anne Edelstein Literary Agency (*US*)
Judith Ehrlich Literary Management (*US*)
Einstein Literary Management (*US*)
Elise Dillsworth Agency (EDA) (*UK*)
Felicia Eth Literary Representation (*US*)
Ethan Ellenberg Literary Agency (*US*)
The Feldstein Agency (*UK*)
Diana Finch Literary Agency (*US*)
FinePrint Literary Management (*US*)
Fletcher & Company (*US*)
Folio Literary Management, LLC (*US*)
Foundry Literary + Media (*US*)
Frances Collin Literary Agent (*US*)
Sarah Jane Freymann Literary Agency (*US*)
Fredrica S. Friedman and Co. Inc. (*US*)
Furniss Lawton (*UK*)
Gelfman Schneider / ICM Partners (*US*)
The Gernert Company (*US*)
Gina Maccoby Agency (*US*)
Glass Literary Management LLC (*US*)
Frances Goldin Literary Agency, Inc. (*US*)
Goodman Associates (*US*)
Irene Goodman Literary Agency (*US*)
Grace Freedson's Publishing Network (*US*)
Graham Maw Christie Literary Agency (*UK*)
Kathryn Green Literary Agency, LLC (*US*)
Greene & Heaton Ltd (*UK*)
Laura Gross Literary Agency (*US*)
Gunn Media Associates (*UK*)
Hannigan Salky Getzler (HSG) Agency (*US*)
Hardman & Swainson (*UK*)
Joy Harris Literary Agency, Inc. (*US*)
Antony Harwood Limited (*UK*)
Rupert Heath Literary Agency (*UK*)
The Jeff Herman Agency, LLC (*US*)
David Higham Associates Ltd (*UK*)
Hill Nadell Literary Agency (*US*)
Kate Hordern Literary Agency (*UK*)
Andrea Hurst Literary Management (*US*)
J de S Associates Inc. (*US*)
Jane Rotrosen Agency (*US*)
The Jean V. Naggar Literary Agency (*US*)
Jenny Brown Associates (*UK*)
Jill Grinberg Literary Management LLC (*US*)
Johnson & Alcock (*UK*)
Jonathan Pegg Literary Agency (*UK*)
Harvey Klinger, Inc (*US*)
Kneerim & Williams (*US*)
The Knight Agency (*US*)
Barbara S. Kouts, Literary Agent (*US*)
Edite Kroll Literary Agency, Inc. (*US*)
Kuhn Projects (*US*)
L. Perkins Associates (*US*)
The LA Literary Agency (*US*)
Laura Langlie, Literary Agent (*US*)
Larsen Pomada Literary Agents (*US*)
Sarah Lazin Books (*US*)
Robert Lecker Agency (*Can*)
Levine Greenberg Rostan Literary Agency (*US*)
Limelight Management (*UK*)
Linda Roghaar Literary Agency, Inc. (*US*)
Linn Prentis, Literary Agent (*US*)
Lippincott Massie McQuilkin (*US*)
The Lisa Richards Agency (*Ire*)
Literary & Creative Artists Inc. (*US*)
The Literary Group International (*US*)
Julia Lord Literary Management (*US*)
Lowenstein Associates, Inc. (*US*)
The Jennifer Lyons Literary Agency, LLC (*US*)
MacGregor Literary (*US*)
Madeleine Milburn Literary, TV & Film Agency (*UK*)
Kirsten Manges Literary Agency, LLC (*US*)
Manus & Associates Literary Agency, Inc. (*US*)
Maria Carvainis Agency, Inc. (*US*)
The Martell Agency (*US*)
Martin Literary Management (*US*)
Margret McBride Literary Agency (*US*)
Martha Millard Literary Agency (*US*)
Howard Morhaim Literary Agency (*US*)
Niad Management (*US*)
P.S. Literary Agency (*Can*)
The Park Literary Group LLC (*US*)
Pavilion Literary Management (*US*)
The Peters Fraser & Dunlop Group Ltd (PFD) (*UK*)
Prospect Agency (*US*)
Lynne Rabinoff Agency (*US*)
Raines & Raines (*US*)
Rebecca Friedman Literary Agency (*US*)
Redhammer (*UK*)
Rees Literary Agency (*US*)
The Amy Rennert Agency, Inc. (*US*)
Richford Becklow Literary Agency (*UK*)
Robin Straus Agency, Inc. (*US*)
Rosica Colin Ltd (*UK*)
Ross Yoon Agency (*US*)
The Rudy Agency (*US*)
Marly Rusoff & Associates, Inc. (*US*)
Salkind Literary Agency (*US*)
Sandra Dijkstra Literary Agency (*US*)
Sanford J. Greenburger Associates, Inc. (*US*)
Sarah Such Literary Agency (*UK*)
Susan Schulman, A Literary Agency (*US*)

The Science Factory (*UK*)
Scovil Galen Ghosh Literary Agency, Inc. (*US*)
Denise Shannon Literary Agency, Inc. (*US*)
Sheil Land Associates Ltd (*UK*)
Sheila Ableman Literary Agency (*UK*)
Signature Literary Agency (*US*)
Jeffrey Simmons (*UK*)
Robert Smith Literary Agency Ltd (*UK*)
Solow Literary Enterprises, Inc. (*US*)
The Spieler Agency (*US*)
Sterling Lord Literistic, Inc. (*US*)
Stonesong (*US*)
Stuart Krichevsky Literary Agency, Inc. (*US*)
The Stuart Agency (*US*)
Susan Rabiner, Literary Agent, Inc. (*US*)
The Swetky Agency and Associates (*US*)
SYLA – Susan Yearwood Literary Agency (*UK*)
Talcott Notch Literary (*US*)
Tessler Literary Agency (*US*)
Thompson Literary Agency (*US*)
Toby Mundy Associates Ltd (*UK*)
TriadaUS Literary Agency, Inc. (*US*)
Trident Media Group, LLC (*US*)
2M Literary Agency Ltd (*US*)
Veritas Literary Agency (*US*)
Ed Victor Ltd (*UK*)
Victoria Sanders & Associates LLC (*US*)
Watkins / Loomis Agency, Inc. (*US*)
Waxman Leavell Literary Agency (*US*)
The Weingel-Fidel Agency (*US*)
Wendy Sherman Associates, Inc. (*US*)
Westwood Creative Artists (*Can*)
Whispering Buffalo Literary Agency Ltd (*UK*)
William Morris Endeavor (WME) London (*UK*)
Wm Clark Associates (*US*)
Writers House UK (*UK*)
Writers' Representatives, LLC (*US*)
Writers House, LLC (*US*)
Yates & Yates (*US*)
The Zack Company, Inc (*US*)
Karen Gantz Zahler Literary Agency (*US*)
Helen Zimmermann Literary Agency (*US*)
Zoë Pagnamenta Agency, LLC (*US*)

Beauty and Fashion
Artellus Limited (*UK*)
Barbara Braun Associates, Inc. (*US*)
Diane Banks Associates Literary Agency (*UK*)
FinePrint Literary Management (*US*)
Antony Harwood Limited (*UK*)
The Knight Agency (*US*)
Kuhn Projects (*US*)
Levine Greenberg Rostan Literary Agency (*US*)
Rosica Colin Ltd (*UK*)
Sterling Lord Literistic, Inc. (*US*)
Stonesong (*US*)
Thompson Literary Agency (*US*)
2M Literary Agency Ltd (*US*)
Whispering Buffalo Literary Agency Ltd (*UK*)

Biography
Aaron M. Priest Literary Agency (*US*)
Adler & Robin Books, Inc (*US*)
The Ahearn Agency, Inc (*US*)
Alive Communications, Inc (*US*)
Ambassador Speakers Bureau & Literary Agency (*US*)
The Ampersand Agency Ltd (*UK*)
Andrew Lownie Literary Agency Ltd (*UK*)
Ann Rittenberg Literary Agency (*US*)
Arcadia (*US*)
Artellus Limited (*UK*)
Audrey A. Wolf Literary Agency (*US*)
The August Agency LLC (*US*)
Ayesha Pande Literary (*US*)
B.J. Robbins Literary Agency (*US*)
Baldi Agency (*US*)
Bell Lomax Moreton Agency (*UK*)
Betsy Amster Literary Enterprises (*US*)
Vicky Bijur Literary Agency (*US*)
David Black Literary Agency (*US*)
Blake Friedmann Literary Agency Ltd (*UK*)
Bleecker Street Associates, Inc. (*US*)
The Blumer Literary Agency, Inc. (*US*)
The Book Group (*US*)
Barbara Braun Associates, Inc. (*US*)
Bresnick Weil Literary Agency, LLC (*US*)
Rick Broadhead & Associates Literary Agency (*Can*)
Marie Brown Associates, Inc. (*US*)
Browne & Miller Literary Associates (*US*)
Carnicelli Literary Management (*US*)
Carol Mann Agency (*US*)
Caroline Davidson Literary Agency (*UK*)
The Characters Talent Agency (*Can*)
Chartwell (*UK*)
Elyse Cheney Literary Associates, LLC (*US*)
The Choate Agency, LLC (*US*)
Cine/Lit Representation (*US*)
Conville & Walsh Ltd (*UK*)
Coombs Moylett & Maclean Literary Agency (*UK*)
The Cowles-Ryan Literary Agency (*US*)
Creative Authors Ltd (*UK*)
Curtis Brown Group Ltd (*UK*)
Richard Curtis Associates, Inc. (*US*)
Laura Dail Literary Agency (*US*)
David Luxton Associates (*UK*)
The Jennifer DeChiara Literary Agency (*US*)
DeFiore and Company (*US*)
Joëlle Delbourgo Associates, Inc. (*US*)
DHH Literary Agency Ltd (*UK*)
Diamond Kahn and Woods (DKW) Literary Agency Ltd (*UK*)
Dinah Wiener Ltd (*UK*)
Don Congdon Associates, Inc. (*US*)
Donadio & Olson, Inc. (*US*)
Jim Donovan Literary (*US*)
Dunham Literary, Inc. (*US*)
Dunow, Carlson & Lerner Agency (*US*)
Dystel & Goderich Literary Management (*US*)
Edwards Fuglewicz (*UK*)
Judith Ehrlich Literary Management (*US*)
Einstein Literary Management (*US*)
Elise Dillsworth Agency (EDA) (*UK*)
Emily Sweet Associates (*UK*)
Felicia Eth Literary Representation (*US*)
Ethan Ellenberg Literary Agency (*US*)

Fairbank Literary Representation (*US*)
The Feldstein Agency (*UK*)
Felicity Bryan Associates (*UK*)
Diana Finch Literary Agency (*US*)
FinePrint Literary Management (*US*)
Fletcher & Company (*US*)
Foundry Literary + Media (*US*)
Fox & Howard Literary Agency (*UK*)
Frances Collin Literary Agent (*US*)
Fredrica S. Friedman and Co. Inc. (*US*)
Furniss Lawton (*UK*)
Georges Borchardt, Inc. (*US*)
Georgina Capel Associates Ltd (*UK*)
The Gernert Company (*US*)
Gina Maccoby Agency (*US*)
Glass Literary Management LLC (*US*)
Goodman Associates (*US*)
Kathryn Green Literary Agency, LLC (*US*)
Greene & Heaton Ltd (*UK*)
Laura Gross Literary Agency (*US*)
Marianne Gunn O'Connor Literary Agency (*Ire*)
Joy Harris Literary Agency, Inc. (*US*)
Antony Harwood Limited (*UK*)
A M Heath & Company Limited, Author's Agents (*UK*)
Rupert Heath Literary Agency (*UK*)
David Higham Associates Ltd (*UK*)
Hill Nadell Literary Agency (*US*)
International Transactions, Inc. (*US*)
J de S Associates Inc. (*US*)
Jane Turnbull (*UK*)
The Jean V. Naggar Literary Agency (*US*)
Jeanne Fredericks Literary Agency, Inc. (*US*)
Jenny Brown Associates (*UK*)
Jill Grinberg Literary Management LLC (*US*)
Johnson & Alcock (*UK*)
Jonathan Pegg Literary Agency (*UK*)
Kathi J. Paton Literary Agency (*US*)
Keane Kataria Literary Agency (*UK*)
Frances Kelly (*UK*)
Harvey Klinger, Inc (*US*)
Kneerim & Williams (*US*)
Linda Konner Literary Agency (*US*)
Barbara S. Kouts, Literary Agent (*US*)
Edite Kroll Literary Agency, Inc. (*US*)
L. Perkins Associates (*US*)
The LA Literary Agency (*US*)
Laura Langlie, Literary Agent (*US*)
Larsen Pomada Literary Agents (*US*)
Sarah Lazin Books (*US*)
Robert Lecker Agency (*Can*)
Levine Greenberg Rostan Literary Agency (*US*)
Limelight Management (*UK*)
Linda Roghaar Literary Agency, Inc. (*US*)
Lippincott Massie McQuilkin (*US*)
The Lisa Richards Agency (*Ire*)
Literary Management Group, Inc. (*US*)
Literary & Creative Artists Inc. (*US*)
The Literary Group International (*US*)
Julia Lord Literary Management (*US*)
The Jennifer Lyons Literary Agency, LLC (*US*)
MacGregor Literary (*US*)
Maggie Pearlstine Associates Ltd (*UK*)
Manus & Associates Literary Agency, Inc. (*US*)
Maria Carvainis Agency, Inc. (*US*)
Marjacq Scripts Ltd (*UK*)
Martin Literary Management (*US*)
MBA Literary Agents Ltd (*UK*)
Duncan McAra (*UK*)
Margret McBride Literary Agency (*US*)
Martha Millard Literary Agency (*US*)
Howard Morhaim Literary Agency (*US*)
Mulcahy Associates (*UK*)
Niad Management (*US*)
MNLA (Maggie Noach Literary Agency) (*UK*)
Northern Lights Literary Services (*US*)
John Pawsey (*UK*)
Puttick Literary Agency (*UK*)
Lynne Rabinoff Agency (*US*)
Raines & Raines (*US*)
Rees Literary Agency (*US*)
The Amy Rennert Agency, Inc. (*US*)
Richford Becklow Literary Agency (*UK*)
RLR Associates (*US*)
Robert Dudley Agency (*UK*)
Robin Straus Agency, Inc. (*US*)
Rosica Colin Ltd (*UK*)
Ross Yoon Agency (*US*)
The Rudy Agency (*US*)
Marly Rusoff & Associates, Inc. (*US*)
The Sagalyn Literary Agency (*US*)
Salkind Literary Agency (*US*)
Sandra Dijkstra Literary Agency (*US*)
Sanford J. Greenburger Associates, Inc. (*US*)
Sarah Such Literary Agency (*UK*)
The Sayle Literary Agency (*UK*)
Susan Schulman, A Literary Agency (*US*)
The Science Factory (*UK*)
Scovil Galen Ghosh Literary Agency, Inc. (*US*)
Lynn Seligman, Literary Agent (*US*)
Denise Shannon Literary Agency, Inc. (*US*)
Sheil Land Associates Ltd (*UK*)
Sheila Ableman Literary Agency (*UK*)
Sheree Bykofsky Associates, Inc. (*US*)
Signature Literary Agency (*US*)
Dorie Simmonds Agency (*UK*)
Jeffrey Simmons (*UK*)
Sinclair-Stevenson (*UK*)
Robert Smith Literary Agency Ltd (*UK*)
The Spieler Agency (*US*)
Philip G. Spitzer Literary Agency, Inc. (*US*)
Sterling Lord Literistic, Inc. (*US*)
Stuart Krichevsky Literary Agency, Inc. (*US*)
SYLA – Susan Yearwood Literary Agency (*UK*)
Teresa Chris Literary Agency Ltd (*UK*)
Tessler Literary Agency (*US*)
Thompson Literary Agency (*US*)
Toby Mundy Associates Ltd (*UK*)
Tracy Brown Literary Agency (*US*)
TriadaUS Literary Agency, Inc. (*US*)
Trident Media Group, LLC (*US*)
United Agents (*UK*)
Ed Victor Ltd (*UK*)
Victoria Sanders & Associates LLC (*US*)
Watkins / Loomis Agency, Inc. (*US*)
Waxman Leavell Literary Agency (*US*)

The Weingel-Fidel Agency (*US*)
Wendy Sherman Associates, Inc. (*US*)
Westwood Creative Artists (*Can*)
William Morris Endeavor (WME) London (*UK*)
Wm Clark Associates (*US*)
Writers House UK (*UK*)
Writers' Representatives, LLC (*US*)
Writers House, LLC (*US*)
Yates & Yates (*US*)
The Zack Company, Inc (*US*)
Helen Zimmermann Literary Agency (*US*)
Zoë Pagnamenta Agency, LLC (*US*)

Business

Alive Communications, Inc (*US*)
Audrey A. Wolf Literary Agency (*US*)
The August Agency LLC (*US*)
The Authors Care Service ltd (*UK*)
Baldi Agency (*US*)
Bell Lomax Moreton Agency (*UK*)
David Black Literary Agency (*US*)
Bleecker Street Associates, Inc. (*US*)
The Blumer Literary Agency, Inc. (*US*)
BookEnds, LLC (*US*)
Rick Broadhead & Associates Literary Agency (*Can*)
Marie Brown Associates, Inc. (*US*)
Browne & Miller Literary Associates (*US*)
Carnicelli Literary Management (*US*)
Carol Mann Agency (*US*)
Elyse Cheney Literary Associates, LLC (*US*)
Creative Authors Ltd (*UK*)
Richard Curtis Associates, Inc. (*US*)
Liza Dawson Associates (*US*)
Joëlle Delbourgo Associates, Inc. (*US*)
Diane Banks Associates Literary Agency (*UK*)
Jim Donovan Literary (*US*)
Dystel & Goderich Literary Management (*US*)
Ebeling & Associates (*US*)
Judith Ehrlich Literary Management (*US*)
Felicia Eth Literary Representation (*US*)
The Feldstein Agency (*UK*)
Diana Finch Literary Agency (*US*)
FinePrint Literary Management (*US*)
Fletcher & Company (*US*)
Folio Literary Management, LLC (*US*)
Foundry Literary + Media (*US*)
Fox & Howard Literary Agency (*UK*)
Fresh Books Literary Agency (*US*)
Sarah Jane Freymann Literary Agency (*US*)
Fredrica S. Friedman and Co. Inc. (*US*)
Furniss Lawton (*UK*)
Glass Literary Management LLC (*US*)
Goodman Associates (*US*)
Grace Freedson's Publishing Network (*US*)
Graham Maw Christie Literary Agency (*UK*)
Kathryn Green Literary Agency, LLC (*US*)
Hannigan Salky Getzler (HSG) Agency (*US*)
Antony Harwood Limited (*UK*)
The Jeff Herman Agency, LLC (*US*)
Hidden Value Group (*US*)
Kate Hordern Literary Agency (*UK*)
Andrea Hurst Literary Management (*US*)
InkWell Management (*US*)
J de S Associates Inc. (*US*)
Jeanne Fredericks Literary Agency, Inc. (*US*)
Jill Grinberg Literary Management LLC (*US*)
Kathi J. Paton Literary Agency (*US*)
Frances Kelly (*UK*)
Kneerim & Williams (*US*)
The Knight Agency (*US*)
Linda Konner Literary Agency (*US*)
Kuhn Projects (*US*)
The LA Literary Agency (*US*)
Larsen Pomada Literary Agents (*US*)
LaunchBooks Literary Agency (*US*)
Levine Greenberg Rostan Literary Agency (*US*)
Limelight Management (*UK*)
Linda Roghaar Literary Agency, Inc. (*US*)
Literary Management Group, Inc. (*US*)
Literary & Creative Artists Inc. (*US*)
The Literary Group International (*US*)
Lowenstein Associates, Inc. (*US*)
MacGregor Literary (*US*)
Manus & Associates Literary Agency, Inc. (*US*)
Maria Carvainis Agency, Inc. (*US*)
The Martell Agency (*US*)
Martin Literary Management (*US*)
Margret McBride Literary Agency (*US*)
The Michael Greer Literary Agency (*UK*)
Martha Millard Literary Agency (*US*)
Howard Morhaim Literary Agency (*US*)
Northern Lights Literary Services (*US*)
P.S. Literary Agency (*Can*)
Queen Literary Agency, Inc. (*US*)
Lynne Rabinoff Agency (*US*)
Rees Literary Agency (*US*)
The Amy Rennert Agency, Inc. (*US*)
Robert Dudley Agency (*UK*)
Ross Yoon Agency (*US*)
The Rudy Agency (*US*)
Marly Rusoff & Associates, Inc. (*US*)
The Sagalyn Literary Agency (*US*)
Salkind Literary Agency (*US*)
Sandra Dijkstra Literary Agency (*US*)
Sanford J. Greenburger Associates, Inc. (*US*)
Susan Schulman, A Literary Agency (*US*)
Scovil Galen Ghosh Literary Agency, Inc. (*US*)
Lynn Seligman, Literary Agent (*US*)
Denise Shannon Literary Agency, Inc. (*US*)
Sheree Bykofsky Associates, Inc. (*US*)
Solow Literary Enterprises, Inc. (*US*)
The Spieler Agency (*US*)
Sterling Lord Literistic, Inc. (*US*)
Stonesong (*US*)
The Strothman Agency (*US*)
Stuart Krichevsky Literary Agency, Inc. (*US*)
The Stuart Agency (*US*)
The Swetky Agency and Associates (*US*)
SYLA – Susan Yearwood Literary Agency (*UK*)
Talcott Notch Literary (*US*)
Tessler Literary Agency (*US*)
TriadaUS Literary Agency, Inc. (*US*)
Trident Media Group, LLC (*US*)
2M Literary Agency Ltd (*US*)
United Talent Agency (*US*)
Veritas Literary Agency (*US*)

Watson, Little Ltd (*UK*)
Waxman Leavell Literary Agency (*US*)
Writers House UK (*UK*)
Writers' Representatives, LLC (*US*)
Writers House, LLC (*US*)
Yates & Yates (*US*)
Zoë Pagnamenta Agency, LLC (*US*)
Cookery
Baldi Agency (*US*)
Betsy Amster Literary Enterprises (*US*)
Bidnick & Company (*US*)
Vicky Bijur Literary Agency (*US*)
David Black Literary Agency (*US*)
Blake Friedmann Literary Agency Ltd (*UK*)
Bleecker Street Associates, Inc. (*US*)
The Blumer Literary Agency, Inc. (*US*)
Luigi Bonomi Associates Ltd (*UK*)
The Book Group (*US*)
Browne & Miller Literary Associates (*US*)
Caroline Davidson Literary Agency (*UK*)
Chartwell (*UK*)
The Choate Agency, LLC (*US*)
Clare Hulton Literary Agency (*UK*)
Coombs Moylett & Maclean Literary Agency (*UK*)
The Cowles-Ryan Literary Agency (*US*)
Creative Authors Ltd (*UK*)
The Culinary Entertainment Agency (CEA) (*US*)
Laura Dail Literary Agency (*US*)
The Jennifer DeChiara Literary Agency (*US*)
Dinah Wiener Ltd (*UK*)
Don Congdon Associates, Inc. (*US*)
Dystel & Goderich Literary Management (*US*)
Elise Dillsworth Agency (EDA) (*UK*)
Emily Sweet Associates (*UK*)
Ethan Ellenberg Literary Agency (*US*)
Fairbank Literary Representation (*US*)
The Feldstein Agency (*UK*)
FinePrint Literary Management (*US*)
Folio Literary Management, LLC (*US*)
Foundry Literary + Media (*US*)
Sarah Jane Freymann Literary Agency (*US*)
Fredrica S. Friedman and Co. Inc. (*US*)
Furniss Lawton (*UK*)
Goodman Associates (*US*)
Irene Goodman Literary Agency (*US*)
Grace Freedson's Publishing Network (*US*)
Graham Maw Christie Literary Agency (*UK*)
Kathryn Green Literary Agency, LLC (*US*)
Greene & Heaton Ltd (*UK*)
Hannigan Salky Getzler (HSG) Agency (*US*)
Antony Harwood Limited (*UK*)
A M Heath & Company Limited, Author's Agents (*UK*)
David Higham Associates Ltd (*UK*)
Hill Nadell Literary Agency (*US*)
Andrea Hurst Literary Management (*US*)
Jeanne Fredericks Literary Agency, Inc. (*US*)
Frances Kelly (*UK*)
Harvey Klinger, Inc (*US*)
The Knight Agency (*US*)
Linda Konner Literary Agency (*US*)
Kuhn Projects (*US*)
L. Perkins Associates (*US*)
The LA Literary Agency (*US*)
Larsen Pomada Literary Agents (*US*)
Robert Lecker Agency (*Can*)
Levine Greenberg Rostan Literary Agency (*US*)
Limelight Management (*UK*)
The Lisa Ekus Group, LLC (*US*)
Literary & Creative Artists Inc. (*US*)
Lutyens and Rubinstein (*UK*)
Kirsten Manges Literary Agency, LLC (*US*)
Martha Millard Literary Agency (*US*)
Howard Morhaim Literary Agency (*US*)
P.S. Literary Agency (*Can*)
The Peters Fraser & Dunlop Group Ltd (PFD) (*UK*)
Queen Literary Agency, Inc. (*US*)
Richford Becklow Literary Agency (*UK*)
Rita Rosenkranz Literary Agency (*US*)
Robin Straus Agency, Inc. (*US*)
Rosica Colin Ltd (*UK*)
Salkind Literary Agency (*US*)
Sandra Dijkstra Literary Agency (*US*)
Susan Schulman, A Literary Agency (*US*)
Scovil Galen Ghosh Literary Agency, Inc. (*US*)
Lynn Seligman, Literary Agent (*US*)
Sheil Land Associates Ltd (*UK*)
Sheree Bykofsky Associates, Inc. (*US*)
The Spieler Agency (*US*)
Sterling Lord Literistic, Inc. (*US*)
Stonesong (*US*)
The Swetky Agency and Associates (*US*)
Talcott Notch Literary (*US*)
Teresa Chris Literary Agency Ltd (*UK*)
Tessler Literary Agency (*US*)
Thompson Literary Agency (*US*)
TriadaUS Literary Agency, Inc. (*US*)
2M Literary Agency Ltd (*US*)
Ed Victor Ltd (*UK*)
Waxman Leavell Literary Agency (*US*)
Wendy Sherman Associates, Inc. (*US*)
Writers House UK (*UK*)
Writers' Representatives, LLC (*US*)
Writers House, LLC (*US*)
The Zack Company, Inc (*US*)
Karen Gantz Zahler Literary Agency (*US*)
Helen Zimmermann Literary Agency (*US*)
Crafts
David Black Literary Agency (*US*)
The Blumer Literary Agency, Inc. (*US*)
Browne & Miller Literary Associates (*US*)
Creative Authors Ltd (*UK*)
The Gernert Company (*US*)
Grace Freedson's Publishing Network (*US*)
Graham Maw Christie Literary Agency (*UK*)
Hannigan Salky Getzler (HSG) Agency (*US*)
Antony Harwood Limited (*UK*)
Jeanne Fredericks Literary Agency, Inc. (*US*)
Levine Greenberg Rostan Literary Agency (*US*)
Limelight Management (*UK*)
Linda Roghaar Literary Agency, Inc. (*US*)
Julia Lord Literary Management (*US*)
MBA Literary Agents Ltd (*UK*)
Howard Morhaim Literary Agency (*US*)

Salkind Literary Agency (*US*)
Susan Schulman, A Literary Agency (*US*)
Stonesong (*US*)
Talcott Notch Literary (*US*)
Teresa Chris Literary Agency Ltd (*UK*)
TriadaUS Literary Agency, Inc. (*US*)
Crime
Aaron M. Priest Literary Agency (*US*)
The Ahearn Agency, Inc (*US*)
Alive Communications, Inc (*US*)
The Ampersand Agency Ltd (*UK*)
Andrew Lownie Literary Agency Ltd (*UK*)
Artellus Limited (*UK*)
Author Rights Agency (*Ire*)
The Axelrod Agency (*US*)
Ayesha Pande Literary (*US*)
Belcastro Agency (*US*)
Blake Friedmann Literary Agency Ltd (*UK*)
Bleecker Street Associates, Inc. (*US*)
The Blumer Literary Agency, Inc. (*US*)
Luigi Bonomi Associates Ltd (*UK*)
The Book Bureau Literary Agency (*Ire*)
Bresnick Weil Literary Agency, LLC (*US*)
Browne & Miller Literary Associates (*US*)
Chartwell (*UK*)
Mic Cheetham Literary Agency (*UK*)
Conville & Walsh Ltd (*UK*)
The Cooke Agency (*Can*)
Coombs Moylett & Maclean Literary Agency (*UK*)
Creative Authors Ltd (*UK*)
Curtis Brown Group Ltd (*UK*)
Laura Dail Literary Agency (*US*)
The Darley Anderson Agency (*UK*)
Deal Points Ent. (*US*)
DHH Literary Agency Ltd (*UK*)
Diamond Kahn and Woods (DKW) Literary Agency Ltd (*UK*)
Diane Banks Associates Literary Agency (*UK*)
Don Congdon Associates, Inc. (*US*)
Jim Donovan Literary (*US*)
The Dravis Agency, Inc. (*US*)
Dystel & Goderich Literary Management (*US*)
Edwards Fuglewicz (*UK*)
Felicia Eth Literary Representation (*US*)
Ethan Ellenberg Literary Agency (*US*)
The Feldstein Agency (*UK*)
Diana Finch Literary Agency (*US*)
FinePrint Literary Management (*US*)
Fletcher & Company (*US*)
Folio Literary Management, LLC (*US*)
Samuel French, Inc. (*US*)
Sarah Jane Freymann Literary Agency (*US*)
Fredrica S. Friedman and Co. Inc. (*US*)
Furniss Lawton (*UK*)
The Gernert Company (*US*)
Goodman Associates (*US*)
Grace Freedson's Publishing Network (*US*)
Kathryn Green Literary Agency, LLC (*US*)
Greene & Heaton Ltd (*UK*)
Gregory & Company, Authors' Agents (*UK*)
Hardman & Swainson (*UK*)
Antony Harwood Limited (*UK*)
A M Heath & Company Limited, Author's Agents (*UK*)
Rupert Heath Literary Agency (*UK*)
The Jeff Herman Agency, LLC (*US*)
David Higham Associates Ltd (*UK*)
Kate Hordern Literary Agency (*UK*)
Hudson Agency (*US*)
Andrea Hurst Literary Management (*US*)
InkWell Management (*US*)
International Transactions, Inc. (*US*)
J de S Associates Inc. (*US*)
Jenny Brown Associates (*UK*)
Jill Grosjean Literary Agency (*US*)
Johnson & Alcock (*UK*)
Juliet Burton Literary Agency (*UK*)
Keane Kataria Literary Agency (*UK*)
Harvey Klinger, Inc (*US*)
Kneerim & Williams (*US*)
The Knight Agency (*US*)
Barbara S. Kouts, Literary Agent (*US*)
L. Perkins Associates (*US*)
Laura Langlie, Literary Agent (*US*)
Larsen Pomada Literary Agents (*US*)
Robert Lecker Agency (*Can*)
Levine Greenberg Rostan Literary Agency (*US*)
Limelight Management (*UK*)
Lippincott Massie McQuilkin (*US*)
Literary & Creative Artists Inc. (*US*)
The Literary Group International (*US*)
Julia Lord Literary Management (*US*)
Lowenstein Associates, Inc. (*US*)
Donald Maass Literary Agency (*US*)
MacGregor Literary (*US*)
Madeleine Milburn Literary, TV & Film Agency (*UK*)
Andrew Mann Ltd (*UK*)
Maria Carvainis Agency, Inc. (*US*)
Marjacq Scripts Ltd (*UK*)
Martin Literary Management (*US*)
Martha Millard Literary Agency (*US*)
Mulcahy Associates (*UK*)
Judith Murdoch Literary Agency (*UK*)
Niad Management (*US*)
The Peters Fraser & Dunlop Group Ltd (PFD) (*UK*)
Prospect Agency (*US*)
Raines & Raines (*US*)
Redhammer (*UK*)
Richford Becklow Literary Agency (*UK*)
Rocking Chair Books (*UK*)
Rosica Colin Ltd (*UK*)
Salkind Literary Agency (*US*)
The Sayle Literary Agency (*UK*)
Susan Schulman, A Literary Agency (*US*)
Secret Agent Man (*US*)
Lynn Seligman, Literary Agent (*US*)
Sheil Land Associates Ltd (*UK*)
Jeffrey Simmons (*UK*)
Robert Smith Literary Agency Ltd (*UK*)
The Spieler Agency (*US*)
The Swetky Agency and Associates (*US*)
SYLA – Susan Yearwood Literary Agency (*UK*)
Talcott Notch Literary (*US*)

Teresa Chris Literary Agency Ltd (*UK*)
Toby Mundy Associates Ltd (*UK*)
TriadaUS Literary Agency, Inc. (*US*)
Trident Media Group, LLC (*US*)
2M Literary Agency Ltd (*US*)
Veritas Literary Agency (*US*)
Victoria Sanders & Associates LLC (*US*)
Watson, Little Ltd (*UK*)
William Morris Endeavor (WME) London (*UK*)
The Zack Company, Inc (*US*)
Zeno Agency Ltd (*UK*)

Criticism

The Blumer Literary Agency, Inc. (*US*)
Barbara Braun Associates, Inc. (*US*)
Don Congdon Associates, Inc. (*US*)
Dunow, Carlson & Lerner Agency (*US*)
The Feldstein Agency (*UK*)
Goodman Associates (*US*)
Antony Harwood Limited (*UK*)
Signature Literary Agency (*US*)
The Swetky Agency and Associates (*US*)
Trident Media Group, LLC (*US*)
Writers' Representatives, LLC (*US*)

Culture

Aaron M. Priest Literary Agency (*US*)
Adler & Robin Books, Inc (*US*)
Miriam Altshuler Literary Agency (*US*)
Ambassador Speakers Bureau & Literary Agency (*US*)
Andrew Lownie Literary Agency Ltd (*UK*)
Ann Rittenberg Literary Agency (*US*)
Artellus Limited (*UK*)
The August Agency LLC (*US*)
Ayesha Pande Literary (*US*)
B.J. Robbins Literary Agency (*US*)
Baldi Agency (*US*)
Betsy Amster Literary Enterprises (*US*)
Blake Friedmann Literary Agency Ltd (*UK*)
Bleecker Street Associates, Inc. (*US*)
The Blumer Literary Agency, Inc. (*US*)
BookBlast Ltd. (*UK*)
BookEnds, LLC (*US*)
Brandt & Hochman Literary Agents, Inc. (*US*)
Barbara Braun Associates, Inc. (*US*)
Bresnick Weil Literary Agency, LLC (*US*)
Rick Broadhead & Associates Literary Agency (*Can*)
Marie Brown Associates, Inc. (*US*)
Browne & Miller Literary Associates (*US*)
Carnicelli Literary Management (*US*)
Carol Mann Agency (*US*)
Caroline Davidson Literary Agency (*UK*)
Chalberg & Sussman (*US*)
Elyse Cheney Literary Associates, LLC (*US*)
Cine/Lit Representation (*US*)
Clare Hulton Literary Agency (*UK*)
The Cooke Agency (*Can*)
The Cowles-Ryan Literary Agency (*US*)
The Creative Rights Agency (*UK*)
Creative Authors Ltd (*UK*)
David Luxton Associates (*UK*)
Liza Dawson Associates (*US*)
The Jennifer DeChiara Literary Agency (*US*)
DeFiore and Company (*US*)
Joëlle Delbourgo Associates, Inc. (*US*)
Diamond Kahn and Woods (DKW) Literary Agency Ltd (*UK*)
Diane Banks Associates Literary Agency (*UK*)
Don Congdon Associates, Inc. (*US*)
Donadio & Olson, Inc. (*US*)
Jim Donovan Literary (*US*)
Dunham Literary, Inc. (*US*)
Dunow, Carlson & Lerner Agency (*US*)
Dystel & Goderich Literary Management (*US*)
Edwards Fuglewicz (*UK*)
Judith Ehrlich Literary Management (*US*)
Felicia Eth Literary Representation (*US*)
Ethan Ellenberg Literary Agency (*US*)
Mary Evans, Inc. (*US*)
Fairbank Literary Representation (*US*)
Diana Finch Literary Agency (*US*)
FinePrint Literary Management (*US*)
The James Fitzgerald Agency (*US*)
Fletcher & Company (*US*)
Folio Literary Management, LLC (*US*)
Foundry Literary + Media (*US*)
Fox & Howard Literary Agency (*UK*)
Frances Collin Literary Agent (*US*)
Sarah Jane Freymann Literary Agency (*US*)
Fredrica S. Friedman and Co. Inc. (*US*)
Gelfman Schneider / ICM Partners (*US*)
Gina Maccoby Agency (*US*)
Glass Literary Management LLC (*US*)
Frances Goldin Literary Agency, Inc. (*US*)
Goodman Associates (*US*)
Irene Goodman Literary Agency (*US*)
Grace Freedson's Publishing Network (*US*)
Kathryn Green Literary Agency, LLC (*US*)
Greene & Heaton Ltd (*UK*)
Laura Gross Literary Agency (*US*)
Hannigan Salky Getzler (HSG) Agency (*US*)
Joy Harris Literary Agency, Inc. (*US*)
Antony Harwood Limited (*UK*)
Rupert Heath Literary Agency (*UK*)
The Jeff Herman Agency, LLC (*US*)
Hill Nadell Literary Agency (*US*)
Kate Hordern Literary Agency (*UK*)
J de S Associates Inc. (*US*)
The Jean V. Naggar Literary Agency (*US*)
Jenny Brown Associates (*UK*)
Jill Grinberg Literary Management LLC (*US*)
Johnson & Alcock (*UK*)
Jonathan Pegg Literary Agency (*UK*)
Kathi J. Paton Literary Agency (*US*)
Ki Agency Ltd (*UK*)
Harvey Klinger, Inc (*US*)
Kneerim & Williams (*US*)
The Knight Agency (*US*)
Linda Konner Literary Agency (*US*)
Edite Kroll Literary Agency, Inc. (*US*)
Kuhn Projects (*US*)
L. Perkins Associates (*US*)
Laura Langlie, Literary Agent (*US*)
Larsen Pomada Literary Agents (*US*)
LaunchBooks Literary Agency (*US*)
Sarah Lazin Books (*US*)

Robert Lecker Agency (*Can*)
Levine Greenberg Rostan Literary Agency (*US*)
Linda Roghaar Literary Agency, Inc. (*US*)
Lippincott Massie McQuilkin (*US*)
The Lisa Richards Agency (*Ire*)
The Literary Group International (*US*)
MacGregor Literary (*US*)
Kirsten Manges Literary Agency, LLC (*US*)
Manus & Associates Literary Agency, Inc. (*US*)
Maria Carvainis Agency, Inc. (*US*)
Martin Literary Management (*US*)
Margret McBride Literary Agency (*US*)
McIntosh & Otis, Inc (*US*)
Martha Millard Literary Agency (*US*)
Howard Morhaim Literary Agency (*US*)
Nappaland Literary Agency (*US*)
New Leaf Literary & Media, Inc. (*US*)
Niad Management (*US*)
The Park Literary Group LLC (*US*)
The Peters Fraser & Dunlop Group Ltd (PFD) (*UK*)
Puttick Literary Agency (*UK*)
Lynne Rabinoff Agency (*US*)
Renee Zuckerbrot Literary Agency (*US*)
RLR Associates (*US*)
Robin Straus Agency, Inc. (*US*)
Rocking Chair Books (*UK*)
Andy Ross Agency (*US*)
Ross Yoon Agency (*US*)
The Rudy Agency (*US*)
Marly Rusoff & Associates, Inc. (*US*)
The Sagalyn Literary Agency (*US*)
Salkind Literary Agency (*US*)
Sandra Dijkstra Literary Agency (*US*)
Sarah Such Literary Agency (*UK*)
Susan Schulman, A Literary Agency (*US*)
Scovil Galen Ghosh Literary Agency, Inc. (*US*)
Lynn Seligman, Literary Agent (*US*)
Sheree Bykofsky Associates, Inc. (*US*)
Signature Literary Agency (*US*)
Robert Smith Literary Agency Ltd (*UK*)
Solow Literary Enterprises, Inc. (*US*)
The Spieler Agency (*US*)
Sterling Lord Literistic, Inc. (*US*)
Stonesong (*US*)
Stuart Krichevsky Literary Agency, Inc. (*US*)
The Stuart Agency (*US*)
The Swetky Agency and Associates (*US*)
Tessler Literary Agency (*US*)
Thompson Literary Agency (*US*)
TriadaUS Literary Agency, Inc. (*US*)
Trident Media Group, LLC (*US*)
2M Literary Agency Ltd (*US*)
Veritas Literary Agency (*US*)
Victoria Sanders & Associates LLC (*US*)
Watkins / Loomis Agency, Inc. (*US*)
Wendy Sherman Associates, Inc. (*US*)
William Morris Endeavor (WME) London (*UK*)
Wm Clark Associates (*US*)
Wolfson Literary Agency (*US*)
The Zack Company, Inc (*US*)
Helen Zimmermann Literary Agency (*US*)

Current Affairs

Aaron M. Priest Literary Agency (*US*)
The Ahearn Agency, Inc (*US*)
Ambassador Speakers Bureau & Literary Agency (*US*)
The Ampersand Agency Ltd (*UK*)
Andrew Lownie Literary Agency Ltd (*UK*)
Arcadia (*US*)
Artellus Limited (*UK*)
Audrey A. Wolf Literary Agency (*US*)
The August Agency LLC (*US*)
David Black Literary Agency (*US*)
Blake Friedmann Literary Agency Ltd (*UK*)
Bleecker Street Associates, Inc. (*US*)
BookEnds, LLC (*US*)
Brandt & Hochman Literary Agents, Inc. (*US*)
Rick Broadhead & Associates Literary Agency (*Can*)
Browne & Miller Literary Associates (*US*)
Carnicelli Literary Management (*US*)
Carol Mann Agency (*US*)
Elyse Cheney Literary Associates, LLC (*US*)
The Choate Agency, LLC (*US*)
Conville & Walsh Ltd (*UK*)
Coombs Moylett & Maclean Literary Agency (*UK*)
The Cowles-Ryan Literary Agency (*US*)
Liza Dawson Associates (*US*)
DeFiore and Company (*US*)
Joëlle Delbourgo Associates, Inc. (*US*)
Diane Banks Associates Literary Agency (*UK*)
Don Congdon Associates, Inc. (*US*)
Jim Donovan Literary (*US*)
Dunham Literary, Inc. (*US*)
Dunow, Carlson & Lerner Agency (*US*)
Dystel & Goderich Literary Management (*US*)
Judith Ehrlich Literary Management (*US*)
Emily Sweet Associates (*UK*)
Felicia Eth Literary Representation (*US*)
Ethan Ellenberg Literary Agency (*US*)
The Feldstein Agency (*UK*)
Felicity Bryan Associates (*UK*)
Diana Finch Literary Agency (*US*)
Fletcher & Company (*US*)
Foundry Literary + Media (*US*)
Fredrica S. Friedman and Co. Inc. (*US*)
Gelfman Schneider / ICM Partners (*US*)
Georges Borchardt, Inc. (*US*)
The Gernert Company (*US*)
Gina Maccoby Agency (*US*)
Frances Goldin Literary Agency, Inc. (*US*)
Goodman Associates (*US*)
Grace Freedson's Publishing Network (*US*)
Kathryn Green Literary Agency, LLC (*US*)
Greene & Heaton Ltd (*UK*)
Laura Gross Literary Agency (*US*)
Hannigan Salky Getzler (HSG) Agency (*US*)
Antony Harwood Limited (*UK*)
Rupert Heath Literary Agency (*UK*)
David Higham Associates Ltd (*UK*)
Hill Nadell Literary Agency (*US*)
Kate Hordern Literary Agency (*UK*)
Andrea Hurst Literary Management (*US*)

InkWell Management (*US*)
J de S Associates Inc. (*US*)
Jane Turnbull (*UK*)
The Jean V. Naggar Literary Agency (*US*)
Jill Grinberg Literary Management LLC (*US*)
Johnson & Alcock (*UK*)
Jonathan Pegg Literary Agency (*UK*)
Kathi J. Paton Literary Agency (*US*)
Kneerim & Williams (*US*)
Barbara S. Kouts, Literary Agent (*US*)
Edite Kroll Literary Agency, Inc. (*US*)
Kuhn Projects (*US*)
Laura Langlie, Literary Agent (*US*)
Larsen Pomada Literary Agents (*US*)
LaunchBooks Literary Agency (*US*)
Sarah Lazin Books (*US*)
Lippincott Massie McQuilkin (*US*)
Literary & Creative Artists Inc. (*US*)
Julia Lord Literary Management (*US*)
The Jennifer Lyons Literary Agency, LLC (*US*)
MacGregor Literary (*US*)
Maggie Pearlstine Associates Ltd (*UK*)
Manus & Associates Literary Agency, Inc. (*US*)
Martin Literary Management (*US*)
McIntosh & Otis, Inc (*US*)
Martha Millard Literary Agency (*US*)
P.S. Literary Agency (*Can*)
The Park Literary Group LLC (*US*)
Puttick Literary Agency (*UK*)
Lynne Rabinoff Agency (*US*)
Robert Dudley Agency (*UK*)
Robin Straus Agency, Inc. (*US*)
Rocking Chair Books (*UK*)
Rosica Colin Ltd (*UK*)
Andy Ross Agency (*US*)
Ross Yoon Agency (*US*)
The Rudy Agency (*US*)
Salkind Literary Agency (*US*)
Sandra Dijkstra Literary Agency (*US*)
The Sayle Literary Agency (*UK*)
Susan Schulman, A Literary Agency (*US*)
The Science Factory (*UK*)
Lynn Seligman, Literary Agent (*US*)
Denise Shannon Literary Agency, Inc. (*US*)
Sheree Bykofsky Associates, Inc. (*US*)
Jeffrey Simmons (*UK*)
Sinclair-Stevenson (*UK*)
Robert Smith Literary Agency Ltd (*UK*)
The Spieler Agency (*US*)
Philip G. Spitzer Literary Agency, Inc. (*US*)
Sterling Lord Literistic, Inc. (*US*)
Stonesong (*US*)
The Strothman Agency (*US*)
Stuart Krichevsky Literary Agency, Inc. (*US*)
The Stuart Agency (*US*)
The Swetky Agency and Associates (*US*)
Toby Mundy Associates Ltd (*UK*)
Tracy Brown Literary Agency (*US*)
TriadaUS Literary Agency, Inc. (*US*)
Trident Media Group, LLC (*US*)
Victoria Sanders & Associates LLC (*US*)
Watkins / Loomis Agency, Inc. (*US*)
Westwood Creative Artists (*Can*)
Wm Clark Associates (*US*)
Writers' Representatives, LLC (*US*)
Yates & Yates (*US*)
The Zack Company, Inc (*US*)
Design
The Blumer Literary Agency, Inc. (*US*)
Barbara Braun Associates, Inc. (*US*)
Carol Mann Agency (*US*)
Caroline Davidson Literary Agency (*UK*)
Fairbank Literary Representation (*US*)
Fresh Books Literary Agency (*US*)
Fredrica S. Friedman and Co. Inc. (*US*)
Grace Freedson's Publishing Network (*US*)
Kathryn Green Literary Agency, LLC (*US*)
Hannigan Salky Getzler (HSG) Agency (*US*)
Antony Harwood Limited (*UK*)
Jeanne Fredericks Literary Agency, Inc. (*US*)
Johnson & Alcock (*UK*)
Kuhn Projects (*US*)
Larsen Pomada Literary Agents (*US*)
Martha Millard Literary Agency (*US*)
Howard Morhaim Literary Agency (*US*)
P.S. Literary Agency (*Can*)
Marly Rusoff & Associates, Inc. (*US*)
Salkind Literary Agency (*US*)
Sandra Dijkstra Literary Agency (*US*)
Lynn Seligman, Literary Agent (*US*)
Stonesong (*US*)
The Stuart Agency (*US*)
The Swetky Agency and Associates (*US*)
Whispering Buffalo Literary Agency Ltd (*UK*)
Wm Clark Associates (*US*)
Karen Gantz Zahler Literary Agency (*US*)
Drama
Abrams Artists Agency (*US*)
Cecily Ware Literary Agents (*UK*)
The Characters Talent Agency (*Can*)
The Dravis Agency, Inc. (*US*)
Jill Foster Ltd (JFL) (*UK*)
Antony Harwood Limited (*UK*)
David Higham Associates Ltd (*UK*)
Hudson Agency (*US*)
Literary & Creative Artists Inc. (*US*)
Niad Management (*US*)
PBJ and JBJ Management (*UK*)
Roger Hancock Ltd (*UK*)
Sheil Land Associates Ltd (*UK*)
The Tennyson Agency (*UK*)
Entertainment
Artellus Limited (*UK*)
The August Agency LLC (*US*)
David Black Literary Agency (*US*)
Bleecker Street Associates, Inc. (*US*)
The Blumer Literary Agency, Inc. (*US*)
The Bright Literary Academy (*UK*)
Diane Banks Associates Literary Agency (*UK*)
FinePrint Literary Management (*US*)
Folio Literary Management, LLC (*US*)
Gina Maccoby Agency (*US*)
Glass Literary Management LLC (*US*)
Frances Goldin Literary Agency, Inc. (*US*)
Gunn Media Associates (*UK*)
Antony Harwood Limited (*UK*)

Jane Turnbull (*UK*)
Jill Grinberg Literary Management LLC (*US*)
The Knight Agency (*US*)
Linda Konner Literary Agency (*US*)
Robert Lecker Agency (*Can*)
Julia Lord Literary Management (*US*)
Martin Literary Management (*US*)
New Leaf Literary & Media, Inc. (*US*)
Redhammer (*UK*)
Rocking Chair Books (*UK*)
Roger Hancock Ltd (*UK*)
Sanford J. Greenburger Associates, Inc. (*US*)
Susan Schulman, A Literary Agency (*US*)
Jeffrey Simmons (*UK*)
Susan Rabiner, Literary Agent, Inc. (*US*)
Wendy Sherman Associates, Inc. (*US*)
Whispering Buffalo Literary Agency Ltd (*UK*)
Karen Gantz Zahler Literary Agency (*US*)

Erotic

The Axelrod Agency (*US*)
Belcastro Agency (*US*)
Bleecker Street Associates, Inc. (*US*)
BookEnds, LLC (*US*)
The Characters Talent Agency (*Can*)
Elaine P. English, Attorney & Literary Agent (*US*)
Goodman Associates (*US*)
Antony Harwood Limited (*UK*)
L. Perkins Associates (*US*)
Robert Lecker Agency (*Can*)
New Leaf Literary & Media, Inc. (*US*)
Prospect Agency (*US*)
Rosica Colin Ltd (*UK*)
Spencerhill Associates (*US*)
The Swetky Agency and Associates (*US*)
Veritas Literary Agency (*US*)
The Zack Company, Inc (*US*)

Fantasy

Aaron M. Priest Literary Agency (*US*)
Miriam Altshuler Literary Agency (*US*)
The Ampersand Agency Ltd (*UK*)
Andrew Lownie Literary Agency Ltd (*UK*)
Anubis Literary Agency (*UK*)
Aponte Literary (*US*)
Artellus Limited (*UK*)
Ayesha Pande Literary (*US*)
Baror International, Inc. (*US*)
Belcastro Agency (*US*)
Luigi Bonomi Associates Ltd (*UK*)
BookEnds, LLC (*US*)
Caroline Sheldon Literary Agency (*UK*)
The Characters Talent Agency (*Can*)
Mic Cheetham Literary Agency (*UK*)
Conville & Walsh Ltd (*UK*)
The Cooke Agency (*Can*)
Curtis Brown Group Ltd (*UK*)
Richard Curtis Associates, Inc. (*US*)
Laura Dail Literary Agency (*US*)
Liza Dawson Associates (*US*)
The Jennifer DeChiara Literary Agency (*US*)
Joëlle Delbourgo Associates, Inc. (*US*)
DHH Literary Agency Ltd (*UK*)
Diamond Kahn and Woods (DKW) Literary Agency Ltd (*UK*)
Don Congdon Associates, Inc. (*US*)
Dunham Literary, Inc. (*US*)
Dystel & Goderich Literary Management (*US*)
Judith Ehrlich Literary Management (*US*)
Elaine P. English, Attorney & Literary Agent (*US*)
Ethan Ellenberg Literary Agency (*US*)
FinePrint Literary Management (*US*)
Folio Literary Management, LLC (*US*)
Frances Collin Literary Agent (*US*)
Samuel French, Inc. (*US*)
Furniss Lawton (*UK*)
The Gernert Company (*US*)
Barry Goldblatt Literary Agency, Inc. (*US*)
Irene Goodman Literary Agency (*US*)
Antony Harwood Limited (*UK*)
Hudson Agency (*US*)
Andrea Hurst Literary Management (*US*)
Jabberwocky Literary Agency (*US*)
The Jean V. Naggar Literary Agency (*US*)
Jill Grinberg Literary Management LLC (*US*)
Virginia Kidd Agency, Inc (*US*)
Harvey Klinger, Inc (*US*)
The Knight Agency (*US*)
L. Perkins Associates (*US*)
Larsen Pomada Literary Agents (*US*)
Linn Prentis, Literary Agent (*US*)
Lippincott Massie McQuilkin (*US*)
The Literary Group International (*US*)
London Independent Books (*UK*)
Lowenstein Associates, Inc. (*US*)
Donald Maass Literary Agency (*US*)
Madeleine Milburn Literary, TV & Film Agency (*UK*)
McIntosh & Otis, Inc (*US*)
Martha Millard Literary Agency (*US*)
Howard Morhaim Literary Agency (*US*)
Nelson Literary Agency, LLC (*US*)
New Leaf Literary & Media, Inc. (*US*)
P.S. Literary Agency (*Can*)
Pavilion Literary Management (*US*)
Prospect Agency (*US*)
Raines & Raines (*US*)
Rebecca Friedman Literary Agency (*US*)
Richford Becklow Literary Agency (*UK*)
Rosica Colin Ltd (*UK*)
Salkind Literary Agency (*US*)
Sandra Dijkstra Literary Agency (*US*)
Sanford J. Greenburger Associates, Inc. (*US*)
Scribe Agency LLC (*US*)
Lynn Seligman, Literary Agent (*US*)
Sheil Land Associates Ltd (*UK*)
Signature Literary Agency (*US*)
Spectrum Literary Agency (*US*)
Spencerhill Associates (*US*)
Philip G. Spitzer Literary Agency, Inc. (*US*)
Steph Roundsmith Agent and Editor (*UK*)
Sternig & Byrne Literary Agency (*US*)
Stuart Krichevsky Literary Agency, Inc. (*US*)
The Swetky Agency and Associates (*US*)
Talcott Notch Literary (*US*)

TriadaUS Literary Agency, Inc. (*US*)
Trident Media Group, LLC (*US*)
Veritas Literary Agency (*US*)
Victoria Sanders & Associates LLC (*US*)
Waxman Leavell Literary Agency (*US*)
Writers House UK (*UK*)
Writers House, LLC (*US*)
The Zack Company, Inc (*US*)
Zeno Agency Ltd (*UK*)
Fiction
A for Authors (*UK*)
A & B Personal Management Ltd (*UK*)
A+B Works (*US*)
Aaron M. Priest Literary Agency (*US*)
Dominick Abel Literary Agency, Inc (*US*)
Abner Stein (*UK*)
Adams Literary (*US*)
Agency for the Performing Arts (APA) (*US*)
The Agency (London) Ltd (*UK*)
The Ahearn Agency, Inc (*US*)
Aimee Entertainment Agency (*US*)
Aitken Alexander Associates (*UK*)
Alive Communications, Inc (*US*)
Miriam Altshuler Literary Agency (*US*)
Ambassador Speakers Bureau & Literary Agency (*US*)
The Ampersand Agency Ltd (*UK*)
Andlyn (*UK*)
Andrew Lownie Literary Agency Ltd (*UK*)
Andrew Nurnberg Associates, Ltd (*UK*)
Ann Rittenberg Literary Agency (*US*)
Anne Clark Literary Agency (*UK*)
Anthony Sheil in Association with Aitken Alexander Associates (*UK*)
Anubis Literary Agency (*UK*)
Aponte Literary (*US*)
Artellus Limited (*UK*)
The August Agency LLC (*US*)
Author Rights Agency (*Ire*)
The Authors Care Service ltd (*UK*)
AVAnti Productions & Management (*UK*)
The Axelrod Agency (*US*)
Ayesha Pande Literary (*US*)
B.J. Robbins Literary Agency (*US*)
Baldi Agency (*US*)
Barbara Hogenson Agency (*US*)
Baror International, Inc. (*US*)
Bath Literary Agency (*UK*)
Belcastro Agency (*US*)
Bell Lomax Moreton Agency (*UK*)
Betsy Amster Literary Enterprises (*US*)
Vicky Bijur Literary Agency (*US*)
David Black Literary Agency (*US*)
The Blair Partnership (*UK*)
Blake Friedmann Literary Agency Ltd (*UK*)
Bleecker Street Associates, Inc. (*US*)
The Blumer Literary Agency, Inc. (*US*)
Luigi Bonomi Associates Ltd (*UK*)
The Book Group (*US*)
The Book Bureau Literary Agency (*Ire*)
BookBlast Ltd. (*UK*)
BookEnds, LLC (*US*)
Bookseeker Agency (*UK*)
Brandt & Hochman Literary Agents, Inc. (*US*)
Barbara Braun Associates, Inc. (*US*)
Bresnick Weil Literary Agency, LLC (*US*)
The Bright Literary Academy (*UK*)
Marie Brown Associates, Inc. (*US*)
Browne & Miller Literary Associates (*US*)
Carnicelli Literary Management (*US*)
Carol Mann Agency (*US*)
Caroline Davidson Literary Agency (*UK*)
Caroline Sheldon Literary Agency (*UK*)
The Catchpole Agency (*UK*)
Catherine Pellegrino & Associates (*UK*)
Chalberg & Sussman (*US*)
Chartwell (*UK*)
Mic Cheetham Literary Agency (*UK*)
Elyse Cheney Literary Associates, LLC (*US*)
The Choate Agency, LLC (*US*)
The Christopher Little Literary Agency (*UK*)
The Chudney Agency (*US*)
Cine/Lit Representation (*US*)
Clare Hulton Literary Agency (*UK*)
Conville & Walsh Ltd (*UK*)
The Cooke Agency (*Can*)
Coombs Moylett & Maclean Literary Agency (*UK*)
The Cowles-Ryan Literary Agency (*US*)
The Creative Rights Agency (*UK*)
Creative Trust, Inc. (*US*)
Creative Authors Ltd (*UK*)
Rupert Crew Ltd (*UK*)
Curtis Brown Group Ltd (*UK*)
Richard Curtis Associates, Inc. (*US*)
Curtis Brown Ltd (*US*)
Laura Dail Literary Agency (*US*)
Darhansoff & Verrill Literary Agents (*US*)
The Darley Anderson Agency (*UK*)
David Godwin Associates (*UK*)
Liza Dawson Associates (*US*)
Deal Points Ent. (*US*)
The Jennifer DeChiara Literary Agency (*US*)
DeFiore and Company (*US*)
Joëlle Delbourgo Associates, Inc. (*US*)
DHH Literary Agency Ltd (*UK*)
Diamond Kahn and Woods (DKW) Literary Agency Ltd (*UK*)
Diane Banks Associates Literary Agency (*UK*)
Dinah Wiener Ltd (*UK*)
Don Congdon Associates, Inc. (*US*)
Donadio & Olson, Inc. (*US*)
Jim Donovan Literary (*US*)
Dunham Literary, Inc. (*US*)
Dunow, Carlson & Lerner Agency (*US*)
Dystel & Goderich Literary Management (*US*)
Toby Eady Associates Ltd (*UK*)
East West Literary Agency LLC (*US*)
Eddison Pearson Ltd (*UK*)
Anne Edelstein Literary Agency (*US*)
Edwards Fuglewicz (*UK*)
Judith Ehrlich Literary Management (*US*)
Einstein Literary Management (*US*)
Elaine Markson Literary Agency (*US*)
Elaine Steel (*UK*)
Elise Dillsworth Agency (EDA) (*UK*)

Elizabeth Roy Literary Agency (*UK*)
Emily Sweet Associates (*UK*)
Elaine P. English, Attorney & Literary Agent (*US*)
Felicia Eth Literary Representation (*US*)
Ethan Ellenberg Literary Agency (*US*)
Faith Evans Associates (*UK*)
Mary Evans, Inc. (*US*)
Eve White: Literary Agent (*UK*)
Fairbank Literary Representation (*US*)
The Feldstein Agency (*UK*)
Felicity Bryan Associates (*UK*)
Felix de Wolfe (*UK*)
Film Rights Ltd in association with Laurence Fitch Ltd (*UK*)
Diana Finch Literary Agency (*US*)
FinePrint Literary Management (*US*)
The James Fitzgerald Agency (*US*)
Fletcher & Company (*US*)
Folio Literary Management, LLC (*US*)
Foundry Literary + Media (*US*)
Frances Collin Literary Agent (*US*)
Frank Fahy (*Ire*)
Fraser Ross Associates (*UK*)
Sarah Jane Freymann Literary Agency (*US*)
Fredrica S. Friedman and Co. Inc. (*US*)
Furniss Lawton (*UK*)
Nancy Gallt Literary Agency (*US*)
Gelfman Schneider / ICM Partners (*US*)
Georges Borchardt, Inc. (*US*)
Georgina Capel Associates Ltd (*UK*)
The Gernert Company (*US*)
Gina Maccoby Agency (*US*)
Eric Glass Ltd (*UK*)
Glass Literary Management LLC (*US*)
Global Lion Intellectual Property Management, Inc. (*US*)
Barry Goldblatt Literary Agency, Inc. (*US*)
Frances Goldin Literary Agency, Inc. (*US*)
Goodman Associates (*US*)
Irene Goodman Literary Agency (*US*)
Christine Green Authors' Agent (*UK*)
Kathryn Green Literary Agency, LLC (*US*)
Louise Greenberg Books Ltd (*UK*)
Greene & Heaton Ltd (*UK*)
The Greenhouse Literary Agency (*UK*)
Gregory & Company, Authors' Agents (*UK*)
Blanche C. Gregory Inc. (*US*)
Greyhaus Literary Agency (*US*)
Laura Gross Literary Agency (*US*)
David Grossman Literary Agency Ltd (*UK*)
Marianne Gunn O'Connor Literary Agency (*Ire*)
Gunn Media Associates (*UK*)
Hannigan Salky Getzler (HSG) Agency (*US*)
Hardman & Swainson (*UK*)
Harold Ober Associates, Inc. (*US*)
Joy Harris Literary Agency, Inc. (*US*)
Antony Harwood Limited (*UK*)
A M Heath & Company Limited, Author's Agents (*UK*)
Rupert Heath Literary Agency (*UK*)
The Helen Brann Agency, Inc. (*US*)
The Helen Heller Agency (*Can*)
Hidden Value Group (*US*)
David Higham Associates Ltd (*UK*)
Hill Nadell Literary Agency (*US*)
Vanessa Holt Ltd (*UK*)
Hopkins Literary Associates (*US*)
Kate Hordern Literary Agency (*UK*)
Hunter Profiles (*UK*)
Andrea Hurst Literary Management (*US*)
InkWell Management (*US*)
Intercontinental Literary Agency (*UK*)
International Transactions, Inc. (*US*)
Isabel White Literary Agent (*UK*)
J de S Associates Inc. (*US*)
Jabberwocky Literary Agency (*US*)
Jane Conway-Gordon Ltd (*UK*)
Jane Rotrosen Agency (*US*)
Jane Turnbull (*UK*)
The Jean V. Naggar Literary Agency (*US*)
Jenny Brown Associates (*UK*)
Jill Grinberg Literary Management LLC (*US*)
Jill Grosjean Literary Agency (*US*)
Jo Unwin Literary Agency (*UK*)
The Joan Brandt Agency (*US*)
Johnson & Alcock (*UK*)
Jonathan Clowes Ltd (*UK*)
Jonathan Pegg Literary Agency (*UK*)
Juliet Burton Literary Agency (*UK*)
Michelle Kass Associates (*UK*)
Kathi J. Paton Literary Agency (*US*)
Keane Kataria Literary Agency (*UK*)
Ken Sherman & Associates (*US*)
Ki Agency Ltd (*UK*)
Virginia Kidd Agency, Inc (*US*)
Harvey Klinger, Inc (*US*)
Kneerim & Williams (*US*)
The Knight Agency (*US*)
Barbara S. Kouts, Literary Agent (*US*)
Edite Kroll Literary Agency, Inc. (*US*)
Kuhn Projects (*US*)
L. Perkins Associates (*US*)
The LA Literary Agency (*US*)
Peter Lampack Agency, Inc (*US*)
Laura Langlie, Literary Agent (*US*)
Larsen Pomada Literary Agents (*US*)
The Steve Laube Agency (*US*)
LaunchBooks Literary Agency (*US*)
Sarah Lazin Books (*US*)
Robert Lecker Agency (*Can*)
Levine Greenberg Rostan Literary Agency (*US*)
Barbara Levy Literary Agency (*UK*)
Limelight Management (*UK*)
Linda Chester & Associates (*US*)
Linda Roghaar Literary Agency, Inc. (*US*)
Lindsay Literary Agency (*UK*)
Linn Prentis, Literary Agent (*US*)
Lippincott Massie McQuilkin (*US*)
The Lisa Richards Agency (*Ire*)
Literary & Creative Artists Inc. (*US*)
The Literary Group International (*US*)
London Independent Books (*UK*)
Julia Lord Literary Management (*US*)
Lorella Belli Literary Agency (LBLA) (*UK*)
Lowenstein Associates, Inc. (*US*)

Lutyens and Rubinstein (*UK*)
The Jennifer Lyons Literary Agency, LLC (*US*)
Donald Maass Literary Agency (*US*)
MacGregor Literary (*US*)
Madeleine Milburn Literary, TV & Film Agency (*UK*)
Maggie Pearlstine Associates Ltd (*UK*)
Kirsten Manges Literary Agency, LLC (*US*)
Andrew Mann Ltd (*UK*)
Manus & Associates Literary Agency, Inc. (*US*)
Maria Carvainis Agency, Inc. (*US*)
Marjacq Scripts Ltd (*UK*)
Marly Russoff & Associates (*US*)
The Martell Agency (*US*)
Martin Literary Management (*US*)
Mary Clemmey Literary Agency (*UK*)
MBA Literary Agents Ltd (*UK*)
Duncan McAra (*UK*)
Margret McBride Literary Agency (*US*)
McIntosh & Otis, Inc (*US*)
Meredith Bernstein Literary Agency, Inc. (*US*)
The Michael Greer Literary Agency (*UK*)
Miles Stott Children's Literary Agency (*UK*)
Martha Millard Literary Agency (*US*)
Patricia Moosbrugger Literary Agency (*US*)
Howard Morhaim Literary Agency (*US*)
Mulcahy Associates (*UK*)
Judith Murdoch Literary Agency (*UK*)
Nappaland Literary Agency (*US*)
Nelson Literary Agency, LLC (*US*)
New Leaf Literary & Media, Inc. (*US*)
Niad Management (*US*)
MNLA (Maggie Noach Literary Agency) (*UK*)
Northern Lights Literary Services (*US*)
Deborah Owen Ltd (*UK*)
P.S. Literary Agency (*Can*)
The Park Literary Group LLC (*US*)
Pavilion Literary Management (*US*)
The Peters Fraser & Dunlop Group Ltd (PFD) (*UK*)
Pippin Properties, Inc (*US*)
Shelley Power Literary Agency Ltd (*UK*)
Prospect Agency (*US*)
Queen Literary Agency, Inc. (*US*)
Raines & Raines (*US*)
Rebecca Friedman Literary Agency (*US*)
Redhammer (*UK*)
Rees Literary Agency (*US*)
Renee Zuckerbrot Literary Agency (*US*)
The Amy Rennert Agency, Inc. (*US*)
Richford Becklow Literary Agency (*UK*)
Riverside Literary Agency (*US*)
RLR Associates (*US*)
Robin Jones Literary Agency (*UK*)
Robin Straus Agency, Inc. (*US*)
Rocking Chair Books (*UK*)
Rosica Colin Ltd (*UK*)
Andy Ross Agency (*US*)
The Rudy Agency (*US*)
Marly Rusoff & Associates, Inc. (*US*)
The Sagalyn Literary Agency (*US*)
Salkind Literary Agency (*US*)
Sandra Dijkstra Literary Agency (*US*)
Sanford J. Greenburger Associates, Inc. (*US*)
Sarah Such Literary Agency (*UK*)
The Sayle Literary Agency (*UK*)
Susan Schulman, A Literary Agency (*US*)
The Science Factory (*UK*)
Scott Treimel NY (*US*)
Scovil Galen Ghosh Literary Agency, Inc. (*US*)
Scribe Agency LLC (*US*)
Secret Agent Man (*US*)
Lynn Seligman, Literary Agent (*US*)
Denise Shannon Literary Agency, Inc. (*US*)
Sheil Land Associates Ltd (*UK*)
Sheree Bykofsky Associates, Inc. (*US*)
Signature Literary Agency (*US*)
Dorie Simmonds Agency (*UK*)
Jeffrey Simmons (*UK*)
Sinclair-Stevenson (*UK*)
Sophie Hicks Agency (*UK*)
Spectrum Literary Agency (*US*)
Spencerhill Associates (*US*)
The Spieler Agency (*US*)
Philip G. Spitzer Literary Agency, Inc. (*US*)
Standen Literary Agency (*UK*)
Steph Roundsmith Agent and Editor (*UK*)
Sterling Lord Literistic, Inc. (*US*)
Sternig & Byrne Literary Agency (*US*)
Stonesong (*US*)
The Strothman Agency (*US*)
Stuart Krichevsky Literary Agency, Inc. (*US*)
The Stuart Agency (*US*)
Susan Rabiner, Literary Agent, Inc. (*US*)
Susanna Lea Associates (UK) (*UK*)
The Susijn Agency (*UK*)
The Swetky Agency and Associates (*US*)
SYLA – Susan Yearwood Literary Agency (*UK*)
Talcott Notch Literary (*US*)
Teresa Chris Literary Agency Ltd (*UK*)
Tessler Literary Agency (*US*)
Thompson Literary Agency (*US*)
Toby Mundy Associates Ltd (*UK*)
Tracy Brown Literary Agency (*US*)
Lavinia Trevor Agency (*UK*)
TriadaUS Literary Agency, Inc. (*US*)
Trident Media Group, LLC (*US*)
Uli Rushby-Smith Literary Agency (*UK*)
United Talent Agency (*US*)
United Agents (*UK*)
Veritas Literary Agency (*US*)
Ed Victor Ltd (*UK*)
Victoria Sanders & Associates LLC (*US*)
Wade & Co Literary Agency (*UK*)
Watkins / Loomis Agency, Inc. (*US*)
Watson, Little Ltd (*UK*)
Waxman Leavell Literary Agency (*US*)
The Weingel-Fidel Agency (*US*)
Wendy Sherman Associates, Inc. (*US*)
Wernick & Pratt Agency (*US*)
Westwood Creative Artists (*Can*)
Whispering Buffalo Literary Agency Ltd (*UK*)
William Morris Endeavor (WME) London (*UK*)
William Morris Endeavor Entertainment (*US*)
Wm Clark Associates (*US*)
Wolfson Literary Agency (*US*)

Writers House UK (*UK*)
The Writers' Practice (*UK*)
Writers' Representatives, LLC (*US*)
Writers House, LLC (*US*)
The Wylie Agency (UK) Ltd (*UK*)
Yates & Yates (*US*)
The Zack Company, Inc (*US*)
Karen Gantz Zahler Literary Agency (*US*)
Zeno Agency Ltd (*UK*)
Helen Zimmermann Literary Agency (*US*)
Zoë Pagnamenta Agency, LLC (*US*)
Film
A & B Personal Management Ltd (*UK*)
Above the Line Agency (*US*)
Abrams Artists Agency (*US*)
Bret Adams Ltd (*US*)
Agency for the Performing Arts (APA) (*US*)
The Agency (London) Ltd (*UK*)
Aimee Entertainment Agency (*US*)
Alan Brodie Representation Ltd (*UK*)
Anonymous Content (*US*)
AVAnti Productions & Management (*UK*)
Berlin Associates (*UK*)
Blake Friedmann Literary Agency Ltd (*UK*)
Barbara Braun Associates, Inc. (*US*)
Kelvin C. Bulger and Associates (*US*)
Cecily Ware Literary Agents (*UK*)
The Characters Talent Agency (*Can*)
Creative Trust, Inc. (*US*)
Curtis Brown Group Ltd (*UK*)
The Jennifer DeChiara Literary Agency (*US*)
DHH Literary Agency Ltd (*UK*)
Don Congdon Associates, Inc. (*US*)
The Dravis Agency, Inc. (*US*)
Elaine Steel (*UK*)
Energy Entertainment (*US*)
Felix de Wolfe (*UK*)
Film Rights Ltd in association with Laurence Fitch Ltd (*UK*)
Diana Finch Literary Agency (*US*)
Jill Foster Ltd (JFL) (*UK*)
Fredrica S. Friedman and Co. Inc. (*US*)
Georgina Capel Associates Ltd (*UK*)
Eric Glass Ltd (*UK*)
Frances Goldin Literary Agency, Inc. (*US*)
Goodman Associates (*US*)
Antony Harwood Limited (*UK*)
David Higham Associates Ltd (*UK*)
Valerie Hoskins Associates (*UK*)
Hudson Agency (*US*)
Independent Talent Group Ltd (*UK*)
Janet Fillingham Associates (*UK*)
Johnson & Alcock (*UK*)
Jonathan Clowes Ltd (*UK*)
Michelle Kass Associates (*UK*)
Ken Sherman & Associates (*US*)
Ki Agency Ltd (*UK*)
L. Perkins Associates (*US*)
Laura Langlie, Literary Agent (*US*)
Larsen Pomada Literary Agents (*US*)
Robert Lecker Agency (*Can*)
Linda Seifert Management (*UK*)
Macnaughton Lord Representation (*UK*)
Madeleine Milburn Literary, TV & Film Agency (*UK*)
Marjacq Scripts Ltd (*UK*)
Mary Clemmey Literary Agency (*UK*)
MBA Literary Agents Ltd (*UK*)
Martha Millard Literary Agency (*US*)
Niad Management (*US*)
Paradigm Talent and Literary Agency (*US*)
PBJ and JBJ Management (*UK*)
Peregrine Whittlesey Agency (*US*)
The Peters Fraser & Dunlop Group Ltd (PFD) (*UK*)
Rochelle Stevens & Co. (*UK*)
Rosica Colin Ltd (*UK*)
Sayle Screen Ltd (*UK*)
Susan Schulman, A Literary Agency (*US*)
Lynn Seligman, Literary Agent (*US*)
Sheil Land Associates Ltd (*UK*)
Sheree Bykofsky Associates, Inc. (*US*)
Jeffrey Simmons (*UK*)
The Spieler Agency (*US*)
Stone Manners Salners Agency (*US*)
The Swetky Agency and Associates (*US*)
The Tennyson Agency (*UK*)
Trident Media Group, LLC (*US*)
2M Literary Agency Ltd (*US*)
United Agents (*UK*)
Victoria Sanders & Associates LLC (*US*)
Watson, Little Ltd (*UK*)
Whispering Buffalo Literary Agency Ltd (*UK*)
William Morris Endeavor Entertainment (*US*)
Wm Clark Associates (*US*)
The Zack Company, Inc (*US*)
Finance
Ambassador Speakers Bureau & Literary Agency (*US*)
Andrew Lownie Literary Agency Ltd (*UK*)
Audrey A. Wolf Literary Agency (*US*)
The August Agency LLC (*US*)
Ayesha Pande Literary (*US*)
Baldi Agency (*US*)
David Black Literary Agency (*US*)
Blake Friedmann Literary Agency Ltd (*UK*)
Bleecker Street Associates, Inc. (*US*)
The Blumer Literary Agency, Inc. (*US*)
Browne & Miller Literary Associates (*US*)
Carol Mann Agency (*US*)
Elyse Cheney Literary Associates, LLC (*US*)
Richard Curtis Associates, Inc. (*US*)
Jim Donovan Literary (*US*)
Dystel & Goderich Literary Management (*US*)
Felicia Eth Literary Representation (*US*)
Diana Finch Literary Agency (*US*)
Fresh Books Literary Agency (*US*)
Fredrica S. Friedman and Co. Inc. (*US*)
Goodman Associates (*US*)
Grace Freedson's Publishing Network (*US*)
Kathryn Green Literary Agency, LLC (*US*)
Hannigan Salky Getzler (HSG) Agency (*US*)
Antony Harwood Limited (*UK*)
InkWell Management (*US*)
J de S Associates Inc. (*US*)
Jeanne Fredericks Literary Agency, Inc. (*US*)

Jenny Brown Associates (*UK*)
Jill Grinberg Literary Management LLC (*US*)
Kathi J. Paton Literary Agency (*US*)
Frances Kelly (*UK*)
Kneerim & Williams (*US*)
The Knight Agency (*US*)
Linda Konner Literary Agency (*US*)
Larsen Pomada Literary Agents (*US*)
Levine Greenberg Rostan Literary Agency (*US*)
The Jennifer Lyons Literary Agency, LLC (*US*)
MacGregor Literary (*US*)
Manus & Associates Literary Agency, Inc. (*US*)
Maria Carvainis Agency, Inc. (*US*)
The Martell Agency (*US*)
Martha Millard Literary Agency (*US*)
Howard Morhaim Literary Agency (*US*)
Mulcahy Associates (*UK*)
The Peters Fraser & Dunlop Group Ltd (PFD) (*UK*)
Lynne Rabinoff Agency (*US*)
Raines & Raines (*US*)
The Amy Rennert Agency, Inc. (*US*)
Marly Rusoff & Associates, Inc. (*US*)
The Sagalyn Literary Agency (*US*)
Salkind Literary Agency (*US*)
Susan Schulman, A Literary Agency (*US*)
Lynn Seligman, Literary Agent (*US*)
Solow Literary Enterprises, Inc. (*US*)
The Spieler Agency (*US*)
Stonesong (*US*)
The Strothman Agency (*US*)
Susan Rabiner, Literary Agent, Inc. (*US*)
The Swetky Agency and Associates (*US*)
TriadaUS Literary Agency, Inc. (*US*)
Writers House UK (*UK*)
Writers' Representatives, LLC (*US*)
Writers House, LLC (*US*)
The Zack Company, Inc (*US*)

Gardening

Betsy Amster Literary Enterprises (*US*)
Caroline Davidson Literary Agency (*UK*)
Grace Freedson's Publishing Network (*US*)
Graham Maw Christie Literary Agency (*UK*)
Greene & Heaton Ltd (*UK*)
Hannigan Salky Getzler (HSG) Agency (*US*)
Antony Harwood Limited (*UK*)
Jane Turnbull (*UK*)
Jeanne Fredericks Literary Agency, Inc. (*US*)
Jill Grosjean Literary Agency (*US*)
Levine Greenberg Rostan Literary Agency (*US*)
Linda Roghaar Literary Agency, Inc. (*US*)
Richford Becklow Literary Agency (*UK*)
Rosica Colin Ltd (*UK*)
Sheil Land Associates Ltd (*UK*)
The Spieler Agency (*US*)
The Swetky Agency and Associates (*US*)
Talcott Notch Literary (*US*)
Teresa Chris Literary Agency Ltd (*UK*)
TriadaUS Literary Agency, Inc. (*US*)
The Zack Company, Inc (*US*)

Gothic

Aaron M. Priest Literary Agency (*US*)
Diamond Kahn and Woods (DKW) Literary Agency Ltd (*UK*)
Elaine P. English, Attorney & Literary Agent (*US*)
Antony Harwood Limited (*UK*)
The Jean V. Naggar Literary Agency (*US*)
Richford Becklow Literary Agency (*UK*)
The Swetky Agency and Associates (*US*)

Health

The Ahearn Agency, Inc (*US*)
Ambassador Speakers Bureau & Literary Agency (*US*)
Andrew Lownie Literary Agency Ltd (*UK*)
Arcadia (*US*)
Audrey A. Wolf Literary Agency (*US*)
B.J. Robbins Literary Agency (*US*)
Betsy Amster Literary Enterprises (*US*)
Vicky Bijur Literary Agency (*US*)
David Black Literary Agency (*US*)
Bleecker Street Associates, Inc. (*US*)
The Blumer Literary Agency, Inc. (*US*)
Luigi Bonomi Associates Ltd (*UK*)
Brandt & Hochman Literary Agents, Inc. (*US*)
Bresnick Weil Literary Agency, LLC (*US*)
Rick Broadhead & Associates Literary Agency (*Can*)
Browne & Miller Literary Associates (*US*)
Carnicelli Literary Management (*US*)
Carol Mann Agency (*US*)
Caroline Davidson Literary Agency (*UK*)
Chartwell (*UK*)
Creative Authors Ltd (*UK*)
Richard Curtis Associates, Inc. (*US*)
The Jennifer DeChiara Literary Agency (*US*)
Joëlle Delbourgo Associates, Inc. (*US*)
Diane Banks Associates Literary Agency (*UK*)
Don Congdon Associates, Inc. (*US*)
Jim Donovan Literary (*US*)
Dunow, Carlson & Lerner Agency (*US*)
Dystel & Goderich Literary Management (*US*)
Ebeling & Associates (*US*)
Judith Ehrlich Literary Management (*US*)
Felicia Eth Literary Representation (*US*)
Ethan Ellenberg Literary Agency (*US*)
Diana Finch Literary Agency (*US*)
FinePrint Literary Management (*US*)
Fletcher & Company (*US*)
Folio Literary Management, LLC (*US*)
Foundry Literary + Media (*US*)
Fox & Howard Literary Agency (*UK*)
Fresh Books Literary Agency (*US*)
Sarah Jane Freymann Literary Agency (*US*)
Fredrica S. Friedman and Co. Inc. (*US*)
Gina Maccoby Agency (*US*)
Glass Literary Management LLC (*US*)
Goodman Associates (*US*)
Grace Freedson's Publishing Network (*US*)
Graham Maw Christie Literary Agency (*UK*)
Kathryn Green Literary Agency, LLC (*US*)
Greene & Heaton Ltd (*UK*)
Laura Gross Literary Agency (*US*)
Marianne Gunn O'Connor Literary Agency (*Ire*)
Hannigan Salky Getzler (HSG) Agency (*US*)

Antony Harwood Limited (*UK*)
The Jeff Herman Agency, LLC (*US*)
Hill Nadell Literary Agency (*US*)
InkWell Management (*US*)
J de S Associates Inc. (*US*)
The Jean V. Naggar Literary Agency (*US*)
Jeanne Fredericks Literary Agency, Inc. (*US*)
Jill Grinberg Literary Management LLC (*US*)
Johnson & Alcock (*UK*)
Kathi J. Paton Literary Agency (*US*)
Frances Kelly (*UK*)
Harvey Klinger, Inc (*US*)
Kneerim & Williams (*US*)
The Knight Agency (*US*)
Linda Konner Literary Agency (*US*)
Barbara S. Kouts, Literary Agent (*US*)
Bert P. Krages (*US*)
Edite Kroll Literary Agency, Inc. (*US*)
Kuhn Projects (*US*)
The LA Literary Agency (*US*)
Larsen Pomada Literary Agents (*US*)
Levine Greenberg Rostan Literary Agency (*US*)
Limelight Management (*UK*)
Linda Roghaar Literary Agency, Inc. (*US*)
Lippincott Massie McQuilkin (*US*)
Literary & Creative Artists Inc. (*US*)
Julia Lord Literary Management (*US*)
Lowenstein Associates, Inc. (*US*)
Maggie Pearlstine Associates Ltd (*UK*)
Kirsten Manges Literary Agency, LLC (*US*)
Manus & Associates Literary Agency, Inc. (*US*)
Marjacq Scripts Ltd (*UK*)
The Martell Agency (*US*)
Martin Literary Management (*US*)
MBA Literary Agents Ltd (*UK*)
Margret McBride Literary Agency (*US*)
Martha Millard Literary Agency (*US*)
Howard Morhaim Literary Agency (*US*)
Northern Lights Literary Services (*US*)
P.S. Literary Agency (*Can*)
Puttick Literary Agency (*UK*)
The Amy Rennert Agency, Inc. (*US*)
Rita Rosenkranz Literary Agency (*US*)
Rosica Colin Ltd (*UK*)
The Rudy Agency (*US*)
Marly Rusoff & Associates, Inc. (*US*)
Salkind Literary Agency (*US*)
Sandra Dijkstra Literary Agency (*US*)
Sanford J. Greenburger Associates, Inc. (*US*)
Susan Schulman, A Literary Agency (*US*)
Scovil Galen Ghosh Literary Agency, Inc. (*US*)
Lynn Seligman, Literary Agent (*US*)
Denise Shannon Literary Agency, Inc. (*US*)
Signature Literary Agency (*US*)
Robert Smith Literary Agency Ltd (*UK*)
Solow Literary Enterprises, Inc. (*US*)
The Spieler Agency (*US*)
Sterling Lord Literistic, Inc. (*US*)
Stonesong (*US*)
The Stuart Agency (*US*)
The Swetky Agency and Associates (*US*)
Tessler Literary Agency (*US*)
Thompson Literary Agency (*US*)
Tracy Brown Literary Agency (*US*)
TriadaUS Literary Agency, Inc. (*US*)
Trident Media Group, LLC (*US*)
2M Literary Agency Ltd (*US*)
Veritas Literary Agency (*US*)
Waxman Leavell Literary Agency (*US*)
Wendy Sherman Associates, Inc. (*US*)
Whispering Buffalo Literary Agency Ltd (*UK*)
Wolfson Literary Agency (*US*)
The Zack Company, Inc (*US*)
Helen Zimmermann Literary Agency (*US*)

Historical
Aaron M. Priest Literary Agency (*US*)
Adler & Robin Books, Inc (*US*)
The Ahearn Agency, Inc (*US*)
Alive Communications, Inc (*US*)
Ambassador Speakers Bureau & Literary Agency (*US*)
The Ampersand Agency Ltd (*UK*)
Andrew Lownie Literary Agency Ltd (*UK*)
Ann Rittenberg Literary Agency (*US*)
Aponte Literary (*US*)
Arcadia (*US*)
Artellus Limited (*UK*)
Audrey A. Wolf Literary Agency (*US*)
The August Agency LLC (*US*)
Author Rights Agency (*Ire*)
Ayesha Pande Literary (*US*)
B.J. Robbins Literary Agency (*US*)
Baldi Agency (*US*)
Betsy Amster Literary Enterprises (*US*)
Vicky Bijur Literary Agency (*US*)
David Black Literary Agency (*US*)
Blake Friedmann Literary Agency Ltd (*UK*)
Bleecker Street Associates, Inc. (*US*)
The Blumer Literary Agency, Inc. (*US*)
Luigi Bonomi Associates Ltd (*UK*)
The Book Group (*US*)
BookEnds, LLC (*US*)
Brandt & Hochman Literary Agents, Inc. (*US*)
Barbara Braun Associates, Inc. (*US*)
Bresnick Weil Literary Agency, LLC (*US*)
Rick Broadhead & Associates Literary Agency (*Can*)
Marie Brown Associates, Inc. (*US*)
Browne & Miller Literary Associates (*US*)
Carnicelli Literary Management (*US*)
Carol Mann Agency (*US*)
Caroline Davidson Literary Agency (*UK*)
Caroline Sheldon Literary Agency (*UK*)
Chalberg & Sussman (*US*)
The Characters Talent Agency (*Can*)
Chartwell (*UK*)
Mic Cheetham Literary Agency (*UK*)
Elyse Cheney Literary Associates, LLC (*US*)
The Choate Agency, LLC (*US*)
The Chudney Agency (*US*)
Clare Hulton Literary Agency (*UK*)
Conville & Walsh Ltd (*UK*)
The Cooke Agency (*Can*)
Coombs Moylett & Maclean Literary Agency (*UK*)
The Cowles-Ryan Literary Agency (*US*)

Creative Authors Ltd (*UK*)
Curtis Brown Group Ltd (*UK*)
Richard Curtis Associates, Inc. (*US*)
Laura Dail Literary Agency (*US*)
David Luxton Associates (*UK*)
Liza Dawson Associates (*US*)
The Jennifer DeChiara Literary Agency (*US*)
DeFiore and Company (*US*)
Joëlle Delbourgo Associates, Inc. (*US*)
DHH Literary Agency Ltd (*UK*)
Diamond Kahn and Woods (DKW) Literary Agency Ltd (*UK*)
Diane Banks Associates Literary Agency (*UK*)
Don Congdon Associates, Inc. (*US*)
Donadio & Olson, Inc. (*US*)
Jim Donovan Literary (*US*)
The Dravis Agency, Inc. (*US*)
Dunham Literary, Inc. (*US*)
Dunow, Carlson & Lerner Agency (*US*)
Dystel & Goderich Literary Management (*US*)
Anne Edelstein Literary Agency (*US*)
Edwards Fuglewicz (*UK*)
Judith Ehrlich Literary Management (*US*)
Einstein Literary Management (*US*)
Emily Sweet Associates (*UK*)
Elaine P. English, Attorney & Literary Agent (*US*)
Felicia Eth Literary Representation (*US*)
Ethan Ellenberg Literary Agency (*US*)
Mary Evans, Inc. (*US*)
The Feldstein Agency (*UK*)
Felicity Bryan Associates (*UK*)
Diana Finch Literary Agency (*US*)
FinePrint Literary Management (*US*)
Fletcher & Company (*US*)
Folio Literary Management, LLC (*US*)
Foundry Literary + Media (*US*)
Fox & Howard Literary Agency (*UK*)
Frances Collin Literary Agent (*US*)
Sarah Jane Freymann Literary Agency (*US*)
Fredrica S. Friedman and Co. Inc. (*US*)
Furniss Lawton (*UK*)
Gelfman Schneider / ICM Partners (*US*)
Georges Borchardt, Inc. (*US*)
Georgina Capel Associates Ltd (*UK*)
The Gernert Company (*US*)
Gina Maccoby Agency (*US*)
Glass Literary Management LLC (*US*)
Frances Goldin Literary Agency, Inc. (*US*)
Goodman Associates (*US*)
Irene Goodman Literary Agency (*US*)
Grace Freedson's Publishing Network (*US*)
Graham Maw Christie Literary Agency (*UK*)
Kathryn Green Literary Agency, LLC (*US*)
Greene & Heaton Ltd (*UK*)
Gregory & Company, Authors' Agents (*UK*)
Laura Gross Literary Agency (*US*)
Hannigan Salky Getzler (HSG) Agency (*US*)
Hardman & Swainson (*UK*)
Joy Harris Literary Agency, Inc. (*US*)
Antony Harwood Limited (*UK*)
A M Heath & Company Limited, Author's Agents (*UK*)
Rupert Heath Literary Agency (*UK*)
The Helen Heller Agency (*Can*)
The Jeff Herman Agency, LLC (*US*)
David Higham Associates Ltd (*UK*)
Hill Nadell Literary Agency (*US*)
Hopkins Literary Associates (*US*)
Kate Hordern Literary Agency (*UK*)
Andrea Hurst Literary Management (*US*)
InkWell Management (*US*)
International Transactions, Inc. (*US*)
J de S Associates Inc. (*US*)
Jabberwocky Literary Agency (*US*)
Jane Rotrosen Agency (*US*)
Jane Turnbull (*UK*)
The Jean V. Naggar Literary Agency (*US*)
Jeanne Fredericks Literary Agency, Inc. (*US*)
Jenny Brown Associates (*UK*)
Jill Grinberg Literary Management LLC (*US*)
Jill Grosjean Literary Agency (*US*)
Johnson & Alcock (*UK*)
Jonathan Pegg Literary Agency (*UK*)
Kathi J. Paton Literary Agency (*US*)
Keane Kataria Literary Agency (*UK*)
Frances Kelly (*UK*)
Ki Agency Ltd (*UK*)
Virginia Kidd Agency, Inc (*US*)
Kneerim & Williams (*US*)
The Knight Agency (*US*)
Barbara S. Kouts, Literary Agent (*US*)
Bert P. Krages (*US*)
Kuhn Projects (*US*)
L. Perkins Associates (*US*)
The LA Literary Agency (*US*)
Laura Langlie, Literary Agent (*US*)
Larsen Pomada Literary Agents (*US*)
Sarah Lazin Books (*US*)
Robert Lecker Agency (*Can*)
Levine Greenberg Rostan Literary Agency (*US*)
Limelight Management (*UK*)
Linda Roghaar Literary Agency, Inc. (*US*)
Lippincott Massie McQuilkin (*US*)
The Lisa Richards Agency (*Ire*)
Literary & Creative Artists Inc. (*US*)
The Literary Group International (*US*)
Julia Lord Literary Management (*US*)
The Jennifer Lyons Literary Agency, LLC (*US*)
Donald Maass Literary Agency (*US*)
MacGregor Literary (*US*)
Madeleine Milburn Literary, TV & Film Agency (*UK*)
Maggie Pearlstine Associates Ltd (*UK*)
Kirsten Manges Literary Agency, LLC (*US*)
Andrew Mann Ltd (*UK*)
Maria Carvainis Agency, Inc. (*US*)
Marjacq Scripts Ltd (*UK*)
The Martell Agency (*US*)
MBA Literary Agents Ltd (*UK*)
Duncan McAra (*UK*)
Margret McBride Literary Agency (*US*)
McIntosh & Otis, Inc (*US*)
Martha Millard Literary Agency (*US*)
Howard Morhaim Literary Agency (*US*)
Mulcahy Associates (*UK*)

Nappaland Literary Agency (*US*)
Nelson Literary Agency, LLC (*US*)
New Leaf Literary & Media, Inc. (*US*)
MNLA (Maggie Noach Literary Agency) (*UK*)
Northern Lights Literary Services (*US*)
P.S. Literary Agency (*Can*)
The Park Literary Group LLC (*US*)
Pavilion Literary Management (*US*)
The Peters Fraser & Dunlop Group Ltd (PFD) (*UK*)
Puttick Literary Agency (*UK*)
Queen Literary Agency, Inc. (*US*)
Lynne Rabinoff Agency (*US*)
Raines & Raines (*US*)
Rees Literary Agency (*US*)
Renee Zuckerbrot Literary Agency (*US*)
The Amy Rennert Agency, Inc. (*US*)
Richford Becklow Literary Agency (*UK*)
Rita Rosenkranz Literary Agency (*US*)
RLR Associates (*US*)
Robert Dudley Agency (*UK*)
Robin Straus Agency, Inc. (*US*)
Rocking Chair Books (*UK*)
Rosica Colin Ltd (*UK*)
Andy Ross Agency (*US*)
Ross Yoon Agency (*US*)
The Rudy Agency (*US*)
Marly Rusoff & Associates, Inc. (*US*)
The Sagalyn Literary Agency (*US*)
Salkind Literary Agency (*US*)
Sandra Dijkstra Literary Agency (*US*)
Sanford J. Greenburger Associates, Inc. (*US*)
Sarah Such Literary Agency (*UK*)
The Sayle Literary Agency (*UK*)
Susan Schulman, A Literary Agency (*US*)
The Science Factory (*UK*)
Scovil Galen Ghosh Literary Agency, Inc. (*US*)
Lynn Seligman, Literary Agent (*US*)
Denise Shannon Literary Agency, Inc. (*US*)
Sheil Land Associates Ltd (*UK*)
Sheila Ableman Literary Agency (*UK*)
Signature Literary Agency (*US*)
Dorie Simmonds Agency (*UK*)
Jeffrey Simmons (*UK*)
Sinclair-Stevenson (*UK*)
Robert Smith Literary Agency Ltd (*UK*)
Solow Literary Enterprises, Inc. (*US*)
Spectrum Literary Agency (*US*)
Spencerhill Associates (*US*)
The Spieler Agency (*US*)
Philip G. Spitzer Literary Agency, Inc. (*US*)
Steph Roundsmith Agent and Editor (*UK*)
Sterling Lord Literistic, Inc. (*US*)
The Strothman Agency (*US*)
Stuart Krichevsky Literary Agency, Inc. (*US*)
The Stuart Agency (*US*)
Susan Rabiner, Literary Agent, Inc. (*US*)
The Swetky Agency and Associates (*US*)
Talcott Notch Literary (*US*)
Teresa Chris Literary Agency Ltd (*UK*)
Tessler Literary Agency (*US*)
Thompson Literary Agency (*US*)
Toby Mundy Associates Ltd (*UK*)
Tracy Brown Literary Agency (*US*)
TriadaUS Literary Agency, Inc. (*US*)
Trident Media Group, LLC (*US*)
United Talent Agency (*US*)
Veritas Literary Agency (*US*)
Ed Victor Ltd (*UK*)
Victoria Sanders & Associates LLC (*US*)
Watkins / Loomis Agency, Inc. (*US*)
Watson, Little Ltd (*UK*)
Waxman Leavell Literary Agency (*US*)
Wendy Sherman Associates, Inc. (*US*)
Westwood Creative Artists (*Can*)
William Morris Endeavor (WME) London (*UK*)
Wm Clark Associates (*US*)
Writers House UK (*UK*)
Writers' Representatives, LLC (*US*)
Writers House, LLC (*US*)
The Zack Company, Inc (*US*)
Karen Gantz Zahler Literary Agency (*US*)
Zeno Agency Ltd (*UK*)
Helen Zimmermann Literary Agency (*US*)
Zoë Pagnamenta Agency, LLC (*US*)

Hobbies

The Blumer Literary Agency, Inc. (*US*)
Browne & Miller Literary Associates (*US*)
Grace Freedson's Publishing Network (*US*)
Antony Harwood Limited (*UK*)
Levine Greenberg Rostan Literary Agency (*US*)
Linda Roghaar Literary Agency, Inc. (*US*)
Julia Lord Literary Management (*US*)
Susan Schulman, A Literary Agency (*US*)
Sheree Bykofsky Associates, Inc. (*US*)

Horror

The Ampersand Agency Ltd (*UK*)
Andrew Lownie Literary Agency Ltd (*UK*)
Anubis Literary Agency (*UK*)
Bleecker Street Associates, Inc. (*US*)
The Characters Talent Agency (*Can*)
Elyse Cheney Literary Associates, LLC (*US*)
Cine/Lit Representation (*US*)
Film Rights Ltd in association with Laurence Fitch Ltd (*UK*)
FinePrint Literary Management (*US*)
Folio Literary Management, LLC (*US*)
Samuel French, Inc. (*US*)
Hardman & Swainson (*UK*)
Antony Harwood Limited (*UK*)
The Jean V. Naggar Literary Agency (*US*)
L. Perkins Associates (*US*)
Donald Maass Literary Agency (*US*)
Madeleine Milburn Literary, TV & Film Agency (*UK*)
Maria Carvainis Agency, Inc. (*US*)
McIntosh & Otis, Inc (*US*)
Martha Millard Literary Agency (*US*)
Howard Morhaim Literary Agency (*US*)
The Peters Fraser & Dunlop Group Ltd (PFD) (*UK*)
Richford Becklow Literary Agency (*UK*)
Rocking Chair Books (*UK*)
Rosica Colin Ltd (*UK*)
Lynn Seligman, Literary Agent (*US*)
Sternig & Byrne Literary Agency (*US*)

The Stuart Agency (*US*)
Talcott Notch Literary (*US*)
The Zack Company, Inc (*US*)
Zeno Agency Ltd (*UK*)

How-to

Aaron M. Priest Literary Agency (*US*)
Adler & Robin Books, Inc (*US*)
AHA Talent Ltd (*UK*)
Alive Communications, Inc (*US*)
Miriam Altshuler Literary Agency (*US*)
Ambassador Speakers Bureau & Literary Agency (*US*)
Andrew Lownie Literary Agency Ltd (*UK*)
Baldi Agency (*US*)
Bleecker Street Associates, Inc. (*US*)
The Blumer Literary Agency, Inc. (*US*)
Browne & Miller Literary Associates (*US*)
The Jennifer DeChiara Literary Agency (*US*)
Jim Donovan Literary (*US*)
Judith Ehrlich Literary Management (*US*)
Diana Finch Literary Agency (*US*)
FinePrint Literary Management (*US*)
Folio Literary Management, LLC (*US*)
Foundry Literary + Media (*US*)
Fresh Books Literary Agency (*US*)
Fredrica S. Friedman and Co. Inc. (*US*)
Grace Freedson's Publishing Network (*US*)
Kathryn Green Literary Agency, LLC (*US*)
Antony Harwood Limited (*UK*)
The Jeff Herman Agency, LLC (*US*)
Andrea Hurst Literary Management (*US*)
J de S Associates Inc. (*US*)
Jeanne Fredericks Literary Agency, Inc. (*US*)
The Joan Brandt Agency (*US*)
Harvey Klinger, Inc (*US*)
The Knight Agency (*US*)
Linda Konner Literary Agency (*US*)
L. Perkins Associates (*US*)
Larsen Pomada Literary Agents (*US*)
Robert Lecker Agency (*Can*)
Linda Roghaar Literary Agency, Inc. (*US*)
Literary & Creative Artists Inc. (*US*)
The Literary Group International (*US*)
MacGregor Literary (*US*)
Manus & Associates Literary Agency, Inc. (*US*)
Martin Literary Management (*US*)
Martha Millard Literary Agency (*US*)
Northern Lights Literary Services (*US*)
Rita Rosenkranz Literary Agency (*US*)
Salkind Literary Agency (*US*)
Susan Schulman, A Literary Agency (*US*)
Lynn Seligman, Literary Agent (*US*)
The Swetky Agency and Associates (*US*)
TriadaUS Literary Agency, Inc. (*US*)
Wolfson Literary Agency (*US*)
Writers House UK (*UK*)
Writers House, LLC (*US*)
The Zack Company, Inc (*US*)
Helen Zimmermann Literary Agency (*US*)

Humour

Abrams Artists Agency (*US*)
Adler & Robin Books, Inc (*US*)
AHA Talent Ltd (*UK*)
The Ahearn Agency, Inc (*US*)
Alive Communications, Inc (*US*)
Ayesha Pande Literary (*US*)
David Black Literary Agency (*US*)
Bleecker Street Associates, Inc. (*US*)
The Blumer Literary Agency, Inc. (*US*)
Bresnick Weil Literary Agency, LLC (*US*)
Rick Broadhead & Associates Literary Agency (*Can*)
Browne & Miller Literary Associates (*US*)
Kelvin C. Bulger and Associates (*US*)
Carol Mann Agency (*US*)
Caroline Sheldon Literary Agency (*UK*)
Cecily Ware Literary Agents (*UK*)
The Characters Talent Agency (*Can*)
The Chudney Agency (*US*)
Clare Hulton Literary Agency (*UK*)
Conville & Walsh Ltd (*UK*)
Creative Authors Ltd (*UK*)
Laura Dail Literary Agency (*US*)
Liza Dawson Associates (*US*)
The Jennifer DeChiara Literary Agency (*US*)
Diamond Kahn and Woods (DKW) Literary Agency Ltd (*UK*)
Don Congdon Associates, Inc. (*US*)
The Dravis Agency, Inc. (*US*)
Dunow, Carlson & Lerner Agency (*US*)
Dystel & Goderich Literary Management (*US*)
Edwards Fuglewicz (*UK*)
Judith Ehrlich Literary Management (*US*)
Elaine P. English, Attorney & Literary Agent (*US*)
Fairbank Literary Representation (*US*)
The Feldstein Agency (*UK*)
Diana Finch Literary Agency (*US*)
FinePrint Literary Management (*US*)
Fletcher & Company (*US*)
Folio Literary Management, LLC (*US*)
Jill Foster Ltd (JFL) (*UK*)
Foundry Literary + Media (*US*)
Samuel French, Inc. (*US*)
Fresh Books Literary Agency (*US*)
Sarah Jane Freymann Literary Agency (*US*)
Fredrica S. Friedman and Co. Inc. (*US*)
Furniss Lawton (*UK*)
Grace Freedson's Publishing Network (*US*)
Graham Maw Christie Literary Agency (*UK*)
Kathryn Green Literary Agency, LLC (*US*)
Greene & Heaton Ltd (*UK*)
Hannigan Salky Getzler (HSG) Agency (*US*)
Joy Harris Literary Agency, Inc. (*US*)
Antony Harwood Limited (*UK*)
Rupert Heath Literary Agency (*UK*)
David Higham Associates Ltd (*UK*)
Hudson Agency (*US*)
Andrea Hurst Literary Management (*US*)
Jane Turnbull (*UK*)
The Jean V. Naggar Literary Agency (*US*)
Jenny Brown Associates (*UK*)
Jill Grinberg Literary Management LLC (*US*)
Jill Grosjean Literary Agency (*US*)
Jo Unwin Literary Agency (*UK*)
Kathi J. Paton Literary Agency (*US*)

Harvey Klinger, Inc (*US*)
Edite Kroll Literary Agency, Inc. (*US*)
Kuhn Projects (*US*)
L. Perkins Associates (*US*)
Laura Langlie, Literary Agent (*US*)
Larsen Pomada Literary Agents (*US*)
LaunchBooks Literary Agency (*US*)
Levine Greenberg Rostan Literary Agency (*US*)
Lippincott Massie McQuilkin (*US*)
The Lisa Richards Agency (*Ire*)
The Literary Group International (*US*)
Julia Lord Literary Management (*US*)
Donald Maass Literary Agency (*US*)
MacGregor Literary (*US*)
Madeleine Milburn Literary, TV & Film Agency (*UK*)
Maria Carvainis Agency, Inc. (*US*)
Margret McBride Literary Agency (*US*)
McIntosh & Otis, Inc (*US*)
Howard Morhaim Literary Agency (*US*)
Nappaland Literary Agency (*US*)
Niad Management (*US*)
P.S. Literary Agency (*Can*)
PBJ and JBJ Management (*UK*)
Rita Rosenkranz Literary Agency (*US*)
RLR Associates (*US*)
Roger Hancock Ltd (*UK*)
Rosica Colin Ltd (*UK*)
Salkind Literary Agency (*US*)
Sandra Dijkstra Literary Agency (*US*)
Sanford J. Greenburger Associates, Inc. (*US*)
Sarah Such Literary Agency (*UK*)
Susan Schulman, A Literary Agency (*US*)
Lynn Seligman, Literary Agent (*US*)
Sheil Land Associates Ltd (*UK*)
Sheree Bykofsky Associates, Inc. (*US*)
Robert Smith Literary Agency Ltd (*UK*)
The Spieler Agency (*US*)
Steph Roundsmith Agent and Editor (*UK*)
The Stuart Agency (*US*)
Susan Rabiner, Literary Agent, Inc. (*US*)
The Swetky Agency and Associates (*US*)
TriadaUS Literary Agency, Inc. (*US*)
Trident Media Group, LLC (*US*)
Victoria Sanders & Associates LLC (*US*)
Watson, Little Ltd (*UK*)
Waxman Leavell Literary Agency (*US*)
Whispering Buffalo Literary Agency Ltd (*UK*)
Wolfson Literary Agency (*US*)
Writers' Representatives, LLC (*US*)
The Zack Company, Inc (*US*)
Helen Zimmermann Literary Agency (*US*)

Legal

Ambassador Speakers Bureau & Literary Agency (*US*)
David Black Literary Agency (*US*)
Carol Mann Agency (*US*)
Don Congdon Associates, Inc. (*US*)
Jim Donovan Literary (*US*)
Judith Ehrlich Literary Management (*US*)
Felicia Eth Literary Representation (*US*)
Diana Finch Literary Agency (*US*)
Goodman Associates (*US*)
Grace Freedson's Publishing Network (*US*)
Laura Gross Literary Agency (*US*)
Antony Harwood Limited (*UK*)
Hill Nadell Literary Agency (*US*)
J de S Associates Inc. (*US*)
Jeanne Fredericks Literary Agency, Inc. (*US*)
Jill Grinberg Literary Management LLC (*US*)
Kneerim & Williams (*US*)
Edite Kroll Literary Agency, Inc. (*US*)
Laura Langlie, Literary Agent (*US*)
Larsen Pomada Literary Agents (*US*)
Literary & Creative Artists Inc. (*US*)
Margret McBride Literary Agency (*US*)
Lynne Rabinoff Agency (*US*)
Susan Schulman, A Literary Agency (*US*)
Jeffrey Simmons (*UK*)
The Spieler Agency (*US*)
The Swetky Agency and Associates (*US*)
Victoria Sanders & Associates LLC (*US*)
Writers' Representatives, LLC (*US*)
Yates & Yates (*US*)

Leisure

Conville & Walsh Ltd (*UK*)
The Feldstein Agency (*UK*)
Goodman Associates (*US*)
Grace Freedson's Publishing Network (*US*)
Antony Harwood Limited (*UK*)
Jeanne Fredericks Literary Agency, Inc. (*US*)
Levine Greenberg Rostan Literary Agency (*US*)
Rosica Colin Ltd (*UK*)
The Swetky Agency and Associates (*US*)
Watson, Little Ltd (*UK*)

Lifestyle

Adler & Robin Books, Inc (*US*)
The Ahearn Agency, Inc (*US*)
Alive Communications, Inc (*US*)
Ambassador Speakers Bureau & Literary Agency (*US*)
Andrew Lownie Literary Agency Ltd (*UK*)
Arcadia (*US*)
Audrey A. Wolf Literary Agency (*US*)
Baldi Agency (*US*)
Betsy Amster Literary Enterprises (*US*)
David Black Literary Agency (*US*)
Bleecker Street Associates, Inc. (*US*)
Luigi Bonomi Associates Ltd (*UK*)
The Book Group (*US*)
BookEnds, LLC (*US*)
Brandt & Hochman Literary Agents, Inc. (*US*)
Bresnick Weil Literary Agency, LLC (*US*)
Rick Broadhead & Associates Literary Agency (*Can*)
Browne & Miller Literary Associates (*US*)
Carol Mann Agency (*US*)
Caroline Davidson Literary Agency (*UK*)
Chartwell (*UK*)
Clare Hulton Literary Agency (*UK*)
Conville & Walsh Ltd (*UK*)
The Culinary Entertainment Agency (CEA) (*US*)
Liza Dawson Associates (*US*)
The Jennifer DeChiara Literary Agency (*US*)
DeFiore and Company (*US*)
Joëlle Delbourgo Associates, Inc. (*US*)

Diane Banks Associates Literary Agency (*UK*)
Don Congdon Associates, Inc. (*US*)
Jim Donovan Literary (*US*)
Dunham Literary, Inc. (*US*)
Dystel & Goderich Literary Management (*US*)
Judith Ehrlich Literary Management (*US*)
Felicia Eth Literary Representation (*US*)
Fairbank Literary Representation (*US*)
The Feldstein Agency (*UK*)
Diana Finch Literary Agency (*US*)
FinePrint Literary Management (*US*)
Fletcher & Company (*US*)
Folio Literary Management, LLC (*US*)
Foundry Literary + Media (*US*)
Fox & Howard Literary Agency (*UK*)
Fresh Books Literary Agency (*US*)
Sarah Jane Freymann Literary Agency (*US*)
Fredrica S. Friedman and Co. Inc. (*US*)
Gina Maccoby Agency (*US*)
Irene Goodman Literary Agency (*US*)
Grace Freedson's Publishing Network (*US*)
Graham Maw Christie Literary Agency (*UK*)
Kathryn Green Literary Agency, LLC (*US*)
Laura Gross Literary Agency (*US*)
Hannigan Salky Getzler (HSG) Agency (*US*)
Antony Harwood Limited (*UK*)
The Jeff Herman Agency, LLC (*US*)
Hidden Value Group (*US*)
J de S Associates Inc. (*US*)
Jane Turnbull (*UK*)
The Jean V. Naggar Literary Agency (*US*)
Jeanne Fredericks Literary Agency, Inc. (*US*)
Jill Grinberg Literary Management LLC (*US*)
Johnson & Alcock (*UK*)
Jonathan Pegg Literary Agency (*UK*)
Kathi J. Paton Literary Agency (*US*)
Frances Kelly (*UK*)
Kneerim & Williams (*US*)
The Knight Agency (*US*)
Linda Konner Literary Agency (*US*)
Barbara S. Kouts, Literary Agent (*US*)
The LA Literary Agency (*US*)
Larsen Pomada Literary Agents (*US*)
Levine Greenberg Rostan Literary Agency (*US*)
Limelight Management (*UK*)
Linda Roghaar Literary Agency, Inc. (*US*)
The Lisa Richards Agency (*Ire*)
Literary Management Group, Inc. (*US*)
Literary & Creative Artists Inc. (*US*)
The Literary Group International (*US*)
Julia Lord Literary Management (*US*)
Lowenstein Associates, Inc. (*US*)
MacGregor Literary (*US*)
Manus & Associates Literary Agency, Inc. (*US*)
Martin Literary Management (*US*)
MBA Literary Agents Ltd (*UK*)
The Michael Greer Literary Agency (*UK*)
Martha Millard Literary Agency (*US*)
Mulcahy Associates (*UK*)
Nappaland Literary Agency (*US*)
Northern Lights Literary Services (*US*)
P.S. Literary Agency (*Can*)
The Amy Rennert Agency, Inc. (*US*)
Richford Becklow Literary Agency (*UK*)
Rita Rosenkranz Literary Agency (*US*)
Robin Straus Agency, Inc. (*US*)
Rocking Chair Books (*UK*)
Rosica Colin Ltd (*UK*)
The Rudy Agency (*US*)
Salkind Literary Agency (*US*)
Sandra Dijkstra Literary Agency (*US*)
Sanford J. Greenburger Associates, Inc. (*US*)
Susan Schulman, A Literary Agency (*US*)
Lynn Seligman, Literary Agent (*US*)
Sheil Land Associates Ltd (*UK*)
Sheree Bykofsky Associates, Inc. (*US*)
Robert Smith Literary Agency Ltd (*UK*)
The Spieler Agency (*US*)
Sterling Lord Literistic, Inc. (*US*)
Stonesong (*US*)
The Stuart Agency (*US*)
SYLA – Susan Yearwood Literary Agency (*UK*)
Talcott Notch Literary (*US*)
Teresa Chris Literary Agency Ltd (*UK*)
TriadaUS Literary Agency, Inc. (*US*)
Trident Media Group, LLC (*US*)
2M Literary Agency Ltd (*US*)
Veritas Literary Agency (*US*)
Wendy Sherman Associates, Inc. (*US*)
Whispering Buffalo Literary Agency Ltd (*UK*)
Wolfson Literary Agency (*US*)
Writers House UK (*UK*)
Writers House, LLC (*US*)
Karen Gantz Zahler Literary Agency (*US*)
Helen Zimmermann Literary Agency (*US*)
Literature
Andrew Lownie Literary Agency Ltd (*UK*)
Baldi Agency (*US*)
The Blumer Literary Agency, Inc. (*US*)
The Bright Literary Academy (*UK*)
Elyse Cheney Literary Associates, LLC (*US*)
The Cowles-Ryan Literary Agency (*US*)
The Jennifer DeChiara Literary Agency (*US*)
DeFiore and Company (*US*)
Don Congdon Associates, Inc. (*US*)
Donadio & Olson, Inc. (*US*)
Georges Borchardt, Inc. (*US*)
Goodman Associates (*US*)
Antony Harwood Limited (*UK*)
Michelle Kass Associates (*UK*)
Kneerim & Williams (*US*)
Laura Langlie, Literary Agent (*US*)
Robert Lecker Agency (*Can*)
Lowenstein Associates, Inc. (*US*)
Patricia Moosbrugger Literary Agency (*US*)
P.S. Literary Agency (*Can*)
Renee Zuckerbrot Literary Agency (*US*)
The Amy Rennert Agency, Inc. (*US*)
Richford Becklow Literary Agency (*UK*)
Rocking Chair Books (*UK*)
Susan Schulman, A Literary Agency (*US*)
Scribe Agency LLC (*US*)
Steph Roundsmith Agent and Editor (*UK*)
The Swetky Agency and Associates (*US*)
Victoria Sanders & Associates LLC (*US*)
Writers' Representatives, LLC (*US*)

Media
Andrew Lownie Literary Agency Ltd (*UK*)
The August Agency LLC (*US*)
The Feldstein Agency (*UK*)
Folio Literary Management, LLC (*US*)
Glass Literary Management LLC (*US*)
Joy Harris Literary Agency, Inc. (*US*)
Antony Harwood Limited (*UK*)
The Knight Agency (*US*)
Martin Literary Management (*US*)

Medicine
Ambassador Speakers Bureau & Literary Agency (*US*)
Andrew Lownie Literary Agency Ltd (*UK*)
Betsy Amster Literary Enterprises (*US*)
The Blumer Literary Agency, Inc. (*US*)
Rick Broadhead & Associates Literary Agency (*Can*)
Browne & Miller Literary Associates (*US*)
Carol Mann Agency (*US*)
Caroline Davidson Literary Agency (*UK*)
Richard Curtis Associates, Inc. (*US*)
Liza Dawson Associates (*US*)
DeFiore and Company (*US*)
Don Congdon Associates, Inc. (*US*)
Jim Donovan Literary (*US*)
Judith Ehrlich Literary Management (*US*)
Felicia Eth Literary Representation (*US*)
Mary Evans, Inc. (*US*)
Diana Finch Literary Agency (*US*)
Goodman Associates (*US*)
Grace Freedson's Publishing Network (*US*)
Laura Gross Literary Agency (*US*)
Antony Harwood Limited (*UK*)
InkWell Management (*US*)
International Transactions, Inc. (*US*)
J de S Associates Inc. (*US*)
Jeanne Fredericks Literary Agency, Inc. (*US*)
Jill Grinberg Literary Management LLC (*US*)
Frances Kelly (*UK*)
Harvey Klinger, Inc (*US*)
Kneerim & Williams (*US*)
Edite Kroll Literary Agency, Inc. (*US*)
Larsen Pomada Literary Agents (*US*)
Literary & Creative Artists Inc. (*US*)
The Martell Agency (*US*)
Margret McBride Literary Agency (*US*)
Northern Lights Literary Services (*US*)
Robert Dudley Agency (*UK*)
The Rudy Agency (*US*)
Marly Rusoff & Associates, Inc. (*US*)
Susan Schulman, A Literary Agency (*US*)
The Science Factory (*UK*)
The Swetky Agency and Associates (*US*)
2M Literary Agency Ltd (*US*)
Wolfson Literary Agency (*US*)
The Zack Company, Inc (*US*)

Men's Interests
Andrew Lownie Literary Agency Ltd (*UK*)
Conville & Walsh Ltd (*UK*)
The Creative Rights Agency (*UK*)
Sarah Jane Freymann Literary Agency (*US*)
Antony Harwood Limited (*UK*)
Hidden Value Group (*US*)
Rosica Colin Ltd (*UK*)

Military
Andrew Lownie Literary Agency Ltd (*UK*)
Artellus Limited (*UK*)
David Black Literary Agency (*US*)
Blake Friedmann Literary Agency Ltd (*UK*)
Bleecker Street Associates, Inc. (*US*)
Rick Broadhead & Associates Literary Agency (*Can*)
The Choate Agency, LLC (*US*)
Conville & Walsh Ltd (*UK*)
Liza Dawson Associates (*US*)
DeFiore and Company (*US*)
Don Congdon Associates, Inc. (*US*)
Jim Donovan Literary (*US*)
Dystel & Goderich Literary Management (*US*)
The Feldstein Agency (*UK*)
Diana Finch Literary Agency (*US*)
FinePrint Literary Management (*US*)
Folio Literary Management, LLC (*US*)
Goodman Associates (*US*)
Grace Freedson's Publishing Network (*US*)
Antony Harwood Limited (*UK*)
J de S Associates Inc. (*US*)
The Literary Group International (*US*)
Duncan McAra (*UK*)
Lynne Rabinoff Agency (*US*)
Raines & Raines (*US*)
Rees Literary Agency (*US*)
Robert Dudley Agency (*UK*)
Rosica Colin Ltd (*UK*)
The Rudy Agency (*US*)
Sheil Land Associates Ltd (*UK*)
Robert Smith Literary Agency Ltd (*UK*)
The Swetky Agency and Associates (*US*)
The Zack Company, Inc (*US*)

Music
Abrams Artists Agency (*US*)
Andrew Lownie Literary Agency Ltd (*UK*)
Arcadia (*US*)
Bresnick Weil Literary Agency, LLC (*US*)
Marie Brown Associates, Inc. (*US*)
Carol Mann Agency (*US*)
Clare Hulton Literary Agency (*UK*)
DeFiore and Company (*US*)
Don Congdon Associates, Inc. (*US*)
Jim Donovan Literary (*US*)
Dunham Literary, Inc. (*US*)
Dunow, Carlson & Lerner Agency (*US*)
The Feldstein Agency (*UK*)
Diana Finch Literary Agency (*US*)
FinePrint Literary Management (*US*)
Folio Literary Management, LLC (*US*)
Foundry Literary + Media (*US*)
Fredrica S. Friedman and Co. Inc. (*US*)
Goodman Associates (*US*)
Antony Harwood Limited (*UK*)
The Jean V. Naggar Literary Agency (*US*)
Jenny Brown Associates (*UK*)
Johnson & Alcock (*UK*)
Harvey Klinger, Inc (*US*)
L. Perkins Associates (*US*)

Larsen Pomada Literary Agents (*US*)
Sarah Lazin Books (*US*)
Robert Lecker Agency (*Can*)
Linda Roghaar Literary Agency, Inc. (*US*)
The Literary Group International (*US*)
Julia Lord Literary Management (*US*)
Margret McBride Literary Agency (*US*)
McIntosh & Otis, Inc (*US*)
Martha Millard Literary Agency (*US*)
Rita Rosenkranz Literary Agency (*US*)
Sandra Dijkstra Literary Agency (*US*)
Sanford J. Greenburger Associates, Inc. (*US*)
The Sayle Literary Agency (*UK*)
Susan Schulman, A Literary Agency (*US*)
The Science Factory (*UK*)
Lynn Seligman, Literary Agent (*US*)
The Spieler Agency (*US*)
The Stuart Agency (*US*)
Thompson Literary Agency (*US*)
TriadaUS Literary Agency, Inc. (*US*)
Trident Media Group, LLC (*US*)
2M Literary Agency Ltd (*US*)
Victoria Sanders & Associates LLC (*US*)
Watson, Little Ltd (*UK*)
The Weingel-Fidel Agency (*US*)
Whispering Buffalo Literary Agency Ltd (*UK*)
Wm Clark Associates (*US*)
The Zack Company, Inc (*US*)
Helen Zimmermann Literary Agency (*US*)

Mystery

Aaron M. Priest Literary Agency (*US*)
Abrams Artists Agency (*US*)
The Ahearn Agency, Inc (*US*)
Alive Communications, Inc (*US*)
Andrew Lownie Literary Agency Ltd (*UK*)
Ann Rittenberg Literary Agency (*US*)
The Axelrod Agency (*US*)
Ayesha Pande Literary (*US*)
B.J. Robbins Literary Agency (*US*)
Belcastro Agency (*US*)
Betsy Amster Literary Enterprises (*US*)
David Black Literary Agency (*US*)
Blake Friedmann Literary Agency Ltd (*UK*)
Bleecker Street Associates, Inc. (*US*)
The Blumer Literary Agency, Inc. (*US*)
BookEnds, LLC (*US*)
Brandt & Hochman Literary Agents, Inc. (*US*)
Barbara Braun Associates, Inc. (*US*)
The Bright Literary Academy (*UK*)
Browne & Miller Literary Associates (*US*)
The Characters Talent Agency (*Can*)
Chartwell (*UK*)
The Choate Agency, LLC (*US*)
The Chudney Agency (*US*)
Cine/Lit Representation (*US*)
Conville & Walsh Ltd (*UK*)
Coombs Moylett & Maclean Literary Agency (*UK*)
The Cowles-Ryan Literary Agency (*US*)
Richard Curtis Associates, Inc. (*US*)
Laura Dail Literary Agency (*US*)
Darhansoff & Verrill Literary Agents (*US*)
Liza Dawson Associates (*US*)
The Jennifer DeChiara Literary Agency (*US*)
Joëlle Delbourgo Associates, Inc. (*US*)
Don Congdon Associates, Inc. (*US*)
Jim Donovan Literary (*US*)
The Dravis Agency, Inc. (*US*)
Dunham Literary, Inc. (*US*)
Dunow, Carlson & Lerner Agency (*US*)
Dystel & Goderich Literary Management (*US*)
Edwards Fuglewicz (*UK*)
Judith Ehrlich Literary Management (*US*)
Einstein Literary Management (*US*)
Elaine P. English, Attorney & Literary Agent (*US*)
Ethan Ellenberg Literary Agency (*US*)
Fairbank Literary Representation (*US*)
The Feldstein Agency (*UK*)
FinePrint Literary Management (*US*)
Folio Literary Management, LLC (*US*)
Samuel French, Inc. (*US*)
Gelfman Schneider / ICM Partners (*US*)
Gina Maccoby Agency (*US*)
Goodman Associates (*US*)
Irene Goodman Literary Agency (*US*)
Laura Gross Literary Agency (*US*)
Hannigan Salky Getzler (HSG) Agency (*US*)
Joy Harris Literary Agency, Inc. (*US*)
Antony Harwood Limited (*UK*)
Hudson Agency (*US*)
InkWell Management (*US*)
International Transactions, Inc. (*US*)
J de S Associates Inc. (*US*)
Jane Rotrosen Agency (*US*)
The Jean V. Naggar Literary Agency (*US*)
Jill Grosjean Literary Agency (*US*)
The Joan Brandt Agency (*US*)
Virginia Kidd Agency, Inc (*US*)
Harvey Klinger, Inc (*US*)
The Knight Agency (*US*)
Barbara S. Kouts, Literary Agent (*US*)
L. Perkins Associates (*US*)
Laura Langlie, Literary Agent (*US*)
Larsen Pomada Literary Agents (*US*)
Robert Lecker Agency (*Can*)
Levine Greenberg Rostan Literary Agency (*US*)
Limelight Management (*UK*)
Linn Prentis, Literary Agent (*US*)
The Literary Group International (*US*)
Julia Lord Literary Management (*US*)
Donald Maass Literary Agency (*US*)
MacGregor Literary (*US*)
Madeleine Milburn Literary, TV & Film Agency (*UK*)
Manus & Associates Literary Agency, Inc. (*US*)
Maria Carvainis Agency, Inc. (*US*)
The Martell Agency (*US*)
McIntosh & Otis, Inc (*US*)
Meredith Bernstein Literary Agency, Inc. (*US*)
Martha Millard Literary Agency (*US*)
Niad Management (*US*)
Northern Lights Literary Services (*US*)
P.S. Literary Agency (*Can*)
Pavilion Literary Management (*US*)
Prospect Agency (*US*)

Queen Literary Agency, Inc. (*US*)
Raines & Raines (*US*)
Rebecca Friedman Literary Agency (*US*)
Redhammer (*UK*)
Rees Literary Agency (*US*)
Renee Zuckerbrot Literary Agency (*US*)
The Amy Rennert Agency, Inc. (*US*)
Rocking Chair Books (*UK*)
Rosica Colin Ltd (*UK*)
Salkind Literary Agency (*US*)
Sandra Dijkstra Literary Agency (*US*)
Sanford J. Greenburger Associates, Inc. (*US*)
Susan Schulman, A Literary Agency (*US*)
Secret Agent Man (*US*)
Lynn Seligman, Literary Agent (*US*)
Sheil Land Associates Ltd (*UK*)
Sheree Bykofsky Associates, Inc. (*US*)
Signature Literary Agency (*US*)
Spectrum Literary Agency (*US*)
Spencerhill Associates (*US*)
The Spieler Agency (*US*)
Philip G. Spitzer Literary Agency, Inc. (*US*)
Steph Roundsmith Agent and Editor (*UK*)
Sternig & Byrne Literary Agency (*US*)
The Swetky Agency and Associates (*US*)
Talcott Notch Literary (*US*)
TriadaUS Literary Agency, Inc. (*US*)
Trident Media Group, LLC (*US*)
Veritas Literary Agency (*US*)
Victoria Sanders & Associates LLC (*US*)
Waxman Leavell Literary Agency (*US*)
Westwood Creative Artists (*Can*)
Wolfson Literary Agency (*US*)
Writers' Representatives, LLC (*US*)
The Zack Company, Inc (*US*)
Helen Zimmermann Literary Agency (*US*)

Nature

The Ahearn Agency, Inc (*US*)
Arcadia (*US*)
Bleecker Street Associates, Inc. (*US*)
The Blumer Literary Agency, Inc. (*US*)
Rick Broadhead & Associates Literary Agency (*Can*)
Browne & Miller Literary Associates (*US*)
Carol Mann Agency (*US*)
Caroline Davidson Literary Agency (*UK*)
The Choate Agency, LLC (*US*)
Cine/Lit Representation (*US*)
The Cooke Agency (*Can*)
The Cowles-Ryan Literary Agency (*US*)
Creative Authors Ltd (*UK*)
DeFiore and Company (*US*)
Don Congdon Associates, Inc. (*US*)
Donadio & Olson, Inc. (*US*)
Jim Donovan Literary (*US*)
Dunham Literary, Inc. (*US*)
Felicia Eth Literary Representation (*US*)
Diana Finch Literary Agency (*US*)
FinePrint Literary Management (*US*)
Frances Collin Literary Agent (*US*)
Sarah Jane Freymann Literary Agency (*US*)
Gina Maccoby Agency (*US*)
Frances Goldin Literary Agency, Inc. (*US*)
Goodman Associates (*US*)
Grace Freedson's Publishing Network (*US*)
Antony Harwood Limited (*UK*)
A M Heath & Company Limited, Author's Agents (*UK*)
Rupert Heath Literary Agency (*UK*)
David Higham Associates Ltd (*UK*)
Hill Nadell Literary Agency (*US*)
Jane Turnbull (*UK*)
Jeanne Fredericks Literary Agency, Inc. (*US*)
Jill Grinberg Literary Management LLC (*US*)
Jill Grosjean Literary Agency (*US*)
Johnson & Alcock (*UK*)
Jonathan Pegg Literary Agency (*UK*)
Kneerim & Williams (*US*)
Barbara S. Kouts, Literary Agent (*US*)
Laura Langlie, Literary Agent (*US*)
Larsen Pomada Literary Agents (*US*)
Levine Greenberg Rostan Literary Agency (*US*)
Limelight Management (*UK*)
Linda Roghaar Literary Agency, Inc. (*US*)
Literary & Creative Artists Inc. (*US*)
Manus & Associates Literary Agency, Inc. (*US*)
McIntosh & Otis, Inc (*US*)
P.S. Literary Agency (*Can*)
The Peters Fraser & Dunlop Group Ltd (PFD) (*UK*)
Robin Straus Agency, Inc. (*US*)
Rocking Chair Books (*UK*)
Rosica Colin Ltd (*UK*)
Sandra Dijkstra Literary Agency (*US*)
Sanford J. Greenburger Associates, Inc. (*US*)
Susan Schulman, A Literary Agency (*US*)
Scovil Galen Ghosh Literary Agency, Inc. (*US*)
Lynn Seligman, Literary Agent (*US*)
Solow Literary Enterprises, Inc. (*US*)
The Spieler Agency (*US*)
Sterling Lord Literistic, Inc. (*US*)
The Strothman Agency (*US*)
Stuart Krichevsky Literary Agency, Inc. (*US*)
The Swetky Agency and Associates (*US*)
Talcott Notch Literary (*US*)
Veritas Literary Agency (*US*)
Watkins / Loomis Agency, Inc. (*US*)
Wendy Sherman Associates, Inc. (*US*)
Whispering Buffalo Literary Agency Ltd (*UK*)
The Zack Company, Inc (*US*)
Helen Zimmermann Literary Agency (*US*)

New Age

Bleecker Street Associates, Inc. (*US*)
The Blumer Literary Agency, Inc. (*US*)
Dystel & Goderich Literary Management (*US*)
Ethan Ellenberg Literary Agency (*US*)
Antony Harwood Limited (*UK*)
J de S Associates Inc. (*US*)
Larsen Pomada Literary Agents (*US*)
Levine Greenberg Rostan Literary Agency (*US*)
Martha Millard Literary Agency (*US*)
Northern Lights Literary Services (*US*)

Nonfiction

A for Authors (*UK*)
A & B Personal Management Ltd (*UK*)
Aaron M. Priest Literary Agency (*US*)

Dominick Abel Literary Agency, Inc (*US*)
Abner Stein (*UK*)
Adler & Robin Books, Inc (*US*)
Agency for the Performing Arts (APA) (*US*)
The Agency (London) Ltd (*UK*)
AHA Talent Ltd (*UK*)
The Ahearn Agency, Inc (*US*)
Aitken Alexander Associates (*UK*)
Alive Communications, Inc (*US*)
Miriam Altshuler Literary Agency (*US*)
Ambassador Speakers Bureau & Literary Agency (*US*)
The Ampersand Agency Ltd (*UK*)
Andlyn (*UK*)
Andrew Lownie Literary Agency Ltd (*UK*)
Andrew Nurnberg Associates, Ltd (*UK*)
Ann Rittenberg Literary Agency (*US*)
Anthony Sheil in Association with Aitken Alexander Associates (*UK*)
Aponte Literary (*US*)
Arcadia (*US*)
Artellus Limited (*UK*)
Audrey A. Wolf Literary Agency (*US*)
The August Agency LLC (*US*)
Author Rights Agency (*Ire*)
The Authors Care Service ltd (*UK*)
AVAnti Productions & Management (*UK*)
Ayesha Pande Literary (*US*)
B.J. Robbins Literary Agency (*US*)
Baldi Agency (*US*)
Barbara Hogenson Agency (*US*)
Baror International, Inc. (*US*)
Bath Literary Agency (*UK*)
Bell Lomax Moreton Agency (*UK*)
Betsy Amster Literary Enterprises (*US*)
Bidnick & Company (*US*)
Vicky Bijur Literary Agency (*US*)
David Black Literary Agency (*US*)
The Blair Partnership (*UK*)
Blake Friedmann Literary Agency Ltd (*UK*)
Bleecker Street Associates, Inc. (*US*)
The Blumer Literary Agency, Inc. (*US*)
Luigi Bonomi Associates Ltd (*UK*)
The Book Group (*US*)
The Book Bureau Literary Agency (*Ire*)
BookBlast Ltd. (*UK*)
BookEnds, LLC (*US*)
Brandt & Hochman Literary Agents, Inc. (*US*)
Barbara Braun Associates, Inc. (*US*)
Bresnick Weil Literary Agency, LLC (*US*)
Rick Broadhead & Associates Literary Agency (*Can*)
Marie Brown Associates, Inc. (*US*)
Browne & Miller Literary Associates (*US*)
Carnicelli Literary Management (*US*)
Carol Mann Agency (*US*)
Caroline Davidson Literary Agency (*UK*)
Caroline Sheldon Literary Agency (*UK*)
Chalberg & Sussman (*US*)
Chartwell (*UK*)
Mic Cheetham Literary Agency (*UK*)
Elyse Cheney Literary Associates, LLC (*US*)
The Choate Agency, LLC (*US*)
The Christopher Little Literary Agency (*UK*)
Cine/Lit Representation (*US*)
Clare Hulton Literary Agency (*UK*)
Conville & Walsh Ltd (*UK*)
The Cooke Agency (*Can*)
Coombs Moylett & Maclean Literary Agency (*UK*)
The Cowles-Ryan Literary Agency (*US*)
The Creative Rights Agency (*UK*)
Creative Trust, Inc. (*US*)
Creative Authors Ltd (*UK*)
Rupert Crew Ltd (*UK*)
The Culinary Entertainment Agency (CEA) (*US*)
Curtis Brown Group Ltd (*UK*)
Richard Curtis Associates, Inc. (*US*)
Curtis Brown Ltd (*US*)
Laura Dail Literary Agency (*US*)
Daniel Literary Group (*US*)
Darhansoff & Verrill Literary Agents (*US*)
David Luxton Associates (*UK*)
David Godwin Associates (*UK*)
Liza Dawson Associates (*US*)
Deal Points Ent. (*US*)
The Jennifer DeChiara Literary Agency (*US*)
DeFiore and Company (*US*)
Joëlle Delbourgo Associates, Inc. (*US*)
DHH Literary Agency Ltd (*UK*)
Diamond Kahn and Woods (DKW) Literary Agency Ltd (*UK*)
Diane Banks Associates Literary Agency (*UK*)
Dinah Wiener Ltd (*UK*)
Don Congdon Associates, Inc. (*US*)
Donadio & Olson, Inc. (*US*)
Jim Donovan Literary (*US*)
Dunham Literary, Inc. (*US*)
Dunow, Carlson & Lerner Agency (*US*)
Dystel & Goderich Literary Management (*US*)
Toby Eady Associates Ltd (*UK*)
East West Literary Agency LLC (*US*)
Ebeling & Associates (*US*)
Eddison Pearson Ltd (*UK*)
Anne Edelstein Literary Agency (*US*)
Edwards Fuglewicz (*UK*)
Judith Ehrlich Literary Management (*US*)
Einstein Literary Management (*US*)
Elaine Markson Literary Agency (*US*)
Elaine Steel (*UK*)
Elise Dillsworth Agency (EDA) (*UK*)
Elizabeth Roy Literary Agency (*UK*)
Emily Sweet Associates (*UK*)
Felicia Eth Literary Representation (*US*)
Ethan Ellenberg Literary Agency (*US*)
Faith Evans Associates (*UK*)
Mary Evans, Inc. (*US*)
Eve White: Literary Agent (*UK*)
Fairbank Literary Representation (*US*)
The Feldstein Agency (*UK*)
Felicity Bryan Associates (*UK*)
Diana Finch Literary Agency (*US*)
FinePrint Literary Management (*US*)
The James Fitzgerald Agency (*US*)
Fletcher & Company (*US*)
Folio Literary Management, LLC (*US*)

Foundry Literary + Media (*US*)
Fox & Howard Literary Agency (*UK*)
Frances Collin Literary Agent (*US*)
Fresh Books Literary Agency (*US*)
Sarah Jane Freymann Literary Agency (*US*)
Fredrica S. Friedman and Co. Inc. (*US*)
Furniss Lawton (*UK*)
Gelfman Schneider / ICM Partners (*US*)
Georges Borchardt, Inc. (*US*)
Georgina Capel Associates Ltd (*UK*)
The Gernert Company (*US*)
Gina Maccoby Agency (*US*)
Eric Glass Ltd (*UK*)
Glass Literary Management LLC (*US*)
Global Lion Intellectual Property Management, Inc. (*US*)
Frances Goldin Literary Agency, Inc. (*US*)
Goodman Associates (*US*)
Irene Goodman Literary Agency (*US*)
Grace Freedson's Publishing Network (*US*)
Graham Maw Christie Literary Agency (*UK*)
Christine Green Authors' Agent (*UK*)
Kathryn Green Literary Agency, LLC (*US*)
Louise Greenberg Books Ltd (*UK*)
Greene & Heaton Ltd (*UK*)
Blanche C. Gregory Inc. (*US*)
Laura Gross Literary Agency (*US*)
David Grossman Literary Agency Ltd (*UK*)
Marianne Gunn O'Connor Literary Agency (*Ire*)
Gunn Media Associates (*UK*)
Hannigan Salky Getzler (HSG) Agency (*US*)
Hardman & Swainson (*UK*)
Harold Ober Associates, Inc. (*US*)
Joy Harris Literary Agency, Inc. (*US*)
Antony Harwood Limited (*UK*)
A M Heath & Company Limited, Author's Agents (*UK*)
Rupert Heath Literary Agency (*UK*)
The Helen Brann Agency, Inc. (*US*)
The Helen Heller Agency (*Can*)
The Jeff Herman Agency, LLC (*US*)
Hidden Value Group (*US*)
David Higham Associates Ltd (*UK*)
Hill Nadell Literary Agency (*US*)
Vanessa Holt Ltd (*UK*)
Kate Hordern Literary Agency (*UK*)
Hunter Profiles (*UK*)
Andrea Hurst Literary Management (*US*)
InkWell Management (*US*)
Intercontinental Literary Agency (*UK*)
International Transactions, Inc. (*US*)
Isabel White Literary Agent (*UK*)
Jabberwocky Literary Agency (*US*)
Jane Conway-Gordon Ltd (*UK*)
Jane Rotrosen Agency (*US*)
Jane Turnbull (*UK*)
The Jean V. Naggar Literary Agency (*US*)
Jeanne Fredericks Literary Agency, Inc. (*US*)
Jenny Brown Associates (*UK*)
Jill Grinberg Literary Management LLC (*US*)
Jo Unwin Literary Agency (*UK*)
The Joan Brandt Agency (*US*)
Johnson & Alcock (*UK*)
Jonathan Clowes Ltd (*UK*)
Jonathan Pegg Literary Agency (*UK*)
Juliet Burton Literary Agency (*UK*)
Kathi J. Paton Literary Agency (*US*)
Keane Kataria Literary Agency (*UK*)
Frances Kelly (*UK*)
Ken Sherman & Associates (*US*)
Ki Agency Ltd (*UK*)
Harvey Klinger, Inc (*US*)
Kneerim & Williams (*US*)
Linda Konner Literary Agency (*US*)
Bert P. Krages (*US*)
Edite Kroll Literary Agency, Inc. (*US*)
Kuhn Projects (*US*)
L. Perkins Associates (*US*)
The LA Literary Agency (*US*)
Peter Lampack Agency, Inc (*US*)
Laura Langlie, Literary Agent (*US*)
Larsen Pomada Literary Agents (*US*)
The Steve Laube Agency (*US*)
LaunchBooks Literary Agency (*US*)
Sarah Lazin Books (*US*)
Robert Lecker Agency (*Can*)
Levine Greenberg Rostan Literary Agency (*US*)
Barbara Levy Literary Agency (*UK*)
Limelight Management (*UK*)
Linda Chester & Associates (*US*)
Linda Roghaar Literary Agency, Inc. (*US*)
Lindsay Literary Agency (*UK*)
Linn Prentis, Literary Agent (*US*)
Lippincott Massie McQuilkin (*US*)
The Lisa Ekus Group, LLC (*US*)
The Lisa Richards Agency (*Ire*)
Literary Management Group, Inc. (*US*)
Literary & Creative Artists Inc. (*US*)
The Literary Group International (*US*)
London Independent Books (*UK*)
Julia Lord Literary Management (*US*)
Lorella Belli Literary Agency (LBLA) (*UK*)
Lowenstein Associates, Inc. (*US*)
Lutyens and Rubinstein (*UK*)
The Jennifer Lyons Literary Agency, LLC (*US*)
MacGregor Literary (*US*)
Madeleine Milburn Literary, TV & Film Agency (*UK*)
Maggie Pearlstine Associates Ltd (*UK*)
Kirsten Manges Literary Agency, LLC (*US*)
Manus & Associates Literary Agency, Inc. (*US*)
Maria Carvainis Agency, Inc. (*US*)
Marjacq Scripts Ltd (*UK*)
Marly Russoff & Associates (*US*)
The Martell Agency (*US*)
Martin Literary Management (*US*)
Mary Clemmey Literary Agency (*UK*)
MBA Literary Agents Ltd (*UK*)
Duncan McAra (*UK*)
Margret McBride Literary Agency (*US*)
McIntosh & Otis, Inc (*US*)
Meredith Bernstein Literary Agency, Inc. (*US*)
The Michael Greer Literary Agency (*UK*)
Martha Millard Literary Agency (*US*)
Patricia Moosbrugger Literary Agency (*US*)
Howard Morhaim Literary Agency (*US*)

Mulcahy Associates (*UK*)
Nappaland Literary Agency (*US*)
New Leaf Literary & Media, Inc. (*US*)
Niad Management (*US*)
MNLA (Maggie Noach Literary Agency) (*UK*)
Northern Lights Literary Services (*US*)
Deborah Owen Ltd (*UK*)
P.S. Literary Agency (*Can*)
The Park Literary Group LLC (*US*)
Pavilion Literary Management (*US*)
John Pawsey (*UK*)
The Peters Fraser & Dunlop Group Ltd (PFD) (*UK*)
Shelley Power Literary Agency Ltd (*UK*)
Prospect Agency (*US*)
Puttick Literary Agency (*UK*)
Queen Literary Agency, Inc. (*US*)
Lynne Rabinoff Agency (*US*)
Raines & Raines (*US*)
Rebecca Friedman Literary Agency (*US*)
Redhammer (*UK*)
Renee Zuckerbrot Literary Agency (*US*)
The Amy Rennert Agency, Inc. (*US*)
Richford Becklow Literary Agency (*UK*)
Rita Rosenkranz Literary Agency (*US*)
Riverside Literary Agency (*US*)
RLR Associates (*US*)
Robert Dudley Agency (*UK*)
Robin Jones Literary Agency (*UK*)
Robin Straus Agency, Inc. (*US*)
Rocking Chair Books (*UK*)
Rosica Colin Ltd (*UK*)
Andy Ross Agency (*US*)
Ross Yoon Agency (*US*)
The Rudy Agency (*US*)
Marly Rusoff & Associates, Inc. (*US*)
The Sagalyn Literary Agency (*US*)
Salkind Literary Agency (*US*)
Sandra Dijkstra Literary Agency (*US*)
Sanford J. Greenburger Associates, Inc. (*US*)
Sarah Such Literary Agency (*UK*)
The Sayle Literary Agency (*UK*)
Susan Schulman, A Literary Agency (*US*)
The Science Factory (*UK*)
Scott Treimel NY (*US*)
Scovil Galen Ghosh Literary Agency, Inc. (*US*)
Secret Agent Man (*US*)
Lynn Seligman, Literary Agent (*US*)
Seventh Avenue Literary Agency (*Can*)
Denise Shannon Literary Agency, Inc. (*US*)
Sheil Land Associates Ltd (*UK*)
Sheila Ableman Literary Agency (*UK*)
Sheree Bykofsky Associates, Inc. (*US*)
Signature Literary Agency (*US*)
Dorie Simmonds Agency (*UK*)
Jeffrey Simmons (*UK*)
Sinclair-Stevenson (*UK*)
SLW Literary Agency (*US*)
Robert Smith Literary Agency Ltd (*UK*)
Solow Literary Enterprises, Inc. (*US*)
Sophie Hicks Agency (*UK*)
Spectrum Literary Agency (*US*)
Spencerhill Associates (*US*)
The Spieler Agency (*US*)
Philip G. Spitzer Literary Agency, Inc. (*US*)
Standen Literary Agency (*UK*)
Sterling Lord Literistic, Inc. (*US*)
Sternig & Byrne Literary Agency (*US*)
Stonesong (*US*)
The Strothman Agency (*US*)
Stuart Krichevsky Literary Agency, Inc. (*US*)
The Stuart Agency (*US*)
Susan Rabiner, Literary Agent, Inc. (*US*)
Susanna Lea Associates (UK) (*UK*)
The Susijn Agency (*UK*)
The Swetky Agency and Associates (*US*)
SYLA – Susan Yearwood Literary Agency (*UK*)
Talcott Notch Literary (*US*)
Teresa Chris Literary Agency Ltd (*UK*)
Tessler Literary Agency (*US*)
Thompson Literary Agency (*US*)
Toby Mundy Associates Ltd (*UK*)
Tracy Brown Literary Agency (*US*)
Lavinia Trevor Agency (*UK*)
TriadaUS Literary Agency, Inc. (*US*)
Trident Media Group, LLC (*US*)
2M Literary Agency Ltd (*US*)
Uli Rushby-Smith Literary Agency (*UK*)
United Talent Agency (*US*)
United Agents (*UK*)
Veritas Literary Agency (*US*)
Ed Victor Ltd (*UK*)
Victoria Sanders & Associates LLC (*US*)
Wade & Co Literary Agency (*UK*)
Watkins / Loomis Agency, Inc. (*US*)
Watson, Little Ltd (*UK*)
Waxman Leavell Literary Agency (*US*)
The Weingel-Fidel Agency (*US*)
Wendy Sherman Associates, Inc. (*US*)
Wernick & Pratt Agency (*US*)
Westwood Creative Artists (*Can*)
Whispering Buffalo Literary Agency Ltd (*UK*)
William Morris Endeavor (WME) London (*UK*)
William Morris Endeavor Entertainment (*US*)
Wm Clark Associates (*US*)
Wolfson Literary Agency (*US*)
Writers House UK (*UK*)
The Writers' Practice (*UK*)
Writers' Representatives, LLC (*US*)
Writers House, LLC (*US*)
The Wylie Agency (UK) Ltd (*UK*)
Yates & Yates (*US*)
The Zack Company, Inc (*US*)
Karen Gantz Zahler Literary Agency (*US*)
Helen Zimmermann Literary Agency (*US*)
Zoë Pagnamenta Agency, LLC (*US*)

Philosophy

Clare Hulton Literary Agency (*UK*)
DeFiore and Company (*US*)
The Feldstein Agency (*UK*)
Georges Borchardt, Inc. (*US*)
Frances Goldin Literary Agency, Inc. (*US*)
Goodman Associates (*US*)
Grace Freedson's Publishing Network (*US*)
Graham Maw Christie Literary Agency (*UK*)
Greene & Heaton Ltd (*UK*)

Hardman & Swainson (*UK*)
Antony Harwood Limited (*UK*)
Literary & Creative Artists Inc. (*US*)
Puttick Literary Agency (*UK*)
The Swetky Agency and Associates (*US*)
Wm Clark Associates (*US*)
Writers' Representatives, LLC (*US*)

Photography

The Blumer Literary Agency, Inc. (*US*)
Barbara Braun Associates, Inc. (*US*)
Diana Finch Literary Agency (*US*)
Fresh Books Literary Agency (*US*)
Fredrica S. Friedman and Co. Inc. (*US*)
Hannigan Salky Getzler (HSG) Agency (*US*)
Antony Harwood Limited (*UK*)
Jeanne Fredericks Literary Agency, Inc. (*US*)
Martha Millard Literary Agency (*US*)
P.S. Literary Agency (*Can*)
Salkind Literary Agency (*US*)
Susan Schulman, A Literary Agency (*US*)
Lynn Seligman, Literary Agent (*US*)
The Spieler Agency (*US*)
The Swetky Agency and Associates (*US*)

Poetry

AVAnti Productions & Management (*UK*)
Bookseeker Agency (*UK*)
Eddison Pearson Ltd (*UK*)
Johnson & Alcock (*UK*)
The Spieler Agency (*US*)
Writers' Representatives, LLC (*US*)

Politics

Aaron M. Priest Literary Agency (*US*)
Ambassador Speakers Bureau & Literary Agency (*US*)
Andrew Lownie Literary Agency Ltd (*UK*)
Aponte Literary (*US*)
Arcadia (*US*)
Audrey A. Wolf Literary Agency (*US*)
The August Agency LLC (*US*)
Vicky Bijur Literary Agency (*US*)
David Black Literary Agency (*US*)
Blake Friedmann Literary Agency Ltd (*UK*)
Bleecker Street Associates, Inc. (*US*)
Barbara Braun Associates, Inc. (*US*)
Bresnick Weil Literary Agency, LLC (*US*)
Rick Broadhead & Associates Literary Agency (*Can*)
Carol Mann Agency (*US*)
Caroline Davidson Literary Agency (*UK*)
Elyse Cheney Literary Associates, LLC (*US*)
The Choate Agency, LLC (*US*)
The Cooke Agency (*Can*)
David Luxton Associates (*UK*)
Liza Dawson Associates (*US*)
DeFiore and Company (*US*)
Diamond Kahn and Woods (DKW) Literary Agency Ltd (*UK*)
Don Congdon Associates, Inc. (*US*)
Jim Donovan Literary (*US*)
Dunham Literary, Inc. (*US*)
Dystel & Goderich Literary Management (*US*)
Judith Ehrlich Literary Management (*US*)
Felicia Eth Literary Representation (*US*)
Mary Evans, Inc. (*US*)
The Feldstein Agency (*UK*)
Diana Finch Literary Agency (*US*)
Fletcher & Company (*US*)
Folio Literary Management, LLC (*US*)
Fredrica S. Friedman and Co. Inc. (*US*)
Furniss Lawton (*UK*)
Gelfman Schneider / ICM Partners (*US*)
Georges Borchardt, Inc. (*US*)
The Gernert Company (*US*)
Gina Maccoby Agency (*US*)
Goodman Associates (*US*)
Greene & Heaton Ltd (*UK*)
Laura Gross Literary Agency (*US*)
Hannigan Salky Getzler (HSG) Agency (*US*)
Antony Harwood Limited (*UK*)
Rupert Heath Literary Agency (*UK*)
Hill Nadell Literary Agency (*US*)
Andrea Hurst Literary Management (*US*)
J de S Associates Inc. (*US*)
Jill Grinberg Literary Management LLC (*US*)
Kathi J. Paton Literary Agency (*US*)
Ki Agency Ltd (*UK*)
Kneerim & Williams (*US*)
Edite Kroll Literary Agency, Inc. (*US*)
Kuhn Projects (*US*)
Laura Langlie, Literary Agent (*US*)
Larsen Pomada Literary Agents (*US*)
LaunchBooks Literary Agency (*US*)
Sarah Lazin Books (*US*)
Levine Greenberg Rostan Literary Agency (*US*)
Lippincott Massie McQuilkin (*US*)
Literary & Creative Artists Inc. (*US*)
Julia Lord Literary Management (*US*)
P.S. Literary Agency (*Can*)
The Park Literary Group LLC (*US*)
Lynne Rabinoff Agency (*US*)
The Rudy Agency (*US*)
Salkind Literary Agency (*US*)
Sandra Dijkstra Literary Agency (*US*)
Sanford J. Greenburger Associates, Inc. (*US*)
Susan Schulman, A Literary Agency (*US*)
The Science Factory (*UK*)
Scovil Galen Ghosh Literary Agency, Inc. (*US*)
Lynn Seligman, Literary Agent (*US*)
Denise Shannon Literary Agency, Inc. (*US*)
Sheil Land Associates Ltd (*UK*)
Signature Literary Agency (*US*)
Jeffrey Simmons (*UK*)
The Spieler Agency (*US*)
Philip G. Spitzer Literary Agency, Inc. (*US*)
Sterling Lord Literistic, Inc. (*US*)
Stuart Krichevsky Literary Agency, Inc. (*US*)
Susan Rabiner, Literary Agent, Inc. (*US*)
The Swetky Agency and Associates (*US*)
Thompson Literary Agency (*US*)
Toby Mundy Associates Ltd (*UK*)
TriadaUS Literary Agency, Inc. (*US*)
Trident Media Group, LLC (*US*)
2M Literary Agency Ltd (*US*)
Ed Victor Ltd (*UK*)
Victoria Sanders & Associates LLC (*US*)
Watkins / Loomis Agency, Inc. (*US*)

Whispering Buffalo Literary Agency Ltd (*UK*)
Writers' Representatives, LLC (*US*)
Yates & Yates (*US*)
The Zack Company, Inc (*US*)
Karen Gantz Zahler Literary Agency (*US*)
Psychology
Miriam Altshuler Literary Agency (*US*)
Andrew Lownie Literary Agency Ltd (*UK*)
Arcadia (*US*)
Betsy Amster Literary Enterprises (*US*)
Vicky Bijur Literary Agency (*US*)
David Black Literary Agency (*US*)
Blake Friedmann Literary Agency Ltd (*UK*)
Bleecker Street Associates, Inc. (*US*)
The Blumer Literary Agency, Inc. (*US*)
The Book Group (*US*)
Barbara Braun Associates, Inc. (*US*)
Bresnick Weil Literary Agency, LLC (*US*)
Browne & Miller Literary Associates (*US*)
Carnicelli Literary Management (*US*)
Carol Mann Agency (*US*)
Caroline Davidson Literary Agency (*UK*)
Chalberg & Sussman (*US*)
Chartwell (*UK*)
Conville & Walsh Ltd (*UK*)
The Cowles-Ryan Literary Agency (*US*)
Liza Dawson Associates (*US*)
DeFiore and Company (*US*)
Joëlle Delbourgo Associates, Inc. (*US*)
Diane Banks Associates Literary Agency (*UK*)
Don Congdon Associates, Inc. (*US*)
Dystel & Goderich Literary Management (*US*)
Anne Edelstein Literary Agency (*US*)
Judith Ehrlich Literary Management (*US*)
Felicia Eth Literary Representation (*US*)
Ethan Ellenberg Literary Agency (*US*)
Diana Finch Literary Agency (*US*)
Folio Literary Management, LLC (*US*)
Foundry Literary + Media (*US*)
Fox & Howard Literary Agency (*UK*)
Sarah Jane Freymann Literary Agency (*US*)
Fredrica S. Friedman and Co. Inc. (*US*)
Furniss Lawton (*UK*)
Goodman Associates (*US*)
Grace Freedson's Publishing Network (*US*)
Kathryn Green Literary Agency, LLC (*US*)
Laura Gross Literary Agency (*US*)
Hannigan Salky Getzler (HSG) Agency (*US*)
Antony Harwood Limited (*UK*)
A M Heath & Company Limited, Author's Agents (*UK*)
The Jeff Herman Agency, LLC (*US*)
Andrea Hurst Literary Management (*US*)
InkWell Management (*US*)
The Jean V. Naggar Literary Agency (*US*)
Jeanne Fredericks Literary Agency, Inc. (*US*)
Jill Grinberg Literary Management LLC (*US*)
Johnson & Alcock (*UK*)
Jonathan Pegg Literary Agency (*UK*)
Harvey Klinger, Inc (*US*)
Kneerim & Williams (*US*)
The Knight Agency (*US*)
Linda Konner Literary Agency (*US*)
Barbara S. Kouts, Literary Agent (*US*)
Bert P. Krages (*US*)
Edite Kroll Literary Agency, Inc. (*US*)
Kuhn Projects (*US*)
L. Perkins Associates (*US*)
The LA Literary Agency (*US*)
Laura Langlie, Literary Agent (*US*)
Larsen Pomada Literary Agents (*US*)
Levine Greenberg Rostan Literary Agency (*US*)
Lippincott Massie McQuilkin (*US*)
The Literary Group International (*US*)
Lowenstein Associates, Inc. (*US*)
Madeleine Milburn Literary, TV & Film Agency (*UK*)
Kirsten Manges Literary Agency, LLC (*US*)
Manus & Associates Literary Agency, Inc. (*US*)
Maria Carvainis Agency, Inc. (*US*)
The Martell Agency (*US*)
McIntosh & Otis, Inc (*US*)
The Michael Greer Literary Agency (*UK*)
Martha Millard Literary Agency (*US*)
Northern Lights Literary Services (*US*)
P.S. Literary Agency (*Can*)
The Peters Fraser & Dunlop Group Ltd (PFD) (*UK*)
Queen Literary Agency, Inc. (*US*)
Lynne Rabinoff Agency (*US*)
Raines & Raines (*US*)
Rees Literary Agency (*US*)
Robin Straus Agency, Inc. (*US*)
Rosica Colin Ltd (*UK*)
Ross Yoon Agency (*US*)
Marly Rusoff & Associates, Inc. (*US*)
Salkind Literary Agency (*US*)
Sanford J. Greenburger Associates, Inc. (*US*)
Susan Schulman, A Literary Agency (*US*)
Scovil Galen Ghosh Literary Agency, Inc. (*US*)
Lynn Seligman, Literary Agent (*US*)
Sheil Land Associates Ltd (*UK*)
Sheree Bykofsky Associates, Inc. (*US*)
Signature Literary Agency (*US*)
Jeffrey Simmons (*UK*)
Solow Literary Enterprises, Inc. (*US*)
Stonesong (*US*)
The Stuart Agency (*US*)
The Swetky Agency and Associates (*US*)
SYLA – Susan Yearwood Literary Agency (*UK*)
Tessler Literary Agency (*US*)
Tracy Brown Literary Agency (*US*)
TriadaUS Literary Agency, Inc. (*US*)
2M Literary Agency Ltd (*US*)
Victoria Sanders & Associates LLC (*US*)
Watson, Little Ltd (*UK*)
The Weingel-Fidel Agency (*US*)
Wendy Sherman Associates, Inc. (*US*)
Writers House UK (*UK*)
Writers House, LLC (*US*)
Karen Gantz Zahler Literary Agency (*US*)
Radio
The Agency (London) Ltd (*UK*)
Alan Brodie Representation Ltd (*UK*)
Berlin Associates (*UK*)
Blake Friedmann Literary Agency Ltd (*UK*)

Curtis Brown Group Ltd (*UK*)
Elaine Steel (*UK*)
Felix de Wolfe (*UK*)
Film Rights Ltd in association with Laurence Fitch Ltd (*UK*)
Jill Foster Ltd (JFL) (*UK*)
Georgina Capel Associates Ltd (*UK*)
Antony Harwood Limited (*UK*)
Valerie Hoskins Associates (*UK*)
Independent Talent Group Ltd (*UK*)
Jonathan Clowes Ltd (*UK*)
Marjacq Scripts Ltd (*UK*)
Mary Clemmey Literary Agency (*UK*)
MBA Literary Agents Ltd (*UK*)
PBJ and JBJ Management (*UK*)
The Peters Fraser & Dunlop Group Ltd (PFD) (*UK*)
Rochelle Stevens & Co. (*UK*)
Rosica Colin Ltd (*UK*)
Sayle Screen Ltd (*UK*)
Sheil Land Associates Ltd (*UK*)
The Tennyson Agency (*UK*)
United Agents (*UK*)

Reference

Adler & Robin Books, Inc (*US*)
Baldi Agency (*US*)
BookEnds, LLC (*US*)
Caroline Davidson Literary Agency (*UK*)
David Luxton Associates (*UK*)
Joëlle Delbourgo Associates, Inc. (*US*)
Jim Donovan Literary (*US*)
Fairbank Literary Representation (*US*)
FinePrint Literary Management (*US*)
Folio Literary Management, LLC (*US*)
Fox & Howard Literary Agency (*UK*)
Fresh Books Literary Agency (*US*)
Graham Maw Christie Literary Agency (*UK*)
The Jeff Herman Agency, LLC (*US*)
Kate Hordern Literary Agency (*UK*)
Jeanne Fredericks Literary Agency, Inc. (*US*)
Frances Kelly (*UK*)
Linda Konner Literary Agency (*US*)
Julia Lord Literary Management (*US*)
Rita Rosenkranz Literary Agency (*US*)
Sanford J. Greenburger Associates, Inc. (*US*)
Sheree Bykofsky Associates, Inc. (*US*)
Signature Literary Agency (*US*)
Writers' Representatives, LLC (*US*)
The Zack Company, Inc (*US*)

Religious

Alive Communications, Inc (*US*)
Ambassador Speakers Bureau & Literary Agency (*US*)
The Authors Care Service ltd (*UK*)
Bleecker Street Associates, Inc. (*US*)
The Blumer Literary Agency, Inc. (*US*)
Marie Brown Associates, Inc. (*US*)
Browne & Miller Literary Associates (*US*)
Kelvin C. Bulger and Associates (*US*)
Carol Mann Agency (*US*)
Liza Dawson Associates (*US*)
Dystel & Goderich Literary Management (*US*)
Anne Edelstein Literary Agency (*US*)
FinePrint Literary Management (*US*)
Folio Literary Management, LLC (*US*)
Foundry Literary + Media (*US*)
Georges Borchardt, Inc. (*US*)
Grace Freedson's Publishing Network (*US*)
Antony Harwood Limited (*UK*)
Hidden Value Group (*US*)
Andrea Hurst Literary Management (*US*)
Kathi J. Paton Literary Agency (*US*)
Kneerim & Williams (*US*)
The Knight Agency (*US*)
Edite Kroll Literary Agency, Inc. (*US*)
Larsen Pomada Literary Agents (*US*)
The Steve Laube Agency (*US*)
Levine Greenberg Rostan Literary Agency (*US*)
Linda Roghaar Literary Agency, Inc. (*US*)
Literary Management Group, Inc. (*US*)
Literary & Creative Artists Inc. (*US*)
The Literary Group International (*US*)
MacGregor Literary (*US*)
Martin Literary Management (*US*)
Nappaland Literary Agency (*US*)
Lynne Rabinoff Agency (*US*)
Rosica Colin Ltd (*UK*)
Andy Ross Agency (*US*)
Salkind Literary Agency (*US*)
Sandra Dijkstra Literary Agency (*US*)
Susan Schulman, A Literary Agency (*US*)
Scovil Galen Ghosh Literary Agency, Inc. (*US*)
Secret Agent Man (*US*)
Signature Literary Agency (*US*)
The Stuart Agency (*US*)
The Swetky Agency and Associates (*US*)
Trident Media Group, LLC (*US*)
Wm Clark Associates (*US*)
Yates & Yates (*US*)
The Zack Company, Inc (*US*)
Karen Gantz Zahler Literary Agency (*US*)

Romance

Abrams Artists Agency (*US*)
The Ahearn Agency, Inc (*US*)
Andrew Lownie Literary Agency Ltd (*UK*)
The Axelrod Agency (*US*)
Ayesha Pande Literary (*US*)
Belcastro Agency (*US*)
David Black Literary Agency (*US*)
Bleecker Street Associates, Inc. (*US*)
Luigi Bonomi Associates Ltd (*UK*)
BookEnds, LLC (*US*)
The Characters Talent Agency (*Can*)
Elyse Cheney Literary Associates, LLC (*US*)
The Cooke Agency (*Can*)
Richard Curtis Associates, Inc. (*US*)
The Darley Anderson Agency (*UK*)
Liza Dawson Associates (*US*)
DeFiore and Company (*US*)
The Dravis Agency, Inc. (*US*)
Dystel & Goderich Literary Management (*US*)
Edwards Fuglewicz (*UK*)
Judith Ehrlich Literary Management (*US*)
Einstein Literary Management (*US*)
Elaine P. English, Attorney & Literary Agent (*US*)

Ethan Ellenberg Literary Agency (*US*)
FinePrint Literary Management (*US*)
Folio Literary Management, LLC (*US*)
Irene Goodman Literary Agency (*US*)
Kathryn Green Literary Agency, LLC (*US*)
Greene & Heaton Ltd (*UK*)
Greyhaus Literary Agency (*US*)
Antony Harwood Limited (*UK*)
Hopkins Literary Associates (*US*)
Hudson Agency (*US*)
Andrea Hurst Literary Management (*US*)
Jane Rotrosen Agency (*US*)
The Jean V. Naggar Literary Agency (*US*)
Jenny Brown Associates (*UK*)
Jill Grinberg Literary Management LLC (*US*)
Jill Grosjean Literary Agency (*US*)
Keane Kataria Literary Agency (*UK*)
Harvey Klinger, Inc (*US*)
The Knight Agency (*US*)
L. Perkins Associates (*US*)
Larsen Pomada Literary Agents (*US*)
Levine Greenberg Rostan Literary Agency (*US*)
The Literary Group International (*US*)
Donald Maass Literary Agency (*US*)
MacGregor Literary (*US*)
Madeleine Milburn Literary, TV & Film Agency (*UK*)
Manus & Associates Literary Agency, Inc. (*US*)
Maria Carvainis Agency, Inc. (*US*)
McIntosh & Otis, Inc (*US*)
Meredith Bernstein Literary Agency, Inc. (*US*)
Martha Millard Literary Agency (*US*)
Howard Morhaim Literary Agency (*US*)
Nelson Literary Agency, LLC (*US*)
New Leaf Literary & Media, Inc. (*US*)
Niad Management (*US*)
Northern Lights Literary Services (*US*)
P.S. Literary Agency (*Can*)
Prospect Agency (*US*)
Rebecca Friedman Literary Agency (*US*)
Rees Literary Agency (*US*)
Richford Becklow Literary Agency (*UK*)
RLR Associates (*US*)
Rocking Chair Books (*UK*)
Rosica Colin Ltd (*UK*)
Sandra Dijkstra Literary Agency (*US*)
Sanford J. Greenburger Associates, Inc. (*US*)
Lynn Seligman, Literary Agent (*US*)
Sheil Land Associates Ltd (*UK*)
Signature Literary Agency (*US*)
Spectrum Literary Agency (*US*)
Spencerhill Associates (*US*)
The Swetky Agency and Associates (*US*)
TriadaUS Literary Agency, Inc. (*US*)
Trident Media Group, LLC (*US*)
Waxman Leavell Literary Agency (*US*)
Whispering Buffalo Literary Agency Ltd (*UK*)
Wolfson Literary Agency (*US*)
The Zack Company, Inc (*US*)
Science
Aaron M. Priest Literary Agency (*US*)
The Ampersand Agency Ltd (*UK*)
Andrew Lownie Literary Agency Ltd (*UK*)
Aponte Literary (*US*)
Arcadia (*US*)
Artellus Limited (*UK*)
B.J. Robbins Literary Agency (*US*)
Baldi Agency (*US*)
Vicky Bijur Literary Agency (*US*)
David Black Literary Agency (*US*)
Blake Friedmann Literary Agency Ltd (*UK*)
Bleecker Street Associates, Inc. (*US*)
Luigi Bonomi Associates Ltd (*UK*)
Brandt & Hochman Literary Agents, Inc. (*US*)
Bresnick Weil Literary Agency, LLC (*US*)
Rick Broadhead & Associates Literary Agency (*Can*)
Browne & Miller Literary Associates (*US*)
Carnicelli Literary Management (*US*)
Caroline Davidson Literary Agency (*UK*)
Chalberg & Sussman (*US*)
The Characters Talent Agency (*Can*)
Chartwell (*UK*)
Elyse Cheney Literary Associates, LLC (*US*)
The Choate Agency, LLC (*US*)
Conville & Walsh Ltd (*UK*)
The Cooke Agency (*Can*)
The Cowles-Ryan Literary Agency (*US*)
Curtis Brown Group Ltd (*UK*)
Richard Curtis Associates, Inc. (*US*)
Laura Dail Literary Agency (*US*)
Liza Dawson Associates (*US*)
The Jennifer DeChiara Literary Agency (*US*)
DeFiore and Company (*US*)
Joëlle Delbourgo Associates, Inc. (*US*)
Diane Banks Associates Literary Agency (*UK*)
Dinah Wiener Ltd (*UK*)
Don Congdon Associates, Inc. (*US*)
Donadio & Olson, Inc. (*US*)
Jim Donovan Literary (*US*)
Dunham Literary, Inc. (*US*)
Dunow, Carlson & Lerner Agency (*US*)
Dystel & Goderich Literary Management (*US*)
Judith Ehrlich Literary Management (*US*)
Felicia Eth Literary Representation (*US*)
Ethan Ellenberg Literary Agency (*US*)
Mary Evans, Inc. (*US*)
Fairbank Literary Representation (*US*)
Felicity Bryan Associates (*UK*)
Diana Finch Literary Agency (*US*)
FinePrint Literary Management (*US*)
Fletcher & Company (*US*)
Folio Literary Management, LLC (*US*)
Foundry Literary + Media (*US*)
Fresh Books Literary Agency (*US*)
Sarah Jane Freymann Literary Agency (*US*)
Furniss Lawton (*UK*)
Gelfman Schneider / ICM Partners (*US*)
Georges Borchardt, Inc. (*US*)
The Gernert Company (*US*)
Frances Goldin Literary Agency, Inc. (*US*)
Goodman Associates (*US*)
Irene Goodman Literary Agency (*US*)
Grace Freedson's Publishing Network (*US*)
Graham Maw Christie Literary Agency (*UK*)
Greene & Heaton Ltd (*UK*)

Hannigan Salky Getzler (HSG) Agency (*US*)
Hardman & Swainson (*UK*)
Antony Harwood Limited (*UK*)
Rupert Heath Literary Agency (*UK*)
Hill Nadell Literary Agency (*US*)
Andrea Hurst Literary Management (*US*)
Jabberwocky Literary Agency (*US*)
The Jean V. Naggar Literary Agency (*US*)
Jeanne Fredericks Literary Agency, Inc. (*US*)
Jenny Brown Associates (*UK*)
Jill Grinberg Literary Management LLC (*US*)
Johnson & Alcock (*UK*)
Jonathan Pegg Literary Agency (*UK*)
Kathi J. Paton Literary Agency (*US*)
Ki Agency Ltd (*UK*)
Harvey Klinger, Inc (*US*)
Kneerim & Williams (*US*)
Linda Konner Literary Agency (*US*)
Bert P. Krages (*US*)
Kuhn Projects (*US*)
L. Perkins Associates (*US*)
The LA Literary Agency (*US*)
Larsen Pomada Literary Agents (*US*)
LaunchBooks Literary Agency (*US*)
Robert Lecker Agency (*Can*)
Levine Greenberg Rostan Literary Agency (*US*)
Limelight Management (*UK*)
Lippincott Massie McQuilkin (*US*)
The Literary Group International (*US*)
Julia Lord Literary Management (*US*)
Lowenstein Associates, Inc. (*US*)
The Jennifer Lyons Literary Agency, LLC (*US*)
Madeleine Milburn Literary, TV & Film Agency (*UK*)
Kirsten Manges Literary Agency, LLC (*US*)
Manus & Associates Literary Agency, Inc. (*US*)
Maria Carvainis Agency, Inc. (*US*)
P.S. Literary Agency (*Can*)
The Park Literary Group LLC (*US*)
Pavilion Literary Management (*US*)
The Peters Fraser & Dunlop Group Ltd (PFD) (*UK*)
Prospect Agency (*US*)
Puttick Literary Agency (*UK*)
Queen Literary Agency, Inc. (*US*)
Lynne Rabinoff Agency (*US*)
Rees Literary Agency (*US*)
Renee Zuckerbrot Literary Agency (*US*)
Rita Rosenkranz Literary Agency (*US*)
Robin Straus Agency, Inc. (*US*)
Rosica Colin Ltd (*UK*)
Andy Ross Agency (*US*)
Ross Yoon Agency (*US*)
The Rudy Agency (*US*)
The Sagalyn Literary Agency (*US*)
Salkind Literary Agency (*US*)
Sandra Dijkstra Literary Agency (*US*)
Sanford J. Greenburger Associates, Inc. (*US*)
The Sayle Literary Agency (*UK*)
Susan Schulman, A Literary Agency (*US*)
The Science Factory (*UK*)
Scovil Galen Ghosh Literary Agency, Inc. (*US*)
Lynn Seligman, Literary Agent (*US*)
Sheil Land Associates Ltd (*UK*)
Sheila Ableman Literary Agency (*UK*)
Signature Literary Agency (*US*)
Solow Literary Enterprises, Inc. (*US*)
The Spieler Agency (*US*)
Sterling Lord Literistic, Inc. (*US*)
Stonesong (*US*)
The Strothman Agency (*US*)
Stuart Krichevsky Literary Agency, Inc. (*US*)
The Stuart Agency (*US*)
Susan Rabiner, Literary Agent, Inc. (*US*)
The Swetky Agency and Associates (*US*)
Talcott Notch Literary (*US*)
Tessler Literary Agency (*US*)
Thompson Literary Agency (*US*)
Toby Mundy Associates Ltd (*UK*)
Lavinia Trevor Agency (*UK*)
TriadaUS Literary Agency, Inc. (*US*)
Trident Media Group, LLC (*US*)
2M Literary Agency Ltd (*US*)
United Talent Agency (*US*)
Veritas Literary Agency (*US*)
Watson, Little Ltd (*UK*)
Waxman Leavell Literary Agency (*US*)
The Weingel-Fidel Agency (*US*)
Westwood Creative Artists (*Can*)
Wm Clark Associates (*US*)
Writers House UK (*UK*)
Writers' Representatives, LLC (*US*)
Writers House, LLC (*US*)
The Zack Company, Inc (*US*)
Helen Zimmermann Literary Agency (*US*)
Zoë Pagnamenta Agency, LLC (*US*)

Sci-Fi

The Ampersand Agency Ltd (*UK*)
Andrew Lownie Literary Agency Ltd (*UK*)
Anubis Literary Agency (*UK*)
Aponte Literary (*US*)
Artellus Limited (*UK*)
Ayesha Pande Literary (*US*)
Baror International, Inc. (*US*)
Belcastro Agency (*US*)
Luigi Bonomi Associates Ltd (*UK*)
BookEnds, LLC (*US*)
The Bright Literary Academy (*UK*)
Mic Cheetham Literary Agency (*UK*)
Conville & Walsh Ltd (*UK*)
The Cooke Agency (*Can*)
Richard Curtis Associates, Inc. (*US*)
Laura Dail Literary Agency (*US*)
Liza Dawson Associates (*US*)
Joëlle Delbourgo Associates, Inc. (*US*)
DHH Literary Agency Ltd (*UK*)
Diamond Kahn and Woods (DKW) Literary Agency Ltd (*UK*)
The Dravis Agency, Inc. (*US*)
Dunham Literary, Inc. (*US*)
Dystel & Goderich Literary Management (*US*)
Ethan Ellenberg Literary Agency (*US*)
FinePrint Literary Management (*US*)
Folio Literary Management, LLC (*US*)
Foundry Literary + Media (*US*)
Frances Collin Literary Agent (*US*)

The Gernert Company (*US*)
Barry Goldblatt Literary Agency, Inc. (*US*)
Greene & Heaton Ltd (*UK*)
Antony Harwood Limited (*UK*)
Rupert Heath Literary Agency (*UK*)
Andrea Hurst Literary Management (*US*)
Jabberwocky Literary Agency (*US*)
Jill Grinberg Literary Management LLC (*US*)
Johnson & Alcock (*UK*)
Virginia Kidd Agency, Inc (*US*)
Harvey Klinger, Inc (*US*)
The Knight Agency (*US*)
L. Perkins Associates (*US*)
LaunchBooks Literary Agency (*US*)
Linn Prentis, Literary Agent (*US*)
Lowenstein Associates, Inc. (*US*)
Donald Maass Literary Agency (*US*)
Madeleine Milburn Literary, TV & Film Agency (*UK*)
Marjacq Scripts Ltd (*UK*)
Margret McBride Literary Agency (*US*)
McIntosh & Otis, Inc (*US*)
Martha Millard Literary Agency (*US*)
Howard Morhaim Literary Agency (*US*)
Nelson Literary Agency, LLC (*US*)
New Leaf Literary & Media, Inc. (*US*)
P.S. Literary Agency (*Can*)
Prospect Agency (*US*)
Raines & Raines (*US*)
Rebecca Friedman Literary Agency (*US*)
Richford Becklow Literary Agency (*UK*)
Salkind Literary Agency (*US*)
Sandra Dijkstra Literary Agency (*US*)
Sanford J. Greenburger Associates, Inc. (*US*)
Scribe Agency LLC (*US*)
Lynn Seligman, Literary Agent (*US*)
Sheil Land Associates Ltd (*UK*)
Signature Literary Agency (*US*)
Spectrum Literary Agency (*US*)
Philip G. Spitzer Literary Agency, Inc. (*US*)
Steph Roundsmith Agent and Editor (*UK*)
Sternig & Byrne Literary Agency (*US*)
Stuart Krichevsky Literary Agency, Inc. (*US*)
The Swetky Agency and Associates (*US*)
Talcott Notch Literary (*US*)
TriadaUS Literary Agency, Inc. (*US*)
Trident Media Group, LLC (*US*)
United Talent Agency (*US*)
Veritas Literary Agency (*US*)
Whispering Buffalo Literary Agency Ltd (*UK*)
Writers House UK (*UK*)
Writers House, LLC (*US*)
The Zack Company, Inc (*US*)
Zeno Agency Ltd (*UK*)

Scripts

A & B Personal Management Ltd (*UK*)
Above the Line Agency (*US*)
Abrams Artists Agency (*US*)
Bret Adams Ltd (*US*)
Agency for the Performing Arts (APA) (*US*)
The Agency (London) Ltd (*UK*)
AHA Talent Ltd (*UK*)
Aimee Entertainment Agency (*US*)
Alan Brodie Representation Ltd (*UK*)
Anonymous Content (*US*)
AVAnti Productions & Management (*UK*)
Barbara Hogenson Agency (*US*)
Berlin Associates (*UK*)
Blake Friedmann Literary Agency Ltd (*UK*)
Kelvin C. Bulger and Associates (*US*)
Cecily Ware Literary Agents (*UK*)
The Characters Talent Agency (*Can*)
Creative Trust, Inc. (*US*)
Curtis Brown Group Ltd (*UK*)
Deal Points Ent. (*US*)
DHH Literary Agency Ltd (*UK*)
The Dravis Agency, Inc. (*US*)
Elaine Steel (*UK*)
Energy Entertainment (*US*)
Felix de Wolfe (*UK*)
Film Rights Ltd in association with Laurence Fitch Ltd (*UK*)
Jill Foster Ltd (JFL) (*UK*)
Samuel French, Inc. (*US*)
Noel Gay (*UK*)
Eric Glass Ltd (*UK*)
David Higham Associates Ltd (*UK*)
Valerie Hoskins Associates (*UK*)
Hudson Agency (*US*)
Independent Talent Group Ltd (*UK*)
Janet Fillingham Associates (*UK*)
Jonathan Clowes Ltd (*UK*)
Michelle Kass Associates (*UK*)
Ken Sherman & Associates (*US*)
Ki Agency Ltd (*UK*)
Linda Seifert Management (*UK*)
The Lisa Richards Agency (*Ire*)
Macnaughton Lord Representation (*UK*)
Madeleine Milburn Literary, TV & Film Agency (*UK*)
Marjacq Scripts Ltd (*UK*)
Mary Clemmey Literary Agency (*UK*)
MBA Literary Agents Ltd (*UK*)
The Michael Greer Literary Agency (*UK*)
Niad Management (*US*)
Paradigm Talent and Literary Agency (*US*)
PBJ and JBJ Management (*UK*)
Peregrine Whittlesey Agency (*US*)
The Peters Fraser & Dunlop Group Ltd (PFD) (*UK*)
Rochelle Stevens & Co. (*UK*)
Roger Hancock Ltd (*UK*)
Rosica Colin Ltd (*UK*)
Sayle Screen Ltd (*UK*)
Susan Schulman, A Literary Agency (*US*)
Sheil Land Associates Ltd (*UK*)
Stone Manners Salners Agency (*US*)
The Swetky Agency and Associates (*US*)
The Tennyson Agency (*UK*)
United Agents (*UK*)
William Morris Endeavor Entertainment (*US*)

Self-Help

Adler & Robin Books, Inc (*US*)
Alive Communications, Inc (*US*)
Miriam Altshuler Literary Agency (*US*)

Ambassador Speakers Bureau & Literary Agency (*US*)
Andrew Lownie Literary Agency Ltd (*UK*)
Arcadia (*US*)
Audrey A. Wolf Literary Agency (*US*)
The Authors Care Service ltd (*UK*)
Baldi Agency (*US*)
Betsy Amster Literary Enterprises (*US*)
Vicky Bijur Literary Agency (*US*)
David Black Literary Agency (*US*)
Bleecker Street Associates, Inc. (*US*)
The Blumer Literary Agency, Inc. (*US*)
The Bright Literary Academy (*UK*)
Rick Broadhead & Associates Literary Agency (*Can*)
Browne & Miller Literary Associates (*US*)
Carol Mann Agency (*US*)
Chalberg & Sussman (*US*)
Clare Hulton Literary Agency (*UK*)
The Cowles-Ryan Literary Agency (*US*)
Liza Dawson Associates (*US*)
The Jennifer DeChiara Literary Agency (*US*)
Diane Banks Associates Literary Agency (*UK*)
Ebeling & Associates (*US*)
Judith Ehrlich Literary Management (*US*)
Diana Finch Literary Agency (*US*)
FinePrint Literary Management (*US*)
Fletcher & Company (*US*)
Folio Literary Management, LLC (*US*)
Fox & Howard Literary Agency (*UK*)
Fresh Books Literary Agency (*US*)
Sarah Jane Freymann Literary Agency (*US*)
Fredrica S. Friedman and Co. Inc. (*US*)
Gina Maccoby Agency (*US*)
Grace Freedson's Publishing Network (*US*)
Graham Maw Christie Literary Agency (*UK*)
Kathryn Green Literary Agency, LLC (*US*)
Antony Harwood Limited (*UK*)
The Jeff Herman Agency, LLC (*US*)
Hidden Value Group (*US*)
Andrea Hurst Literary Management (*US*)
InkWell Management (*US*)
J de S Associates Inc. (*US*)
Jeanne Fredericks Literary Agency, Inc. (*US*)
Johnson & Alcock (*UK*)
Frances Kelly (*UK*)
Ki Agency Ltd (*UK*)
Harvey Klinger, Inc (*US*)
The Knight Agency (*US*)
Linda Konner Literary Agency (*US*)
Edite Kroll Literary Agency, Inc. (*US*)
Larsen Pomada Literary Agents (*US*)
Levine Greenberg Rostan Literary Agency (*US*)
Linda Roghaar Literary Agency, Inc. (*US*)
The Lisa Richards Agency (*Ire*)
The Literary Group International (*US*)
Julia Lord Literary Management (*US*)
MacGregor Literary (*US*)
Madeleine Milburn Literary, TV & Film Agency (*UK*)
Manus & Associates Literary Agency, Inc. (*US*)
The Martell Agency (*US*)
Martin Literary Management (*US*)
MBA Literary Agents Ltd (*UK*)
Margret McBride Literary Agency (*US*)
McIntosh & Otis, Inc (*US*)
Martha Millard Literary Agency (*US*)
Northern Lights Literary Services (*US*)
Puttick Literary Agency (*UK*)
Rees Literary Agency (*US*)
Richford Becklow Literary Agency (*UK*)
Robert Dudley Agency (*UK*)
Salkind Literary Agency (*US*)
Sandra Dijkstra Literary Agency (*US*)
Sanford J. Greenburger Associates, Inc. (*US*)
Susan Schulman, A Literary Agency (*US*)
Lynn Seligman, Literary Agent (*US*)
Sheil Land Associates Ltd (*UK*)
Sheree Bykofsky Associates, Inc. (*US*)
Robert Smith Literary Agency Ltd (*UK*)
Sterling Lord Literistic, Inc. (*US*)
Stonesong (*US*)
The Swetky Agency and Associates (*US*)
TriadaUS Literary Agency, Inc. (*US*)
Veritas Literary Agency (*US*)
Watson, Little Ltd (*UK*)
Waxman Leavell Literary Agency (*US*)
Wendy Sherman Associates, Inc. (*US*)
Whispering Buffalo Literary Agency Ltd (*UK*)
Writers House UK (*UK*)
Writers' Representatives, LLC (*US*)
Writers House, LLC (*US*)
The Zack Company, Inc (*US*)

Short Stories

The Ahearn Agency, Inc (*US*)
Alive Communications, Inc (*US*)
The Bright Literary Academy (*UK*)
DeFiore and Company (*US*)
Georges Borchardt, Inc. (*US*)
Joy Harris Literary Agency, Inc. (*US*)
Antony Harwood Limited (*UK*)
International Transactions, Inc. (*US*)
MacGregor Literary (*US*)
Martha Millard Literary Agency (*US*)
Renee Zuckerbrot Literary Agency (*US*)
Sandra Dijkstra Literary Agency (*US*)
Scribe Agency LLC (*US*)
Philip G. Spitzer Literary Agency, Inc. (*US*)
The Swetky Agency and Associates (*US*)
Watkins / Loomis Agency, Inc. (*US*)
Zoë Pagnamenta Agency, LLC (*US*)

Sociology

Miriam Altshuler Literary Agency (*US*)
Ann Rittenberg Literary Agency (*US*)
The August Agency LLC (*US*)
Betsy Amster Literary Enterprises (*US*)
Vicky Bijur Literary Agency (*US*)
Blake Friedmann Literary Agency Ltd (*UK*)
Bleecker Street Associates, Inc. (*US*)
Barbara Braun Associates, Inc. (*US*)
Browne & Miller Literary Associates (*US*)
Carol Mann Agency (*US*)
Liza Dawson Associates (*US*)
The Jennifer DeChiara Literary Agency (*US*)
DeFiore and Company (*US*)

Diamond Kahn and Woods (DKW) Literary Agency Ltd (*UK*)
Judith Ehrlich Literary Management (*US*)
Felicia Eth Literary Representation (*US*)
Mary Evans, Inc. (*US*)
The Feldstein Agency (*UK*)
Fredrica S. Friedman and Co. Inc. (*US*)
Furniss Lawton (*UK*)
The Gernert Company (*US*)
Frances Goldin Literary Agency, Inc. (*US*)
Goodman Associates (*US*)
Irene Goodman Literary Agency (*US*)
Hannigan Salky Getzler (HSG) Agency (*US*)
Antony Harwood Limited (*UK*)
Kate Hordern Literary Agency (*UK*)
J de S Associates Inc. (*US*)
Kneerim & Williams (*US*)
Larsen Pomada Literary Agents (*US*)
LaunchBooks Literary Agency (*US*)
Levine Greenberg Rostan Literary Agency (*US*)
Lippincott Massie McQuilkin (*US*)
The Literary Group International (*US*)
Lowenstein Associates, Inc. (*US*)
Sandra Dijkstra Literary Agency (*US*)
Sanford J. Greenburger Associates, Inc. (*US*)
Susan Schulman, A Literary Agency (*US*)
Scovil Galen Ghosh Literary Agency, Inc. (*US*)
Lynn Seligman, Literary Agent (*US*)
Denise Shannon Literary Agency, Inc. (*US*)
The Spieler Agency (*US*)
The Swetky Agency and Associates (*US*)
Victoria Sanders & Associates LLC (*US*)
The Weingel-Fidel Agency (*US*)
Wm Clark Associates (*US*)
Karen Gantz Zahler Literary Agency (*US*)

Spiritual
Alive Communications, Inc (*US*)
Miriam Altshuler Literary Agency (*US*)
Arcadia (*US*)
Baldi Agency (*US*)
David Black Literary Agency (*US*)
Bleecker Street Associates, Inc. (*US*)
Carnicelli Literary Management (*US*)
Carol Mann Agency (*US*)
The Cooke Agency (*Can*)
The Cowles-Ryan Literary Agency (*US*)
Liza Dawson Associates (*US*)
Dunham Literary, Inc. (*US*)
Dystel & Goderich Literary Management (*US*)
Felicia Eth Literary Representation (*US*)
Ethan Ellenberg Literary Agency (*US*)
FinePrint Literary Management (*US*)
Folio Literary Management, LLC (*US*)
Foundry Literary + Media (*US*)
Fox & Howard Literary Agency (*UK*)
Sarah Jane Freymann Literary Agency (*US*)
Joy Harris Literary Agency, Inc. (*US*)
Antony Harwood Limited (*UK*)
The Jeff Herman Agency, LLC (*US*)
Jill Grinberg Literary Management LLC (*US*)
Harvey Klinger, Inc (*US*)
Kuhn Projects (*US*)
Levine Greenberg Rostan Literary Agency (*US*)
Linda Roghaar Literary Agency, Inc. (*US*)
Literary Management Group, Inc. (*US*)
Literary & Creative Artists Inc. (*US*)
Lowenstein Associates, Inc. (*US*)
Kirsten Manges Literary Agency, LLC (*US*)
McIntosh & Otis, Inc (*US*)
The Amy Rennert Agency, Inc. (*US*)
Rita Rosenkranz Literary Agency (*US*)
Salkind Literary Agency (*US*)
Susan Schulman, A Literary Agency (*US*)
Sheree Bykofsky Associates, Inc. (*US*)
Signature Literary Agency (*US*)
The Spieler Agency (*US*)
Thompson Literary Agency (*US*)
Wendy Sherman Associates, Inc. (*US*)
The Zack Company, Inc (*US*)
Karen Gantz Zahler Literary Agency (*US*)
Helen Zimmermann Literary Agency (*US*)

Sport
Alive Communications, Inc (*US*)
The Ampersand Agency Ltd (*UK*)
Andrew Lownie Literary Agency Ltd (*UK*)
Audrey A. Wolf Literary Agency (*US*)
B.J. Robbins Literary Agency (*US*)
Bell Lomax Moreton Agency (*UK*)
David Black Literary Agency (*US*)
Bleecker Street Associates, Inc. (*US*)
Bresnick Weil Literary Agency, LLC (*US*)
Browne & Miller Literary Associates (*US*)
Carnicelli Literary Management (*US*)
Carol Mann Agency (*US*)
The Characters Talent Agency (*Can*)
Elyse Cheney Literary Associates, LLC (*US*)
Conville & Walsh Ltd (*UK*)
The Creative Rights Agency (*UK*)
David Luxton Associates (*UK*)
The Jennifer DeChiara Literary Agency (*US*)
Don Congdon Associates, Inc. (*US*)
Jim Donovan Literary (*US*)
Dunow, Carlson & Lerner Agency (*US*)
Judith Ehrlich Literary Management (*US*)
Fairbank Literary Representation (*US*)
The Feldstein Agency (*UK*)
Diana Finch Literary Agency (*US*)
Fletcher & Company (*US*)
Folio Literary Management, LLC (*US*)
Foundry Literary + Media (*US*)
Sarah Jane Freymann Literary Agency (*US*)
Furniss Lawton (*UK*)
The Gernert Company (*US*)
Glass Literary Management LLC (*US*)
Frances Goldin Literary Agency, Inc. (*US*)
Goodman Associates (*US*)
Grace Freedson's Publishing Network (*US*)
Kathryn Green Literary Agency, LLC (*US*)
Laura Gross Literary Agency (*US*)
Antony Harwood Limited (*UK*)
A M Heath & Company Limited, Author's Agents (*UK*)
J de S Associates Inc. (*US*)
Jeanne Fredericks Literary Agency, Inc. (*US*)
Jenny Brown Associates (*UK*)
Jill Grinberg Literary Management LLC (*US*)

Johnson & Alcock (*UK*)
Kathi J. Paton Literary Agency (*US*)
Ki Agency Ltd (*UK*)
Harvey Klinger, Inc (*US*)
Kneerim & Williams (*US*)
The LA Literary Agency (*US*)
Larsen Pomada Literary Agents (*US*)
LaunchBooks Literary Agency (*US*)
Levine Greenberg Rostan Literary Agency (*US*)
Limelight Management (*UK*)
Lippincott Massie McQuilkin (*US*)
The Lisa Richards Agency (*Ire*)
The Literary Group International (*US*)
Julia Lord Literary Management (*US*)
The Jennifer Lyons Literary Agency, LLC (*US*)
MacGregor Literary (*US*)
Kirsten Manges Literary Agency, LLC (*US*)
Marjacq Scripts Ltd (*UK*)
McIntosh & Otis, Inc (*US*)
The Michael Greer Literary Agency (*UK*)
Howard Morhaim Literary Agency (*US*)
Mulcahy Associates (*UK*)
Niad Management (*US*)
P.S. Literary Agency (*Can*)
John Pawsey (*UK*)
Queen Literary Agency, Inc. (*US*)
The Amy Rennert Agency, Inc. (*US*)
RLR Associates (*US*)
Robert Dudley Agency (*UK*)
Rosica Colin Ltd (*UK*)
Sandra Dijkstra Literary Agency (*US*)
Sanford J. Greenburger Associates, Inc. (*US*)
Susan Schulman, A Literary Agency (*US*)
Scovil Galen Ghosh Literary Agency, Inc. (*US*)
Jeffrey Simmons (*UK*)
SLW Literary Agency (*US*)
Philip G. Spitzer Literary Agency, Inc. (*US*)
The Stuart Agency (*US*)
Susan Rabiner, Literary Agent, Inc. (*US*)
The Swetky Agency and Associates (*US*)
Thompson Literary Agency (*US*)
TriadaUS Literary Agency, Inc. (*US*)
Trident Media Group, LLC (*US*)
2M Literary Agency Ltd (*US*)
Watson, Little Ltd (*UK*)
Waxman Leavell Literary Agency (*US*)
Wendy Sherman Associates, Inc. (*US*)
Yates & Yates (*US*)
The Zack Company, Inc (*US*)
Helen Zimmermann Literary Agency (*US*)

Suspense

Aaron M. Priest Literary Agency (*US*)
Abrams Artists Agency (*US*)
The Ahearn Agency, Inc (*US*)
Alive Communications, Inc (*US*)
Andrew Lownie Literary Agency Ltd (*UK*)
B.J. Robbins Literary Agency (*US*)
Belcastro Agency (*US*)
Blake Friedmann Literary Agency Ltd (*UK*)
The Blumer Literary Agency, Inc. (*US*)
BookEnds, LLC (*US*)
Caroline Sheldon Literary Agency (*UK*)
Chalberg & Sussman (*US*)
Chartwell (*UK*)
Elyse Cheney Literary Associates, LLC (*US*)
The Chudney Agency (*US*)
Conville & Walsh Ltd (*UK*)
Coombs Moylett & Maclean Literary Agency (*UK*)
Curtis Brown Group Ltd (*UK*)
Darhansoff & Verrill Literary Agents (*US*)
The Darley Anderson Agency (*UK*)
Liza Dawson Associates (*US*)
The Jennifer DeChiara Literary Agency (*US*)
Diamond Kahn and Woods (DKW) Literary Agency Ltd (*UK*)
Don Congdon Associates, Inc. (*US*)
Jim Donovan Literary (*US*)
The Dravis Agency, Inc. (*US*)
Dunow, Carlson & Lerner Agency (*US*)
Dystel & Goderich Literary Management (*US*)
FinePrint Literary Management (*US*)
Folio Literary Management, LLC (*US*)
Furniss Lawton (*UK*)
Gelfman Schneider / ICM Partners (*US*)
Gina Maccoby Agency (*US*)
Goodman Associates (*US*)
Irene Goodman Literary Agency (*US*)
Kathryn Green Literary Agency, LLC (*US*)
Laura Gross Literary Agency (*US*)
Hannigan Salky Getzler (HSG) Agency (*US*)
Joy Harris Literary Agency, Inc. (*US*)
Antony Harwood Limited (*UK*)
A M Heath & Company Limited, Author's Agents (*UK*)
J de S Associates Inc. (*US*)
Jane Rotrosen Agency (*US*)
The Jean V. Naggar Literary Agency (*US*)
Jill Grosjean Literary Agency (*US*)
The Joan Brandt Agency (*US*)
Johnson & Alcock (*UK*)
Virginia Kidd Agency, Inc (*US*)
Harvey Klinger, Inc (*US*)
The Knight Agency (*US*)
Barbara S. Kouts, Literary Agent (*US*)
Laura Langlie, Literary Agent (*US*)
Larsen Pomada Literary Agents (*US*)
Robert Lecker Agency (*Can*)
Levine Greenberg Rostan Literary Agency (*US*)
Limelight Management (*UK*)
Lippincott Massie McQuilkin (*US*)
Donald Maass Literary Agency (*US*)
MacGregor Literary (*US*)
Madeleine Milburn Literary, TV & Film Agency (*UK*)
Manus & Associates Literary Agency, Inc. (*US*)
Maria Carvainis Agency, Inc. (*US*)
The Martell Agency (*US*)
Margret McBride Literary Agency (*US*)
McIntosh & Otis, Inc (*US*)
Martha Millard Literary Agency (*US*)
Nappaland Literary Agency (*US*)
Niad Management (*US*)
Northern Lights Literary Services (*US*)
P.S. Literary Agency (*Can*)

The Peters Fraser & Dunlop Group Ltd (PFD) (*UK*)
Prospect Agency (*US*)
Raines & Raines (*US*)
Rebecca Friedman Literary Agency (*US*)
Rees Literary Agency (*US*)
Rosica Colin Ltd (*UK*)
Salkind Literary Agency (*US*)
Sandra Dijkstra Literary Agency (*US*)
Susan Schulman, A Literary Agency (*US*)
Secret Agent Man (*US*)
Spectrum Literary Agency (*US*)
Philip G. Spitzer Literary Agency, Inc. (*US*)
Sternig & Byrne Literary Agency (*US*)
The Swetky Agency and Associates (*US*)
Talcott Notch Literary (*US*)
TriadaUS Literary Agency, Inc. (*US*)
Trident Media Group, LLC (*US*)
Victoria Sanders & Associates LLC (*US*)
Waxman Leavell Literary Agency (*US*)
Wendy Sherman Associates, Inc. (*US*)
Wolfson Literary Agency (*US*)
The Zack Company, Inc (*US*)
Helen Zimmermann Literary Agency (*US*)

Technology

Andrew Lownie Literary Agency Ltd (*UK*)
Arcadia (*US*)
The August Agency LLC (*US*)
Baldi Agency (*US*)
Blake Friedmann Literary Agency Ltd (*UK*)
Bleecker Street Associates, Inc. (*US*)
Browne & Miller Literary Associates (*US*)
Chartwell (*UK*)
Richard Curtis Associates, Inc. (*US*)
Laura Dail Literary Agency (*US*)
DeFiore and Company (*US*)
Don Congdon Associates, Inc. (*US*)
Dunham Literary, Inc. (*US*)
Dystel & Goderich Literary Management (*US*)
Felicia Eth Literary Representation (*US*)
Mary Evans, Inc. (*US*)
Diana Finch Literary Agency (*US*)
FinePrint Literary Management (*US*)
Folio Literary Management, LLC (*US*)
Fresh Books Literary Agency (*US*)
Frances Goldin Literary Agency, Inc. (*US*)
Goodman Associates (*US*)
Grace Freedson's Publishing Network (*US*)
Antony Harwood Limited (*UK*)
Jill Grinberg Literary Management LLC (*US*)
Kathi J. Paton Literary Agency (*US*)
Harvey Klinger, Inc (*US*)
Kneerim & Williams (*US*)
Kuhn Projects (*US*)
LaunchBooks Literary Agency (*US*)
Levine Greenberg Rostan Literary Agency (*US*)
Julia Lord Literary Management (*US*)
Kirsten Manges Literary Agency, LLC (*US*)
Maria Carvainis Agency, Inc. (*US*)
New Leaf Literary & Media, Inc. (*US*)
Lynne Rabinoff Agency (*US*)
Robert Dudley Agency (*UK*)
The Rudy Agency (*US*)
The Sagalyn Literary Agency (*US*)
Salkind Literary Agency (*US*)
Susan Schulman, A Literary Agency (*US*)
The Science Factory (*UK*)
Signature Literary Agency (*US*)
Sterling Lord Literistic, Inc. (*US*)
Stuart Krichevsky Literary Agency, Inc. (*US*)
The Swetky Agency and Associates (*US*)
Talcott Notch Literary (*US*)
Trident Media Group, LLC (*US*)
Watkins / Loomis Agency, Inc. (*US*)
Watson, Little Ltd (*UK*)
The Weingel-Fidel Agency (*US*)
Wm Clark Associates (*US*)
The Zack Company, Inc (*US*)
Helen Zimmermann Literary Agency (*US*)

Theatre

A & B Personal Management Ltd (*UK*)
Bret Adams Ltd (*US*)
Agency for the Performing Arts (APA) (*US*)
The Agency (London) Ltd (*UK*)
Alan Brodie Representation Ltd (*UK*)
AVAnti Productions & Management (*UK*)
Barbara Hogenson Agency (*US*)
Berlin Associates (*UK*)
Curtis Brown Group Ltd (*UK*)
Liza Dawson Associates (*US*)
The Jennifer DeChiara Literary Agency (*US*)
DHH Literary Agency Ltd (*UK*)
Don Congdon Associates, Inc. (*US*)
Felix de Wolfe (*UK*)
Film Rights Ltd in association with Laurence Fitch Ltd (*UK*)
Diana Finch Literary Agency (*US*)
Jill Foster Ltd (JFL) (*UK*)
Samuel French, Inc. (*US*)
Eric Glass Ltd (*UK*)
Goodman Associates (*US*)
Antony Harwood Limited (*UK*)
David Higham Associates Ltd (*UK*)
Independent Talent Group Ltd (*UK*)
Janet Fillingham Associates (*UK*)
Jonathan Clowes Ltd (*UK*)
Ki Agency Ltd (*UK*)
L. Perkins Associates (*US*)
Laura Langlie, Literary Agent (*US*)
Robert Lecker Agency (*Can*)
The Lisa Richards Agency (*Ire*)
Macnaughton Lord Representation (*UK*)
Mary Clemmey Literary Agency (*UK*)
MBA Literary Agents Ltd (*UK*)
Martha Millard Literary Agency (*US*)
Niad Management (*US*)
Paradigm Talent and Literary Agency (*US*)
PBJ and JBJ Management (*UK*)
Peregrine Whittlesey Agency (*US*)
The Peters Fraser & Dunlop Group Ltd (PFD) (*UK*)
Rochelle Stevens & Co. (*UK*)
Rosica Colin Ltd (*UK*)
Sayle Screen Ltd (*UK*)
Susan Schulman, A Literary Agency (*US*)
Sheil Land Associates Ltd (*UK*)

Jeffrey Simmons (*UK*)
The Spieler Agency (*US*)
The Swetky Agency and Associates (*US*)
The Tennyson Agency (*UK*)
United Agents (*UK*)
Victoria Sanders & Associates LLC (*US*)
Wm Clark Associates (*US*)

Thrillers

Aaron M. Priest Literary Agency (*US*)
The Ahearn Agency, Inc (*US*)
Alive Communications, Inc (*US*)
The Ampersand Agency Ltd (*UK*)
Andrew Lownie Literary Agency Ltd (*UK*)
Ann Rittenberg Literary Agency (*US*)
The Axelrod Agency (*US*)
Ayesha Pande Literary (*US*)
B.J. Robbins Literary Agency (*US*)
Belcastro Agency (*US*)
Betsy Amster Literary Enterprises (*US*)
David Black Literary Agency (*US*)
Blake Friedmann Literary Agency Ltd (*UK*)
Bleecker Street Associates, Inc. (*US*)
The Blumer Literary Agency, Inc. (*US*)
Luigi Bonomi Associates Ltd (*UK*)
The Book Bureau Literary Agency (*Ire*)
Brandt & Hochman Literary Agents, Inc. (*US*)
Barbara Braun Associates, Inc. (*US*)
The Bright Literary Academy (*UK*)
Chalberg & Sussman (*US*)
The Characters Talent Agency (*Can*)
Chartwell (*UK*)
Mic Cheetham Literary Agency (*UK*)
Elyse Cheney Literary Associates, LLC (*US*)
The Choate Agency, LLC (*US*)
Cine/Lit Representation (*US*)
Conville & Walsh Ltd (*UK*)
Coombs Moylett & Maclean Literary Agency (*UK*)
The Creative Rights Agency (*UK*)
Curtis Brown Group Ltd (*UK*)
Richard Curtis Associates, Inc. (*US*)
Laura Dail Literary Agency (*US*)
The Darley Anderson Agency (*UK*)
Liza Dawson Associates (*US*)
The Jennifer DeChiara Literary Agency (*US*)
DeFiore and Company (*US*)
Joëlle Delbourgo Associates, Inc. (*US*)
DHH Literary Agency Ltd (*UK*)
Diamond Kahn and Woods (DKW) Literary Agency Ltd (*UK*)
Diane Banks Associates Literary Agency (*UK*)
Don Congdon Associates, Inc. (*US*)
Jim Donovan Literary (*US*)
The Dravis Agency, Inc. (*US*)
Dunham Literary, Inc. (*US*)
Dunow, Carlson & Lerner Agency (*US*)
Dystel & Goderich Literary Management (*US*)
Edwards Fuglewicz (*UK*)
Judith Ehrlich Literary Management (*US*)
Einstein Literary Management (*US*)
Ethan Ellenberg Literary Agency (*US*)
Fairbank Literary Representation (*US*)
The Feldstein Agency (*UK*)
Diana Finch Literary Agency (*US*)
FinePrint Literary Management (*US*)
Folio Literary Management, LLC (*US*)
Foundry Literary + Media (*US*)
Samuel French, Inc. (*US*)
Sarah Jane Freymann Literary Agency (*US*)
Furniss Lawton (*UK*)
Gelfman Schneider / ICM Partners (*US*)
The Gernert Company (*US*)
Gina Maccoby Agency (*US*)
Goodman Associates (*US*)
Irene Goodman Literary Agency (*US*)
Kathryn Green Literary Agency, LLC (*US*)
Greene & Heaton Ltd (*UK*)
Gregory & Company, Authors' Agents (*UK*)
Laura Gross Literary Agency (*US*)
Gunn Media Associates (*UK*)
Hannigan Salky Getzler (HSG) Agency (*US*)
Hardman & Swainson (*UK*)
Antony Harwood Limited (*UK*)
A M Heath & Company Limited, Author's Agents (*UK*)
Rupert Heath Literary Agency (*UK*)
The Helen Heller Agency (*Can*)
David Higham Associates Ltd (*UK*)
Hill Nadell Literary Agency (*US*)
Kate Hordern Literary Agency (*UK*)
Andrea Hurst Literary Management (*US*)
InkWell Management (*US*)
International Transactions, Inc. (*US*)
J de S Associates Inc. (*US*)
Jane Rotrosen Agency (*US*)
The Jean V. Naggar Literary Agency (*US*)
Jenny Brown Associates (*UK*)
Jill Grosjean Literary Agency (*US*)
Johnson & Alcock (*UK*)
Jonathan Pegg Literary Agency (*UK*)
Harvey Klinger, Inc (*US*)
The Knight Agency (*US*)
Barbara S. Kouts, Literary Agent (*US*)
L. Perkins Associates (*US*)
Laura Langlie, Literary Agent (*US*)
Larsen Pomada Literary Agents (*US*)
LaunchBooks Literary Agency (*US*)
Robert Lecker Agency (*Can*)
Levine Greenberg Rostan Literary Agency (*US*)
Limelight Management (*UK*)
Lippincott Massie McQuilkin (*US*)
The Literary Group International (*US*)
Julia Lord Literary Management (*US*)
Lowenstein Associates, Inc. (*US*)
The Jennifer Lyons Literary Agency, LLC (*US*)
MacGregor Literary (*US*)
Madeleine Milburn Literary, TV & Film Agency (*UK*)
Andrew Mann Ltd (*UK*)
Manus & Associates Literary Agency, Inc. (*US*)
Maria Carvainis Agency, Inc. (*US*)
Marjacq Scripts Ltd (*UK*)
The Martell Agency (*US*)
Margret McBride Literary Agency (*US*)
McIntosh & Otis, Inc (*US*)
Meredith Bernstein Literary Agency, Inc. (*US*)

Martha Millard Literary Agency (*US*)
Howard Morhaim Literary Agency (*US*)
Mulcahy Associates (*UK*)
New Leaf Literary & Media, Inc. (*US*)
Niad Management (*US*)
P.S. Literary Agency (*Can*)
Pavilion Literary Management (*US*)
The Peters Fraser & Dunlop Group Ltd (PFD) (*UK*)
Prospect Agency (*US*)
Queen Literary Agency, Inc. (*US*)
Raines & Raines (*US*)
Rebecca Friedman Literary Agency (*US*)
Redhammer (*UK*)
Rees Literary Agency (*US*)
Renee Zuckerbrot Literary Agency (*US*)
Rocking Chair Books (*UK*)
Rosica Colin Ltd (*UK*)
The Rudy Agency (*US*)
Salkind Literary Agency (*US*)
Sandra Dijkstra Literary Agency (*US*)
Sanford J. Greenburger Associates, Inc. (*US*)
Susan Schulman, A Literary Agency (*US*)
Secret Agent Man (*US*)
Sheil Land Associates Ltd (*UK*)
Spencerhill Associates (*US*)
The Spieler Agency (*US*)
Philip G. Spitzer Literary Agency, Inc. (*US*)
The Stuart Agency (*US*)
The Swetky Agency and Associates (*US*)
SYLA – Susan Yearwood Literary Agency (*UK*)
Talcott Notch Literary (*US*)
Toby Mundy Associates Ltd (*UK*)
TriadaUS Literary Agency, Inc. (*US*)
Trident Media Group, LLC (*US*)
Veritas Literary Agency (*US*)
Victoria Sanders & Associates LLC (*US*)
Westwood Creative Artists (*Can*)
Whispering Buffalo Literary Agency Ltd (*UK*)
William Morris Endeavor (WME) London (*UK*)
Wolfson Literary Agency (*US*)
Writers' Representatives, LLC (*US*)
Yates & Yates (*US*)
The Zack Company, Inc (*US*)
Zeno Agency Ltd (*UK*)
Helen Zimmermann Literary Agency (*US*)

Translations

Aaron M. Priest Literary Agency (*US*)
Andrew Lownie Literary Agency Ltd (*UK*)
Diana Finch Literary Agency (*US*)
Goodman Associates (*US*)
Joy Harris Literary Agency, Inc. (*US*)
Antony Harwood Limited (*UK*)
Intercontinental Literary Agency (*UK*)
J de S Associates Inc. (*US*)
Madeleine Milburn Literary, TV & Film Agency (*UK*)
Rocking Chair Books (*UK*)
The Swetky Agency and Associates (*US*)
Victoria Sanders & Associates LLC (*US*)
Wm Clark Associates (*US*)

Travel

B.J. Robbins Literary Agency (*US*)
Baldi Agency (*US*)
Betsy Amster Literary Enterprises (*US*)
Blake Friedmann Literary Agency Ltd (*UK*)
The Blumer Literary Agency, Inc. (*US*)
BookBlast Ltd. (*UK*)
Bresnick Weil Literary Agency, LLC (*US*)
Cine/Lit Representation (*US*)
Conville & Walsh Ltd (*UK*)
The Jennifer DeChiara Literary Agency (*US*)
Don Congdon Associates, Inc. (*US*)
Dunham Literary, Inc. (*US*)
Elise Dillsworth Agency (EDA) (*UK*)
Felicia Eth Literary Representation (*US*)
The Feldstein Agency (*UK*)
FinePrint Literary Management (*US*)
Fletcher & Company (*US*)
Foundry Literary + Media (*US*)
Frances Collin Literary Agent (*US*)
Sarah Jane Freymann Literary Agency (*US*)
Goodman Associates (*US*)
Greene & Heaton Ltd (*UK*)
Hannigan Salky Getzler (HSG) Agency (*US*)
Antony Harwood Limited (*UK*)
Jeanne Fredericks Literary Agency, Inc. (*US*)
Jill Grinberg Literary Management LLC (*US*)
Jill Grosjean Literary Agency (*US*)
Larsen Pomada Literary Agents (*US*)
Robert Lecker Agency (*Can*)
Levine Greenberg Rostan Literary Agency (*US*)
Limelight Management (*UK*)
The Literary Group International (*US*)
Kirsten Manges Literary Agency, LLC (*US*)
Marjacq Scripts Ltd (*UK*)
Duncan McAra (*UK*)
Margret McBride Literary Agency (*US*)
McIntosh & Otis, Inc (*US*)
MNLA (Maggie Noach Literary Agency) (*UK*)
Robert Dudley Agency (*UK*)
Rocking Chair Books (*UK*)
Rosica Colin Ltd (*UK*)
Salkind Literary Agency (*US*)
Sandra Dijkstra Literary Agency (*US*)
The Sayle Literary Agency (*UK*)
Susan Schulman, A Literary Agency (*US*)
The Science Factory (*UK*)
Sheil Land Associates Ltd (*UK*)
Sinclair-Stevenson (*UK*)
The Spieler Agency (*US*)
Philip G. Spitzer Literary Agency, Inc. (*US*)
Sterling Lord Literistic, Inc. (*US*)
The Swetky Agency and Associates (*US*)
Tessler Literary Agency (*US*)
Tracy Brown Literary Agency (*US*)
TriadaUS Literary Agency, Inc. (*US*)
Ed Victor Ltd (*UK*)
Watkins / Loomis Agency, Inc. (*US*)

TV

A & B Personal Management Ltd (*UK*)
Above the Line Agency (*US*)
Abrams Artists Agency (*US*)
Bret Adams Ltd (*US*)
Agency for the Performing Arts (APA) (*US*)
The Agency (London) Ltd (*UK*)

Alan Brodie Representation Ltd (*UK*)
Anonymous Content (*US*)
Berlin Associates (*UK*)
Blake Friedmann Literary Agency Ltd (*UK*)
Luigi Bonomi Associates Ltd (*UK*)
The Bright Literary Academy (*UK*)
Kelvin C. Bulger and Associates (*US*)
Cecily Ware Literary Agents (*UK*)
The Characters Talent Agency (*Can*)
Clare Hulton Literary Agency (*UK*)
Curtis Brown Group Ltd (*UK*)
DHH Literary Agency Ltd (*UK*)
The Dravis Agency, Inc. (*US*)
Elaine Steel (*UK*)
Energy Entertainment (*US*)
Felix de Wolfe (*UK*)
Film Rights Ltd in association with Laurence Fitch Ltd (*UK*)
Jill Foster Ltd (JFL) (*UK*)
Georgina Capel Associates Ltd (*UK*)
Eric Glass Ltd (*UK*)
Antony Harwood Limited (*UK*)
David Higham Associates Ltd (*UK*)
Valerie Hoskins Associates (*UK*)
Hudson Agency (*US*)
Independent Talent Group Ltd (*UK*)
Jane Turnbull (*UK*)
Janet Fillingham Associates (*UK*)
Jonathan Clowes Ltd (*UK*)
Michelle Kass Associates (*UK*)
Ken Sherman & Associates (*US*)
Ki Agency Ltd (*UK*)
Linda Seifert Management (*UK*)
Macnaughton Lord Representation (*UK*)
Madeleine Milburn Literary, TV & Film Agency (*UK*)
Marjacq Scripts Ltd (*UK*)
Mary Clemmey Literary Agency (*UK*)
MBA Literary Agents Ltd (*UK*)
Niad Management (*US*)
Paradigm Talent and Literary Agency (*US*)
PBJ and JBJ Management (*UK*)
Peregrine Whittlesey Agency (*US*)
The Peters Fraser & Dunlop Group Ltd (PFD) (*UK*)
Rochelle Stevens & Co. (*UK*)
Rosica Colin Ltd (*UK*)
Sayle Screen Ltd (*UK*)
Sheil Land Associates Ltd (*UK*)
Sheila Ableman Literary Agency (*UK*)
Stone Manners Salners Agency (*US*)
The Swetky Agency and Associates (*US*)
The Tennyson Agency (*UK*)
United Agents (*UK*)
William Morris Endeavor Entertainment (*US*)
The Zack Company, Inc (*US*)

Westerns

Alive Communications, Inc (*US*)
Andrew Lownie Literary Agency Ltd (*UK*)
The Characters Talent Agency (*Can*)
Richard Curtis Associates, Inc. (*US*)
Jim Donovan Literary (*US*)
Antony Harwood Limited (*UK*)
Hudson Agency (*US*)
Andrea Hurst Literary Management (*US*)
J de S Associates Inc. (*US*)
L. Perkins Associates (*US*)
Donald Maass Literary Agency (*US*)
Margret McBride Literary Agency (*US*)
Prospect Agency (*US*)
Raines & Raines (*US*)
Secret Agent Man (*US*)
The Swetky Agency and Associates (*US*)

Women's Interests

Aaron M. Priest Literary Agency (*US*)
The Ahearn Agency, Inc (*US*)
Alive Communications, Inc (*US*)
Ambassador Speakers Bureau & Literary Agency (*US*)
The Ampersand Agency Ltd (*UK*)
Ann Rittenberg Literary Agency (*US*)
Aponte Literary (*US*)
Arcadia (*US*)
The August Agency LLC (*US*)
The Axelrod Agency (*US*)
Ayesha Pande Literary (*US*)
Belcastro Agency (*US*)
Betsy Amster Literary Enterprises (*US*)
David Black Literary Agency (*US*)
Blake Friedmann Literary Agency Ltd (*UK*)
Bleecker Street Associates, Inc. (*US*)
The Blumer Literary Agency, Inc. (*US*)
Luigi Bonomi Associates Ltd (*UK*)
The Book Bureau Literary Agency (*Ire*)
BookEnds, LLC (*US*)
Barbara Braun Associates, Inc. (*US*)
Bresnick Weil Literary Agency, LLC (*US*)
The Bright Literary Academy (*UK*)
Marie Brown Associates, Inc. (*US*)
Browne & Miller Literary Associates (*US*)
Carol Mann Agency (*US*)
Caroline Sheldon Literary Agency (*UK*)
Chalberg & Sussman (*US*)
The Characters Talent Agency (*Can*)
Chartwell (*UK*)
Elyse Cheney Literary Associates, LLC (*US*)
Conville & Walsh Ltd (*UK*)
Coombs Moylett & Maclean Literary Agency (*UK*)
Creative Authors Ltd (*UK*)
Laura Dail Literary Agency (*US*)
The Darley Anderson Agency (*UK*)
Liza Dawson Associates (*US*)
The Jennifer DeChiara Literary Agency (*US*)
Joëlle Delbourgo Associates, Inc. (*US*)
DHH Literary Agency Ltd (*UK*)
Diane Banks Associates Literary Agency (*UK*)
Don Congdon Associates, Inc. (*US*)
Jim Donovan Literary (*US*)
Dunham Literary, Inc. (*US*)
Dunow, Carlson & Lerner Agency (*US*)
Dystel & Goderich Literary Management (*US*)
Judith Ehrlich Literary Management (*US*)
Einstein Literary Management (*US*)
Elaine P. English, Attorney & Literary Agent (*US*)

Felicia Eth Literary Representation (*US*)
Ethan Ellenberg Literary Agency (*US*)
The Feldstein Agency (*UK*)
Diana Finch Literary Agency (*US*)
FinePrint Literary Management (*US*)
Fletcher & Company (*US*)
Folio Literary Management, LLC (*US*)
Foundry Literary + Media (*US*)
Frances Collin Literary Agent (*US*)
Sarah Jane Freymann Literary Agency (*US*)
Fredrica S. Friedman and Co. Inc. (*US*)
Furniss Lawton (*UK*)
Gelfman Schneider / ICM Partners (*US*)
The Gernert Company (*US*)
Gina Maccoby Agency (*US*)
Goodman Associates (*US*)
Irene Goodman Literary Agency (*US*)
Grace Freedson's Publishing Network (*US*)
Kathryn Green Literary Agency, LLC (*US*)
Greyhaus Literary Agency (*US*)
Laura Gross Literary Agency (*US*)
Hannigan Salky Getzler (HSG) Agency (*US*)
Hardman & Swainson (*UK*)
Joy Harris Literary Agency, Inc. (*US*)
Antony Harwood Limited (*UK*)
A M Heath & Company Limited, Author's Agents (*UK*)
Hidden Value Group (*US*)
Hill Nadell Literary Agency (*US*)
Hopkins Literary Associates (*US*)
Kate Hordern Literary Agency (*UK*)
Andrea Hurst Literary Management (*US*)
International Transactions, Inc. (*US*)
Jane Rotrosen Agency (*US*)
Jeanne Fredericks Literary Agency, Inc. (*US*)
Jenny Brown Associates (*UK*)
Jill Grinberg Literary Management LLC (*US*)
Jill Grosjean Literary Agency (*US*)
Jo Unwin Literary Agency (*UK*)
The Joan Brandt Agency (*US*)
Johnson & Alcock (*UK*)
Juliet Burton Literary Agency (*UK*)
Keane Kataria Literary Agency (*UK*)
Virginia Kidd Agency, Inc (*US*)
Harvey Klinger, Inc (*US*)
Kneerim & Williams (*US*)
The Knight Agency (*US*)
Linda Konner Literary Agency (*US*)
Barbara S. Kouts, Literary Agent (*US*)
Edite Kroll Literary Agency, Inc. (*US*)
Laura Langlie, Literary Agent (*US*)
Larsen Pomada Literary Agents (*US*)
Levine Greenberg Rostan Literary Agency (*US*)
Limelight Management (*UK*)
Linda Roghaar Literary Agency, Inc. (*US*)
Linn Prentis, Literary Agent (*US*)
Lippincott Massie McQuilkin (*US*)
The Literary Group International (*US*)
Julia Lord Literary Management (*US*)
Lowenstein Associates, Inc. (*US*)
Donald Maass Literary Agency (*US*)
MacGregor Literary (*US*)
Madeleine Milburn Literary, TV & Film Agency (*UK*)
Kirsten Manges Literary Agency, LLC (*US*)
Manus & Associates Literary Agency, Inc. (*US*)
Maria Carvainis Agency, Inc. (*US*)
Marjacq Scripts Ltd (*UK*)
The Martell Agency (*US*)
Martin Literary Management (*US*)
Margret McBride Literary Agency (*US*)
McIntosh & Otis, Inc (*US*)
Martha Millard Literary Agency (*US*)
Howard Morhaim Literary Agency (*US*)
Mulcahy Associates (*UK*)
Judith Murdoch Literary Agency (*UK*)
Nappaland Literary Agency (*US*)
Nelson Literary Agency, LLC (*US*)
New Leaf Literary & Media, Inc. (*US*)
Northern Lights Literary Services (*US*)
P.S. Literary Agency (*Can*)
The Park Literary Group LLC (*US*)
Prospect Agency (*US*)
Lynne Rabinoff Agency (*US*)
Rebecca Friedman Literary Agency (*US*)
Rees Literary Agency (*US*)
Renee Zuckerbrot Literary Agency (*US*)
Richford Becklow Literary Agency (*UK*)
RLR Associates (*US*)
Robin Straus Agency, Inc. (*US*)
Rocking Chair Books (*UK*)
Rosica Colin Ltd (*UK*)
Salkind Literary Agency (*US*)
Sandra Dijkstra Literary Agency (*US*)
Sanford J. Greenburger Associates, Inc. (*US*)
Susan Schulman, A Literary Agency (*US*)
Scovil Galen Ghosh Literary Agency, Inc. (*US*)
Lynn Seligman, Literary Agent (*US*)
Sheil Land Associates Ltd (*UK*)
Sheree Bykofsky Associates, Inc. (*US*)
Dorie Simmonds Agency (*UK*)
The Spieler Agency (*US*)
Sterling Lord Literistic, Inc. (*US*)
The Swetky Agency and Associates (*US*)
SYLA – Susan Yearwood Literary Agency (*UK*)
Talcott Notch Literary (*US*)
Teresa Chris Literary Agency Ltd (*UK*)
Tessler Literary Agency (*US*)
Tracy Brown Literary Agency (*US*)
TriadaUS Literary Agency, Inc. (*US*)
Trident Media Group, LLC (*US*)
Veritas Literary Agency (*US*)
Victoria Sanders & Associates LLC (*US*)
Watson, Little Ltd (*UK*)
Waxman Leavell Literary Agency (*US*)
The Weingel-Fidel Agency (*US*)
Wendy Sherman Associates, Inc. (*US*)
Wolfson Literary Agency (*US*)
Writers House UK (*UK*)
Writers House, LLC (*US*)
Yates & Yates (*US*)
The Zack Company, Inc (*US*)
Zeno Agency Ltd (*UK*)
Helen Zimmermann Literary Agency (*US*)

US Publishers

For the most up-to-date listings of these and hundreds of other publishers, visit https://www.firstwriter.com/publishers

*To claim your **free** access to the site, please see the back of this book.*

Abdo Publishing Co

8000 W. 78th St.
Suite 310
Edina
MN 55439
Tel: +1 (800) 800-1312
Fax: +1 (952) 831-1632
Email: fiction@abdopublishing.com
Website: http://abdopublishing.com

Publishes: Fiction; Nonfiction; *Areas:* Anthropology; Arts; Biography; Cookery; Crafts; Culture; Current Affairs; Design; Entertainment; Historical; Hobbies; Medicine; Military; Politics; Religious; Science; Sociology; Sport; Technology; Travel; *Markets:* Children's

Contact: Paul Abdo

Publishes nonfiction, educational material for children up to the 12th grade, plus fiction series for children. Not accepting nonfiction submissions as at May 2017 (see website for current situation). Writers with a concept for a fiction series should send samples of manuscripts by email.

Abrams ComicArts

115 West 18th Street, 6th Floor
New York, NY 10011
Tel: +1 (212) 206-7715
Fax: +1 (212) 519-1210
Email: abrams@abramsbooks.com
Website: http://www.abramsbooks.com

Publishes: Fiction; Nonfiction; *Markets:* Adult; Children's

Contact: Abrams ComicArts Editorial

Publishes graphic novels, illustrated books, and nonfiction books about comics and comic history. Send submissions by post with SASE.

Academy Chicago

814 North Franklin Street
Chicago, Illinois 60610
Tel: +1 (312) 337-0747
Fax: +1 (312) 337-5110
Email: csherry@chicagoreviewpress.com
Website: http://www.chicagoreviewpress.com

Publishes: Fiction; Nonfiction; *Areas:* Autobiography; Mystery; *Markets:* Adult; *Treatments:* Contemporary; Mainstream

Contact: Cynthia Sherry

Send query by email with one-sentence description of your novel, a brief synopsis (a couple of paragraphs), word count, author bio, market info, and a few sample chapters. No mind/body/spirit, religion, diet/fitness/nutrition, family memoir, self-help, business, poetry, or photography.

ACTA Publications

4848 N. Clark Street
Chicago, IL 60640

Tel: +1 (800) 397-2282
Fax: +1 (800) 397-0079
Email: acta@actapublications.com
Website: http://www.actapublications.com

Publishes: Nonfiction; *Areas:* Religious; Self-Help; Spiritual; *Markets:* Adult

Send query with SASE, outline, table of contents, and one sample chapter. Publishes religious books, particularly Catholic, for a mainstream nonacademic audience. Do not submit unless you have read catalog or one of the books published by this company.

Ahsahta Press

Department of English
Boise State University
1910 University Drive
Boise, ID 83725-1525
Tel: +1 (208) 426-3134
Email: ahsahta@boisestate.edu
Website: http://ahsahtapress.org

Publishes: Poetry; *Markets:* Adult; *Treatments:* Literary

Contact: Janet Holmes

Submit poetry manuscripts between 50 and 100 pages long via online submissions system. Accepts open submissions during March each year only. Charges $5 per submission. Also runs poetry competitions at other times of the year.

Albert Whitman & Company

250 South Northwest Highway, Suite 320
Park Ridge, Illinois 60068
Tel: +1 (800) 255-7675
Fax: +1 (847) 581-0039
Email: submissions@albertwhitman.com
Website: http://www.albertwhitman.com

Publishes: Fiction; Nonfiction; *Markets:* Children's; Youth

Contact: Kathleen Tucker, Editor-in-Chief

Publishes picture books, middle-grade fiction, and young adult novels. Will consider fiction and nonfiction manuscripts for picture books for children ages 1 to 8, up to 1,000 words; fiction queries and sample pages for middle-grade novels up to 35,000 words for children up to the age of 12; and fiction queries and sample pages for young adult novels up to 70,000 words for ages 12-18. See website for full submission guidelines.

Algora Publishing

1732 1st Ave #20330
New York, NY 10128
Tel: +1 (212) 678-0232
Fax: +1 (212) 202-5488
Website: http://www.algora.com

Publishes: Nonfiction; *Areas:* Anthropology; Archaeology; Finance; Historical; Literature; Military; Music; Nature; Philosophy; Politics; Psychology; Religious; Science; Sociology; Translations; Women's Interests; *Markets:* Academic; Adult

Describes itself as an "academic-type press, publishing general nonfiction for the educated reader". Accepts proposal packages by post. An email query may optionally be sent prior to the proposal package. See website for full guidelines.

Alice James Books

114 Prescott Street
Farmington, ME 04938
Tel: +1 (207) 778-7071
Fax: +1 (207) 778-7766
Email: info@alicejamesbooks.org
Website: http://alicejamesbooks.org

Publishes: Poetry; *Markets:* Adult

Poetry press accepting submissions through its various competitions only. Competitions include large cash prizes and reasonable entry fees.

Allyn and Bacon / Merrill Education

445 Hutchinson Avenue
Columbus, OH 43235
Email: education.service@pearson.com
Website: http://www.allynbaconmerrill.com

Publishes: Nonfiction; *Markets:* Academic; Professional

Publishes books focused on the professional development of teachers, that effectively blend academic research and practical application for today's K-12 educators.

Alpine Publications, Inc.

38262 Linman Road
Crawford, CO 81415
Email: editorialdept@alpinepub.com
Website: http://www.alpinepub.com

Publishes: Nonfiction; *Areas:* Biography; Hobbies; Nature; *Markets:* Adult

Publishes books on dogs and horses. Welcomes submissions. Send query by post or by email with synopsis, chapter outline, author bio, market analysis, and 1-3 sample chapters.

Amakella Publishing

Arlington, VA
Email: info@amakella.com
Website: http://www.amakella.com

Publishes: Fiction; Nonfiction; *Areas:* Adventure; Anthropology; Biography; Business; Culture; Current Affairs; Historical; Hobbies; How-to; Leisure; Lifestyle; Literature; Media; Men's Interests; Nature; Psychology; Romance; Self-Help; Short Stories; Sociology; Spiritual; Travel; Women's Interests; *Markets:* Academic; Family; Professional; *Treatments:* Commercial; Contemporary; Literary; Mainstream; Niche; Popular; Positive; Progressive; Serious

An independent publisher currently particularly interested in publishing books in areas such as social sciences, international development, environmental conservation, and current affairs.

American Counseling Association

6101 Stevenson Avenue
Alexandria, VA 22304
Tel: +1 (703) 823-9800
Fax: +1 (703) 823-0252
Email: cbaker@counseling.org
Website: https://www.counseling.org

Publishes: Nonfiction; *Areas:* Health; *Markets:* Academic; Professional

Publishes books on mental health for the professional and academic markets.

American Psychiatric Association Publishing

1000 Wilson Boulevard, Suite 1825
Arlington, VA 22209
Tel: +1 (703) 907-7871
Email: hkoch@psych.org
Website: https://www.appi.org

Publishes: Nonfiction; *Areas:* Health; Psychology; Science; *Markets:* Academic; Adult; Professional

Contact: Heidi Koch (Editorial Support Services Manager)

Publishes books, journals, and multimedia on psychiatry, mental health and behavioral science, geared toward psychiatrists, other mental health professionals, psychiatric residents, medical students and the general public.

American Quilter's Society

5801 Kentucky Dam Road
Paducah, KY 42003-9323
Tel: +1 (270) 898-7903
Fax: +1 (270) 898-1173
Email: editor@aqsquilt.com
Website: http://www.americanquilter.com

Publishes: Fiction; Nonfiction; *Areas:* Crafts; Hobbies; How-to; Humour; Mystery; Romance; *Markets:* Adult

Publishes nonfiction and fiction related to quilts. Send proposal by post. See website for complete guidelines.

AMG Publishers

6815 Shallowford Road
Chattanooga, TN 37421
Tel: +1 (423) 894-6060 (ext. 275)
Fax: +1 (423) 894-9511
Email: ricks@amgpublishers.com
Website: http://www.amgpublishers.com

Publishes: Fiction; Nonfiction; Reference; *Areas:* Fantasy; Lifestyle; Politics; Religious; Spiritual; *Markets:* Adult

Contact: Rick Steele

Publishes biblically oriented books including: Biblical Reference, Applied Theology and Apologetics, Christian Ministry, Bible Study Books in the Following God series format, Christian Living, Women/Men/Family Issues, Single/Divorce Issues, Contemporary Issues, (unique) Devotionals, Inspirational, Prayer, and Gift books. Introducing young adult fiction titles. Send query letter by email or by post, including proposed page count, brief description of the proposed book, market info, and author details. See website for full guidelines.

Amira Press

Email: submissions@amirapress.com
Website: http://www.amirapress.com

Publishes: Fiction; *Areas:* Erotic; Fantasy; Historical; Horror; Romance; Sci-Fi; Suspense; Travel; Westerns; *Markets:* Adult; *Treatments:* Contemporary

Contact: Y. Lynn; Dahlia Rose

Small ebook publisher of erotic romance. Send complete ms by email. See website for more details.

Andrews McMeel Publishing

attn: Book Submissions
1130 Walnut Street
Kansas City, MO 64106
Tel: +1 (816) 581-8921
Website: http://www.andrewsmcmeel.com

Publishes: Fiction; Nonfiction; Poetry; *Areas:* Cookery; Humour; Lifestyle; *Markets:* Adult; Children's

Publishes humour, inspiration, middle grade children's books, and calendars. Will consider submissions via a literary agent or direct from authors, if submission guidelines on website are adhered to.

Ankerwycke

American Bar Association
321 North Clark Street
Chicago, IL 60654
Tel: +1 (312) 988-5000
Website: http://www.ababooks.org

Publishes: Fiction; Nonfiction; *Areas:* Crime; Legal; *Markets:* Adult; *Treatments:* Popular

Publishes books that bring law to the general public, including legal fiction, true crime, popular legal histories, handbooks, and guides.

Appalachian Mountain Club Books

5 Joy Street
Boston, MA 02108
Tel: +1 (617) 523-0636
Fax: +1 (617) 523-0722
Email: amcbooks@outdoors.org
Website: http://www.outdoors.org

Publishes: Nonfiction; *Areas:* Leisure; Nature; Travel; *Markets:* Adult

Publishes books for people interested in outdoor recreation, conservation, nature, and the outdoor world of the American north east in general.

Arbordale Publishing

612 Johnnie Dodds., Suite A2
Mount Pleasant, SC 29464
Email: katie@arbordalepublishing.com
Website: http://www.arbordalepublishing.com

Publishes: Fiction; Nonfiction; *Areas:* Science; *Markets:* Children's

Contact: Katie Hall, Associate Editor

Publishes picture books that aim to get children excited about science and maths. Publishes mainly fiction with nonfiction facts woven into the story, but will also consider nonfiction stories. Submit by email only. See website for full submission guidelines.

Arch Street Press

1429 South 9th Street
Philadelphia, PA 19147
Tel: +1 (877) 732-ARCH
Email: contact@archstreetpress.org
Website: http://archstreetpress.org

Publishes: Fiction; Nonfiction; *Areas:* Arts; Autobiography; Biography; Business;

Criticism; Culture; Finance; Historical; Legal; Literature; Music; Nature; Philosophy; Politics; Sociology; Spiritual; Translations; Women's Interests; *Markets:* Adult; *Treatments:* Contemporary; Literary

Independent nonprofit publisher dedicated to the collaborative work of creative visionaries, social entrepreneurs and leading scholars worldwide. Send query with SASE, outline, and three sample chapters.

Arrow Publications, LLC

20411 Sawgrass Drive
Montgomery Village, MD 20886
Tel: +1 (301) 299-9422
Fax: +1 (301) 632-8477
Email: arrow_info@arrowpub.com
Website: http://www.arrowpub.com

Publishes: Fiction; *Areas:* Adventure; Crime; Fantasy; Humour; Mystery; Romance; Suspense; Women's Interests; *Markets:* Adult

Contact: Tom King; Maryan Gibson

Publishes romance fiction and selective nonfiction, including women's interests. Also considers supernatural, mystery, crime and other genres if the story has a strong romance element. Send query by email with outline, word count, brief description, one chapter (usually the first), and promotional plan. See website for full guidelines.

Arthur A. Levine Books

557 Broadway
New York, NY 10012
Email: arthuralevinebooks@scholastic.com
Website: http://www.arthuralevinebooks.com

Publishes: Fiction; Nonfiction; *Markets:* Children's; Youth

Publishes books for children and young adults. Send query with full text (picture books), first two chapters and synopsis (novels), or ten sample pages (nonfiction), via online submission system. Monthly submission quota, so if submission system is not accepting submissions check back next month.

Asabi Publishing

Email: apsubmit@asabipublishing.com
Website: http://www.asabipublishing.com

Publishes: Fiction; Nonfiction; *Areas:* Autobiography; Biography; Crime; Culture; Erotic; Historical; Horror; Mystery; Thrillers; *Markets:* Adult; Children's; Youth

Check website for submission windows. Submit query by email or through form on website, with table of contents and three sample chapters. No religious or spiritual books of any kind.

ASCE Press

1801 Alexander Bell Drive
Reston, VA 20191
Tel: +1 (703) 295-6300
Email: ascepress@asce.org
Website: http://www.asce.org

Publishes: Nonfiction; *Areas:* Architecture; Design; Science; Technology; *Markets:* Professional

Publishes books for professional civil engineers. Send proposal by email or by post. See website for full submission guidelines.

Association for Supervision and Curriculum Development (ASCD)

1703 North Beauregard Street
Alexandria, VA 22311
Tel: +1 (703) 578-9600
Email: acquisitions@ascd.org
Website: http://www.ascd.org

Publishes: Nonfiction; *Markets:* Professional

Publishes books for educators. Continually searching for writers with new ideas, fresh voices, and diverse backgrounds. Submit via online submission system on website.

Astragal Press

5995 149th Street West, Suite 105
Apple Valley, MN 55124
Tel: +1 (866) 543-3045
Fax: +1 (800) 330-6232
Email: info@finneyco.com
Website: http://www.astragalpress.com

Publishes: Nonfiction; *Areas:* Antiques; Crafts; Historical; Science; Technology; *Markets:* Adult; *Treatments:* Niche

Send query with SASE, one-page overview, table of contents, introduction, at least three chapters, market info, and details of your background and qualifications. Publishes books for a niche market on subjects such as antique tools, early sciences, the history of the railroad, etc. See website for more details.

Augsburg Fortress

PO Box 1209
Minneapolis, MN 55440-1209
Tel: +1 (800) 328-4648
Fax: +1 (800) 722-7766
Website: https://www.augsburgfortress.org

Publishes: Fiction; Nonfiction; *Areas:* Culture; Historical; Lifestyle; Religious; *Markets:* Adult; Children's

Publishes bibles, adult nonfiction, and children's fiction for a Lutheran audience.

Avatar Press

515 N. Century Blvd,
Rantoul, IL 61866
Fax: +1 (217) 893-9671
Email: submissions@avatarpress.net
Website: http://www.avatarpress.com

Publishes: Fiction; *Markets:* Adult; Youth

Comic book publisher. Accepts submissions from artists, but no script-only submissions at this time. See website for current status and full submission guidelines.

The Backwater Press

3502 North 52nd Street
Omaha, NE 68104-3506
Tel: +1 (402) 451-4052
Email: thebackwaterspress@gmail.com
Website: http://thebackwaterspress.com

Publishes: Poetry; *Markets:* Adult; *Treatments:* Literary

Publishes poetry. Currently closed to general submissions, and is accepting work only through its poetry competition, for which there is a reading fee of $25. Submit online via website.

Baen Books

PO Box 1188
Wake Forest, NC 27588
Email: info@baen.com
Website: http://www.baen.com

Publishes: Fiction; *Areas:* Fantasy; Sci-Fi; *Markets:* Adult; *Treatments:* Contemporary

Publishes only science fiction and fantasy. Interested in science fiction with powerful plots and solid scientific and philosophical underpinnings. For fantasy, any magical system must be both rigorously coherent and integral to the plot. Work must at least strive for originality. Prefers manuscripts between 100,000 and 130,000 words. No submissions via mail or email. Full manuscripts can be submitted online, in rtf format, via an electronic submission system.

Bailiwick Press

309 East Mulberry Street
Fort Collins, Colorado 80524
Tel: +1 (970) 672-4878
Fax: +1 (970) 672-4731
Email: aldozelnick@gmail.com
Website: http://www.bailiwickpress.com

Publishes: Fiction; *Areas:* Humour; *Markets:* Children's; Youth

Publishes smart, funny, and layered writing for children and young adult. Looking for hysterically funny. Illustrated fiction is desired but not required. Approach through online form, where you will be required to submit the funniest part of your book, and display a knowledge of the publisher's existing work.

Baker Publishing Group

6030 East Fulton Road
Ada, MI 49301
Tel: +1 (616) 676-9185
Fax: +1 (616) 676-9573
Email: submissions@bakeracademic.com
Website: http://bakerpublishinggroup.com

Publishes: Nonfiction; *Areas:* Religious; *Markets:* Academic; Adult; Professional

Publishes Christian books. No unsolicited mss. Accepts approaches only through literary agent, writers' conferences, or third part manuscript submission services (see website for details).

Ball Publishing

622 Town Road
PO Box 1660
West Chicago, IL 60186
Tel: +1 (630) 231-3675
Fax: +1 (630) 231-5254
Email: cbeytes@ballpublishing.com
Website: http://www.ballpublishing.com

Publishes: Nonfiction; *Areas:* Gardening; *Markets:* Adult; Professional

Contact: Chris Beytes (Editor)

Send query describing book and its "hook" with SASE. Include your qualifications to write the book (possibly in the form of a CV), market overview (including details of competing books, and how your book is different and superior), details of contents (table of contents, word count, illustrations), estimated completion time, and two or three sample chapters. See website for full guidelines. Publishes books on gardening and horticulture for both professionals and home gardeners.

Barron's Educational Series, Inc.

250 Wireless Blvd
Hauppauge, NY 11788
Tel: +1 (800) 645-3476
Email: waynebarr@barronseduc.com
Website: http://www.barronseduc.com

Publishes: Fiction; Nonfiction; *Areas:* Arts; Beauty and Fashion; Business; Cookery; Crafts; Finance; Health; Hobbies; Legal; Lifestyle; New Age; Photography; Sport; Travel; *Markets:* Adult; Children's; Youth

Contact: Wayne Barr, Acquisitions Editor

Particularly interested in children and young adult fiction and nonfiction books, foreign language learning books, New Age books, cookbooks, business and financial advice books, parenting advice books, art instruction books, sports, fashion, crafts, and study guides. No poetry. Send query by email or by post with SASE (if return of materials required). Only queries accepted by email. See website for full guidelines.

Beacon Hill Press of Kansas City

PO Box 419527
Kansas City, MO 64141
Tel: +1 (816) 931-1900
Fax: +1 (816) 753-4071
Email: customerservice@beaconhillbooks.com
Website: http://beaconhillbooks.com

Publishes: Nonfiction; *Areas:* Religious; *Markets:* Adult

Publishes Wesleyan Christian books, Bible studies, and Bible commentaries. Send query by email.

Beacon Press

24 Farnsworth Street
Boston, MA 02210
Tel: +1 (617) 742-2110
Fax: +1 (617) 723-3097
Email: editorial@beacon.org
Website: http://www.beacon.org

Publishes: Nonfiction; *Areas:* Arts; Autobiography; Biography; Current Affairs; Historical; Lifestyle; Literature; Medicine; Nature; Politics; Religious; Science; Sociology; Women's Interests; *Markets:* Adult

Contact: Editorial Department

Publishes general trade nonfiction, in particular religion, history, current affairs, political science, gay/lesbian/gender studies, education, African-American studies, women's studies, child and family issues and nature and the environment. No poetry, fiction, or self-help books. Send query by email with 250-word description of your proposal. If interested, a full proposal will be requested within three weeks. Response not guaranteed.

BearManor Media

PO Box 71426
Albany, GA 31708

Tel: +1 (580) 252-3547
Fax: +1 (800) 332-8092
Email: books@benohmart.com
Website: http://www.bearmanormedia.com

Publishes: Fiction; Nonfiction; *Areas:* Autobiography; Biography; Film; Humour; Radio; TV; *Markets:* Adult

Contact: Ben Ohmart

Publisher of books on the past of TV, film, and radio. Particularly interested in books on voice actors and supporting actors. Also expanding ebook-only range to include such areas as fiction, humour, etc. Send query by email.

Belle Lutte Press

PO Box 49858
Austin, TX 78765
Email: Inquiries@BelleLutte.com
Website: http://bellelutte.com

Publishes: Fiction; *Markets:* Adult; *Treatments:* Literary

Publishes fiction. Send cover letter and up to 30 pages or three chapters of your work via online submission system.

BelleBooks

PO Box 300921
Memphis, TN 38130
Tel: +1 (901) 344-9024
Fax: +1 (901) 344-9068
Email: query@BelleBooks.com
Website: http://www.bellebooks.com

Publishes: Fiction; *Areas:* Fantasy; Historical; Horror; Mystery; Romance; Sci-Fi; Short Stories; Suspense; Thrillers; Women's Interests; *Markets:* Adult; Children's; Youth

Publishes women's fiction, cozy mysteries, well-researched civil war fiction, young adult fiction, urban fantasy and horror, young adult fantasy fiction, and fantasy. Send query by email with brief synopsis and credentials/credits. See website for full guidelines.

Bellevue Literary Press

Department of Medicine
NYU School of Medicine
550 First Avenue, OBV A612
New York, NY 10016
Tel: +1 (212) 263-7802
Email: blpsubmissions@gmail.com
Website: http://blpress.org

Publishes: Fiction; Nonfiction; *Markets:* Adult; *Treatments:* Literary

Contact: Erika Goldman, Publisher and Editorial Director

Publisher of literary fiction and narrative nonfiction. No poetry, single short stories, plays, screenplays, or self-help/instructional books. Send submissions by email. For fiction submissions, attach complete ms. For nonfiction, send complete ms or proposal. See website for full guidelines.

BenBella Books

10300 North Central Expy, Suite 530 Dallas, TX 75231
Tel: +1 (214) 750-3600
Email: glenn@benbellabooks.com
Website: http://www.benbellabooks.com

Publishes: Nonfiction; *Areas:* Autobiography; Biography; Business; Cookery; Culture; Health; Lifestyle; Politics; Science; Self-Help; Sociology; Sport; *Markets:* Adult; *Treatments:* Popular

Contact: Glenn Yeffeth

Marketing-focussed publishing house, publishing 30-40 titles a year. Actively acquiring strong nonfiction manuscripts. Send pitch of no more than a few pages describing your book, how it differs from others, your qualifications to write it, and explaining why you think the book will sell.

Bethany House Publishers

Baker Publishing Group
6030 East Fulton Road
Ada, MI 49301
Tel: +1 (616) 676-9185
Fax: +1 (616) 676-9573
Website: http://bakerpublishinggroup.com/bethanyhouse

Publishes: Fiction; Nonfiction; *Areas:* Fantasy; Historical; Mystery; Religious; Romance; Suspense; Women's Interests; *Markets:* Adult; Children's; Youth; *Treatments:* Contemporary; Literary

Publishes Christian fiction and nonfiction. No poetry, memoirs, picture books, Western, End-Times, Spiritual Warfare, or Chick-Lit. No unsolicited manuscripts, proposals or queries by mail, telephone, email, or fax. Approach through a literary agent, at a conference, or through an online manuscript service (see website for more details).

Bilingual Review Press

Hispanic Research Center
Arizona State University
PO Box 875303
Tempe, AZ 85287-5303
Email: brp@asu.edu
Website: http://bilingualpress.clas.asu.edu/

Publishes: Fiction; Nonfiction; Poetry; Scripts; *Areas:* Short Stories; Translations; *Markets:* Academic; Adult; *Treatments:* Literary; Serious

Contact: Gary Francisco Keller

Publishes hardcover and paperback originals and reprints on US Hispanic themes, including creative literature (novels, short story collections, poetry, drama, translations), scholarly monographs and edited compilations, and other nonfiction. Particularly interested in Chicano, Puerto Rican, Cuban American, and other US Hispanic themes with strong and serious literary qualities and distinctive and intellectually important topics. Send query by post with SASE and sample chapter or sample poems, plot summary / TOC, marketing info and brief bio. Accepts simultaneous submissions, but no electronic submissions. See website for full guidelines.

Black Lyon Publishing, LLC

PO Box 567
Baker City, OR 97814
Email: Queries@BlackLyonPublishing.com
Website: http://www.blacklyonpublishing.com

Publishes: Fiction; Nonfiction; *Areas:* Adventure; Historical; Romance; Self-Help; Women's Interests; *Markets:* Adult; *Treatments:* Contemporary; Literary

Small, independent publishing house, publishing mainly romance (contemporary, paranormal, historical, inspirational, adventure, literary, and novellas), as well as self-help. Send query by email. See website for full submission guidelines.

Black Ocean

Email: carrie@blackocean.org
Website: http://www.blackocean.org

Publishes: Poetry; Translations; *Markets:* Adult; *Treatments:* Literary

Contact: Carrie O. Adams (Poetry Editor)

Publishes new poetry, and out-of-print or translated texts. Reading period runs from June 1 to June 30 each year. During reading period, submit via link on website.

Black Rose Writing

PO Box 1540
Castroville, TX 78009
Email: creator@blackrosewriting.com
Website: http://www.blackrosewriting.com

Publishes: Fiction; Nonfiction; *Markets:* Adult; Children's

Accepts all fiction and nonfiction for adults. Accepts children's books with full illustrations only. No poetry or short story collections. Submit via online submission system.

BlazeVOX [books]

Email: editor@blazevox.org
Website: http://www.blazevox.org

Publishes: Fiction; Nonfiction; Poetry; *Areas:* Criticism; Literature; Short Stories; *Markets:* Adult; *Treatments:* Experimental; Literary

Contact: Geoffrey Gatza

Publishes poetry, short stories, experimental fiction, literary criticism (including companions, studies and histories).

Blue Light Press

1563 – 45th Avenue
San Francisco, CA 94122
Email: bluelightpress@aol.com
Website: http://www.bluelightpress.com

Publishes: Poetry; *Markets:* Adult; *Treatments:* Literary

Contact: Diane Frank

Co-operative press run by a collective of poets and artists. Publishes chapbooks with print runs of 50-200 and full-length books that are printed on demand. Committed to the publication of poetry which is "imagistic, inventive, emotionally honest, and pushes the language to a deeper level of insight". Relies on poets to actively promote their books.

Blue River Press

2402 N. Shadeland Ave., Ste. A
Indianapolis, IN 46219
Tel: +1 (317) 352-8200
Fax: +1 (317) 352-8200
Email: proposals@brpressbooks.com
Website: http://www.brpressbooks.com

Publishes: Nonfiction; *Areas:* Culture; Health; Sport; Travel; *Markets:* Adult; *Treatments:* Popular

Publishes nonfiction for a general or specialised audience. Interested in both series products and stand-alone books. Seeks knowledgeable authors with a passion for their subject and a willingness to promote their ideas and books. Send proposals by email.

BLVNP Incorporated

Email: info@blvnp.com
Website: http://www.blvnp.com

Publishes: Fiction; *Areas:* Fantasy; Humour; Literature; Mystery; Romance; Sci-Fi; Self-Help; Short Stories; *Markets:* Adult; Family; Youth; *Treatments:* Contemporary; Light; Positive

So here's what we do:

When a book is getting published it is read by our team of Grammar Nazis/Ninjas (they're both) who will literally cut out any misspelled words and grammar errors (it was really hard on laptop screens until we got them touch screens and padded swords).

Once the author approves the edits, our team of Graphic Ninjas meditate and visualize deep into the cosmic group mind and create eye-catching covers, ready to blind an innocent book reader.

Our Marketing Ninjas step in to make sure that the book would be seen by the people who want your book for and make sure they buy it!

Of course being ninjas we have grown quickly with thousands of books and now magazines.

Honestly, we love this. It is so much more fun than killing people in their sleep. Of course killing monsters (especially gorgons) is still pretty fun. Look behind the scenes in some of the team photos, and you will see a bit of gorgon blood.

Plus, we all love being with one another. We're all fun, crazy, and we patch ourselves up whenever someone hits someone else with their sword accidentally.

BookFish Books

Email: bookfishbooks@gmail.com
Website: http://www.bookfishbooks.com

Publishes: Fiction; *Markets:* Adult; Children's; Youth

Publishes novels and novellas for middle grade, young adult, and new adult, in all subgenres. Novels should be between 40,000 and 80,000 words, and novellas between 20,000 and 35,000 words. Send query by email with synopsis up to two pages and first three chapters as Word attachment. See website for full guidelines.

Boyds Mills Press

815 Church Street
Honesdale, Pennsylvania 18431
Tel: +1 (570) 253-1164
Email: marketing@boydsmillspress.com
Website: http://www.boydsmillspress.com

Publishes: Fiction; Nonfiction; Poetry; *Markets:* Children's

Publishes a range of books for children, from pre-school to young adult, including fiction, nonfiction, and poetry. Send query with SASE, synopsis, and three sample chapters for middle grade fiction, or complete ms for picture books and collections of poetry.

Bucknell University Press

Bucknell University, One Dent Drive, Lewisburg, PA 17837
Tel: +1 (570) 577-3674
Email: clingham@bucknell.edu
Website: http://www.bucknell.edu/universitypress

Publishes: Nonfiction; *Areas:* Anthropology; Architecture; Arts; Criticism; Culture; Historical; Legal; Literature; Medicine; Philosophy; Politics; Psychology; Religious; Science; Sociology; *Markets:* Academic

Contact: Greg Clingham

Publishes scholarship in the humanities and social sciences, particularly literary criticism, Modern Languages, Classics, theory, cultural studies, historiography (including the history of law, of medicine, and of science), philosophy, psychology and psychoanalysis, religion, political science, cultural and political geography, and interdisciplinary combinations of the above. Send proposal by post or by email.

Butte Publications, Inc.

PO Box 1328
Hillsboro, OR 97123-1328
Tel: +1 (503) 648-9791
Email: service@buttepublications.com
Website: http://www.buttepublications.com

Publishes: Nonfiction; *Markets:* Academic; Professional

Publishes special educational resources. All titles must be useful to Deaf and Hard of Hearing, Speech and Hearing, Special Education, English as a Second Language, or Early Intervention and Early Childhood. See website for submission guidelines.

Capstone Professional

Capstone Nonfiction
1710 Roe Crest Drive
North Mankato, MN 56003
Tel: +1 (312) 324-5200
Fax: +1 (312) 324-5201
Email: info@maupinhouse.com
Website: http://www.capstonepub.com/classroom/professional-development/

Publishes: Nonfiction; *Markets:* Academic; Professional

Publishes books for teaching professionals, written by classroom practitioners with vast experiences. Send query by US mail only, with cover letter, CV, and up to three writing samples.

CATO Institute

1000 Massachusetts Ave, NW
Washington, DC 20001-5403
Tel: +1 (202) 842 0200
Website: http://www.cato.org

Publishes: Nonfiction; *Areas:* Philosophy; Politics; Sociology; *Markets:* Adult

Public policy think tank promoting individual liberty, limited government, free markets and peace. Send query by post with SASE.

Cave Books

277 Clamer Road
Trenton, NJ 08628
Tel: +1 (609) 530-9743
Email: editor@cavebooks.com
Website: http://www.cavebooks.com

Publishes: Fiction; Nonfiction; *Areas:* Adventure; Anthropology; Archaeology; Biography; Historical; Leisure; Nature; Photography; Science; Sport; Travel; *Markets: Treatments:* Literary; Serious

Contact: Elizabeth Winkler

!! Books about caves ONLY!!

Small press devoted to books on caves, karst, and speleology.

Fiction: novels about cave exploration only. Publishes hardcover and trade paperback originals and reprints.

Books: acid-free paper, offset printing.

Published two debut authors within the last year.

Needs: Adventure, historical, literary, caves, karst, speleology.

How to Contact: Accepts unsolicited mss. Query with SASE or submit complete ms. Accepts queries by email. Send SASE for return of ms or send a disposable ms and SASE for reply only. Responds in 2 weeks to queries; 3 months to mss. Accepts simultaneous submissions, electronic submissions.

Sometimes comments on rejected mss.

Terms: Pays 10% royalty on retail price.

Publishes ms 18 months after acceptance.

Advice: "In the last three years we have received only three novels about caves, and we have published one of them. We get dozens of inappropriate submissions."

Cave Hollow Press

PO Drawer J
Warrensburg, MO 64093
Email: gbcrump@cavehollowpress.com
Website: http://www.cavehollowpress.com

Publishes: Fiction; *Markets:* Adult; *Treatments:* Mainstream

Contact: Georgia R. Nagel; R.M. Kinder

Note: Not accepting new material as at April 2016

Actively seeking mainstream novels between 60,000 and 80,000 words by authors from Missouri, the Midwest, and surrounding regions. Send query with SASE, 1-3 page synopsis, and first three chapters or 30-40 pages of the completed MS.

Chelsea Green Publishing, Inc.

85 North Main Street, Suite 120
White River Junction, VT 05001
Tel: +1 (802) 295-6300
Fax: +1 (802) 295-6444
Email: web@chelseagreen.com
Website: http://www.chelseagreen.com

Publishes: Nonfiction; *Areas:* Cookery; Finance; Gardening; How-to; Lifestyle; Nature; New Age; Politics; Science; Spiritual; *Markets:* Academic; Adult; Professional

Publishes books on organic gardening and market farming, from home to professional scale, and related topics, including renewable energy, food politics, and alternative economic models. Will only occasionally publish academic, new age, or spiritual, and does not publish fiction, poetry, or books for children. See website for submission guidelines.

Children's Brains are Yummy (CBAY) Books

PO Box 670296
Dallas, TX 75367
Email: madeline@cbaybooks.com
Website: http://cbaybooks.com

Publishes: Fiction; *Areas:* Adventure; Fantasy; Mystery; Sci-Fi; Short Stories; Suspense; *Markets:* Children's; Youth

Contact: Madeline Smoot

Publishes fiction for children. Closed to approaches for chapter books, midgrade or YA novels as at September 2015, but open to anthology submissions of short fiction. See website for details.

Cinco Puntos Press

701 Texas Avenue
El Paso, Texas 79901
Tel: +1 (915) 838-1625
Fax: +1 (915) 838-1635
Email: info@cincopuntos.com
Website: http://www.cincopuntos.com

Publishes: Fiction; Nonfiction; Poetry; *Markets:* Adult; Children's; Youth

Contact: Lee Byrd, Acquisitions Editor,

Small independent publishing company, publishing fiction, poetry, nonfiction and graphic novels for adults, young adults, and children. Review books on website to see if yours is a fit, and if so query Acquisitions Editor by phone. See website for more details.

Cleveland State University Poetry Center

2121 Euclid Avenue
Rhodes Tower, Room 1841
Cleveland, OH 44115
Email: poetrycenter@csuohio.edu
Website: http://www.csupoetrycenter.com

Publishes: Poetry; *Markets:* Adult

Most books published are received through competitions run by the press, for which there is an entry fee. Also publishes books solicited from authors, but no unsolicited mss, other than via the competitions or for occasional anthologies (see website).

Concordia Publishing House

3558 S. Jefferson
St. Louis, MO 63118-3968
Tel: +1 (314) 268-1000
Fax: +1 (800) 490 9889
Email: ideas@cph.org
Website: http://www.cph.org

Publishes: Nonfiction; *Areas:* Culture; Lifestyle; Religious; Spiritual; *Markets:* Adult; Children's; Family; Youth

No Christian fiction, autobiographies, poetry, or children's picture books. Send query by email.

Covenant Communications Inc.

920 E State Road
American Fork, UT 84003
Tel: +1 (801) 756-1041
Fax: +1 (801) 756-1049
Email: submissionsdesk@covenant-lds.com
Website: http://www.covenant-lds.com

Publishes: Fiction; Nonfiction; Reference; *Areas:* Adventure; Biography; Historical; Humour; Mystery; Religious; Romance; Spiritual; Suspense; *Markets:* Academic; Adult; Children's; Family; Youth; *Treatments:* Contemporary; Literary; Mainstream

Only publishes work that supports the doctrines and / or values of The Church of Jesus Christ of Latter-day Saints. Books should be original and well written, appeal to a broad readership, be consistent with the standards and principles of the restored gospel of Jesus Christ, and promote the faith of members of the Church and inspire them to lead better lives. Not generally interested in poetry, family histories, or personal journals. Send complete MS by email or by post. See website for full submission guidelines.

CQ Press

2455 Teller Road
Thousand Oaks, CA 91320
Tel: +1 (800) 818-7243
Fax: +1 (800) 583-2665
Email: michael.kerns@sagepub.com
Website: http://www.cqpress.com

Publishes: Nonfiction; Reference; *Areas:* Historical; Politics; *Markets:* Academic; Adult; Professional

Contact: Michael Kerns

Publishes books on American and international politics and people, including academic text books on political science, directories on governments, elections, etc. See website for full submission guidelines and individual Acquisition Editor contact details.

Creative With Words (CWW)

PO Box 223226
Carmel, CA 93922
Fax: +1 (831) 655-8627
Email: geltrich@mbay.net
Website: http://creativewithwords.tripod.com

Publishes: Fiction; Poetry; *Areas:* Short Stories; *Markets:* Adult; Children's; Family; Youth

Contact: Brigitta Geltrich

Publishes themed anthologies of fiction and prose by adults and children. See website for details.

Creston Books

PO Box 9369
Berkeley, CA 94709
Email: submissions@crestonbooks.co
Website: http://crestonbooks.co

Publishes: Fiction; *Markets:* Children's

Publishes novels and picture books for children. Send query by email with full text (for picture books) or first chapters (novels) pasted into the body of the email. Accepts multiple submissions, but no more than one project per month from the same author.

Cricket Books

70 East Lake Street, Suite 300
Chicago, IL 60601
Tel: +1 (603) 924-7209
Fax: +1 (603) 924-7380
Website: http://www.cricketmag.com

Publishes: Fiction; *Areas:* Adventure; Fantasy; Historical; Horror; Mystery; Sci-Fi; Sport; Suspense; Westerns; *Markets:* Children's; Youth

Publishes books for children from 6 months to teenagers 14+.

Crimson Romance

Email: editorcrimson@gmail.com
Website: http://www.crimsonromance.com

Publishes: Fiction; *Areas:* Historical; Romance; Suspense; *Markets:* Adult; *Treatments:* Contemporary

Digital-first romance publisher open to submissions in five sub-genres: romantic suspense, contemporary, paranormal, historical, and spicy romance. Willing to consider novels between 55,000 words and 90,000 words, and novellas between 20,000 and 50,000 words. See website for full submission guidelines and specific submission calls.

Crystal Spirit Publishing, Inc.

PO Box 12506
Durham, NC 27709
Email: submissions@crystalspiritinc.com
Website: http://www.crystalspiritinc.com

Publishes: Fiction; Nonfiction; Poetry; Adventure; Business; Erotic; Religious; Romance; Self-Help; Short Stories; *Markets:* Adult; Children's

Send query by post with SASE or by email, with synopsis and 30-page sample. Will not consider one-page proposals or full mss. No historical novels, science fiction, fantasy, westerns, horror, plays, scientific or technical reference, or books intended as textbooks. See website for full details.

Curiosity Quills Press

PO Box 2160
Reston, VA 20195
Tel: +1 (800) 998-2509
Email: info@curiosityquills.com
Website: https://curiosityquills.com

Publishes: Fiction; *Areas:* Crime; Fantasy; Horror; Mystery; Romance; Thrillers; Women's Interests; *Markets:* Adult; Children's; Youth; *Treatments:* Contemporary; Dark

Publishes hard-hitting dark sci-fi, speculative fiction, and paranormal works aimed at adults, young adults, and new adults. Send query with first three chapters using online submission form.

Dark Horse Comics

10956 SE Main Street
Milwaukie, OR 97222
Email: prose@darkhorse.com
Website: http://www.darkhorse.com

Publishes: Fiction; *Areas:* Fantasy; Horror; *Markets:* Adult; Youth; *Treatments:* Dark

Publishes comics and prose books in the genres of horror, dark fantasy, and other genres tangential to or overlapping those. Targets adult and young adult markets. Send query by post with CV, synopsis, and up to three sample chapters (up to about 10,000 words). See website for full submission guidelines.

Darkhouse Books

Email: submissions@darkhousebooks.com
Website: http://darkhousebooks.com

Publishes: Fiction; *Areas:* Crime; Mystery; Short Stories; *Markets:* Adult

Publishes crime and mystery novels and anthologies. See website for current calls for submissions.

David R. Godine, Publisher

Fifteen Court Square, Suite 320
Boston, MA 02108-2536
Tel: +1 (617) 451-9600
Fax: +1 (617) 350-0250
Email: info@godine.com
Website: http://www.godine.com

Publishes: Fiction; Nonfiction; Poetry; *Areas:* Architecture; Arts; Biography; Criticism; Gardening; Historical; Humour; Literature; Nature; Photography; Translations; *Markets:* Adult; *Treatments:* Literary

Recommends writers make approaches via agents. Any unsolicited material received without return postage will be disposed of. No telephone calls or email submissions.

Dawn Publications

12402 Bitney Springs Road
Nevada City, CA 95959
Tel: +1 (530) 274-7775
Fax: +1 (530) 274-7778
Email: submission@dawnpub.com
Website: http://www.dawnpub.com

Publishes: Nonfiction; *Areas:* Nature; *Markets:* Adult; Children's

Contact: Glenn Hovemann, Editor & Co-Publisher

Publisher of nature awareness titles for adults and children. Send complete MS by email or by post with SASE, with description of your work, including: audience age; previous publications (if any); your motivation; relevant background. No response to postal submissions without SASE.

Divertir Publishing LLC

PO Box 232
North Salem, NH 03073
Email: query@divertirpublishing.com
Website: http://divertirpublishing.com

Publishes: Fiction; Nonfiction; Poetry; *Areas:* Crafts; Current Affairs; Fantasy; Historical; Hobbies; Humour; Mystery; Politics; Religious; Romance; Sci-Fi; Self-Help; Short Stories; Spiritual; Suspense; *Markets:* Adult; Youth; *Treatments:* Contemporary; Satirical

Publishes full-length fiction, short fiction, poetry, and nonfiction. No erotica or material which is disrespectful to the opinions of others. Accepts queries and submissions by email only. See website for full guidelines.

Dreamriver Press

19 Grace Court, Apt.2D
Brooklyn, NY 11201
Tel: +1 (215) 253-4621
Email: info@dreamriverpress.com
Website: http://www.dreamriverpress.com

Publishes: Fiction; Nonfiction; *Areas:* Adventure; Anthropology; Arts; Autobiography; Biography; Cookery; Crafts; Culture; Current Affairs; Drama; Gardening; Health; Historical; How-to; Lifestyle; Literature; Medicine; Nature; New Age; Philosophy; Politics; Psychology; Religious; Science; Self-Help; Sociology; Spiritual; Technology; *Markets:* Adult; Family; Youth; *Treatments:* Light; Literary; Positive; Progressive

Contact: Theodore Poulis

Closed to submissions as at September 2016. Check website for current situation.

An independent publishing house that aims to print books in the fields of mind-body-spirit and spirituality, holistic health, environment and sustainable living, as well as inspirational fables for all age groups.

We prefer to receive submission inquiries by email. Queries can include a synopsis of the work, the first three chapters as well as a short bio of the writer.

Please visit our web site for further information.

Duquesne University Press

600 Forbes Avenue
Pittsburgh, PA 15282
Tel: +1 (800) 666-2211
Email: wadsworth@duq.edu
Website: http://www.dupress.duq.edu

Publishes: Nonfiction; *Areas:* Literature; Philosophy; Psychology; Religious; Sociology; Spiritual; *Markets:* Academic

Contact: Susan Wadsworth-Booth, Director

Publishes monographs and collections in the humanities and social sciences, particularly literature studies (Medieval and Renaissance), philosophy, psychology, religious studies and theology, plus spirituality. No fiction, poetry, children's books, technical or "hard" science works, or unrevised theses or dissertations. Send query with outline, table of contents, sample chapter or introduction, author CV, and details of any previous publications. Submit by post (with SASE if return of material required) or by email (in the body of the email only – no attachments).

Eagle's View Publishing

6756 North Fork Road
Liberty, UT 84310
Tel: +1 (801) 393-4555
Email: sales@eaglefeathertrading.com
Website: http://www.eaglesviewpub.com

Publishes: Nonfiction; *Areas:* Anthropology; Archaeology; Crafts; Culture; Historical; Hobbies; How-to; *Markets:* Adult

Contact: Denise Knight

Publishes books on Native American crafts, history, and culture. Send outline with one or two sample chapters.

Edward Elgar Publishing Inc.

The William Pratt House
9 Dewey Court
Northampton, MA 01060-3815
Tel: +1 (413) 584-5551
Fax: +1 (413) 584-9933
Email: elgarinfo@e-elgar.com
Website: http://www.e-elgar.com

Publishes: Nonfiction; *Areas:* Business; Finance; Legal; Sociology; Travel; *Markets:* Academic; Professional

Contact: Alan Sturmer; Stephen Gutierrez

International academic and professional publisher with a strong focus on the social sciences and legal fields. Actively commissioning new titles and happy to consider and advise on ideas for monograph books, textbooks, professional law books and academic journals at any stage. See website for more details and proposal forms.

Ellysian Press

Email: submissions@ellysianpress.com
Website: http://www.ellysianpress.com

Publishes: Fiction; *Areas:* Fantasy; Horror; Romance; Sci-Fi; *Markets:* Adult; Youth

Publishes novels between 60,000 and 120,000 words. Send query by email with synopsis and first ten pages in the body of the email. See website for full guidelines.

Entangled Teen

Website: http://www.entangledteen.com

Publishes: Fiction; *Areas:* Fantasy; Historical; Romance; Sci-Fi; Thrillers; *Markets:* Youth; *Treatments:* Contemporary

Publishes young adult romances between 50,000 and 100,000 words, aimed at ages 16-19. Submit via website using online submission system.

FalconGuides

246 Goose Lane
Guilford, CT 06357
Tel: +1 (203) 458-4500
Email: info@rowman.com
Website: http://www.falcon.com

Publishes: Nonfiction; *Areas:* Adventure; Nature; Travel; *Markets:* Adult

Publishes outdoor guidebooks covering hiking, climbing, paddling, and outdoor adventure.

Familius

1254 Commerce Way
Sanger, CA 93657
Tel: +1 (559) 876-2170
Fax: +1 (559) 876-2180
Email: bookideas@familius.com
Website: http://familius.com

Publishes: Fiction; Nonfiction; *Areas:* Autobiography; Cookery; Finance; Health; Hobbies; Humour; Lifestyle; Medicine; Self-Help; *Markets:* Adult; Children's; Youth

Publishes fiction and nonfiction for adults, young adults, and children, focussed on family as the fundamental unit of society. Submit by post or using online submission system. See website for full details.

Fantagraphics

7563 Lake City Way NE
Seattle, WA 98115
Tel: +1 (206) 524-1967
Fax: +1 (206) 524-2104
Email: FBIComix@fantagraphics.com
Website: http://www.fantagraphics.com

Publishes: Fiction; *Areas:* Arts; Autobiography; Culture; Humour; *Markets:* Adult; *Treatments:* Literary

Publishes comics for thinking readers. Previous work has covered autobiographical journalism, surrealism, arts, culture, etc. No mainstream comic genres or material aimed at children. Submit by post only. No response unless interested. See website for full guidelines.

Farrar, Straus and Giroux Books for Younger Readers

175 Fifth Avenue
New York, NY 10010
Email: childrens.editorial@fsgbooks.com
Website: http://us.macmillan.com/publishers/farrar-straus-giroux#FYR

Publishes: Fiction; Nonfiction; *Markets:* Children's; Youth

Publishes fiction, nonfiction, and picture books for children and teenagers. Send query by post only with first 50 pages.

Ferguson Publishing

132 West 31st Street, 17th Floor
New York, NY 10001
Tel: +1 (800) 322-8755
Fax: +1 (800) 678-3633
Email: editorial@factsonfile.com
Website: http://ferguson.infobasepublishing.com

Publishes: Nonfiction; Reference; *Areas:* How-to; Lifestyle; Self-Help; *Markets:* Academic; Adult; Children's; Professional; Youth

Publishes career education books aimed at the middle school, high school, and public library markets. Send query or outline with one sample chapter. See website for full submission guidelines.

Finney Company

5995 149th Street West, Suite 105
Apple Valley, MN 55124
Tel: +1 (952) 469-6699
Fax: +1 (952) 469-1968
Email: info@finneyco.com
Website: http://www.finneyco.com

Publishes: Nonfiction; *Areas:* Arts; Crafts; Culture; Gardening; Historical; Leisure; Nature; Science; Sport; Technology; Travel; *Markets:* Adult; Children's

Independent publisher, distributor, and manufacturer of educational materials. No mysteries, romances, science fiction, poems, collections of short stories, religious material, or recipe/cookbooks. Send query outlining your MS and background with SASE, one-page outline, table of contents, at least the first three chapters, and market info. No submissions by email. See website for full guidelines.

Floating Bridge Press

909 NE 43rd Street, #205
Seattle, WA 98105
Email: floatingbridgepress@yahoo.com
Website: http://www.floatingbridgepress.org

Publishes: Poetry; *Markets:* Adult

Publishes books of poetry by Washington State poets. All submissions must be made through the annual competition, entry fee: $12. Submit online.

Folded Word LLC

Attn: Barbara Flaherty, Submissions Editor
79 Tracy Way
Meredith, NH 03253
Website: https://folded.wordpress.com

Publishes: Fiction; Nonfiction; Poetry; *Areas:* Humour; Literature; Nature; Translations; Travel; *Markets:* Adult; *Treatments:* Literary

Publishes fiction, poetry, literary essays, travel narratives, translation, and novels in verse / flash. Only accepting queries for chapbook-length manuscripts as at March 2016. Check website for current status. Send query by post only, with cover letter, three sample pages, and SASE (writers outside the US may omit the stamp). See website for full guidelines.

Fonthill Media LLC

60 Thoreau Street #204
Concord, MA 01742

UK OFFICE:
Millview House
Toadsmoor Road
Stroud
Gloucestershire
GL5 2TB
Email: submissions@fonthillmedia.com
Website: http://fonthillmedia.com

Publishes: Nonfiction; *Areas:* Archaeology; Biography; Historical; Military; Sociology; Sport; Travel; *Markets:* Adult

Independent publisher with offices in the UK and US. Publishes nonfiction only. Send query through website submissions form or by email, providing your project's title, description up to 200 words, description of yourself up to 100 words, proposed word count, and nature and number of illustrations.

Fordham University Press

2546 Belmont Avenue
University Box L
Bronx, NY 10458
Tel: +1 (718) 817-4795
Fax: +1 (718) 817-4785
Email: tlay@fordham.edu
Website: http://fordhampress.com

Publishes: Nonfiction; *Areas:* Anthropology; Architecture; Arts; Biography; Business; Culture; Finance; Historical; Legal; Literature; Media; Medicine; Music; Philosophy; Photography; Politics; Religious; Science; Sociology; Women's Interests; *Markets:* Academic; Adult

Contact: Tom Lay, Acquisitions Editor

Publishes scholarly books in the humanities and social sciences, as well as trade books of interest to the general public. Particularly interested in philosophy, religion, theology, literature, history, media studies, and books of both scholarly and general appeal about New York City and the Hudson Valley. Send proposal by post only (see website for list of appropriate contacts for different subjects). No fiction, or submissions by email.

4th Level Indie

Email: 4thlevelindie@gmail.com
Website: http://www.4thlevelindie.com

Publishes: Nonfiction; *Areas:* Crafts; Hobbies; *Markets:* Adult

Small publisher publishing 1-2 books a year on alternative crafts and hobbies.

FutureCycle Press

Email: dkistner@gmail.com
Website: http://www.futurecycle.org

Publishes: Poetry; *Markets:* Adult

Publishes contemporary English language poetry books and chapbooks. Submit via website through online submission system. $15 reading fee.

Gallaudet University Press

800 Florida Avenue, NE
Washington, DC 20002
Email: ivey.wallace@gallaudet.edu
Website: http://gupress.gallaudet.edu

Publishes: Nonfiction; *Areas:* Biography; Culture; Historical; Literature; Psychology; Sociology; *Markets:* Academic; Adult

Contact: Ivey Pittle Wallace

Publishes books about deaf and hard of hearing people, their languages, their communities, their history, and their education. Publishes scholarly and trade books in fields such as biography by and about deaf adults, culture, deaf studies, disability studies, education, history, interpretation, linguistics, literary works by deaf authors, psychology, sign language, and sociology. See website for full guidelines.

Genealogical Publishing Company

3600 Clipper Mill Road, Suite 260
Baltimore, Maryland 21211
Tel: +1 (410) 837-8271
Fax: +1 (410) 752-8492
Email: info@genealogical.com
Website: http://www.genealogical.com

Publishes: Nonfiction; *Areas:* Historical; Hobbies; How-to; *Markets:* Adult

Publishes books for amateur genealogists.

Golden West Books

PO Box 80250
San Marino, CA 91118-8250
Tel: +1 (626) 458-8148
Fax: +1 (626) 458-8148
Website: http://www.goldenwestbooks.com

Publishes: Nonfiction; *Areas:* Historical; Travel; *Markets:* Adult

Publishes books on railroad history. Send query via online form on website in first instance.

Goosebottom Books LLC

543 Trinidad Lane
Foster City, CA 94404
Tel: +1 (800) 788-3123
Fax: +1 (888) 407-5286
Email: submissions@goosebottombooks.com
Website: http://goosebottombooks.com

Publishes: Fiction; Nonfiction; *Areas:* Adventure; Historical; *Markets:* Children's; Youth

Publishes books for children and young adults, including fiction and nonfiction, particularly historical. All work is commissioned. Send writing samples if you would like to be considered as a writer for future projects.

Grayson Books

Email: gconnors@graysonbooks.com
Website: http://www.graysonbooks.com

Publishes: Poetry; *Markets:* Adult

Small poetry publisher, publishing a few books each year. Send query by email with Word document attachment with a sample of 6-10 poems.

Greenhaven Publishing

Attn: Publisher – Greenhaven Press
27500 Drake Rd.
Farmington Hills, MI 48331
Tel: +1 (800) 877-4253
Website: http://www.gale.cengage.com/greenhaven

Publishes: Nonfiction; Reference; *Areas:* Arts; Current Affairs; Health; Historical; Literature; Medicine; Music; Nature; Politics; Science; Sociology; *Markets:* Academic

Publishes young adult academic reference titles. No submissions of mss, but will hire writers to produce material. Send query by email with CV and list of published works by email.

Gryphon House, Inc.

PO Box 10
Lewisville, NC 27023
Tel: +1 (800) 638-0928
Fax: +1 (877) 638-7576
Email: info@ghbooks.com
Website: http://www.gryphonhouse.com

Publishes: Nonfiction; *Areas:* How-to; *Markets:* Adult; Children's; Professional

Publishes books intended to help teachers and parents enrich the lives of children from birth to age eight. See website for proposal submission guidelines.

Hachai Publishing

527 Empire Boulevard
Brooklyn, NY 11225
Tel: +1 (718) 633-0100
Fax: +1 (718) 633-0103
Email: editor@hachai.com
Website: http://hachai.com

Publishes: Fiction; Nonfiction; *Areas:* Historical; Religious; *Markets:* Children's

Publishes children's fiction and nonfiction relating to the Jewish experience. No animal stories, romance, violence, preachy sermonising, or elements that violate Jewish Law. See website for full submission guidelines.

Hanser Publications

6915 Valley Avenue
Cincinnati, OH 45244-3029
Tel: +1 (800) 950-8977
Fax: +1 (513) 527-8801
Email: info@hanserpublications.com
Website: http://www.hanserpublications.com

Publishes: Nonfiction; Reference; *Areas:* Business; Science; Technology; *Markets:* Academic; Professional

Publisher of plastics technology and metalworking titles for manufacturers and educators. Send query with proposal, CV, and brief writing sample.

Harken Media

Seattle, WA
Email: hmeditors@gmail.com
Website: http://www.harkenmedia.com

Publishes: Fiction; *Areas:* Fantasy; Historical; Humour; Mystery; Sci-Fi; *Markets:* Adult; Youth; *Treatments:* Literary

Publishes books with unique insights or compelling themes for young adult, new adult, and adult audiences. Send query by email only. See website for full guidelines.

Harlequin American Romance

PO Box 5190
Buffalo, NY 14240-5190
Email: submisssions@harlequin.com
Website: http://www.harlequin.com

Publishes: Fiction; *Areas:* Romance; Westerns; *Markets: Treatments:* Contemporary

Contact: Kathleen Scheibling

Publishes heart-warming contemporary romances featuring small town America and cowboys, up to 55,000 words. See website for more details and to submit.

Harmony Ink Press

5032 Capital Circle SW, Ste 2 PMB 279
Tallahassee, FL 32305-7886
Tel: +1 (800) 970-3759
Fax: +1 (888) 308-3739
Email: submissions@harmonyinkpress.com
Website: https://www.harmonyinkpress.com

Publishes: Fiction; *Areas:* Fantasy; Mystery; Romance; Sci-Fi; *Markets:* Youth

Publishes Teen and New Adult fiction featuring significant personal growth of unforgettable characters across the LGBTQ+ spectrum. Closed to general submissions as at May 2016.

Hartman Publishing, Inc.

1313 Iron Ave SW
Albuquerque, NM 87102
Tel: +1 (800) 999-9534
Fax: +1 (800) 474-6106
Email: info@hartmanonline.com
Website: http://www.hartmanonline.com

Publishes: Nonfiction; *Areas:* Health; *Markets:* Professional

Contact: Susan Alvare

Provides in-service education materials for health professionals delivering long-term care, plus textbooks for training nursing assistants and home health aides. See website for more details, and online query form or PDF query form to return by post.

Health Communications, Inc.

3201 S.W. 15th Street
Deerfield Beach, Florida 33442
Tel: +1 (954) 360-0909
Fax: +1 (954) 360-0034
Email: Editorial@hcibooks.com
Website: http://www.hcibooks.com

Publishes: Nonfiction; *Areas:* Autobiography; Biography; Cookery; Health; How-to; Lifestyle; Medicine; Men's Interests; Psychology; Religious; Self-Help; Spiritual; Women's Interests; *Markets:* Adult; Youth; *Treatments:* Contemporary; Popular; Positive

Contact: Editorial Committee

Life issues publisher, publishing books on self improvement, personal health and development, recovery, etc. Authors should be experts in the field or write from experience. Books should be affirming, readable, and offer positive long-term life-changing solutions. See website for full requirements and proposal guidelines.

Helicon Nine Editions

PO Box 22412
Kansas City, MO 64113
Tel: +1 (816) 753-1095
Fax: +1 (816) 753-1016
Email: helicon9@aol.com
Website: http://www.heliconnine.com

Publishes: Fiction; Poetry; *Areas:* Short Stories; *Markets:* Adult; *Treatments:* Literary

Independent small, literary publisher, publishing books, chapbooks, and magazines of poetry and fiction.

Hendrickson Publishers

PO Box 3473
Peabody, MA 01961-3473
Tel: +1 (978) 532-6546
Fax: +1 (978) 573-8111
Email: editorial@hendrickson.com
Website: http://www.hendrickson.com

Publishes: Nonfiction; Reference; *Areas:* Religious; *Markets:* Academic; Adult

Christian publisher. Publishes bibles and academic, trade, and reference books. Accepts approaches only from literary agents or through conferences.

Heyday Books

PO Box 9145
Berkeley, CA 94709
Tel: +1 (510) 549-3564
Fax: +1 (510) 549-1889
Email: heyday@heydaybooks.com
Website: http://www.heydaybooks.com

Publishes: Fiction; Nonfiction; Poetry; *Areas:* Arts; Culture; Historical; Literature; Nature; *Markets:* Adult; Children's; *Treatments:* Literary

Small publisher of natural and cultural history, literature, and arts, concentrating on California and the West. Consult website to see if your book is appropriate, then send query by post with author details, outline, table of contents and list of illustrations, market details, sample chapter, and SASE. Submissions for children's books may be sent by email. See website for full details.

Hipso Media

8151 East 29th Avenue
Denver, CO 80238
Email: rob@hipsomedia.com
Website: http://www.hipsomedia.com

Publishes: Fiction; Nonfiction; *Areas:* Cookery; Culture; Erotic; Health; How-to; Humour; Lifestyle; Medicine; Mystery; Self-Help; Short Stories; Travel; *Markets:* Adult; Youth

Contact: Rob Simon, Publisher

Digital-first publisher. Particularly keen on work that lends itself to media enhancements such as illustrations, videos, music, sound effects, animations, hyperlinks, etc. Send query by email with synopsis and author bio. See website for full guidelines.

Hohm Press

PO Box 4410
Chino Valley, AZ 86323
Tel: +1 (800) 381-2700
Fax: +1 (928) 636-7519

Email: publisher@hohmpress.com
Website: http://www.hohmpress.com

Publishes: Nonfiction; *Areas:* Arts; Health; Lifestyle; Literature; Nature; Religious; Women's Interests; *Markets:* Adult

Publishes books that provide readers with alternatives to the materialistic values of the current culture and promote self-awareness, the recognition of interdependence and compassion. Send query by post with small sample.

Holiday House, Inc.

425 Madison Ave
New York, NY 10017
Tel: +1 (212) 688-0085
Fax: +1 (212) 421-6134
Email: info@holidayhouse.com
Website: http://www.holidayhouse.com

Publishes: Fiction; Nonfiction; *Markets:* Children's; Youth

Contact: Editorial Department

Independent publisher of children's books, from picture books to young adult fiction and nonfiction. Send complete ms by post only. No need to include SASE. No submissions by fax or email.

Humanix Books

Tel: +1 (855) 371-7810
Email: sherries@humanixbooks.com
Website: http://www.humanixbooks.com

Publishes: Nonfiction; *Areas:* Autobiography; Business; Finance; Health; Historical; Politics; Science; *Markets:* Adult

Contact: Sherrie Slopianka

Publishes books for independent thinkers from acclaimed experts in health and wellness, finance and investing, and politics and history.

ICS Publications

ICS Editorial
11041 Broken Woods Drive
Miamisburg, OH 45342
Email: editor@icspublications.org
Website: http://www.icspublications.org

Publishes: Nonfiction; *Areas:* Historical; Religious; Spiritual; Translations; *Markets:* Adult

Publishes books in the field of Carmelite spirituality, particularly Carmelite saints and related topics.

Illusio & Baqer

Email: submissions@zharmae.com
Website: https://illusiobaqer.com

Publishes: Fiction; *Markets:* Children's; Youth

Contact: T Denise Clary; Emily Stanford; Cynthia Kumancik

Publishes Young Adult, New Adult, and Middle Grade. Always on the lookout for new, dynamic, and fresh voices. Send query by email with word count, brief author bio (100-200 words), one-page synopsis, and first 3-5 chapters. See website for full guidelines.

Image Comics

Submissions
c/o Image Comics
2001 Center Street, Sixth Floor
Berkeley, CA 94704
Email: submissions@imagecomics.com
Website: http://www.imagecomics.com

Publishes: Fiction; *Markets:* Adult; Youth

Third largest comic book publisher in the United States. Publishes comics and graphic novels. Only interested in creator-owned comics. Does not acquire any rights. Looking for comics that are well written and well drawn, by people who are dedicated and can meet deadlines, not any specific genre or type of comic book. See website for full submission guidelines.

Incentive Publications

2400 Crestmoor Road
Nashville, TN 37215
Tel: +1 (800) 967-5325
Email: incentive@worldbook.com
Website: http://incentivepublications.com

Publishes: Nonfiction; *Markets:* Academic; Children's; Professional

Publishes supplemental resources for student use and instruction and classroom management improvement materials for teachers. Always looking for talented authors and illustrators with a love of entertaining and educating children. Send manuscripts by email.

Interlink Publishing Group, Inc.

46 Crosby Street
Northampton, MA 01060
Tel: +1 (413) 582 7054
Fax: +1 (413) 582 7057
Email: info@interlinkbooks.com
Website: http://www.interlinkbooks.com

Publishes: Fiction; Nonfiction; Reference; *Areas:* Arts; Cookery; Film; Historical; Leisure; Literature; Music; Photography; Politics; Sport; Translations; Travel; *Markets:* Adult; Children's

Research the types of books published by reading examples first. If you think your work is suitable, send query by email. In fiction, only publishes work by authors born outside the US, bringing it to the American audience. All children's books are aimed at ages between three and eight, and are illustrated. Manuscripts that do not have illustrations already included are not considered.

Publishes fiction, travel, Children's, politics, cookbooks, and specialises in Middle East titles and ethnicity. No poetry, plays, unsolicited MSS, or queries by fax or email. See website for full guidelines.

International Wealth Success (IWS) Inc.

24 Canterbury Road
Rockville Centre, NY 11570
Tel: +1 (516) 766-5850
Fax: +1 (516) 766-5919
Email: admin@iwsmoney.com
Website: http://www.iwsmoney.com

Publishes: Nonfiction; *Areas:* Business; Finance; How-to; Self-Help; *Markets:* Adult

Publishes books that help people become more independent and wealthy through real estate and small businesses.

Italica Press

595 Main Street, Suite 605
New York, NY 10044
Tel: +1 (917) 371-0563
Email: inquiries@ItalicaPress.com
Website: http://www.italicapress.com

Publishes: Fiction; Nonfiction; Poetry; Scripts; *Areas:* Arts; Drama; Historical; Translations; Travel; *Markets:* Adult

Publishes English translations of medieval, Renaissance and early-modern texts, historical travel, English translations of modern Italian fiction, dual-language poetry, drama, and a series of studies in art and history. Welcomes submissions and enquiries regarding possible projects in these areas. See website for full guidelines.

Jolly Fish Press

PO Box 1773
Provo, UT 84603-1773
Email: submit@jollyfishpress.com
Website: http://www.jollyfishpress.com

Publishes: Fiction; *Areas:* Autobiography; Biography; Fantasy; Historical; Horror; Humour; Mystery; Sci-Fi; Self-Help; Suspense; Thrillers; *Markets:* Adult; Children's; Youth; *Treatments:* Commercial; Literary

Accepts submissions by email only. For fiction, send one-page query, one-page synopsis, and first three chapters, in the body of your email. For nonfiction, send one-page query and book proposal. No attachments. No children's picture books, novellas, gift books, poetry, or religious books. See website for full details.

Judaica Press

Tel: +1 (718) 972-6200
Email: submissions@judaicapress.com
Website: https://www.judaicapress.com

Publishes: Fiction; Nonfiction; *Areas:* Biography; Historical; Religious; Self-Help;

Short Stories; *Markets:* Adult; Children's; Family; Youth

Publishes books for a varied audience, that conform to Torah-observant Jewish values. Send complete ms by email as Word, DavkaWriter, RTF, or PDF files, with cover letter and author contact details. See website for full details.

Kaeden Books

PO Box 16190
Rocky River, OH 44116
Email: sales@kaeden.com
Website: http://www.kaeden.com

Publishes: Fiction; Nonfiction; *Areas:* Science; *Markets:* Academic; Children's

Publishes reading materials for primary teachers to use with children in their first years of the reading experience.

Kansas City Star Quilts

C&T Publishing
1651 Challenge Drive
Concord, CA 94520
Email: roxanec@ctpub.com
Website: http://www.kansascitystarquilts.com

Publishes: Nonfiction; *Areas:* Crafts; Hobbies; *Markets:* Adult

Contact: Roxane Cerda

Publishes quilt books.

Kar-Ben Publishing

1251 Washington Ave N
Minneapolis, MN 55401
Tel: +1 (800) 452-7236
Email: editorial@karben.com
Website: http://www.karben.com

Publishes: Fiction; Nonfiction; *Areas:* Religious; *Markets:* Children's; Family

Publishes fiction and nonfiction on Jewish themes for children and families. No adult, young adult, games, textbooks, or books in Hebrew. Send submissions by email and allow 6-8 weeks for reply.

Kathy Dawson Books

Penguin Group
375 Hudson Street
New York, NY 10014
Website: http://kathydawsonbooks.tumblr.com

Publishes: Fiction; *Markets:* Children's; Youth

Publishes middle grade and young adult fiction. Submit query by post only, with first 10 pages and details of any relevant publishing history. Do not include SASE – all submissions are recycled. Response only if interested.

Lee & Low Books

95 Madison Avenue, suite 1205
New York, NY 10016
Tel: +1 (212) 779-4400
Fax: +1 (212) 532-6035
Email: general@leeandlow.com
Website: http://www.leeandlow.com

Publishes: Fiction; Nonfiction; *Areas:* Culture; *Markets:* Children's; *Treatments:* Positive

Contact: Submissions Editor

Publisher of multicultural books featuring people of colour, aimed at ages 5 to 12. For picture books submit complete MS, but do not include artwork unless you are a professional illustrator. Fiction picture books should be no more than 1,500 words, while nonfiction picture books should be no more than 3,000 words. For middlegrade MSS more than 10,000 words send query with short synopsis and chapter outline (do not send complete MS). All submissions must include SASE. No folklore or animal stories.

Leisure Arts, Inc.

104 Champs Boulevard, Suite 100
Maumelle, AR 72113
Tel: +1 (800) 643-8030
Email: submissions@leisurearts.com
Website: http://www.leisurearts.com

Publishes: Nonfiction; *Areas:* Crafts; Hobbies; How-to; Lifestyle; *Markets:* Adult

Publisher of lifestyle and instructional craft publications. Publishes books and leaflets in virtually all craft categories. Send photographs, swatches, sketches, outlines, charts, artwork by post or by email, but do not send actual designs or instructions unless requested. See website for full details.

LexisNexis

230 Park Avenue, Suite 7
New York, NY 10169
Tel: +1 (212) 309-8100
Fax: +1 (800) 437-8674
Website: http://www.lexisnexis.com

Publishes: Nonfiction; Reference; *Areas:* Legal; *Markets:* Professional

Publishes books and online materials for the professional legal market.

Limitless Publishing

Email: submissions@limitlesspublishing.com
Website: http://www.limitlesspublishing.net

Publishes: Fiction; Nonfiction; *Areas:* Military; Mystery; Romance; Suspense; Thrillers; *Markets:* Adult; Youth

Send submissions by email with brief bio, writing background and publishing history, social networks used, decsription of your book, and the first four chapters as a Microsoft Word attachment.

Little Pickle Press, Inc.

3701 Sacramento Street #494
San Francisco, CA 94118
Tel: +1 (800) 788-3123
Email: info@littlepicklepress.com
Website: http://www.littlepicklepress.com

Publishes: Fiction; Nonfiction; *Markets:* Children's; Youth

Publishes books that foster kindness in young people. Submit via website through online submission system.

Livingston Press

University of West Alabama
100 North Washington Street, Station 22
University of West Alabama
Livingston, AL 35470
Email: jwt@uwa.edu
Website: http://www.livingstonpress.uwa.edu

Publishes: Fiction; *Areas:* Short Stories; *Markets:* Adult; *Treatments:* Contemporary; Literary; Progressive

Publishes off-beat (as opposed to mainstream) and southern literature; both novels and short story collections (but strong preference given to novels, as short story collections are generally published through annual short story contest). Send query by post with SASE and about 30 pages of work in June only.

Lonely Planet Publications

150 Linden Street
Oakland, CA 94607
Tel: +1 (510) 250-6400
Fax: +1 (510) 893-8572
Email: info@lonelyplanet.com
Website: http://www.lonelyplanet.com

Publishes: Nonfiction; Reference; *Areas:* Travel; *Markets:* Adult

Publisher of travel guides and other travel-related material.

LSU Press

338 Johnston Hall
Louisiana State University
Baton Rouge, LA 70803
Tel: +1 (225) 578-6294
Email: mkc@lsu.edu
Website: http://lsupress.org

Publishes: Fiction; Nonfiction; Poetry; *Areas:* Archaeology; Culture; Historical; Literature; Media; Military; Music; Nature; *Markets:* Academic; Adult; *Treatments:* Literary

Academic publisher publishing scholarly monographs and general interest books about Louisiana and the South. Approach by post only. Send query with CV and proposal for nonfiction; one-page summary and brief sample for fiction; and 4-5 sample pages for poetry. See website for full details.

The Lyons Press Inc.

The Globe Pequot Press, Inc.
Box 480
246 Goose Lane
Guilford, CT 06437
Tel: +1 (203) 458-4500
Fax: +1 (203) 458-4668
Email: info@globepequot.com
Website: http://www.lyonspress.com

Publishes: Nonfiction; Reference; *Areas:* Autobiography; Cookery; Culture; Current Affairs; Historical; Nature; Sport; *Markets:* Adult; *Treatments:* Popular

Publishes history, current affairs, popular culture, memoir, sports, cooking, nature, pets, fishing, hunting, reference and equestrian books. Not accepting submissions or proposals as at January 2015. Check website for current situation.

M P Publishing USA

Email: mark@mpassociates.co.uk
Website: http://mppublishingusa.com

Publishes: Fiction; Nonfiction; *Areas:* Adventure; Crime; Fantasy; Gothic; Literature; Mystery; Romance; Sci-Fi; Short Stories; Suspense; Thrillers; Women's Interests; *Markets:* Adult; Youth; *Treatments:* Commercial; Contemporary; Dark; Experimental; In-depth; Light; Literary; Mainstream; Niche; Popular; Progressive; Satirical; Serious; Traditional

Contact: Mark Pearce

Publishes fiction and nonfiction. Not accepting submissions for print publication or American distribution as at March 2015. Submitters should have bought or borrowed one of the publisher's books prior to submitting. Accepts submissions by post, but prefers electronic submissions via form on website.

Mage Publishers

1780 Crossroads Drive
Odenton, MD 21113
Tel: +1 (202) 342-1642
Fax: +1 (202) 342-9269
Email: as@mage.com
Website: http://www.mage.com

Publishes: Fiction; Nonfiction; Poetry; *Areas:* Anthropology; Archaeology; Architecture; Arts; Autobiography; Biography; Cookery; Culture; Historical; Literature; Music; Short Stories; Translations; *Markets:* Adult; Children's; *Treatments:* Contemporary; Literary; Mainstream

Contact: Amin Sepehri

Publishes English language books about Persian culture, including nonfiction, cookbooks, translations of literature, history, children's tales, biography and autobiography, architectural studies, and books on music and poetry. Send query by email with brief biographical statement.

Maven House Press

4 Snead Court
Palmyra, VA 22963
Tel: +1 (610) 883-7988
Email: jim@mavenhousepress.com
Website: http://mavenhousepress.com

Publishes: Nonfiction; *Areas:* Business; *Markets:* Professional

Publishes business books for executives and managers to help them lead their organisations to greatness. Download proposal form from website and submit proposal by email. See website for full submission guidelines.

McFarland & Company, Inc.

Box 611
Jefferson, NC 28640
Tel: +1 (336) 246-4460
Fax: +1 (336) 246-5018
Email: info@mcfarlandpub.com
Website: http://www.mcfarlandpub.com

Publishes: Nonfiction; Reference; *Areas:* Architecture; Arts; Culture; Current Affairs; Film; Health; Historical; Leisure; Literature; Medicine; Military; Music; Sport; Women's Interests; *Markets:* Adult

Publishes Pop Culture, Sports, Military History, Transportation, Body amp; Mind, History, Literature, Medieval Studies, and Graphic Novels. Send query with SASE, outline, and sample chapters. No fiction, poetry, or children's.

Melange Books, LLC

Email: submissions-nancy@melange-books.com
Website: http://www.melange-books.com

Publishes: Fiction; *Areas:* Erotic; Romance; Short Stories; *Markets:* Adult; Youth; *Treatments:* Mainstream

Contact: Nancy Schumacher

Publishes mainstream general fiction, romance, and erotica. Send first three chapters or complete short story if under 15,000 words, as RFT file by email. See website for full guidelines.

Metal Powder Industries Federation (MPIF)

105 College Road East
Princeton, NJ 08540
Tel: +1 (609) 452-7700
Fax: +1 (609) 987-8523
Email: info@mpif.org
Website: http://www.mpif.org

Publishes: Nonfiction; *Areas:* Technology; *Markets:* Professional

Publishes books on powder metallurgy and particulate materials.

Mitchell Lane Publishers, Inc.

PO Box 196
Hockessin, DE 19707
Tel: +1 (302) 234-9426
Fax: +1 (302) 234-4742
Email: customerservice@mitchelllane.com
Website: http://www.mitchelllane.com

Publishes: Nonfiction; *Areas:* Arts; Biography; Crafts; Health; Historical; Literature; Music; Politics; Science; Technology; *Markets:* Children's

Publishes nonfiction for children. No unsolicited mss. Send query by post with SASE.

Museum of Northern Arizona

3101 North Fort Valley Road
Flagstaff, AZ 86001
Tel: +1 (928) 774-5213
Email: publications@mna.mus.az.us
Website: http://musnaz.org

Publishes: Nonfiction; *Areas:* Historical; Nature; *Markets:* Adult

Publishes natural history relating to Northern Arizona.

New Directions Publishing

80 Eighth Avenue
New York, NY 10011
Email: editorial@ndbooks.com
Website: http://www.ndbooks.com

Publishes: Fiction; Poetry; *Areas:* Historical; Humour; Short Stories; Suspense; Translations; *Markets:* Adult; *Treatments:* Experimental; Literary

Literary publisher of poetry and fiction. Unable to accept unsolicited mss, but will make an effort to answer all brief queries.

New York University (NYU) Press

838 Broadway, 3rd Floor
New York, NY 10003-4812
Email: information@nyupress.org
Website: http://nyupress.org

Publishes: Nonfiction; *Areas:* Anthropology; Crime; Culture; Historical; Legal; Literature; Media; Politics; Psychology; Religious; Sociology; Women's Interests; *Markets:* Academic

Publishes mainly for the academic market. Send proposals by post only. See website for full guidelines.

Nightboat Books

PO Box 10
Callicoon, NY 12723
Email: info@nightboat.org
Website: http://nightboat.org

Publishes: Fiction; Nonfiction; Poetry; *Areas:* Translations; *Markets:* Adult; *Treatments:* Literary

Publishes poetry, fiction, essay, intergenre, and translations. Currently only accepting submissions for poetry, and then only through its annual poetry competition (closes in November; $28 entry fee), open to poetry manuscripts between 60 and 90 pages. For status on prose and translation submissions check website after start of 2017.

Nolo

950 Parker Street
Berkeley, CA 94710
Tel: +1 (510) 549-1976
Fax: +1 (510) 859-0025
Email: mantha@nolo.com
Website: http://www.nolo.com

Publishes: Nonfiction; Reference; *Areas:* Business; Finance; How-to; Legal; Self-Help; *Markets:* Adult; Professional

Publishes books that help individuals, small businesses, and other organisations handle their own legal matters.Send query with SASE, outline, and sample chapter.

Nomad Press

2456 Christian Street
White River Junction, VT 05001
Email: info@nomadpress.net
Website: http://nomadpress.net

Publishes: Nonfiction; *Areas:* Historical; Science; Sociology; *Markets:* Academic; Children's

Publishes educational activity books for children exploring the science and history behind a wide variety of topics, using hands-on projects to provide experiential education. Send query by post or by email. No unsolicited mss.

NursesBooks

American Nurses Association
8515 Georgia Avenue, Suite 400
Silver Spring, MD 20910-3492
Tel: +1 (800) 637-0323
Email: joseph.vallina@ana.org
Website: http://www.nursesbooks.org

Publishes: Nonfiction; *Areas:* Health; *Markets:* Professional

Publishes books for nurses. Send proposal, saved as a Word file, by email.

Oak Knoll Press

310 Delaware Street
New Castle, DE 19720
Tel: +1 (302) 328-7232
Email: publishing@oakknoll.com
Website: http://www.oakknoll.com

Publishes: Nonfiction; *Areas:* Antiques; Historical; Literature; *Markets:* Academic

Contact: Robert Fleck

Publishes academic titles about printed books: book selling; book collecting; typography; antique books; book binding; etc.

Oceanview Publishing

CEO Center at Mediterranean Plaza
595 Bay Isles Road, Suite 120-G
Longboat Key, FL 34228
Tel: +1 (941) 387-8500
Email: submissions@oceanviewpub.com
Website: http://oceanviewpub.com

Publishes: Fiction; *Areas:* Mystery; Thrillers; *Markets:* Adult

Publishes adult fiction, with a primary interest in the mystery/thriller genre. No children's or young adult literature, poetry, memoirs, cookbooks, technical manuals, or short stories. Accepts submissions only from authors who either have a literary agent; have been previously published by a traditional publishing house; or have been specifically invited to submit by a representative or author of the publishing house. See website for more details.

Oregon State University Press

Oregon State University Press
121 The Valley Library, Room 3733
Corvallis, OR 97331-4501
Tel: +1 (541) 737-3873
Fax: +1 (541) 737-3170
Email: mary.braun@oregonstate.edu
Website: http://osupress.oregonstate.edu

Publishes: Nonfiction; *Areas:* Biography; Culture; Historical; Literature; Nature; Science; *Markets:* Academic

Published academic books of importance to the Pacific Northwest, particularly those dealing with the history, natural history, cultures, and literature of the region. Send query by post. No unsolicited mss or queries by phone or email. See website for full guidelines.

The Overmountain Press

PO Box 1261
Johnson City, TN 37605
Tel: +1 (423) 926-2691
Fax: +1 (423) 232-1252
Email: submissions@overmtn.com
Website: http://overmtn.com

Publishes: Fiction; Nonfiction; *Areas:* Cookery; Historical; Travel; *Markets:* Adult; Children's; Youth

Contact: Beth Wright (Publisher); Daniel Lewis (Managing Editor)

Primarily a publisher of Southern Appalachian nonfiction. Publishes fiction in the form of picture books for children only. Publishes nonfiction for children and adults, including histories, cookery, guidebooks, ghost lore and folk lore. No email submissions.

O'Reilly Media

1005 Gravenstein Hwy N
Sebastopol, CA 95472
Tel: +1 (707) 827-7019
Fax: +1 (707) 824-8268
Email: workwithus@oreilly.com
Website: http://www.oreilly.com

Publishes: Nonfiction; *Areas:* Business; Design; Health; Photography; Science; Self-Help; Technology; *Markets:* Adult

Publishes informative books written by smart people, for smart people, on topics such as technology, programming, business, health, etc. Send query or proposal by email.

Page Street Publishing Co.

27 Congress Street, Suite 103
Salem, MA 01970
Tel: +1 (978) 594-8758
Email: submissions@pagestreetpublishing.com
Website: http://www.pagestreetpublishing.com

Publishes: Fiction; Nonfiction; *Areas:* Cookery; Crafts; Design; Fantasy; Historical; Lifestyle; Mystery; Nature; Science; Sport; *Markets:* Adult; Youth; *Treatments:* Literary

Publishes nonfiction and young adult fiction. Send query by email, stating "YA" or "NONFICTION" in the subject line, and "AGENTED" if being submitted by a literary agent. For fiction, include 1-2 page query with synopsis and bio. Fiction should be 60-90,000 words with a protagonist aged 15-18. For nonfiction, send one-page synopsis with writing sample and details of any media exposure. See website for full guidelines.

Paladin Press

5540 Central Avenue, Suite 200
Boulder, CO 80301
Tel: +1 (303) 443-7250
Fax: +1 (303) 442-8741
Email: editorial@paladin-press.com
Website: http://www.paladin-press.com

Publishes: Nonfiction; *Areas:* Historical; How-to; Military; Politics; Technology; *Markets:* Adult

Publishes books and videos on personal freedom, survival and preparedness, firearms and shooting, martial arts and self-defense, military and police tactics, knives and knife fighting, etc. Send outline with one or two sample chapters or complete MS.

Paragon House

3600 Labore Road, Suite 1
St Paul, Minnesota 55110-4144
Tel: +1 (651) 644-3087
Fax: +1 (651) 644-0997
Email: submissions@paragonhouse.com
Website: http://www.paragonhouse.com

Publishes: Nonfiction; Reference; *Areas:* Biography; Current Affairs; Finance;

Historical; Philosophy; Politics; Psychology; Religious; Spiritual; *Markets:* Academic; Adult

Submit by email only, as an attachment. Include abstract of your project (summary of your premise, main arguments, and conclusions); table of contents; sample chapter; CV; estimated number of diagrams, figures, pictures or drawings; estimated number of double-spaced manuscript pages, in your completed project; tentative schedule for completion; copies of any endorsements or reviews; list of competing books, and a brief note on how your book compares to each; and SASE for entire MS.

Parallax Press

PO Box 7355
Berkeley, CA 94707
Tel: +1 (510) 540-6411
Email: rachel.neumann@parallax.org
Website: http://www.parallax.org

Publishes: Nonfiction; Markets

Buddhist publisher of books on mindfulness in daily life. Committed to making these teachings accessible to everyone and preserving them for future generations. Proposals accepted by post or by email. See website for full guidelines.

Pelican Publishing Company

1000 Burmaster Street
Gretna, Louisiana 70053-2246
Tel: +1 (800) 843-1724
Fax: +1 (504) 368-1195
Email: editorial@pelicanpub.com
Website: http://www.pelicanpub.com

Publishes: Fiction; Nonfiction; Poetry; *Areas:* Antiques; Architecture; Arts; Autobiography; Biography; Business; Cookery; Crafts; Crime; Criticism; Gardening; Health; Historical; Hobbies; Humour; Legal; Leisure; Lifestyle; Literature; Medicine; Music; Nature; Photography; Politics; Psychology; Religious; Science; Self-Help; Sociology; Sport; Travel; *Markets:* Adult; Children's

Publishes nonfiction for all ages and fiction for children only. No adult fiction. Send query briefly describing the project with SASE, author bio and CV, and optionally a synopsis and one or two sample chapters. Query should outline the length of the book, its intended market, the author's writing and professional background, etc. See website for full guidelines. No queries or submissions by email.

Pen Books

Email: info@open-bks.com
Website: http://www.open-bks.com

Publishes: Fiction; Nonfiction; *Areas:* Adventure; Anthropology; Autobiography; Biography; Crime; Culture; Current Affairs; Drama; Entertainment; Fantasy; Film; Finance; Health; Historical; Horror; Humour; Legal; Leisure; Lifestyle; Literature; Media; Mystery; Philosophy; Politics; Psychology; Sci-Fi; Sociology; Sport; Suspense; Technology; Theatre; Thrillers; Translations; Travel; Women's Interests; *Markets:* Adult; *Treatments:* Contemporary; Literary; Mainstream; Niche; Popular; Progressive; Satirical; Serious; Traditional

Contact: D. Ross, K. Huddleston

Publishes high quality fiction, nonfiction and poetry in paperback and all eBook formats

Our focus is on high quality literary and contemporary fiction, timely and entertaining nonfiction and avant-garde poetry. It is our aim to present the very best of a new generation of authors to readers who are looking for fresh voices.

A fully integrated royalty publisher. All our publications are published in trade paperback and eBook editions. Paperback editions are available from the publisher and at many high quality booksellers around the world. eBook editions are multi-format and available to read on all popular eReaders including Amazon Kindle, Barnes amp; Noble Nook, Sony Reader, Kobo Reader, Apple iPad and others, as well as in PDF for your PC.

Where to find and purchase our books

All titles can be purchased from our online store. All transactions at are secure. Delivery for paperback editions is within 7 -10 days. Delivery is immediate for eBooks. All relevant file formats are offered, so simply choose the format that corresponds to the device on which you will be reading. All downloads are DRM free so you can share your book with family and friends. And remember, authors earn higher royalties when you buy direct from the publisher.

Titles are also available from most of your favorite online retailers including Amazon.com, Amazon.co.uk, Barnes amp; Noble, Books-A-Million, Waterstones, WH Smith, Kobo, Diesel eBooks, Sony ebooks, Apple, Google eBooks, Angus amp; Robertson and Smashwords, as well as many others. You may also find titles at your local library. If you do not find the title of your choice listed there, please request that your library acquire the book you want.

Penguin Group (USA) Inc.

375 Hudson Street
New York, NY 10014
Tel: +1 (212) 366-2000
Fax: +1 (212) 366-2666
Email: online@us.penguingroup.com
Website: http://www.penguin.com

Publishes: Fiction; Nonfiction; *Markets:* Adult; Children's

Generally closed to submissions except through an agent, however some specific imprints may be accepting unsolicited material. See website for information and submission guidelines in these cases.

Pflaum Publishing Group

2621 Dryden Road
Dayton, OH 45439
Tel: +1 (800) 543-4383
Email: Service@Pflaum.com
Website: http://www.pflaum.com

Publishes: Nonfiction; *Areas:* Religious; *Markets:* Academic

Publisher of religious education material, mainly catholic. Send query with SASE.

Philosophy Documentation Center

PO Box 7147
Charlottesville, VA 22906-7147
Tel: +1 (434) 220-3300
Email: leaman@pdcnet.org
Website: https://www.pdcnet.org

Publishes: Nonfiction; Reference; *Areas:* Philosophy; *Markets:* Academic

Contact: George Leaman, Director

Publishes books, journals, and reference materials on philosophy and related fields.

Picton Press

814 East Elkcam Circle
Marco Island, FL 34145
Email: sales@pictonpress.com
Website: http://www.pictonpress.com

Publishes: Nonfiction; Reference; *Areas:* Historical; Hobbies; *Markets:* Adult

Publishes genealogical and historical books, specialising in research tools for the 17th-19th centuries. Send query with SASE and outline.

Pinata Books

Arte Publico Press
University of Houston
4902 Gulf Fwy, Bldg 19, Rm100
Houston, TX 77204-2004
Tel: +1 (713) 743-2843
Fax: +1 (713) 743-2847
Email: submapp@uh.edu
Website: https://artepublicopress.com/contact/

Publishes: Fiction; *Areas:* Culture; *Markets:* Children's; Youth

Publishes children's and young adult literature that authentically and realistically portrays themes, characters, and customs unique to US Hispanic culture. Submit via form on website.

Polis Books

Email: submissions@polisbooks.com
Website: http://polisbooks.com

Publishes: Fiction; *Areas:* Crime; Erotic; Fantasy; Horror; Humour; Mystery; Romance; Sci-Fi; Suspense; Thrillers; Women's Interests; *Markets:* Adult; Youth; *Treatments:* Commercial; Literary

Send query by email with author bio and three sample chapters. No children's picture books, graphic novels, short stories, stand-alone novellas, or religious-based titles.

Professional Publications, Inc. (PPI)

1250 Fifth Ave
Belmont, CA 94002
Tel: +1 (650) 593-9119
Fax: +1 (650) 592-4519
Email: acquisitions@ppi2pass.com
Website: http://ppi2pass.com

Publishes: Nonfiction; Reference; *Areas:* Architecture; Design; Science; *Markets:* Professional

Publishes books relating to architecture, engineering, design, matematics, science etc. and provides products and information for FE/EIT, PE, FS/PS, ARE, NCIDQ and LARE exam preparation. Send proposal with MS and market analysis, etc. Seeks technical, detailed material.

Prometheus Books

59 John Glenn Drive
Amherst, New York 14228-2197
Tel: +1 (716) 691-0133
Fax: +1 (716) 691-0137
Email: editorial@prometheusbooks.com
Website: http://www.prometheusbooks.com

Publishes: Nonfiction; *Areas:* Business; Current Affairs; Health; Philosophy; Science; Sociology; *Markets:* Adult

Send query by email in first instance. Do not send full proposal or complete MS unless requested, and then only by post. See website for full details.

Quill Driver Books

2006 South Mary Street
Fresno, CA 93721
Email: kent@lindenpub.com
Website: http://quilldriverbooks.com

Publishes: Nonfiction; *Areas:* Architecture; Arts; Biography; Business; Crime; Health; Hobbies; Humour; Lifestyle; Self-Help; Spiritual; Technology; Travel; *Markets:* Adult

Contact: Kent Sorsky

Publishes nonfiction only. Send a book proposal including synopsis; commercial info; author platform; and sample chapters or supporting materials. See website for full guidelines.

Quirk Books

215 Church Street
Philadelphia, PA 19106
Email: jason@quirkbooks.com
Website: http://www.quirkbooks.com

Publishes: Fiction; Nonfiction; *Areas:* Culture; Historical; Humour; Mystery; Science; Sci-Fi; Women's Interests; *Markets:* Adult; Children's; Youth; *Treatments:* Experimental; Literary; Popular

Publishes unconventional books across a broad range of categories. Query one editor directly (see website for list of interests and specific contact details) by post with SASE or by email. Limit query to one page and include sample chapters if available.

Rainbow Publishers

PO Box 261129
San Diego, CA 92196
Email: info@rainbowpublishers.com
Website: http://www.rainbowpublishers.com

Publishes: Nonfiction; *Areas:* Religious; *Markets:* Children's

Publishes reproducible classroom resource books for Sunday School. See website for submission guidelines. No academics, poetry, picture books, or fiction.

Red Empress Publishing

Email: submissions@redempresspublishing.com
Website: http://redempresspublishing.com

Publishes: Fiction; *Areas:* Adventure; Culture; Fantasy; Gothic; Historical; Mystery; Romance; Translations; Women's

Interests; *Markets:* Adult; *Treatments:* Commercial; Light; Literary; Mainstream; Niche; Popular; Positive; Progressive; Traditional

A full-service publisher offering traditional and new services for our authors to help them succeed and stand out in an ever-changing market. Here are some of the benefits our authors enjoy.

Professional preparation – editing, cover design, layout, etc.
Digital book distribution through all major outlets – Amazon, Barns and Noble, iBooks, Kobo and more.
Physical book distribution at higher returns than CreateSpace or any other POD publisher because we invest in large print runs of our authors' books.
Audiobook creation and distribution.
Negotiate foreign rights with our partner publishers around the world.
Book launch tours with hundreds of book bloggers to get your book in front of as many readers as possible.

Red Wheel

65 Parker Street, Suite 7
Newburyport, MA 01950
Tel: +1 (978) 465-0504
Fax: +1 (978) 465-0243
Email: submissions@rwwbooks.com
Website: http://www.redwheelweiser.com

Publishes: Nonfiction; *Areas:* Arts; Business; Cookery; Culture; Design; Health; Historical; Humour; Lifestyle; Nature; New Age; Philosophy; Psychology; Religious; Self-Help; Spiritual; Women's Interests; *Markets:* Adult; Children's; Youth

Publishes "Spunky Self-Help", Self-Help/Inspiration, Spirituality/Self-Help, Magic, Wicca, Tarot, Astrology, Qabalah, Spirituality, Personal Growth, Parenting, and Social Issues. Send query by email only. See website for full guidelines.

Redleaf Press

10 Yorkton Court
St. Paul, MN 55117-1065
Tel: +1 (800) 423-8309
Fax: +1 (800) 641-0115
Email: acquisitions@redleafpress.org
Website: http://www.redleafpress.org

Publishes: Nonfiction; *Markets:* Professional

Publishes resources for early childhood professionals. Send proposals by post or by email. See website for guidelines.

Reference Service Press

2310 Homestead Road, Suite C1 #219
Los Altos, CA 94024
Tel: +1 (650) 861-3170
Fax: +1 (650) 861-3171
Email: info@rspfunding.com
Website: http://www.rspfunding.com

Publishes: Nonfiction; Reference; *Areas:* Architecture; Arts; Business; Culture; Health; Historical; Medicine; Religious; Science; Sociology; Women's Interests; *Markets:* Professional

Contact: Stuart Hauser, Acquisitions Editor

Publishes financial aid publications for librarians, counselors, researchers, students, re-entry women, scholars, and other fundseekers. Send outline with sample chapters.

River City Publishing

1719 Mulberry Street
Montgomery, AL 36106
Tel: +1 (334) 265-6753
Fax: +1 (334) 265-8880
Email: fnorris@rivercitypublishing.com
Website: http://www.rivercitypublishing.com

Publishes: Fiction; Nonfiction; *Areas:* Autobiography; Biography; Culture; Historical; Humour; Short Stories; Thrillers; Travel; *Markets:* Adult; *Treatments:* Contemporary

Contact: Fran Norris, Editor

Publishes novels, short story collections, nonfiction, poetry, and children's books of national appeal, usually with an emphasis on Southern writers and Southern stories. Send query by post with SASE, or in the body of an email (no attachments or sample chapters). Not accepting poetry or children's books as at January 2017. See website for current situation.

Roberts Press

685 Spring Street, PMB 161
Friday Harbor, WA 98250
Email: submit-robertspress@falsebaybooks.com
Website: https://robertsbookpressdotcom.wordpress.com

Publishes: Fiction; *Areas:* Fantasy; Mystery; Short Stories; Suspense; Women's Interests; *Markets:* Adult; Children's; Youth; *Treatments:* Literary; Mainstream

Small indie book publisher, publishing works of fiction only. Publishes novels between 45,000 and 80,000 words. Also has specific calls for anthologies. Send complete ms by email. See website for full guidelines.

The Rosen Publishing Group, Inc.

29 East 21st Street
New York, NY 10010
Tel: +1 (800) 237-9932
Fax: +1 (888) 436-4643
Website: http://www.rosenpublishing.com

Publishes: Nonfiction; *Areas:* Arts; Biography; Crafts; Culture; Health; Historical; Religious; Science; Self-Help; Sociology; Sport; *Markets:* Academic; Children's; Youth

Independent educational publishing house serving the needs of students in grades Pre-K -12 with high interest, curriculum-correlated materials.

Running Press

2300 Chestnut Street
Philadelphia, PA 19103
Tel: +1 (215) 567-5080
Fax: +1 (215) 568-2919
Email: perseus.promos@perseusbooks.com
Website: http://www.runningpress.com

Publishes: Fiction; Nonfiction; *Areas:* Arts; Beauty and Fashion; Cookery; Crafts; Culture; Health; Hobbies; Humour; Leisure; Lifestyle; Self-Help; Sport; *Markets:* Adult

Publisher of nonfiction and fiction. No unsolicited submissions.

Saddleback Educational Publishing

Submissions
3120-A Pullman Street
Costa Mesa, CA 92626
Email: contact@sdlback.com
Website: http://www.sdlback.com

Publishes: Fiction; *Markets:* Children's; Youth

Publishes books in all genres and subjects for children aged 12-18, but focusses on original fiction. No K-3 elementary submissions. Submit by post or email. See website for full guidelines.

SAE International

400 Commonwealth Drive
Warrendale, PA 15096-0001
Tel: +1 (724) 776-4970
Fax: +1 (724) 776-0790
Email: writeabook@sae.org
Website: https://www.sae.org

Publishes: Nonfiction; *Areas:* Technology; *Markets:* Professional

Seeks authors who can write books for automotive, aerospace and commercial vehicle engineers. See website for guidelines.

Saguaro Books, LLC

16201 E. Keymar Drive
Fountain Hills, AZ 85268
Tel: +1 (602) 309-7670
Fax: +1 (480) 284-4855
Email: mjnickum@saguarobooks.com
Website: http://www.saguarobooks.com

Publishes: Fiction; *Markets:* Children's; Youth

Contact: Mary Nickum

Publishes books for children and young adults aged 10-18, but first-time authors over the age of 18. Send query by email describing your submission in first instance.

Salvo Press

101 Hudson Street, 37th Floor, Suite 3705
Jersey City, NJ 07302

Tel: +1 (212) 431-5455
Email: info@salvopress.com
Website: http://salvopress.com

Publishes: Fiction; *Areas:* Mystery; Thrillers; *Markets:* Adult; *Treatments:* Literary

Publishes quality mysteries, thrillers, and literary books in eBook and audiobook formats.

Scarecrow Press Inc.

4501 Forbes Blvd, Suite 200
Lanham, MD 20706
Tel: +1 (717) 794-3800 ext. 3557
Email: asnider@scarecrowpress.com
Website: http://www.scarecrowpress.com

Publishes: Nonfiction; Reference; *Areas:* Culture; Film; Historical; Literature; Music; Philosophy; Religious; Sport; Theatre; *Markets:* Academic

Contact: April Snider, Acquisitions Editor

Publishes historical dictionaries; reference and general interest in history, philosophy, religion and related areas.

Scholastic Library Publishing

PO Box 3765
Jefferson City, MO 65102-3765
Tel: +1 (800) 621-1115
Fax: +1 (866) 783-4361
Email: slpservice@scholastic.com
Website: http://scholasticlibrary.digital.scholastic.com

Publishes: Fiction; Nonfiction; Reference; *Markets:* Children's

Publishes children's fiction, nonfiction, and reference.

School Guide Publications

606 Halstead Avenue
Mamaroneck, NY 10543
Tel: +1 (800) 433-7771
Email: mridder@schoolguides.com
Website: http://www.schoolguides.com

Publishes: Nonfiction; Reference; *Markets:* Adult

Publishes directories and guides on 4 amp; 2-year colleges, Nursing Schools, Business Schools and Military Programs.

Scribner

1230 Avenue of the Americas, 12th Floor
New York, NY 10020
Tel: +1 (212) 698-7000
Email: info@simonsays.com
Website: http://www.simonandschusterpublishing.com/scribner/

Publishes: Fiction; Nonfiction; *Areas:* Historical; Mystery; Philosophy; Psychology; Religious; Science; Suspense; *Markets:* Adult; *Treatments:* Literary

Accepts submissions via literary agents only.

Seven Stories Press

140 Watts Street
New York, NY 10013
Tel: +1 (212) 226-8760
Fax: +1 (212) 226-1411
Email: info@sevenstories.com
Website: http://www.sevenstories.com

Publishes: Fiction; Nonfiction; *Areas:* Autobiography; Current Affairs; Health; Historical; Politics; Translations; *Treatments:* Literary

Publishes works of the imagination and political titles by voices of conscience. Send query by post with two sample chapters and 46 cent SASE or postcard for reply. If you require submission materials returned to you, include adequate return postage. No unsolicited mss and no email submissions.

Shape & Nature Press

76 Hastings Street
Greenfield, MA 01301
Email: submission@shapeandnature.com
Website: http://www.shapeandnature.com

Publishes: Fiction; Poetry; *Areas:* Short Stories; *Markets:* Adult; *Treatments:* Literary

Publishes manuscripts of poetry, cross-genre work, and fiction (including novels, novellas, long stories, and short story collections). Open to submissions September to

December. See website for full submission guidelines.

Sibling Rivalry Press, LLC

PO Box 26147
Little Rock, AR 72221
Tel: +1 (870) 723-6008
Email: info@siblingrivalrypress.com
Website: https://siblingrivalrypress.com

Publishes: Poetry; *Markets:* Adult; *Treatments:* Literary

Contact: Bryan Borland, Publisher; Seth Pennington, Editor

Publishes poetry that disturbs and enraptures. Has had award-winning success publishing LGBTIQ authors, but is an inclusive publishing house welcoming all authors, regardless of sexual orientation or identity. Open to submissions from march 1 to June 1 annually.

Sidestreet Cookie Publishing

357 Hillandale rd Apt 82
Greenville, SC 39609
Tel: +1 (864) 990- 6502
Email: sscpsubmissions@Gmail.com
Website: http://www.sidestreetcookiepublishing.com

Publishes: Fiction; *Areas:* Adventure; Anthropology; Drama; Entertainment; Erotic; Fantasy; Gothic; Historical; Horror; Humour; Literature; Military; Mystery; Romance; Sci-Fi; Suspense; Thrillers; Women's Interests; *Markets:* Adult; Youth

Contact: Brenda Mcleod

Founded in September of 2012 to help new independent authors navigate the muddy waters of publishing. Intends to make independent publishing equal in quality and ease as traditional publishing by coaching authors through the process and finding the right and affordable services to make sure their work is the best it can be. We provide authors with a consulting service to help them through the process of publishing and we even do project management for those who want us to take the work out of publishing.

Sierra Club Books

85 Second Street, 2nd Floor
San Francisco, CA 94105
Tel: +1 (415) 977-5500
Fax: +1 (415) 977-5797
Email: books.publishing@sierraclub.org
Website: http://www.sierraclub.org

Publishes: Nonfiction; Nature; Travel; *Markets:* Adult

Publishes books on the natural world, exploring nature, and environmental issues. Send query with SASE.

Silver Lake Publishing, LLC

PO Box 173
Aberdeen, WA 98520
Tel: +1 (360) 532-5758
Fax: +1 (360) 532-5728
Email: publisher@silverlakepub.com
Website: http://www.silverlakepub.com

Publishes: Nonfiction; Reference; *Areas:* Business; Finance; How-to; Legal; Lifestyle; Medicine; Politics; *Markets:* Adult

Publishes books that give readers tools for making smart, aggressive decisions about risk, security and financial matters. Send query with synopsis, two sample chapters, and author CV. No fiction or poetry, or submissions by email.

Sky Pony Press

307 West 36th Street, 11th Floor
New York, NY 10018
Tel: +1 (212) 643-6816
Fax: +1 (212) 643-6819
Email: skyponysubmissions@skyhorsepublishing.com
Website: http://skyponypress.com

Publishes: Fiction; Nonfiction; *Markets:* Children's; Youth

Publishes picture books, chapter books, middle grade, and YA fiction and nonfiction, in any genre or style. Send proposal or complete ms by email as a Word attachment. Do not send hard copy unless requested.

Southern Illinois University Press

1915 University Press Drive
Carbondale, IL 62901-4323
Tel: +1 (618) 453-2281
Fax: +1 (618) 453-1221
Email: kageff@siu.edu
Website: http://www.siupress.com

Publishes: Fiction; Nonfiction; Poetry; *Areas:* Arts; Biography; Crime; Film; Health; Historical; Legal; Philosophy; Photography; Politics; Theatre; Women's Interests; *Markets:* Academic

Contact: Karl Kageff

Publishes nonfiction books for academic and general audiences. No fiction, conference proceedings, edited primary sources, unrevised dissertations, or festschriften. See website for full guidelines.

St Pauls

2187 Victory Boulevard
Staten Island, NY 10314
Tel: +1 (718) 698-2759
Fax: +1 (718) 698-8390
Email: sales@stpauls.us
Website: http://www.stpaulsusa.com

Publishes: Nonfiction; *Areas:* Biography; Religious; Self-Help; Spiritual; *Markets:* Adult

Publishes books for a Roman Catholic readership.

St. Johann Press

PO Box 241
Haworth, NJ 07641
Email: d.biesel@verizon.net
Website: http://stjohannpress.com

Publishes: Fiction; Nonfiction; Poetry; *Areas:* Autobiography; Biography; Hobbies; Religious; Short Stories; Sport; *Markets:* Adult

Contact: David Biesel

Small, independent press located in Northern New Jersey specialising in niche publishing of nonfiction titles, though also some poetry and fiction collections. Send query with SASE.

Standard Publishing

8805 Governor's Hill Drive, Suite 400
Cincinnati, OH 45249
Tel: +1 (800) 543-1353
Email: customerservice@standardpub.com
Website: http://standardpub.com

Publishes: Nonfiction; *Areas:* Religious; *Markets:* Adult; Children's; Youth

Publisher serving Christian churches worldwide. Most widely known as a publisher of Children's and Adult resources. See website for submission guidelines.

Star Bright Books

13 Landsdowne Street
Cambridge, MA 02139
Tel: +1 (617) 354-1300
Fax: +1 (617) 354-1399
Email: info@starbrightbooks.com
Website: https://starbrightbooks.org

Publishes: Fiction; Nonfiction; *Markets:* Children's

Publishes books that are entertaining, meaningful and sensitive to the needs of all children. Welcomes submissions for picture books and longer works, both fiction and nonfiction. See website for full submission guidelines.

STC Craft

115 West 18th Street, 6th Floor
New York, NY 10011
Tel: +1 (212) 206-7715
Fax: +1 (212) 519-1210
Email: stccraft@abramsbooks.com
Website: http://www.abramsbooks.com

Publishes: Nonfiction; *Areas:* Crafts; Hobbies; *Markets:* Adult

Publishes books on crafts, such as knitting, sewing, felting, quilting, etc.

Sterling Publishing Co. Inc.

1166 Avenue of the Americas, Floor 17
New York, NY 10036
Tel: +1 (212) 532-7160

Fax: +1 (212) 213-2495
Email: editorial@sterlingpublishing.com
Website: https://www.sterlingpublishing.com

Publishes: Fiction; Nonfiction; Reference; *Areas:* Arts; Crafts; Crime; Finance; Gardening; Health; Hobbies; How-to; Humour; Lifestyle; Literature; Music; Mystery; Nature; New Age; Photography; Science; Spiritual; Sport; Travel; *Markets:* Adult; Children's; Youth

Publishes mainly adult nonfiction, reference, and how-to, plus fiction for children. No adult fiction. Send query with SASE, outline of idea, sample chapter, sample illustrations (where appropriate), and details about yourself, including any publishing history. No submissions by email.

Storey Publishing

210 MASS MoCA Way
North Adams, MA 01247
Tel: +1 (413) 346-2100
Fax: +1 (413) 346-2199
Email: feedback@storey.com
Website: http://www.storey.com

Publishes: Nonfiction; *Areas:* Business; Cookery; Crafts; Gardening; Health; Nature; Spiritual; *Markets:* Adult

Contact: Deborah Balmuth: Building and mind/body/spirit; Deborah Burns: Equine, animals, nature; Gwen Steege: Crafts; Carleen Madigan: Gardening; Margaret Sutherland: Cooking, wine, and beer.

Send query by post with description, market info, author details, table of contents, details of final length and any photos/illustrations, writing sample from previous books or magazines, and sample chapter. Address material to appropriate Acquiring Editor. See website for more details.

Sunscribe

1735 Heckle Blvd
Suite 103
Rock Hill, SC 29732
Tel: +1 (704) 467-4067
Email: sunscribepublishers@gmail.com
Website: http://sunscribe.net

Publishes: Fiction; Nonfiction; Poetry; Reference; Scripts; *Areas:* Adventure; Anthropology; Antiques; Archaeology; Architecture; Arts; Autobiography; Beauty and Fashion; Biography; Business; Cookery; Crafts; Crime; Criticism; Culture; Current Affairs; Design; Drama; Entertainment; Fantasy; Film; Finance; Gardening; Gothic; Health; Historical; Hobbies; How-to; Humour; Legal; Leisure; Lifestyle; Literature; Media; Medicine; Men's Interests; Military; Music; Mystery; Nature; New Age; Philosophy; Photography; Politics; Psychology; Radio; Religious; Romance; Science; Sci-Fi; Self-Help; Short Stories; Sociology; Spiritual; Sport; Suspense; Technology; Theatre; Thrillers; Translations; Travel; TV; Westerns; Women's Interests; *Markets:* Academic; Adult; Children's; Family; Professional; Youth; *Treatments:* Commercial; Contemporary; Experimental; In-depth; Light; Literary; Mainstream; Niche; Popular; Positive; Progressive; Serious; Traditional

Contact: Roxanne Hanna

Traditional publishing company with three imprints, partnering with writers: we are proud members of AAP and IBPA. Our works adhere to our philosophy of pairing our expertise with excellent writing by establishing a culture of collaboration, focusing on talent and text. Our mission is to offer writers an opportunity to write: we handle editing, marketing, and distribution. Our standard is excellence, and we strive to team with writers passionate about their craft.

Sunstone Press

Box 2321
Santa Fe, NM 87504-2321
Tel: +1 (800) 243-5644
Fax: +1 (505) 988-1025
Website: http://www.sunstonepress.com

Publishes: Fiction; Nonfiction; Poetry; Reference; *Areas:* Adventure; Archaeology; Architecture; Arts; Autobiography; Biography; Business; Cookery; Crafts; Crime; Fantasy; Gardening; Health; Historical; How-to; Humour; Legal; Military; Music; Mystery; Nature; Photography; Politics; Religious; Romance;

Sci-Fi; Short Stories; Spiritual; Sport; Theatre; Travel; Westerns; Women's Interests; *Markets:* Adult; Children's; Family

Began in the 1970s with a focus on nonfiction about the American Southwest, but has since expanded its focus to include mainstream themes and categories in both fiction and nonfiction. Send query by post only with short summary, author bio, one sample chapter, table of contents, marketing plan, and statement on why this is the right publisher for your book.

Swedenborg Foundation

320 North Church Street
West Chester, PA 19380
Tel: +1 (610) 430-3222
Fax: +1 (610) 430-7982
Email: info@swedenborg.com
Website: http://www.swedenborg.com

Publishes: Nonfiction; *Areas:* Philosophy; Psychology; Religious; Science; *Markets:* Adult

Publishes books by and about Emanuel Swedenborg, and/or related to his ideas. Send query by post with SASE or by email, including synopsis, sample chapters, and outline.

Syracuse University Press

Syracuse University Press
621 Skytop Road, Suite 110
Syracuse, NY 13244-5290
Tel: +1 (315) 443-5534
Fax: +1 (315) 443-5545
Email: supress@syr.edu
Website: http://www.
syracuseuniversitypress.syr.edu

Publishes: Nonfiction; *Areas:* Anthropology; Biography; Culture; Current Affairs; Entertainment; Historical; Literature; Politics; Religious; Sociology; Sport; Translations; TV; Women's Interests; *Markets:* Academic

Publishes scholarly books on international affairs, the Middle East, women and religion, politics, Irish studies, medieaval history, television, translations of Middle Eastern literature, etc. Complete book proposal form (available on website) and submit by email with CV and preliminary table of contents. No unsolicited mss.

Teachers College Press

1234 Amsterdam Avenue
New York, NY 10027
Tel: +1 (212) 678-3929
Fax: +1 (212) 678-4149
Email: tcpress@tc.columbia.edu
Website: http://www.
teacherscollegepress.com

Publishes: Nonfiction; *Areas:* Film; Historical; Philosophy; Politics; Sociology; Technology; Theatre; Women's Interests; *Markets:* Academic

Publishes educational titles for all levels of students.

Temple University Press

1852 North 10th Street
Philadelphia, PA 19122
Tel: +1 (215) 204-8787
Email: tempress@temple.edu
Website: http://www.temple.edu/tempress/

Publishes: Nonfiction; *Areas:* Anthropology; Arts; Biography; Business; Crime; Culture; Drama; Film; Finance; Health; Historical; Legal; Leisure; Lifestyle; Literature; Media; Nature; Photography; Politics; Psychology; Religious; Science; Sociology; Sport; Technology; Women's Interests; *Markets:* Academic

Send query with brief outline, including email address for response. Publishes scholarly books, usually authored by academics. Best known for publishing in the areas of the social sciences and humanities.

ThunderStone Books

Email: info@thunderstonebooks.com
Website: http://thunderstonebooks.com

Publishes: Fiction; Nonfiction; *Markets:* Children's

Publish children's fiction and nonfiction that has an educational aspect. Send query by email with up to first 50 pages as Word attachment.

Tia Chucha Press

PO Box 328
San Fernando, CA 91341
Tel: +1 (818) 528-4511
Fax: +1 (818) 367-5600
Email: tcpress@tiachucha.org
Website: http://www.tiachucha.com

Publishes: Poetry; *Areas: Markets:* Adult

Contact: Luis J. Rodriguez, Editor

Publishes all types of poetic expression and are not bound by poetic style, form, school, or era. Cross-cultural – published poets have included Chicano, African American, Jamaican American, Native American, Irish American, Italian American, Korean American, Japanese American, Puerto Rican, Cuban American, and more. All ages, genders, sexual orientations, disabilities, and spiritual persuasions are welcome, but publishes only two books per year (1% of submissions). Send complete poetry ms between 60 and 120 pages by hard copy only. See website for full guidelines.

Torah Aura Productions

2710 Supply Avenue
Los Angeles CA, 90040
Tel: +1 (800) 238-6724
Fax: +1 (323) 585-0327
Email: misrad@torahaura.com
Website: http://www.torahaura.com

Publishes: Nonfiction; *Areas:* Historical; Lifestyle; Religious; *Markets:* Academic; Children's; Youth

Contact: Jane Golub, Acquisitions

Publisher of educational materials for Jewish classrooms. No picture books.

Tower Publishing

588 Saco Road
Standish, ME 04084
Tel: +1 (800) 969-8693
Fax: +1 (800) 264-3870
Email: info@towerpub.com
Website: http://www.towerpub.com

Publishes: Nonfiction; Reference; *Areas:* Business; Legal; *Markets:* Professional

Contact: Michael Lyons (michaell@towerpub.com)

Independent publisher of legal publications, business directories, and data lists. Send query by email or by post with SASE, with sample chapters, proposed chapter outline, marketing plan, details of competing books, and ideas for business development. See website for full details.

Triangle Square

140 Watts Street
New York, NY 10013
Tel: +1 (212) 226-8760
Fax: +1 (212) 226-1411
Email: info@sevenstories.com
Website: https://www.sevenstories.com/imprints/triangle-square

Publishes: Fiction; Nonfiction; *Areas:* Autobiography; Biography; Health; Historical; Music; Nature; Philosophy; Politics; Religious; *Markets:* Children's; Youth

Publishes fiction and nonfiction for children and young adults, on such subjects as environmentalism, human rights, gender and feminism, etc.

Triumph Books

814 North Franklin Street
Chicago, IL 60610
Tel: +1 (312) 337-0747
Fax: +1 (312) 337-5985
Email: orders@ipgbook.com
Website: http://www.triumphbooks.com

Publishes: Nonfiction; *Areas:* Autobiography; Biography; Sport; *Markets:* Adult

Describes itself as the nation's leading sports book publisher. Send query with SASE.

Truman State University Press

100 East Normal Avenue
Kirksville, MO 63501-4221
Tel: +1 (660) 785-7336
Fax: +1 (660) 785-4480
Email: tsup@truman.edu
Website: http://tsup.truman.edu

Publishes: Nonfiction; *Areas:* Anthropology; Archaeology; Architecture; Arts; Autobiography; Biography; Criticism; Historical; Literature; Nature; Religious; Translations; Travel; *Markets:* Academic; Adult

Publishes peer-reviewed research and literature for the scholarly community and the reading public. See website for full submission guidelines.

Tumblehome Learning, Inc.

Boston, MA
Tel: +1 (781) 924-5036
Email: submissions@tumblehomelearning.com
Website: http://tumblehomelearning.com

Publishes: Fiction; *Areas:* Adventure; Science; *Markets:* Children's

Publishes books that allow kids to experience science through adventure and discovery. Submit complete ms by email.

Tyrus Books

1213 N. Sherman Ave. #306
Madison, WI 53704
Tel: +1 (508) 427-7100
Email: submissions@tyrusbooks.com
Website: http://www.tyrusbooks.com

Publishes: Fiction; *Areas:* Crime; *Markets:* Adult; *Treatments:* Literary

Publishes crime and literary fiction. Not interested in books that are heavy on explosions, violence, or cliched plots or characters. Stories should be approximately 60,000 to 100,000 words. See website for full guidelines. Send query by email with synopsis and optionally up to 20 pages in the body of the email. No attachments. If no response after a few months, assume rejection.

University of Alabama Press

Box 870380
Tuscaloosa, AL 35487-0380
Tel: +1 (205) 348-5180
Fax: +1 (205) 348-9201

Publishes: Nonfiction; Anthropology; Archaeology; Biography; Criticism; Historical; Literature; Military; Politics; Religious; Technology; Theatre; *Markets:* Academic

Publishes American history and religious history, Latin American history, as well as African-American, Judaic, Native-American, and theatre studies. No poetry, fiction, or drama.

University of Alaska Press

Editorial Department
University of Alaska Press
PO Box 756240
104 Eielson Building
Fairbanks, AK 99775-6240
Tel: +1 (907) 474-5831
Fax: +1 (907) 474-5502
Email: bauer@alaska.edu
Website: http://www.alaska.edu/uapress/

Publishes: Fiction; Nonfiction; Poetry; *Areas:* Autobiography; Biography; Culture; Historical; Nature; Politics; Science; Sport; Translations; *Markets:* Academic; Adult

Publisher based in Alaska, publishing academic and general trade books on an expanding range of subject areas, including politics and history, Native languages and cultures, science and natural history, biography and memoir, poetry, fiction and anthologies, and original translations. Send proposals by post. No unsolicited mss.

University of Chicago Press

Editorial Department
The University of Chicago Press
1427 East 60th Street
Chicago, IL 60637
Tel: +1 (773) 702-7700
Fax: +1 (773) 702-9756
Email: chenry@uchicago.edu
Website: http://www.press.uchicago.edu

Publishes: Nonfiction; Reference; *Areas:* Anthropology; Archaeology; Architecture; Arts; Biography; Film; Gardening; Historical; Legal; Medicine; Music; Philosophy; Politics; Psychology; Religious; Science; Sociology; Technology; Translations; Travel; *Markets:* Academic

Contact: See website for appropriate editorial contact.

Send query by post or email, with CV, table of contents, brief prospectus including a description of the work and intended audience, expected length and number of illustrations, and information on the schedule for completion of the manuscript. A sample chapter may be included. Consult website for appropriate editorial contact. No fiction, poetry, or unsolicited MSS.

The University of Michigan Press

839 Greene Street
Ann Arbor, MI 48104-3209
Tel: +1 (734) 764-4388
Fax: +1 (734) 615-1540
Email: scottom@umich.edu
Website: http://www.press.umich.edu

Publishes: Fiction; Nonfiction; Reference; *Areas:* Anthropology; Archaeology; Arts; Autobiography; Biography; Business; Cookery; Culture; Finance; Historical; Legal; Literature; Media; Music; Nature; Philosophy; Politics; Psychology; Religious; Sociology; Sport; Theatre; Travel; Women's Interests; *Markets:* Academic

Send query with table of contents, outline of chapters, overview, and CV. Queries should include statements on the rationale of your book, similar and competing books in the field, your target audience, why you think it is right for this list, the length of MS, number of illustrations, and what your anticipated date of completion is. Send queries and proposals by email to specific editor (guidelines on website). See website for particular guidelines realting to fiction and certain series published by the press.

University of Pittsburgh Press

7500 Thomas Boulevard
Pittsburgh, PA 15260
Tel: +1 (412) 383-2456
Fax: +1 (412) 383-2466
Email: info@upress.pitt.edu
Website: http://www.upress.pitt.edu

Publishes: Nonfiction; Poetry; *Areas:* Architecture; Historical; Philosophy; Science; *Markets:* Academic

Publishes books on Latin American studies, Russian and East European studies, international relations, poetry, Pittsburgh and Western Pennsylvania regional studies, environmental studies, architecture and landscape history, urban studies, composition and literacy, the history of science, and the philosophy of science. No hard sciences, memoirs, or fiction. Only considers poetry manuscripts from poets who have already published full-length collections of at least 48 pages. Poets who have not may submit to the first-book competition run by the press. See website for full guidelines.

University of South Carolina Press

1600 Hampton Street, 5th Floor
Columbia, SC 29208
Email: lfogle@mailbox.sc.edu
Website: http://www.sc.edu/uscpress

Publishes: Fiction; Nonfiction; Poetry; *Areas:* Architecture; Arts; Cookery; Culture; Gardening; Historical; Literature; Military; Nature; Religious; Women's Interests; *Markets:* Academic; Adult

Publishes works of original scholarship and regional general interest, as well as poetry and original fiction, focussed on the American South. See website for full details.

University of Washington Press

4333 Brooklyn Avenue NE
Seattle, WA 98105
Tel: +1 (206) 543-4050
Fax: +1 (206) 543-3932
Email: uwapress@uw.edu
Website: http://www.washington.edu/uwpress/

Publishes: Nonfiction; *Areas:* Anthropology; Arts; Biography; Culture; Historical; Nature; *Markets:* Academic

Publishes scholarly books and distinguished works of regional nonfiction in the Pacific

Northwest. Particularly known for Asian studies, Middle East studies, anthropology, Western history and biography, environmental studies, and natural history.

Urban Ministries, Inc.

PO Box 87618
Chicago, IL 60680-0618
Tel: +1 (800) 860-8642
Website: http://urbanministries.com

Publishes: Nonfiction; *Areas:* Religious; *Markets:* Academic; Adult; Children's

Publishes Christian education resources, including Bible studies, Sunday School and Vacation Bible School curriculum books, movies, and websites designed for African American churches and individuals.

Utah State University Press

3078 Old Main Hill
Logan, UT 84322-3078
Tel: +1 (720) 406-8849
Fax: +1 (720) 406-8849
Email: jessica@upcolorado.com
Website: http://www.usu.edu/usupress

Publishes: Nonfiction; *Areas:* Anthropology; Archaeology; Culture; Historical; Nature; Science; *Markets:* Academic

Contact: Jessica d'Arbonne, Acquisitions Editor

Academic publisher. Prefers to receive submissions through online submission system. See website for details.

Venture Publishing, Inc.

1807 N. Federal Drive
Urbana, IL 61801
Tel: +1 (217) 359-5940
Fax: +1 (217) 359-5975
Email: books@sagamorepub.com
Website: http://www.sagamorepub.com

Publishes: Nonfiction; *Areas:* Leisure; Nature; Sociology; *Markets:* Adult; Professional

Publishes educational material for the park and recreation industry.

Veritas Publications

7-8 Lower Abbey Street
Dublin 1
Email: donna.doherty@veritas.ie
Website: http://www.veritasbooksonline.com

Publishes: Nonfiction; *Areas:* Psychology; Religious; Self-Help; Sociology; Spiritual; *Markets:* Adult

Contact: Donna Doherty, Commissioning Editor

Publishes theology, philosophy, spirituality, psychology, self-help, family, social issues, parish and church resources, bible study, etc. Send proposal or complete ms by post or by email. See website for full guidelines.

Verso

Editorial Dept.
20 Jay Street, Suite 1010
Brooklyn, NY 11201
Tel: +1 (718) 246-8160
Fax: +1 (718) 246-8165
Email: submissions@versobooks.com
Website: http://www.versobooks.com

Publishes: Nonfiction; *Areas:* Business; Finance; Historical; Philosophy; Politics; Sociology; Women's Interests; *Markets:* Adult

Queries from North America should be directed to the US address. Queries from elswhere in the world should be directed to the UK address (see separate listing). Send query with overview, list of contents, author info, market info, and timetable. 15 pages maximum. See website for full guidelines.

Walch Education

40 Walch Drive
PO Box 658
Portland, ME 04104-0658
Tel: +1 (207) 772-2846
Fax: +1 (207) 772-3105
Email: customerservice@walch.com
Website: http://www.walch.com

Publishes: Nonfiction; *Areas:* Arts; Science; Sociology; *Markets:* Academic

Publishes high school math curriculum and resources aligned to the Common Core and selected state and district standards.

Wannabee Books

750 Pinehurst Drive
Rio Vista, CA 94571
Tel: +1 (707) 398-6430
Email: Books@WannabeeBooks.com
Website: http://www.wannabeebooks.com

Publishes: Nonfiction; *Areas:* Anthropology; Archaeology; Architecture; Arts; Criticism; Gardening; Health; Legal; Literature; Medicine; Music; Nature; Photography; Psychology; Science; Sport; Technology; *Markets:* Children's

Publishes nonfiction for children, organised around what they might want to be when they grow up.

WaterBrook & Multnomah

10807 New Allegiance Drive Suite 500
Colorado Springs, CO 80921
Tel: +1 (719) 590-4999
Fax: +1 (719) 590-8977
Email: info@waterbrookpress.com
Website: http://waterbrookmultnomah.com

Publishes: Fiction; Nonfiction; *Areas:* Adventure; Historical; Mystery; Religious; Romance; Sci-Fi; Spiritual; Suspense; *Markets:* Adult; Children's

Publishes fiction and nonfiction with a Christian perspective. Agented submissions only.

Wave Books

1938 Fairview Avenue East, Suite 201
Seattle, WA 98102
Tel: +1 (206) 676-5337
Email: info@wavepoetry.com
Website: https://www.wavepoetry.com

Publishes: Poetry; *Markets:* Adult; *Treatments:* Contemporary

Contact: Charlie Wright, Publisher

Independent poetry press based in Seattle. Accepts submissions only in response to specific calls for submissions posted on the website (see the submissions page).

Wesleyan Publishing House

PO Box 50434
Indianapolis, IN 46250
Tel: +1 (800) 493-7539
Email: submissions@wesleyan.org
Website: https://www.wesleyan.org

Publishes: Nonfiction; *Areas:* Religious; Spiritual; *Markets:* Adult

Publishes topical, adult, Christian nonfiction titles on Discipleship Group Study; Deeper Devotion; Christian Living; Spiritual Growth; Social Issues; and Ministry Leadership. No fiction, children's books, Bible studies, biographies, autobiographies, poetry, academic works, or textbooks. Send all proposals by email. No queries.

Wesleyan University Press

215 Long Lane
Middletown, CT 06459
Tel: +1 (860) 685-7730
Fax: +1 (860) 685-7712
Email: stamminen@wesleyan.edu
Website: http://www.wesleyan.edu/wespress

Publishes: Nonfiction; Poetry; *Areas:* Culture; Film; Historical; Media; Music; Sci-Fi; TV; *Markets:* Academic

Publishes nonfiction in the areas of dance, music/culture, film/TV and media studies, science fiction studies, and Connecticut history and culture. See website for submission guidelines. Also publishes poetry, but accepts submission by invitation only.

Western Psychological Services

625 Alaska Avenue
Torrance, CA 90503-5124
Tel: +1 (800) 648-8857
Email: review@wpspublish.com
Website: http://www.wpspublish.com

Publishes: Fiction; Nonfiction; Reference; *Areas:* Psychology; Sociology; *Markets:* Children's; Professional

Publishes books for professionals in the areas of psychology and education, and children's fiction dealing with feelings, anger, social skills, autism, family problems, etc. for use by professionals when dealing with children. Send complete ms.

Whitaker House

1030 Hunt Valley Circle
New Kensington, PA 15068
Tel: +1 (724) 334-7000
Fax: +1 (724) 334-1200
Email: publisher@whitakerhouse.com
Website: http://www.whitakerhouse.com

Publishes: Fiction; Nonfiction; *Areas:* Autobiography; Biography; Historical; How-to; Lifestyle; Men's Interests; Religious; Self-Help; Spiritual; Women's Interests; *Markets:* Adult

Publisher of inspiring and uplifting Christian fiction and nonfiction. Establish contact with a representative prior to submitting a manuscript or proposal.

John Wiley & Sons, Inc.

111 River Street
Hoboken, NJ 07030
Tel: +1 (212) 850-6000
Fax: +1 (212) 850-6088
Email: info@wiley.com
Website: http://www.wiley.com

Publishes: Nonfiction; Reference; *Areas:* Architecture; Business; Cookery; Design; Finance; Medicine; Psychology; Religious; Science; Sociology; Technology; *Markets:* Academic; Adult; Professional

Publishes professional, trade, and educational material as print books, journals, and in electronic format.

Willow Creek Press, Inc.

PO Box 147
Minocqua, WI 54548
Tel: +1 (800) 850-9453
Fax: +1 (715) 358-2807
Email: andread@willowcreekpress.com
Website: http://www.willowcreekpress.com

Publishes: Nonfiction; Reference; *Areas:* Cookery; Gardening; How-to; Leisure; Nature; Sport; *Markets:* Adult

Send query with SASE, outline / table of contents, one or two sample chapters, author bio, and indication as to whether the proposal is simultaneously under consideration elsewhere. See website for full details. May consider but will generally not accept personal memoirs, children's books, or MSS dealing with limited regional subject matter.

Wilshire Book Company

9731 Variel Avenue
Chatsworth, CA 91311-4315
Tel: +1 (818) 700-1522
Fax: +1 (818) 700-1527
Email: mpowers@mpowers.com
Website: http://www.mpowers.com

Publishes: Fiction; Nonfiction; *Areas:* How-to; Humour; Psychology; Self-Help; Spiritual; *Markets:* Adult; *Treatments:* Commercial

Publishes psychology and self help nonfiction, plus adult allegories that teach principles of psychological and spiritual growth. Advises writers to read the bestsellers listed on their website and duplicate their winning elements in your own style with a creative new approach and fresh material. Submissions should be conceived and developed with market potential uppermost in your mind. Send synopsis for fiction or detailed chapter outline for nonfiction with three sample chapters, SASE, and contact email address (however no email submissions). Queries accepted by telephone for instant feedback on ideas.

WordSong

815 Church Street
Honesdale, PA 18431
Tel: +1 (570) 253-1164
Email: submissions@boydsmillspress.com
Website: https://www.boydsmillspress.com

Publishes: Poetry; *Markets:* Children's

Describes itself as "the only children's imprint in the United States specifically dedicated to poetry". Send book-length collection of poetry by post with SASE. Do not make initial query prior to submission.

World Book, Inc.

233 North Michigan Avenue, Suite 2000
Chicago, IL 60601
Tel: +1 (312) 729-5800
Fax: +1 (312) 729-5600
Email: service@worldbook.com
Website: http://www.worldbook.com

Publishes: Nonfiction; Reference; *Areas:* Health; Historical; Science; Sociology; *Markets:* Children's

Publishes nonfiction and reference for children aged 3-14. No poetry or fiction.

World Weaver Press

Email: publisher@worldweaverpress.com
Website: http://www.worldweaverpress.com

Publishes: Fiction; *Areas:* Fantasy; Romance; Sci-Fi; Short Stories; *Markets:* Adult

Publishes speculative romance, including Paranormal Romance, Epic Fantasy, Urban Fantasy, Fairy Tale, Hard Science Fiction, Soft Science Fiction, Space Opera, Solarpunk, Steampunk, Dieselpunk, Decopunk, Fantasy Romance, Science Fiction Romance, Paranormal Mystery, and Time Travel Romance. No horror, grimdark, or dystopia. Accepts submissions in specific submission windows only (see website for details). Also publishes anthologies of short stories. See website for current opportunities.

WorthyKids / Ideals

6100 Tower Circle, Suite 210
Franklin, TN 37067
Tel: +1 (615) 932-7600
Email: idealsinfo@worthy-ideals.com
Website: https://www.idealsbooks.com

Publishes: Fiction; Nonfiction; *Areas:* Lifestyle; Religious; *Markets:* Children's

Publishes fiction and nonfiction board books, novelty books, and picture books for children aged 0-8. Subjects include inspiration/faith, patriotism, and holidays, particularly Easter and Christmas; relationships and values; and general fiction. Board book manuscripts should be no longer than 250 words. Picture book manuscripts should be no longer than 800 words. Submit complete ms by post only – no queries or proposals or submissions by email. See website for full submission guidelines.

Yale University Press

PO Box 209040
New Haven, CT 06520-9040
Tel: +1 (203) 432-0960
Fax: +1 (203) 432-0948
Email: Sarah.Miller@yale.edu
Website: http://yalepress.yale.edu/yupbooks

Publishes: Nonfiction; Poetry; *Areas:* Architecture; Arts; Current Affairs; Historical; Legal; Literature; Medicine; Nature; Philosophy; Politics; Psychology; Religious; Science; *Markets:* Academic; Adult

Publishes nonfiction and one book of poetry a year. Poetry must be submitted through annual contest. For nonfiction, see website for list of editors and submit to one editor only, by post or by email. See website for full guidelines.

YMAA Publication Center, Inc.

PO Box 480
Wolfeboro, NH 03894
Tel: +1 (603) 569-7988
Fax: +1 (603) 569-1889
Website: https://ymaa.com

Publishes: Nonfiction; *Areas:* Health; Medicine; Philosophy; Spiritual; Sport; *Markets:* Adult

Publishes books on martial arts, Eastern philosophy, Chinese medicine, etc.

Zebra

Kensington Publishing Corp.
119 West 40th Street
New York, New York, 10018
Tel: +1 (800) 221-2647
Email: esogah@kensingtonbooks.com
Website: http://www.kensingtonbooks.com

Publishes: Fiction; *Areas:* Romance; Women's Interests; *Markets:* Adult

Contact: Esi Sogah, Senior Editor

Publishes women's fiction, including romance. Send query only by email. No attachments or proposals. Response only if interested. See website for full guidelines.

Zenith Press

400 First Avenue North, Suite 400
Minneapolis, MN 55401
Tel: +1 (612) 344-8100
Fax: +1 (612) 344-8691
Email: erik.gilg@quartous.com
Website: http://www.zenithpress.com

Publishes: Nonfiction; *Areas:* Culture; Historical; Military; Science; Sociology; Technology; Travel; *Markets:* Adult

Contact: Erik Gilg, Editorial Director

Publishes engaging American stories with a firm historical foundation; particularly in the areas of military history and aviation. Accepts submissions by post, but prefers them by email. See website for full guidelines.

Zumaya Publications

3209 S. Interstate 35 #1086
Austin, TX 78741
Email: acquisitions@zumayapublications.com
Website: http://www.zumayapublications.com

Publishes: Fiction; Nonfiction; *Areas:* Autobiography; Crime; Fantasy; Gothic; Historical; Horror; Mystery; Romance; Sci-Fi; Short Stories; Thrillers; Westerns; *Markets:* Adult; Children's; Youth; *Treatments:* Mainstream; Niche

Contact: Adrienne Rose

Publishes adult fiction of at least 50,000 words, and juvenile fiction of at least 40,000 words. Send queries by email only, with sample as an attachment, with a brief synopsis up to 1,000 words at its start. See website for full submission guidelines.

UK Publishers

For the most up-to-date listings of these and hundreds of other publishers, visit https://www.firstwriter.com/publishers

*To claim your **free** access to the site, please see the back of this book.*

A Swift Exit

Email: aswiftexit@gmail.com
Website: http://aswiftexit.co.uk

Publishes: Fiction; Nonfiction; Poetry; *Areas:* Short Stories; *Markets:* Adult; *Treatments:* Literary

Contact: Jim Ladd and Will Vigar

Publishes new collections of poetry and prose from the finest new writers as ebooks and in print. Currently working on a strict back end profit share basis. See website for current calls for submissions and guidelines.

ACC Art Books Ltd

Sandy Lane
Old Martlesham
Woodbridge
Suffolk
IP12 4SD
Tel: +44 (0) 1394 389950
Fax: +44 (0) 1394 389999
Email: submissions@antique-acc.com
Website: http://www.antiquecollectorsclub.com

Publishes: Nonfiction; *Areas:* Antiques; Architecture; Arts; Beauty and Fashion; Business; Crafts; Design; Gardening; Historical; Photography; Travel; *Markets:* Adult; Children's

Publishes books on antiques and decorative arts. Send queries or submit manuscripts by post or by email.

J.A. Allen

Clerkenwell House
45–47 Clerkenwell Green
London
EC1R 0HT
Tel: +44 (0) 20 7251 2661
Fax: +44 (0) 20 7490 4958
Email: allen@halebooks.com
Website: http://halebooks.com/jaallen/

Publishes: Nonfiction; *Areas:* How-to; *Markets:* Adult

Contact: Lesley Gowers

Publishes books on horses and horsemanship. Send proposal with SASE, outline, aim, background and market, detailed synopsis, and three sample chapters.

Allison & Busby Ltd

12 Fitzroy Mews
London
W1T 6DW
Tel: +44 (0) 20 7580 1080
Fax: +44 (0) 20 7580 1180
Email: susie@allisonandbusby.com
Website: http://www.allisonandbusby.com

Publishes: Fiction; Nonfiction; *Areas:* Autobiography; Biography; Crime; Culture;

Fantasy; Historical; Military; Mystery; Sci-Fi; Self-Help; Short Stories; Thrillers; Travel; Women's Interests; *Markets:* Adult; Youth; *Treatments:* Contemporary; Literary

Contact: Susie Dunlop, Publishing Director

Accepts approaches via a literary agent only. No unsolicited MSS or queries from authors. In field of nonfiction publishes guides for writers. No horror, romance, spirituality, short stories, self-help, poetry or plays.

Alma Books Ltd

3 Castle Yard
Richmond
TW10 6TF
Tel: +44 (0) 20 8940 6917
Fax: +44 (0) 20 8948 5599
Email: info@almabooks.com
Website: http://www.almabooks.com

Publishes: Fiction; Nonfiction; *Areas:* Historical; Literature; *Markets:* Adult; *Treatments:* Contemporary; Literary

Publishes literary fiction and a small number of nonfiction titles with a strong literary or historical connotation. No novellas, short stories, children's books, poetry, academic works, science fiction, horror, or fantasy. Accepts unsolicited MSS by post with synopsis, two sample chapters, and SAE if return of material required. No submissions by email, or submissions from outside the UK. Submissions received from outside the UK will not receive a response.

Alma Classics

3 Castle Yard
Richmond
TW10 6TF
Tel: +44 (0) 20 8940 6917
Fax: +44 (0) 20 8948 5599
Email: info@almabooks.com
Website: http://www.almaclassics.com

Publishes: Fiction; Poetry; Scripts; *Areas:* Arts; Autobiography; Biography; Literature; Sociology; Translations; *Markets:* Adult; *Treatments:* Literary

Publishes classic European literature. Welcomes suggestions and ideas for the list, as well as proposals from translators. Send proposals by email.

Amberley Publishing

The Hill
Merrywalks
Stroud
GL5 4EP
Tel: +44 (0) 1453 847800
Fax: +44 (0) 1453 847820
Email: submissions@amberley-books.com
Website: http://www.amberleybooks.com

Publishes: Nonfiction; *Areas:* Archaeology; Biography; Historical; Military; Sport; Travel; *Markets:* Adult

Publishes local interest and niche history. Send query by email, with one-page proposal describing the book; reason for writing the book; proposed word count; proposed number of images; and any other relevant information.

And Other Stories

88 Easton Street
High Wycombe
Bucks
HP11 1LT
Email: info@andotherstories.org
Website: http://www.andotherstories.org

Publishes: Fiction; Nonfiction; Poetry; *Areas:* Translations; *Markets:* Adult; *Treatments:* Contemporary; Literary

Focuses on fiction, but will consider nonfiction (especially creative nonfiction) and poetry. Welcomes unsolicited submissions from authors and keen to consider debut writers writing in English. Also accepts translations of published writers from other languages. Accepts paper submissions only, and asks submissions to include a receipt showing that you have purchased one of their books or are a subscriber.

Andersen Press Ltd

20 Vauxhall Bridge Road
London
SW1V 2SA
Tel: +44 (0) 20 7840 8701
Email: anderseneditorial@

penguinrandomhouse.co.uk
Website: http://www.andersenpress.co.uk

Publishes: Fiction; *Markets:* Children's

Publishes picture books and longer children's fiction up to 75,000 words. Publishes rhyming stories, but no poetry, adult fiction, nonfiction, or short story collections. Send query with complete ms for picture books, or synopsis and first three chapters by post only, with SAE if return of work required. See website for full guidelines.

Anness Publishing Ltd

108 Great Russell Street
London
WC1B 3NA
Email: info@anness.com
Website: http://www.aquamarinebooks.com

Publishes: Nonfiction; Reference; *Areas:* Arts; Cookery; Crafts; Design; Gardening; Health; Historical; Hobbies; Leisure; Lifestyle; Military; Music; New Age; Photography; Spiritual; Sport; Travel; *Markets:* Adult; Children's

Publishes co-edition books in the above-listed areas; usually heavily illustrated.

Arc Publications

Nanholme Mill
Shaw Wood Road
Todmorden
Lancs
OL14 6DA
Tel: +44 (0) 1706 812338
Email: info@arcpublications.co.uk
Website: http://www.arcpublications.co.uk/submissions

Publishes: Poetry; *Areas:* Music; Translations; *Markets:* Adult; *Treatments:* Contemporary

Send 16-24 poems by email as a Word / PDF attachment, maximum one poem per page, during December or June only. Submissions from outside the UK and Ireland should be sent to specific address for international submissions, available on website. Cover letter should include short bio and details of the contemporary poets you read. See website for full guidelines.

The Armchair Traveller at the bookHaus

Haus Publishing Ltd
70 Cadogan Place
London
SW1X 9AH
Tel: +44 (0) 20 7838 9055
Email: emma@hauspublishing.com
Website: http://www.thearmchairtraveller.com

Publishes: Nonfiction; *Areas:* Travel; *Markets:* Adult

Contact: Emma Henderson

Publishes travel writing. Send query by email only with book proposal, and sample three chapters if book has already been written.

Arrowhead Press

70 Clifton Road
Darlington
Co. Durham
DL1 5DX
Email: editor@arrowheadpress.co.uk
Website: http://www.arrowheadpress.co.uk

Publishes: Poetry; *Markets:* Adult

Contact: Joanna Boulter, Poetry Editor

Publishes poetry books and pamphlets. Not accepting unsolicited submissions as at February 2016.

Ashgate Publishing Limited

Taylor & Francis Group Ltd
2 Park Square
Milton Park
Abingdon
Oxford
OX14 4RN
Tel: +44 (0) 20 7017-6000
Fax: +44 (0) 20 7017-6699
Email: heidi.bishop@tandf.co.uk
Website: http://www.ashgate.com

Publishes: Nonfiction; *Areas:* Architecture; Arts; Business; Culture; Historical; Legal; Literature; Music; Philosophy; Politics;

Religious; Sociology; *Markets:* Academic; Professional

Contact: Heidi Bishop, Senior Editor

Publishes books in the Social Sciences, Arts, and Humanities. See website for full submission guidelines.

Ashmolean Museum Publications

Ashmolean Museum
Beaumont Street
Oxford
OX1 2PH
Tel: +44 (0) 1865 278010
Email: publications@ashmus.ox.ac.uk
Website: http://www.ashmolean.org

Publishes: Nonfiction; *Areas:* Archaeology; Arts; Historical; *Markets:* Adult; Children's

Contact: Declan McCarthy

Publications mainly based on in-house collections. Publishes both adult and Children's on the subjects of European archeology and ancient history, European and Oriental arts, Egyptology and numismatics. No fiction, African / American / modern art, post-medieval history, ethnography, or unsolicited MSS.

Aureus Publishing Limited

Email: info@aureus.co.uk
Website: http://www.aureus.co.uk

Publishes: Nonfiction; *Areas:* Biography; Music; Sport; *Markets:* Academic; Adult

Publishes books on music, sport, biography and education.

Aurora Metro Press

67 Grove Avenue
Twickenham
TW1 4HX
Tel: +44 (0) 20 3261 0000
Email: submissions@aurorametro.com
Website: http://www.aurorametro.com

Publishes: Fiction; Nonfiction; Scripts; *Areas:* Arts; Biography; Cookery; Culture; Drama; Film; Humour; Literature; Music; Short Stories; Theatre; Translations; Women's Interests; *Markets:* Adult; Children's; Youth

Contact: Neil Gregory (Submissions Manager)

Publishes fiction, plays/theatre texts, and both general and specialist nonfiction books across theatre, film, music, literature, and popular culture. Send synopsis and complete ms by email only. For play submissions, if a production is scheduled then the full script must be sent at least 6 weeks before opening night.

Authentic Media

PO Box 6326
Bletchley
Milton Keynes
MK1 9GG
Tel: +44 (0) 1908 268500
Email: submissions@authenticmedia.co.uk
Website: http://www.authenticmedia.co.uk

Publishes: Nonfiction; *Areas:* Biography; Religious; Spiritual; *Markets:* Academic; Adult

Publisher of Christian books, journals, and other media. Particularly interested in biographies and church and personal spiritual growth. No fiction, poetry, Phds, or children's books. Download and complete pitch form from website and return it by email.

Award Publications Limited

The Old Riding School
The Welbeck Estate
Worksop
Nottinghamshire
S80 3LR
Tel: +44 (0) 1909 478170
Fax: +44 (0) 1909 484632
Email: info@awardpublications.co.uk
Website: http://www.awardpublications.co.uk

Publishes: Fiction; Nonfiction; Reference; *Markets:* Children's

Publishes children's fiction, nonfiction, and reference.

Barefoot Books Ltd

294 Banbury Road
Oxford
OX2 7ED
Tel: +44 (0) 1865 311100
Fax: +44 (0) 1865 514965
Email: help@barefootbooks.com
Website: http://www.barefootbooks.com

Publishes: Fiction; *Markets:* Children's

Publishing program currently full as at June 2015. Check website for current status and notify via Error Report if situation has changed.

Publishes high-quality picture-books for children. Particularly interested in both new and traditional stories from a variety of cultures. Submit material via submission form on website.

Barrington Stoke

18 Walker Street
Edinburgh
EH3 7LP
Tel: +44 (0) 131 225 4113
Fax: +44 (0) 131 225 4140
Email: info@barringtonstoke.co.uk
Website: http://www.barringtonstoke.co.uk

Publishes: Fiction; Nonfiction; Reference; *Markets:* Children's; Professional

Commissions books via literary agents only. No unsolicited material. Publishes books for "reluctant, dyslexic, disenchanted and under-confident" readers and their teachers.

Bennion Kearny

6 Woodside
Churnet View Road
Oakamoor
ST10 3AE
Tel: +44 (0) 1538 703 591
Email: editorial@BennionKearny.com
Website: http://www.bennionkearny.com

Publishes: Nonfiction; *Areas:* Business; Sport; Travel; Markets

Nonfiction publisher. Particularly interested in sport, business, and travel.

Berlitz Publishing

1st Floor West
Magdalen House
136-148 Tooley Street
London
SE1 2TU
Tel: +44 (0) 20 7403 0284
Email: london@berlitzpublishing.com
Website: http://www.berlitzpublishing.com

Publishes: Nonfiction; Reference; *Areas:* Travel; *Markets:* Adult

Publishes books on travel and language.

BFI Publishing

Palgrave Macmillan Ltd
4 Crinan St
London
N1 9XW
Tel: +44 (0) 20 7418 5804
Email: j.steventon@palgrave.com
Website: http://www.palgrave.com/bfi

Publishes: Nonfiction; Reference; *Areas:* Film; Media; TV; *Markets:* Academic

Contact: Jenna Steventon, Senior Commissioning Editor and Head of Higher Education Humanities and BFI Publishing

Welcomes book proposals. Publishes film and television-related books and resources, both for schools and academic readerships, and more generally. See website for publishing proposal forms, and lists of editorial contacts to submit them to.

Birlinn Ltd

West Newington House
10 Newington Road
Edinburgh
EH9 1QS
Tel: +44 (0) 131 668 4371
Fax: +44 (0) 131 668 4466
Email: info@birlinn.co.uk
Website: http://www.birlinn.co.uk

Publishes: Fiction; Nonfiction; Poetry; Reference; *Areas:* Adventure; Architecture; Arts; Autobiography; Biography; Culture; Current Affairs; Finance; Historical; Humour; Legal; Medicine; Military; Nature; Politics; Sociology; Sport; Travel; *Markets:* Adult; Children's

Focuses on Scottish material: local, military, and Highland history; humour, adventure; reference, guidebooks, and folklore. Not currently accepting romantic fiction, science fiction, or short stories. Send query by post with SAE, synopsis, three sample chapters, and explanation of why you have chosen this publisher. No submissions by fax, email, or on disk. See website for full details.

Black & White Publishing Ltd

29 Ocean Drive
Edinburgh
EH6 6JL
Tel: +44 (0) 01316 254500
Email: mail@blackandwhitepublishing.com
Website: http://www.blackandwhitepublishing.com

Publishes: Fiction; Nonfiction; *Areas:* Autobiography; Biography; Cookery; Crime; Humour; Psychology; Romance; Sport; Thrillers; Women's Interests; *Markets:* Academic; Adult; Children's; Youth; *Treatments:* Commercial

Contact: Campbell Brown; Alison McBride

Publisher of general fiction and nonfiction. See website for an idea of the kind of books normally published, and to submit via online submission system. No poetry, short stories, or work in languages other than English.

Black Dog Publishing London UK

10A Acton Street
London
WC1X 9NG
Tel: +44 (0) 20 7713 5097
Fax: +44 (0) 20 7713 8682
Email: info@blackdogonline.com
Website: http://blackdogonline.com

Publishes: Nonfiction; Reference; *Areas:* Architecture; Arts; Beauty and Fashion; Crafts; Culture; Design; Film; Music; Nature; Photography; *Markets:* Adult; *Treatments:* Contemporary

Publishes illustrated books with a fresh, eclectic take on contemporary culture. Originally focused on art and architecture, but now includes subjects as varied as design, fashion, music and environmental concerns.

John Blake Publishing

3 Bramber Court
2 Bramber Road
London
W14 9PB
Tel: +44 (0) 20 7381 0666
Fax: +44 (0) 20 7381 6868
Email: submissions@johnblakebooks.com
Website: https://johnblakebooks.com

Publishes: Fiction; Nonfiction; *Areas:* Autobiography; Biography; Business; Cookery; Crime; Entertainment; Film; Health; Historical; Humour; Legal; Military; Music; Nature; Politics; Science; Self-Help; Sport; Travel; TV; *Markets:* Adult; *Treatments:* Commercial; Mainstream; Popular

Welcomes synopses and ideas for nonfiction. Send query with chapter-by-chapter synopsis, personal details, publishing history, sample chapters, and SAE for response. Always looking for inspiring/shocking real life stories from ordinary people. Not currently accepting fiction. No unsolicited MSS. If submitting by email, attachments should be no larger than 1MB and be saved in .rtf format. See website for full submission guidelines.

Bloodaxe Books Ltd

Eastburn
South Park
Hexham
Northumberland
NE46 1BS
Tel: +44 (0) 01434 611581
Email: editor@bloodaxebooks.com
Website: http://www.bloodaxebooks.com

Publishes: Poetry; *Markets:* Adult

Contact: Neil Astley, Managing/Editorial Director

Submit poetry only if you have a track record of publication in magazines. If so, send sample of up to a dozen poems with SAE, or email address for response if outside the UK. No submissions by email or on disk. Poems from the UK sent without return postage will be recycled unread; submissions by email will be deleted unread. No longer accepting poets who have already published a full-length collection with another publisher. See website for full details.

Bloomsbury Publishing Plc

50 Bedford Square
London
WC1B 3DP
Tel: +44 (0) 20 7631 5600
Fax: +44 (0) 20 7631 5800
Email: contact@bloomsbury.com
Website: http://www.bloomsbury.com

Publishes: Fiction; Nonfiction; Reference; *Areas:* Arts; Historical; Hobbies; Music; Nature; Sport; *Markets:* Academic; Adult; Children's; Professional

No longer accepting submissions of fiction, or nonfiction other than in the following areas: Education, Music, Military History, Natural History, Nautical and Sport. See website for full submission guidelines.

Bloomsbury Spark

Email: BloomsburySparkUK@bloomsbury.com
Website: http://www.bloomsbury.com/spark

Publishes: Fiction; *Areas:* Historical; Mystery; Romance; Sci-Fi; Thrillers; *Markets:* Children's; Youth; *Treatments:* Contemporary

Global, digital imprint from a major international publisher. Publishes ebooks for teen, young adult, and new adult readers. Willing to consider all genres, including romance, contemporary, dystopian, paranormal, sci-fi, mystery, and thrillers. Accepts unsolicited mss between 25,000 and 60,000 words. Submit by email (see website for specific email addresses for different geographic locations) along with query and author bio. See website for full details.

Blue Guides Limited

27 John Street
London
WC1N 2BX
Email: editorial@blueguides.com
Website: http://blueguides.com

Publishes: Nonfiction; *Areas:* Culture; Travel; *Markets:* Adult

Publishes travel guides. Always on the lookout for new authors. Contact by email in first instance, giving an indication of your areas of interest.

Boydell & Brewer Ltd

Bridge Farm Business Park
Top Street
Martlesham
Suffolk
IP12 4RB
Tel: +44 (0) 1394 411320
Email: cpalmer@boydell.co.uk
Website: http://www.boydellandbrewer.com

Publishes: Nonfiction; *Areas:* Archaeology; Arts; Historical; Literature; Military; Music; Religious; *Markets:* Academic; Adult

Contact: Caroline Palmer (Medieval Studies); Michael Middeke (Modern History and Music); Peter Sowden (Maritime History)

Publishes nonfiction in the areas of medieval studies; music; early modern and modern history. Specialist areas include Arthurian studies; the history of religion; military history; and local history. Send proposals by post or by email. See website for specific contacts and individual email addresses.

Bradt Travel Guides

1st Floor IDC House
The Vale
Chalfont St Peter, Bucks
England
SL9 9RZ
Tel: +44 (0) 1753 893444
Fax: +44 (0) 1753 892333
Email: rachel.fielding@bradtguides.com
Website: http://www.bradtguides.com

Publishes: Nonfiction; *Areas:* Travel; *Markets:* Adult

Contact: Rachel Fielding, Commissioning Editor

Publishes travel guides to off-beat places. Send query by email with CV, details of any writing and travel experience, and proposal.

Brilliant Publications

Unit 10, Sparrow Hall Farm
Edlesborough
Dunstable
Bedfordshire
LU6 2ES
Tel: +44 (0) 1525 222292
Fax: +44 (0) 1525 222720
Email: info@brilliantpublications.co.uk
Website: https://www.brilliantpublications.co.uk

Publishes: Nonfiction; *Markets:* Professional

Contact: Priscilla Hannaford

Independent educational publisher specialising in books for teachers. See FAQ section of website for instructions on submitting a new book proposal.

Calisi Press

Tel: +44 (0) 1303 272216
Email: info@calisipress.com
Website: http://www.calisipress.com

Publishes: Fiction; *Areas:* Translations; Women's Interests; *Markets:* Adult

Contact: Franca Simpson

Publishes English translations of books by female Italian writers.

Candy Jar Books

Mackintosh House
136 Newport Road
Cardiff
CF24 1DJ
Tel: +44 (0) 29 2115 7202
Email: shaun@candyjarbooks.co.uk
Website: http://www.candyjarbooks.co.uk

Publishes: Fiction; Nonfiction; *Areas:* Biography; Fantasy; Historical; Military; Sci-Fi; TV; *Markets:* Adult; Children's; Youth

Contact: Shaun Russell (Head of Publishing)

Award-winning independent book publisher, publishing a wide variety of books, from nonfiction, general fiction and children's, through to a range of cult TV books. Submit by post or using online submission form. No children's picture books. See website for full guidelines.

Canongate Books

14 High Street
Edinburgh
EH1 1TE
Tel: +44 (0) 1315 575111
Email: support@canongate.co.uk
Website: http://www.canongate.net

Publishes: Fiction; Nonfiction; *Areas:* Autobiography; Biography; Culture; Historical; Humour; Politics; Science; Translations; Travel; *Markets:* Adult; *Treatments:* Literary

Publisher of a wide range of literary fiction and nonfiction, with a traditionally Scottish slant but becoming increasingly international. Publishes fiction in translation under its international imprint. No children's books, poetry, or drama. Send synopsis with three sample chapters and info about yourself. No submissions by fax, email or on disk.

Canopus Publishing Ltd

15 Nelson Parade
Bdeminster
Bristol
BS3 4HY
Tel: +44 (0) 7970 153217
Email: robin@canopusbooks.com
Website: http://www.canopusbooks.com

Publishes: Nonfiction; *Areas:* Science; Technology; *Markets:* Academic; Adult; *Treatments:* Popular

Contact: Robin Rees

Welcomes book proposals for both academic and popular branches of aerospace and astronomy. Send query by email with author bio, two-page summary outlining concept, coverage, and readership level. See website for more details.

Carcanet Press Ltd

4th Floor
Alliance House
Cross Street
Manchester

M2 7AP
Tel: +44 (0) 161 834 8730
Fax: +44 (0) 161 832 0084
Email: info@carcanet.co.uk
Website: http://www.carcanet.co.uk

Publishes: Nonfiction; Poetry; *Areas:* Biography; Literature; Translations; *Markets:* Academic; Adult; *Treatments:* Literary

Award-winning small press, publishing mainly poetry and academic material. Authors should familiarise themselves with the publisher's list, then, if appropriate, submit 6-10 pages of poetry or translations, with SAE. For other projects, send a full synopsis and covering letter, with sample pages, having first ascertained from the website that the kind of book proposed is suitable. No phone calls. No short stories, childrens prose/poetry or non-poetry related titles.

Carina UK

Harlequin
1 London Bridge Street
London
SE1 9GF
Email: CarinaUKSubs@hqnuk.co.uk
Website: https://www.millsandboon.co.uk

Publishes: Fiction; *Areas:* Adventure; Crime; Erotic; Fantasy; Gothic; Historical; Horror; Humour; Literature; Men's Interests; Mystery; Romance; Sci-Fi; Short Stories; Suspense; Thrillers; Westerns; Women's Interests; *Markets:* Adult; Children's; Family; Youth

Digital imprint from a major publisher, considering all genres of writing, whether novels, novellas, serials, or a series. Particularly interested in authors from the UK, Ireland, South Africa and India. Send submissions by email with any type of attachment.

Chapman Publishing

4 Broughton Place
Edinburgh
EH1 3RX
Tel: +44 (0) 131 557 2207
Email: chapman-pub@blueyonder.co.uk
Website: http://www.chapman-pub.co.uk

Publishes: Fiction; Poetry; Scripts; *Areas:* Drama; Short Stories; *Markets:* Adult; *Treatments:* Literary

Contact: Joy Hendry

Note: No new books being undertaken as at April 2017. Check website for current status.

Publishes one or two books of short stories, drama, and (mainly) poetry by established and rising Scottish writers per year. No novels. Only considers writers who have previously been published in the press's magazine (see entry in magazines database). Only publishes plays that have been previously performed. No unsolicited MSS.

Churchwarden Publications Ltd

PO Box 420
WARMINSTER
BA12 9XB
Tel: +44 (0) 1985 840189
Fax: +44 (0) 1985 840243
Email: enquiries@churchwardenbooks.co.uk
Website: http://www.churchwardenbooks.co.uk

Publishes: Nonfiction; Reference; *Areas:* Religious; *Markets:* Professional

Contact: John Stidolph

Publisher of books and stationery for churchwardens and church administrators.

Cicerone Press

2 Police Square
Milnthorpe
Cumbria
LA7 7PY
Tel: +44 (0) 1539 562069
Email: info@cicerone.co.uk
Website: http://www.cicerone.co.uk

Publishes: Nonfiction; Reference; *Areas:* Hobbies; Leisure; Travel; *Markets:* Adult

Considers synopses and ideas. Publishes guidebooks for outdoor enthusiasts. No poetry, fiction, or unsolicited MSS.

Classical Comics Limited

PO Box 177
Ludlow
SY8 9DL
Tel: +44 (0) 845 812 3000
Fax: +44 (0) 845 812 3005
Email: info@classicalcomics.com
Website: http://www.classicalcomics.com

Publishes: Fiction; *Areas:* Literature; *Markets:* Children's

Contact: Gary Bryant (Managing Director); Jo Wheeler (Creative Director)

Publishes graphic novel adaptations of classical literature.

Co & Bear Productions

63 Edith Grove
London
SW10 0LB
Email: info@cobear.co.uk
Website: http://www.scriptumeditions.co.uk

Publishes: Nonfiction; *Areas:* Arts; Beauty and Fashion; Design; Lifestyle; Nature; Photography; *Markets:* Adult

Publishes illustrated books on interior design, lifestyle, fashion and photography, botanical art, natural history and exploration.

Comma Press

Studio 510a, 5th Floor
Hope Mill
113 Pollard Street
Manchester
M4 7JA
Tel: +44 (0) 7792 564747
Email: info@commapress.co.uk
Website: http://commapress.co.uk

Publishes: Fiction; *Areas:* Short Stories; *Markets:* Adult

Short story publisher aiming to put the short story at the heart of contemporary narrative culture. Stories should be between 1,500 and 8,000 words. No micro-fiction or novellas. See website for full submission guidelines.

Connections Book Publishing Ltd

St. Chad's House
148 King's Cross Road
London
WC1X 9DH
Tel: +44 (0) 20 7837 1968
Fax: +44 (0) 20 7837 2025
Email: info@connections-publishing.com
Website: http://www.connections-publishing.com

Publishes: Nonfiction; Reference; *Areas:* Health; Leisure; Lifestyle; Men's Interests; New Age; Philosophy; Psychology; Religious; Self-Help; Spiritual; Women's Interests; *Markets:* Adult; Family; Youth; *Treatments:* Light; Mainstream; Positive

Contact: Ian Jackson – Editorial Director

Specialises in New Age and spiritual. Emphasis on oracles and self help approach. Interest in martial arts and yoga as well as new healing and physical well being techniques. No academic. Most authors are well known from previous success and widely published books.

Council for British Archaeology (CBA) Publishing

Council for British Archaeology
Beatrice de Cardi House
66 Bootham
York
YO30 7BZ
Tel: +44 (0) 1904 671417
Fax: +44 (0) 1904 671384
Email: webenquiry@archaeologyUK.org
Website: http://new.archaeologyuk.org/

Publishes: Nonfiction; *Areas:* Archaeology; *Markets:* Academic

Publisher of academic books on archaeology. Query by telephone in first instance.

Crescent Moon Publishing

PO Box 1312
Maidstone
Kent
ME14 5XU
Tel: +44 (0) 1622 729593

Email: cresmopub@yahoo.co.uk
Website: http://www.crmoon.com

Publishes: Fiction; Nonfiction; Poetry; *Areas:* Arts; Criticism; Culture; Film; Literature; Media; Music; Philosophy; Politics; Women's Interests; *Markets:* Adult; *Treatments:* Contemporary; Literary

Contact: Jeremy Robinson

Publishes nonfiction on literature, culture, media, and the arts; as well as poetry and some fiction. Non-rhyming poetry is preferred. Send query with one or two sample chapters or up to six poems, with author bio and appropriate return postage for response. Material is only returned if requested and if adequate postage is provided.

Cressrelles Publishing Co. Ltd

10 Station Road Industrial Estate
Colwall
Malvern
WR13 6RN
Tel: +44 (0) 1684 540154
Fax: +44 (0) 1684 540154
Email: simon@cressrelles.co.uk
Website: http://www.cressrelles.co.uk

Publishes: Nonfiction; Scripts; *Areas:* Drama; *Markets:* Academic; Adult

Contact: Simon Smith

Welcomes submissions. Publishes plays, theatre and drama textbooks, and local interest books. Accepts scripts by post or by email.

Crown House Publishing

Submissions
Crown Buildings
Bancyfelin
Carmarthen
SA33 5ND
Tel: +44 (0) 1267 211345
Fax: +44 (0) 1267 211882
Email: submissions@crownhouse.co.uk
Website: http://www.crownhouse.co.uk

Publishes: Nonfiction; *Areas:* Business; Health; Humour; Psychology; Self-Help; Spiritual; *Markets:* Academic; Adult; Children's; *Treatments:* Popular

Publishes books on Mind Body Spirit; Business Training and Development; Education
Psychotherapy; Personal Growth; and Health and Wellbeing. Send email up to 300 words only describing your ideas in the first instance.

CTS (Catholic Truth Society)

40 Harleyford Road
Vauxhall
London
SE11 5AY
Tel: +44 (0) 20 7640 0042
Fax: +44 (0) 20 7640 0046
Email: f.martin@cts-online.org.uk
Website: http://www.cts-online.org.uk

Publishes: Nonfiction; *Areas:* Religious; *Markets:* Adult

Contact: Fergal Martin (Publisher)

Publisher of Roman Catholic religious books. Publishes a range of books in this area, including Vatican documents and sources, as well as moral, doctrinal, liturgical, and biographical books. Welcomes appropriate ideas, synopses, and unsolicited MSS. Send query with 1-2 page synopsis or a sample text.

Curious Fox

Brunel Road
Handmills
Basingstoke Hants
RG21 6XS
Tel: +44 (0) 845 070 5656
Fax: +44 (0) 1256 812558
Email: submissions@curious-fox.com
Website: http://www.curious-fox.com

Publishes: Fiction; *Areas:* Adventure; Crime; Fantasy; Historical; Humour; Nature; Romance; Sci-Fi; Thrillers; *Markets:* Children's

Publishes fiction for children. Send query by email with CV, sample chapters, and list of any previous writing credits in the body of the email.

DB Publishing

29 Clarence Road
Attenborough
Nottingham
NG9 5HY
Tel: +44 (0) 1332 384235
Fax: +44 (0) 1332 292755
Email: submissions@jmdmedia.co.uk
Website: http://www.dbpublishing.co.uk

Publishes: Fiction; Nonfiction; *Areas:* Autobiography; Biography; Crime; Health; Historical; Sociology; Sport; Travel; *Markets:* Adult

Contact: Steve Caron

Considers all types of books, but focuses on local interest, sport, biography, autobiography and social history. Approach by email or phone – no submissions by post. See website for full guidelines.

DC Thomson

2 Albert Square
Dundee
DD1 9QJ
Tel: +44 (0) 1382 223131
Email: innovation@dcthomson.co.uk
Website: http://www.dcthomson.co.uk

Publishes: Fiction; Nonfiction; *Markets:* Adult; Children's

Publisher of newspapers, magazines, comics, and books, with offices in Dundee, Aberdeen, Glasgow, and London. For fiction guidelines send large SAE marked for the attention of the Central Fiction Department.

Dedalus Ltd

Langford Lodge
St Judith's Lane
Sawtry
PE28 5XE
Tel: +44 (0) 1487 832382
Fax: +44 (0) 1487 832382
Email: info@dedalusbooks.com
Website: http://www.dedalusbooks.com

Publishes: Fiction; *Areas:* Literature; Translations; *Markets:* Adult; *Treatments:* Contemporary; Literary

Send query letter describing yourself along with SAE, synopsis, three sample chapters, and explanation of why you think this publisher in particular is right for you – essential to be familiar with and have read other books on this publisher's list before submitting, as most material received is entirely inappropriate. Welcomes submissions of suitable original fiction and is particularly interested in intellectually clever and unusual fiction, however undertakes only between one and three new projects a year. No email or disk submissions, or collections of short stories by unknown authors. Novels should be over 40,000 words – ideally over 50,000. Most books are translations.

Dino Books

3 Bramber Court
2 Bramber Road
London
W14 9PB
Tel: +44 (0) 20 7381 0666
Email: help@dinobooks.co.uk
Website: https://dinobooks.co.uk

Publishes: Nonfiction; *Areas:* Humour; Sport; *Markets:* Children's

Publishes nonfiction for children aged 9-12, that aim to entertain, educate, and "turn your way of thinking upside down".

Discovery Walking Guides Ltd

Email: ask.discovery@ntlworld.com
Website: http://www.dwgwalking.co.uk

Publishes: Nonfiction; *Areas:* Travel; *Markets:* Adult

Publishes walking guidebooks and maps. Welcomes proposals for new projects. Send query by email. No attachments.

Dodo Ink

Email: sam@dodoink.com
Website: http://www.dodoink.com

Publishes: Fiction; *Markets:* Adult; *Treatments:* Literary

Contact: Sam Mills

Independent UK publisher aiming to publish three novels per year, in paperback and digital formats. Publishes risk-taking, imaginative novels, that don't fall into easy marketing categories. Closed to submissions as at June 2017.

Dref Wen

28 Church Road
Whitchurch
Cardiff
CF14 2EA
Tel: +44 (0) 2920 617860
Fax: +44 (0) 2920 610507
Email: post@drefwen.com
Website: http://www.drefwen.com

Publishes: Fiction; Nonfiction; *Areas:* Autobiography; *Markets:* Academic; Adult; Children's

Publishes bilingual and Welsh language books for children, as well as Welsh and English educational books for those learning Welsh. Also moving into adult publishing, in particular autobiographies of Welsh personalities.

Dunedin Academic Press Ltd

Hudson House
8 Albany Street
Edinburgh
EH1 3QB

LONDON OFICE:
352 Cromwell Tower,
Barbican,
London
EC2Y 8NB
Tel: +44 (0) 1314 732397
Fax: +44 (0) 1250 770088
Email: mail@dunedinacademicpress.co.uk
Website: http://www.dunedinacademicpress.co.uk

Publishes: Nonfiction; *Areas:* Anthropology; Biography; Current Affairs; Finance; Health; Historical; Legal; Medicine; Music; Nature; Philosophy; Religious; Science; Sociology; *Markets:* Academic; Professional

Publishes academic works, mainly at levels from first year undergraduate to postgraduate and research levels.

Dynasty Press

36 Ravensdon Street
Kennington
London
SE11 4AR
Tel: +44 (0) 7970 066894
Email: admin@dynastypress.co.uk
Website: http://www.dynastypress.co.uk

Publishes: Nonfiction; *Areas:* Biography; Historical; *Markets:* Adult

Publishes books connected to royalty, dynasties and people of influence.

Edinburgh University Press

The Tun – Holyrood Road
12 (2f) Jackson's Entry
Edinburgh
EH8 8PJ
Tel: +44 (0) 1316 504218
Fax: +44 (0) 1316 503286
Email: editorial@eup.ed.ac.uk
Website: http://www.euppublishing.com

Publishes: Nonfiction; Reference; *Areas:* Archaeology; Architecture; Culture; Film; Historical; Legal; Literature; Media; Philosophy; Politics; Religious; Science; Sociology; *Markets:* Academic

Publishes academic and scholarly nonfiction and reference across the humanities and social sciences.

Edward Elgar Publishing Ltd

The Lypiatts
15 Lansdown Road
Cheltenham
Glos
GL50 2JA
Tel: +44 (0) 1242 226934
Fax: +44 (0) 1242 262111
Email: info@e-elgar.com
Website: http://www.e-elgar.co.uk

Publishes: Nonfiction; *Areas:* Business; Culture; Finance; Legal; Nature; Politics; Sociology; *Markets:* Academic; Professional

Contact: [See website for contact details for different areas]

Academic and professional publisher of books and journals, with a strong focus on the social sciences and legal fields. Actively commissioning new titles. See website for contact details and proposal forms.

Egmont UK Ltd

First Floor
The Yellow Building
1 Nicholas Road
London
W11 4AN
Tel: +44 (0) 20 3220 0400
Fax: +44 (0) 20 3220 0401
Email: service@egmont.co.uk
Website: http://www.egmont.co.uk

Publishes: Fiction; *Markets:* Children's

Publishes picture books and children's fiction. Agented submissions only.

Eland Publishing Ltd

61 Exmouth Market
Clerkenwell
London
EC1R 4QL
Tel: +44 (0) 20 7833 0762
Fax: +44 (0) 20 7833 4434
Email: info@travelbooks.co.uk
Website: http://www.travelbooks.co.uk

Publishes: Nonfiction; Poetry; *Areas:* Travel; *Markets:* Adult

Contact: Rose Baring; John Hatt; Barnaby Rogerson; Stephanie Allen

Specialises in keeping the classics of travel literature in print. Also publishes books of poetry relating to particular places.

The Emma Press Ltd

Email: queries@theemmapress.com
Website: http://theemmapress.com

Publishes: Fiction; Nonfiction; Poetry; *Markets:* Adult; Children's

Contact: Emma Wright

Publishes themed anthologies of poetry, stories, and essays. See website for themes of current calls for submissions. In order to submit, must have been previously accepted by or purchased from the press.

Encyclopedia Britannica (UK) Ltd

2nd Floor, Unity Wharf
Mill Street
London
SE1 2BH
Tel: +44 (0) 20 7500 7800
Fax: +44 (0) 20 7500 7878
Email: enquiries@britannica.co.uk
Website: https://britannica.co.uk

Publishes: Nonfiction; Reference; *Markets:* Academic; Adult; Family

Global digital educational publisher, publishing information and instructional products used in schools, universities, homes, libraries and workplaces throughout the world.

Euromonitor

60-61 Britton Street
London
EC1M 5UX
Tel: +44 (0) 20 7251 8024
Fax: +44 (0) 20 7608 3149
Email: info@euromonitor.com
Website: http://www.euromonitor.com

Publishes: Nonfiction; Reference; *Areas:* Business; *Markets:* Professional

International publisher of business reference and nonfiction, including market reports, directories, etc. for the professional market.

Exley Publications

16 Chalk Hill
Watford
WD19 4BG
Tel: +44 (0) 1923 474480
Website: https://www.helenexley.com

Publishes: Nonfiction; *Markets:* Adult; *Treatments:* Popular

Publishes gift books.

Eye Books

Tel: +44 (0) 7973 861869
Email: dan@eye-books.com
Website: http://eye-books.com

Publishes: Nonfiction; *Areas:* Travel; *Markets:* Adult

Contact: Dan Hiscocks

Small independent publisher, publishing books about ordinary people doing extraordinary things. Often includes strong travel element. See website for detailed submission guidelines and online submission system.

Fabian Society

61 Petty France
Westminster
London
SW1H 9EU
Tel: +44 (0) 20 7227 4900
Email: info@fabians.org.uk
Website: http://www.fabians.org.uk

Publishes: Nonfiction; *Areas:* Current Affairs; Finance; Nature; Politics; Sociology; *Markets:* Adult

Left-leaning political think tank publishing books on current affairs, politics, economics, environment, social policy, etc.

Famous Seamus

83 Ducie Street
Manchester
M1 2JQ
Email: submissions@thefamousseamus.com
Website: http://www.famousseamuspublishing.com

Publishes: Fiction; Nonfiction; Poetry; Reference; Scripts; *Areas:* Adventure; Anthropology; Arts; Biography; Cookery; Crime; Criticism; Culture; Current Affairs; Drama; Entertainment; Erotic; Fantasy; Film; Gothic; Health; Historical; Hobbies; Horror; How-to; Humour; Leisure; Lifestyle; Literature; Media; Medicine; Men's Interests; Music; Mystery; Nature; New Age; Philosophy; Photography; Politics; Psychology; Romance; Science; Sci-Fi; Self-Help; Short Stories; Spiritual; Suspense; Thrillers; Women's Interests; *Markets:* Academic; Adult; Children's; Family; Professional; Youth; *Treatments:* Contemporary; Cynical; Dark; Experimental; In-depth; Light; Literary; Niche; Popular; Positive; Progressive; Satirical; Serious; Traditional

Contact: Famous Seamus

An all round publisher that looks for the unusual, the challenging, controversial, subversive, fetishistic and down right strange.

Findhorn Press Ltd

Delft Cottage
Dyke
Forres
IV36 2TF
Tel: +44 (0) 1309 690582
Email: submissions@findhornpress.com
Website: http://www.findhornpress.com

Publishes: Nonfiction; *Areas:* Health; New Age; Spiritual; *Markets:* Adult

Publishes books on mind, body, spirit, New Age and healing. Approach by email only. Send 1-2 page synopsis, word count, number of illustrations, table of contents, page describing intended readership, brief personal bio including any previous publications, and details on ways you can help promote your book. See website for more information.

Fingerpress UK

Email: firstwriter@fingerpress.co.uk
Website: http://www.fingerpress.co.uk

Publishes: Fiction; *Areas:* Historical; Sci-Fi; Thrillers; *Markets:* Adult; *Treatments:* Commercial

Note: Not accepting submissions as at May 2016 – check website for current status.

*** Please read the submissions page on our website before submitting anything... ***

Only open to submissions at certain times. Check website for current status. When open to submissions, this will be announced on our Facebook and Twitter pages.

We're an independent publisher based in London; we publish high quality Historical Fiction and Science Fiction. We're building a range of savvy, entertaining titles that are both thought-provoking and a good read. The ideal novel will have memorable characters with good plot development and pacing.

If your book isn't either Historical Fiction or Science Fiction, please don't submit it to us -- many thanks for your understanding.

We look for:

* submissions of completed, professionally edited, commercial-grade novels

Please check out our sister website – a virtual reality Facebook for authors, publishers and readers.

Fisherton Press

Email: general@fishertonpress.co.uk
Website: http://fishertonpress.co.uk

Publishes: Fiction; *Markets:* Children's

Contact: Eleanor Levenson

Aims to publish books for children that adults will also enjoy reading, whether for the first time or the hundredth. Send query with ideas or fully written or illustrated texts with short bio, by email.

Fitzrovia Press Limited

10 Grafton Mews
London
W1T 5JG
Tel: +44 (0) 20 7380 0749
Email: info@fitzroviapress.co.uk
Website: http://www.fitzroviapress.com

Publishes: Fiction; Nonfiction; *Areas:* Philosophy; Spiritual; *Markets:* Adult

Contact: Ranchor Prime

Publishes fiction and nonfiction on Hinduism, spirituality, and Eastern philosophy. No unsolicited mss. Send query with outline and sample chapter.

Fleming Publications

134 Renfrew Street
Glasgow
G3 6ST
Email: info@ettadunn.com
Website: http://www.flemingpublications.com

Publishes: Fiction; Nonfiction; Poetry; *Areas:* Biography; Historical; Photography; Self-Help; *Markets:* Adult

Contact: Etta Dunn

Publishes nonfiction, fiction, and poetry for "mindful individuals".

Floris Books

15 Harrison Gardens
Edinburgh
EH11 1SH
Tel: +44 (0) 1313 372372
Fax: +44 (0) 1313 479919
Email: floris@florisbooks.co.uk
Website: http://www.florisbooks.co.uk

Publishes: Fiction; Nonfiction; *Areas:* Architecture; Arts; Biography; Crafts; Health; Historical; Literature; Philosophy; Religious; Science; Self-Help; Sociology; Spiritual; *Markets:* Adult; Children's; Youth

Publishes a wide range of books including adult nonfiction, picture books and children's novels. No poetry or verse, fiction for people over the age of 15, or autobiography, unless it specifically relates to a relevant nonfiction subject area. No submissions by email. See website for full details of areas covered and submission guidelines.

Fonthill Media Ltd

Millview House
Toadsmoor Road
Stroud
Gloucestershire
GL5 2TB

US OFFICE:
60 Thoreau Street #204
Concord, MA 01742
Email: submissions@fonthillmedia.com
Website: http://fonthillmedia.com

Publishes: Nonfiction; *Areas:* Archaeology; Biography; Historical; Military; Sociology; Sport; Travel; *Markets:* Adult

Independent publisher with offices in the UK and US. Publishes nonfiction only. Send query through website submissions form or by email, providing your project's title, description up to 200 words, description of yourself up to 100 words, proposed word count, and nature and number of illustrations.

Frances Lincoln Children's Books

74-77 White Lion Street
London
N1 9PF
Tel: +44 (0) 20 7284 9300
Fax: +44 (0) 20 7485 0490
Email: QuartoKidsSubmissions@Quarto.com
Website: http://www.quartoknows.com/Frances-Lincoln-Childrens-Books

Publishes: Fiction; Nonfiction; Poetry; *Areas:* Culture; *Markets:* Children's

Contact: Rachel Williams, Publisher; Janetta Otter-Barry, Publisher; Katie Cotton, Editor

Publishes picture books, multicultural books, poetry, picture books and information books. Submit by email. See website for full guidelines.

Frontinus

4 The Links
Cambridge Road
Newmarket
Suffolk
CB8 0TG
Tel: +44 (0) 1638 663456
Email: info@frontinus.org.uk
Website: http://www.frontinus.org.uk

Publishes: Nonfiction; *Areas:* Design; Technology; *Markets:* Academic; Professional

Publishes academic and professional nonfiction for engineers.

Galley Beggar Press

37 Dover Street
Norwich
NR2 3LG
Email: info@galleybeggar.co.uk
Website: http://galleybeggar.co.uk

Publishes: Fiction; Nonfiction; *Areas:* Literature; Sci-Fi; Short Stories; *Markets:* Adult; *Treatments:* Literary

Publishing company specifically set up to act as a sponsor to writers who have struggled to either find or retain a publisher, and whose writing shows great ambition and literary merit. Publishes a wide range of nonfiction and fiction, including quality SF, but no poetry, children's, young adult, or specialist nonfiction. When submitting, authors must be able to prove that they have read something published by the press. Closed to submissions as at November 2015, but due to re-open soon. See website for current status and full submission guidelines.

GEY Books

Email: geybooks@gmail.com

Publishes: Fiction; Nonfiction; Poetry; *Areas:* Culture; Drama; Entertainment; Erotic; Fantasy; Men's Interests; Romance; Short Stories; Thrillers; Travel; *Markets:* Adult; *Treatments:* Contemporary; Experimental; Literary

Contact: Thomas Moore

We are interested in publishing writers who identify on the LGBTQIA spectrum. The work we publish represents the many complexities of human relationships within the crazy, brilliant and beautiful LGBTQIA community.

We are interested in publishing: Fiction, Non-fiction, Poetry, Photography, Art and Comics. We are open to all types of media so long as we can create a product out of the work.

We will only publish original and previously unpublished works.

As a standard we pay our authors 50% of profits made from all sales.

We will not accept a full submission in the first instance. Please send over a brief outline of the project attaching a small sample of the work no more then 2 sides of A4 in PDF form. We will not accept any submissions via any other form besides email or any attachments other then PDFs.

Gibson Square Books Ltd

Tel: +44 (0) 20 7096 1100
Fax: +44 (0) 20 7993 2214
Email: info@gibsonsquare.com
Website: http://www.gibsonsquare.com

Publishes: Nonfiction; *Areas:* Arts; Biography; Criticism; Culture; Current Affairs; Historical; Philosophy; Politics; Psychology; Travel; Women's Interests; *Markets:* Adult

Publishes books which contribute to a general debate. Send proposals by email. See website for full guidelines.

Gingko Library

70 Cadogan Place
London
SW1X 9AH
Tel: +44 (0) 20 7838 9055
Email: aran@thegingkolibrary.com
Website: http://www.gingkolibrary.com

Publishes: Nonfiction; *Areas:* Architecture; Arts; Biography; Finance; Historical; Literature; Music; Philosophy; Politics; Religious; Science; Technology; *Markets:* Academic; Adult

Publisher promoting dialogue between the West and the Middle East and North Africa. Publishes collected articles and academic monographs, peer-reviewed by scholars and academic advisors. See website for submission guidelines.

GL Assessment

1st Floor Vantage London
Great West Road
Brentford
TW8 9AG
Tel: +44 (0) 20 8996 3333
Fax: +44 (0) 20 8742 8767
Email: info@gl-assessment.co.uk
Website: https://www.gl-assessment.co.uk

Publishes: Nonfiction; *Markets:* Academic

Publishes educational testing and assessment material.

Gomer Press

Llandysul Enterprise Park
Llandysul
Ceredigion
SA44 4JL
Tel: +44 (0) 1559 362371
Fax: +44 (0) 1559 363758
Email: gwasg@gomer.co.uk
Website: http://www.gomer.co.uk

Publishes: Fiction; Nonfiction; Poetry; Reference; Scripts; *Areas:* Arts; Autobiography; Biography; Culture; Drama; Historical; Leisure; Literature; Music; Nature; Religious; Sport; Theatre; Travel; *Markets:* Academic; Adult; Children's

Publishes fiction, nonfiction, plays, poetry, language books, and educational material, for adults and children, in English and in Welsh. See website for contact details of editors and query appropriate editor with sample chapter, synopsis, CV, and sales strengths of your proposal. Do not send complete MS in first instance.

Granta Books

12 Addison Avenue
London
W11 4QR
Tel: +44 (0) 20 7605 1360
Fax: +44 (0) 20 7605 1361
Email: info@grantabooks.com
Website: http://www.grantabooks.com

Publishes: Fiction; Nonfiction; *Areas:* Autobiography; Biography; Criticism; Culture; Historical; Nature; Politics; Sociology; Travel; *Markets:* Adult; *Treatments:* Literary; Serious

Publishes around 70% nonfiction / 30% fiction. In nonfiction publishes serious cultural, political and social history, narrative history, or memoir. Rarely publishes straightforward biographies. No genre fiction. Accepts submissions via literary agent only.

Gresham Books Ltd

The Carriage House
Ningwood Manor
Isle of Wight
PO30 4NJ
Tel: +44 (0) 1983 761389
Email: info@gresham-books.co.uk
Website: http://www.gresham-books.co.uk

Publishes: Nonfiction; *Areas:* Religious; *Markets:* Academic; Adult; Children's

Contact: Paul Lewis

Publishes bespoke books for schools, including hymn books, plus text books to help teach British values.

Guild of Master Craftsman (GMC) Publications Ltd

166 High Street
Lewes
BN7 1XU
Tel: +44 (0) 1273 477374
Fax: +44 (0) 1273 402866
Email: pubs@thegmcgroup.com
Website: http://www.gmcbooks.com

Publishes: Nonfiction; Reference; *Areas:* Architecture; Arts; Cookery; Crafts; Film; Gardening; Hobbies; How-to; Humour; Photography; TV; *Markets:* Adult; Children's

Publishes books on the above topics, plus woodworking, dolls houses, and miniatures. Also publishes magazines and videos. No fiction.

Halban Publishers

22 Golden Square
London
W1F 9JW
Tel: +44 (0) 20 7437 9300
Fax: +44 (0) 20 7437 9512
Email: books@halbanpublishers.com
Website: http://www.halbanpublishers.com

Publishes: Fiction; Nonfiction; *Areas:* Autobiography; Biography; Criticism; Historical; Literature; Philosophy; Politics; Religious; *Markets:* Adult

Contact: Peter Halban; Martine Halban

Independent publisher of fiction, memoirs, history, biography, and books of Jewish interest. Send query by post or by email. No unsolicited MSS. Unsolicited emails deleted unread.

Haldane Mason Ltd

PO Box 34196
London
NW10 3YB
Tel: +44 (0) 20 8459 2131
Fax: +44 (0) 20 8728 1216
Email: sfrancis@haldanemason.com
Website: http://haldanemason.com

Publishes: Nonfiction; *Areas:* Crafts; Health; Historical; Lifestyle; Science; *Markets:* Adult; Children's; Youth

Publishes books and box-sets – mainly for children through children's imprint, but also for adults, covering such topics as alternative health, yoga, henna body art, Feng Shui, etc. Children's books include crafts, puzzles, history, science, maths, etc. Send query by email in first instance.

Halsgrove

Halsgrove House
Ryelands Business Park
Bagley Road
Wellington
Somerset
TA21 9PZ
Tel: +44 (0) 1823 653777
Fax: +44 (0) 1823 216796
Email: sales@halsgrove.com
Website: http://www.halsgrove.com

Publishes: Nonfiction; *Areas:* Arts; Biography; Historical; Photography; *Markets:* Adult

Publishes regional material covering various regions in the areas of history, biography, photography, and art. No fiction or poetry. Send query by email with brief synopsis in first instance.

Harlequin Mills & Boon Ltd

Harlequin
1 London Bridge Street
London
SE1 9GF

Email: submissions@harlequin.com
Website: http://www.millsandboon.co.uk

Publishes: Fiction; *Areas:* Crime; Historical; Romance; *Markets:* Adult; *Treatments:* Commercial; Contemporary

Major publisher with extensive romance list and various romance imprints. Submit via online submission system.

Also includes digital imprint accepting submissions in any genre, and particularly interested in authors from rapidly expanding digital markets in the UK, Ireland, South Africa and India. See website for separate submission guidelines and specific email address for this imprint. Commercial fiction and crime imprint accepts submissions via literary agents only.

HarperCollins Publishers Ltd

The News Building
1 London Bridge Street
London
SE1 9GF
Tel: +44 (0) 20 8741 7070
Fax: +44 (0) 20 8307 4440
Email: enquiries@harpercollins.co.uk
Website: http://www.harpercollins.co.uk

Publishes: Fiction; Nonfiction; Reference; *Areas:* Autobiography; Biography; Cookery; Crafts; Crime; Entertainment; Fantasy; Film; Gardening; Health; Historical; Leisure; Lifestyle; Media; Military; Science; Sci-Fi; Sport; Thrillers; *Markets:* Adult; Children's; *Treatments:* Literary

One of the UK's three largest publishers, with one of the broadest ranges of material published. Authors include many award-winning bestsellers, and significant figures of literary history. Accepts approaches through agents and from published authors only, or if accompanied by a positive assessment from a manuscript assessment agency. No unsolicited MSS.

HarperImpulse

Email: romance@harpercollins.co.uk
Website: http://www.harperimpulseromance.com

Publishes: Fiction; *Areas:* Erotic; Historical; Romance; Short Stories; *Markets:* Adult; *Treatments:* Contemporary; Experimental; Mainstream

Contact: Kimberley Young, Publishing Director

Digital-first romance publisher publishing fun and fast Adult and New Adult genre fiction to more mainstream novels; particularly contemporary, historical, paranormal and erotic fiction. Will consider work of any length (including short form fiction targetted at mobile devices), and is keen to see work that experiements with length, genre, and form, etc. Submit complete ms with covering letter and synopsis by email. See website for full guidelines.

Hart Publishing Ltd

Kemp House
Chawley Park
Cumnor Hill
Oxford
OX2 9PH
Tel: +44 (0) 1865 598648
Fax: +44 (0) 1865 727017
Email: sinead@hartpub.co.uk
Website: http://www.hartpub.co.uk

Publishes: Nonfiction; *Areas:* Legal; *Markets:* Academic; Professional

Contact: Sinead Moloney; Bill Asquith

Publisher or legal books and journals for the professional and academic markets. See website for submission guidelines and specific editor subject areas and contact details.

Haus Publishing

70 Cadogan Place
London
SW1X 9AH
Tel: +44 (0) 20 7838 9055
Fax: +44 (0) 20 7584 9501
Email: emma@hauspublishing.com
Website: http://www.hauspublishing.com

Publishes: Fiction; Nonfiction; *Areas:* Arts; Biography; Film; Historical; Music;

Photography; Politics; Theatre; Travel; *Markets:* Adult; *Treatments:* Literary

Contact: Emma Henderson

Publishes non-academic biographies of historical figures, and literary travel accounts (not guides). No autobiographies, fiction for children or young adults, or biographies of living people. Send query by email only, with synopsis, author bio, sample chapter headings, and the first three chapters. If the book is not yet written, send a proposal and sample chapter of your writing. Allow 6-8 weeks for response.

Hawthorn Press

1 Lansdown Lane
Stroud
Gloucestershire
GL5 1BJ
Tel: +44 (0) 1453 757040
Fax: +44 (0) 1453 751138
Email: info@hawthornpress.com
Website: http://www.hawthornpress.com

Publishes: Nonfiction; *Areas:* Lifestyle; Self-Help; *Markets:* Adult

Publisher aiming to contribute to a more creative, peaceful and sustainable world through its publishing. Publishes mainly commissioned work, but will consider approaches. Send first two chapters with introduction, full table of contents/book plan, brief author biography and/or CV, and SAE. Allow at least 2–4 months for response. Accepts email enquiries, but full submissions should be made by post.

Hay House Publishers

33 Notting Hill Gate
London
W11 3JQ
Tel: +44 (0) 20 3675 2450
Fax: +44 (0) 20 3675 2451
Email: submissions@hayhouse.co.uk
Website: http://www.hayhouse.co.uk

Publishes: Nonfiction; *Areas:* Biography; Business; Current Affairs; Finance; Health; Lifestyle; Medicine; Men's Interests; Nature; Philosophy; Psychology; Religious; Self-Help; Sociology; Spiritual; Women's Interests; *Markets:* Adult; *Treatments:* Positive

Describes itself as the world's leading mind body and spirit publisher. Open to submissions from April 4, 2016. Accepts proposals as hard copy by post or by email, but prefers email approaches. See website for full submission guidelines.

Haynes Publishing

Sparkford
Near Yeovil
Somerset
BA22 7JJ
Tel: +44 (0) 1963 440635
Fax: +44 (0) 1963 440023
Email: bookseditorial@haynes.co.uk
Website: http://www.haynes.co.uk

Publishes: Nonfiction; Reference; *Areas:* How-to; Leisure; Sport; Technology; *Markets:* Adult

Contact: John H. Haynes OBE (Chairman)

Mostly publishes motoring and transport titles, including DIY service and repair manuals for cars and motorbikes, motoring in general (including Motor Sports), but also home, DIY, and leisure titles. Unsolicited MSS welcome, if on one of the above areas of interest.

Head of Zeus

Clerkenwell House
45-47 Clerkenwell Green
London
EC1R 0HT
Email: info@headofzeus.com
Website: http://www.headofzeus.com

Publishes: Fiction; Nonfiction; *Areas:* Biography; Crime; Fantasy; Historical; Mystery; Philosophy; Romance; Sci-Fi; Short Stories; Sociology; Sport; Suspense; Thrillers; *Markets:* Adult; Youth; *Treatments:* Commercial; Literary

Publishes general and literary fiction, genre fiction, and nonfiction. Submit via online submission system.

Headland Publications

38 York Avenue
West Kirby
Wirral
CH48 3JF
Tel: +44 (0) 01516 259128
Email: headlandpublications@hotmail.co.uk
Website: http://www.headlandpublications.co.uk

Publishes: Fiction; Nonfiction; Poetry; *Areas:* Biography; Short Stories; *Markets:* Adult

Specialises in poetry, but has expanded scope to include short stories and biography.

Headline Publishing Group

Carmelite House
50 Victoria Embankment
London
EC4Y 0DZ
Tel: +44 (0) 20 3122 7222
Email: enquiries@headline.co.uk
Website: https://www.headline.co.uk

Publishes: Fiction; Nonfiction; *Areas:* Autobiography; Biography; Cookery; Gardening; Historical; Science; Sport; TV; *Markets:* Adult; *Treatments:* Commercial; Literary; Popular

Publishes hardback and paperback commercial and literary fiction, as well as popular nonfiction.

Hesperus Press Limited

28 Mortimer Street
London
W1W 7RD
Tel: +44 (0) 20 7436 0869
Email: info@hesperuspress.com
Website: http://www.hesperuspress.com

Publishes: Fiction; Nonfiction; Poetry; Reference; *Areas:* Autobiography; Biography; Crime; Culture; Erotic; Fantasy; Historical; Literature; Romance; Sci-Fi; Thrillers; Translations; Travel; *Markets:* Adult; Children's; *Treatments:* Contemporary; Literary; Traditional

Publishes the lesser known works of classical authors, both in English and in translation. No unsolicited MSS and no submissions.

Hippopotamus Press

22 Whitewell Road
Frome
Somerset BA11 4EL
Tel: +44 (0) 1373 466653
Email: rjhippopress@aol.com

Publishes: Poetry; *Markets:* Adult; *Treatments:* Literary

Contact: Roland John

Publishes first collections of poetry by poets who have an established track-record of publication in poetry magazines.

The History Press

The Mill,
Brimscombe Port
Stroud
Gloucestershire
GL5 2QG
Email: web@thehistorypress.co.uk
Website: http://www.thehistorypress.co.uk

Publishes: Nonfiction; *Areas:* Archaeology; Biography; Crime; Historical; Military; Sport; *Markets:* Adult

Publishes books on history, from local to international. Send query by email. No unsolicited mss. See website for full guidelines.

Hodder Education

338 Euston Road
London
NW1 3BH
Tel: +44 (0) 20 7873 6000
Fax: +44 (0) 20 7873 6299
Email: educationenquiries@hodder.co.uk
Website: http://www.hoddereducation.co.uk

Publishes: Nonfiction; Reference; *Areas:* Health; Medicine; Science; Self-Help; *Markets:* Academic; Adult

Publishes educational and reference books including home learning and school textbooks. See website for more details and for specific submission addresses for different types of books.

Hodder Faith

Carmelite House
50 Victoria Embankment
London
EC4Y 0DZ
Tel: +44 (0) 20 3122 6777
Email: hodderfaith@hodder.co.uk
Website: http://www.hodderfaith.com

Publishes: Nonfiction; *Areas:* Religious; *Markets:* Adult

Seeks to provide a platform for Christian views to be expressed across all denominations, races and ages.

Honno Welsh Women's Press

Honno
Unit 14, Creative Units
Aberystwyth Arts Centre
Aberystwyth
Ceredigion
SY23 3GL
Tel: +44 (0) 1970 623150
Fax: +44 (0) 1970 623150
Email: post@honno.co.uk
Website: http://www.honno.co.uk

Publishes: Fiction; Nonfiction; Poetry; *Areas:* Autobiography; Crime; Fantasy; Short Stories; Women's Interests; *Markets:* Adult; Children's; Youth; *Treatments:* Literary

Contact: Caroline Oakley

Welcomes MSS and ideas for books from women born in, living in, or significantly connected to Wales, only. Publishes fiction, autobiographical writing and reprints of classic titles in English and Welsh, as well as anthologies of poetry and short stories. Particularly looking for more literary, crime, and fantasy titles, among others. All submissions must be sent as hard copy; no email submissions. Send query with synopsis and first 50 pages. Not currently accepting children/teenage novels or poetry or short story collections by a single author.

Hopscotch

St Jude's Church
Dulwich Road
Herne Hill
London
SE24 0PB
Tel: +44 (0) 20 7501 6736
Fax: +44 (0) 20 7738 9718
Email: hopscotch@bebc.co.uk
Website: http://www.hopscotchbooks.com

Publishes: Nonfiction; *Areas:* Historical; Science; Technology; *Markets:* Professional

Publishes teaching resources for primary school teachers.

House of Lochar

Isle of Colonsay
PA61 7YR
Tel: +44 (0) 1951 200232
Fax: +44 (0) 1951 200232
Email: sales@houseoflochar.com
Website: http://www.houseoflochar.com

Publishes: Fiction; Nonfiction; *Areas:* Biography; Historical; Literature; Travel; *Markets:* Adult; Children's

Publishes fiction and nonfiction related to Scotland and / or Celtic themes, including history, fiction, transport, maritime, genealogy, Gaelic, and books for children. No poetry or books unrelated to Scottish or Celtic themes.

Hymns Ancient & Modern Ltd

3rd Floor, Invicta House
108-114 Golden Lane
London
EC1Y 0TG
Tel: +44 (0) 20 7776 7548
Fax: +44 (0) 20 7776 7556
Email: mary@hymnsam.co.uk
Website: http://www.hymnsam.co.uk

Publishes: Nonfiction; Reference; *Areas:* Biography; Humour; Music; Religious; Spiritual; *Markets:* Academic; Adult

Contact: Mary Matthews, Editorial Manager

Publishes religious books including hymn books, liturgical material, and schoolbooks. No proposals for dissertations, fiction, poetry, drama, children's books, books of specialist local interest, or (generally) multi-authored collections of essays or symposium papers. Send query with contents page, synopsis, and first chapter with SAE.

Imprint Academic

PO Box 200
Exeter
EX5 5YX
Tel: +44 (0) 1392 851550
Fax: +44 (0) 1392 851178
Email: keith@imprint.co.uk
Website: http://www.imprint-academic.com

Publishes: Nonfiction; *Areas:* Criticism; Philosophy; Politics; Psychology; *Markets:* Academic; Adult

Contact: Keith Sutherland

Publisher of books on politics, psychology, and philosophy for both academic and general readership. Welcomes ideas and unsolicited MSS by email or by post, provided return postage is included.

Independent Music Press

PO Box 69
Church Stretton
Shropshire
SY6 6WZ
Email: info@impbooks.com
Website: http://www.impbooks.com

Publishes: Nonfiction; *Areas:* Biography; Culture; Music; *Markets:* Adult; Youth

Contact: Martin Roach

Publishes biographies of music stars, and books on youth culture.

Indigo Dreams Publishing

24 Forest Houses
Halwill
Beaworthy
Devon
EX21 5UU
Email: publishing@indigodreams.co.uk
Website: http://www.indigodreams.co.uk

Publishes: Poetry; *Markets:* Adult; *Treatments:* Literary

Contact: Ronnie Goodyer

Publishes poetry collections up to 60/70 pages and poetry pamphlets up to 36 pages. See website for submission guidelines.

Infinite Ideas

36 St Giles
Oxford
OX1 3LD
Tel: +44 (0) 1865 514888
Email: richard@infideas.com
Website: http://www.infideas.com

Publishes: Nonfiction; *Areas:* Autobiography; Biography; Business; Cookery; Culture; Current Affairs; Entertainment; Gardening; Hobbies; Lifestyle; Media; Politics; Self-Help; Travel; *Markets:* Professional; *Treatments:* Commercial; Contemporary; Progressive; Traditional

Contact: Richard Burton

Set up in 2004. We were on a mission to create a publishing business like no other. In a world that is teeming with books, good and bad (mainly bad), we set out to publish books of real value to the reader. Every page has something that might change readers' lives for the better, for ever.

160 plus books later, we like to think that we've achieved some of our ambitions. We've developed great book series.

We've worked with top brands including Marks and Spencer, Sainsbury's Champneys, Simple and Anne Summers who value our ability to produce great content in a beautiful package.

We've worked too with a number of new authors to help them get their masterpieces into the market.

We love great content, we love great books and we love great ideas.

Do feel free to get in touch to with us if you'd like to hear more. Send short synopsis by email.

Iron Press

5 Marden Terrace
Cullercoats
North Shields
Northumberland
NE30 4PD
Tel: +44 (0) 191 253 1901

Fax: +44 (0) 191 253 1901
Email: contact@ironpress.co.uk
Website: http://www.ironpress.co.uk

Publishes: Fiction; Poetry; *Areas:* Short Stories; *Markets:* Adult; *Treatments:* Literary

Contact: Peter Mortimer

Poetry and fiction publisher championing quality new writing since 1973. Publishes poetry, (including haiku), collections of short stories, and anthologies of verse and prose. No novels or unsolicited mss. Send query by email in first instance.

IWM (Imperial War Museums)

IWM London
Lambeth Road
London
SE1 6HZ
Tel: +44 (0) 20 7416 5000
Email: publishing@iwm.org.uk
Website: http://www.iwm.org.uk/commercial/publishing

Publishes: Nonfiction; *Areas:* Historical; Military; *Markets:* Adult

Publishes books linked to its exhibitions and archives. Send query by email with brief outline and sample material.

Jacaranda Books Art Music Ltd

Unit 304 Metal Box Factory
30 Great Guildford Street
London
SE1 0HS
Email: office@jacarandabooksartmusic.co.uk
Website: http://www.jacarandabooksartmusic.co.uk

Publishes: Fiction; Nonfiction; *Areas:* Arts; Autobiography; Beauty and Fashion; Biography; Crime; Photography; Romance; *Markets:* Adult; *Treatments:* Contemporary

Contact: Valerie Brandes, Founder & Publisher

Publishes adult fiction and nonfiction, including crime, romance, illustrated books, biography, memoir, and autobiography. Particularly interested in books where the central character or theme relates to minority groups and/or has strong female protagonists. Also interested in original works from or about African, African-American, Caribbean and black British artists working in the fields of photography, fine art, fashion, and contemporary and modern art, and artists of calibre from the soul, blues, Ramp;B and reggae traditions. Send query by email with writer CV, detailed synopsis, and two sample chapters. See website for full submission guidelines.

Jane's Information Group

Sentinel House
163 Brighton Road
Coulsdon
Surrey
CR5 2YH
Tel: +44 (0) 1344 328300
Fax: +44 (0) 20 8763 1006
Website: http://www.janes.com

Publishes: Nonfiction; Reference; *Areas:* Military; *Markets:* Adult

Publisher of magazines, books, reference works, online material, and yearbooks related to defence, aerospace, security, and transport topics.

Joffe Books Ltd

Unit 3, 7a Plough Yard
London
EC2A 3LP
Email: submissions@joffebooks.com
Website: http://www.joffebooks.com

Publishes: Fiction; *Areas:* Crime; Mystery; Romance; Suspense; *Markets:* Adult

Contact: Jasper Joffe

Publishes full-length mysteries, romances, thrillers, detective stories, and suspense. No kids books, sci-fi, nonfiction, conspiracy theories, or erotic. Send query by email with complete ms as an attachment, a synopsis in the body of the email, and 100 words about yourself. Include "submission" in the subject line. See website for full guidelines.

Jordan Publishing

21 St Thomas Street
Bristol
BS1 6JS

20-22 Bedford Row
London
WC1R 4JS
Tel: +44 (0) 1179 230600
Fax: +44 (0) 1179 250486
Email: editor@jordanpublishing.co.uk
Website: http://www.jordanpublishing.co.uk

Publishes: Nonfiction; *Areas:* Legal; *Markets:* Professional

Legal publisher specialising in family law, company and commercial, insolvency, private client, civil litigation and personal injury. Welcomes proposals in these and other areas of legal practice. Submit query via website.

Josef Weinberger Ltd

12-14 Mortimer Street
London
W1T 3JJ
Tel: +44 (0) 20 7580 2827
Fax: +44 (0) 20 7436 9616
Email: general.info@jwmail.co.uk
Website: http://www.josef-weinberger.com

Publishes: Scripts; *Areas:* Theatre; *Markets:* Adult

Publishes theatre scripts for musicals, plays, pantomimes, operas, and operettas.

Kube Publishing

MCC, Ratby Lane
Markfield
Leicestershire
LE67 9SY
Tel: +44 (0) 1530 249230
Fax: +44 (0) 1530 249656
Email: info@kubepublishing.com
Website: http://www.kubepublishing.com

Publishes: Fiction; Nonfiction; Poetry; *Areas:* Biography; Culture; Historical; Lifestyle; Politics; Religious; Sociology; Spiritual; *Markets:* Academic; Adult; Children's; Youth

Independent publisher of general interest, academic, and children's books on Islam and the Muslim experience. Publishes nonfiction for children, young people, and adults, but fiction and poetry for children and teens only. See website for full guidelines.

Kyle Books

192-198 Vauxhall Bridge Road
London
SW1V 1DX
Tel: +44 (0) 20 7692 7215
Fax: +44 (0) 20 7692 7260
Email: general.enquiries@kylebooks.com
Website: http://www.kylebooks.com

Publishes: Nonfiction; Reference; *Areas:* Beauty and Fashion; Cookery; Gardening; Health; Lifestyle; *Markets:* Adult

Describes itself as "one of the UK's leading publishers in the areas of cookery, health, lifestyle and gardening."

Laurence King Publishing Ltd

361-373 City Road
London
EC1V 1LR
Tel: +44 (0) 20 7841 6900
Fax: +44 (0) 20 7841 6910
Email: commissioning@laurenceking.com
Website: http://www.laurenceking.co.uk

Publishes: Nonfiction; *Areas:* Architecture; Arts; Beauty and Fashion; Design; Film; Historical; Photography; *Markets:* Academic; Adult

Publisher of books on the creative arts. Send proposal by email.

Lawrence & Wishart

Central Books Building
Freshwater Road
Chadwell Heath
RM8 1RX
Tel: +44 (0) 20 8597 0090
Email: submissions@lwbooks.co.uk
Website: http://www.lwbooks.co.uk

Publishes: Nonfiction; *Areas:* Culture; Current Affairs; Historical; Politics; *Markets:* Adult

Contact: Katharine Harris

Independent publisher of books on current affairs and political history and culture. Formed through a merger in the 1930s of the Communist Party's press and a liberal and anti-fascist publisher.

Legend Business

175-185 Gray's Inn Road
London
WC1X 8UE
Tel: +44 (0) 20 7812 0641
Email: submissions@legend-paperbooks.co.uk
Website: http://www.legendtimesgroup.co.uk/legend-business

Publishes: Nonfiction; *Areas:* Business; *Markets:* Professional

Publishes a wide-ranging list of business titles. Welcomes proposals and finished manuscripts. Submit synopsis and first three chapters through online submission system. See website for more details.

Legend Press

175-185 Gray's Inn Road
London
WC1X 8UE
Tel: +44 (0) 20 7812 0641
Email: info@legend-paperbooks.co.uk
Website: http://www.legendpress.co.uk

Publishes: Fiction; *Markets:* Adult; *Treatments:* Commercial; Contemporary; Mainstream

Contact: Tom Chalmers

Publishes a diverse list of contemporary adult novels. No historical fiction, children's books, poetry or travel writing. See website for full submission guidelines and online submission system.

Lion Hudson Plc

Wilkinson House
Jordan Hill Road
Oxford
OX2 8DR
Tel: +44 (0) 1865 302750
Fax: +44 (0) 1865 302757
Email: SubmissionstoLionBooksMonarchLionFiction@LionHudson.com
Website: http://www.lionhudson.com

Publishes: Fiction; Nonfiction; Reference; *Areas:* Autobiography; Biography; Health; Religious; Spiritual; *Markets:* Adult; Children's; *Treatments:* Positive

Publishes books that reflect Christian values or are inspired by a Christian world view, including adult nonfiction / reference, and children's fiction and nonfiction. See website for specific submission guidelines for different imprints.

Liverpool University Press

4 Cambridge Street
Liverpool
L69 7ZU
Tel: +44 (0) 1517 942233
Fax: +44 (0) 1517 942235
Email: lup@liv.ac.uk
Website: http://www.liverpooluniversitypress.co.uk

Publishes: Nonfiction; *Areas:* Archaeology; Architecture; Arts; Culture; Historical; Literature; Politics; Sci-Fi; Sociology; *Markets:* Academic

Contact: Alison Welsby; Anthony Cond

Publishes books and journals, specialising in Modern Languages, Postcolonial, Slavery and Migration Studies, Irish History, Labour History, Science Fiction Studies and Art History. Download proposal submission form from website.

Lonely Planet

240 Blackfriars Road
London
SE1 8NW
Tel: +44 (0) 20 3771 5100
Fax: +44 (0) 20 3771 5101
Email: recruitingcontributors@lonelyplanet.com
Website: http://www.lonelyplanet.com

Publishes: Nonfiction; *Areas:* Travel; *Markets:* Adult

Publishes international travel guides. Send query by email with speculative CV or resume.

Lost Tower Publications

Email: losttowerpublications@yahoo.com
Website: http://losttowerpublications.jigsy.com

Publishes: Fiction; Poetry; *Areas:* Adventure; Autobiography; Crime; Fantasy; Gothic; Horror; Leisure; Lifestyle; Mystery; Sci-Fi; Spiritual; Suspense; Thrillers; Women's Interests; *Markets:* Adult; Children's; Family; Youth; *Treatments:* Contemporary; Dark; Experimental; Niche; Positive; Progressive

Contact: Harry Yang

Formed in 2011 as part of a poetry book publishing campaign to promote poetry world wide as an attractive and entertaining art form for the twenty first century. We print 3-4 books a year collecting the best photographs and poetry from around the world, to produce high quality books for people to enjoy. Our books are available to buy worldwide either from Amazon or to order through your local bookshop.

In March 2013 we published a journey of hope through poems and photographs which have been collected from around the world. The work in this anthology has been collected from every continent of our planet and illustrates ideas of hope from many of the world religions; looks at the different forms hope can take and how hope can always be found if you look carefully into the world which surrounds you.

Luath Press Ltd

543/2 Castlehill
The Royal Mile
Edinburgh
EH1 2ND
Tel: +44 (0) 131 225 4326
Fax: +44 (0) 131 225 4324
Email: sales@luath.co.uk
Website: http://www.luath.co.uk

Publishes: Fiction; Nonfiction; Poetry; *Areas:* Arts; Beauty and Fashion; Biography; Crime; Current Affairs; Drama; Historical; Leisure; Lifestyle; Nature; Photography; Politics; Sociology; Sport; Thrillers; Travel; *Markets:* Adult; Children's; Youth

Contact: G.H. MacDougall, Managing Editor

Publishes a range of books, usually with a Scottish connection. Check upcoming publishing schedule on website, and – if you think your book fits – send query with SAE, synopsis up to 250 words, manuscript or sample chapters, author bio, and any other relevant material. See website for full submission guidelines. Approaches by email will not be considered.

Luna Press Publishing

149/4 Morrison Street
Edinburgh
EH3 8AG
Email: lunapress@outlook.com
Website: http://www.lunapresspublishing.com

Publishes: Fiction; *Areas:* Fantasy; Sci-Fi; Short Stories; *Markets:* Academic; Adult; *Treatments:* Dark

Publishes Science Fiction, Fantasy, and Dark Fantasy (including their sub-genres). Will consider short stories, novelettes, novellas, novels, graphic novels, academic material. See website for submission guidelines.

Note: not accepting novel submissions as at May 2016 – check website for current status.

Lund Humphries Limited

Office 3, Book House
261A City Road
London
EC1V 1JX
Tel: +44 (0) 20 7440 7530
Email: lclark@lundhumphries.com
Website: http://www.lundhumphries.com

Publishes: Nonfiction; *Areas:* Architecture; Arts; Design; Historical; *Markets:* Adult

Contact: Lucy Clark

Publishes books on art, art history, and design. See website for guidelines on submitting a proposal.

Macmillan

The Macmillan Building
4 Crinan Street
London
N1 9XW
Tel: +44 (0) 20 7833 4000
Fax: +44 (0) 20 7843 4640
Website: http://www.macmillan.com

Publishes: Fiction; Nonfiction; Poetry; Reference; *Areas:* Autobiography; Biography; Business; Cookery; Crime; Culture; Current Affairs; Fantasy; Film; Finance; Gardening; Health; Historical; Horror; Humour; Military; Music; Nature; Philosophy; Politics; Psychology; Romance; Science; Sci-Fi; Sport; Theatre; Thrillers; Travel; TV; *Markets:* Academic; Adult; Children's; Family; Professional; Youth; *Treatments:* Commercial; Literary; Popular

Large publishing company publishing a wide range of titles through its various divisions and imprints. Policies towards submissions and material published varies across these divisions and imprints (as does the address to contact), so further research essential.

Management Books 2000 Ltd

36 Western Road
Oxford
OX1 4LG
Tel: +44 (0) 1865 600738
Email: info@mb2000.com
Website: http://www.mb2000.com

Publishes: Nonfiction; *Areas:* Business; Finance; Lifestyle; Self-Help; *Markets:* Adult

Send outline of book, including why it was written, where it would be sold and read, etc. synopsis or detailed contents page, and a couple of sample chapters. Publishes books on management, business, finance, and related topics. Welcomes new ideas.

Manchester University Press

Floor J, Renold Building
Altrincham Street
Manchester
M1 7JA
Tel: +44 (0) 1612 752310
Fax: +44 (0) 1612 757711
Email: mup@manchester.ac.uk
Website: http://www.manchesteruniversitypress.co.uk

Publishes: Nonfiction; Reference; *Areas:* Arts; Business; Criticism; Culture; Design; Film; Finance; Historical; Legal; Literature; Media; Politics; Theatre; TV; *Markets:* Academic

Publishes mainly textbooks for undergraduates and A-level students, plus research monographs.

Mandrake of Oxford

PO Box 250
Oxford
OX1 1AP
Email: mandrake@mandrake.uk.net
Website: http://mandrake.uk.net

Publishes: Fiction; Nonfiction; *Areas:* Arts; Crime; Culture; Erotic; Health; Horror; Lifestyle; Mystery; Philosophy; Sci-Fi; Self-Help; Spiritual; *Markets:* Adult

Send query by post or by email. May also include synopsis. See website for full guidelines, and for examples of the kind of material published.

Mantra Lingua Ltd

Global House
303 Ballards Lane
London
N12 8NP
Tel: +44 (0) 20 8445 5123
Fax: +44 (0) 20 8446 7745
Email: info@mantralingua.com
Website: http://www.mantralingua.com

Publishes: Fiction; Nonfiction; *Areas:* Translations; *Markets:* Children's

Multilingual educational publishers of nonfiction and picture books for children up to 12 years. 1,400 words maximum (800 for children up to 7). All books are print products which are sound enabled, playing back audio narrations or music, etc. Send submissions by email. See website for more details.

Marion Boyars Publishers

26 Parke Road
London
SW13 9NG
Tel: +44 (0) 20 8788 9522
Fax: +44 (0) 20 8789 8122
Email: catheryn@marionboyars.com
Website: http://www.marionboyars.co.uk

Publishes: Fiction; Nonfiction; *Areas:* Anthropology; Autobiography; Biography; Criticism; Culture; Drama; Film; Literature; Music; Philosophy; Psychology; Sociology; Theatre; Women's Interests; *Markets:* Adult

Contact: Catheryn Kilgarriff (Director), catheryn@marionboyars.com; Rebecca Gillieron (Fiction Editor), rebecca@marionboyars.com; Amy Christian (Nonfiction Editor), amy@marionboyars.com

Note: Not accepting new submissions as at June 2015. Check website for current status.

For nonfiction, send synopses and ideas with SAE. Particularly interested in music, film, and contemporary culture. Fiction submissions via a literary agent only. No poetry submissions or approaches by email.

Maverick Reads

124 Cromwell Road
Kensington
London
SW7 4ET
Email: Editor@maverick-reads.com
Website: http://www.maverick-reads.com

Publishes: Fiction; Nonfiction; Poetry; Reference; *Areas:* Adventure; Criticism; Culture; Fantasy; Gothic; Historical; Literature; Media; Music; Mystery; Nature; New Age; Philosophy; Psychology; Religious; Romance; Science; Sci-Fi; Self-Help; Short Stories; Spiritual; Suspense; Theatre; Thrillers; Women's Interests; *Markets:* Academic; Adult; Children's; Family; Professional; Youth; *Treatments:* Contemporary; Dark; Experimental; In-depth; Literary; Niche; Positive; Progressive; Satirical; Serious

Contact: The Editor, Adriano Bulla

Please submit:
A bio and description of book.
- 6-10 short poems or a long one of about 10 pages for Poetry
- 2-4 chapters for prose (max 15 pages)
- A sample, a plan and qualifications for nonfiction.

Kevin Mayhew Publishers

Buxhall
Stowmarket
Suffolk
IP14 3BW
Tel: +44 (0) 845 3881634
Fax: +44 (0) 1449 737834
Email: submissions@kevinmayhew.com
Website: http://www.kevinmayhew.com

Publishes: Nonfiction; *Areas:* Music; Religious; Spiritual; *Markets:* Academic; Adult; Children's

Contact: Manuscript Submissions Department

Publishes books relating to Christianity and music, for adults, children, schools, etc. Send query by email only, with first three chapters, full contents list, sales pitch, summary, market info, bio, and details of any previous publications. See website for full details.

The Merlin Press

99b Wallis Road
London
E9 5LN
Tel: +44 (0) 20 8533 5800
Email: info@merlinpress.co.uk
Website: http://www.merlinpress.co.uk

Publishes: Nonfiction; *Areas:* Historical; Philosophy; Politics; *Markets:* Adult

Publisher based in London specialising in history, philosophy, and politics.

Merlin Unwin Books

Palmers House
7 Corve Street
Ludlow
Shropshire
SY8 1DB
Tel: +44 (0) 1584 877456

Fax: +44 (0) 1584 877457
Email: books@merlinunwin.co.uk
Website: http://www.merlinunwin.co.uk

Publishes: Nonfiction; *Areas:* Autobiography; Cookery; Humour; Leisure; Nature; Sport; *Markets:* Adult

Publishes books on the countryside and countryside pursuits, covering such topics as nature, fishing, shooting, etc.

Merrell Publishers Limited

70 Cowcross Street
London
EC1M 6EJ
Tel: +44 (0) 20 7928 8880
Fax: +44 (0) 20 7928 1199
Email: hm@merrellpublishers.com
Website: http://www.merrellpublishers.com

Publishes: Nonfiction; *Areas:* Architecture; Arts; Beauty and Fashion; Culture; Design; Photography; *Markets:* Adult

Contact: Hugh Merrell, Publisher

Send query, preferably by email, with one-page synopsis of the project, highlighting its subject-matter, scope, approach and purpose, and indicating why you believe it to be commercially viable; an annotated table of contents to indicate how the book will be structured and what each chapter will contain in terms of subject-matter, numbers of words and numbers of illustrations; a single chapter of sample text, if already written; photocopies or printouts of sample images from the book, if available; a brief (one-paragraph) biography of each author, which should highlight, in particular, why they are qualified to write on the subject of the proposed book and provide details of any previous publications; an annotated list of related or competing works currently in print, highlighting how the proposed book differs from anything already available.

Methodist Publishing

Methodist Church House
25 Marylebone Road
London
NW1 5JR
Tel: +44 (0) 20 7486 5502
Email: helpdesk@methodistchurch.org.uk
Website: http://www.mph.org.uk

Publishes: Nonfiction; *Areas:* Philosophy; Religious; *Markets:* Adult

Publishes resources for the Methodist Church in Britain. No unsolicited mss.

Metro Publications Ltd

Po Box 6336
London
N1 6PY
Tel: +44 (0) 20 8533 7777
Fax: +44 (0) 20 8533 7777
Email: info@metropublications.com
Website: https://metropublications.com

Publishes: Nonfiction; *Areas:* Architecture; Arts; Leisure; Travel; *Markets:* Adult

Publisher of guide books on many aspects of London life.

Michael Terence Publishing (MTP)

Two Brewers House
2A Wellington Street
Thame
OX9 3BN

Tel: +44 (0) 20 3582 2002
Email: admin@mtp.agency
Website: https://www.mtp.agency

Publishes: Fiction; Nonfiction; *Markets:* Adult

Contact: Keith Abbott

A dynamic publisher offering quick responses to MSS and queries with a fast time to market for accepted works. Submissions always welcome. Please send your first 3 chapters, synopsis and a brief bio by email or via our website.

Milo Books Ltd

The Old Weighbridge
Station Road
Wrea Green
Lancashire
PR4 2PH
Email: publish@milobooks.com
Website: http://www.milobooks.com

Publishes: Nonfiction; *Areas:* Autobiography; Biography; Crime; Culture; Current Affairs; Sport; *Markets:* Adult; Youth

Will consider books in any nonfiction genre, but specialises in true crime, autobiography/biography, sports, current affairs and youth culture. Send query by post (with return postage if return required) or by email, with first couple of chapters.

Monarch Books

Lion Hudson Plc.
Wilkinson House
Jordan Hill Road
Oxford
OX2 8DR
Tel: +44 (0) 1865 302750
Fax: +44 (0) 1865 302757
Email: SubmissionstoLionBooksMonarchLionFiction@LionHudson.com
Website: http://www.lionhudson.com/page.asp?pid=monarch_books

Publishes: Fiction; Nonfiction; *Areas:* Politics; Psychology; Religious; Spiritual; *Markets:* Adult

Publishes a wide range of Christian books. Accepts unsolicited MSS, synopses, and ideas. Accepts submissions by email. See website for full guidelines. Response not guaranteed unless interested. If no response after three months assume rejection.

Monsoon Books Pte Ltd

No.1 Duke of Windsor Suite
Burrough Court
Burrough on the Hill
Leics
LE14 2QS
Email: customerservice@monsoonbooks.com.sg
Website: http://www.monsoonbooks.com.sg

Publishes: Fiction; Nonfiction; *Areas:* Autobiography; Biography; Crime; Erotic; Fantasy; Historical; Horror; Military; Politics; Romance; Short Stories; Thrillers; Travel; *Markets:* Adult; Children's; Youth

A Singapore-registered award-winning independent publisher of English-language books and ebooks on Asia, with its editorial office in the UK. Welcomes submissions with Asian (particularly Southeast Asian) themes from agents direct, or from published and unpublished authors via online submission system via website.

Mudfog Press

C/o Arts and Events
Culture and Tourism
P.O Box 99A
Civic Centre
Middlesbrough
TS1 2QQ
Email: contact@mudfog.co.uk
Website: http://www.mudfog.co.uk

Publishes: Fiction; Poetry; *Areas:* Short Stories; *Markets:* Adult

Publishes poetry and short fiction by writers in the Tees Valley area. Send query with 15-20 poems or 2-3 stories. See website for full details. No email submissions.

Natural History Museum Publishing

The Natural History Museum
Cromwell Road
London
SW7 5BD
Tel: +44 (0) 20 7942 5336
Email: publishing@nhm.ac.uk
Website: http://www.nhm.ac.uk/business-services/publishing.html

Publishes: Nonfiction; *Areas:* Arts; Nature; Science; *Markets:* Adult; *Treatments:* Popular

Publishes accessible, fully illustrated books about the natural world.

Neil Wilson Publishing Ltd

226 King Street
Castle Douglas
DG7 1DS
Tel: +44 (0) 1556 504119
Fax: +44 (0) 1556 504065
Email: submissions@nwp.co.uk
Website: http://www.nwp.co.uk

Publishes: Nonfiction; Reference; *Areas:* Biography; Cookery; Crime; Culture;

Historical; Humour; Music; Nature; Travel; *Markets:* Adult

Welcomes approaches by email only. Publishes books of Scottish interest through a variety of imprints, including history, hill-walking, humour, food and drink (including whisky), biography, true crime, and reference. Has published fiction in the past, but longer does so. No academic, political, fiction, or technical. See website for full guidelines.

New Holland Publishers (UK) Ltd

The Chandlery Unit 009
50 Westminster Road
London
SE1 7QY
Tel: +44 (0) 20 7953 7565
Email: enquiries@nhpub.co.uk
Website: http://www.newhollandpublishers.com

Publishes: Nonfiction; Reference; *Areas:* Arts; Biography; Cookery; Crafts; Design; Gardening; Health; Historical; How-to; Humour; Lifestyle; Nature; Photography; Self-Help; Spiritual; Sport; Travel; *Markets:* Adult

International publisher of nonfiction and reference. Send query with SAE, synopsis, CV, and sample chapters.

New Playwrights' Network (NPN)

10 Station Road Industrial Estate
Colwall
Herefordshire
WR13 6RN
Tel: +44 (0) 1684 540154
Email: simon@cressrelles.co.uk
Website: http://www.cressrelles.co.uk

Publishes: Scripts; *Areas:* Drama; Theatre; *Markets:* Adult

Contact: Simon Smith

Established in the 1970s to promote scripts by new writers. Send scripts by email or by post.

Michael O'Mara Books Ltd

9 Lion Yard
Tremadoc Road
London
SW4 7NQ
Tel: +44 (0) 20 7720 8643
Fax: +44 (0) 20 7627 4900
Email: enquiries@mombooks.com
Website: http://www.mombooks.com

Publishes: Nonfiction; *Areas:* Biography; Historical; Humour; *Markets:* Adult; Children's

Independent publisher dealing in general nonfiction, royal and celebrity biographies, humour, and anthologies, and books for children through its imprint (including quirky nonfiction, humour, novelty, picture, and board books). Welcomes ideas, and prefers synopses and sample text to unsolicited mss. No fiction. See website for full details.

Oberon Books

521 Caledonian Road
London
N7 9RH
Tel: +44 (0) 20 7607 3637
Fax: +44 (0) 20 7607 3629
Email: george@oberonbooks.com
Website: http://www.oberonbooks.com

Publishes: Nonfiction; Scripts; *Areas:* Drama; Theatre; *Markets:* Adult; Professional

Contact: George Spender, Senior Editor

Publishes play texts, and books on dance and theatre. Specialises in translations of European classics and contemporary plays, though also publishes edited performance versions of classics including Shakespeare. Play texts are usually published in conjunction with a production. Play scripts may be submitted by post or by email. Book proposals for trade and professional titles should include summary, table of contents, estimate word count, and sample chapter.

Octopus Publishing Group Limited

Carmelite House
50 Victoria Embankment
London
EC4Y 0DZ
Tel: +44 (0) 20 3122 6400
Email: info@octopusbooks.co.uk
Website: https://www.octopusbooks.co.uk

Publishes: Nonfiction; Reference; *Areas:* Antiques; Architecture; Arts; Beauty and Fashion; Cookery; Crafts; Culture; Design; Film; Gardening; Health; Historical; Humour; Lifestyle; Music; Psychology; Spiritual; Sport; Travel; *Markets:* Adult; Children's

Publisher with wide range of imprints dealing with a variety of nonfiction and reference subjects. See website for specific email addresses dedicated to each individual imprint.

Oneworld Publications

10 Bloomsbury Street
London
WC1B 3SR
Tel: +44 (0) 20 7307 8900
Email: submissions@oneworld-publications.com
Website: http://www.oneworld-publications.com

Publishes: Fiction; Nonfiction; *Areas:* Anthropology; Arts; Biography; Business; Current Affairs; Historical; Literature; Nature; Philosophy; Politics; Psychology; Religious; Science; Self-Help; Translations; *Markets:* Adult; *Treatments:* Commercial; Literary; Popular

Not accepting fiction submissions as at July 2016, but hopes this will change in the near future. Check website for current status.

Nonfiction authors must be academics and/or experts in their field. Approaches for fiction must provide a clear and concise synopsis, outlining the novel's main themes. See website for full submission guidelines, and forms for fiction and nonfiction, which may be submitted by email.

Ouen Press

Email: submissions@ouenpress.com
Website: http://www.ouenpress.com

Publishes: Fiction; Nonfiction; *Areas:* Biography; Short Stories; Travel; *Markets:* Adult; *Treatments:* Contemporary

Publishes contemporary fiction, travel literature, short story collections and biography, if edgy. No genre, children's books, poetry, single short stories, guide books or recipe books. Send query by email only with outline, brief resume of your writing experience, and first 4,000 words, all in the body of the email. Do not include a cover letter. No attachments, or submissions by post. If no reponse within 60 days, assume rejection.

Oversteps Books

6 Halwell House
South Pool
Nr Kingsbridge
Devon
TQ7 2RX
Email: alwynmarriage@overstepsbooks.com
Website: http://www.overstepsbooks.com

Publishes: Poetry; *Markets:* Adult

Poetry publisher. Send email with copies of six poems that have been published in magazines or won competitions, along with details of dates or issue numbers and email addresses of the editors. Include poems and information in the body of your email. No submissions by post.

Pandora Press

144 Hemingford Road
London
N1 1DE
Tel: +44 (0) 20 7607 0823
Fax: +44 (0) 20 7609 2776
Email: ro@riversoram.com
Website: http://www.riversoram.com

Publishes: Nonfiction; Reference; *Areas:* Arts; Biography; Current Affairs; Health; Media; Politics; Women's Interests; *Markets:* Adult

Feminist press publishing general nonfiction, including arts, biography, current affairs, media, reference, and sexual politics.

PaperBooks

The Old Fire Station
140 Tabernacle Street
London
EC2A 4SD
Tel: +44 (0) 20 7300 7370
Email: submissions@legend-paperbooks.co.uk
Website: http://www.legendtimesgroup.co.uk/paperbooks

Publishes: Nonfiction; *Areas:* Autobiography; Cookery; *Markets:* Adult

Former fiction publisher now relaunched as a nonfiction publisher. Publishes cookery and memoir, and looking to extend this list. Submit online using online submission system.

Parthian Books

426 Grove Extension
Swansea University
Singleton Park
Swansea
SA2 8PP
Tel: +44 (0) 1792 606605
Email: susieparthian@gmail.com
Website: http://www.parthianbooks.co.uk

Publishes: Fiction; Poetry; Scripts; *Areas:* Drama; Short Stories; Translations; *Markets:* Adult

Contact: Susie Wild

Publisher of poetry, drama, and fiction, of Welsh origin, in the English language. Also publishes English language translations of Welsh language work. Not accepting poetry submissions as at June 2015 (check website for current situation). Send query with SAE, one-page synopsis, and first 30 pages. No email submissions. See website for full submission guidelines.

Pavilion Publishing

Rayford House
School Road
Hove
East Sussex
BN3 5HX
Tel: +44 (0) 1273 434943
Fax: +44 (0) 1273 227308
Email: info@pavpub.com
Website: http://www.pavpub.com

Publishes: Nonfiction; Reference; *Areas:* Health; Sociology; *Markets:* Professional

Publishes books and resources for public, private and voluntary workers in the health, social care, education and community safety sectors. Welcomes submissions from both new and established authors, and organisations that are developing training materials.

Phaidon Press Limited

Regent's Wharf
All Saints Street
London
N1 9PA
Tel: +44 (0) 20 7843 1000
Fax: +44 (0) 20 7843 1010
Email: submissions@phaidon.com
Website: http://www.phaidon.com

Publishes: Nonfiction; *Areas:* Architecture; Arts; Beauty and Fashion; Cookery; Culture; Design; Film; Historical; Music; Photography; Travel; *Markets:* Academic; Adult; Children's

Publishes books in the areas of art, architecture, design, photography, film, fashion, contemporary culture, decorative arts, music, performing arts, cultural history, food and cookery, travel and books for children. No fiction or approaches by post. Send query by email only, with CV and short description of the project. Response only if interested.

Phoenix Yard Books

65 King's Cross Road
London
WC1X 9LW
Tel: +44 (0) 20 7239 4968
Email: submissions@phoenixyardbooks.com
Website: http://www.phoenixyardbooks.com

Publishes: Fiction; Nonfiction; Poetry; *Markets:* Children's; Youth; *Treatments:* Literary

Contact: Emma Langley

Publishes picture books, fiction, poetry, nonfiction and illustration for children aged around three to thirteen. Considers books of all genres, but leans more towards the literary and of the fiction spectrum. Particularly interested in character-based series, and fiction appealing to boys aged 6-9. Does not concentrate on young adult fiction, but will consider older fiction as part of epic series, sagas or trilogies. Accepts queries through literary agents, foreign publishers, and literary translators only.

The Policy Press

1-9 Old Park Hill
Bristol
BS2 8BB
Tel: +44 (0) 1179 545940
Email: pp-info@bristol.ac.uk
Website: http://www.policypress.co.uk

Publishes: Nonfiction; *Areas:* Politics; Sociology; *Markets:* Academic; Professional

Publishes monographs, texts and journals for scholars internationally; reports for policy makers, professionals and researchers; and practice guides for practitioners and user groups. Aims to publish the latest policy research for the whole policy studies community, including academics, policy makers, practitioners and students. Welcomes proposals for books, reports, guides or journals. Author guidelines available on website.

Polity Press

65 Bridge Street
Cambridge
CB2 1UR
Tel: +44 (0) 1223 324315
Fax: +44 (0) 1223 461385
Email: editorial@politybooks.com
Website: http://www.polity.co.uk

Publishes: Nonfiction; Reference; *Areas:* Anthropology; Archaeology; Business; Crime; Culture; Finance; Health; Historical; Literature; Media; Medicine; Nature; Philosophy; Politics; Psychology; Religious; Sociology; Women's Interests; *Markets:* Adult

Contact: Appropriate commissioning editor (see website)

Describes itself as one of the world's leading publishers of social sciences and humanities. Welcomes synopses and ideas for books. See website for appropriate commissioning editor to contact, and details of what your proposal should include.

Professional and Higher Partnership

4 The Links
Cambridge Road
Newmarket
Suffolk
CB8 0TG
Tel: +44 (0) 1638 663456
Email: info@frontinus.org.uk
Website: http://pandhp.com

Publishes: Nonfiction; *Markets:* Academic; Professional

Publishes nonfiction for the academic and professional markets, including books on higher education and creative writing studies.

Psychology Press

2 Park Square
Milton Park
Abingdon
Oxford
OX14 4RN
Tel: +44 (0) 1235 400400
Fax: +44 (0) 1235 400401
Email: russell.george@tandf.co.uk
Website: https://www.routledge.com/psychology

Publishes: Nonfiction; *Areas:* Psychology; *Markets:* Academic; Professional

Contact: Russell George

Publishes academic and professional books and journals on psychology. Send query by email to appropriate editor (see website for specific addresses).

Pushkin Press

71-75 Shelton Street
London

WC2H 9JQ
Tel: +44 (0) 20 7470 8830
Email: books@pushkinpress.com
Website: http://pushkinpress.com

Publishes: Fiction; Nonfiction; *Areas:* Autobiography; *Markets:* Adult; Children's; *Treatments:* Contemporary; Traditional

Publishes novels, essays, memoirs, children's books, including timeless classics and contemporary.

Quadrille Publishing Ltd

Pentagon House
52-54 Southwark Street
London
SE1 1UN
Tel: +44 (0) 20 7601 7500
Email: enquiries@quadrille.co.uk
Website: http://www.quadrille.co.uk

Publishes: Nonfiction; *Areas:* Beauty and Fashion; Cookery; Crafts; Design; Gardening; Health; Humour; *Markets:* Adult

Publishes quality illustrated nonfiction. No fiction or books for children.

Quiller Publishing Ltd

Wykey House
Wykey
Shrewsbury
Shropshire
SY4 1JA
Tel: +44 (0) 1939 261616
Email: info@quillerbooks.com
Website: http://www.quillerpublishing.com

Publishes: Nonfiction; Reference; *Areas:* Architecture; Biography; Business; Cookery; Gardening; Humour; Sport; Travel; *Markets:* Adult

Contact: Andrew Johnston

Publishes books for all lovers of fishing, shooting, equestrian and country pursuits. Accepts unsolicited MSS from authors. Send submissions as hard copy only, with email address for reply or SAE if return of ms is required. Proposals may be sent by email. Suggestions may be made by post, email, or phone.

Radcliffe Publishing Ltd

5 Thomas More Square
London
E1W 1YW
Tel: +44 (0) 844 887 1380
Email: jonathan.mckenna@radcliffepublishing.com
Website: http://www.radcliffehealth.com

Publishes: Nonfiction; *Areas:* Health; Medicine; *Markets:* Professional

Contact: Jonathan McKenna; Katrina Hulme-Cross

Publishes books on medicine, including health care policy and management, and also training materials. Welcomes synopses, ideas, and unsolicited MSS.

Ragged Bears Limited

Unit 14A
Bennett's Field Trading Estate
Southgate Road
Wincanton
Somerset
BA9 9DT
Tel: +44 (0) 1963 34300
Email: books@ragged-bears.co.uk
Website: http://www.ragged-bears.co.uk

Publishes: Fiction; *Markets:* Children's; Youth

Publishes picture books and novelty books, up to young teen fiction. Accepts submissions by post with SAE (no original artwork), but prefers submissions by email.

Ransom Publishing Ltd

Radley House
8 St Cross Road
Winchester
Hampshire
SO23 9HX
Tel: +44 (0) 1962 862307
Fax: +44 (0) 5601 148881
Email: ransom@ransom.co.uk
Website: http://www.ransom.co.uk

Publishes: Fiction; Nonfiction; *Markets:* Adult; Children's; Professional; Youth

An independent specialist publisher of high quality, inspirational books that encourage and help children, young adults, and adults to develop their reading skills. Books are intended to have content which is age appropriate and engaging, but reading levels that would normally be appropriate for younger readers. Also publishes resources for both the library and classroom. Will consider unsolicited mss. Email in first instance.

Reaktion Books

33 Great Sutton Street
London
EC1V 0DX
Tel: +44 (0) 20 7253 1071
Fax: +44 (0) 20 7253 1208
Email: info@reaktionbooks.co.uk
Website: http://www.reaktionbooks.co.uk

Publishes: Nonfiction; *Areas:* Architecture; Arts; Beauty and Fashion; Biography; Culture; Current Affairs; Design; Film; Finance; Gardening; Historical; Literature; Medicine; Music; Nature; Philosophy; Photography; Science; Sport; Travel; *Markets:* Adult; *Treatments:* Popular

Send 4-5 page book proposal by post or email, including title, synopsis, outline, details of illustrations, your CV, details of the market and competition, and your anticipated date of data delivery. See website for more details.

Reality Street Editions

63 All Saints Street
Hastings
East Sussex
TN34 3BN
Tel: +44 (0) 7706 189253
Email: info@realitystreet.co.uk
Website: http://www.realitystreet.co.uk

Publishes: Fiction; Poetry; *Markets:* Adult; *Treatments:* Experimental; Literary

Contact: Ken Edwards

Not planning to publish any new titles after 2016, when existing commitments are fulfilled. Not accepting any new material.

Small poetry press which has in recent years also published experimental prose, both narrative and non-narrative. Publishes only a few books each year, so usually heavily committed: "if you are not familiar with any of those writers we have published and/or are unwilling to research further by buying and reading our books, then it's highly unlikely you have anything to interest us."

Red Rattle Books

Email: editor@redrattlebooks.co.uk
Website: http://www.redrattlebooks.co.uk

Publishes: Fiction; Nonfiction; *Areas:* Crime; Horror; *Markets:* Adult

Independent, family run company, publishing new crime, horror and nonfiction books. Submit via website using online submission form.

Robert Hale Publishers

The Crowood Press
The Stable Block
Crowood Lane
Ramsbury
Wiltshire
SN8 2HR
Tel: +44 (0) 20 7251 2661
Fax: +44 (0) 20 7490 4958
Email: enquiries@crowood.com
Website: http://www.halebooks.com

Publishes: Fiction; Nonfiction; Reference; *Areas:* Arts; Biography; Crime; Design; Health; Historical; Leisure; Lifestyle; Nature; Romance; Spiritual; Sport; Westerns; *Markets:* Adult

Contact: Editorial Department

See website for full submission guidelines, and list of material not currently being accepted. Send query with synopsis and three sample chapters.

Rose and Crown Books

36 Salmons Leap
Calne
Wiltshire
SN11 9EU
Tel: +44 (0) 1508 480087
Email: query@roseandcrownbooks.com
Website: http://www.
roseandcrownbooks.com/

Publishes: Fiction; *Areas:* Historical; Military; Religious; Romance; Travel; *Markets:* Adult; Family; *Treatments:* Commercial; Contemporary; Light; Literary; Mainstream; Niche; Popular; Positive; Serious; Traditional

Imprint with launch date in 2009. Our focus is on romance with an inspirational flavour. Intended to complement American brands such as the Steeple Hill, Thorndike and Bethany House imprints, we would seem to be the first publisher in the United Kingdom to take up the banner for this genre.

We believe strongly that Inspirational Romance has a role to play in the lives of today's women, of all ages, races and creeds around the world – a role of pure reading enjoyment as well as food for their imaginations and their feminine spirits and minds. We are concentrating on strong writing and intelligent stories that speak to women across the board, with characters and situations they can identify with – tales that fit many age groups and categories: tender young love, later life meetings, families, and romance for the more senior of us, too.

Some will have more Christian influence than others; some will be contemporary, others historical, with locations all around the world. They will vary in style from straight romance to historical fiction, contemporary novels, humour, travel, adventure, crime/detective, Western, military, etc. As long as they have a romance at their heart and Christian characters, with a greater or lesser Christian implication, they fit what we are looking for.

Query first please, with single para description of book, brief author bio, email address and postal address, and synopsis. For full guidelines and more information on how we work as a company, please visit the web site, and please take the time to read and follow the guidelines. If you want us to show interest in you, please show enough interest in us to submit correctly; we thank you!

RotoVision

Sheridan House
112-116A Western Road
Hove
East Sussex
BN3 1DD
Tel: +44 (0) 1273 727268
Fax: +44 (0) 1273 727269
Email: alison.morris@quarto.com
Website: http://www.rotovision.com

Publishes: Nonfiction; *Areas:* Architecture; Arts; Design; Film; Photography; *Markets:* Adult

Contact: Alison Morris (Commissioning Editor)

Publisher of books on the visual arts.

Route Publishing

PO Box 167
Pontefract
WF8 4WW
Tel: +44 (0) 845 158 1565
Email: info@route-online.com
Website: http://www.route-online.com

Publishes: Fiction; Poetry; *Areas:* Culture; Short Stories; *Markets:* Adult; *Treatments:* Contemporary

Contact: Ian Daley; Isabel Galan

Publisher of novels, short stories, and poetry. Open door for new writing submissions is currently unsupported. Any new books considered must be self-supporting. This consideration must be addressed in any proposals.

Ryland Peters & Small

20-21 Jockey's Fields
London
WC1R 4BW
Tel: +44 (0) 20 7025 2200
Fax: +44 (0) 20 7025 2201
Email: enquiries@rps.co.uk
Website: http://www.rylandpeters.com

Publishes: Nonfiction; *Areas:* Cookery; Crafts; Gardening; Health; Lifestyle; *Markets:* Adult

Contact: David Peters (Managing Director); Alison Starling (Publishing Director)

Publishes highly illustrated books on homes and gardens, crafts, food and drink, health and well-being, weddings, and mother and baby. Also has a vibrant gift and stationery list. Welcomes synopses and ideas, but no unsolicited MSS.

Saffron Books

EAPGROUP
PO Box 13666
London
SW14 8WF
Tel: +44 (0) 20 8392 1122
Fax: +44 (0) 20 8392 1422
Email: info@eapgroup.com
Website: http://www.saffronbooks.com

Publishes: Fiction; Nonfiction; *Areas:* Archaeology; Arts; Business; Culture; Current Affairs; Finance; Historical; Sociology; *Markets:* Adult

Publishes books on art, archaeology and architecture, art history, current affairs and linguistics, with a particular emphasis on Asia, Africa, and the Middle East. Also publishes fiction. Welcomes proposals for books and monongraphs from new or established authors. Send query by email, post, or fax (not preferred for long documents). See website for full guidelines.

The Salariya Book Company

25 Marlborough Place
Brighton
East Sussex
BN1 1UB
Tel: +44 (0) 1273 603306
Fax: +44 (0) 1273 621619
Email: salariya@salariya.com
Website: http://www.salariya.com

Publishes: Fiction; Nonfiction; *Areas:* Adventure; Fantasy; Historical; Nature; Science; *Markets:* Children's

Publishes books of fiction and nonfiction for children.

Salt Publishing Ltd

12 Norwich Road
CROMER
Norfolk
NR27 0AX
Tel: +44 (0) 1263 511011
Email: submissions@saltpublishing.com
Website: http://www.saltpublishing.com

Publishes: Fiction; *Areas:* Crime; Gothic; Literature; Thrillers; *Markets:* Adult; *Treatments:* Dark; Literary; Mainstream; Traditional

Accepts print fiction submissions via agents only. Accepts direct submissions from authors for ebooks – novellas 20,000 to 30,000 words long, dealing explicitly with lives of young people in modern Britain and the US. Full submission guidelines on website. No poetry (adult or children's), biography or autobiography, plays or nonfiction.

Samuel French Ltd

Performing Rights Department
52 Fitzroy Street
London
W1T 5JR
Tel: +44 (0) 20 7387 9373
Fax: +44 (0) 20 7387 2161
Email: submissions@samuelfrench-london.co.uk
Website: http://www.samuelfrench-london.co.uk

Publishes: Scripts; *Areas:* Drama; *Markets:* Adult

Publishes plays only. Send query by email only, following the guidelines in the FAQ section of the website. No unsolicited MSS.

Sandstone Press Ltd

PO Box 5725
One High Street
Dingwall
Ross-shire
IV15 9WJ
Tel: +44 (0) 1349 862583
Fax: +44 (0) 1349 862583
Email: moira@sandstonepress.com
Website: http://www.sandstonepress.com

Publishes: Fiction; Nonfiction; *Areas:* Crime; Thrillers; *Markets:* Adult; *Treatments:* Literary

Contact: Moira Forsyth, Commissioning Editor

Publishes fiction and nonfiction and adults. Interested in literary fiction, crime novels, and thrillers, set in the past, present, or future. Welcomes proposals – send introductory email query in first instance, including outline and bio, including publishing history. No children's, young adult, poetry, short story collections, science fiction, fantasy, general historical fiction, or horror. See website for more details and submission form.

Schofield & Sims

Unit 11, The Piano Works
113-117 Farringdon Road
London
EC1R 3BX
Tel: +44 (0) 1484 607080
Fax: +44 (0) 1484 606815
Email: editorial@schofieldandsims.co.uk
Website: http://www.schofieldandsims.co.uk

Publishes: Nonfiction; *Areas:* Historical; Literature; Science; *Markets:* Academic; Children's

Publishes educational material for children at nursery, infants, and primary school, covering such topics as phonics, reading, maths, science, etc. Send manuscripts and ideas for educational resources by post or by email.

Scripture Union

Queensway House
207-209 Queensway
Bletchley
Milton Keynes
MK2 2EB
Email: info@scriptureunion.org.uk
Website: http://www.scriptureunion.org.uk

Publishes: Fiction; Nonfiction; *Areas:* Religious; *Markets:* Adult; Children's; Family; Youth

Publishes Christian nonfiction books for people of all ages. Also Christian fiction for children only.

Search Press Ltd

Wellwood
North Farm Road
Tunbridge Wells
Kent
TN2 3DR
Tel: +44 (0) 1892 510850
Fax: +44 (0) 1892 515903
Email: katie@searchpress.com
Website: http://www.searchpress.com

Publishes: Nonfiction; *Areas:* Arts; Crafts; Hobbies; How-to; Leisure; *Markets:* Adult; Children's

Contact: Katie French, Commissioning Editor

Publishes books on fine art, textiles, general crafts and children's crafts. Send query by post or by email with summary, synopsis, samples, and author information. See website for full guidelines.

Seren Books

57 Nolton Street
Bridgend
Wales
CF31 3AE
Tel: +44 (0) 1656 663018
Fax: +44 (0) 1656 649226
Email: Seren@SerenBooks.com
Website: http://www.serenbooks.com

Publishes: Fiction; Nonfiction; Poetry; *Areas:* Anthropology; Arts; Biography; Criticism; Current Affairs; Drama; Historical; Music; Photography; Politics; Sport; Translations; Travel; *Markets:* Adult; Children's; *Treatments:* Literary

Contact: Penny Thomas (Fiction Editor); Amy Wack (Poetry Editor); Mick Felton (Nonfiction Editor)

Publishes fiction, nonfiction, and poetry. Specialises in English-language writing from Wales and aims to bring Welsh culture, art, literature, and politics to a wider audience. Accepts nonfiction submissions only by email; no poetry or fiction submissions by email. See website for complete submission guidelines.

Serpent's Tail

3 Holford Yard
Bevin Way
London
WC1X 9HD

Tel: +44 (0) 20 7841 6300
Email: info@profilebooks.com
Website: http://www.serpentstail.com

Publishes: Fiction; Nonfiction; *Areas:* Autobiography; Biography; Crime; Culture; Current Affairs; Music; Politics; *Markets:* Adult

Prefers to receive approaches through a literary agent, but will also accept queries by email (up to 250 words) with sample text (10 pages or the first chapter only). See website for full submission guidelines. No Romance, Science Fiction, YA or children's books, or translations.

Responds to all queries, but may take up to three months. If no response after 6 weeks, email to request an update.

Severn House Publishers

Salatin House
19 Cedar Road
Sutton
Surrey
SM2 5DA
Tel: +44 (0) 20 8770 3930
Fax: +44 (0) 20 8770 3850
Email: sales@severnhouse.com
Website: http://severnhouse.com

Publishes: Fiction; *Areas:* Crime; Historical; Horror; Mystery; Romance; Sci-Fi; Thrillers; Markets

Accepts submissions via literary agents only. Targets the UK and US fiction library markets, and considers only authors with a significant background in these markets.

Shearsman Books

50 Westons Hill Drive
Emersons Green
Bristol
BS16 7DF
Tel: +44 (0) 1179 572957
Email: editor@shearsman.com
Website: http://www.shearsman.com

Publishes: Nonfiction; Poetry; *Areas:* Autobiography; Criticism; Literature; Translations; *Markets:* Adult

Contact: Tony Frazer

Publishes poetry books of at least 64 A5 pages. Publishes mainly poetry by British, Irish, North American and Australian/New Zealand poets, plus poetry in translation from any language—although particular interest in German, Spanish and Latin American poetry.

Submit only if MS is of appropriate length and most of it has already appeared in UK or US magazines of some repute. Send selection of 6-10 pages by post with SASE or by email with material embedded in the text or as PDF attachment. No other kind of attachments accepted.

Also sometimes publishes literary criticism on poetry, and essays or memoirs by poets.

Short Books

Unit 316
ScreenWorks
22 Highbury Grove
London
N5 2EF
Tel: +44 (0) 20 7833 9429
Email: info@shortbooks.co.uk
Website: http://shortbooks.co.uk

Publishes: Fiction; Nonfiction; *Markets:* Adult

Send submissions via literary agent only. Send cover letter with synopsis and first three chapters / roughly 30 pages.

Singing Dragon

73 Collier Street
London
N1 9BE
Tel: +44 (0) 20 7833 2307
Email: hello@singingdragon.com
Website: http://singingdragon.com

Publishes: Nonfiction; *Areas:* Health; Leisure; Medicine; Self-Help; Spiritual; *Markets:* Academic; Adult; Professional

Publishes authoritative books on complementary and alternative health, Tai Chi, Qigong and ancient wisdom traditions for health, wellbeing, and professional and personal development, for parents, professionals, academics and the general reader. Welcomes ideas for new books. Send query by email with CV and completed proposal form (available on website).

Siri Scientific Press

Arrow Mill (Office 41)
Queensway
Rochdale
OL11 2YW
Email: books@siriscientificpress.co.uk
Website: http://siriscientificpress.co.uk

Publishes: Nonfiction; Reference; *Areas:* Science; *Markets:* Academic; Adult

Contact: Dave Penney

Publishes short run science books for the academic market (but also accessible to the general public) which are of scientific value, but which might not have a large enough market to be attractive to more mainstream publishers. Send query by email to discuss ideas, or arrange face-to-face meeting.

Snowbooks

Chiltern House
Thame Road
Haddenham
HP17 8BY
Tel: +44 (0) 1865 600995
Email: emma@snowbooks.com
Website: http://www.snowbooks.com

Publishes: Fiction; Nonfiction; *Areas:* Crafts; Crime; Fantasy; Historical; Horror; Leisure; Sci-Fi; Sport; Thrillers; *Markets:* Adult

Contact: Emma Barnes, Managing Director

Open to submissions of horror, science fiction, and fantasy novels over 70,000 words. Named joint Small Publisher of the Year at the 2006 British book Trade Awards. Friendly attitude towards authors and unsolicited approaches. See website for guidelines. Approach via web submission system only – postal submissions will neither be read nor returned, even if sent through an agent. £2 submission fee.

Society for Promoting Christian Knowledge (SPCK)

36 Causton Street
London
SW1P 4ST
Tel: +44 (0) 20 7592 3900
Fax: +44 (0) 20 7592 3939
Email: submissions@spck.org.uk
Website: http://www.spck.org.uk

Publishes: Nonfiction; *Areas:* Health; Lifestyle; Medicine; Psychology; Religious; Self-Help; Sociology; Spiritual; *Markets:* Academic; Adult

Publisher of Christian books, including liturgy, prayer, biblical studies, educational resources, etc. Imprints handle general spirituality and topics such as popular medicine, self-help, health, etc. Send query by post with SAE or by email. See website for full guidelines.

Souvenir Press Ltd

43 Great Russell Street
London
WC1B 3PA
Tel: +44 (0) 20 7580 9307 / +44 (0) 20 7637 5711
Fax: +44 (0) 20 7580 5064
Email: souvenirpress@souvenirpress.co.uk
Website: http://www.souvenirpress.co.uk

Publishes: Fiction; Nonfiction; *Areas:* Antiques; Archaeology; Autobiography; Beauty and Fashion; Biography; Business; Cookery; Crafts; Crime; Gardening; Health; Historical; Hobbies; Humour; Lifestyle; Literature; Medicine; Military; Music; Mystery; Nature; Philosophy; Politics; Psychology; Religious; Science; Self-Help; Sociology; Spiritual; Sport; Theatre; Travel; Women's Interests; *Markets:* Academic; Adult

Contact: Ernest Hecht

Independent publisher publishing an eclectic mixture of bestsellers and books intended for more limited audiences. Send query letter with outline in first instance.

Speechmark Publishing Limited

5 Thomas More Square
St Katharine Docks
London
E1W 1YW
Tel: +44 (0) 1869 244644
Email: Ben.Hulme-Cross@speechmark.net
Website: http://www.speechmark.net

Publishes: Nonfiction; *Areas:* Health; Psychology; *Markets:* Academic; Professional

Contact: Ben Hulme-Cross

Publishes books, games, and other resources for use by professionals and students in the fields of special needs; speech amp; language therapy; mental health; groupwork; elderly care; and early development. Welcomes unsolicited MSS, synopses, and ideas. Download Author Submission Form from website.

St David's Press

PO Box 733
Cardiff
CF14 7ZY
Tel: +44 (0) 2920 218187
Email: post@welsh-academic-press.com
Website: http://www.welsh-academic-press.com

Publishes: Nonfiction; Reference; *Areas:* Historical; Leisure; Sport; Travel; *Markets:* Adult

Publisher focussing primarily on books for the Welsh market. Publishes books on sport, including boxing, cricket, football, and rugby; books on walking; reference; and local history and Celtic interest titles. Proposal submission form available on website.

Stenlake Publishing

54-58 Mill Square
Catrine
Ayrshire
KA5 6RD
Tel: +44 (0) 1290 552233
Fax: +44 (0) 1290 551122
Email: info@stenlake.co.uk
Website: http://stenlake.co.uk

Publishes: Nonfiction; *Areas:* Architecture; Arts; Cookery; Crafts; Historical; Hobbies; Literature; Travel; *Markets:* Adult; Children's

Publishes books of local interest, highly illustrated with old photographs, and usually accompanied by informative text. Also publishes industrial and transport-related titles – railways, canals, road transport, coastal shipping, mining, and aviation, covering Scotland, Wales, Northern Ireland, England, the Isle of Man and the Republic of Ireland. Also publishes books on Robert Burns, ceramics, horticulture, bee-keeping, building conservation, and china painting. Send outline by email in first instance.

Stonewood Press

Submissions
Stonewood Press
97 Benefield Road
Oundle
PE8 4EU
Email: stonewoodpress@gmail.com
Website: http://www.stonewoodpress.co.uk

Publishes: Fiction; Poetry; *Areas:* Short Stories; *Markets:* Adult; *Treatments:* Contemporary

Contact: Martin Parker

Independent publisher dedicated to promoting new writing, with an emphasis on contemporary short stories and poetry. Send query with biography, publishing history, and either one story and a brief outline of the others in the collection, or up to 10 poems and details of how many other poems are in the collection. Submit by post only. No children's books, creative nonfiction, novels, or drama.

Stripes Publishing

1 The Coda Centre
189 Munster Road
London
SW6 6AW
Tel: +44 (0) 20 7385 6333
Email: editorial@stripespublishing.co.uk
Website: http://www.stripespublishing.co.uk

Publishes: Fiction; *Markets:* Children's

Publishes fiction for children aged 6-12 and teendagers. No books for adults, educational books, poetry, graphic novels, comics, multimedia, scripts, screenplays, short stories, nonfiction or picture books for babies and toddlers. No longer accepting submissions by post. Send queries by email only, with one-page synopsis and 1,000-word extract.

Summersdale Publishers Ltd

46 West Street
Chichester
West Sussex
PO19 1RP
Tel: +44 (0) 1243 771107
Fax: +44 (0) 1243 786300
Email: submissions@summersdale.com
Website: http://www.summersdale.com

Publishes: Nonfiction; *Areas:* Crime; Health; Humour; Lifestyle; Travel; *Markets:* Adult

Contact: Submissions Team

Publisher of books on travel, humour, health, and general nonfiction. No fiction, poetry, children's books, or autobiography. Send query with cover letter, synopsis, and two sample chapters, by post or by email.

Sweet Cherry Publishing

Unit E Vulcan Business Complex
Vulcan Road
Leicester
LE5 3EB
Email: submissions@sweetcherrypublishing.com
Website: http://www.sweetcherrypublishing.com

Publishes: Fiction; *Markets:* Children's

Contact: Abdul Thadha

Publishes books for children of all ages. Looking for talented new authors of children's series and collections. Send submissions by email or by post with SASE. See website for full submission guidelines.

Tarquin

Suite 74
17 Holywell Hill
St Albans
Hertfordshire
AL1 1DT
Tel: +44 (0) 1727 833866
Fax: +44 (0) 8454 566385
Email: info@tarquinbooks.com
Website: http://www.tarquinbooks.com

Publishes: Nonfiction; *Markets:* Children's

Publishes books for children on mathematical models, puzzles, and paper engineering. Aims to combine fun with education. Send query by email.

The Templar Company Limited

Deepdene Lodge
Deepdene Avenue
Dorking
Surrey
RH5 4AT
Tel: +44 (0) 1306 876361
Fax: +44 (0) 1306 889097
Email: submissions@templarco.co.uk
Website: http://www.templarco.co.uk

Publishes: Fiction; Nonfiction; *Markets:* Children's

Publishes children's fiction and picture and novelty books. Currently closed to fiction submissions, but welcomes novelty and picture book submissions, in hard copy by post only. Include SAE if return of work required. Artwork submissions accepted by email.

Templar Poetry

58 Dale Road
Matlock
Derbyshire
DE4 3NB
Tel: +44 (0) 1629 582500
Email: info@templarpoetry.com
Website: http://templarpoetry.com

Publishes: Poetry; *Markets:* Adult; *Treatments:* Contemporary; Literary

Publishes poetry acquired through a numebr of competitions, ranging from short selections of poems up to a full collection. See website for guidelines and to submit online. Note that entering the competitions requires the payment of an entry fee.

Think Publishing

Capital House
25 Chapel Street
London
NW1 5DH
Tel: +44 (0) 20 3771 7200
Fax: +44 (0) 20 7723 1035
Email: ian@thinkpublishing.co.uk
Website: http://www.thinkpublishing.co.uk

Publishes: Nonfiction; *Areas:* Gardening; Nature; *Markets:* Adult

Contact: Ian Mcauliffe

Publishes nonfiction in partnership with clients that are seeking to use books as a medium for their brand to reach new audiences and potentially provide a commercial revenue stream. Query by email in first instance.

Thistle Publishing

London
Email: info@thistlepublishing.co.uk
Website: http://www.thistlepublishing.co.uk

Publishes: Fiction; Nonfiction; *Markets:* Adult

London-based publisher of quality fiction and nonfiction. Welcomes submissions. For nonfiction, send synopsis, author profile, sample chapter, and brief chapter summaries; for fiction, send synopsis and three sample chapters.

Tiny Owl

1 Repton House
London
SW1V 2LD

Email: info@tinyowl.co.uk
Website: http://tinyowl.co.uk

Publishes: Fiction; *Markets:* Children's

Publisher of books for children.

Titan Books

Titan House
144 Southwark Street
London
SE1 0UP
Tel: +44 (0) 20 7620 0200
Email: editorial@titanemail.com
Website: http://www.titanbooks.com

Publishes: Fiction; Nonfiction; *Areas:* Entertainment; Film; Humour; Sci-Fi; Short Stories; TV; *Markets:* Adult; Youth

Contact: Commissioning Editor

Publisher of graphic novels, particularly with film or television tie-ins, and books related to film and TV. No unsolicited fiction or books for children, but will consider ideas for licensed projects they have already contracted. Send query with synopsis by post only. No email submissions.

Top That! Publishing

Marine House
Tide Mill Way
Woodbridge
Suffolk
IP12 1AP
Tel: +44 (0) 1394 386651
Email: josh@topthatpublishing.com
Website: http://topthatpublishing.com

Publishes: Fiction; Nonfiction; Reference; *Areas:* Cookery; Humour; *Markets:* Adult; Children's

Contact: Josh Simpkin-Betts

Publishes Activity Books, Character Books, Cookery Books, Felt Books, Fiction, Humour, Magnetic Books, Novelty Books, Phonics Books, Picture Storybooks, Pop-Up Books, Press Out amp; Play, Reference Books, and Sticker Books. Does not currently publish "regular" children's or adults fiction. See online book catalogue for the kinds of books published. If suitable for the list, send submissions by email (preferred), ideally under 1MB, or by post (mss not returned). See website for full guidelines. Responds within 8 weeks if interested. No simultaneous submissions.

Trentham Books Limited

Institute of Education
University of London
20 Bedford Way
London
WC1H 0AL
Tel: +44 (0) 20 7911 5563
Email: g.klein@ioe.ac.uk
Website: http://www.trentham-books.co.uk

Publishes: Nonfiction; *Areas:* Design; Science; Sociology; Technology; Women's Interests; *Markets:* Academic

Contact: Dr Gillian Klein

Publishes academic and professional books. No fiction, biography, or poetry. No unsolicited MSS, but accepts queries by email. See website for full guidelines and for downloadable book proposal guidelines, which you should fill in as thoroughly as possible before submitting it by email.

Troika Books

Well House
Green Lane
Ardleigh
Essex
CO7 7PD
Tel: +44 (0) 1206 233 333
Email: info@troikabooks.com
Website: http://www.troikabooks.com

Publishes: Fiction; Poetry; *Markets:* Children's

Contact: Martin West

Publishes picture books, fiction, and poetry for children.

Twenty First Century Publishers Ltd

Email: tfcp@btinternet.com
Website: http://www.twentyfirstcenturypublishers.com

Publishes: Fiction; *Areas:* Crime; Finance; Historical; Psychology; Thrillers; *Markets:* Adult

Publishes general fiction written thoughtfully and with insight, plot driven original works, and knowledgeably written financial thrillers, in English, French, and German. Send submissions by email, with a brief 1-2 page synopsis or overview in the body of the email, and the full ms, or as many chapters as you wish, in a file attachment.

Two Rivers Press

7 Denmark Road
Reading
RG1 5PA
Email: tworiverspress@gmail.com
Website: http://tworiverspress.com

Publishes: Nonfiction; Poetry; *Areas:* Arts; Culture; *Markets:* Adult; *Treatments:* Literary

Publishes poetry, art, culture, and local interest books, focusing on Reading and the surrounding area.

Ulric Publishing

PO Box 55
Church Stretton
Shropshire
SY6 6WR
Tel: +44 (0) 1694 781354
Email: enquiries@ulricpublishing.com
Website: http://www.ulricpublishing.com

Publishes: Nonfiction; *Areas:* Military; Technology; Travel; *Markets:* Adult

Publishes military and motoring history. Sister company provides publishing services to companies and individuals. Send synopsis (not exceeding two A4 pages) by email.

Unbound Press

Unit 18, Waterside
44-48 Wharf Road
London
N1 7UX
Tel: +44 (0) 20 7821 6561
Email: support@unbound.com
Website: https://unbound.com

Publishes: Fiction; Nonfiction; *Markets:* Adult

Crowdfunding publisher. Submit manuscripts via form on website.

Vallentine Mitchell & Co., Limited

Catalyst House
720 Centennial Court
Centennial Park
Elstree
Herts
WD6 3SY
Tel: +44 (0) 20 8736 4596
Email: editor@vmbooks.com
Website: http://www.vmbooksuk.com

Publishes: Nonfiction; *Areas:* Culture; Historical; Philosophy; Religious; *Markets:* Academic; Adult

Publishes books on Jewish history, culture and heritage, Jewish thought, Middle Eastern history, politics and culture and the Holocaust, for both academic and general readerships. Offices in London and Portland, Oregon. Send proposals by email.

Valley Press

Woodend
The Crescent
Scarborough
YO11 2PW
Email: jamie@valleypressuk.com
Website: http://www.valleypressuk.com

Publishes: Fiction; Nonfiction; Poetry; *Areas:* Autobiography; Short Stories; Travel; *Markets:* Adult

Accepts submissions of poetry, fiction, and nonfiction, accompanied by SASE and submission form, which can be acquired by purchasing a book from the website.

Verso

6 Meard Street
London
W1F 0EG
Tel: +44 (0) 20 7437 3546
Fax: +44 (0) 20 7734 0059
Email: submissions@verso.co.uk
Website: http://www.versobooks.com

Publishes: Fiction; Nonfiction; *Areas:* Anthropology; Architecture; Arts; Autobiography; Biography; Culture; Film; Finance; Historical; Media; Philosophy; Politics; Sociology; *Markets:* Academic; Adult

"Radical" publisher of the political left. Publishes mainly nonfiction and does not consider unsolicited fiction submissions. For nonfiction, send proposal up to 15 pages, including overview, contents / chapter outline, author background, market info, and your timetable, by email only. No unsolicited MSS, or hard copy submissions. If no response within two months, assume rejection.

Virago Press

Carmelite House
50 Victoria Embankment
LONDON
EC4Y 0DZ
Tel: +44 (0) 20 3122 7000
Email: virago@littlebrown.co.uk
Website: http://www.virago.co.uk

Publishes: Fiction; Nonfiction; *Areas:* Literature; Women's Interests; *Markets:* Adult; *Treatments:* Literary

Publishes fiction and nonfiction women's literature. No poetry. Accepts approaches via literary agents only.

Wooden Books

8A Market Place
Glastonbury
BA6 8LT
Email: info@woodenbooks.com
Website: http://www.woodenbooks.com

Publishes: Nonfiction; *Areas:* Historical; Science; Spiritual; *Markets:* Adult

Publishes illustration-heavy books on such topics as ancient sciences, magic, mathematics, etc. Prospective authors will need to provide high quality illustrations. Essential to query before commencing work. Send query by email or by post. See website for full details.

W.W. Norton & Company Ltd

75-76 Wells Street
London
W1T 3QT
Tel: +44 (0) 20 7323 1579

Fax: +44 (0) 20 7436 4553
Email: office@wwnorton.co.uk
Website: http://wwnorton.co.uk

Publishes: Fiction; Nonfiction; Poetry; *Areas:* Adventure; Anthropology; Archaeology; Architecture; Autobiography; Biography; Business; Crafts; Crime; Current Affairs; Design; Drama; Film; Finance; Health; Historical; Hobbies; Humour; Legal; Leisure; Lifestyle; Literature; Medicine; Music; Nature; Philosophy; Politics; Psychology; Religious; Science; Self-Help; Sociology; Sport; Technology; Travel; Women's Interests; *Markets:* Academic; Adult; Professional

UK branch of a US publisher. No editorial office in the UK – contact the main office in New York (see separate listing).

Walker Books Ltd

87 Vauxhall Walk
London
SE11 5HJ
Tel: +44 (0) 20 7793 0909
Fax: +44 (0) 20 7587 1123
Email: editorial@walker.co.uk
Website: http://www.walkerbooks.co.uk

Publishes: Fiction; Nonfiction; *Markets:* Children's

Publishes fiction and nonfiction for children, including illustrated books. Does not accept full-length fiction manuscripts, but accepts illustrated picture-book stories and/or artwork samples via post or email.

Ward Lock Educational Ltd

BIC Ling Kee House
1 Christopher Road
East Grinstead
West Sussex
RH19 3BT
Tel: +44 (0) 1342 318980
Fax: +44 (0) 1342 410980
Email: wle@lingkee.com
Website: http://wle.lingkee.com

Publishes: Nonfiction; *Areas:* Drama; Literature; Music; Science; *Markets:* Academic; Children's; Professional

Publishes school text books and books for teachers, covering a range of school subjects at Key Stages 1-4 as well as resource materials.

Waverley Books

Academy Park
Building 4000
Glasgow
G51 1PR
Email: info@waverley-books.co.uk
Website: http://www.waverley-books.co.uk

Publishes: Fiction; Nonfiction; *Areas:* Cookery; Historical; Humour; *Markets:* Adult; Children's

Publishes history, fiction, nostalgia, food and drink, humour, children's, graphic novels, and Scottish interest.

Weidenfeld & Nicolson

3rd Floor, Carmelite House
50 Victoria Embankment
London
EC4Y 0DZ
Website: http://www.wnblog.co.uk

Publishes: Fiction; Nonfiction; *Areas:* Autobiography; Biography; Cookery; Current Affairs; Finance; Historical; Military; Travel; *Markets:* Adult; *Treatments:* Literary

Publishers of high quality, prize-winning fiction and nonfiction across a range of categories, including autobiography, business, cookery, economics, history and more.

Welsh Academic Press

PO Box 733
Caerdydd
Cardiff
CF14 7ZY
Tel: +44 (0) 29 2021 8187
Email: post@welsh-academic-press.com
Website: http://www.welsh-academic-press.com

Publishes: Nonfiction; *Areas:* Historical; Politics; *Markets:* Academic

Publishes academic monographs, reference works, text books and popular scholarly titles in the fields of education, history, political studies, Scandinavian and Baltic studies, contemporary work and employment, and medieval Wales. Complete questionnaire available on website.

Philip Wilson Publishers Ltd

6 Salem Road
London
W2 4BU
Tel: +44 (0) 20 7243 1225
Fax: +44 (0) 20 7243 1226
Email: philipwilso@gmail.com
Website: http://www.philip-wilson.co.uk

Publishes: Nonfiction; *Areas:* Architecture; Arts; Design; Historical; *Markets:* Adult

Contact: Philip Wilson; Anne Jackson

Publishes books on art, art history, andtiques, and collectibles. See website and contact for further details.

WIT Press

Ashurst Lodge
Ashurst
Southampton
SO40 7AA
Tel: +44 (0) 23 8029 3223
Fax: +44 (0) 23 8029 2853
Email: witpress@witpress.com
Website: http://www.witpress.com

Publishes: Nonfiction; *Areas:* Architecture; Nature; Science; Technology; *Markets:* Academic; Adult

Contact: Professor C.A. Brebbia

Publisher of scientific and technical material in such fields as architecture, environmental engineering and bioengineering. Target market is generally postgraduate and above. No school or college texts, or material not of a scientific or technical nature. Potential authors should contact the Chairman by email in the first instance (see website for specific email address).

Wordsworth Editions

8B, East Street
Ware
Hertfordshire
SG12 9HJ
Tel: +44 (0) 1920 465167
Fax: +44 (0) 1920 462267
Email: enquiries@wordsworth-editions.com
Website: http://www.wordsworth-editions.com

Publishes: Fiction; *Areas:* Adventure; Biography; Gothic; Mystery; Romance; Sci-Fi; *Markets:* Adult; Family; Professional; Youth; *Treatments:* Mainstream; Niche; Popular

Contact: Managing Director, Helen Trayler

Publishes out-of-copyright titles. No submissions of new material.

The X Press

PO Box 25694
London
N17 6FP
Tel: +44 (0) 20 8801 2100
Fax: +44 (0) 20 8885 1322
Email: vibes@xpress.co.uk
Website: http://www.xpress.co.uk

Publishes: Fiction; *Areas:* Culture; *Markets:* Adult; Children's; *Treatments:* Contemporary; Literary; Popular

Contact: Dotun Adebayo (Editorial Director); Steve Pope (Marketing Director)

Europe's largest publisher of Black interest books. Publishes popular contemporary fiction, children's fiction, and black classics, though scope is expanding. Send SAE with MS, rather than synopses or ideas. No poetry.

Yale University Press (London)

47 Bedford Square
London
WC1B 3DP
Tel: +44 (0) 20 7079 4900
Fax: +44 (0) 20 7079 4901
Email: sales@yaleup.co.uk
Website: http://www.yalebooks.co.uk

Publishes: Nonfiction; Reference; *Areas:* Architecture; Arts; Autobiography; Beauty and Fashion; Biography; Business; Criticism; Current Affairs; Finance; Health; Historical; Legal; Literature; Medicine; Music; Philosophy; Politics; Religious; Science; Sociology; Technology; Translations; *Markets:* Adult

Welcomes unsolicited MSS and synopses in specified subject areas.

Zed Books Ltd

The Foundry
17 Oval Way
London
SE11 5RR
Tel: +44 (0) 20 3752 5830
Email: editorial@zedbooks.net
Website: http://www.zedbooks.co.uk

Publishes: Nonfiction; *Areas:* Anthropology; Architecture; Autobiography; Biography; Business; Culture; Current Affairs; Finance; Health; Historical; Media; Medicine; Nature; Politics; Sociology; *Markets:* Academic; Adult

Publishes academic works and books for a general audience. See website for information on submitting a proposal.

Canadian Publishers

For the most up-to-date listings of these and hundreds of other publishers, visit https://www.firstwriter.com/publishers

*To claim your **free** access to the site, please see the back of this book.*

Arsenal Pulp Press

202-211 East Georgia Street
Vancouver, BC, V6A 1Z6
Tel: +1 (604) 687-4233
Fax: +1 (604) 687-4283
Email: info@arsenalpulp.com
Website: http://www.arsenalpulp.com

Publishes: Fiction; Nonfiction; *Areas:* Arts; Cookery; Crafts; Culture; Health; Lifestyle; Politics; Sociology; *Markets:* Adult; Children's; Youth; *Treatments:* Literary

Publishes Cultural studies, Political/sociological studies, Regional studies and guides, in particular for British Columbia, Cookbooks, Gay and lesbian fiction and non-fiction (including young adult and children's), Visual art, Multicultural fiction and non-fiction, Literary fiction and nonfiction (no genre fiction, such as mysteries, thriller, or romance), Youth culture, Health, and books for children (especially those that emphasise diversity). Send query with synopsis, chapter by chapter outline for nonfiction, writing credentials, 50-page excerpt, and marketing analysis. Include self-addressed envelope and appropriate return postage (either Canadian postage or IRCs), or email address for response. See website for full details. No submissions by fax or email, or queries by phone.

Carswell

One Corporate Plaza
2075 Kennedy Road
Toronto, ON
M1T 3V4
Tel: +1 (416) 298-5007
Email: jayne.jackson@thomsonreuters.com
Website: http://www.carswell.com

Publishes: Nonfiction; Reference; *Areas:* Finance; Legal; *Markets:* Professional

Publishes material for legal, tax, and accounting professionals.

Dragon Moon Press

Email: dmpsubmissions@gmail.com
Website: http://dragonmoonpress.com

Publishes: Fiction; Nonfiction; *Areas:* Fantasy; Horror; How-to; Romance; Sci-Fi; *Markets:* Adult; Youth

Publishes novel-length fantasy, science fiction, and gentle horror for adults and the upper end of the YA spectrum. No middle grade or children's, or short story collections. Particularly interested in traditional fantasy (quests / dragons rather than werewolves and vampires). Also publishes how-to titles on how to write / sell writing. See website for submission guidelines.

ECW Press

665 Gerrard Street East
Toronto, ON M4M 1Y2
Tel: +1 (416) 694-3348
Fax: +1 (416) 698-9906
Email: info@ecwpress.com
Website: http://www.ecwpress.com

Publishes: Fiction; Nonfiction; Poetry; *Areas:* Autobiography; Biography; Business; Culture; Finance; Health; Historical; Humour; Literature; Mystery; Politics; Religious; Sport; Suspense; TV; Women's Interests; *Markets:* Adult; *Treatments:* Commercial; Literary; Mainstream

Publishes only Canadian-authored fiction and poetry. Non-fiction proposals accepted from anywhere. Proposal should be made by post and include: cover letter; biog; sample of the manuscript (for poetry, 10-15 pages, for fiction and nonfiction, 15-25 pages); synopsis.

Fitzhenry & Whiteside Ltd

195 Allstate Parkway
Markham, Ontario L3R 4T8
Tel: +1 (905) 477-9700
Fax: +1 (800) 260-9777
Email: godwit@fitzhenry.ca
Website: http://www.fitzhenry.ca

Publishes: Fiction; Nonfiction; *Markets:* Adult; Children's; Youth

Contact: Sharon Fitzhenry (Adult); Cheryl Chen (Children's)

Publishes fiction and nonfiction for adults, children, and young adults. See website for submission guidelines.

Insomniac Press

520 Princess Avenue
London, ON N6B 2B8
Email: mike@insomniacpress.com
Website: http://www.insomniacpress.com

Publishes: Fiction; Nonfiction; Poetry; Reference; *Areas:* Business; Crime; Criticism; Culture; Finance; Gardening; Health; Humour; Legal; Lifestyle; Literature; Medicine; Music; Mystery; Politics; Religious; Self-Help; Short Stories; Spiritual; Sport; Suspense; Travel; *Markets:* Adult; *Treatments:* Commercial; Experimental; Literary; Mainstream

Contact: Mike O'Connor

Particularly interested in creative nonfiction on business / personal finance; gay and lesbian studies; black canadian studies and others. No science fiction, cookbooks, romance, or children's books. Poetry list is booked up for the foreseeable future. Send query by email or post in first instance. Approaches by authors who have had work published elsewhere (e.g. short stories in magazines) will receive closer attention.

On The Mark Press

15 Dairy Avenue
Napanee, ON, K7R 1M4
Tel: +1 (800) 463-6367
Email: productdevelopment@onthemarkpress.com
Website: http://www.onthemarkpress.com

Publishes: Nonfiction; *Markets:* Academic; Professional

Publishes workbooks and resources to support teachers in the classroom. Send samples with resume by post or by email.

Penguin Canada

Penguin Group (Canada)
90 Eglinton Avenue East, Suite 700
Toronto, Ontario M4P 2Y3
Tel: +1 (416) 925-2249
Fax: +1 (416) 925-0068
Email: customerservicescanada@penguinrandomhouse.com
Website: http://penguinrandomhouse.ca

Publishes: Fiction; Nonfiction; *Markets:* Adult

Publishes fiction and nonfiction by Canadian authors on Canadian subjects. Accepts submissions through literary agents only.

Rebelight Publishing Inc.

Email: submit@rebelight.com
Website: http://rebelight.com

Publishes: Fiction; *Markets:* Children's; Youth

Publishes fiction of any genre for Middle Grade and Young Adult audiences. Accepts submissions from Canadian writers only, but seeks to appeal to a worldwide market. No adult fiction, holiday stories, graphic novels, poetry, short stories, illustrations, picture books, nonfiction, erotica, or previously published work (including self-published material). Send query with CV, one-page synopsis, and first three chapters by email. See website for full guidelines.

TouchWood Editions

103 – 1075 Pendergast Street
Victoria, BC V8V 0A1
Tel: +1 (250) 360-0829
Fax: +1 (250) 386-0829
Email: edit@touchwoodeditions.com
Website: http://www.touchwoodeditions.com

Publishes: Fiction; Nonfiction; *Areas:* Arts; Biography; Cookery; Culture; Gardening; Historical; Mystery; Nature; Suspense; Travel; *Markets:* Adult

Accepts submissions as hard copy by post and digitally by email. Publishes Canadian authors only. See website for full guidelines.

Vehicule Press

P.O.B. 42094 BP Roy
Montreal, Quebec H2W 2T3
Tel: +1 (514) 844-6073
Fax: +1 (514) 844-7543
Email: admin@vehiculepress.com
Website: http://www.vehiculepress.com

Publishes: Fiction; Nonfiction; Poetry; *Areas:* Historical; Music; Religious; Sociology; Translations; *Markets:* Adult

Publishes poetry, literary novels, novellas, short story collections, and translations, primarily from Canadian authors. Not accepting poetry manuscripts as at April 2017. See website for current status, and full fiction submission guidelines.

Irish Publishers

For the most up-to-date listings of these and hundreds of other publishers, visit https://www.firstwriter.com/publishers

*To claim your **free** access to the site, please see the back of this book.*

CJ Fallon

Ground Floor – Block B
Liffey Valley Office Campus
Dublin 22
Tel: 01 6166400
Fax: 01 6166499
Email: editorial@cjfallon.ie
Website: http://www.cjfallon.ie

Publishes: Nonfiction; Reference; Business; Finance; Historical; Literature; Music; Religious; Science; Technology; *Markets:* Academic; Children's; Professional; Youth

Publishes teaching resources written by teachers, for teachers. Send proposal to the Managing Editor in the first instance.

Flyleaf Press

4 Spencer Villas
Glenageary
Co. Dublin
Tel: +353 1 2854658
Email: books@flyleaf.ie
Website: http://flyleaf.ie

Publishes: Nonfiction; Reference; *Areas:* Historical; How-to; *Markets:* Adult

Publishes family history and genealogy titles, how-to guides for researching family history, and reference workds on Church Records, Census records and wills.

Four Courts Press

7 Malpas Street
Dublin
D08 YD81
Tel: 353-1-453-4668
Email: info@fourcourtspress.ie
Website: http://www.fourcourtspress.ie

Publishes: Nonfiction; *Areas:* Archaeology; Architecture; Arts; Criticism; Historical; Legal; Literature; Philosophy; Religious; *Markets:* Academic

Academic press, originally focusing on theology, now also publishing books on history, art, literature, and law. Send query by email in first instance.

The Gallery Press

Loughcrew
Oldcastle
County Meath
Tel: +353 (0) 49 8541779
Fax: +353 (0) 49 8541779
Email: gallery@indigo.ie
Website: http://www.gallerypress.com

Publishes: Fiction; Nonfiction; Poetry; Scripts; *Areas:* Theatre; *Markets:* Adult; *Treatments:* Literary

Contact: Peter Fallon

Publishes poetry, drama, and prose by Ireland's leading contemporary writers. See website for submission guidelines. No submissions by fax or email. Accepts work from Irish or Irish-based authors only.

Gill & Macmillan

Hume Avenue
Park West
Dublin 12
Tel: +353 (01) 500 9500
Email: dmarsh@gillmacmillan.ie
Website: http://www.gillmacmillanbooks.ie

Publishes: Fiction; Nonfiction; Reference; *Areas:* Biography; Cookery; Crime; Current Affairs; Historical; Hobbies; Humour; Leisure; Lifestyle; Nature; Sport; *Markets:* Adult; Children's

Contact: Deborah Marsh, Editorial Administrator

Publishes adult nonfiction and children's fiction and nonfiction. No adult fiction, poetry, short stories or plays. Prefers proposals by email, but will also accept proposals by post. See website for full submission guidelines.

The Lilliput Press

62-63 Sitric Road
Arbour Hill
Dublin 7
Tel: +353 (01) 671 16 47
Fax: +353 (01) 671 12 33
Email: info@lilliputpress.ie
Website: http://www.lilliputpress.ie

Publishes: Fiction; Nonfiction; Poetry; Reference; Scripts; *Areas:* Architecture; Arts; Autobiography; Biography; Business; Cookery; Criticism; Culture; Current Affairs; Drama; Historical; Literature; Music; Nature; Philosophy; Photography; Politics; Sociology; Sport; Travel; *Markets:* Adult; *Treatments:* Literary; Popular

Contact: Submissions Editor

Publishes books broadly focused on Irish themes. Send query by post with one-page synopsis and complete ms or three sample chapters. Include SASE if response required. No submissions by email. See website for full guidelines.

The O'Brien Press

12 Terenure Road East
Rathgar
Dublin 6
D06 HD27
Tel: +353-1-4923333
Fax: +353-1-4922777
Email: books@obrien.ie
Website: http://www.obrien.ie

Publishes: Fiction; Nonfiction; Reference; *Areas:* Architecture; Arts; Autobiography; Biography; Business; Cookery; Crafts; Crime; Drama; Historical; Humour; Lifestyle; Literature; Music; Nature; Photography; Politics; Religious; Sport; Travel; *Markets:* Adult; Children's; Youth

Mainly publishes children's fiction, children's nonfiction and adult nonfiction. Generally doesn't publish poetry, academic works or adult fiction. Send synopsis and two or three sample chapters. If fewer than 1,000 words, send complete ms. See website for full guidelines.

Oak Tree Press

33 Rochestown Rise
Rochestown
Cork
Tel: +353 86 244 1633
Fax: +353 86 330 7694
Email: info@oaktreepress.com
Website: http://oaktreepress.eu

Publishes: Nonfiction; *Areas:* Business; Finance; Legal; *Markets:* Professional

Publishes books on business, particularly for small business owners and managers.

Onstream Publications Ltd

Currabaha
Cloghroe
Blarney
Co. Cork
Tel: +353 21 4385798
Email: info@onstream.ie
Website: http://www.onstream.ie

Publishes: Fiction; Nonfiction; *Areas:* Cookery; Historical; Travel; *Markets:* Academic; Adult

Publisher of mainly nonfiction, although some fiction published. Also offers services to authors.

Somerville Press

Dromore
Bantry
Co. Cork
Tel: 353 (0) 28 32873
Fax: 353 (0) 28 328
Email: somervillepress@eircom.net
Website: http://www.somervillepress.com

Publishes: Fiction; Nonfiction; *Markets:* Adult

Publishes fiction and nonfiction, mainly of Irish interest.

Publishers Subject Index

This section lists publishers by their subject matter, with directions to the section of the book where the full listing can be found.

You can create your own customised lists of publishers using different combinations of these subject areas, plus over a dozen other criteria, instantly online at https://www.firstwriter.com.

*To claim your **free** access to the site, please see the back of this book.*

Adventure
Amakella Publishing (*US*)
Arrow Publications, LLC (*US*)
Birlinn Ltd (*UK*)
Black Lyon Publishing, LLC (*US*)
Carina UK (*UK*)
Cave Books (*US*)
Children's Brains are Yummy (CBAY) Books (*US*)
Covenant Communications Inc. (*US*)
Cricket Books (*US*)
Crystal Spirit Publishing, Inc. (*US*)
Curious Fox (*UK*)
Dreamriver Press (*US*)
FalconGuides (*US*)
Famous Seamus (*UK*)
Goosebottom Books LLC (*US*)
Lost Tower Publications (*UK*)
M P Publishing USA (*US*)
Maverick Reads (*UK*)
Pen Books (*US*)
Red Empress Publishing (*US*)
The Salariya Book Company (*UK*)
Sidestreet Cookie Publishing (*US*)
Sunscribe (*US*)
Sunstone Press (*US*)
Tumblehome Learning, Inc. (*US*)
W.W. Norton & Company Ltd (*UK*)
WaterBrook & Multnomah (*US*)
Wordsworth Editions (*UK*)

Anthropology
Abdo Publishing Co (*US*)
Algora Publishing (*US*)
Amakella Publishing (*US*)
Bucknell University Press (*US*)
Cave Books (*US*)
Dreamriver Press (*US*)
Dunedin Academic Press Ltd (*UK*)
Eagle's View Publishing (*US*)
Famous Seamus (*UK*)
Fordham University Press (*US*)
Mage Publishers (*US*)
Marion Boyars Publishers (*UK*)
New York University (NYU) Press (*US*)
Oneworld Publications (*UK*)
Pen Books (*US*)
Polity Press (*UK*)
Seren Books (*UK*)
Sidestreet Cookie Publishing (*US*)
Sunscribe (*US*)
Syracuse University Press (*US*)
Temple University Press (*US*)
Truman State University Press (*US*)
University of Alabama Press (*US*)
University of Chicago Press (*US*)
The University of Michigan Press (*US*)
University of Washington Press (*US*)
Utah State University Press (*US*)
Verso (*UK*)
W.W. Norton & Company Ltd (*UK*)
Wannabee Books (*US*)
Zed Books Ltd (*UK*)

Antiques
ACC Art Books Ltd (*UK*)
Astragal Press (*US*)
Oak Knoll Press (*US*)
Octopus Publishing Group Limited (*UK*)
Pelican Publishing Company (*US*)

Souvenir Press Ltd (*UK*)
Sunscribe (*US*)

Archaeology

Algora Publishing (*US*)
Amberley Publishing (*UK*)
Ashmolean Museum Publications (*UK*)
Boydell & Brewer Ltd (*UK*)
Cave Books (*US*)
Council for British Archaeology (CBA) Publishing (*UK*)
Eagle's View Publishing (*US*)
Edinburgh University Press (*UK*)
Fonthill Media LLC (*US*)
Fonthill Media Ltd (*UK*)
Four Courts Press (*Ire*)
The History Press (*UK*)
Liverpool University Press (*UK*)
LSU Press (*US*)
Mage Publishers (*US*)
Polity Press (*UK*)
Saffron Books (*UK*)
Souvenir Press Ltd (*UK*)
Sunscribe (*US*)
Sunstone Press (*US*)
Truman State University Press (*US*)
University of Alabama Press (*US*)
University of Chicago Press (*US*)
The University of Michigan Press (*US*)
Utah State University Press (*US*)
W.W. Norton & Company Ltd (*UK*)
Wannabee Books (*US*)

Architecture

ACC Art Books Ltd (*UK*)
ASCE Press (*US*)
Ashgate Publishing Limited (*UK*)
Birlinn Ltd (*UK*)
Black Dog Publishing London UK (*UK*)
Bucknell University Press (*US*)
David R. Godine, Publisher (*US*)
Edinburgh University Press (*UK*)
Floris Books (*UK*)
Fordham University Press (*US*)
Four Courts Press (*Ire*)
Gingko Library (*UK*)
Guild of Master Craftsman (GMC) Publications Ltd (*UK*)
Laurence King Publishing Ltd (*UK*)
The Lilliput Press (*Ire*)
Liverpool University Press (*UK*)
Lund Humphries Limited (*UK*)
Mage Publishers (*US*)
McFarland & Company, Inc. (*US*)
Merrell Publishers Limited (*UK*)
Metro Publications Ltd (*UK*)
The O'Brien Press (*Ire*)
Octopus Publishing Group Limited (*UK*)
Pelican Publishing Company (*US*)
Phaidon Press Limited (*UK*)
Professional Publications, Inc. (PPI) (*US*)
Quill Driver Books (*US*)
Quiller Publishing Ltd (*UK*)
Reaktion Books (*UK*)
Reference Service Press (*US*)
RotoVision (*UK*)
Stenlake Publishing (*UK*)
Sunscribe (*US*)
Sunstone Press (*US*)
Truman State University Press (*US*)
University of Chicago Press (*US*)
University of Pittsburgh Press (*US*)
University of South Carolina Press (*US*)
Verso (*UK*)
W.W. Norton & Company Ltd (*UK*)
Wannabee Books (*US*)
John Wiley & Sons, Inc. (*US*)
Philip Wilson Publishers Ltd (*UK*)
WIT Press (*UK*)
Yale University Press (*US*)
Yale University Press (London) (*UK*)
Zed Books Ltd (*UK*)

Arts

Abdo Publishing Co (*US*)
ACC Art Books Ltd (*UK*)
Alma Classics (*UK*)
Anness Publishing Ltd (*UK*)
Arch Street Press (*US*)
Arsenal Pulp Press (*Can*)
Ashgate Publishing Limited (*UK*)
Ashmolean Museum Publications (*UK*)
Aurora Metro Press (*UK*)
Barron's Educational Series, Inc. (*US*)
Beacon Press (*US*)
Birlinn Ltd (*UK*)
Black Dog Publishing London UK (*UK*)
Bloomsbury Publishing Plc (*UK*)
Boydell & Brewer Ltd (*UK*)
Bucknell University Press (*US*)
Co & Bear Productions (*UK*)
Crescent Moon Publishing (*UK*)
David R. Godine, Publisher (*US*)
Dreamriver Press (*US*)
Famous Seamus (*UK*)
Fantagraphics (*US*)
Finney Company (*US*)
Floris Books (*UK*)
Fordham University Press (*US*)
Four Courts Press (*Ire*)
Gibson Square Books Ltd (*UK*)
Gingko Library (*UK*)
Gomer Press (*UK*)
Greenhaven Publishing (*US*)
Guild of Master Craftsman (GMC) Publications Ltd (*UK*)
Halsgrove (*UK*)
Haus Publishing (*UK*)
Heyday Books (*US*)
Hohm Press (*US*)
Interlink Publishing Group, Inc. (*US*)
Italica Press (*US*)
Jacaranda Books Art Music Ltd (*UK*)
Laurence King Publishing Ltd (*UK*)
The Lilliput Press (*Ire*)
Liverpool University Press (*UK*)
Luath Press Ltd (*UK*)
Lund Humphries Limited (*UK*)
Mage Publishers (*US*)

Manchester University Press (*UK*)
Mandrake of Oxford (*UK*)
McFarland & Company, Inc. (*US*)
Merrell Publishers Limited (*UK*)
Metro Publications Ltd (*UK*)
Mitchell Lane Publishers, Inc. (*US*)
Natural History Museum Publishing (*UK*)
New Holland Publishers (UK) Ltd (*UK*)
The O'Brien Press (*Ire*)
Octopus Publishing Group Limited (*UK*)
Oneworld Publications (*UK*)
Pandora Press (*UK*)
Pelican Publishing Company (*US*)
Phaidon Press Limited (*UK*)
Quill Driver Books (*US*)
Reaktion Books (*UK*)
Red Wheel (*US*)
Reference Service Press (*US*)
Robert Hale Publishers (*UK*)
The Rosen Publishing Group, Inc. (*US*)
RotoVision (*UK*)
Running Press (*US*)
Saffron Books (*UK*)
Search Press Ltd (*UK*)
Seren Books (*UK*)
Southern Illinois University Press (*US*)
Stenlake Publishing (*UK*)
Sterling Publishing Co. Inc. (*US*)
Sunscribe (*US*)
Sunstone Press (*US*)
Temple University Press (*US*)
TouchWood Editions (*Can*)
Truman State University Press (*US*)
Two Rivers Press (*UK*)
University of Chicago Press (*US*)
The University of Michigan Press (*US*)
University of South Carolina Press (*US*)
University of Washington Press (*US*)
Verso (*UK*)
Walch Education (*US*)
Wannabee Books (*US*)
Philip Wilson Publishers Ltd (*UK*)
Yale University Press (*US*)
Yale University Press (London) (*UK*)

Autobiography
Academy Chicago (*US*)
Allison & Busby Ltd (*UK*)
Alma Classics (*UK*)
Arch Street Press (*US*)
Asabi Publishing (*US*)
Beacon Press (*US*)
BearManor Media (*US*)
BenBella Books (*US*)
Birlinn Ltd (*UK*)
Black & White Publishing Ltd (*UK*)
John Blake Publishing (*UK*)
Canongate Books (*UK*)
DB Publishing (*UK*)
Dreamriver Press (*US*)
Dref Wen (*UK*)
ECW Press (*Can*)
Familius (*US*)
Fantagraphics (*US*)
Gomer Press (*UK*)
Granta Books (*UK*)
Halban Publishers (*UK*)
HarperCollins Publishers Ltd (*UK*)
Headline Publishing Group (*UK*)
Health Communications, Inc. (*US*)
Hesperus Press Limited (*UK*)
Honno Welsh Women's Press (*UK*)
Humanix Books (*US*)
Infinite Ideas (*UK*)
Jacaranda Books Art Music Ltd (*UK*)
Jolly Fish Press (*US*)
The Lilliput Press (*Ire*)
Lion Hudson Plc (*UK*)
Lost Tower Publications (*UK*)
The Lyons Press Inc. (*US*)
Macmillan (*UK*)
Mage Publishers (*US*)
Marion Boyars Publishers (*UK*)
Merlin Unwin Books (*UK*)
Milo Books Ltd (*UK*)
Monsoon Books Pte Ltd (*UK*)
The O'Brien Press (*Ire*)
PaperBooks (*UK*)
Pelican Publishing Company (*US*)
Pen Books (*US*)
Pushkin Press (*UK*)
River City Publishing (*US*)
Serpent's Tail (*UK*)
Seven Stories Press (*US*)
Shearsman Books (*UK*)
Souvenir Press Ltd (*UK*)
St. Johann Press (*US*)
Sunscribe (*US*)
Sunstone Press (*US*)
Triangle Square (*US*)
Triumph Books (*US*)
Truman State University Press (*US*)
University of Alaska Press (*US*)
The University of Michigan Press (*US*)
Valley Press (*UK*)
Verso (*UK*)
W.W. Norton & Company Ltd (*UK*)
Weidenfeld & Nicolson (*UK*)
Whitaker House (*US*)
Yale University Press (London) (*UK*)
Zed Books Ltd (*UK*)
Zumaya Publications (*US*)

Beauty and Fashion
ACC Art Books Ltd (*UK*)
Barron's Educational Series, Inc. (*US*)
Black Dog Publishing London UK (*UK*)
Co & Bear Productions (*UK*)
Jacaranda Books Art Music Ltd (*UK*)
Kyle Books (*UK*)
Laurence King Publishing Ltd (*UK*)
Luath Press Ltd (*UK*)
Merrell Publishers Limited (*UK*)
Octopus Publishing Group Limited (*UK*)
Phaidon Press Limited (*UK*)
Quadrille Publishing Ltd (*UK*)
Reaktion Books (*UK*)
Running Press (*US*)

Souvenir Press Ltd (*UK*)
Sunscribe (*US*)
Yale University Press (London) (*UK*)

Biography

Abdo Publishing Co (*US*)
Allison & Busby Ltd (*UK*)
Alma Classics (*UK*)
Alpine Publications, Inc. (*US*)
Amakella Publishing (*US*)
Amberley Publishing (*UK*)
Arch Street Press (*US*)
Asabi Publishing (*US*)
Aureus Publishing Limited (*UK*)
Aurora Metro Press (*UK*)
Authentic Media (*UK*)
Beacon Press (*US*)
BearManor Media (*US*)
BenBella Books (*US*)
Birlinn Ltd (*UK*)
Black & White Publishing Ltd (*UK*)
John Blake Publishing (*UK*)
Candy Jar Books (*UK*)
Canongate Books (*UK*)
Carcanet Press Ltd (*UK*)
Cave Books (*US*)
Covenant Communications Inc. (*US*)
David R. Godine, Publisher (*US*)
DB Publishing (*UK*)
Dreamriver Press (*US*)
Dunedin Academic Press Ltd (*UK*)
Dynasty Press (*UK*)
ECW Press (*Can*)
Famous Seamus (*UK*)
Fleming Publications (*UK*)
Floris Books (*UK*)
Fonthill Media LLC (*US*)
Fonthill Media Ltd (*UK*)
Fordham University Press (*US*)
Gallaudet University Press (*US*)
Gibson Square Books Ltd (*UK*)
Gill & Macmillan (*Ire*)
Gingko Library (*UK*)
Gomer Press (*UK*)
Granta Books (*UK*)
Halban Publishers (*UK*)
Halsgrove (*UK*)
HarperCollins Publishers Ltd (*UK*)
Haus Publishing (*UK*)
Hay House Publishers (*UK*)
Head of Zeus (*UK*)
Headland Publications (*UK*)
Headline Publishing Group (*UK*)
Health Communications, Inc. (*US*)
Hesperus Press Limited (*UK*)
The History Press (*UK*)
House of Lochar (*UK*)
Hymns Ancient & Modern Ltd (*UK*)
Independent Music Press (*UK*)
Infinite Ideas (*UK*)
Jacaranda Books Art Music Ltd (*UK*)
Jolly Fish Press (*US*)
Judaica Press (*US*)
Kube Publishing (*UK*)
The Lilliput Press (*Ire*)
Lion Hudson Plc (*UK*)
Luath Press Ltd (*UK*)
Macmillan (*UK*)
Mage Publishers (*US*)
Marion Boyars Publishers (*UK*)
Milo Books Ltd (*UK*)
Mitchell Lane Publishers, Inc. (*US*)
Monsoon Books Pte Ltd (*UK*)
Neil Wilson Publishing Ltd (*UK*)
New Holland Publishers (UK) Ltd (*UK*)
The O'Brien Press (*Ire*)
Michael O'Mara Books Ltd (*UK*)
Oneworld Publications (*UK*)
Oregon State University Press (*US*)
Ouen Press (*UK*)
Pandora Press (*UK*)
Paragon House (*US*)
Pelican Publishing Company (*US*)
Pen Books (*US*)
Quill Driver Books (*US*)
Quiller Publishing Ltd (*UK*)
Reaktion Books (*UK*)
River City Publishing (*US*)
Robert Hale Publishers (*UK*)
The Rosen Publishing Group, Inc. (*US*)
Seren Books (*UK*)
Serpent's Tail (*UK*)
Southern Illinois University Press (*US*)
Souvenir Press Ltd (*UK*)
St Pauls (*US*)
St. Johann Press (*US*)
Sunscribe (*US*)
Sunstone Press (*US*)
Syracuse University Press (*US*)
Temple University Press (*US*)
TouchWood Editions (*Can*)
Triangle Square (*US*)
Triumph Books (*US*)
Truman State University Press (*US*)
University of Alabama Press (*US*)
University of Alaska Press (*US*)
University of Chicago Press (*US*)
The University of Michigan Press (*US*)
University of Washington Press (*US*)
Verso (*UK*)
W.W. Norton & Company Ltd (*UK*)
Weidenfeld & Nicolson (*UK*)
Whitaker House (*US*)
Wordsworth Editions (*UK*)
Yale University Press (London) (*UK*)
Zed Books Ltd (*UK*)

Business

ACC Art Books Ltd (*UK*)
Amakella Publishing (*US*)
Arch Street Press (*US*)
Ashgate Publishing Limited (*UK*)
Barron's Educational Series, Inc. (*US*)
BenBella Books (*US*)
Bennion Kearny (*UK*)
John Blake Publishing (*UK*)
CJ Fallon (*Ire*)
Crown House Publishing (*UK*)

Crystal Spirit Publishing, Inc. (*US*)
ECW Press (*Can*)
Edward Elgar Publishing Inc. (*US*)
Edward Elgar Publishing Ltd (*UK*)
Euromonitor (*UK*)
Fordham University Press (*US*)
Hanser Publications (*US*)
Hay House Publishers (*UK*)
Humanix Books (*US*)
Infinite Ideas (*UK*)
Insomniac Press (*Can*)
International Wealth Success (IWS) Inc. (*US*)
Legend Business (*UK*)
The Lilliput Press (*Ire*)
Macmillan (*UK*)
Management Books 2000 Ltd (*UK*)
Manchester University Press (*UK*)
Maven House Press (*US*)
Nolo (*US*)
The O'Brien Press (*Ire*)
Oak Tree Press (*Ire*)
Oneworld Publications (*UK*)
O'Reilly Media (*US*)
Pelican Publishing Company (*US*)
Polity Press (*UK*)
Prometheus Books (*US*)
Quill Driver Books (*US*)
Quiller Publishing Ltd (*UK*)
Red Wheel (*US*)
Reference Service Press (*US*)
Saffron Books (*UK*)
Silver Lake Publishing, LLC (*US*)
Souvenir Press Ltd (*UK*)
Storey Publishing (*US*)
Sunscribe (*US*)
Sunstone Press (*US*)
Temple University Press (*US*)
Tower Publishing (*US*)
The University of Michigan Press (*US*)
Verso (*US*)
W.W. Norton & Company Ltd (*UK*)
John Wiley & Sons, Inc. (*US*)
Yale University Press (London) (*UK*)
Zed Books Ltd (*UK*)

Cookery

Abdo Publishing Co (*US*)
Andrews McMeel Publishing (*US*)
Anness Publishing Ltd (*UK*)
Arsenal Pulp Press (*Can*)
Aurora Metro Press (*UK*)
Barron's Educational Series, Inc. (*US*)
BenBella Books (*US*)
Black & White Publishing Ltd (*UK*)
John Blake Publishing (*UK*)
Chelsea Green Publishing, Inc. (*US*)
Dreamriver Press (*US*)
Familius (*US*)
Famous Seamus (*UK*)
Gill & Macmillan (*Ire*)
Guild of Master Craftsman (GMC) Publications Ltd (*UK*)
HarperCollins Publishers Ltd (*UK*)
Headline Publishing Group (*UK*)
Health Communications, Inc. (*US*)
Hipso Media (*US*)
Infinite Ideas (*UK*)
Interlink Publishing Group, Inc. (*US*)
Kyle Books (*UK*)
The Lilliput Press (*Ire*)
The Lyons Press Inc. (*US*)
Macmillan (*UK*)
Mage Publishers (*US*)
Merlin Unwin Books (*UK*)
Neil Wilson Publishing Ltd (*UK*)
New Holland Publishers (UK) Ltd (*UK*)
The O'Brien Press (*Ire*)
Octopus Publishing Group Limited (*UK*)
Onstream Publications Ltd (*Ire*)
The Overmountain Press (*US*)
Page Street Publishing Co. (*US*)
PaperBooks (*UK*)
Pelican Publishing Company (*US*)
Phaidon Press Limited (*UK*)
Quadrille Publishing Ltd (*UK*)
Quiller Publishing Ltd (*UK*)
Red Wheel (*US*)
Running Press (*US*)
Ryland Peters & Small (*UK*)
Souvenir Press Ltd (*UK*)
Stenlake Publishing (*UK*)
Storey Publishing (*US*)
Sunscribe (*US*)
Sunstone Press (*US*)
Top That! Publishing (*UK*)
TouchWood Editions (*Can*)
The University of Michigan Press (*US*)
University of South Carolina Press (*US*)
Waverley Books (*UK*)
Weidenfeld & Nicolson (*UK*)
John Wiley & Sons, Inc. (*US*)
Willow Creek Press, Inc. (*US*)

Crafts

Abdo Publishing Co (*US*)
ACC Art Books Ltd (*UK*)
American Quilter's Society (*US*)
Anness Publishing Ltd (*UK*)
Arsenal Pulp Press (*Can*)
Astragal Press (*US*)
Barron's Educational Series, Inc. (*US*)
Black Dog Publishing London UK (*UK*)
Divertir Publishing LLC (*US*)
Dreamriver Press (*US*)
Eagle's View Publishing (*US*)
Finney Company (*US*)
Floris Books (*UK*)
4th Level Indie (*US*)
Guild of Master Craftsman (GMC) Publications Ltd (*UK*)
Haldane Mason Ltd (*UK*)
HarperCollins Publishers Ltd (*UK*)
Kansas City Star Quilts (*US*)
Leisure Arts, Inc. (*US*)
Mitchell Lane Publishers, Inc. (*US*)
New Holland Publishers (UK) Ltd (*UK*)
The O'Brien Press (*Ire*)
Octopus Publishing Group Limited (*UK*)

Page Street Publishing Co. (*US*)
Pelican Publishing Company (*US*)
Quadrille Publishing Ltd (*UK*)
The Rosen Publishing Group, Inc. (*US*)
Running Press (*US*)
Ryland Peters & Small (*UK*)
Search Press Ltd (*UK*)
Snowbooks (*UK*)
Souvenir Press Ltd (*UK*)
STC Craft (*US*)
Stenlake Publishing (*UK*)
Sterling Publishing Co. Inc. (*US*)
Storey Publishing (*US*)
Sunscribe (*US*)
Sunstone Press (*US*)
W.W. Norton & Company Ltd (*UK*)

Crime

Allison & Busby Ltd (*UK*)
Ankerwycke (*US*)
Arrow Publications, LLC (*US*)
Asabi Publishing (*US*)
Black & White Publishing Ltd (*UK*)
John Blake Publishing (*UK*)
Carina UK (*UK*)
Curiosity Quills Press (*US*)
Curious Fox (*UK*)
Darkhouse Books (*US*)
DB Publishing (*UK*)
Famous Seamus (*UK*)
Gill & Macmillan (*Ire*)
Harlequin Mills & Boon Ltd (*UK*)
HarperCollins Publishers Ltd (*UK*)
Head of Zeus (*UK*)
Hesperus Press Limited (*UK*)
The History Press (*UK*)
Honno Welsh Women's Press (*UK*)
Insomniac Press (*Can*)
Jacaranda Books Art Music Ltd (*UK*)
Joffe Books Ltd (*UK*)
Lost Tower Publications (*UK*)
Luath Press Ltd (*UK*)
M P Publishing USA (*US*)
Macmillan (*UK*)
Mandrake of Oxford (*UK*)
Milo Books Ltd (*UK*)
Monsoon Books Pte Ltd (*UK*)
Neil Wilson Publishing Ltd (*UK*)
New York University (NYU) Press (*US*)
The O'Brien Press (*Ire*)
Pelican Publishing Company (*US*)
Pen Books (*US*)
Polis Books (*US*)
Polity Press (*UK*)
Quill Driver Books (*US*)
Red Rattle Books (*UK*)
Robert Hale Publishers (*UK*)
Salt Publishing Ltd (*UK*)
Sandstone Press Ltd (*UK*)
Serpent's Tail (*UK*)
Severn House Publishers (*UK*)
Snowbooks (*UK*)
Southern Illinois University Press (*US*)
Souvenir Press Ltd (*UK*)
Sterling Publishing Co. Inc. (*US*)
Summersdale Publishers Ltd (*UK*)
Sunscribe (*US*)
Sunstone Press (*US*)
Temple University Press (*US*)
Twenty First Century Publishers Ltd (*UK*)
Tyrus Books (*US*)
W.W. Norton & Company Ltd (*UK*)
Zumaya Publications (*US*)

Criticism

Arch Street Press (*US*)
BlazeVOX [books] (*US*)
Bucknell University Press (*US*)
Crescent Moon Publishing (*UK*)
David R. Godine, Publisher (*US*)
Famous Seamus (*UK*)
Four Courts Press (*Ire*)
Gibson Square Books Ltd (*UK*)
Granta Books (*UK*)
Halban Publishers (*UK*)
Imprint Academic (*UK*)
Insomniac Press (*Can*)
The Lilliput Press (*Ire*)
Manchester University Press (*UK*)
Marion Boyars Publishers (*UK*)
Maverick Reads (*UK*)
Pelican Publishing Company (*US*)
Seren Books (*UK*)
Shearsman Books (*UK*)
Sunscribe (*US*)
Truman State University Press (*US*)
University of Alabama Press (*US*)
Wannabee Books (*US*)
Yale University Press (London) (*UK*)

Culture

Abdo Publishing Co (*US*)
Allison & Busby Ltd (*UK*)
Amakella Publishing (*US*)
Arch Street Press (*US*)
Arsenal Pulp Press (*Can*)
Asabi Publishing (*US*)
Ashgate Publishing Limited (*UK*)
Augsburg Fortress (*US*)
Aurora Metro Press (*UK*)
BenBella Books (*US*)
Birlinn Ltd (*UK*)
Black Dog Publishing London UK (*UK*)
Blue Guides Limited (*UK*)
Blue River Press (*US*)
Bucknell University Press (*US*)
Canongate Books (*UK*)
Concordia Publishing House (*US*)
Crescent Moon Publishing (*UK*)
Dreamriver Press (*US*)
Eagle's View Publishing (*US*)
ECW Press (*Can*)
Edinburgh University Press (*UK*)
Edward Elgar Publishing Ltd (*UK*)
Famous Seamus (*UK*)
Fantagraphics (*US*)
Finney Company (*US*)
Fordham University Press (*US*)
Frances Lincoln Children's Books (*UK*)

Gallaudet University Press (*US*)
GEY Books (*UK*)
Gibson Square Books Ltd (*UK*)
Gomer Press (*UK*)
Granta Books (*UK*)
Hesperus Press Limited (*UK*)
Heyday Books (*US*)
Hipso Media (*US*)
Independent Music Press (*UK*)
Infinite Ideas (*UK*)
Insomniac Press (*Can*)
Kube Publishing (*UK*)
Lawrence & Wishart (*UK*)
Lee & Low Books (*US*)
The Lilliput Press (*Ire*)
Liverpool University Press (*UK*)
LSU Press (*US*)
The Lyons Press Inc. (*US*)
Macmillan (*UK*)
Mage Publishers (*US*)
Manchester University Press (*UK*)
Mandrake of Oxford (*UK*)
Marion Boyars Publishers (*UK*)
Maverick Reads (*UK*)
McFarland & Company, Inc. (*US*)
Merrell Publishers Limited (*UK*)
Milo Books Ltd (*UK*)
Neil Wilson Publishing Ltd (*UK*)
New York University (NYU) Press (*US*)
Octopus Publishing Group Limited (*UK*)
Oregon State University Press (*US*)
Pen Books (*US*)
Phaidon Press Limited (*UK*)
Pinata Books (*US*)
Polity Press (*UK*)
Quirk Books (*US*)
Reaktion Books (*UK*)
Red Empress Publishing (*US*)
Red Wheel (*US*)
Reference Service Press (*US*)
River City Publishing (*US*)
The Rosen Publishing Group, Inc. (*US*)
Route Publishing (*UK*)
Running Press (*US*)
Saffron Books (*UK*)
Scarecrow Press Inc. (*US*)
Serpent's Tail (*UK*)
Sunscribe (*US*)
Syracuse University Press (*US*)
Temple University Press (*US*)
TouchWood Editions (*Can*)
Two Rivers Press (*UK*)
University of Alaska Press (*US*)
The University of Michigan Press (*US*)
University of South Carolina Press (*US*)
University of Washington Press (*US*)
Utah State University Press (*US*)
Vallentine Mitchell & Co., Limited (*UK*)
Verso (*UK*)
Wesleyan University Press (*US*)
The X Press (*UK*)
Zed Books Ltd (*UK*)
Zenith Press (*US*)

Current Affairs
Abdo Publishing Co (*US*)
Amakella Publishing (*US*)
Beacon Press (*US*)
Birlinn Ltd (*UK*)
Divertir Publishing LLC (*US*)
Dreamriver Press (*US*)
Dunedin Academic Press Ltd (*UK*)
Fabian Society (*UK*)
Famous Seamus (*UK*)
Gibson Square Books Ltd (*UK*)
Gill & Macmillan (*Ire*)
Greenhaven Publishing (*US*)
Hay House Publishers (*UK*)
Infinite Ideas (*UK*)
Lawrence & Wishart (*UK*)
The Lilliput Press (*Ire*)
Luath Press Ltd (*UK*)
The Lyons Press Inc. (*US*)
Macmillan (*UK*)
McFarland & Company, Inc. (*US*)
Milo Books Ltd (*UK*)
Oneworld Publications (*UK*)
Pandora Press (*UK*)
Paragon House (*US*)
Pen Books (*US*)
Prometheus Books (*US*)
Reaktion Books (*UK*)
Saffron Books (*UK*)
Seren Books (*UK*)
Serpent's Tail (*UK*)
Seven Stories Press (*US*)
Sunscribe (*US*)
Syracuse University Press (*US*)
W.W. Norton & Company Ltd (*UK*)
Weidenfeld & Nicolson (*UK*)
Yale University Press (*US*)
Yale University Press (London) (*UK*)
Zed Books Ltd (*UK*)

Design
Abdo Publishing Co (*US*)
ACC Art Books Ltd (*UK*)
Anness Publishing Ltd (*UK*)
ASCE Press (*US*)
Black Dog Publishing London UK (*UK*)
Co & Bear Productions (*UK*)
Frontinus (*UK*)
Laurence King Publishing Ltd (*UK*)
Lund Humphries Limited (*UK*)
Manchester University Press (*UK*)
Merrell Publishers Limited (*UK*)
New Holland Publishers (UK) Ltd (*UK*)
Octopus Publishing Group Limited (*UK*)
O'Reilly Media (*US*)
Page Street Publishing Co. (*US*)
Phaidon Press Limited (*UK*)
Professional Publications, Inc. (PPI) (*US*)
Quadrille Publishing Ltd (*UK*)
Reaktion Books (*UK*)
Red Wheel (*US*)
Robert Hale Publishers (*UK*)
RotoVision (*UK*)
Sunscribe (*US*)

Trentham Books Limited (*UK*)
W.W. Norton & Company Ltd (*UK*)
John Wiley & Sons, Inc. (*US*)
Philip Wilson Publishers Ltd (*UK*)

Drama
Aurora Metro Press (*UK*)
Chapman Publishing (*UK*)
Cressrelles Publishing Co. Ltd (*UK*)
Dreamriver Press (*US*)
Famous Seamus (*UK*)
GEY Books (*UK*)
Gomer Press (*UK*)
Italica Press (*US*)
The Lilliput Press (*Ire*)
Luath Press Ltd (*UK*)
Marion Boyars Publishers (*UK*)
New Playwrights' Network (NPN) (*UK*)
The O'Brien Press (*Ire*)
Oberon Books (*UK*)
Parthian Books (*UK*)
Pen Books (*US*)
Samuel French Ltd (*UK*)
Seren Books (*UK*)
Sidestreet Cookie Publishing (*US*)
Sunscribe (*US*)
Temple University Press (*US*)
W.W. Norton & Company Ltd (*UK*)
Ward Lock Educational Ltd (*UK*)

Entertainment
Abdo Publishing Co (*US*)
John Blake Publishing (*UK*)
Famous Seamus (*UK*)
GEY Books (*UK*)
HarperCollins Publishers Ltd (*UK*)
Infinite Ideas (*UK*)
Pen Books (*US*)
Sidestreet Cookie Publishing (*US*)
Sunscribe (*US*)
Syracuse University Press (*US*)
Titan Books (*UK*)

Erotic
Amira Press (*US*)
Asabi Publishing (*US*)
Carina UK (*UK*)
Crystal Spirit Publishing, Inc. (*US*)
Famous Seamus (*UK*)
GEY Books (*UK*)
HarperImpulse (*UK*)
Hesperus Press Limited (*UK*)
Hipso Media (*US*)
Mandrake of Oxford (*UK*)
Melange Books, LLC (*US*)
Monsoon Books Pte Ltd (*UK*)
Polis Books (*US*)
Sidestreet Cookie Publishing (*US*)

Fantasy
Allison & Busby Ltd (*UK*)
AMG Publishers (*US*)
Amira Press (*US*)
Arrow Publications, LLC (*US*)
Baen Books (*US*)
BelleBooks (*US*)
Bethany House Publishers (*US*)
BLVNP Incorporated (*US*)
Candy Jar Books (*UK*)
Carina UK (*UK*)
Children's Brains are Yummy (CBAY) Books (*US*)
Cricket Books (*US*)
Curiosity Quills Press (*US*)
Curious Fox (*UK*)
Dark Horse Comics (*US*)
Divertir Publishing LLC (*US*)
Dragon Moon Press (*Can*)
Ellysian Press (*US*)
Entangled Teen (*US*)
Famous Seamus (*UK*)
GEY Books (*UK*)
Harken Media (*US*)
Harmony Ink Press (*US*)
HarperCollins Publishers Ltd (*UK*)
Head of Zeus (*UK*)
Hesperus Press Limited (*UK*)
Honno Welsh Women's Press (*UK*)
Jolly Fish Press (*US*)
Lost Tower Publications (*UK*)
Luna Press Publishing (*UK*)
M P Publishing USA (*US*)
Macmillan (*UK*)
Maverick Reads (*UK*)
Monsoon Books Pte Ltd (*UK*)
Page Street Publishing Co. (*US*)
Pen Books (*US*)
Polis Books (*US*)
Red Empress Publishing (*US*)
Roberts Press (*US*)
The Salariya Book Company (*UK*)
Sidestreet Cookie Publishing (*US*)
Snowbooks (*UK*)
Sunscribe (*US*)
Sunstone Press (*US*)
World Weaver Press (*US*)
Zumaya Publications (*US*)

Fiction
A Swift Exit (*UK*)
Abdo Publishing Co (*US*)
Abrams ComicArts (*US*)
Academy Chicago (*US*)
Albert Whitman & Company (*US*)
Allison & Busby Ltd (*UK*)
Alma Books Ltd (*UK*)
Alma Classics (*UK*)
Amakella Publishing (*US*)
American Quilter's Society (*US*)
AMG Publishers (*US*)
Amira Press (*US*)
And Other Stories (*UK*)
Andersen Press Ltd (*UK*)
Andrews McMeel Publishing (*US*)
Ankerwycke (*US*)
Arbordale Publishing (*US*)
Arch Street Press (*US*)
Arrow Publications, LLC (*US*)
Arsenal Pulp Press (*Can*)
Arthur A. Levine Books (*US*)
Asabi Publishing (*US*)

Augsburg Fortress (*US*)
Aurora Metro Press (*UK*)
Avatar Press (*US*)
Award Publications Limited (*UK*)
Baen Books (*US*)
Bailiwick Press (*US*)
Barefoot Books Ltd (*UK*)
Barrington Stoke (*UK*)
Barron's Educational Series, Inc. (*US*)
BearManor Media (*US*)
Belle Lutte Press (*US*)
BelleBooks (*US*)
Bellevue Literary Press (*US*)
Bethany House Publishers (*US*)
Bilingual Review Press (*US*)
Birlinn Ltd (*UK*)
Black & White Publishing Ltd (*UK*)
Black Lyon Publishing, LLC (*US*)
Black Rose Writing (*US*)
John Blake Publishing (*UK*)
BlazeVOX [books] (*US*)
Bloomsbury Publishing Plc (*UK*)
Bloomsbury Spark (*UK*)
BLVNP Incorporated (*US*)
BookFish Books (*US*)
Boyds Mills Press (*US*)
Calisi Press (*UK*)
Candy Jar Books (*UK*)
Canongate Books (*UK*)
Carina UK (*UK*)
Cave Books (*US*)
Cave Hollow Press (*US*)
Chapman Publishing (*UK*)
Children's Brains are Yummy (CBAY) Books (*US*)
Cinco Puntos Press (*US*)
Classical Comics Limited (*UK*)
Comma Press (*UK*)
Covenant Communications Inc. (*US*)
Creative With Words (CWW) (*US*)
Crescent Moon Publishing (*UK*)
Creston Books (*US*)
Cricket Books (*US*)
Crimson Romance (*US*)
Crystal Spirit Publishing, Inc. (*US*)
Curiosity Quills Press (*US*)
Curious Fox (*UK*)
Dark Horse Comics (*US*)
Darkhouse Books (*US*)
David R. Godine, Publisher (*US*)
DB Publishing (*UK*)
DC Thomson (*UK*)
Dedalus Ltd (*UK*)
Divertir Publishing LLC (*US*)
Dodo Ink (*UK*)
Dragon Moon Press (*Can*)
Dreamriver Press (*US*)
Dref Wen (*UK*)
ECW Press (*Can*)
Egmont UK Ltd (*UK*)
Ellysian Press (*US*)
The Emma Press Ltd (*UK*)
Entangled Teen (*US*)
Familius (*US*)
Famous Seamus (*UK*)
Fantagraphics (*US*)
Farrar, Straus and Giroux Books for Younger Readers (*US*)
Fingerpress UK (*UK*)
Fisherton Press (*UK*)
Fitzhenry & Whiteside Ltd (*Can*)
Fitzrovia Press Limited (*UK*)
Fleming Publications (*UK*)
Floris Books (*UK*)
Folded Word LLC (*US*)
Frances Lincoln Children's Books (*UK*)
The Gallery Press (*Ire*)
Galley Beggar Press (*UK*)
GEY Books (*UK*)
Gill & Macmillan (*Ire*)
Gomer Press (*UK*)
Goosebottom Books LLC (*US*)
Granta Books (*UK*)
Hachai Publishing (*US*)
Halban Publishers (*UK*)
Harken Media (*US*)
Harlequin American Romance (*US*)
Harlequin Mills & Boon Ltd (*UK*)
Harmony Ink Press (*US*)
HarperCollins Publishers Ltd (*UK*)
HarperImpulse (*UK*)
Haus Publishing (*UK*)
Head of Zeus (*UK*)
Headland Publications (*UK*)
Headline Publishing Group (*UK*)
Helicon Nine Editions (*US*)
Hesperus Press Limited (*UK*)
Heyday Books (*US*)
Hipso Media (*US*)
Holiday House, Inc. (*US*)
Honno Welsh Women's Press (*UK*)
House of Lochar (*UK*)
Illusio & Baqer (*US*)
Image Comics (*US*)
Insomniac Press (*Can*)
Interlink Publishing Group, Inc. (*US*)
Iron Press (*UK*)
Italica Press (*US*)
Jacaranda Books Art Music Ltd (*UK*)
Joffe Books Ltd (*UK*)
Jolly Fish Press (*US*)
Judaica Press (*US*)
Kaeden Books (*US*)
Kar-Ben Publishing (*US*)
Kathy Dawson Books (*US*)
Kube Publishing (*UK*)
Lee & Low Books (*US*)
Legend Press (*UK*)
The Lilliput Press (*Ire*)
Limitless Publishing (*US*)
Lion Hudson Plc (*UK*)
Little Pickle Press, Inc. (*US*)
Livingston Press (*US*)
Lost Tower Publications (*UK*)
LSU Press (*US*)
Luath Press Ltd (*UK*)

Luna Press Publishing (*UK*)
M P Publishing USA (*US*)
Macmillan (*UK*)
Mage Publishers (*US*)
Mandrake of Oxford (*UK*)
Mantra Lingua Ltd (*UK*)
Marion Boyars Publishers (*UK*)
Maverick Reads (*UK*)
Melange Books, LLC (*US*)
Michael Terence Publishing (MTP) (*UK*)
Monarch Books (*UK*)
Monsoon Books Pte Ltd (*UK*)
Mudfog Press (*UK*)
New Directions Publishing (*US*)
Nightboat Books (*US*)
The O'Brien Press (*Ire*)
Oceanview Publishing (*US*)
Oneworld Publications (*UK*)
Onstream Publications Ltd (*Ire*)
Ouen Press (*UK*)
The Overmountain Press (*US*)
Page Street Publishing Co. (*US*)
Parthian Books (*UK*)
Pelican Publishing Company (*US*)
Pen Books (*US*)
Penguin Canada (*Can*)
Penguin Group (USA) Inc. (*US*)
Phoenix Yard Books (*UK*)
Pinata Books (*US*)
Polis Books (*US*)
Pushkin Press (*UK*)
Quirk Books (*US*)
Ragged Bears Limited (*UK*)
Ransom Publishing Ltd (*UK*)
Reality Street Editions (*UK*)
Rebelight Publishing Inc. (*Can*)
Red Empress Publishing (*US*)
Red Rattle Books (*UK*)
River City Publishing (*US*)
Robert Hale Publishers (*UK*)
Roberts Press (*US*)
Rose and Crown Books (*UK*)
Route Publishing (*UK*)
Running Press (*US*)
Saddleback Educational Publishing (*US*)
Saffron Books (*UK*)
Saguaro Books, LLC (*US*)
The Salariya Book Company (*UK*)
Salt Publishing Ltd (*UK*)
Salvo Press (*US*)
Sandstone Press Ltd (*UK*)
Scholastic Library Publishing (*US*)
Scribner (*US*)
Scripture Union (*UK*)
Seren Books (*UK*)
Serpent's Tail (*UK*)
Seven Stories Press (*US*)
Severn House Publishers (*UK*)
Shape & Nature Press (*US*)
Short Books (*UK*)
Sidestreet Cookie Publishing (*US*)
Sky Pony Press (*US*)
Snowbooks (*UK*)
Somerville Press (*Ire*)
Southern Illinois University Press (*US*)
Souvenir Press Ltd (*UK*)
St. Johann Press (*US*)
Star Bright Books (*US*)
Sterling Publishing Co. Inc. (*US*)
Stonewood Press (*UK*)
Stripes Publishing (*UK*)
Sunscribe (*US*)
Sunstone Press (*US*)
Sweet Cherry Publishing (*UK*)
The Templar Company Limited (*UK*)
Thistle Publishing (*UK*)
ThunderStone Books (*US*)
Tiny Owl (*UK*)
Titan Books (*UK*)
Top That! Publishing (*UK*)
TouchWood Editions (*Can*)
Triangle Square (*US*)
Troika Books (*UK*)
Tumblehome Learning, Inc. (*US*)
Twenty First Century Publishers Ltd (*UK*)
Tyrus Books (*US*)
Unbound Press (*UK*)
University of Alaska Press (*US*)
The University of Michigan Press (*US*)
University of South Carolina Press (*US*)
Valley Press (*UK*)
Vehicule Press (*Can*)
Verso (*UK*)
Virago Press (*UK*)
W.W. Norton & Company Ltd (*UK*)
Walker Books Ltd (*UK*)
WaterBrook & Multnomah (*US*)
Waverley Books (*UK*)
Weidenfeld & Nicolson (*UK*)
Western Psychological Services (*US*)
Whitaker House (*US*)
Wilshire Book Company (*US*)
Wordsworth Editions (*UK*)
World Weaver Press (*US*)
WorthyKids / Ideals (*US*)
The X Press (*UK*)
Zebra (*US*)
Zumaya Publications (*US*)

Film

Aurora Metro Press (*UK*)
BearManor Media (*US*)
BFI Publishing (*UK*)
Black Dog Publishing London UK (*UK*)
John Blake Publishing (*UK*)
Crescent Moon Publishing (*UK*)
Edinburgh University Press (*UK*)
Famous Seamus (*UK*)
Guild of Master Craftsman (GMC) Publications Ltd (*UK*)
HarperCollins Publishers Ltd (*UK*)
Haus Publishing (*UK*)
Interlink Publishing Group, Inc. (*US*)
Laurence King Publishing Ltd (*UK*)
Macmillan (*UK*)
Manchester University Press (*UK*)
Marion Boyars Publishers (*UK*)

McFarland & Company, Inc. (*US*)
Octopus Publishing Group Limited (*UK*)
Pen Books (*US*)
Phaidon Press Limited (*UK*)
Reaktion Books (*UK*)
RotoVision (*UK*)
Scarecrow Press Inc. (*US*)
Southern Illinois University Press (*US*)
Sunscribe (*US*)
Teachers College Press (*US*)
Temple University Press (*US*)
Titan Books (*UK*)
University of Chicago Press (*US*)
Verso (*UK*)
W.W. Norton & Company Ltd (*UK*)
Wesleyan University Press (*US*)

Finance
Algora Publishing (*US*)
Arch Street Press (*US*)
Barron's Educational Series, Inc. (*US*)
Birlinn Ltd (*UK*)
Carswell (*Can*)
Chelsea Green Publishing, Inc. (*US*)
CJ Fallon (*Ire*)
Dunedin Academic Press Ltd (*UK*)
ECW Press (*Can*)
Edward Elgar Publishing Inc. (*US*)
Edward Elgar Publishing Ltd (*UK*)
Fabian Society (*UK*)
Familius (*US*)
Fordham University Press (*US*)
Gingko Library (*UK*)
Hay House Publishers (*UK*)
Humanix Books (*US*)
Insomniac Press (*Can*)
International Wealth Success (IWS) Inc. (*US*)
Macmillan (*UK*)
Management Books 2000 Ltd (*UK*)
Manchester University Press (*UK*)
Nolo (*US*)
Oak Tree Press (*Ire*)
Paragon House (*US*)
Pen Books (*US*)
Polity Press (*UK*)
Reaktion Books (*UK*)
Saffron Books (*UK*)
Silver Lake Publishing, LLC (*US*)
Sterling Publishing Co. Inc. (*US*)
Sunscribe (*US*)
Temple University Press (*US*)
Twenty First Century Publishers Ltd (*UK*)
The University of Michigan Press (*US*)
Verso (*US*)
Verso (*UK*)
W.W. Norton & Company Ltd (*UK*)
Weidenfeld & Nicolson (*UK*)
John Wiley & Sons, Inc. (*US*)
Yale University Press (London) (*UK*)
Zed Books Ltd (*UK*)

Gardening
ACC Art Books Ltd (*UK*)
Anness Publishing Ltd (*UK*)
Ball Publishing (*US*)
Chelsea Green Publishing, Inc. (*US*)
David R. Godine, Publisher (*US*)
Dreamriver Press (*US*)
Finney Company (*US*)
Guild of Master Craftsman (GMC) Publications Ltd (*UK*)
HarperCollins Publishers Ltd (*UK*)
Headline Publishing Group (*UK*)
Infinite Ideas (*UK*)
Insomniac Press (*Can*)
Kyle Books (*UK*)
Macmillan (*UK*)
New Holland Publishers (UK) Ltd (*UK*)
Octopus Publishing Group Limited (*UK*)
Pelican Publishing Company (*US*)
Quadrille Publishing Ltd (*UK*)
Quiller Publishing Ltd (*UK*)
Reaktion Books (*UK*)
Ryland Peters & Small (*UK*)
Souvenir Press Ltd (*UK*)
Sterling Publishing Co. Inc. (*US*)
Storey Publishing (*US*)
Sunscribe (*US*)
Sunstone Press (*US*)
Think Publishing (*UK*)
TouchWood Editions (*Can*)
University of Chicago Press (*US*)
University of South Carolina Press (*US*)
Wannabee Books (*US*)
Willow Creek Press, Inc. (*US*)

Gothic
Carina UK (*UK*)
Famous Seamus (*UK*)
Lost Tower Publications (*UK*)
M P Publishing USA (*US*)
Maverick Reads (*UK*)
Red Empress Publishing (*US*)
Salt Publishing Ltd (*UK*)
Sidestreet Cookie Publishing (*US*)
Sunscribe (*US*)
Wordsworth Editions (*UK*)
Zumaya Publications (*US*)

Health
American Counseling Association (*US*)
American Psychiatric Association Publishing (*US*)
Anness Publishing Ltd (*UK*)
Arsenal Pulp Press (*Can*)
Barron's Educational Series, Inc. (*US*)
BenBella Books (*US*)
John Blake Publishing (*UK*)
Blue River Press (*US*)
Connections Book Publishing Ltd (*UK*)
Crown House Publishing (*UK*)
DB Publishing (*UK*)
Dreamriver Press (*US*)
Dunedin Academic Press Ltd (*UK*)
ECW Press (*Can*)
Familius (*US*)
Famous Seamus (*UK*)
Findhorn Press Ltd (*UK*)
Floris Books (*UK*)
Greenhaven Publishing (*US*)

Haldane Mason Ltd (*UK*)
HarperCollins Publishers Ltd (*UK*)
Hartman Publishing, Inc. (*US*)
Hay House Publishers (*UK*)
Health Communications, Inc. (*US*)
Hipso Media (*US*)
Hodder Education (*UK*)
Hohm Press (*US*)
Humanix Books (*US*)
Insomniac Press (*Can*)
Kyle Books (*UK*)
Lion Hudson Plc (*UK*)
Macmillan (*UK*)
Mandrake of Oxford (*UK*)
McFarland & Company, Inc. (*US*)
Mitchell Lane Publishers, Inc. (*US*)
New Holland Publishers (UK) Ltd (*UK*)
NursesBooks (*US*)
Octopus Publishing Group Limited (*UK*)
O'Reilly Media (*US*)
Pandora Press (*UK*)
Pavilion Publishing (*UK*)
Pelican Publishing Company (*US*)
Pen Books (*US*)
Polity Press (*UK*)
Prometheus Books (*US*)
Quadrille Publishing Ltd (*UK*)
Quill Driver Books (*US*)
Radcliffe Publishing Ltd (*UK*)
Red Wheel (*US*)
Reference Service Press (*US*)
Robert Hale Publishers (*UK*)
The Rosen Publishing Group, Inc. (*US*)
Running Press (*US*)
Ryland Peters & Small (*UK*)
Seven Stories Press (*US*)
Singing Dragon (*UK*)
Society for Promoting Christian Knowledge (SPCK) (*UK*)
Southern Illinois University Press (*US*)
Souvenir Press Ltd (*UK*)
Speechmark Publishing Limited (*UK*)
Sterling Publishing Co. Inc. (*US*)
Storey Publishing (*US*)
Summersdale Publishers Ltd (*UK*)
Sunscribe (*US*)
Sunstone Press (*US*)
Temple University Press (*US*)
Triangle Square (*US*)
W.W. Norton & Company Ltd (*UK*)
Wannabee Books (*US*)
World Book, Inc. (*US*)
Yale University Press (London) (*UK*)
YMAA Publication Center, Inc. (*US*)
Zed Books Ltd (*UK*)

Historical

Abdo Publishing Co (*US*)
ACC Art Books Ltd (*UK*)
Algora Publishing (*US*)
Allison & Busby Ltd (*UK*)
Alma Books Ltd (*UK*)
Amakella Publishing (*US*)
Amberley Publishing (*UK*)
Amira Press (*US*)
Anness Publishing Ltd (*UK*)
Arch Street Press (*US*)
Asabi Publishing (*US*)
Ashgate Publishing Limited (*UK*)
Ashmolean Museum Publications (*UK*)
Astragal Press (*US*)
Augsburg Fortress (*US*)
Beacon Press (*US*)
BelleBooks (*US*)
Bethany House Publishers (*US*)
Birlinn Ltd (*UK*)
Black Lyon Publishing, LLC (*US*)
John Blake Publishing (*UK*)
Bloomsbury Publishing Plc (*UK*)
Bloomsbury Spark (*UK*)
Boydell & Brewer Ltd (*UK*)
Bucknell University Press (*US*)
Candy Jar Books (*UK*)
Canongate Books (*UK*)
Carina UK (*UK*)
Cave Books (*US*)
CJ Fallon (*Ire*)
Covenant Communications Inc. (*US*)
CQ Press (*US*)
Cricket Books (*US*)
Crimson Romance (*US*)
Curious Fox (*UK*)
David R. Godine, Publisher (*US*)
DB Publishing (*UK*)
Divertir Publishing LLC (*US*)
Dreamriver Press (*US*)
Dunedin Academic Press Ltd (*UK*)
Dynasty Press (*UK*)
Eagle's View Publishing (*US*)
ECW Press (*Can*)
Edinburgh University Press (*UK*)
Entangled Teen (*US*)
Famous Seamus (*UK*)
Fingerpress UK (*UK*)
Finney Company (*US*)
Fleming Publications (*UK*)
Floris Books (*UK*)
Flyleaf Press (*Ire*)
Fonthill Media LLC (*US*)
Fonthill Media Ltd (*UK*)
Fordham University Press (*US*)
Four Courts Press (*Ire*)
Gallaudet University Press (*US*)
Genealogical Publishing Company (*US*)
Gibson Square Books Ltd (*UK*)
Gill & Macmillan (*Ire*)
Gingko Library (*UK*)
Golden West Books (*US*)
Gomer Press (*UK*)
Goosebottom Books LLC (*US*)
Granta Books (*UK*)
Greenhaven Publishing (*US*)
Hachai Publishing (*US*)
Halban Publishers (*UK*)
Haldane Mason Ltd (*UK*)
Halsgrove (*UK*)
Harken Media (*US*)

Harlequin Mills & Boon Ltd (*UK*)
HarperCollins Publishers Ltd (*UK*)
HarperImpulse (*UK*)
Haus Publishing (*UK*)
Head of Zeus (*UK*)
Headline Publishing Group (*UK*)
Hesperus Press Limited (*UK*)
Heyday Books (*US*)
The History Press (*UK*)
Hopscotch (*UK*)
House of Lochar (*UK*)
Humanix Books (*US*)
ICS Publications (*US*)
Interlink Publishing Group, Inc. (*US*)
Italica Press (*US*)
IWM (Imperial War Museums) (*UK*)
Jolly Fish Press (*US*)
Judaica Press (*US*)
Kube Publishing (*UK*)
Laurence King Publishing Ltd (*UK*)
Lawrence & Wishart (*UK*)
The Lilliput Press (*Ire*)
Liverpool University Press (*UK*)
LSU Press (*US*)
Luath Press Ltd (*UK*)
Lund Humphries Limited (*UK*)
The Lyons Press Inc. (*US*)
Macmillan (*UK*)
Mage Publishers (*US*)
Manchester University Press (*UK*)
Maverick Reads (*UK*)
McFarland & Company, Inc. (*US*)
The Merlin Press (*UK*)
Mitchell Lane Publishers, Inc. (*US*)
Monsoon Books Pte Ltd (*UK*)
Museum of Northern Arizona (*US*)
Neil Wilson Publishing Ltd (*UK*)
New Directions Publishing (*US*)
New Holland Publishers (UK) Ltd (*UK*)
New York University (NYU) Press (*US*)
Nomad Press (*US*)
The O'Brien Press (*Ire*)
Michael O'Mara Books Ltd (*UK*)
Oak Knoll Press (*US*)
Octopus Publishing Group Limited (*UK*)
Oneworld Publications (*UK*)
Onstream Publications Ltd (*Ire*)
Oregon State University Press (*US*)
The Overmountain Press (*US*)
Page Street Publishing Co. (*US*)
Paladin Press (*US*)
Paragon House (*US*)
Pelican Publishing Company (*US*)
Pen Books (*US*)
Phaidon Press Limited (*UK*)
Picton Press (*US*)
Polity Press (*UK*)
Quirk Books (*US*)
Reaktion Books (*UK*)
Red Empress Publishing (*US*)
Red Wheel (*US*)
Reference Service Press (*US*)
River City Publishing (*US*)
Robert Hale Publishers (*UK*)
Rose and Crown Books (*UK*)
The Rosen Publishing Group, Inc. (*US*)
Saffron Books (*UK*)
The Salariya Book Company (*UK*)
Scarecrow Press Inc. (*US*)
Schofield & Sims (*UK*)
Scribner (*US*)
Seren Books (*UK*)
Seven Stories Press (*US*)
Severn House Publishers (*UK*)
Sidestreet Cookie Publishing (*US*)
Snowbooks (*UK*)
Southern Illinois University Press (*US*)
Souvenir Press Ltd (*UK*)
St David's Press (*UK*)
Stenlake Publishing (*UK*)
Sunscribe (*US*)
Sunstone Press (*US*)
Syracuse University Press (*US*)
Teachers College Press (*US*)
Temple University Press (*US*)
Torah Aura Productions (*US*)
TouchWood Editions (*Can*)
Triangle Square (*US*)
Truman State University Press (*US*)
Twenty First Century Publishers Ltd (*UK*)
University of Alabama Press (*US*)
University of Alaska Press (*US*)
University of Chicago Press (*US*)
The University of Michigan Press (*US*)
University of Pittsburgh Press (*US*)
University of South Carolina Press (*US*)
University of Washington Press (*US*)
Utah State University Press (*US*)
Vallentine Mitchell & Co., Limited (*UK*)
Vehicule Press (*Can*)
Verso (*US*)
Verso (*UK*)
Wooden Books (*UK*)
W.W. Norton & Company Ltd (*UK*)
WaterBrook & Multnomah (*US*)
Waverley Books (*UK*)
Weidenfeld & Nicolson (*UK*)
Welsh Academic Press (*UK*)
Wesleyan University Press (*US*)
Whitaker House (*US*)
Philip Wilson Publishers Ltd (*UK*)
World Book, Inc. (*US*)
Yale University Press (*US*)
Yale University Press (London) (*UK*)
Zed Books Ltd (*UK*)
Zenith Press (*US*)
Zumaya Publications (*US*)

Hobbies

Abdo Publishing Co (*US*)
Alpine Publications, Inc. (*US*)
Amakella Publishing (*US*)
American Quilter's Society (*US*)
Anness Publishing Ltd (*UK*)
Barron's Educational Series, Inc. (*US*)
Bloomsbury Publishing Plc (*UK*)
Cicerone Press (*UK*)

Divertir Publishing LLC (*US*)
Eagle's View Publishing (*US*)
Familius (*US*)
Famous Seamus (*UK*)
4th Level Indie (*US*)
Genealogical Publishing Company (*US*)
Gill & Macmillan (*Ire*)
Guild of Master Craftsman (GMC) Publications Ltd (*UK*)
Infinite Ideas (*UK*)
Kansas City Star Quilts (*US*)
Leisure Arts, Inc. (*US*)
Pelican Publishing Company (*US*)
Picton Press (*US*)
Quill Driver Books (*US*)
Running Press (*US*)
Search Press Ltd (*UK*)
Souvenir Press Ltd (*UK*)
St. Johann Press (*US*)
STC Craft (*US*)
Stenlake Publishing (*UK*)
Sterling Publishing Co. Inc. (*US*)
Sunscribe (*US*)
W.W. Norton & Company Ltd (*UK*)

Horror

Amira Press (*US*)
Asabi Publishing (*US*)
BelleBooks (*US*)
Carina UK (*UK*)
Cricket Books (*US*)
Curiosity Quills Press (*US*)
Dark Horse Comics (*US*)
Dragon Moon Press (*Can*)
Ellysian Press (*US*)
Famous Seamus (*UK*)
Jolly Fish Press (*US*)
Lost Tower Publications (*UK*)
Macmillan (*UK*)
Mandrake of Oxford (*UK*)
Monsoon Books Pte Ltd (*UK*)
Pen Books (*US*)
Polis Books (*US*)
Red Rattle Books (*UK*)
Severn House Publishers (*UK*)
Sidestreet Cookie Publishing (*US*)
Snowbooks (*UK*)
Zumaya Publications (*US*)

How-to

J.A. Allen (*UK*)
Amakella Publishing (*US*)
American Quilter's Society (*US*)
Chelsea Green Publishing, Inc. (*US*)
Dragon Moon Press (*Can*)
Dreamriver Press (*US*)
Eagle's View Publishing (*US*)
Famous Seamus (*UK*)
Ferguson Publishing (*US*)
Flyleaf Press (*Ire*)
Genealogical Publishing Company (*US*)
Gryphon House, Inc. (*US*)
Guild of Master Craftsman (GMC) Publications Ltd (*UK*)
Haynes Publishing (*UK*)
Health Communications, Inc. (*US*)
Hipso Media (*US*)
International Wealth Success (IWS) Inc. (*US*)
Leisure Arts, Inc. (*US*)
New Holland Publishers (UK) Ltd (*UK*)
Nolo (*US*)
Paladin Press (*US*)
Search Press Ltd (*UK*)
Silver Lake Publishing, LLC (*US*)
Sterling Publishing Co. Inc. (*US*)
Sunscribe (*US*)
Sunstone Press (*US*)
Whitaker House (*US*)
Willow Creek Press, Inc. (*US*)
Wilshire Book Company (*US*)

Humour

American Quilter's Society (*US*)
Andrews McMeel Publishing (*US*)
Arrow Publications, LLC (*US*)
Aurora Metro Press (*UK*)
Bailiwick Press (*US*)
BearManor Media (*US*)
Birlinn Ltd (*UK*)
Black & White Publishing Ltd (*UK*)
John Blake Publishing (*UK*)
BLVNP Incorporated (*US*)
Canongate Books (*UK*)
Carina UK (*UK*)
Covenant Communications Inc. (*US*)
Crown House Publishing (*UK*)
Curious Fox (*UK*)
David R. Godine, Publisher (*US*)
Dino Books (*UK*)
Divertir Publishing LLC (*US*)
ECW Press (*Can*)
Familius (*US*)
Famous Seamus (*UK*)
Fantagraphics (*US*)
Folded Word LLC (*US*)
Gill & Macmillan (*Ire*)
Guild of Master Craftsman (GMC) Publications Ltd (*UK*)
Harken Media (*US*)
Hipso Media (*US*)
Hymns Ancient & Modern Ltd (*UK*)
Insomniac Press (*Can*)
Jolly Fish Press (*US*)
Macmillan (*UK*)
Merlin Unwin Books (*UK*)
Neil Wilson Publishing Ltd (*UK*)
New Directions Publishing (*US*)
New Holland Publishers (UK) Ltd (*UK*)
The O'Brien Press (*Ire*)
Michael O'Mara Books Ltd (*UK*)
Octopus Publishing Group Limited (*UK*)
Pelican Publishing Company (*US*)
Pen Books (*US*)
Polis Books (*US*)
Quadrille Publishing Ltd (*UK*)
Quill Driver Books (*US*)
Quiller Publishing Ltd (*UK*)
Quirk Books (*US*)
Red Wheel (*US*)

River City Publishing (*US*)
Running Press (*US*)
Sidestreet Cookie Publishing (*US*)
Souvenir Press Ltd (*UK*)
Sterling Publishing Co. Inc. (*US*)
Summersdale Publishers Ltd (*UK*)
Sunscribe (*US*)
Sunstone Press (*US*)
Titan Books (*UK*)
Top That! Publishing (*UK*)
W.W. Norton & Company Ltd (*UK*)
Waverley Books (*UK*)
Wilshire Book Company (*US*)

Legal

Ankerwycke (*US*)
Arch Street Press (*US*)
Ashgate Publishing Limited (*UK*)
Barron's Educational Series, Inc. (*US*)
Birlinn Ltd (*UK*)
John Blake Publishing (*UK*)
Bucknell University Press (*US*)
Carswell (*Can*)
Dunedin Academic Press Ltd (*UK*)
Edinburgh University Press (*UK*)
Edward Elgar Publishing Inc. (*US*)
Edward Elgar Publishing Ltd (*UK*)
Fordham University Press (*US*)
Four Courts Press (*Ire*)
Hart Publishing Ltd (*UK*)
Insomniac Press (*Can*)
Jordan Publishing (*UK*)
LexisNexis (*US*)
Manchester University Press (*UK*)
New York University (NYU) Press (*US*)
Nolo (*US*)
Oak Tree Press (*Ire*)
Pelican Publishing Company (*US*)
Pen Books (*US*)
Silver Lake Publishing, LLC (*US*)
Southern Illinois University Press (*US*)
Sunscribe (*US*)
Sunstone Press (*US*)
Temple University Press (*US*)
Tower Publishing (*US*)
University of Chicago Press (*US*)
The University of Michigan Press (*US*)
W.W. Norton & Company Ltd (*UK*)
Wannabee Books (*US*)
Yale University Press (*US*)
Yale University Press (London) (*UK*)

Leisure

Amakella Publishing (*US*)
Anness Publishing Ltd (*UK*)
Appalachian Mountain Club Books (*US*)
Cave Books (*US*)
Cicerone Press (*UK*)
Connections Book Publishing Ltd (*UK*)
Famous Seamus (*UK*)
Finney Company (*US*)
Gill & Macmillan (*Ire*)
Gomer Press (*UK*)
HarperCollins Publishers Ltd (*UK*)
Haynes Publishing (*UK*)
Interlink Publishing Group, Inc. (*US*)
Lost Tower Publications (*UK*)
Luath Press Ltd (*UK*)
McFarland & Company, Inc. (*US*)
Merlin Unwin Books (*UK*)
Metro Publications Ltd (*UK*)
Pelican Publishing Company (*US*)
Pen Books (*US*)
Robert Hale Publishers (*UK*)
Running Press (*US*)
Search Press Ltd (*UK*)
Singing Dragon (*UK*)
Snowbooks (*UK*)
St David's Press (*UK*)
Sunscribe (*US*)
Temple University Press (*US*)
Venture Publishing, Inc. (*US*)
W.W. Norton & Company Ltd (*UK*)
Willow Creek Press, Inc. (*US*)

Lifestyle

Amakella Publishing (*US*)
AMG Publishers (*US*)
Andrews McMeel Publishing (*US*)
Anness Publishing Ltd (*UK*)
Arsenal Pulp Press (*Can*)
Augsburg Fortress (*US*)
Barron's Educational Series, Inc. (*US*)
Beacon Press (*US*)
BenBella Books (*US*)
Chelsea Green Publishing, Inc. (*US*)
Co & Bear Productions (*UK*)
Concordia Publishing House (*US*)
Connections Book Publishing Ltd (*UK*)
Dreamriver Press (*US*)
Familius (*US*)
Famous Seamus (*UK*)
Ferguson Publishing (*US*)
Gill & Macmillan (*Ire*)
Haldane Mason Ltd (*UK*)
HarperCollins Publishers Ltd (*UK*)
Hawthorn Press (*UK*)
Hay House Publishers (*UK*)
Health Communications, Inc. (*US*)
Hipso Media (*US*)
Hohm Press (*US*)
Infinite Ideas (*UK*)
Insomniac Press (*Can*)
Kube Publishing (*UK*)
Kyle Books (*UK*)
Leisure Arts, Inc. (*US*)
Lost Tower Publications (*UK*)
Luath Press Ltd (*UK*)
Management Books 2000 Ltd (*UK*)
Mandrake of Oxford (*UK*)
New Holland Publishers (UK) Ltd (*UK*)
The O'Brien Press (*Ire*)
Octopus Publishing Group Limited (*UK*)
Page Street Publishing Co. (*US*)
Pelican Publishing Company (*US*)
Pen Books (*US*)
Quill Driver Books (*US*)
Red Wheel (*US*)
Robert Hale Publishers (*UK*)

Running Press (*US*)
Ryland Peters & Small (*UK*)
Silver Lake Publishing, LLC (*US*)
Society for Promoting Christian Knowledge (SPCK) (*UK*)
Souvenir Press Ltd (*UK*)
Sterling Publishing Co. Inc. (*US*)
Summersdale Publishers Ltd (*UK*)
Sunscribe (*US*)
Temple University Press (*US*)
Torah Aura Productions (*US*)
W.W. Norton & Company Ltd (*UK*)
Whitaker House (*US*)
WorthyKids / Ideals (*US*)

Literature
Algora Publishing (*US*)
Alma Books Ltd (*UK*)
Alma Classics (*UK*)
Amakella Publishing (*US*)
Arch Street Press (*US*)
Ashgate Publishing Limited (*UK*)
Aurora Metro Press (*UK*)
Beacon Press (*US*)
BlazeVOX [books] (*US*)
BLVNP Incorporated (*US*)
Boydell & Brewer Ltd (*UK*)
Bucknell University Press (*US*)
Carcanet Press Ltd (*UK*)
Carina UK (*UK*)
CJ Fallon (*Ire*)
Classical Comics Limited (*UK*)
Crescent Moon Publishing (*UK*)
David R. Godine, Publisher (*US*)
Dedalus Ltd (*UK*)
Dreamriver Press (*US*)
Duquesne University Press (*US*)
ECW Press (*Can*)
Edinburgh University Press (*UK*)
Famous Seamus (*UK*)
Floris Books (*UK*)
Folded Word LLC (*US*)
Fordham University Press (*US*)
Four Courts Press (*Ire*)
Gallaudet University Press (*US*)
Galley Beggar Press (*UK*)
Gingko Library (*UK*)
Gomer Press (*UK*)
Greenhaven Publishing (*US*)
Halban Publishers (*UK*)
Hesperus Press Limited (*UK*)
Heyday Books (*US*)
Hohm Press (*US*)
House of Lochar (*UK*)
Insomniac Press (*Can*)
Interlink Publishing Group, Inc. (*US*)
The Lilliput Press (*Ire*)
Liverpool University Press (*UK*)
LSU Press (*US*)
M P Publishing USA (*US*)
Mage Publishers (*US*)
Manchester University Press (*UK*)
Marion Boyars Publishers (*UK*)
Maverick Reads (*UK*)
McFarland & Company, Inc. (*US*)
Mitchell Lane Publishers, Inc. (*US*)
New York University (NYU) Press (*US*)
The O'Brien Press (*Ire*)
Oak Knoll Press (*US*)
Oneworld Publications (*UK*)
Oregon State University Press (*US*)
Pelican Publishing Company (*US*)
Pen Books (*US*)
Polity Press (*UK*)
Reaktion Books (*UK*)
Salt Publishing Ltd (*UK*)
Scarecrow Press Inc. (*US*)
Schofield & Sims (*UK*)
Shearsman Books (*UK*)
Sidestreet Cookie Publishing (*US*)
Souvenir Press Ltd (*UK*)
Stenlake Publishing (*UK*)
Sterling Publishing Co. Inc. (*US*)
Sunscribe (*US*)
Syracuse University Press (*US*)
Temple University Press (*US*)
Truman State University Press (*US*)
University of Alabama Press (*US*)
The University of Michigan Press (*US*)
University of South Carolina Press (*US*)
Virago Press (*UK*)
W.W. Norton & Company Ltd (*UK*)
Wannabee Books (*US*)
Ward Lock Educational Ltd (*UK*)
Yale University Press (*US*)
Yale University Press (London) (*UK*)

Media
Amakella Publishing (*US*)
BFI Publishing (*UK*)
Crescent Moon Publishing (*UK*)
Edinburgh University Press (*UK*)
Famous Seamus (*UK*)
Fordham University Press (*US*)
HarperCollins Publishers Ltd (*UK*)
Infinite Ideas (*UK*)
LSU Press (*US*)
Manchester University Press (*UK*)
Maverick Reads (*UK*)
New York University (NYU) Press (*US*)
Pandora Press (*UK*)
Pen Books (*US*)
Polity Press (*UK*)
Sunscribe (*US*)
Temple University Press (*US*)
The University of Michigan Press (*US*)
Verso (*UK*)
Wesleyan University Press (*US*)
Zed Books Ltd (*UK*)

Medicine
Abdo Publishing Co (*US*)
Beacon Press (*US*)
Birlinn Ltd (*UK*)
Bucknell University Press (*US*)
Dreamriver Press (*US*)
Dunedin Academic Press Ltd (*UK*)
Familius (*US*)
Famous Seamus (*UK*)

Fordham University Press (*US*)
Greenhaven Publishing (*US*)
Hay House Publishers (*UK*)
Health Communications, Inc. (*US*)
Hipso Media (*US*)
Hodder Education (*UK*)
Insomniac Press (*Can*)
McFarland & Company, Inc. (*US*)
Pelican Publishing Company (*US*)
Polity Press (*UK*)
Radcliffe Publishing Ltd (*UK*)
Reaktion Books (*UK*)
Reference Service Press (*US*)
Silver Lake Publishing, LLC (*US*)
Singing Dragon (*UK*)
Society for Promoting Christian Knowledge (SPCK) (*UK*)
Souvenir Press Ltd (*UK*)
Sunscribe (*US*)
University of Chicago Press (*US*)
W.W. Norton & Company Ltd (*UK*)
Wannabee Books (*US*)
John Wiley & Sons, Inc. (*US*)
Yale University Press (*US*)
Yale University Press (London) (*UK*)
YMAA Publication Center, Inc. (*US*)
Zed Books Ltd (*UK*)

Men's Interests

Amakella Publishing (*US*)
Carina UK (*UK*)
Connections Book Publishing Ltd (*UK*)
Famous Seamus (*UK*)
GEY Books (*UK*)
Hay House Publishers (*UK*)
Health Communications, Inc. (*US*)
Sunscribe (*US*)
Whitaker House (*US*)

Military

Abdo Publishing Co (*US*)
Algora Publishing (*US*)
Allison & Busby Ltd (*UK*)
Amberley Publishing (*UK*)
Anness Publishing Ltd (*UK*)
Birlinn Ltd (*UK*)
John Blake Publishing (*UK*)
Boydell & Brewer Ltd (*UK*)
Candy Jar Books (*UK*)
Fonthill Media LLC (*US*)
Fonthill Media Ltd (*UK*)
HarperCollins Publishers Ltd (*UK*)
The History Press (*UK*)
IWM (Imperial War Museums) (*UK*)
Jane's Information Group (*UK*)
Limitless Publishing (*US*)
LSU Press (*US*)
Macmillan (*UK*)
McFarland & Company, Inc. (*US*)
Monsoon Books Pte Ltd (*UK*)
Paladin Press (*US*)
Rose and Crown Books (*UK*)
Sidestreet Cookie Publishing (*US*)
Souvenir Press Ltd (*UK*)
Sunscribe (*US*)
Sunstone Press (*US*)
Ulric Publishing (*UK*)
University of Alabama Press (*US*)
University of South Carolina Press (*US*)
Weidenfeld & Nicolson (*UK*)
Zenith Press (*US*)

Music

Algora Publishing (*US*)
Anness Publishing Ltd (*UK*)
Arc Publications (*UK*)
Arch Street Press (*US*)
Ashgate Publishing Limited (*UK*)
Aureus Publishing Limited (*UK*)
Aurora Metro Press (*UK*)
Black Dog Publishing London UK (*UK*)
John Blake Publishing (*UK*)
Bloomsbury Publishing Plc (*UK*)
Boydell & Brewer Ltd (*UK*)
CJ Fallon (*Ire*)
Crescent Moon Publishing (*UK*)
Dunedin Academic Press Ltd (*UK*)
Famous Seamus (*UK*)
Fordham University Press (*US*)
Gingko Library (*UK*)
Gomer Press (*UK*)
Greenhaven Publishing (*US*)
Haus Publishing (*UK*)
Hymns Ancient & Modern Ltd (*UK*)
Independent Music Press (*UK*)
Insomniac Press (*Can*)
Interlink Publishing Group, Inc. (*US*)
The Lilliput Press (*Ire*)
LSU Press (*US*)
Macmillan (*UK*)
Mage Publishers (*US*)
Marion Boyars Publishers (*UK*)
Maverick Reads (*UK*)
Kevin Mayhew Publishers (*UK*)
McFarland & Company, Inc. (*US*)
Mitchell Lane Publishers, Inc. (*US*)
Neil Wilson Publishing Ltd (*UK*)
The O'Brien Press (*Ire*)
Octopus Publishing Group Limited (*UK*)
Pelican Publishing Company (*US*)
Phaidon Press Limited (*UK*)
Reaktion Books (*UK*)
Scarecrow Press Inc. (*US*)
Seren Books (*UK*)
Serpent's Tail (*UK*)
Souvenir Press Ltd (*UK*)
Sterling Publishing Co. Inc. (*US*)
Sunscribe (*US*)
Sunstone Press (*US*)
Triangle Square (*US*)
University of Chicago Press (*US*)
The University of Michigan Press (*US*)
Vehicule Press (*Can*)
W.W. Norton & Company Ltd (*UK*)
Wannabee Books (*US*)
Ward Lock Educational Ltd (*UK*)
Wesleyan University Press (*US*)
Yale University Press (London) (*UK*)

Mystery

Academy Chicago (*US*)
Allison & Busby Ltd (*UK*)
American Quilter's Society (*US*)
Arrow Publications, LLC (*US*)
Asabi Publishing (*US*)
BelleBooks (*US*)
Bethany House Publishers (*US*)
Bloomsbury Spark (*UK*)
BLVNP Incorporated (*US*)
Carina UK (*UK*)
Children's Brains are Yummy (CBAY) Books (*US*)
Covenant Communications Inc. (*US*)
Cricket Books (*US*)
Curiosity Quills Press (*US*)
Darkhouse Books (*US*)
Divertir Publishing LLC (*US*)
ECW Press (*Can*)
Famous Seamus (*UK*)
Harken Media (*US*)
Harmony Ink Press (*US*)
Head of Zeus (*UK*)
Hipso Media (*US*)
Insomniac Press (*Can*)
Joffe Books Ltd (*UK*)
Jolly Fish Press (*US*)
Limitless Publishing (*US*)
Lost Tower Publications (*UK*)
M P Publishing USA (*US*)
Mandrake of Oxford (*UK*)
Maverick Reads (*UK*)
Oceanview Publishing (*US*)
Page Street Publishing Co. (*US*)
Pen Books (*US*)
Polis Books (*US*)
Quirk Books (*US*)
Red Empress Publishing (*US*)
Roberts Press (*US*)
Salvo Press (*US*)
Scribner (*US*)
Severn House Publishers (*UK*)
Sidestreet Cookie Publishing (*US*)
Souvenir Press Ltd (*UK*)
Sterling Publishing Co. Inc. (*US*)
Sunscribe (*US*)
Sunstone Press (*US*)
TouchWood Editions (*Can*)
WaterBrook & Multnomah (*US*)
Wordsworth Editions (*UK*)
Zumaya Publications (*US*)

Nature

Algora Publishing (*US*)
Alpine Publications, Inc. (*US*)
Amakella Publishing (*US*)
Appalachian Mountain Club Books (*US*)
Arch Street Press (*US*)
Beacon Press (*US*)
Birlinn Ltd (*UK*)
Black Dog Publishing London UK (*UK*)
John Blake Publishing (*UK*)
Bloomsbury Publishing Plc (*UK*)
Cave Books (*US*)
Chelsea Green Publishing, Inc. (*US*)
Co & Bear Productions (*UK*)
Curious Fox (*UK*)
David R. Godine, Publisher (*US*)
Dawn Publications (*US*)
Dreamriver Press (*US*)
Dunedin Academic Press Ltd (*UK*)
Edward Elgar Publishing Ltd (*UK*)
Fabian Society (*UK*)
FalconGuides (*US*)
Famous Seamus (*UK*)
Finney Company (*US*)
Folded Word LLC (*US*)
Gill & Macmillan (*Ire*)
Gomer Press (*UK*)
Granta Books (*UK*)
Greenhaven Publishing (*US*)
Hay House Publishers (*UK*)
Heyday Books (*US*)
Hohm Press (*US*)
The Lilliput Press (*Ire*)
LSU Press (*US*)
Luath Press Ltd (*UK*)
The Lyons Press Inc. (*US*)
Macmillan (*UK*)
Maverick Reads (*UK*)
Merlin Unwin Books (*UK*)
Museum of Northern Arizona (*US*)
Natural History Museum Publishing (*UK*)
Neil Wilson Publishing Ltd (*UK*)
New Holland Publishers (UK) Ltd (*UK*)
The O'Brien Press (*Ire*)
Oneworld Publications (*UK*)
Oregon State University Press (*US*)
Page Street Publishing Co. (*US*)
Pelican Publishing Company (*US*)
Polity Press (*UK*)
Reaktion Books (*UK*)
Red Wheel (*US*)
Robert Hale Publishers (*UK*)
The Salariya Book Company (*UK*)
Sierra Club Books (*US*)
Souvenir Press Ltd (*UK*)
Sterling Publishing Co. Inc. (*US*)
Storey Publishing (*US*)
Sunscribe (*US*)
Sunstone Press (*US*)
Temple University Press (*US*)
Think Publishing (*UK*)
TouchWood Editions (*Can*)
Triangle Square (*US*)
Truman State University Press (*US*)
University of Alaska Press (*US*)
The University of Michigan Press (*US*)
University of South Carolina Press (*US*)
University of Washington Press (*US*)
Utah State University Press (*US*)
Venture Publishing, Inc. (*US*)
W.W. Norton & Company Ltd (*UK*)
Wannabee Books (*US*)
Willow Creek Press, Inc. (*US*)
WIT Press (*UK*)
Yale University Press (*US*)
Zed Books Ltd (*UK*)

New Age
Anness Publishing Ltd (*UK*)
Barron's Educational Series, Inc. (*US*)
Chelsea Green Publishing, Inc. (*US*)
Connections Book Publishing Ltd (*UK*)
Dreamriver Press (*US*)
Famous Seamus (*UK*)
Findhorn Press Ltd (*UK*)
Maverick Reads (*UK*)
Red Wheel (*US*)
Sterling Publishing Co. Inc. (*US*)
Sunscribe (*US*)
Nonfiction
A Swift Exit (*UK*)
Abdo Publishing Co (*US*)
Abrams ComicArts (*US*)
Academy Chicago (*US*)
ACC Art Books Ltd (*UK*)
ACTA Publications (*US*)
Albert Whitman & Company (*US*)
Algora Publishing (*US*)
J.A. Allen (*UK*)
Allison & Busby Ltd (*UK*)
Allyn and Bacon / Merrill Education (*US*)
Alma Books Ltd (*UK*)
Alpine Publications, Inc. (*US*)
Amakella Publishing (*US*)
Amberley Publishing (*UK*)
American Counseling Association (*US*)
American Psychiatric Association Publishing (*US*)
American Quilter's Society (*US*)
AMG Publishers (*US*)
And Other Stories (*UK*)
Andrews McMeel Publishing (*US*)
Ankerwycke (*US*)
Anness Publishing Ltd (*UK*)
Appalachian Mountain Club Books (*US*)
Arbordale Publishing (*US*)
Arch Street Press (*US*)
The Armchair Traveller at the bookHaus (*UK*)
Arsenal Pulp Press (*Can*)
Arthur A. Levine Books (*US*)
Asabi Publishing (*US*)
ASCE Press (*US*)
Ashgate Publishing Limited (*UK*)
Ashmolean Museum Publications (*UK*)
Association for Supervision and Curriculum Development (ASCD) (*US*)
Astragal Press (*US*)
Augsburg Fortress (*US*)
Aureus Publishing Limited (*UK*)
Aurora Metro Press (*UK*)
Authentic Media (*UK*)
Award Publications Limited (*UK*)
Baker Publishing Group (*US*)
Ball Publishing (*US*)
Barrington Stoke (*UK*)
Barron's Educational Series, Inc. (*US*)
Beacon Hill Press of Kansas City (*US*)
Beacon Press (*US*)
BearManor Media (*US*)
Bellevue Literary Press (*US*)
BenBella Books (*US*)
Bennion Kearny (*UK*)
Berlitz Publishing (*UK*)
Bethany House Publishers (*US*)
BFI Publishing (*UK*)
Bilingual Review Press (*US*)
Birlinn Ltd (*UK*)
Black & White Publishing Ltd (*UK*)
Black Dog Publishing London UK (*UK*)
Black Lyon Publishing, LLC (*US*)
Black Rose Writing (*US*)
John Blake Publishing (*UK*)
BlazeVOX [books] (*US*)
Bloomsbury Publishing Plc (*UK*)
Blue Guides Limited (*UK*)
Blue River Press (*US*)
Boydell & Brewer Ltd (*UK*)
Boyds Mills Press (*US*)
Bradt Travel Guides (*UK*)
Brilliant Publications (*UK*)
Bucknell University Press (*US*)
Butte Publications, Inc. (*US*)
Candy Jar Books (*UK*)
Canongate Books (*UK*)
Canopus Publishing Ltd (*UK*)
Capstone Professional (*US*)
Carcanet Press Ltd (*UK*)
Carswell (*Can*)
CATO Institute (*US*)
Cave Books (*US*)
Chelsea Green Publishing, Inc. (*US*)
Churchwarden Publications Ltd (*UK*)
Cicerone Press (*UK*)
Cinco Puntos Press (*US*)
CJ Fallon (*Ire*)
Co & Bear Productions (*UK*)
Concordia Publishing House (*US*)
Connections Book Publishing Ltd (*UK*)
Council for British Archaeology (CBA) Publishing (*UK*)
Covenant Communications Inc. (*US*)
CQ Press (*US*)
Crescent Moon Publishing (*UK*)
Cressrelles Publishing Co. Ltd (*UK*)
Crown House Publishing (*UK*)
Crystal Spirit Publishing, Inc. (*US*)
CTS (Catholic Truth Society) (*UK*)
David R. Godine, Publisher (*US*)
Dawn Publications (*US*)
DB Publishing (*UK*)
DC Thomson (*UK*)
Dino Books (*UK*)
Discovery Walking Guides Ltd (*UK*)
Divertir Publishing LLC (*US*)
Dragon Moon Press (*Can*)
Dreamriver Press (*US*)
Dref Wen (*UK*)
Dunedin Academic Press Ltd (*UK*)
Duquesne University Press (*US*)
Dynasty Press (*UK*)
Eagle's View Publishing (*US*)
ECW Press (*Can*)
Edinburgh University Press (*UK*)

Edward Elgar Publishing Inc. (*US*)
Edward Elgar Publishing Ltd (*UK*)
Eland Publishing Ltd (*UK*)
The Emma Press Ltd (*UK*)
Encyclopedia Britannica (UK) Ltd (*UK*)
Euromonitor (*UK*)
Exley Publications (*UK*)
Eye Books (*UK*)
Fabian Society (*UK*)
FalconGuides (*US*)
Familius (*US*)
Famous Seamus (*UK*)
Farrar, Straus and Giroux Books for Younger Readers (*US*)
Ferguson Publishing (*US*)
Findhorn Press Ltd (*UK*)
Finney Company (*US*)
Fitzhenry & Whiteside Ltd (*Can*)
Fitzrovia Press Limited (*UK*)
Fleming Publications (*UK*)
Floris Books (*UK*)
Flyleaf Press (*Ire*)
Folded Word LLC (*US*)
Fonthill Media LLC (*US*)
Fonthill Media Ltd (*UK*)
Fordham University Press (*US*)
Four Courts Press (*Ire*)
4th Level Indie (*US*)
Frances Lincoln Children's Books (*UK*)
Frontinus (*UK*)
Gallaudet University Press (*US*)
The Gallery Press (*Ire*)
Galley Beggar Press (*UK*)
Genealogical Publishing Company (*US*)
GEY Books (*UK*)
Gibson Square Books Ltd (*UK*)
Gill & Macmillan (*Ire*)
Gingko Library (*UK*)
GL Assessment (*UK*)
Golden West Books (*US*)
Gomer Press (*UK*)
Goosebottom Books LLC (*US*)
Granta Books (*UK*)
Greenhaven Publishing (*US*)
Gresham Books Ltd (*UK*)
Gryphon House, Inc. (*US*)
Guild of Master Craftsman (GMC) Publications Ltd (*UK*)
Hachai Publishing (*US*)
Halban Publishers (*UK*)
Haldane Mason Ltd (*UK*)
Halsgrove (*UK*)
Hanser Publications (*US*)
HarperCollins Publishers Ltd (*UK*)
Hart Publishing Ltd (*UK*)
Hartman Publishing, Inc. (*US*)
Haus Publishing (*UK*)
Hawthorn Press (*UK*)
Hay House Publishers (*UK*)
Haynes Publishing (*UK*)
Head of Zeus (*UK*)
Headland Publications (*UK*)
Headline Publishing Group (*UK*)
Health Communications, Inc. (*US*)
Hendrickson Publishers (*US*)
Hesperus Press Limited (*UK*)
Heyday Books (*US*)
Hipso Media (*US*)
The History Press (*UK*)
Hodder Education (*UK*)
Hodder Faith (*UK*)
Hohm Press (*US*)
Holiday House, Inc. (*US*)
Honno Welsh Women's Press (*UK*)
Hopscotch (*UK*)
House of Lochar (*UK*)
Humanix Books (*US*)
Hymns Ancient & Modern Ltd (*UK*)
ICS Publications (*US*)
Imprint Academic (*UK*)
Incentive Publications (*US*)
Independent Music Press (*UK*)
Infinite Ideas (*UK*)
Insomniac Press (*Can*)
Interlink Publishing Group, Inc. (*US*)
International Wealth Success (IWS) Inc. (*US*)
Italica Press (*US*)
IWM (Imperial War Museums) (*UK*)
Jacaranda Books Art Music Ltd (*UK*)
Jane's Information Group (*UK*)
Jordan Publishing (*UK*)
Judaica Press (*US*)
Kaeden Books (*US*)
Kansas City Star Quilts (*US*)
Kar-Ben Publishing (*US*)
Kube Publishing (*UK*)
Kyle Books (*UK*)
Laurence King Publishing Ltd (*UK*)
Lawrence & Wishart (*UK*)
Lee & Low Books (*US*)
Legend Business (*UK*)
Leisure Arts, Inc. (*US*)
LexisNexis (*US*)
The Lilliput Press (*Ire*)
Limitless Publishing (*US*)
Lion Hudson Plc (*UK*)
Little Pickle Press, Inc. (*US*)
Liverpool University Press (*UK*)
Lonely Planet (*UK*)
Lonely Planet Publications (*US*)
LSU Press (*US*)
Luath Press Ltd (*UK*)
Lund Humphries Limited (*UK*)
The Lyons Press Inc. (*US*)
M P Publishing USA (*US*)
Macmillan (*UK*)
Mage Publishers (*US*)
Management Books 2000 Ltd (*UK*)
Manchester University Press (*UK*)
Mandrake of Oxford (*UK*)
Mantra Lingua Ltd (*UK*)
Marion Boyars Publishers (*UK*)
Maven House Press (*US*)
Maverick Reads (*UK*)
Kevin Mayhew Publishers (*UK*)
McFarland & Company, Inc. (*US*)

The Merlin Press (*UK*)
Merlin Unwin Books (*UK*)
Merrell Publishers Limited (*UK*)
Metal Powder Industries Federation (MPIF) (*US*)
Methodist Publishing (*UK*)
Metro Publications Ltd (*UK*)
Michael Terence Publishing (MTP) (*UK*)
Milo Books Ltd (*UK*)
Mitchell Lane Publishers, Inc. (*US*)
Monarch Books (*UK*)
Monsoon Books Pte Ltd (*UK*)
Museum of Northern Arizona (*US*)
Natural History Museum Publishing (*UK*)
Neil Wilson Publishing Ltd (*UK*)
New Holland Publishers (UK) Ltd (*UK*)
New York University (NYU) Press (*US*)
Nightboat Books (*US*)
Nolo (*US*)
Nomad Press (*US*)
NursesBooks (*US*)
The O'Brien Press (*Ire*)
Michael O'Mara Books Ltd (*UK*)
Oak Knoll Press (*US*)
Oak Tree Press (*Ire*)
Oberon Books (*UK*)
Octopus Publishing Group Limited (*UK*)
On The Mark Press (*Can*)
Oneworld Publications (*UK*)
Onstream Publications Ltd (*Ire*)
Oregon State University Press (*US*)
Ouen Press (*UK*)
The Overmountain Press (*US*)
O'Reilly Media (*US*)
Page Street Publishing Co. (*US*)
Paladin Press (*US*)
Pandora Press (*UK*)
PaperBooks (*UK*)
Paragon House (*US*)
Parallax Press (*US*)
Pavilion Publishing (*UK*)
Pelican Publishing Company (*US*)
Pen Books (*US*)
Penguin Canada (*Can*)
Penguin Group (USA) Inc. (*US*)
Pflaum Publishing Group (*US*)
Phaidon Press Limited (*UK*)
Philosophy Documentation Center (*US*)
Phoenix Yard Books (*UK*)
Picton Press (*US*)
The Policy Press (*UK*)
Polity Press (*UK*)
Professional and Higher Partnership (*UK*)
Professional Publications, Inc. (PPI) (*US*)
Prometheus Books (*US*)
Psychology Press (*UK*)
Pushkin Press (*UK*)
Quadrille Publishing Ltd (*UK*)
Quill Driver Books (*US*)
Quiller Publishing Ltd (*UK*)
Quirk Books (*US*)
Radcliffe Publishing Ltd (*UK*)
Rainbow Publishers (*US*)
Ransom Publishing Ltd (*UK*)
Reaktion Books (*UK*)
Red Rattle Books (*UK*)
Red Wheel (*US*)
Redleaf Press (*US*)
Reference Service Press (*US*)
River City Publishing (*US*)
Robert Hale Publishers (*UK*)
The Rosen Publishing Group, Inc. (*US*)
RotoVision (*UK*)
Running Press (*US*)
Ryland Peters & Small (*UK*)
SAE International (*US*)
Saffron Books (*UK*)
The Salariya Book Company (*UK*)
Sandstone Press Ltd (*UK*)
Scarecrow Press Inc. (*US*)
Schofield & Sims (*UK*)
Scholastic Library Publishing (*US*)
School Guide Publications (*US*)
Scribner (*US*)
Scripture Union (*UK*)
Search Press Ltd (*UK*)
Seren Books (*UK*)
Serpent's Tail (*UK*)
Seven Stories Press (*US*)
Shearsman Books (*UK*)
Short Books (*UK*)
Sierra Club Books (*US*)
Silver Lake Publishing, LLC (*US*)
Singing Dragon (*UK*)
Siri Scientific Press (*UK*)
Sky Pony Press (*US*)
Snowbooks (*UK*)
Society for Promoting Christian Knowledge (SPCK) (*UK*)
Somerville Press (*Ire*)
Southern Illinois University Press (*US*)
Souvenir Press Ltd (*UK*)
Speechmark Publishing Limited (*UK*)
St David's Press (*UK*)
St Pauls (*US*)
St. Johann Press (*US*)
Standard Publishing (*US*)
Star Bright Books (*US*)
STC Craft (*US*)
Stenlake Publishing (*UK*)
Sterling Publishing Co. Inc. (*US*)
Storey Publishing (*US*)
Summersdale Publishers Ltd (*UK*)
Sunscribe (*US*)
Sunstone Press (*US*)
Swedenborg Foundation (*US*)
Syracuse University Press (*US*)
Tarquin (*UK*)
Teachers College Press (*US*)
The Templar Company Limited (*UK*)
Temple University Press (*US*)
Think Publishing (*UK*)
Thistle Publishing (*UK*)
ThunderStone Books (*US*)
Titan Books (*UK*)
Top That! Publishing (*UK*)

Torah Aura Productions (*US*)
TouchWood Editions (*Can*)
Tower Publishing (*US*)
Trentham Books Limited (*UK*)
Triangle Square (*US*)
Triumph Books (*US*)
Truman State University Press (*US*)
Two Rivers Press (*UK*)
Ulric Publishing (*UK*)
Unbound Press (*UK*)
University of Alabama Press (*US*)
University of Alaska Press (*US*)
University of Chicago Press (*US*)
The University of Michigan Press (*US*)
University of Pittsburgh Press (*US*)
University of South Carolina Press (*US*)
University of Washington Press (*US*)
Urban Ministries, Inc. (*US*)
Utah State University Press (*US*)
Vallentine Mitchell & Co., Limited (*UK*)
Valley Press (*UK*)
Vehicule Press (*Can*)
Venture Publishing, Inc. (*US*)
Veritas Publications (*US*)
Verso (*US*)
Verso (*UK*)
Virago Press (*UK*)
Wooden Books (*UK*)
W.W. Norton & Company Ltd (*UK*)
Walch Education (*US*)
Walker Books Ltd (*UK*)
Wannabee Books (*US*)
Ward Lock Educational Ltd (*UK*)
WaterBrook & Multnomah (*US*)
Waverley Books (*UK*)
Weidenfeld & Nicolson (*UK*)
Welsh Academic Press (*UK*)
Wesleyan Publishing House (*US*)
Wesleyan University Press (*US*)
Western Psychological Services (*US*)
Whitaker House (*US*)
John Wiley & Sons, Inc. (*US*)
Willow Creek Press, Inc. (*US*)
Wilshire Book Company (*US*)
Philip Wilson Publishers Ltd (*UK*)
WIT Press (*UK*)
World Book, Inc. (*US*)
WorthyKids / Ideals (*US*)
Yale University Press (*US*)
Yale University Press (London) (*UK*)
YMAA Publication Center, Inc. (*US*)
Zed Books Ltd (*UK*)
Zenith Press (*US*)
Zumaya Publications (*US*)

Philosophy

Algora Publishing (*US*)
Arch Street Press (*US*)
Ashgate Publishing Limited (*UK*)
Bucknell University Press (*US*)
CATO Institute (*US*)
Connections Book Publishing Ltd (*UK*)
Crescent Moon Publishing (*UK*)
Dreamriver Press (*US*)
Dunedin Academic Press Ltd (*UK*)
Duquesne University Press (*US*)
Edinburgh University Press (*UK*)
Famous Seamus (*UK*)
Fitzrovia Press Limited (*UK*)
Floris Books (*UK*)
Fordham University Press (*US*)
Four Courts Press (*Ire*)
Gibson Square Books Ltd (*UK*)
Gingko Library (*UK*)
Halban Publishers (*UK*)
Hay House Publishers (*UK*)
Head of Zeus (*UK*)
Imprint Academic (*UK*)
The Lilliput Press (*Ire*)
Macmillan (*UK*)
Mandrake of Oxford (*UK*)
Marion Boyars Publishers (*UK*)
Maverick Reads (*UK*)
The Merlin Press (*UK*)
Methodist Publishing (*UK*)
Oneworld Publications (*UK*)
Paragon House (*US*)
Pen Books (*US*)
Philosophy Documentation Center (*US*)
Polity Press (*UK*)
Prometheus Books (*US*)
Reaktion Books (*UK*)
Red Wheel (*US*)
Scarecrow Press Inc. (*US*)
Scribner (*US*)
Southern Illinois University Press (*US*)
Souvenir Press Ltd (*UK*)
Sunscribe (*US*)
Swedenborg Foundation (*US*)
Teachers College Press (*US*)
Triangle Square (*US*)
University of Chicago Press (*US*)
The University of Michigan Press (*US*)
University of Pittsburgh Press (*US*)
Vallentine Mitchell & Co., Limited (*UK*)
Verso (*US*)
Verso (*UK*)
W.W. Norton & Company Ltd (*UK*)
Yale University Press (*US*)
Yale University Press (London) (*UK*)
YMAA Publication Center, Inc. (*US*)

Photography

ACC Art Books Ltd (*UK*)
Anness Publishing Ltd (*UK*)
Barron's Educational Series, Inc. (*US*)
Black Dog Publishing London UK (*UK*)
Cave Books (*US*)
Co & Bear Productions (*UK*)
David R. Godine, Publisher (*US*)
Famous Seamus (*UK*)
Fleming Publications (*UK*)
Fordham University Press (*US*)
Guild of Master Craftsman (GMC) Publications Ltd (*UK*)
Halsgrove (*UK*)
Haus Publishing (*UK*)
Interlink Publishing Group, Inc. (*US*)

Jacaranda Books Art Music Ltd (*UK*)
Laurence King Publishing Ltd (*UK*)
The Lilliput Press (*Ire*)
Luath Press Ltd (*UK*)
Merrell Publishers Limited (*UK*)
New Holland Publishers (UK) Ltd (*UK*)
The O'Brien Press (*Ire*)
O'Reilly Media (*US*)
Pelican Publishing Company (*US*)
Phaidon Press Limited (*UK*)
Reaktion Books (*UK*)
RotoVision (*UK*)
Seren Books (*UK*)
Southern Illinois University Press (*US*)
Sterling Publishing Co. Inc. (*US*)
Sunscribe (*US*)
Sunstone Press (*US*)
Temple University Press (*US*)
Wannabee Books (*US*)

Poetry

A Swift Exit (*UK*)
Ahsahta Press (*US*)
Alice James Books (*US*)
Alma Classics (*UK*)
And Other Stories (*UK*)
Andrews McMeel Publishing (*US*)
Arc Publications (*UK*)
Arrowhead Press (*UK*)
The Backwater Press (*US*)
Bilingual Review Press (*US*)
Birlinn Ltd (*UK*)
Black Ocean (*US*)
BlazeVOX [books] (*US*)
Bloodaxe Books Ltd (*UK*)
Blue Light Press (*US*)
Boyds Mills Press (*US*)
Carcanet Press Ltd (*UK*)
Chapman Publishing (*UK*)
Cinco Puntos Press (*US*)
Cleveland State University Poetry Center (*US*)
Creative With Words (CWW) (*US*)
Crescent Moon Publishing (*UK*)
Crystal Spirit Publishing, Inc. (*US*)
David R. Godine, Publisher (*US*)
Divertir Publishing LLC (*US*)
ECW Press (*Can*)
Eland Publishing Ltd (*UK*)
The Emma Press Ltd (*UK*)
Famous Seamus (*UK*)
Fleming Publications (*UK*)
Floating Bridge Press (*US*)
Folded Word LLC (*US*)
Frances Lincoln Children's Books (*UK*)
FutureCycle Press (*US*)
The Gallery Press (*Ire*)
GEY Books (*UK*)
Gomer Press (*UK*)
Grayson Books (*US*)
Headland Publications (*UK*)
Helicon Nine Editions (*US*)
Hesperus Press Limited (*UK*)
Heyday Books (*US*)
Hippopotamus Press (*UK*)
Honno Welsh Women's Press (*UK*)
Indigo Dreams Publishing (*UK*)
Insomniac Press (*Can*)
Iron Press (*UK*)
Italica Press (*US*)
Kube Publishing (*UK*)
The Lilliput Press (*Ire*)
Lost Tower Publications (*UK*)
LSU Press (*US*)
Luath Press Ltd (*UK*)
Macmillan (*UK*)
Mage Publishers (*US*)
Maverick Reads (*UK*)
Mudfog Press (*UK*)
New Directions Publishing (*US*)
Nightboat Books (*US*)
Oversteps Books (*UK*)
Parthian Books (*UK*)
Pelican Publishing Company (*US*)
Phoenix Yard Books (*UK*)
Reality Street Editions (*UK*)
Route Publishing (*UK*)
Seren Books (*UK*)
Shape & Nature Press (*US*)
Shearsman Books (*UK*)
Sibling Rivalry Press, LLC (*US*)
Southern Illinois University Press (*US*)
St. Johann Press (*US*)
Stonewood Press (*UK*)
Sunscribe (*US*)
Sunstone Press (*US*)
Templar Poetry (*UK*)
Tia Chucha Press (*US*)
Troika Books (*UK*)
Two Rivers Press (*UK*)
University of Alaska Press (*US*)
University of Pittsburgh Press (*US*)
University of South Carolina Press (*US*)
Valley Press (*UK*)
Vehicule Press (*Can*)
W.W. Norton & Company Ltd (*UK*)
Wave Books (*US*)
Wesleyan University Press (*US*)
WordSong (*US*)
Yale University Press (*US*)

Politics

Abdo Publishing Co (*US*)
Algora Publishing (*US*)
AMG Publishers (*US*)
Arch Street Press (*US*)
Arsenal Pulp Press (*Can*)
Ashgate Publishing Limited (*UK*)
Beacon Press (*US*)
BenBella Books (*US*)
Birlinn Ltd (*UK*)
John Blake Publishing (*UK*)
Bucknell University Press (*US*)
Canongate Books (*UK*)
CATO Institute (*US*)
Chelsea Green Publishing, Inc. (*US*)
CQ Press (*US*)
Crescent Moon Publishing (*UK*)
Divertir Publishing LLC (*US*)

Dreamriver Press (*US*)
ECW Press (*Can*)
Edinburgh University Press (*UK*)
Edward Elgar Publishing Ltd (*UK*)
Fabian Society (*UK*)
Famous Seamus (*UK*)
Fordham University Press (*US*)
Gibson Square Books Ltd (*UK*)
Gingko Library (*UK*)
Granta Books (*UK*)
Greenhaven Publishing (*US*)
Halban Publishers (*UK*)
Haus Publishing (*UK*)
Humanix Books (*US*)
Imprint Academic (*UK*)
Infinite Ideas (*UK*)
Insomniac Press (*Can*)
Interlink Publishing Group, Inc. (*US*)
Kube Publishing (*UK*)
Lawrence & Wishart (*UK*)
The Lilliput Press (*Ire*)
Liverpool University Press (*UK*)
Luath Press Ltd (*UK*)
Macmillan (*UK*)
Manchester University Press (*UK*)
The Merlin Press (*UK*)
Mitchell Lane Publishers, Inc. (*US*)
Monarch Books (*UK*)
Monsoon Books Pte Ltd (*UK*)
New York University (NYU) Press (*US*)
The O'Brien Press (*Ire*)
Oneworld Publications (*UK*)
Paladin Press (*US*)
Pandora Press (*UK*)
Paragon House (*US*)
Pelican Publishing Company (*US*)
Pen Books (*US*)
The Policy Press (*UK*)
Polity Press (*UK*)
Seren Books (*UK*)
Serpent's Tail (*UK*)
Seven Stories Press (*US*)
Silver Lake Publishing, LLC (*US*)
Southern Illinois University Press (*US*)
Souvenir Press Ltd (*UK*)
Sunscribe (*US*)
Sunstone Press (*US*)
Syracuse University Press (*US*)
Teachers College Press (*US*)
Temple University Press (*US*)
Triangle Square (*US*)
University of Alabama Press (*US*)
University of Alaska Press (*US*)
University of Chicago Press (*US*)
The University of Michigan Press (*US*)
Verso (*US*)
Verso (*UK*)
W.W. Norton & Company Ltd (*UK*)
Welsh Academic Press (*UK*)
Yale University Press (*US*)
Yale University Press (London) (*UK*)
Zed Books Ltd (*UK*)

Psychology
Algora Publishing (*US*)
Amakella Publishing (*US*)
American Psychiatric Association Publishing (*US*)
Black & White Publishing Ltd (*UK*)
Bucknell University Press (*US*)
Connections Book Publishing Ltd (*UK*)
Crown House Publishing (*UK*)
Dreamriver Press (*US*)
Duquesne University Press (*US*)
Famous Seamus (*UK*)
Gallaudet University Press (*US*)
Gibson Square Books Ltd (*UK*)
Hay House Publishers (*UK*)
Health Communications, Inc. (*US*)
Imprint Academic (*UK*)
Macmillan (*UK*)
Marion Boyars Publishers (*UK*)
Maverick Reads (*UK*)
Monarch Books (*UK*)
New York University (NYU) Press (*US*)
Octopus Publishing Group Limited (*UK*)
Oneworld Publications (*UK*)
Paragon House (*US*)
Pelican Publishing Company (*US*)
Pen Books (*US*)
Polity Press (*UK*)
Psychology Press (*UK*)
Red Wheel (*US*)
Scribner (*US*)
Society for Promoting Christian Knowledge (SPCK) (*UK*)
Souvenir Press Ltd (*UK*)
Speechmark Publishing Limited (*UK*)
Sunscribe (*US*)
Swedenborg Foundation (*US*)
Temple University Press (*US*)
Twenty First Century Publishers Ltd (*UK*)
University of Chicago Press (*US*)
The University of Michigan Press (*US*)
Veritas Publications (*US*)
W.W. Norton & Company Ltd (*UK*)
Wannabee Books (*US*)
Western Psychological Services (*US*)
John Wiley & Sons, Inc. (*US*)
Wilshire Book Company (*US*)
Yale University Press (*US*)

Radio
BearManor Media (*US*)
Sunscribe (*US*)

Reference
AMG Publishers (*US*)
Anness Publishing Ltd (*UK*)
Award Publications Limited (*UK*)
Barrington Stoke (*UK*)
Berlitz Publishing (*UK*)
BFI Publishing (*UK*)
Birlinn Ltd (*UK*)
Black Dog Publishing London UK (*UK*)
Bloomsbury Publishing Plc (*UK*)
Carswell (*Can*)
Churchwarden Publications Ltd (*UK*)

Cicerone Press (*UK*)
CJ Fallon (*Ire*)
Connections Book Publishing Ltd (*UK*)
Covenant Communications Inc. (*US*)
CQ Press (*US*)
Edinburgh University Press (*UK*)
Encyclopedia Britannica (UK) Ltd (*UK*)
Euromonitor (*UK*)
Famous Seamus (*UK*)
Ferguson Publishing (*US*)
Flyleaf Press (*Ire*)
Gill & Macmillan (*Ire*)
Gomer Press (*UK*)
Greenhaven Publishing (*US*)
Guild of Master Craftsman (GMC) Publications Ltd (*UK*)
Hanser Publications (*US*)
HarperCollins Publishers Ltd (*UK*)
Haynes Publishing (*UK*)
Hendrickson Publishers (*US*)
Hesperus Press Limited (*UK*)
Hodder Education (*UK*)
Hymns Ancient & Modern Ltd (*UK*)
Insomniac Press (*Can*)
Interlink Publishing Group, Inc. (*US*)
Jane's Information Group (*UK*)
Kyle Books (*UK*)
LexisNexis (*US*)
The Lilliput Press (*Ire*)
Lion Hudson Plc (*UK*)
Lonely Planet Publications (*US*)
The Lyons Press Inc. (*US*)
Macmillan (*UK*)
Manchester University Press (*UK*)
Maverick Reads (*UK*)
McFarland & Company, Inc. (*US*)
Neil Wilson Publishing Ltd (*UK*)
New Holland Publishers (UK) Ltd (*UK*)
Nolo (*US*)
The O'Brien Press (*Ire*)
Octopus Publishing Group Limited (*UK*)
Pandora Press (*UK*)
Paragon House (*US*)
Pavilion Publishing (*UK*)
Philosophy Documentation Center (*US*)
Picton Press (*US*)
Polity Press (*UK*)
Professional Publications, Inc. (PPI) (*US*)
Quiller Publishing Ltd (*UK*)
Reference Service Press (*US*)
Robert Hale Publishers (*UK*)
Scarecrow Press Inc. (*US*)
Scholastic Library Publishing (*US*)
School Guide Publications (*US*)
Silver Lake Publishing, LLC (*US*)
Siri Scientific Press (*UK*)
St David's Press (*UK*)
Sterling Publishing Co. Inc. (*US*)
Sunscribe (*US*)
Sunstone Press (*US*)
Top That! Publishing (*UK*)
Tower Publishing (*US*)
University of Chicago Press (*US*)
The University of Michigan Press (*US*)
Western Psychological Services (*US*)
John Wiley & Sons, Inc. (*US*)
Willow Creek Press, Inc. (*US*)
World Book, Inc. (*US*)
Yale University Press (London) (*UK*)

Religious

Abdo Publishing Co (*US*)
ACTA Publications (*US*)
Algora Publishing (*US*)
AMG Publishers (*US*)
Ashgate Publishing Limited (*UK*)
Augsburg Fortress (*US*)
Authentic Media (*UK*)
Baker Publishing Group (*US*)
Beacon Hill Press of Kansas City (*US*)
Beacon Press (*US*)
Bethany House Publishers (*US*)
Boydell & Brewer Ltd (*UK*)
Bucknell University Press (*US*)
Churchwarden Publications Ltd (*UK*)
CJ Fallon (*Ire*)
Concordia Publishing House (*US*)
Connections Book Publishing Ltd (*UK*)
Covenant Communications Inc. (*US*)
Crystal Spirit Publishing, Inc. (*US*)
CTS (Catholic Truth Society) (*UK*)
Divertir Publishing LLC (*US*)
Dreamriver Press (*US*)
Dunedin Academic Press Ltd (*UK*)
Duquesne University Press (*US*)
ECW Press (*Can*)
Edinburgh University Press (*UK*)
Floris Books (*UK*)
Fordham University Press (*US*)
Four Courts Press (*Ire*)
Gingko Library (*UK*)
Gomer Press (*UK*)
Gresham Books Ltd (*UK*)
Hachai Publishing (*US*)
Halban Publishers (*UK*)
Hay House Publishers (*UK*)
Health Communications, Inc. (*US*)
Hendrickson Publishers (*US*)
Hodder Faith (*UK*)
Hohm Press (*US*)
Hymns Ancient & Modern Ltd (*UK*)
ICS Publications (*US*)
Insomniac Press (*Can*)
Judaica Press (*US*)
Kar-Ben Publishing (*US*)
Kube Publishing (*UK*)
Lion Hudson Plc (*UK*)
Maverick Reads (*UK*)
Kevin Mayhew Publishers (*UK*)
Methodist Publishing (*UK*)
Monarch Books (*UK*)
New York University (NYU) Press (*US*)
The O'Brien Press (*Ire*)
Oneworld Publications (*UK*)
Paragon House (*US*)
Pelican Publishing Company (*US*)
Pflaum Publishing Group (*US*)

Polity Press (*UK*)
Rainbow Publishers (*US*)
Red Wheel (*US*)
Reference Service Press (*US*)
Rose and Crown Books (*UK*)
The Rosen Publishing Group, Inc. (*US*)
Scarecrow Press Inc. (*US*)
Scribner (*US*)
Scripture Union (*UK*)
Society for Promoting Christian Knowledge (SPCK) (*UK*)
Souvenir Press Ltd (*UK*)
St Pauls (*US*)
St. Johann Press (*US*)
Standard Publishing (*US*)
Sunscribe (*US*)
Sunstone Press (*US*)
Swedenborg Foundation (*US*)
Syracuse University Press (*US*)
Temple University Press (*US*)
Torah Aura Productions (*US*)
Triangle Square (*US*)
Truman State University Press (*US*)
University of Alabama Press (*US*)
University of Chicago Press (*US*)
The University of Michigan Press (*US*)
University of South Carolina Press (*US*)
Urban Ministries, Inc. (*US*)
Vallentine Mitchell & Co., Limited (*UK*)
Vehicule Press (*Can*)
Veritas Publications (*US*)
W.W. Norton & Company Ltd (*UK*)
WaterBrook & Multnomah (*US*)
Wesleyan Publishing House (*US*)
Whitaker House (*US*)
John Wiley & Sons, Inc. (*US*)
WorthyKids / Ideals (*US*)
Yale University Press (*US*)
Yale University Press (London) (*UK*)

Romance

Amakella Publishing (*US*)
American Quilter's Society (*US*)
Amira Press (*US*)
Arrow Publications, LLC (*US*)
BelleBooks (*US*)
Bethany House Publishers (*US*)
Black & White Publishing Ltd (*UK*)
Black Lyon Publishing, LLC (*US*)
Bloomsbury Spark (*UK*)
BLVNP Incorporated (*US*)
Carina UK (*UK*)
Covenant Communications Inc. (*US*)
Crimson Romance (*US*)
Crystal Spirit Publishing, Inc. (*US*)
Curiosity Quills Press (*US*)
Curious Fox (*UK*)
Divertir Publishing LLC (*US*)
Dragon Moon Press (*Can*)
Ellysian Press (*US*)
Entangled Teen (*US*)
Famous Seamus (*UK*)
GEY Books (*UK*)
Harlequin American Romance (*US*)
Harlequin Mills & Boon Ltd (*UK*)
Harmony Ink Press (*US*)
HarperImpulse (*UK*)
Head of Zeus (*UK*)
Hesperus Press Limited (*UK*)
Jacaranda Books Art Music Ltd (*UK*)
Joffe Books Ltd (*UK*)
Limitless Publishing (*US*)
M P Publishing USA (*US*)
Macmillan (*UK*)
Maverick Reads (*UK*)
Melange Books, LLC (*US*)
Monsoon Books Pte Ltd (*UK*)
Polis Books (*US*)
Red Empress Publishing (*US*)
Robert Hale Publishers (*UK*)
Rose and Crown Books (*UK*)
Severn House Publishers (*UK*)
Sidestreet Cookie Publishing (*US*)
Sunscribe (*US*)
Sunstone Press (*US*)
WaterBrook & Multnomah (*US*)
Wordsworth Editions (*UK*)
World Weaver Press (*US*)
Zebra (*US*)
Zumaya Publications (*US*)

Science

Abdo Publishing Co (*US*)
Algora Publishing (*US*)
American Psychiatric Association Publishing (*US*)
Arbordale Publishing (*US*)
ASCE Press (*US*)
Astragal Press (*US*)
Beacon Press (*US*)
BenBella Books (*US*)
John Blake Publishing (*UK*)
Bucknell University Press (*US*)
Canongate Books (*UK*)
Canopus Publishing Ltd (*UK*)
Cave Books (*US*)
Chelsea Green Publishing, Inc. (*US*)
CJ Fallon (*Ire*)
Dreamriver Press (*US*)
Dunedin Academic Press Ltd (*UK*)
Edinburgh University Press (*UK*)
Famous Seamus (*UK*)
Finney Company (*US*)
Floris Books (*UK*)
Fordham University Press (*US*)
Gingko Library (*UK*)
Greenhaven Publishing (*US*)
Haldane Mason Ltd (*UK*)
Hanser Publications (*US*)
HarperCollins Publishers Ltd (*UK*)
Headline Publishing Group (*UK*)
Hodder Education (*UK*)
Hopscotch (*UK*)
Humanix Books (*US*)
Kaeden Books (*US*)
Macmillan (*UK*)
Maverick Reads (*UK*)
Mitchell Lane Publishers, Inc. (*US*)

Natural History Museum Publishing (*UK*)
Nomad Press (*US*)
Oneworld Publications (*UK*)
Oregon State University Press (*US*)
O'Reilly Media (*US*)
Page Street Publishing Co. (*US*)
Pelican Publishing Company (*US*)
Professional Publications, Inc. (PPI) (*US*)
Prometheus Books (*US*)
Quirk Books (*US*)
Reaktion Books (*UK*)
Reference Service Press (*US*)
The Rosen Publishing Group, Inc. (*US*)
The Salariya Book Company (*UK*)
Schofield & Sims (*UK*)
Scribner (*US*)
Siri Scientific Press (*UK*)
Souvenir Press Ltd (*UK*)
Sterling Publishing Co. Inc. (*US*)
Sunscribe (*US*)
Swedenborg Foundation (*US*)
Temple University Press (*US*)
Trentham Books Limited (*UK*)
Tumblehome Learning, Inc. (*US*)
University of Alaska Press (*US*)
University of Chicago Press (*US*)
University of Pittsburgh Press (*US*)
Utah State University Press (*US*)
Wooden Books (*UK*)
W.W. Norton & Company Ltd (*UK*)
Walch Education (*US*)
Wannabee Books (*US*)
Ward Lock Educational Ltd (*UK*)
John Wiley & Sons, Inc. (*US*)
WIT Press (*UK*)
World Book, Inc. (*US*)
Yale University Press (*US*)
Yale University Press (London) (*UK*)
Zenith Press (*US*)

Sci-Fi
Allison & Busby Ltd (*UK*)
Amira Press (*US*)
Baen Books (*US*)
BelleBooks (*US*)
Bloomsbury Spark (*UK*)
BLVNP Incorporated (*US*)
Candy Jar Books (*UK*)
Carina UK (*UK*)
Children's Brains are Yummy (CBAY) Books (*US*)
Cricket Books (*US*)
Curious Fox (*UK*)
Divertir Publishing LLC (*US*)
Dragon Moon Press (*Can*)
Ellysian Press (*US*)
Entangled Teen (*US*)
Famous Seamus (*UK*)
Fingerpress UK (*UK*)
Galley Beggar Press (*UK*)
Harken Media (*US*)
Harmony Ink Press (*US*)
HarperCollins Publishers Ltd (*UK*)
Head of Zeus (*UK*)
Hesperus Press Limited (*UK*)
Jolly Fish Press (*US*)
Liverpool University Press (*UK*)
Lost Tower Publications (*UK*)
Luna Press Publishing (*UK*)
M P Publishing USA (*US*)
Macmillan (*UK*)
Mandrake of Oxford (*UK*)
Maverick Reads (*UK*)
Pen Books (*US*)
Polis Books (*US*)
Quirk Books (*US*)
Severn House Publishers (*UK*)
Sidestreet Cookie Publishing (*US*)
Snowbooks (*UK*)
Sunscribe (*US*)
Sunstone Press (*US*)
Titan Books (*UK*)
WaterBrook & Multnomah (*US*)
Wesleyan University Press (*US*)
Wordsworth Editions (*UK*)
World Weaver Press (*US*)
Zumaya Publications (*US*)

Scripts
Alma Classics (*UK*)
Aurora Metro Press (*UK*)
Bilingual Review Press (*US*)
Chapman Publishing (*UK*)
Cressrelles Publishing Co. Ltd (*UK*)
Famous Seamus (*UK*)
The Gallery Press (*Ire*)
Gomer Press (*UK*)
Italica Press (*US*)
Josef Weinberger Ltd (*UK*)
The Lilliput Press (*Ire*)
New Playwrights' Network (NPN) (*UK*)
Oberon Books (*UK*)
Parthian Books (*UK*)
Samuel French Ltd (*UK*)
Sunscribe (*US*)

Self-Help
ACTA Publications (*US*)
Allison & Busby Ltd (*UK*)
Amakella Publishing (*US*)
BenBella Books (*US*)
Black Lyon Publishing, LLC (*US*)
John Blake Publishing (*UK*)
BLVNP Incorporated (*US*)
Connections Book Publishing Ltd (*UK*)
Crown House Publishing (*UK*)
Crystal Spirit Publishing, Inc. (*US*)
Divertir Publishing LLC (*US*)
Dreamriver Press (*US*)
Familius (*US*)
Famous Seamus (*UK*)
Ferguson Publishing (*US*)
Fleming Publications (*UK*)
Floris Books (*UK*)
Hawthorn Press (*UK*)
Hay House Publishers (*UK*)
Health Communications, Inc. (*US*)
Hipso Media (*US*)
Hodder Education (*UK*)

Infinite Ideas (*UK*)
Insomniac Press (*Can*)
International Wealth Success (IWS) Inc. (*US*)
Jolly Fish Press (*US*)
Judaica Press (*US*)
Management Books 2000 Ltd (*UK*)
Mandrake of Oxford (*UK*)
Maverick Reads (*UK*)
New Holland Publishers (UK) Ltd (*UK*)
Nolo (*US*)
Oneworld Publications (*UK*)
O'Reilly Media (*US*)
Pelican Publishing Company (*US*)
Quill Driver Books (*US*)
Red Wheel (*US*)
The Rosen Publishing Group, Inc. (*US*)
Running Press (*US*)
Singing Dragon (*UK*)
Society for Promoting Christian Knowledge (SPCK) (*UK*)
Souvenir Press Ltd (*UK*)
St Pauls (*US*)
Sunscribe (*US*)
Veritas Publications (*US*)
W.W. Norton & Company Ltd (*UK*)
Whitaker House (*US*)
Wilshire Book Company (*US*)

Short Stories

A Swift Exit (*UK*)
Allison & Busby Ltd (*UK*)
Amakella Publishing (*US*)
Aurora Metro Press (*UK*)
BelleBooks (*US*)
Bilingual Review Press (*US*)
BlazeVOX [books] (*US*)
BLVNP Incorporated (*US*)
Carina UK (*UK*)
Chapman Publishing (*UK*)
Children's Brains are Yummy (CBAY) Books (*US*)
Comma Press (*UK*)
Creative With Words (CWW) (*US*)
Crystal Spirit Publishing, Inc. (*US*)
Darkhouse Books (*US*)
Divertir Publishing LLC (*US*)
Famous Seamus (*UK*)
Galley Beggar Press (*UK*)
GEY Books (*UK*)
HarperImpulse (*UK*)
Head of Zeus (*UK*)
Headland Publications (*UK*)
Helicon Nine Editions (*US*)
Hipso Media (*US*)
Honno Welsh Women's Press (*UK*)
Insomniac Press (*Can*)
Iron Press (*UK*)
Judaica Press (*US*)
Livingston Press (*US*)
Luna Press Publishing (*UK*)
M P Publishing USA (*US*)
Mage Publishers (*US*)
Maverick Reads (*UK*)
Melange Books, LLC (*US*)
Monsoon Books Pte Ltd (*UK*)
Mudfog Press (*UK*)
New Directions Publishing (*US*)
Ouen Press (*UK*)
Parthian Books (*UK*)
River City Publishing (*US*)
Roberts Press (*US*)
Route Publishing (*UK*)
Shape & Nature Press (*US*)
St. Johann Press (*US*)
Stonewood Press (*UK*)
Sunscribe (*US*)
Sunstone Press (*US*)
Titan Books (*UK*)
Valley Press (*UK*)
World Weaver Press (*US*)
Zumaya Publications (*US*)

Sociology

Abdo Publishing Co (*US*)
Algora Publishing (*US*)
Alma Classics (*UK*)
Amakella Publishing (*US*)
Arch Street Press (*US*)
Arsenal Pulp Press (*Can*)
Ashgate Publishing Limited (*UK*)
Beacon Press (*US*)
BenBella Books (*US*)
Birlinn Ltd (*UK*)
Bucknell University Press (*US*)
CATO Institute (*US*)
DB Publishing (*UK*)
Dreamriver Press (*US*)
Dunedin Academic Press Ltd (*UK*)
Duquesne University Press (*US*)
Edinburgh University Press (*UK*)
Edward Elgar Publishing Inc. (*US*)
Edward Elgar Publishing Ltd (*UK*)
Fabian Society (*UK*)
Floris Books (*UK*)
Fonthill Media LLC (*US*)
Fonthill Media Ltd (*UK*)
Fordham University Press (*US*)
Gallaudet University Press (*US*)
Granta Books (*UK*)
Greenhaven Publishing (*US*)
Hay House Publishers (*UK*)
Head of Zeus (*UK*)
Kube Publishing (*UK*)
The Lilliput Press (*Ire*)
Liverpool University Press (*UK*)
Luath Press Ltd (*UK*)
Marion Boyars Publishers (*UK*)
New York University (NYU) Press (*US*)
Nomad Press (*US*)
Pavilion Publishing (*UK*)
Pelican Publishing Company (*US*)
Pen Books (*US*)
The Policy Press (*UK*)
Polity Press (*UK*)
Prometheus Books (*US*)
Reference Service Press (*US*)
The Rosen Publishing Group, Inc. (*US*)
Saffron Books (*UK*)

Society for Promoting Christian Knowledge (SPCK) (*UK*)
Souvenir Press Ltd (*UK*)
Sunscribe (*US*)
Syracuse University Press (*US*)
Teachers College Press (*US*)
Temple University Press (*US*)
Trentham Books Limited (*UK*)
University of Chicago Press (*US*)
The University of Michigan Press (*US*)
Vehicule Press (*Can*)
Venture Publishing, Inc. (*US*)
Veritas Publications (*US*)
Verso (*US*)
Verso (*UK*)
W.W. Norton & Company Ltd (*UK*)
Walch Education (*US*)
Western Psychological Services (*US*)
John Wiley & Sons, Inc. (*US*)
World Book, Inc. (*US*)
Yale University Press (London) (*UK*)
Zed Books Ltd (*UK*)
Zenith Press (*US*)

Spiritual
ACTA Publications (*US*)
Amakella Publishing (*US*)
AMG Publishers (*US*)
Anness Publishing Ltd (*UK*)
Arch Street Press (*US*)
Authentic Media (*UK*)
Chelsea Green Publishing, Inc. (*US*)
Concordia Publishing House (*US*)
Connections Book Publishing Ltd (*UK*)
Covenant Communications Inc. (*US*)
Crown House Publishing (*UK*)
Divertir Publishing LLC (*US*)
Dreamriver Press (*US*)
Duquesne University Press (*US*)
Famous Seamus (*UK*)
Findhorn Press Ltd (*UK*)
Fitzrovia Press Limited (*UK*)
Floris Books (*UK*)
Hay House Publishers (*UK*)
Health Communications, Inc. (*US*)
Hymns Ancient & Modern Ltd (*UK*)
ICS Publications (*US*)
Insomniac Press (*Can*)
Kube Publishing (*UK*)
Lion Hudson Plc (*UK*)
Lost Tower Publications (*UK*)
Mandrake of Oxford (*UK*)
Maverick Reads (*UK*)
Kevin Mayhew Publishers (*UK*)
Monarch Books (*UK*)
New Holland Publishers (UK) Ltd (*UK*)
Octopus Publishing Group Limited (*UK*)
Paragon House (*US*)
Quill Driver Books (*US*)
Red Wheel (*US*)
Robert Hale Publishers (*UK*)
Singing Dragon (*UK*)
Society for Promoting Christian Knowledge (SPCK) (*UK*)
Souvenir Press Ltd (*UK*)
St Pauls (*US*)
Sterling Publishing Co. Inc. (*US*)
Storey Publishing (*US*)
Sunscribe (*US*)
Sunstone Press (*US*)
Veritas Publications (*US*)
Wooden Books (*UK*)
WaterBrook & Multnomah (*US*)
Wesleyan Publishing House (*US*)
Whitaker House (*US*)
Wilshire Book Company (*US*)
YMAA Publication Center, Inc. (*US*)

Sport
Abdo Publishing Co (*US*)
Amberley Publishing (*UK*)
Anness Publishing Ltd (*UK*)
Aureus Publishing Limited (*UK*)
Barron's Educational Series, Inc. (*US*)
BenBella Books (*US*)
Bennion Kearny (*UK*)
Birlinn Ltd (*UK*)
Black & White Publishing Ltd (*UK*)
John Blake Publishing (*UK*)
Bloomsbury Publishing Plc (*UK*)
Blue River Press (*US*)
Cave Books (*US*)
Cricket Books (*US*)
DB Publishing (*UK*)
Dino Books (*UK*)
ECW Press (*Can*)
Finney Company (*US*)
Fonthill Media LLC (*US*)
Fonthill Media Ltd (*UK*)
Gill & Macmillan (*Ire*)
Gomer Press (*UK*)
HarperCollins Publishers Ltd (*UK*)
Haynes Publishing (*UK*)
Head of Zeus (*UK*)
Headline Publishing Group (*UK*)
The History Press (*UK*)
Insomniac Press (*Can*)
Interlink Publishing Group, Inc. (*US*)
The Lilliput Press (*Ire*)
Luath Press Ltd (*UK*)
The Lyons Press Inc. (*US*)
Macmillan (*UK*)
McFarland & Company, Inc. (*US*)
Merlin Unwin Books (*UK*)
Milo Books Ltd (*UK*)
New Holland Publishers (UK) Ltd (*UK*)
The O'Brien Press (*Ire*)
Octopus Publishing Group Limited (*UK*)
Page Street Publishing Co. (*US*)
Pelican Publishing Company (*US*)
Pen Books (*US*)
Quiller Publishing Ltd (*UK*)
Reaktion Books (*UK*)
Robert Hale Publishers (*UK*)
The Rosen Publishing Group, Inc. (*US*)
Running Press (*US*)
Scarecrow Press Inc. (*US*)
Seren Books (*UK*)

Snowbooks (*UK*)
Souvenir Press Ltd (*UK*)
St David's Press (*UK*)
St. Johann Press (*US*)
Sterling Publishing Co. Inc. (*US*)
Sunscribe (*US*)
Sunstone Press (*US*)
Syracuse University Press (*US*)
Temple University Press (*US*)
Triumph Books (*US*)
University of Alaska Press (*US*)
The University of Michigan Press (*US*)
W.W. Norton & Company Ltd (*UK*)
Wannabee Books (*US*)
Willow Creek Press, Inc. (*US*)
YMAA Publication Center, Inc. (*US*)

Suspense

Amira Press (*US*)
Arrow Publications, LLC (*US*)
BelleBooks (*US*)
Bethany House Publishers (*US*)
Carina UK (*UK*)
Children's Brains are Yummy (CBAY) Books (*US*)
Covenant Communications Inc. (*US*)
Cricket Books (*US*)
Crimson Romance (*US*)
Divertir Publishing LLC (*US*)
ECW Press (*Can*)
Famous Seamus (*UK*)
Head of Zeus (*UK*)
Insomniac Press (*Can*)
Joffe Books Ltd (*UK*)
Jolly Fish Press (*US*)
Limitless Publishing (*US*)
Lost Tower Publications (*UK*)
M P Publishing USA (*US*)
Maverick Reads (*UK*)
New Directions Publishing (*US*)
Pen Books (*US*)
Polis Books (*US*)
Roberts Press (*US*)
Scribner (*US*)
Sidestreet Cookie Publishing (*US*)
Sunscribe (*US*)
TouchWood Editions (*Can*)
WaterBrook & Multnomah (*US*)

Technology

Abdo Publishing Co (*US*)
ASCE Press (*US*)
Astragal Press (*US*)
Canopus Publishing Ltd (*UK*)
CJ Fallon (*Ire*)
Dreamriver Press (*US*)
Finney Company (*US*)
Frontinus (*UK*)
Gingko Library (*UK*)
Hanser Publications (*US*)
Haynes Publishing (*UK*)
Hopscotch (*UK*)
Metal Powder Industries Federation (MPIF) (*US*)
Mitchell Lane Publishers, Inc. (*US*)
O'Reilly Media (*US*)
Paladin Press (*US*)
Pen Books (*US*)
Quill Driver Books (*US*)
SAE International (*US*)
Sunscribe (*US*)
Teachers College Press (*US*)
Temple University Press (*US*)
Trentham Books Limited (*UK*)
Ulric Publishing (*UK*)
University of Alabama Press (*US*)
University of Chicago Press (*US*)
W.W. Norton & Company Ltd (*UK*)
Wannabee Books (*US*)
John Wiley & Sons, Inc. (*US*)
WIT Press (*UK*)
Yale University Press (London) (*UK*)
Zenith Press (*US*)

Theatre

Aurora Metro Press (*UK*)
The Gallery Press (*Ire*)
Gomer Press (*UK*)
Haus Publishing (*UK*)
Josef Weinberger Ltd (*UK*)
Macmillan (*UK*)
Manchester University Press (*UK*)
Marion Boyars Publishers (*UK*)
Maverick Reads (*UK*)
New Playwrights' Network (NPN) (*UK*)
Oberon Books (*UK*)
Pen Books (*US*)
Scarecrow Press Inc. (*US*)
Southern Illinois University Press (*US*)
Souvenir Press Ltd (*UK*)
Sunscribe (*US*)
Sunstone Press (*US*)
Teachers College Press (*US*)
University of Alabama Press (*US*)
The University of Michigan Press (*US*)

Thrillers

Allison & Busby Ltd (*UK*)
Asabi Publishing (*US*)
BelleBooks (*US*)
Black & White Publishing Ltd (*UK*)
Bloomsbury Spark (*UK*)
Carina UK (*UK*)
Curiosity Quills Press (*US*)
Curious Fox (*UK*)
Entangled Teen (*US*)
Famous Seamus (*UK*)
Fingerpress UK (*UK*)
GEY Books (*UK*)
HarperCollins Publishers Ltd (*UK*)
Head of Zeus (*UK*)
Hesperus Press Limited (*UK*)
Jolly Fish Press (*US*)
Limitless Publishing (*US*)
Lost Tower Publications (*UK*)
Luath Press Ltd (*UK*)
M P Publishing USA (*US*)
Macmillan (*UK*)
Maverick Reads (*UK*)
Monsoon Books Pte Ltd (*UK*)

Oceanview Publishing (*US*)
Pen Books (*US*)
Polis Books (*US*)
River City Publishing (*US*)
Salt Publishing Ltd (*UK*)
Salvo Press (*US*)
Sandstone Press Ltd (*UK*)
Severn House Publishers (*UK*)
Sidestreet Cookie Publishing (*US*)
Snowbooks (*UK*)
Sunscribe (*US*)
Twenty First Century Publishers Ltd (*UK*)
Zumaya Publications (*US*)

Translations

Algora Publishing (*US*)
Alma Classics (*UK*)
And Other Stories (*UK*)
Arc Publications (*UK*)
Arch Street Press (*US*)
Aurora Metro Press (*UK*)
Bilingual Review Press (*US*)
Black Ocean (*US*)
Calisi Press (*UK*)
Canongate Books (*UK*)
Carcanet Press Ltd (*UK*)
David R. Godine, Publisher (*US*)
Dedalus Ltd (*UK*)
Folded Word LLC (*US*)
Hesperus Press Limited (*UK*)
ICS Publications (*US*)
Interlink Publishing Group, Inc. (*US*)
Italica Press (*US*)
Mage Publishers (*US*)
Mantra Lingua Ltd (*UK*)
New Directions Publishing (*US*)
Nightboat Books (*US*)
Oneworld Publications (*UK*)
Parthian Books (*UK*)
Pen Books (*US*)
Red Empress Publishing (*US*)
Seren Books (*UK*)
Seven Stories Press (*US*)
Shearsman Books (*UK*)
Sunscribe (*US*)
Syracuse University Press (*US*)
Truman State University Press (*US*)
University of Alaska Press (*US*)
University of Chicago Press (*US*)
Vehicule Press (*Can*)
Yale University Press (London) (*UK*)

Travel

Abdo Publishing Co (*US*)
ACC Art Books Ltd (*UK*)
Allison & Busby Ltd (*UK*)
Amakella Publishing (*US*)
Amberley Publishing (*UK*)
Amira Press (*US*)
Anness Publishing Ltd (*UK*)
Appalachian Mountain Club Books (*US*)
The Armchair Traveller at the bookHaus (*UK*)
Barron's Educational Series, Inc. (*US*)
Bennion Kearny (*UK*)
Berlitz Publishing (*UK*)
Birlinn Ltd (*UK*)
John Blake Publishing (*UK*)
Blue Guides Limited (*UK*)
Blue River Press (*US*)
Bradt Travel Guides (*UK*)
Canongate Books (*UK*)
Cave Books (*US*)
Cicerone Press (*UK*)
DB Publishing (*UK*)
Discovery Walking Guides Ltd (*UK*)
Edward Elgar Publishing Inc. (*US*)
Eland Publishing Ltd (*UK*)
Eye Books (*UK*)
FalconGuides (*US*)
Finney Company (*US*)
Folded Word LLC (*US*)
Fonthill Media LLC (*US*)
Fonthill Media Ltd (*UK*)
GEY Books (*UK*)
Gibson Square Books Ltd (*UK*)
Golden West Books (*US*)
Gomer Press (*UK*)
Granta Books (*UK*)
Haus Publishing (*UK*)
Hesperus Press Limited (*UK*)
Hipso Media (*US*)
House of Lochar (*UK*)
Infinite Ideas (*UK*)
Insomniac Press (*Can*)
Interlink Publishing Group, Inc. (*US*)
Italica Press (*US*)
The Lilliput Press (*Ire*)
Lonely Planet (*UK*)
Lonely Planet Publications (*US*)
Luath Press Ltd (*UK*)
Macmillan (*UK*)
Metro Publications Ltd (*UK*)
Monsoon Books Pte Ltd (*UK*)
Neil Wilson Publishing Ltd (*UK*)
New Holland Publishers (UK) Ltd (*UK*)
The O'Brien Press (*Ire*)
Octopus Publishing Group Limited (*UK*)
Onstream Publications Ltd (*Ire*)
Ouen Press (*UK*)
The Overmountain Press (*US*)
Pelican Publishing Company (*US*)
Pen Books (*US*)
Phaidon Press Limited (*UK*)
Quill Driver Books (*US*)
Quiller Publishing Ltd (*UK*)
Reaktion Books (*UK*)
River City Publishing (*US*)
Rose and Crown Books (*UK*)
Seren Books (*UK*)
Sierra Club Books (*US*)
Souvenir Press Ltd (*UK*)
St David's Press (*UK*)
Stenlake Publishing (*UK*)
Sterling Publishing Co. Inc. (*US*)
Summersdale Publishers Ltd (*UK*)
Sunscribe (*US*)
Sunstone Press (*US*)
TouchWood Editions (*Can*)

Truman State University Press (*US*)
Ulric Publishing (*UK*)
University of Chicago Press (*US*)
The University of Michigan Press (*US*)
Valley Press (*UK*)
W.W. Norton & Company Ltd (*UK*)
Weidenfeld & Nicolson (*UK*)
Zenith Press (*US*)

TV

BearManor Media (*US*)
BFI Publishing (*UK*)
John Blake Publishing (*UK*)
Candy Jar Books (*UK*)
ECW Press (*Can*)
Guild of Master Craftsman (GMC) Publications Ltd (*UK*)
Headline Publishing Group (*UK*)
Macmillan (*UK*)
Manchester University Press (*UK*)
Sunscribe (*US*)
Syracuse University Press (*US*)
Titan Books (*UK*)
Wesleyan University Press (*US*)

Westerns

Amira Press (*US*)
Carina UK (*UK*)
Cricket Books (*US*)
Harlequin American Romance (*US*)
Robert Hale Publishers (*UK*)
Sunscribe (*US*)
Sunstone Press (*US*)
Zumaya Publications (*US*)

Women's Interests

Algora Publishing (*US*)
Allison & Busby Ltd (*UK*)
Amakella Publishing (*US*)
Arch Street Press (*US*)
Arrow Publications, LLC (*US*)
Aurora Metro Press (*UK*)
Beacon Press (*US*)
BelleBooks (*US*)
Bethany House Publishers (*US*)
Black & White Publishing Ltd (*UK*)
Black Lyon Publishing, LLC (*US*)
Calisi Press (*UK*)
Carina UK (*UK*)
Connections Book Publishing Ltd (*UK*)
Crescent Moon Publishing (*UK*)
Curiosity Quills Press (*US*)
ECW Press (*Can*)
Famous Seamus (*UK*)
Fordham University Press (*US*)
Gibson Square Books Ltd (*UK*)
Hay House Publishers (*UK*)
Health Communications, Inc. (*US*)
Hohm Press (*US*)
Honno Welsh Women's Press (*UK*)
Lost Tower Publications (*UK*)
M P Publishing USA (*US*)
Marion Boyars Publishers (*UK*)
Maverick Reads (*UK*)
McFarland & Company, Inc. (*US*)
New York University (NYU) Press (*US*)
Pandora Press (*UK*)
Pen Books (*US*)
Polis Books (*US*)
Polity Press (*UK*)
Quirk Books (*US*)
Red Empress Publishing (*US*)
Red Wheel (*US*)
Reference Service Press (*US*)
Roberts Press (*US*)
Sidestreet Cookie Publishing (*US*)
Southern Illinois University Press (*US*)
Souvenir Press Ltd (*UK*)
Sunscribe (*US*)
Sunstone Press (*US*)
Syracuse University Press (*US*)
Teachers College Press (*US*)
Temple University Press (*US*)
Trentham Books Limited (*UK*)
The University of Michigan Press (*US*)
University of South Carolina Press (*US*)
Verso (*US*)
Virago Press (*UK*)
W.W. Norton & Company Ltd (*UK*)
Whitaker House (*US*)
Zebra (*US*)

Get Free Access to the firstwriter.com Website

To claim your free access to the firstwriter.com website simply go to the website at https://www.firstwriter.com/subscribe and begin the subscription process as normal. On the second page, enter the required details (such as your name and address, etc.) then for "Voucher / coupon number" enter the following promotional code:

- **JT79-F1CT**

This will reduce the cost of creating a subscription by up to $15 / £10 / €15, making it free to create a monthly, quarterly, or combination subscription. Alternatively, you can use the discount to take out an annual or life subscription at a reduced rate.

Continue the process until your account is created. Please note that you will need to provide your payment details, even if there is no up-front payment. This is in case you choose to leave your subscription running after the free initial period, but there is no obligation for you to do so.

When you use this code to take out a free subscription you are under no obligation to make any payments whatsoever and you are free to cancel your account before you make any payments if you wish.

If you need any assistance, please email support@firstwriter.com.

If you have found this book useful, please consider leaving a review on the website where you bought it!

What you get

Once you have set up access to ths site you will be able to benefit from all the following features:

Databases

All our databases are updated almost every day, and include powerful search facilities to help you find exactly what you need. Searches that used to take you hours or even days in print books or on search engines can now be done in seconds, and produce more accurate and up-to-date information. Our agents database also includes independent reports from at least three separate sources, showing you which are the top agencies and helping you avoid the scams that are all over the internet. You can try out any of our databases before you subscribe:

- Search dozens of **current competitions**
- Search **over 2,200 magazines**

- Search **over 650 literary agencies**
- Search **over 1,900 book publishers** that **don't** charge fees

PLUS advanced features to help you with your search:

- Save searches and save time – set up to 15 search parameters specific to your work, save them, and then access the search results with a single click whenever you log in. You can even save multiple different searches if you have different types of work you are looking to place.
- Add personal notes to listings, visible only to you and fully searchable – helping you to organise your actions.
- Set reminders on listings to notify you when to submit your work, when to follow up, when to expect a reply, or any other custom action.
- Track which listings you've viewed and when, to help you organise your search – any listings which have changed since you last viewed them will be highlighted for your attention!

Daily email updates

As a subscriber you will be able to take advantage of our email alert service, meaning you can specify your particular interests and we'll send you automatic email updates when we change or add a listing that matches them. So if you're interested in agents dealing in romantic fiction in the United States you can have us send you emails with the latest updates about them – keeping you up to date without even having to log in.

User feedback

Our agent, publisher, and magazine databases all include a user feedback feature that allows our subscribers to leave feedback on each listing – giving you not only the chance to have your say about the markets you contact, but giving a unique authors' perspective on the listings.

Save on copyright protection fees

If you're sending your work away to publishers, competitions, or literary agents, it's vital that you first protect your copyright. As a subscriber to firstwriter.com you can do this through our site and save 10% on the copyright registration fees normally payable for protecting your work internationally through the Intellectual Property Rights Office.

firstwriter.magazine

firstwriter.magazine showcases the best in new poetry and fiction from around the world. If you're interested in writing and want to get published, the most important thing you can do is read contemporary writing that's getting into print now. firstwriter.magazine helps you do that.

Monthly newsletter

When you subscribe to firstwriter.com you also receive our monthly email newsletter – described by one publishing company as "the best in the business" – including articles, news, and interviews for writers. And the best part is that you can continue to receive the newsletter even after you stop your paid subscription – at no cost!

Terms and conditions

The promotional code contained in this publication may be used by the owner of the book only to create one subscription to firstwriter.com at a reduced cost, or for free. It may not be used by or disseminated to third parties. Should the code be misused then the owner of the book will be liable for any costs incurred, including but not limited to payment in full at the standard rate for the subscription in question. The code may be used at any time until the end of the calendar year named in the title of the publication, after which time it will become invalid. The code may be redeemed against the creation of a new account only – it cannot be redeemed against the ongoing costs of keeping a subscription open. In order to create a subscription a method of payment must be provided, but there is no obligation to make any payment. Subscriptions may be cancelled at any time, and if an account is cancelled before any payment becomes due then no payment will be made. Once a subscription has been created, the normal schedule of payments will begin on a monthly, quarterly, or annual basis, unless a life Subscription is selected, or the subscription is cancelled prior to the first payment becoming due. Subscriptions may be cancelled at any time, but if they are left open beyond the date at which the first payment becomes due and is processed then payments will not be refundable.

CPSIA information can be obtained
at www.ICGtesting.com
Printed in the USA
LVHW04s1534090818
586500LV00012B/670/P

9 781909 935181